ANGELA'S ASHES & 'TIS

FRANK McCOURT taught for thirty years in various New York City high schools and in city colleges. His play, *The Irish and How They Got That Way*, has been produced in New York, Boston, Chicago and Melbourne, Australia. He lives in New York.

Praise for Frank McCourt:

Angela's Ashes

'Autobiography at its best. McCourt is a silver-tongued storyteller and you'll laugh as much as you'll cry.'   *Sun-Herald* (Sydney)

'A stunning memoir ... Writing in prose that's pictorial and tactile, lyrical but streetwise, McCourt does for the town of Limerick what the young Joyce did for Dublin: he conjures the place for us with such intimacy that we feel we've walked its streets and crawled its pubs.'   *New York Times*

'Our first Irish Dickens ... Big, strong, unashamed sentiment ... the thing Irish people run away from, afraid of their own hearts. But in some hands sentimentality is powerful and an instrument of the truth. I think the sentiment in *Angela's Ashes* is something the reader will be the richer for opening towards.'   *Irish Times*

'A jewel of a book ... A story as sad as this one should make hard reading. But the younger Frank's resilience, and the older Frank's ability to weave a yarn that contains not a few threads of humour, urge the reader on.'   *Belfast Telegraph*

'Tis

'Full of the narrative brio, the intuitive feel for character and above all the love of language that made *Angela's Ashes* such a success.'   *Los Angeles Times*

''*Tis* is the update of Frankie's story – his life as a bellhop, toilet cleaner, soldier, warehouseman and finally teacher. His many fans will want to catch up with his family story, and it is all here, too, funny-sad and bittersweet. Frank McCourt readers will never have enough of their master's voice.'   *Express*

'Exhilarating ... bursting with gusto, unflinchingly direct and with subject matter so rich it would have done for three volumes.'   *Literary Review*

''*Tis* feels like a friend, telling the tales of his life over a pint, with charm and humour, economy and pace. There is a sense of loss when you have to close the pages and sleep, or go on to other things. McCourt is a masterful writer ... All who read *Angela's Ashes* will read '*Tis*. They will love it, and so did I.'

Independent on Sunday

Flamingo
An imprint of HarperCollins*Publishers*
77−85 Fulham Palace Road,
Hammersmith, London w6 8jb

Flamingo is a registered trademark of HarperCollins*Publishers*

www.**fire**and**water**.com

This special omnibus edition of *Angela's Ashes* and *'Tis*
published by Flamingo 2001

1 3 5 7 9 8 6 4 2

Angela's Ashes first published in Great Britain by
HarperCollins*Publishers* 1996
Copyright © Frank McCourt 1996

'Tis first published in Great Britain by Flamingo 1999
Copyright © Frank McCourt 1999

The Author and Publishers are grateful to John Murray
(Publishers) Ltd for permission to reproduce (in *Angela's Ashes*)
an extract from 'The Highwayman' by Alfred Noyes, from their
edition of his *Collected Poems*

Some of the names in *'Tis* have been changed.

Frank McCourt asserts the moral right to
be identified as the author of this work.

ISBN 0 00 713125 9

Printed and bound by Griffin Press, Netley, Australia

Frank McCourt

Angela's Ashes

A MEMOIR OF A CHILDHOOD

Flamingo
An Imprint of HarperCollins*Publishers*

This book is dedicated to my brothers,
Malachy, Michael, Alphonsus.
I learn from you, I admire you and I love you.

ACKNOWLEDGEMENTS

This is a small hymn to an exaltation of women.

R'lene Dahlberg fanned the embers.
Lisa Schwarzbaum read early pages and encouraged me.
Mary Breasted Smyth, elegant novelist herself, read the first third
and passed it on to
Molly Friedrich, who became my agent and thought that
Nan Graham, Editor-in-Chief at Scribner, would be just the
right person to put the book on the road.
And Molly was right.

My daughter, Maggie, has shown me how life can be
a grand adventure, while exquisite moments with
my granddaughter, Chiara, have helped me recall
a small child's wonder.
My wife, Ellen, listened while I read and cheered me
to the final page.

I am blessed among men.

ANGELA'S ASHES

I

My father and mother should have stayed in New York where they met and married and where I was born. Instead, they returned to Ireland when I was four, my brother, Malachy, three, the twins, Oliver and Eugene, barely one, and my sister, Margaret, dead and gone.

When I look back on my childhood I wonder how I survived at all. It was, of course, a miserable childhood: the happy childhood is hardly worth your while. Worse than the ordinary miserable childhood is the miserable Irish childhood, and worse yet is the miserable Irish Catholic childhood.

People everywhere brag and whimper about the woes of their early years, but nothing can compare with the Irish version: the poverty; the shiftless loquacious alcoholic father; the pious defeated mother moaning by the fire; pompous priests; bullying schoolmasters; the English and the terrible things they did to us for eight hundred long years.

Above all—we were wet.

Out in the Atlantic Ocean great sheets of rain gathered to drift slowly up the River Shannon and settle forever in Limerick. The rain dampened the city from the Feast of the Circumcision to New Year's Eve. It created a cacophony of hacking coughs, bronchial rattles, asthmatic wheezes, consumptive croaks. It turned noses into fountains, lungs into bacterial sponges. It provoked cures galore; to ease the catarrh you boiled onions in milk blackened with pepper; for the congested passages you made a paste of boiled flour and nettles, wrapped it in a rag, and slapped it, sizzling, on the chest.

From October to April the walls of Limerick glistened with the damp. Clothes never dried: tweed and woolen coats housed living things, sometimes sprouted mysterious vegetations. In pubs, steam rose from damp bodies and garments to be inhaled with cigarette and pipe smoke laced with the stale fumes of spilled stout and whiskey and tinged with the odor of piss wafting in from the outdoor jakes where many a man puked up his week's wages.

The rain drove us into the church—our refuge, our strength, our only dry place. At Mass, Benediction, novenas, we huddled in great damp clumps, dozing through priest drone, while steam rose again from our clothes to mingle with the sweetness of incense, flowers and candles.

Limerick gained a reputation for piety, but we knew it was only the rain.

My father, Malachy McCourt, was born on a farm in Toome, County Antrim. Like his father before, he grew up wild, in trouble with the English, or the Irish, or both. He fought with the Old IRA and for some desperate act he wound up a fugitive with a price on his head.

When I was a child I would look at my father, the thinning hair, the collapsing teeth, and wonder why anyone would give money for a head like that. When I was thirteen my father's mother told me a secret: as a wee lad your poor father was dropped on his head. It was an accident, he was never the same after, and you must remember that people dropped on their heads can be a bit peculiar.

Because of the price on the head he had been dropped on, he had to be spirited out of Ireland via cargo ship from Galway. In New York, with Prohibition in full swing, he thought he had died and gone to hell for his sins. Then he discovered speakeasies and he rejoiced.

After wandering and drinking in America and England he yearned for peace in his declining years. He returned to Belfast, which erupted all around him. He said, A pox on all their houses, and chatted with the ladies of Andersontown. They tempted him with delicacies but he waved them away and drank his tea. He no longer smoked or touched alcohol, so what was the use? It was time to go and he died in the Royal Victoria Hospital.

My mother, the former Angela Sheehan, grew up in a Limerick slum with her mother, two brothers, Thomas and Patrick, and a sister, Agnes. She never saw her father, who had run off to Australia weeks before her birth.

After a night of drinking porter in the pubs of Limerick he staggers down the lane singing his favorite song,

> *Who threw the overalls in Mrs. Murphy's chowder?*
> *Nobody spoke so he said it all the louder*
> *It's a dirty Irish trick and I can lick the Mick*
> *Who threw the overalls in Murphy's chowder.*

He's in great form altogether and he thinks he'll play a while with little Patrick, one year old. Lovely little fella. Loves his daddy. Laughs when Daddy throws him up in the air. Upsy daisy, little Paddy, upsy daisy, up in the air in the dark, so dark, oh, Jasus, you miss the child on the way down and poor little Patrick lands on his head, gurgles a bit, whimpers, goes quiet. Grandma heaves herself from the bed, heavy with the child in her belly, my mother. She's barely able to lift little Patrick from the floor. She moans a long moan over the child and turns on Grandpa. Get out of it. Out. If you stay here a minute longer I'll take the hatchet to you, you drunken lunatic. By Jesus, I'll swing at the end of a rope for you. Get out.

Grandpa stands his ground like a man. I have a right, he says, to stay in me own house.

She runs at him and he melts before this whirling dervish with a damaged child in her arms and a healthy one stirring inside. He stumbles from the house, up the lane, and doesn't stop till he reaches Melbourne in Australia.

Little Pat, my uncle, was never the same after. He grew up soft in the head with a left leg that went one way, his body the other. He never learned to read or write but God blessed him in another way. When he started to sell newspapers at the age of eight he could count money better than the Chancellor of the Exchequer himself. No one knew why he was called Ab Sheehan, The Abbot, but all Limerick loved him.

My mother's troubles began the night she was born. There is my grandmother in the bed heaving and gasping with the labor pains, praying to St. Gerard Majella, patron saint of expectant mothers. There is Nurse O'Halloran, the midwife, all dressed up in her finery. It's New Year's Eve and Mrs. O'Halloran is anxious for this child to be born so that she can rush off to the parties and celebrations. She tells my grandmother: Will you push, will you, push. Jesus, Mary and holy St. Joseph, if you don't hurry with this child it won't be born till the New Year and what good is that to me with me new dress? Never mind St. Gerard Majella. What can a man do for a woman at a time like this even if he is a saint? St. Gerard Majella my arse.

My grandmother switches her prayers to St. Ann, patron saint of difficult labor. But the child won't come. Nurse O'Halloran tells my grandmother, Pray to St. Jude, patron saint of desperate cases.

St. Jude, patron of desperate cases, help me. I'm desperate. She grunts and pushes and the infant's head appears, only the head, my mother, and it's the stroke of midnight, the New Year. Limerick City erupts with whistles, horns, sirens, brass bands, people calling and singing, Happy New Year. Should auld acquaintance be forgot, and church bells all over ring out the Angelus and Nurse O'Halloran weeps for the waste of a dress, that child still in there and me in me finery. Will you come out, child, will you? Grandma gives a great push and the child is in the world, a lovely girl with black curly hair and sad blue eyes.

Ah, Lord above, says Nurse O'Halloran, this child is a time straddler, born with her head in the New Year and her arse in the Old or was it her head in the Old Year and her arse in the New. You'll have to write to the Pope, missus, to find out what year this child was born in and I'll save this dress for next year.

And the child was named Angela for the Angelus which rang the midnight hour, the New Year, the minute of her coming and because she was a little angel anyway.

> Love her as in childhood
> Though feeble, old and grey.
> For you'll never miss a mother's love
> Till she's buried beneath the clay.

At the St. Vincent de Paul School, Angela learned to read, write, and calculate and by her ninth year her schooling was done. She tried her hand at being a charwoman, a skivvy, a maid with a little white hat opening doors, but she could not manage the little curtsy that is required and her mother said, You don't have the knack of it. You're pure useless. Why don't you go to America where there's room for all sorts of uselessness? I'll give you the fare.

She arrived in New York just in time for the first Thanksgiving Day of the Great Depression. She met Malachy at a party given by Dan MacAdorey and his wife, Minnie, on Classon Avenue in Brooklyn. Malachy liked Angela and she liked him. He had a hangdog look, which came from the three months he had just spent in jail for hijacking a truck. He and his friend John McErlaine believed what they were told in the speakeasy, that the truck was packed to the roof with cases of canned pork and beans. Neither knew how to drive and when the police saw the truck lurch and jerk along Myrtle Avenue they pulled it over. The police searched the truck and wondered why anyone would hijack a truck containing, not pork and beans, but cases of buttons.

With Angela drawn to the hangdog look and Malachy lonely after three months in jail, there was bound to be a knee-trembler.

A knee-trembler is the act itself done up against a wall, man and woman up on their toes, straining so hard their knees tremble with the excitement that's in it.

That knee-trembler put Angela in an interesting condition and, of course, there was talk. Angela had cousins, the MacNamara sisters, Delia and Philomena, married, respectively, to Jimmy Fortune of County Mayo, and Tommy Flynn, of Brooklyn itself.

Delia and Philomena were large women, great-breasted and fierce. When they sailed along the sidewalks of Brooklyn lesser creatures stepped aside, respect was shown. The sisters knew what was right and they knew what was wrong and any doubts could be resolved by the One, Holy, Roman, Catholic and Apostolic Church. They knew that Angela, unmarried, had no right to be in an interesting condition and they would take steps.

Steps they took. With Jimmy and Tommy in tow they marched to the speakeasy on Atlantic Avenue where Malachy could be found on Friday, payday when he had a job. The man in the speak, Joey Cacciamani, did not want to admit the sisters but Philomena told him that if he wanted to keep the nose on his face and that door on its hinges he'd better open up for they were there on God's business. Joey said, Awright, awright, you Irish. Jeezoz! Trouble, trouble.

Malachy, at the far end of the bar, turned pale, gave the great-breasted ones a sickly smile, offered them a drink. They resisted the smile and spurned the offer. Delia said, We don't know what class of a tribe you come from in the North of Ireland.

Philomena said, There is a suspicion you might have Presbyterians in your family, which would explain what you did to our cousin.

Jimmy said, Ah, now, ah, now. 'Tisn't his fault if there's Presbyterians in his family.

Delia said, You shuddup.

Tommy had to join in. What you did to that poor unfortunate girl is a disgrace to the Irish race and you should be ashamed of yourself.

Och, I am, said Malachy. I am.

Nobody asked you to talk, said Philomena. You done enough damage with your blather, so shut your yap.

And while your yap is shut, said Delia, we're here to see you do the right thing by our poor cousin, Angela Sheehan.

Malachy said, Och, indeed, indeed. The right thing is the right thing and I'd be glad to buy you all a drink while we have this little talk.

Take the drink, said Tommy, and shove it up your ass.

Philomena said, Our little cousin no sooner gets off the boat than you are at her. We have morals in Limerick, you know, morals. We're not like jackrabbits from Antrim, a place crawling with Presbyterians.

Jimmy said, He don't look like a Presbyterian.

You shuddup, said Delia.

Another thing we noticed, said Philomena. You have a very odd manner.

Malachy smiled. I do?

You do, says Delia. I think 'tis one of the first things we noticed about you, that odd manner, and it gives us a very uneasy feeling.

'Tis that sneaky little Presbyterian smile, said Philomena.

Och, said Malachy, it's just the trouble I have with my teeth.

Teeth or no teeth, odd manner or no odd manner, you're gonna marry that girl, said Tommy. Up the middle aisle you're going.

Och, said Malachy, I wasn't planning to get married, you know. There's no work and I wouldn't be able to support . . .

Married is what you're going to be, said Delia.

Up the middle aisle, said Jimmy.

You shuddup, said Delia.

. . .

Malachy watched them leave. I'm in a desperate pickle, he told Joey Cacciamani.

Bet your ass, said Joey. I see them babes comin' at me I jump inna Hudson River.

Malachy considered the pickle he was in. He had a few dollars in his pocket from the last job and he had an uncle in San Francisco or one of the other California Sans. Wouldn't he be better off in California, far from the great-breasted MacNamara sisters and their grim husbands? He would, indeed, and he'd have a drop of the Irish to celebrate his decision and departure. Joey poured and the drink nearly took the lining off Malachy's gullet. Irish, indeed! He told Joey it was a Prohibition concoction from the devil's own still. Joey shrugged. I don't know nothing. I only pour. Still, it was better than nothing and Malachy would have another and one for yourself, Joey, and ask them two decent Italians what they'd like and what are you talking about, of course, I have the money to pay for it.

He awoke on a bench in the Long Island Railroad Station, a cop rapping on his boots with a nightstick, his escape money gone, the Mac-Namara sisters ready to eat him alive in Brooklyn.

On the feast of St. Joseph, a bitter day in March, four months after the knee-trembler, Malachy married Angela and in August the child was born. In November Malachy got drunk and decided it was time to register the child's birth. He thought he might name the child Malachy, after himself, but his North of Ireland accent and the alcoholic mumble confused the clerk so much he simply entered the name Male on the certificate.

Not until late December did they take Male to St. Paul's Church to be baptized and named Francis after his father's father and the lovely saint of Assisi. Angela wanted to give him a middle name, Munchin, after the patron saint of Limerick but Malachy said over his dead body. No son of his would have a Limerick name. It's hard enough going through life with one name. Sticking on middle names was an atrocious American habit and there was no need for a second name when you're christened after the man from Assisi.

There was a delay the day of the baptism when the chosen god-father, John McErlaine, got drunk at the speakeasy and forgot his responsibilities. Philomena told her husband, Tommy, he'd have to be godfather. Child's soul is in danger, she said. Tommy put his head down and grumbled. All right. I'll be godfather but I'm not goin' to be responsible if he grows up like his father causin' trouble and goin' through life with the odd manner for if he does he can go to John McErlaine at the speakeasy. The priest said, True for you, Tom, decent man that you are, fine man that never set foot inside a speakeasy. Malachy, fresh from the speakeasy himself, felt insulted and wanted to argue with the priest, one sacrilege on top of another. Take off that collar and we'll see who's the man. He had to be held back by the great-breasted ones and their husbands grim. Angela, new mother, agitated, forgot she was holding the child and let him slip into the baptismal font, a total immersion of the Protestant type. The altar boy assisting the priest plucked the infant from the font and restored him to Angela, who sobbed and clutched him, dripping, to her bosom. The priest laughed, said he had never seen the likes, that the child was a regular little Baptist now and hardly needed a priest. This maddened Malachy again and he wanted to jump at the priest for calling the child some class of a Protestant. The priest said, Quiet, man, you're in God's house, and when Malachy said, God's house, my arse, he was thrown out on Court Street because you can't say arse in God's house.

After baptism Philomena said she had tea and ham and cakes in her house around the corner. Malachy said, Tea? and she said, Yes, tea, or is it whiskey you want? He said tea was grand but first he'd have to go and deal with John McErlaine, who didn't have the decency to carry out his duties as godfather. Angela said, You're only looking for an excuse to run to the speakeasy, and he said, As God is my witness, the drink is the last thing on my mind. Angela started to cry. Your son's christening day and you have to go drinking. Delia told him he was a disgusting specimen but what could you expect from the North of Ireland.

Malachy looked from one to the other, shifted on his feet, pulled his cap down over his eyes, shoved his hands deep in his trouser pockets, said, Och, aye, the way they do in the far reaches of County Antrim, turned, hurried up Court Street to the speakeasy on Atlantic Avenue where he was sure they'd ply him with free drink in honor of his son's baptism.

At Philomena's house the sisters and their husbands ate and drank while Angela sat in a corner nursing the baby and crying. Philomena stuffed her mouth with bread and ham and rumbled at Angela, That's what you get for being such a fool. Hardly off the boat and you fall for that lunatic. You shoulda stayed single, put the child up for adoption, and you'd be a free woman today. Angela cried harder and Delia took up the attack, Oh, stop it, Angela, stop it. You have nobody to blame but yourself for gettin' into trouble with a drunkard from the North, a man that doesn't even look like a Catholic, him with his odd manner. I'd say that . . . that . . . Malachy has a streak of the Presbyterian in him right enough. You shuddup, Jimmy.

If I was you, said Philomena, I'd make sure there's no more children. He don't have a job, so he don't, an' never will the way he drinks. So . . . no more children, Angela. Are you listenin' to me?

I am, Philomena.

A year later another child was born. Angela called him Malachy after his father and gave him a middle name, Gerard, after his father's brother.

The MacNamara sisters said Angela was nothing but a rabbit and they wanted nothing to do with her till she came to her senses.

Their husbands agreed.

I'm in a playground on Classon Avenue in Brooklyn with my brother, Malachy. He's two, I'm three. We're on the seesaw.

Up, down, up, down.

Malachy goes up.

I get off.

Malachy goes down. Seesaw hits the ground. He screams. His hand is on his mouth and there's blood.

Oh, God. Blood is bad. My mother will kill me.

And here she is, trying to run across the playground. Her big belly slows her.

She says, What did you do? What did you do to the child?

I don't know what to say. I don't know what I did.

She pulls my ear. Go home. Go to bed.

Bed? In the middle of the day?

She pushes me toward the playground gate. Go.

She picks up Malachy and waddles off.

My father's friend, Mr. MacAdorey, is outside our building. He's stand-ing at the edge of the sidewalk with his wife, Minnie, looking at a dog lying in the gutter. There is blood all around the dog's head. It's the color of the blood from Malachy's mouth.

Malachy has dog blood and the dog has Malachy blood.

I pull Mr. MacAdorey's hand. I tell him Malachy has blood like the dog.

Oh, he does, indeed, Francis. Cats have it, too. And Eskimos. All the same blood.

Minnie says, Stop that, Dan. Stop confusing the wee fellow. She tells me the poor wee dog was hit by a car and he crawled all the way from the middle of the street before he died. Wanted to come home, the poor wee creature.

Mr. MacAdorey says, You'd better go home, Francis. I don't know what you did to your wee brother, but your mother took him off to the hos-pital. Go home, child.

Will Malachy die like the dog, Mr. MacAdorey?

Minnie says, He bit his tongue. He won't die.

Why did the dog die?

It was his time, Francis.

The apartment is empty and I wander between the two rooms, the bed-room and the kitchen. My father is out looking for a job and my mother is at the hospital with Malachy. I wish I had something to eat but there's nothing in the icebox but cabbage leaves floating in the melted ice. My father said never eat anything floating in water for the rot that might be in it. I fall asleep on my parents' bed and when my mother shakes me it's nearly dark. Your little brother is going to sleep a while. Nearly bit his tongue off. Stitches galore. Go into the other room.

My father is in the kitchen sipping black tea from his big white enamel mug. He lifts me to his lap.

Dad, will you tell me the story about Coo Coo?

Cuchulain. Say it after me, Coo-hoo-lin. I'll tell you the story when you say the name right. Coo-hoo-lin.

I say it right and he tells me the story of Cuchulain, who had a different name when he was a boy, Setanta. He grew up in Ireland where Dad lived when he was a boy in County Antrim. Setanta had a stick and ball and one day he hit the ball and it went into the mouth of a big dog that belonged to Culain and choked him. Oh, Culain was angry and he said, What am I to do now without my big dog to guard my house and my wife and my ten small children as well as numerous pigs, hens, sheep?

Setanta said, I'm sorry. I'll guard your house with my stick and ball and I'll change my name to Cuchulain, the Hound of Culain. He did. He guarded the house and regions beyond and became a great hero, the Hound of Ulster itself. Dad said he was a greater hero than Hercules or Achilles that the Greeks were always bragging about and he could take on King Arthur and all his knights in a fair fight which, of course, you could never get with an Englishman anyway.

That's my story. Dad can't tell that story to Malachy or any other children down the hall.

He finishes the story and lets me sip his tea. It's bitter, but I'm happy there on his lap.

For days Malachy's tongue is swollen and he can hardly make a sound never mind talk. But even if he could no one is paying any attention to him because we have two new babies who were brought by an angel in the middle of the night. The neighbors say, Ooh, Ah, they're lovely boys, look at those big eyes.

Malachy stands in the middle of the room, looking up at everyone, pointing to his tongue and saying, Uck, uck. When the neighbors say, Can't you see we're looking at your little brothers? he cries, till Dad pats him on the head. Put in your tongue, son, and go out and play with Frankie. Go on.

In the playground I tell Malachy about the dog who died in the street because someone drove a ball into his mouth. Malachy shakes his head. No uck ball. Car uck kill dog. He cries because his tongue hurts and he can hardly talk and it's terrible when you can't talk. He won't let me push him on the swing. He says, You uck kill me uck on seesaw. He gets Freddie Leibowitz to push him and he's happy, laughing when he swings to the sky. Freddie is big, he's seven, and I ask him to push me. He says, No, you tried to kill your brother.

I try to get the swing going myself but all I can do is move it back and forth and I'm angry because Freddie and Malachy are laughing at the way I can't swing. They're great pals now, Freddie, seven, Malachy, two. They laugh every day and Malachy's tongue gets better with all the laughing.

When he laughs you can see how white and small and pretty his teeth are and you can see his eyes shine. He has blue eyes like my mother. He has golden hair and pink cheeks. I have brown eyes like Dad. I have black hair and my cheeks are white in the mirror. My mother tells Mrs. Leibowitz down the hall that Malachy is the happiest child in the world. She tells Mrs. Leibowitz down the hall, Frankie has the odd manner like his father. I wonder what the odd manner is but I can't ask because I'm not supposed to be listening.

I wish I could swing up into the sky, up into the clouds. I might be able to fly around the whole world and not hear my brothers, Oliver and Eugene, cry in the middle of the night anymore. My mother says they're always hungry. She cries in the middle of the night, too. She says she's worn out nursing and feeding and changing and four boys is too much for her. She wishes she had one little girl all for herself. She'd give anything for one little girl.

I'm in the playground with Malachy. I'm four, he's three. He lets me push him on the swing because he's no good at swinging himself and Freddie Leibowitz is in school. We have to stay in the playground because the twins are sleeping and my mother says she's worn out. Go out and play, she says, and give me some rest. Dad is out looking for a job again and sometimes he comes home with the smell of whiskey, singing all the songs about suffering Ireland. Mam gets angry and says Ireland can kiss her arse. He says that's nice language to be using in front of the children and she says never mind the language, food on the table is what she wants, not suffering Ireland. She says it was a sad day Prohibition ended because Dad gets the drink going around to saloons offering to sweep out the bars and lift barrels for a whiskey or a beer. Sometimes he brings home bits of the free lunch, rye bread, corned beef, pickles. He puts the food on the table and drinks tea himself. He says food is a shock to the system and he doesn't know where we get our appetites. Mam says, They get their appetites because they're starving half the time.

When Dad gets a job Mam is cheerful and she sings,

> *Anyone can see why I wanted your kiss,*
> *It had to be and the reason is this*
> *Could it be true, someone like you*
> *Could love me, love me?*

When Dad brings home the first week's wages Mam is delighted she can pay the lovely Italian man in the grocery shop and she can hold her head up again because there's nothing worse in the world than to owe and be beholden to anyone. She cleans the kitchen, washes the mugs and plates, brushes crumbs and bits of food from the table, cleans out the icebox and orders a fresh block of ice from another Italian. She buys toilet paper that we can take down the hall to the lavatory and that, she says, is better than having the headlines from the *Daily News* blackening your arse. She boils water on the stove and spends a day at a great tin tub washing our shirts and socks, diapers for the twins, our two sheets, our three towels. She hangs everything out on the clotheslines behind the apartment house and we can watch the clothes dance in wind and sun. She says you wouldn't want the neighbors to know what you have in the way of a wash but there's nothing like the sweetness of clothes dried by the sun.

When Dad brings home the first week's wages on a Friday night we know the weekend will be wonderful. On Saturday night Mam will boil water on the stove and wash us in the great tin tub and Dad will dry us. Malachy will turn around and show his behind. Dad will pretend to be shocked and we'll all laugh. Mam will make hot cocoa and we'll be able to stay up while Dad tells us a story out of his head. All we have to do is say a name, Mr. MacAdorey or Mr. Leibowitz down the hall, and Dad will have the two of them rowing up a river in Brazil chased by Indians with green noses and puce shoulders. On nights like that we can drift off to sleep knowing there will be a breakfast of eggs, fried tomatoes and fried bread, tea with lashings of sugar and milk and, later in the day, a big dinner of mashed potatoes, peas and ham, and a trifle Mam makes, layers of fruit and warm delicious custard on a cake soaked in sherry.

When Dad brings home the first week's wages and the weather is fine Mam takes us to the playground. She sits on a bench and talks to Minnie MacAdorey. She tells Minnie stories about characters in Limerick and Minnie tells her about characters in Belfast and they laugh because there are funny people in Ireland, North and South. Then they teach each other sad songs and Malachy and I leave the swings and see-saws to sit with them on the bench and sing,

> *A group of young soldiers one night in a camp*
> *Were talking of sweethearts they had.*
> *All seemed so merry except one young lad,*
> *And he was downhearted and sad.*
> *Come and join us, said one of the boys,*
> *Surely there's someone for you.*
> *But Ned shook his head and proudly he said*
> *I am in love with two, Each like a mother to me,*
> *From neither of them shall I part.*
> *For one is my mother, God bless her and love her,*
> *The other is my sweetheart.*

Malachy and I sing that song and Mam and Minnie laugh till they cry at the way Malachy takes a deep bow and holds his arms out to Mam at the end. Dan MacAdorey comes along on his way home from work and says Rudy Vallee better start worrying about the competition.

When we go home Mam makes tea and bread and jam or mashed potatoes with butter and salt. Dad drinks the tea and eats nothing. Mam says, God above, How can you work all day and not eat? He says, The tea is enough. She says, You'll ruin your health, and he tells her again that food is a shock to the system. He drinks his tea and tells us stories and shows us letters and words in the *Daily News* or he smokes a cigarette, stares at the wall, runs his tongue over his lips.

When Dad's job goes into the third week he does not bring home the wages. On Friday night we wait for him and Mam gives us bread and tea. The darkness comes down and the lights come on along Classon Avenue. Other men with jobs are home already and having eggs for dinner because you can't have meat on a Friday. You can hear the families talking upstairs and downstairs and down the hall and Bing Crosby is singing on the radio, Brother, can you spare a dime?

Malachy and I play with the twins. We know Mam won't sing Anyone can see why I wanted your kiss. She sits at the kitchen table talking to herself, What am I going to do? till it's late and Dad rolls up the stairs singing Roddy McCorley. He pushes in the door and calls for us, Where are my troops? Where are my four warriors?

Mam says, Leave those boys alone. They're gone to bed half hungry because you have to fill your belly with whiskey.

He comes to the bedroom door. Up, boys, up. A nickel for everyone who promises to die for Ireland.

> Deep in Canadian woods we met
> From one bright island flown.
> Great is the land we tread, but yet
> Our hearts are with our own.

Up, boys, up. Francis, Malachy, Oliver, Eugene. The Red Branch Knights, the Fenian Men, the IRA. Up, up.

Mam is at the kitchen table, shaking, her hair hanging damp, her face wet. Can't you leave them alone? she says. Jesus, Mary and Joseph, isn't it enough that you come home without a penny in your pocket without making fools of the children on top of it?

She comes to us. Go back to bed, she says.

I want them up, he says. I want them ready for the day Ireland will be free from the center to the sea.

Don't cross me, she says, for if you do it'll be a sorry day in your mother's house.

He pulls his cap down over his face and cries, My poor mother. Poor Ireland. Och, what are we going to do?

Mam says, You're pure stone mad, and she tells us again to go to bed.

On the morning of the fourth Friday of Dad's job Mam asks him if he'll be home tonight with his wages or will he drink everything again? He looks at us and shakes his head at Mam as if to say, Och, you shouldn't talk like that in front of the children.

Mam keeps at him. I'm asking you, Are you coming home so that we can have a bit of supper or will it be midnight with no money in your pocket and you singing Kevin Barry and the rest of the sad songs?

He puts on his cap, shoves his hands into his trouser pockets, sighs and looks up at the ceiling. I told you before I'll be home, he says.

Later in the day Mam dresses us. She puts the twins into the pram and off we go through the long streets of Brooklyn. Sometimes she lets Malachy sit in the pram when he's tired of trotting along beside her. She tells me I'm too big for the pram. I could tell her I have pains in my legs from trying to keep up with her but she's not singing and I know this is not the day to be talking about my pains.

We come to a big gate where there's a man standing in a box with windows all around. Mam talks to the man. She wants to know if she can go inside to where the men are paid and maybe they'd give her some of Dad's wages so he wouldn't spend it in the bars. The man shakes his head. I'm sorry, lady, but if we did that we'd have half the wives in Brooklyn storming the place. Lotta men have the drinking problem but there's nothing we can do long as they show up sober and do their work.

We wait across the street. Mam lets me sit on the sidewalk with my back against the wall. She gives the twins their bottles of water and sugar but Malachy and I have to wait till she gets money from Dad and we can go to the Italian for tea and bread and eggs.

When the whistle blows at half five men in caps and overalls swarm through the gate, their faces and hands black from the work. Mam tells us watch carefully for Dad because she can hardly see across the street herself, her eyes are that bad. There are dozens of men, then a few, then none. Mam is crying, Why couldn't ye see him? Are ye blind or what?

She goes back to the man in the box. Are you sure there wouldn't be one man left inside?

No, lady, he says. They're out. I don't know how he got past you.

We go back through the long streets of Brooklyn. The twins hold up their bottles and cry for more water and sugar. Malachy says he's hungry and Mam tells him wait a little, we'll get money from Dad and we'll all have a nice supper. We'll go to the Italian and get eggs and make toast with the flames on the stove and we'll have jam on it. Oh, we will, and we'll all be nice and warm.

It's dark on Atlantic Avenue and all the bars around the Long Island Railroad Station are bright and noisy. We go from bar to bar looking for Dad. Mam leaves us outside with the pram while she goes in or she sends

7/8/2003

me. There are crowds of noisy men and stale smells that remind me of Dad when he comes home with the smell of the whiskey on him.

The man behind the bar says, Yeah, sonny, whaddya want? You're not supposeta be in here, y'know.

I'm looking for my father. Is my father here?

Naw, sonny, how'd I know dat? Who's your fawdah?

His name is Malachy and he sings Kevin Barry.

Malarkey?

No, Malachy.

Malachy? And he sings Kevin Barry?

He calls out to the men in the bar, Youse guys, youse know guy Malachy what sings Kevin Barry?

Men shake their heads. One says he knew a guy Michael sang Kevin Barry but he died of the drink which he had because of his war wounds.

The barman says, Jeez, Pete, I didn't ax ya to tell me history o' da woild, did I? Naw, kid. We don't let people sing in here. Causes trouble. Specially the Irish. Let 'em sing, next the fists are flying. Besides, I never hoid a name like dat Malachy. Naw, kid, no Malachy here.

The man called Pete holds his glass toward me. Here, kid, have a sip, but the barman says, Whaddya doin', Pete? Tryina get the kid drunk? Do that again, Pete, an' I'll come out an' break y'ass.

Mam tries all the bars around the station before she gives up. She leans against a wall and cries. Jesus, we still have to walk all the way to Classon Avenue and I have four starving children. She sends me back into the bar where Pete offered me the sip to see if the barman would fill the twins' bottles with water and maybe a little sugar in each. The men in the bar think it's very funny that the barman should be filling baby bottles but he's big and he tells them shut their lip. He tells me babies should be drinking milk not water and when I tell him Mam doesn't have the money he empties the baby bottles and fills them with milk. He says, Tell ya mom they need that for the teeth an' bones. Ya drink water an' sugar an' all ya get is rickets. Tell ya Mom.

Mam is happy with the milk. She says she knows all about teeth and bones and rickets but beggars can't be choosers.

When we reach Classon Avenue she goes straight to the Italian grocery shop. She tells the man her husband is late tonight, that he's probably working overtime, and would it be at all possible to get a few things and she'll be sure to see him tomorrow?

The Italian says, Missus, you always pay your bill sooner or later and you can have anything you like in this store.

Oh, she says, I don't want much.

Anything you like, missus, because I know you're an honest woman and you got a bunch o' nice kids there.

We have eggs and toast and jam though we're so weary walking the long streets of Brooklyn we can barely move our jaws to chew. The twins fall asleep after eating and Mam lays them on the bed to change their diapers. She sends me down the hall to rinse the dirty diapers in the lavatory so that they can be hung up to dry and used the next day. Malachy helps her wash the twins' bottoms though he's ready to fall asleep himself.

I crawl into bed with Malachy and the twins. I look out at Mam at the kitchen table, smoking a cigarette, drinking tea, and crying. I want to get up and tell her I'll be a man soon and I'll get a job in the place with the big gate and I'll come home every Friday night with money for eggs and toast and jam and she can sing again Anyone can see why I wanted your kiss.

The next week Dad loses the job. He comes home that Friday night, throws his wages on the table and says to Mam, Are you happy now? You hang around the gate complaining and accusing and they sack me. They were looking for an excuse and you gave it to them.

He takes a few dollars from his wages and goes out. He comes home late roaring and singing. The twins cry and Mam shushes them and cries a long time herself.

We spend hours in the playground when the twins are sleeping, when Mam is tired, and when Dad comes home with the whiskey smell on him, roaring about Kevin Barry getting hanged on a Monday morning or the Roddy McCorley song,

> Up the narrow street he stepped
> Smiling and proud and young
> About the hemp-rope on his neck
> The golden ringlets clung,
> There's never a tear in the blue eyes
> Both glad and bright are they,
> As Roddy McCorley goes to die
> On the bridge of Toome today.

When he sings he marches around the table, Mam cries and the twins howl with her. She says, Go out, Frankie, go out, Malachy. You shouldn't see your father like this. Stay in the playground.

We don't mind going to the playground. We can play with the leaves piling up on the ground and we can push each other on the swings but then winter comes to Classon Avenue and the swings are frozen and won't even move. Minnie MacAdorey says, God help these poor wee boys. They don't have a glove between them. That makes me laugh because I know Malachy and I have four hands between us and one glove would be silly. Malachy doesn't know what I'm laughing at: He won't know anything till he's four going on five.

Minnie brings us in and gives us tea and porridge with jam in it. Mr. MacAdorey sits in an armchair with their new baby, Maisie. He holds her bottle and sings,

> *Clap hands, clap hands,*
> *Till Daddy comes home,*
> *With buns in his pocket*
> *For Maisie alone.*
> *Clap hands, clap hands,*
> *Till Daddy comes home,*
> *For Daddy has money*
> *And Mammy has none.*

Malachy tries to sing that song but I tell him stop, it's Maisie's song. He starts to cry and Minnie says, There, there. You can sing the song. That's a song for all the children. Mr. MacAdorey smiles at Malachy and I wonder what kind of world is it where anyone can sing anyone else's song.

Minnie says, Don't frown, Frankie. It makes your face dark and God knows it's dark enough. Some day you'll have a little sister and you can sing that song to her. Och, aye. You'll have a little sister, surely.

Minnie is right and Mam gets her wish. There's a new baby soon, a little girl, and they call her Margaret. We all love Margaret. She has black curly hair and blue eyes like Mam and she waves her little hands and chirps like any little bird in the trees along Classon Avenue. Minnie says there was a holiday in heaven the day this child was made. Mrs.

Leibowitz says the world never saw such eyes, such a smile, such happiness. She makes me dance, says Mrs. Leibowitz.

When Dad comes home from looking for a job he holds Margaret and sings to her:

> *In a shady nook one moonlit night*
> *A leprechaun I spied.*
> *With scarlet cap and coat of green*
> *A cruiskeen by his side.*
> *'Twas tick tock tick his hammer went*
> *Upon a tiny shoe.*
> *Oh, I laugh to think he was caught at last,*
> *But the fairy was laughing, too.*

He walks around the kitchen with her and talks to her. He tells her how lovely she is with her curly black hair and the blue eyes of her mother. He tells her he'll take her to Ireland and they'll walk the Glens of Antrim and swim in Lough Neagh. He'll get a job soon, so he will, and she'll have dresses of silk and shoes with silver buckles.

The more Dad sings to Margaret the less she cries and as the days pass she even begins to laugh. Mam says, Look at him trying to dance with that child in his arms, him with his two left feet. She laughs and we all laugh.

The twins cried when they were small and Dad and Mam would say Whisht and Hush and feed them and they'd go back to sleep. But when Margaret cries there's a high lonely feeling in the air and Dad is out of bed in a second, holding her to him, doing a slow dance around the table, singing to her, making sounds like a mother. When he passes the window where the streetlight shines in you can see tears on his cheeks and that's strange because he never cries for anyone unless he has the drink taken and he sings the Kevin Barry song and the Roddy McCorley song. Now he cries over Margaret and he has no smell of drink on him.

Mam tells Minnie MacAdorey, He's in heaven over that child. He hasn't touched a drop since she was born. I should've had a little girl a long time ago.

Och, they're lovely, aren't they? says Minnie. The little boys are grand, too, but you need a little girl for yourself.

My mother laughs, For myself? Lord above, if I didn't nurse her I wouldn't be able to get near her the way he wants to be holding her day and night.

Minnie says it's lovely, all the same, to see a man so charmed with his little girl for isn't everyone charmed with her?

Everyone.

The twins are able to stand and walk and they have accidents all the time. Their bottoms are sore because they're always wet and shitty. They put dirty things in their mouths, bits of paper, feathers, shoelaces, and they get sick. Mam says we're all driving her crazy. She dresses the twins, puts them in the pram, and Malachy and I take them to the playground. The cold weather is gone and the trees have green leaves up and down Classon Avenue.

We race the pram around the playground and the twins laugh and make goo-goo sounds till they get hungry and start to cry. There are two bottles in the pram filled with water and sugar and that keeps them quiet for awhile till they're hungry again and they cry so hard I don't know what to do because they're so small and I wish I could give them all kinds of food so that they'd laugh and make the baby sounds. They love the mushy food Mam makes in a pot, bread mashed up in milk and water and sugar. Mam calls it bread and goody.

If I take the twins home now Mam will yell at me for giving her no rest or for waking Margaret. We are to stay in the playground till she sticks her head out the window and calls for us. I make funny faces for the twins to stop their crying. I put a piece of paper on my head and let it fall and they laugh and laugh. I push the pram over to Malachy playing on the swings with Freddie Leibowitz. Malachy is trying to tell Freddie all about the way Setanta became Cuchulain. I tell him stop telling that story, it's my story. He won't stop. I push him and he cries, Waah, waah, I'll tell Mam. Freddie pushes me and everything turns dark in my head and I run at him with fists and knees and feet till he yells, Hey, stop, stop, and I won't because I can't, I don't know how, and if I stop Malachy will go on taking my story from me. Freddie pushes me away and runs off, yelling, Frankie tried to kill me. Frankie tried to kill me. I don't know what to do because I never tried to kill anyone before and now Malachy, on the swing, cries, Don't kill me, Frankie, and he looks so helpless I put my arms around him and help him off the swing. He hugs me. I won't tell your story anymore. I won't tell Freddie about Coo, Coo. I want to laugh but I can't because the twins are crying in the pram and it's dark in the playground and what's the use of trying to make funny faces and letting things fall off your head when they can't see you in the dark?

The Italian grocery shop is across the street and I see bananas, apples, oranges. I know the twins can eat bananas. Malachy loves bananas and I like them myself. But you need money, Italians are not known for giving away bananas especially to the McCourts who owe them money already for groceries.

My mother tells me all the time, Never, never leave that playground except to come home. But what am I to do with the twins bawling with the hunger in the pram? I tell Malachy I'll be back in a minute. I make sure no one is looking, grab a bunch of bananas outside the Italian grocery shop and run down Myrtle Avenue, away from the playground, around the block and back to the other end where there's a hole in the fence. We push the pram to a dark corner and peel the bananas for the twins. There are five bananas in the bunch and we feast on them in the dark corner. The twins slobber and chew and spread banana over their faces, their hair, their clothes. I realize then that questions will be asked. Mam will want to know why the twins are smothered in bananas, where did you get them? I can't tell her about the Italian shop on the corner. I will have to say, A man.

That's what I'll say. A man.

Then the strange thing happens. There's a man at the gate of the playground. He's calling me. Oh, God, it's the Italian. Hey, sonny, come 'ere. Hey, talkin' to ya. Come 'ere.

I go to him.

You the kid wid the little bruddas, right? Twins?

Yes, sir.

Heah. Gotta bag o' fruit. I don' give it to you I trow id out. Right? So, heah, take the bag. Ya got apples, oranges, bananas. Ya like bananas, right? I think ya like bananas, eh? Ha, ha. I know ya like the bananas. Heah, take the bag. Ya gotta nice mother there. Ya father? Well, ya know, he's got the problem, the Irish thing. Give them twins a banana. Shud 'em up. I hear 'em all the way cross the street.

Thank you, sir.

Jeez. Polite kid, eh? Where ja loin dat?

My father told me to say thanks, sir.

Your father? Oh, well.

Dad sits at the table reading the paper. He says that President Roosevelt is a good man and everyone in America will soon have a job. Mam is on the other side of the table feeding Margaret with a bottle. She has the hard look that frightens me.

Where did you get that fruit?

The man.

What man?

The Italian man gave it to me.

Did you steal that fruit?

Malachy says, The man. The man gave Frankie the bag.

And what did you do to Freddie Leibowitz? His mother was here. Lovely woman. I don't know what we'd do without her and Minnie MacAdorey. And you had to attack poor Freddie.

Malachy jumps up and down. He din't. He din't. Din't try to kill Freddie. Din't try to kill me.

Dad says, Whisht, Malachy, whisht. Come over here. And he takes Malachy on his lap.

My mother says, Go down the hall and tell Freddie you're sorry.

But Dad says, Do you want to tell Freddie you're sorry?

I don't.

My parents look at one another. Dad says, Freddie is a good boy. He was only pushing your little brother on the swing. Isn't that right?

He was trying to steal my Cuchulain story.

Och, now. Freddie doesn't care about the Cuchulain story. He has his own story. Hundreds of stories. He's Jewish.

What's Jewish?

Dad laughs. Jewish is, Jewish is people with their own stories. They don't need Cuchulain. They have Moses. They have Samson.

What's Samson?

If you go down and talk to Freddie I'll tell you about Samson later. You can tell Freddie you're sorry and you'll never do it again and you can even ask him about Samson. Anything you like as long as you talk to Freddie. Will you?

The baby gives a little cry in my mother's arms and Dad jumps up, dropping Malachy to the floor. Is she all right? My mother says, Of course she's all right. She's feeding. God above, you're a bundle of nerves.

They're talking about Margaret now and I'm forgotten. I don't care. I'm going down the hall to ask Freddie about Samson, to see if Samson is as good as Cuchulain, to see if Freddie has his own story or if he still wants to steal Cuchulain. Malachy wants to go with me now that my father is standing and doesn't have a lap anymore.

Mrs. Leibowitz says, Oh, Frankie, Frankie, come in, come in. And little Malachy. And tell me, Frankie, what did you do to Freddie? Tried to kill him? Freddie is a good boy, Frankie. Reads his book. Listens to radio with his papa. He swinks you brother on swink. And you try to kill him. Oh, Frankie, Frankie. And you poor mother and her sick baby.

She's not sick, Mrs. Leibowitz.

Sick she is. Zat is one sick baby. I know from sick babies. I work in hoztipal. Don't tell me, Frankie. Come in, come in. Freddie, Freddie, Frankie is here. Come out. Frankie won't kill you no more. You and little Malachy. Nice Chewish name, have piece cake, eh? Why they give you a Chewish name, eh? So, glass milk, piece cake. You boys so thin, Irish don't eat.

We sit at the table with Freddie, eating cake, drinking milk. Mr. Leibowitz sits in an armchair reading the paper, listening to the radio. Sometimes he speaks to Mrs. Leibowitz and I don't understand because strange sounds come from his mouth. Freddie understands. When Mr. Leibowitz makes the strange sounds Freddie gets up and takes him a piece of cake. Mr. Leibowitz smiles at Freddie and pats his head and Freddie smiles back and makes the strange sounds.

Mrs. Leibowitz shakes her head at Malachy and me. Oy, so thin. She says Oy so much Malachy laughs and says Oy and the Leibowitzes laugh and Mr. Leibowitz says words we can understand, When Irish oyes are smiling. Mrs. Leibowitz laughs so hard her body shakes and she holds her stomach and Malachy says Oy again because he knows that makes everyone laugh. I say Oy but no one laughs and I know Oy belongs to Malachy the way Cuchulain belongs to me and Malachy can have his Oy.

Mrs. Leibowitz, my father said Freddie has a favorite story.

Malachy says, Sam, Sam, Oy. Everyone laughs again but I don't because I can't remember what comes after Sam. Freddie mumbles through his cake, Samson, and Mrs. Leibowitz tells him, Don't talk wiz you mouse full, and I laugh because she's grown-up and she says mouse instead of mouth. Malachy laughs because I laugh and the Leibowitzes look at each other and smile. Freddie says, Not Samson. My favorite story is David and the giant, Goliath. David killed him dead with a slingshot, a stone in his head. His brains was on the ground.

Were on the ground, says Mr. Leibowitz.

Yes, Papa.

Papa. That's what Freddie calls his father and Dad is what I call my father.

My mother's whisper wakes me. What's up with the child? It's still early and there isn't much morning in the room but you can see Dad over by the window with Margaret in his arms. He's rocking her and sighing, Och.

Mam says, Is she, is she sick?

Och, she's very quiet and she's a wee bit cold.

My mother is out of the bed, taking the child. Go for the doctor. Go for God's sake, and my father is pulling on his trousers over his shirt, no jacket, shoes, no socks on this bitter day.

We wait in the room, the twins asleep at the bottom of the bed, Malachy stirring beside me. Frankie, I want a drink of water. Mam rocks in her bed with the baby in her arms. Oh, Margaret, Margaret, my own little love. Open your lovely blue eyes, my little leanv.

I fill a cup of water for Malachy and me and my mother wails, Water for you and your brother. Oh, indeed, Water, is it? And nothing for your sister. Your poor little sister. Did you ask if she had a mouth in her head? Did you ask if she'd like a drop of water? Oh, no. Go on and drink your water, you and your brother, as if nothing happened. A regular day for the two of you, isn't it? And the twins sleeping away as if they didn't have a care and their poor little sister sick here in my arms. Sick in my arms. Oh, sweet Jesus in heaven.

Why is she talking like this? She's not talking like my mother today. I want my father. Where is my father?

I get back into bed and start to cry. Malachy says, Why you cry? Why you cry? till Mam is at me again. Your sister is sick in my arms and you're there whining and whinging. If I go over to that bed I'll give you something to whinge about.

Dad is back with the doctor. Dad has the whiskey smell. The doctor examines the baby, prods her, raises her eyelids, feels her neck, arms, legs. He straightens up and shakes his head. She's gone. Mam reaches for the baby, hugs her, turns to the wall. The doctor wants to know, Was there any kind of accident? Did anyone drop the baby? Did the boys play too hard with her? Anything?

My father shakes his head. Doctor says he'll have to take her to examine her and Dad signs a paper. My mother begs for another few minutes with her baby but the doctor says he doesn't have all day. When Dad reaches for Margaret my mother pulls away against the wall. She has the wild look, her black curly hair is damp on her forehead and there is sweat all over her face, her eyes are wide open and her face is shiny with tears, she keeps shaking her head and moaning, Ah, no, ah, no, till Dad eases the baby from her arms. The doctor wraps Margaret completely in a blanket and my mother cries, Oh, Jesus, you'll smother her. Jesus, Mary and Joseph, help me. The doctor leaves. My mother turns to the wall and doesn't make a move or sound. The twins are awake, crying with the hunger, but Dad stands in the middle of the room, staring at the ceiling. His face is white and he beats on his thighs with his fists. He comes to the bed, puts his hand on my head. His hand is shaking. Francis, I'm going out for cigarettes.

Mam stays in the bed all day, hardly moving. Malachy and I fill the twins' bottles with water and sugar. In the kitchen we find a half loaf of stale bread and two cold sausages. We can't have tea because the milk is sour in the icebox where the ice is melted again and everyone knows you can't drink tea without milk unless your father gives it to you out of his mug while he's telling you about Cuchulain.

The twins are hungry again but I know I can't give them water and sugar all day and night. I boil sour milk in a pot, mash in some of the stale bread, and try to feed them from a cup, bread and goody. They make faces and run to Mam's bed, crying. She keeps her face to the wall and they run back to me, still crying. They won't eat the bread and goody till I kill the taste of the sour milk with sugar. Now they eat and smile and rub the goody over their faces. Malachy wants some and if he can eat it, so can I. We all sit on the floor eating the goody and chewing on the cold sausage and drinking water my mother keeps in a milk bottle in the icebox.

After we eat and drink we have to go to the lavatory down the hall but we can't get in because Mrs. Leibowitz is inside, humming and singing. She says, Wait, chiltren, wait, darlinks. Won't be two seconds. Malachy claps his hands and dances around, singing, Wait, chiltren, wait, darlinks. Mrs. Leibowitz opens the lavatory door. Look at him. Little actor awready. So, chiltren, how's you mother?

She's in bed, Mrs. Leibowitz. The doctor took Margaret and my father went for cigarettes.

Oh, Frankie, Frankie. I said that was one sick child.

Malachy is clutching himself. Have to pee. Have to pee.

So, pee awready. You boys pee and we see you mother.

After we pee Mrs. Leibowitz comes to see Mam. Oh, Mrs. McCourt. Oy vey, darlink. Look at this. Look at these twins. Naked. Mrs. McCourt, what is mazzer, eh? The baby she is sick? So talk to me. Poor woman. Here turn around, missus. Talk to me. Oy, this is one mess. Talk to me, Mrs. McCourt.

She helps my mother sit up against the wall. Mam seems smaller. Mrs. Leibowitz says she'll bring some soup and tells me get some water to wash my mother's face. I dip a towel in cold water and pat her forehead. She presses my hand against her cheeks. Oh, Jesus, Frankie. Oh, Jesus. She won't let my hand go and I'm frightened because I've never seen her like this before. She's saying Frankie only because it's my hand she's holding and it's Margaret she's thinking about, not me. Your lovely little sister is dead, Frankie. Dead. And where is your father? She lets my hand drop. I said where is your father? Drinking. That's where he is. There isn't a penny in the house. He can't get a job but he finds money for the drink, money for the drink, money for the drink, money for the drink. She rears back, knocks her head on the wall and screams, Where is she? Where is she? Where is my little girl? Oh, Jesus, Mary and Joseph, help me this night. I'll go mad, so I will, I'll go pure mad.

Mrs. Leibowitz rushes in. Missus, missus, what is it? The little girl. Where is she?

My mother screams again, Dead, Mrs. Leibowitz. Dead. Her head drops and she rocks back and forth. Middle of the night, Mrs. Leibowitz. In her pram. I should have been watching her. Seven weeks she had in this world and died in the middle of the night, alone, Mrs. Leibowitz, all alone in that pram.

Mrs. Leibowitz holds my mother in her arms. Shush, now, shush. Babies go like that. It happens, missus. God takes them.

In the pram, Mrs. Leibowitz. Near my bed. I could have picked her up and she didn't have to die, did she? God doesn't want little babies. What is God going to do with little babies?

I don't know, missus. I don't know from God. Have soup. Good soup. Make you strong. You boys. Get bowls. I give you soup.

What's bowls, Mrs. Leibowitz?

Oh, Frankie. You don't know bowl? For the soup, darlink. You don' have a bowl? So get cups for the soup. I mix pea soup and lentil soup. No ham. Irish like the ham. No ham, Frankie. Drink, missus. Drink you soup.

She spoons the soup into my mother's mouth, wipes the dribble from her chin. Malachy and I sit on the floor drinking from mugs. We spoon the soup into the twins' mouths. It is lovely and hot and tasty. My mother never makes soup like this and I wonder if there's any chance Mrs. Leibowitz could ever be my mother. Freddie could be me and have my mother and my father, too, and he could have Malachy and the twins for brothers. He can't have Margaret anymore because she's like the dog in the street that was taken away. I don't know why she was taken away. My mother said she died in her pram and that must be like getting hit by a car because they take you away.

I wish little Margaret could be here for the soup. I could give it to her with a spoon the way Mrs. Leibowitz is giving it to my mother and she'd gurgle and laugh the way she did with Dad. She wouldn't cry anymore and my mother wouldn't be in the bed day and night and Dad would be telling me Cuchulain stories and I wouldn't want Mrs. Leibowitz to be my mother anymore. Mrs. Leibowitz is nice but I'd rather have my father telling me Cuchulain stories and Margaret chirping and Mam laughing when Dad dances with two left feet.

Minnie MacAdorey comes in to help. Mother o' God, Mrs. Leibowitz, these twins smell to the high heavens.

I don't know about Mother o' God, Minnie, but these twins need a wash. They need clean diapers. Frankie, where are the clean diapers?

I don't know.

Minnie says, They're just wearing rags for diapers. I'll get some of Maisie's. Frankie, you take off those rags and throw them out.

Malachy removes Oliver's rag and I struggle with Eugene. The safety pin is stuck and when he wriggles it comes loose, sticks him in the hip, and starts him screaming for Mam. But Minnie is back with a towel and soap and hot water. I help her wash away the caked shit and she lets me shake talcum powder on the twins' raw sore skin. She says they're good little boys and she has a big surprise for them. She goes down the hall and brings back a pot of mashed potatoes for all of us. There is plenty of salt and butter in the potatoes and I wonder if there's any chance Minnie could be my mother so that I could eat like this all the time. If I could have Mrs. Leibowitz and Minnie for mothers at the same time I'd have no end of soup and mashed potatoes.

Minnie and Mrs. Leibowitz sit at the table. Mrs. Leibowitz says something has to be done. These children are running wild and where is the father? I hear Minnie whisper he's out for the drink. Mrs. Leibowitz says terrible, terrible, the way the Irish drink. Minnie says her Dan doesn't drink. Never touches the stuff and Dan told her that when the baby died that poor man, Malachy McCourt, went mad all over Flatbush Avenue and Atlantic Avenue, that he was thrown out of all the bars around the Long Island Railroad Station, that the cops would have thrown him in jail if it was anything else but the death of that lovely little baby.

Here he has four lovely little boys, says Minnie, but it's no comfort to him. That little girl brought out something in him. You know he didn't even drink after she was born and that was a miracle.

Mrs. Leibowitz wants to know where Mam's cousins are, the big women with the quiet husbands. Minnie will find them and tell them the children are neglected, running wild, sore arses and everything.

Two days later Dad returns from his cigarette hunt. It's the middle of the night but he gets Malachy and me out of the bed. He has the smell of the drink on him. He has us stand at attention in the kitchen. We are soldiers. He tells us we must promise to die for Ireland.

We will, Dad, we will.

All together we sing Kevin Barry,

On Mountjoy one Monday morning,
High upon the gallows tree,
Kevin Barry gave his young life
For the cause of liberty.
Just a lad of eighteen summers
Sure there's no one can deny
As he marched to death that morning
How he held his head on high.

There's a knock at the door, Mr. MacAdorey. Och, Malachy, for God's sake, it's three in the morning. You have the whole house woke with the singing.

Och, Dan, I'm only teaching the boys to die for Ireland.

You can teach them to die for Ireland in the daytime, Malachy.

'Tis urgent, Dan, 'tis urgent.

I know, Malachy, but they're only children. Babies. You go to bed now like a dacent man.

Bed, Dan! What am I to do in bed? Her little face is there day and night, her curly black hair and her lovely blue eyes. Oh, Jesus, Dan, what will I do? Was it the hunger that killed her, Dan?

Of course not. Your missus was nursing her. God took her. He has his reasons.

One more song, Dan, before we go to bed.

Good night, Malachy.

Come on, boys. Sing.

Because he loved the motherland,
Because he loved the green
He goes to meet a martyr's fate
With proud and joyous mien;
True to the last, oh! true to the last
He treads the upward way;
Young Roddy McCorley goes to die
On the bridge at Toome today.

You'll die for Ireland, won't you, boys?

We will, Dad.

And we'll all meet your little sister in heaven, won't we, boys?

We will, Dad.

40

My brother is standing with his face pressed against a leg of the table and he's asleep. Dad lifts him, staggers across the room, places him in the bed by my mother. I climb into bed and my father, still in his clothes, lies beside me. I'm hoping he'll put his arms around me but he goes on singing about Roddy McCorley and talking to Margaret, Oh, my little curly-haired, blue-eyed love, I would dress you in silks and take you to Lough Neagh, till day is at the window and I fall asleep.

That night Cuchulain comes to me. There's a big green bird on his shoulder that keeps singing about Kevin Barry and Roddy McCorley and I don't like that bird because there's blood dripping from his mouth when he sings. In one hand Cuchulain carries the gae bolga, the spear that is so mighty only he can throw it. In the other hand he carries a banana, which he keeps offering to the bird, who just squawks and spits blood at him. You'd wonder why Cuchulain puts up with a bird like that. If the twins ever spat blood at me when I offered them a banana I think I'd hit them on the head with it.

In the morning my father is at the kitchen table and I tell him my dream. He says there were no bananas in Ireland in the old times and even if there were Cuchulain would never offer one to that bird because that was the one that came over from England for the summer and perched on his shoulder when he was dying and propped up against a stone and when the men of Erin which is Ireland wanted to kill him they were afraid till they saw the bird drinking Cuchulain's blood and then they knew it was safe to attack him, the dirty bloody cowards. So you have to be wary of birds, Francis, birds and Englishmen.

Most of the day Mam lies in bed with her face to the wall. If she drinks tea or eats anything she throws up in the bucket under the bed and I have to empty it and rinse it in the lavatory down the hall. Mrs. Leibowitz brings her soup and funny bread that is twisted. Mam tries to slice it but Mrs. Leibowitz laughs and tells her just pull. Malachy calls it pull bread but Mrs. Leibowitz says, No, it's challah, and teaches us how to say it. She shakes her head. Oy, you Irish. You'll live forever but you'll never say challah like a Chew.

Minnie MacAdorey brings potatoes and cabbage and sometimes a piece of meat. Och, times are hard, Angela, but that lovely man, Mr. Roosevelt, will find a job for everyone and your husband will have work. Poor man, it's not his fault there's a Depression. He looks for work day and night. My Dan is lucky, four years with the city and he don't drink. He grew up in Toome with your husband. Some drink. Some don't. Curse of the Irish. Now eat, Angela. Build yourself up after your loss.

Mr. MacAdorey tells Dad there's work with the WPA and when he gets the work there's money for food and Mam leaves the bed to clean the twins and to feed us. When Dad comes home with the drink smell there's no money and Mam screams at him till the twins cry, and Malachy and I run out to the playground. On those nights Mam crawls back into bed and Dad sings the sad songs about Ireland. Why doesn't he hold her and help her sleep the way he did with my little sister who died? Why doesn't he sing a Margaret song or a song that will dry Mam's tears? He still gets Malachy and me out of bed to stand in our shirts promising to die for Ireland. One night he wanted to make the twins promise to die for Ireland but they can't even talk and Mam screamed at him, You mad oul' bastard, can't you leave the children alone?

He'll give us a nickel for ice cream if we promise to die for Ireland and we promise but we never get the nickel.

We get soup from Mrs. Leibowitz and mashed potatoes from Minnie MacAdorey and they show us how to take care of the twins, how to wash their bottoms and how to wash diaper rags after they get them all shitty. Mrs. Leibowitz calls them diapers and Minnie calls them nappies but it doesn't matter what they call them because the twins get them shitty anyway. If Mam stays in the bed and Dad goes out looking for a job we can do what we like all day. We can put the twins in the small swings in the park and swing them till they get hungry and cry. The Italian man calls to me from across the street, Hey, Frankie, c'mere. Watch out crossing da street. Dem twins hungry again? He gives us bits of cheese and ham and bananas but I can't eat bananas anymore after the way the bird spat blood at Cuchulain.

The man says his name is Mr. Dimino and that's his wife, Angela, behind the counter. I tell him that's my mother's name. No kiddin', kid. Your mother is Angela? I didn't know the Irish had any Angelas. Hey, Angela, his mother's name is Angela. She smiles. She says, Thatsa nice.

Mr. Dimino asks me about Mam and Dad and who cooks for us. I tell him we get food from Mrs. Leibowitz and Minnie MacAdorey. I tell him all about the diapers and the nappies and how they get shitty anyway and he laughs. Angela, you listenin' to this? Thank God you're Italian, Angela. He says, Kid, I gotta talk to Mrs. Leibowitz. Ya gotta have relations can take care of you. Ya see Minnie MacAdorey, tell her come in see me. You kids runnin' wild.

Two big women are at the door. They say, Who are you?

I'm Frank.

Frank! How old are you?

I'm four going on five.

You're not very big for your age, are you?

I don't know.

Is your mother here?

She's in the bed.

What is she doing in the bed on a fine day in the middle of the day?

She's sleeping.

Well, we'll come in. We have to talk to your mother.

They brush past me into the room. Jesus, Mary and Joseph, the smell of this place. And who are these children?

Malachy runs smiling to the big women. When he smiles you can see how white and straight and pretty his teeth are and you can see the shiny blue of his eyes, the pink of his cheeks. All that makes the big women smile and I wonder why they didn't smile when they talked to me.

Malachy says, I'm Malachy and this is Oliver and this is Eugene, they're twins, and that's Frankie over there.

The big woman with the brown hair says, Well, you're not a bit shy, are you? I'm your mother's cousin, Philomena, and this is your mother's cousin, Delia. I'm Mrs. Flynn and she's Mrs. Fortune and that's what you call us.

Good God, says Philomena. Those twins are naked. Don't you have clothes for them?

Malachy says, They're all shitty.

Delia barks. See. That's what happens. A mouth like a sewer, and no wonder with a father from the North. Don't use that word. That's a bad word, a curse word. You could go to hell using a word like that.

43

What's hell? says Malachy. You'll know soon enough, says Delia.

The big women sit at the table with Mrs. Leibowitz and Minnie MacAdorey. Philomena says it's terrible what happened to Angela's little baby. They heard all about it and you'd wonder, wouldn't you, what they did with the little body. You might wonder and I might wonder but Tommy Flynn didn't wonder. Tommy said that Malachy from the North got money for that baby. Money? says Mrs. Leibowitz. That's right, says Philomena. Money. They take bodies any age and do experiments on them and there's not much left to give back nor would you want back bits of baby when they can't be buried in consecrated ground in that condition.

That's terrible, says Mrs. Leibowitz. A father or mother would never give the baby for something like that.

They would, says Delia, when they have the craving for the drink. They'd give their own mothers when they have the craving so what's a baby that's dead and gone in the first place?

Mrs. Leibowitz shakes her head and rocks in her chair. Oy, she says, oy, oy, oy. The poor baby. The poor mother. I thank God my husband don' have no what you call it? Craving? Right, craving. It's the Irish have the craving.

Not my husband, says Philomena. I'd break his face if he came home with the craving. Of course, Delia's Jimmy has the craving. Every Friday night you see him slipping into the saloon.

You needn't start insulting my Jimmy, says Delia. He works. He brings home his wages.

You'd want to keep an eye on him, says Philomena. The craving could get the better of him and you'd have another Malachy from the North on your hands.

Mind your own bloody business, says Delia. At least Jimmy is Irish, not born in Brooklyn like your Tommy.

And Philomena has no answer for that.

Minnie is holding her baby and the big women say she's a lovely baby, clean, not like this pack of Angela's running around this place. Philomena says she doesn't know where Angela got her dirty habits because Angela's mother was spotless, so clean you could eat your dinner off her floor.

I wonder why you'd want to eat your dinner off the floor when you had a table and a chair.

Delia says something has to be done about Angela and these children for they are a disgrace, so they are, enough to make you ashamed to be related. A letter has to be written to Angela's mother. Philomena will write it because a teacher in Limerick told her once she had a fine fist. Delia has to tell Mrs. Leibowitz that a fine fist means good handwriting.

Mrs. Leibowitz goes down the hall to borrow her husband's fountain pen, paper and an envelope. The four women sit at the table and make up a letter to send to my mother's mother:

Dear Aunt Margaret,

I take pen in hand to write you this letter and hope this finds you as it leaves us in the best of health. My husband Tommy is in fine form working away and Delia's husband Jimmy is in fine form working away and we hope this finds you in fine form. I am very sorry to tell you that Angela is not in fine form as the baby died, the little girl that was called Margaret after yourself, and Angela has not been the same since lying in the bed with her face to the wall. To make matters worser we think she's expecting again and that's too much altogether. The minute she losses one child there is another one on the way. We don't know how she does it. She's married four years, five children and another on the way. That shows you what can happen when you marry someone from the North for they have no control over themselves up there a bunch of Protestands that they are. He goes out for work every day but we know he spends all his time in the saloons and gets a few dollars for sweeping floors and lifting barrels and spends the money right back on the drink. It's terrible, Aunt Margaret, and we all think Angela and the children would be better off in her native land. We don't have the money to buy the tickets ourselves for times is hard but you might be able to see your way. Hopping this finds you in fine form as it leaves us thank God and His Blessed Mother.

> I remain your loving neice
> Philomena Flynn (what was MacNamara)
> and last but not least your neice
> Delia Fortune (what was MacNamara, too, ha ha ha)

45

Grandma Sheehan sent money to Philomena and Delia. They bought the tickets, found a steamer trunk at the St. Vincent de Paul Society, hired a van to take us to the pier in Manhattan, put us on the ship, said Good-bye and good riddance, and went away.

The ship pulled away from the dock. Mam said, That's the Statue of Liberty and that's Ellis Island where all the immigrants came in. Then she leaned over the side and vomited and the wind from the Atlantic blew it all over us and other happy people admiring the view. Passengers cursed and ran, seagulls came from all over the harbor and Mam hung limp and pale on the ship's rail.

II

In a week we arrived at Moville, County Donegal, where we took a bus to Belfast and from there another bus to Toome in County Antrim. We left the trunk in a shop and set out to walk the two miles up the road to Grandpa McCourt's house. It was dark on the road, the dawn barely stirring on the hills beyond.

Dad carried the twins in his arms and they took turns crying with the hunger. Mam stopped every few minutes to sit and rest on the stone wall along the road. We sat with her and watched the sky turn red and then blue. Birds started to chirp and sing in the trees and as the dawn came up we saw strange creatures in the fields, standing, looking at us. Malachy said, What are they, Dad?

Cows, son.

What are cows, Dad?

Cows are cows, son.

We walked farther along the brightening road and there were other creatures in the fields, white furry creatures.

Malachy said, What are they, Dad?

Sheep, son.

What are sheep, Dad?

My father barked at him, Is there any end to your questions? Sheep are sheep, cows are cows, and that over there is a goat. A goat is a goat.

The goat gives milk, the sheep gives wool, the cow gives everything. What else in God's name do you want to know?

And Malachy yelped with fright because Dad never talked like that, never spoke sharply to us. He might get us up in the middle of the night and make us promise to die for Ireland but he never barked like this. Malachy ran to Mam and she said, There, there, love, don't cry. Your father is just worn out carrying the twins and 'tis hard answering all those questions when you're carting twins through the world.

Dad set the twins on the road and held out his arms to Malachy. Now the twins started to cry and Malachy clung to Mam, sobbing. The cows mooed, the sheep maaed, the goat ehehed, the birds twittered in the trees, and the beep beep of a motor car cut through everything. A man called from the motor car, Good Lord, what are you people doing on this road at this hour of an Easter Sunday morning?

Dad said, Good morning, Father.

Father? I said. Dad, is that your father?

Mam said, Don't ask him any questions.

Dad said, No, no, this is a priest.

Malachy said, What's a—? but Mam put her hand over his mouth.

The priest had white hair and a white collar. He said, Where are you going?

Dad said, Up the road to McCourts of Moneyglass, and the priest took us in his motor car. He said he knew the McCourts, a fine family, good Catholics, some daily communicants, and he hoped he'd see us all at Mass, especially the little Yankees who didn't know what a priest was, God help us.

At the house my mother reaches for the gate latch. Dad says, No, no, not that way. Not the front gate. They use the front door only for visits from the priest or funerals.

We make our way around the house to the kitchen door. Dad pushes in the door and there's Grandpa McCourt drinking tea from a big mug and Grandma McCourt frying something.

Och, says Grandpa, you're here.

Och, we are, says Dad. He points to my mother. This is Angela, he says. Grandpa says, Och, you must be worn out, Angela. Grandma says nothing, she turns back to the frying pan. Grandpa leads us through the kitchen to a large room with a long table and chairs. He says, Sit down and have some tea. Would you like boxty?

Malachy says, What's boxty?

Dad laughs. Pancakes, son. Pancakes made with potatoes.

Grandpa says, We have eggs. It's Easter Sunday and you can have all the eggs you can hold.

We have tea and boxty and boiled eggs and we all fall asleep. I wake up in a bed with Malachy and the twins. My parents are in another bed over by the window. Where am I? It's getting dark. This is not the ship. Mam snores hink, Dad snores honk. I get up and poke at Dad. I have to pee. He says, Use the chamber pot.

What?

Under the bed, son. The chamber pot. It has roses on it and maidens cavorting in the glen. Pee in that, son.

I want to ask him what he's talking about for even if I'm bursting I feel strange peeing into a pot with roses and maidens cavorting, whatever they are. We had nothing like this in Classon Avenue where Mrs. Leibowitz sang in the lavatory while we clutched ourselves in the hall.

Now Malachy has to use the chamber pot but he wants to sit on it. Dad says, No, you can't do that, son. You have to go outside. When he says that I have to go, too, to sit. He leads us downstairs and through the big room where Grandpa is sitting reading by the fire and Grandma is dozing in her chair. It's dark outside, though the moon is bright enough for us to see where we're going. Dad opens the door of a little house that has a seat with a hole in it. He shows Malachy and me how to sit on the hole and how to wipe ourselves with squares of newspaper stuck on a nail. Then he tells us wait while he goes inside, closes the door and grunts. The moon is so bright I can look down the field and see the things called cows and sheep and I wonder why they don't go home.

In the house there are other people in the room with my grandparents. Dad says, These are your aunts: Emily, Nora, Maggie, Vera. Your aunt Eva is in Ballymena with children like you. My aunts are not like Mrs. Leibowitz and Minnie MacAdorey, they nod their heads but they don't hug us or smile. Mam comes into the room with the twins and when Dad tells his sisters, This is Angela and these are the twins, they just nod again.

Grandma goes to the kitchen and soon we have bread and sausages and tea. The only one who speaks at the table is Malachy. He points his spoon at the aunts and asks their names again. When Mam tells him eat his sausage and be quiet his eyes fill with tears and Aunt Nora reaches over to comfort him. She says, There, there, and I wonder why everyone says there there when Malachy cries. I wonder what there there means.

It's quiet at the table till Dad says, Things are terrible in America. Grandma says, Och, aye. I read it in the paper. But they say Mr. Roosevelt is a good man and if you stayed you might have work by now.

Dad shakes his head and Grandma says, I don't know what you're going to do, Malachy. Things are worse here than they are in America. No work here and, God knows, we don't have room in this house for six more people.

Dad says, I thought I might get work on some of the farms. We could get a small place.

Where would you stay in the meantime? says Grandma. And how would you support yourself and your family?

Och, I could go on the dole, I suppose.

You can't get off a ship from America and go on the dole, says Grandpa. They make you wait a while and what would you do while you're waiting?

Dad says nothing and Mam looks straight ahead at the wall.

You'd be better off in the Free State, says Grandma. Dublin is big and surely there's work there or in the farms around.

You're entitled to money from the IRA, too, says Grandpa. You did your bit and they've been handing out money to men all over the Free State. You could go to Dublin and ask for help. We can loan you the bus fare to Dublin. The twins can sit on your lap and you won't have to pay for them.

Dad says, Och, aye, and Mam stares at the wall with tears in her eyes.

After we ate we went back to bed and next morning, all the grown-ups sat around looking sad. Soon a man came in a motor car and took us back down the road to the shop which had our trunk. They lifted the trunk up on the roof of a bus and we got into the bus. Dad said we were going to Dublin. Malachy said, What's Dublin? but no one answered him. Dad held Eugene on his lap and Mam held Oliver. Dad looked out at the fields and told me this is where Cuchulain liked to go for a walk. I asked him where Cuchulain hit the ball into the dog's mouth and he said a few miles away.

Malachy said, Look, look, and we looked. It was a great silvery sheet of water and Dad said it was Lough Neagh, the largest lake in Ireland, the lake where Cuchulain used to swim after his great battles. Cuchulain would get so hot that when he jumped into Lough Neagh it boiled over and warmed the surrounding countryside for days. Some day we'd all come back and go swimming like Cuchulain himself. We'd fish for eels and fry them in a pan not like Cuchulain, who would pluck them from the lough and swallow them, wriggling, because there's great power in an eel.

Is that right, Dad?

'Tis.

Mam didn't look out the window at Lough Neagh. Her cheek rested on top of Oliver's head and she stared at the floor of the bus.

Soon the bus is rolling into a place where there are big houses, motor cars, horses pulling carts, people on bicycles and hundreds walking. Malachy is excited. Dad, Dad, where's the playground, the swings? I want to see Freddie Leibowitz.

Och, son, you're in Dublin now, far from Classon Avenue. You're in Ireland, a long way from New York.

When the bus stops the trunk is lifted down and set on the floor of the bus station. Dad tells Mam she can sit on a bench in the station while he goes to see the IRA man in a place called Terenure. He says there are lavatories in the station for the boys, he won't be long, he'll have money when he returns and we'll all have food. He tells me go with him and Mam says, No, I need him to help. But when Dad says, I'll need help carrying all that money, she laughs and says, All right, go with your Pop.

Your Pop. That means she's in a good mood. If she says your father it means she's in a bad mood.

Dad holds my hand as I trot along beside him. He's a fast walker, it's a long way to Terenure and I'm hoping he'll stop and carry me the way he did with the twins in Toome. But he lopes along and says nothing except to ask people where Terenure is. In awhile he says we're in Terenure and now we have to find Mr. Charles Heggarty of the IRA. A man with a pink patch on his eye tells us we're on the right street, Charlie Heggarty lives at number fourteen, God blast him. The man tells Dad, I can see you're a man that did his bit. Dad says, Och, I did my bit, and the man says, I did me bit, too, and what did it get me but one eye less and a pension that wouldn't feed a canary.

But Ireland is free, says Dad, and that's a grand thing.

Free, my arse, the man says. I think we were better off under the English. Good luck to you anyway, mister, for I think I know what you're here for.

A woman opens the door at number fourteen. I'm afraid, she says, that Mr. Heggarty is busy. Dad tells her he just walked all the way from the middle of Dublin with his small son, that he left wife and three children waiting for him at the bus place, and if Mr. Heggarty is that busy then we'll wait for him on the doorstep.

The woman is back in a minute to say Mr. Heggarty has a little time to spare and would you come this way. Mr. Heggarty is sitting at a desk near a glowing fire. He says, What can I do for you? Dad stands before the desk and says, I have just returned from America with wife and four children. We have nothing. I fought with a Flying Column during the Troubles and I'm hoping you can help me now in the time of need.

Mr. Heggarty takes Dad's name and turns the pages of a big book on his desk. He shakes his head, No, no record of your service here.

Dad makes a long speech. He tells Mr. Heggarty how he fought, where, when, how he had to be smuggled out of Ireland because of the price on his head, how he was raising his sons to love Ireland.

Mr. Heggarty says he's sorry but he can't be handing out money to every man who wanders in claiming he did his bit. Dad says to me, Remember this, Francis. This is the new Ireland. Little men in little chairs with little bits of paper. This is the Ireland men died for.

Mr. Heggarty says he'll look into Dad's claim and he'll be sure to let him know what turns up. He'll let us have money to take the bus back into the city. Dad looks at the coins in Mr. Heggarty's hand and says, You could add to that and make the price of a pint.

Oh, it's the drink you want, is it?

One pint is hardly drink.

You'd walk the miles back and make the boy walk because you want a pint, wouldn't you?

Walking never killed anyone.

I want you to leave this house, says Mr. Heggarty, or I'll call a guard, and you can be sure you'll never hear from me again. We're not handing out money to support the Guinness family.

Night falls along the streets of Dublin. Children laugh and play under streetlights, mothers call from doorways, smells of cooking come at us all the way, through windows we see people around tables, eating. I'm tired and hungry and I want Dad to carry me but I know there's no use asking him now the way his face is tight and set. I let him hold my hand and I run to keep up with him till we reach the bus place where Mam is waiting with my brothers.

They're all asleep on the bench, my mother and three brothers. When Dad tells Mam there's no money she shakes her head and sobs, Oh, Jesus, what are we going to do? A man in a blue uniform comes over and asks her, What's up, missus? Dad tells him we're stranded there at the bus station, we have no money and no place to stay and the children are hungry. The man says he's going off duty now, he'll take us to the police barracks where he has to report anyway, and they'll see what can be done.

The man in uniform tells us we can call him guard. That's what you call policeman in Ireland. He asks us what you call policemen in America and Malachy says, cop. The guard pats him on the head and tells him he's a clever little Yankee.

At the police barracks the sergeant tells us we can spend the night. He's sorry but all he can offer is the floor. It's Thursday and the cells are filled with men who drank their dole money and wouldn't leave the pubs.

The guards give us hot sweet tea and thick slices of bread slathered with butter and jam and we're so happy we run around the barracks, playing. The guards say we're a great bunch of little Yanks and they'd like to take us home but I say, No, Malachy says, No, the twins say, No, No, and all the guards laugh. Men in cells reach out and pat our heads, they smell like Dad when he comes home singing about Kevin Barry and Roddy McCorley going to die. The men say, Jasus, will ye listen to them. They sound like bloody fillum stars. Did yez fall outa the sky or what? Women in cells at the other end tell Malachy he's gorgeous and the twins are dotes. One woman talks to me. C'mere, love, would you like a sweet? I nod, and she says, All right, put your hand out. She takes something sticky from her mouth and puts it on my hand. There you are now, she says, a nice bit of butterscotch. Put that in your mouth. I don't want to put it in my mouth because it's sticky and wet from her mouth but I don't know what you're supposed to do when a woman in a cell offers you sticky butterscotch and I'm about to put it in my mouth when a guard comes, takes the butterscotch and throws it back at the woman. You drunken hoor, he says, leave the child alone, and all the women laugh.

The sergeant gives my mother a blanket and she sleeps stretched out on a bench. The rest of us lie on the floor. Dad sits with his back to the wall, his eyes open under the peak of his cap, and he smokes when the guards give him cigarettes. The guard who threw the butterscotch at the woman says he's from Ballymena in the north and he talks with Dad about people they know there and in other places like Cushendall and Toome. The guard says he'll have a pension some day and he'll live on the shores of Lough Neagh and fish his days away. Eels, he says, eels galore. Jasus, I love a fried eel. I ask Dad, Is this Cuchulain? and the guard laughs till his face turns red. Ah, Mother o' God, did yez hear this? The lad wants to know if I'm Cuchulain. A little Yank and he knows all about Cuchulain.

Dad says, No, he's not Cuchulain but he's a fine man who will live on the shores of Lough Neagh and fish his days away.

Dad is shaking me. Up, Francis, up. It is noisy in the barracks. A boy mopping the floor is singing,

> *Anyone can see why I wanted your kiss,*
> *It had to be and the reason is this,*
> *Could it be true, someone like you*
> *Could love me, love me?*

I tell him that's my mother's song and he's to stop singing it but he just puffs on his cigarette and walks away and I wonder why people have to sing other people's songs. Men and women coming out of the cells are yawning and grunting. The woman who offered me the butterscotch stops and says, I had a drop taken, child. I'm sorry I made a fool of you, but the guard from Ballymena tells her, Move on, you oul' hoor, before I lock you up again.

Oh, lock me up, she says. In, out. What does it matter, you blue-arsed bastard.

Mam is sitting up on the bench, the blanket wrapped around her. A woman with gray hair brings her a mug of tea and tells her, Sure, I'm the sergeant's wife and he said you might need help. Would you like a nice soft-boiled egg, missus?

Mam shakes her head, no.

Ah, now, missus, surely you should have a nice egg in your condition.

But Mam shakes her head and I wonder how she can say no to a soft-boiled egg when there's nothing in the world like it.

All right, ma'am, says the sergeant's wife, a bit of toast, then, and something for the children and your poor husband.

She goes back to another room and soon there's tea and bread. Dad drinks his tea but gives us his bread and Mam says, Will you eat your bread, for God's sake. You won't be much use to us falling down with the hunger. He shakes his head and asks the sergeant's wife is there any chance of a cigarette. She brings him the cigarette and tells Mam the guards in the barracks have taken up a collection to pay our train fares to Limerick. There will be a motor car to pick up our trunk and leave us at Kingsbridge Railway Station and, You'll be in Limerick in three or four hours.

Mam puts up her arms and hugs the sergeant's wife. God bless you and your husband and all the guards, Mam says. I don't know what we'd do without you. God knows 'tis a lovely thing to be back among our own.

'Tis the least we could do, says the sergeant's wife. These are lovely children you have and I'm from Cork meself and I know what 'tis to be in Dublin without two pennies to rub together.

Dad sits at the other end of the bench, smoking his cigarette, drinking his tea. He stays that way till the motor car comes to take us through the streets of Dublin. Dad asks the driver if he'd mind going by way of the G.P.O. and the driver says, Is it a stamp you want or what? No, says Dad. I hear they put up a new statue of Cuchulain to honor the men who died in 1916 and I'd like to show it to my son here who has a great admiration for Cuchulain.

The driver says he has no notion of who this Cuchulain was but he wouldn't mind stopping one bit. He might come in himself and see what the commotion is all about for he hasn't been in the G.P.O. since he was a boy and the English nearly wrecked it with their big guns firing up from the Liffey River. He says you'll see the bullet holes all over the front and they should be left there to remind the Irish of English perfidy. I ask the man what's perfidy and he says ask your father and I would but we're stopping outside a big building with columns and that's the G.P.O.

Mam stays in the motor car while we follow the driver into the G.P.O. There he is, he says, there's your man Cuchulain.

And I feel tears coming because I'm looking at him at last, Cuchulain, there on his pedestal in the G.P.O. He's golden and he has long hair, his head is hanging and there's a big bird perched on his shoulder.

The driver says, Now what in God's name is this all about? What's this fellow doin' with the long hair and the bird on his shoulder? And will you kindly tell me, mister, what this has to do with the men of 1916?

Dad says, Cuchulain fought to the end like the men of Easter Week. His enemies were afraid to go near him till they were sure he was dead and when the bird landed on him and drank his blood they knew.

Well, says the driver, 'tis a sad day for the men of Ireland when they need a bird to tell them a man is dead. I think we better go now or we'll be missing that train to Limerick.

The sergeant's wife said she'd send a telegram to Grandma to meet us in Limerick and there she was on the platform, Grandma, with white hair, sour eyes, a black shawl, and no smile for my mother or any of us, even my brother, Malachy, who had the big smile and the sweet white teeth. Mam pointed to Dad. This is Malachy, she said, and Grandma nodded and looked away. She called two boys who were hanging around the railway station and paid them to carry the trunk. The boys had shaved heads, snotty noses, and no shoes and we followed them through the streets of Limerick. I asked Mam why they had no hair and she said their heads were shaved so that the lice would have no place to hide. Malachy said, What's a lice? and Mam said, Not lice. One of them is a louse. Grandma said, Will ye stop it! What kind o' talk is this? The boys whistled and laughed and trotted along as if they had shoes and Grandma told them, Stop that laughin' or 'tis droppin' an' breakin' that trunk ye'll be. They stopped the whistling and laughing and we followed them into a park with a tall pillar and a statue in the middle and grass so green it dazzled you.

Dad carried the twins, Mam carried a bag in one hand and held Malachy's hand with the other. When she stopped every few minutes to catch her breath, Grandma said, Are you still smokin' them fags? Them fags will be the death of you. There's enough consumption in Limerick without people smokin' fags on top of it an' 'tis a rich man's foolishness.

Along the path through the park there were hundreds of flowers of different colors that excited the twins. They pointed and made squeaky noises and we laughed, everyone except Grandma, who pulled her shawl over her head. Dad stopped and put the twins down so that they could be closer to the flowers. He said, Flowers, and they ran back and forth, pointing, trying to say Flowers. One of the boys with the trunk said, God, are they Americans? and Mam said, They are. They were born in New York. All the boys were born in New York. The boy said to the other boy, God, they're Americans. They put the trunk down and stared at us and we stared back at them till Grandma said, Are ye goin' to stand here all day lookin' at flowers an' gawkin' at each other? And we all moved on again, out of the park, down a narrow lane and into another lane to Grandma's house.

There is a row of small houses on each side of the lane and Grandma lives in one of the small houses. Her kitchen has a shiny polished black iron range with a fire glowing in the grate. There is a table along the wall under the window and a press opposite with cups and saucers and vases. This press is always locked and she keeps the key in her purse because you're not supposed to use anything in there unless someone dies or returns from foreign parts or there's a visit by a priest.

There is a picture on the wall by the range of a man with long brown hair and sad eyes. He is pointing to his chest where there is a big heart with flames coming out of it. Mam tells us, That's the Sacred Heart of Jesus, and I want to know why the man's heart is on fire and why doesn't He throw water on it? Grandma says, Don't these children know anything about their religion? and Mam tells her it's different in America. Grandma says the Sacred Heart is everywhere and there's no excuse for that kind of ignorance.

Under the picture of the man with the burning heart there is a shelf with a red glass holding a flickering candle and next to it a small statue. Mam tells us, That's the Baby Jesus, the Infant of Prague, and if ye ever need anything pray to Him.

Malachy says, Mam, could I tell Him I'm hungry, and Mam puts her finger to her lips.

Grandma grumbles around the kitchen making tea and telling Mam to cut the loaf of bread and don't make the cuts too thick. Mam sits by the table with her breath coming hard and says she'll cut the bread in a minute. Dad takes the knife and starts slicing the bread and you can see Grandma doesn't like that. She frowns at him but says nothing even though he makes thick slices.

There aren't enough chairs for everyone so I sit on the stairs with my brothers to have bread and tea. Dad and Mam sit at the table and Grandma sits under the Sacred Heart with her mug of tea. She says, I don't know under God what I'm goin' to do with ye. There is no room in this house. There isn't room for even one of ye.

Malachy says, Ye, ye, and starts to giggle and I say, Ye, ye, and the twins say, Ye, ye, and we're laughing so hard we can hardly eat our bread.

Grandma glares at us. What are ye laughin' at? There's nothin' to laugh at in this house. Ye better behave yeerselves before I go over to ye.

She won't stop saying Ye, and now Malachy is helpless with laughter, spewing out his bread and tea, his face turning red.

Dad says, Malachy and the rest of you, stop it. But Malachy can't, he goes on laughing till Dad says, Come over here. He rolls up Malachy's sleeve and raises his hand to slap his arm.

Are you going to behave yourself?

Malachy's eyes fill with tears and he nods, I will, because Dad never raised his hand like that before. Dad says, Be a good boy and go sit with your brothers, and he pulls down the sleeve and pats Malachy on the head.

That night Mam's sister, Aunt Aggie, came home from her job in the clothing factory. She was big like the MacNamara sisters, and she had flaming red hair. She wheeled a large bicycle into the little room behind the kitchen and came out to her supper. She was living in Grandma's because she had a fight with her husband, Pa Keating, who told her, when he had drink taken, You're a great fat cow, go home to your mother. That's what Grandma told Mam and that's why there was no room for us in Grandma's house. She had herself, Aunt Aggie, and her son Pat, who was my uncle and who was out selling newspapers.

Aunt Aggie complained when Grandma told her Mam would have to sleep with her that night. Grandma said, Oh, will you shut your gob. 'Tis only for one night an' that won't kill you an' if you don't like it you can go back to your husband where you belong anyway instead of runnin' home to me. Jesus, Mary an' Holy St. Joseph, look at this house—you an' Pat an' Angela and her clatther of Americans. Will I have any peace in the latter end of my life?

She spread coats and rags on the floor of the little back room and we slept there with the bicycle. Dad stayed on a chair in the kitchen, took us to the lavatory in the backyard when we needed it, and in the night hushed the twins when they cried from the cold.

In the morning, Aunt Aggie came for her bicycle telling us, Will ye mind yeerselves, will ye? Will ye get out of my way?

When she left, Malachy kept saying, Will ye mind yeerselves, will ye? Will ye get out of the way, will ye? and I could hear Dad laughing out in the kitchen till Grandma came down the stairs and he had to tell Malachy be quiet.

That day Grandma and Mam went out and found a furnished room on Windmill Street where Aunt Aggie had a flat with her husband, Pa Keating. Grandma paid the rent, ten shillings for two weeks. She gave Mam money for food, loaned us a kettle, a pot, a frying pan, knives and spoons, jam jars to be used for mugs, a blanket and a pillow. She said that was all she could afford anymore, that Dad would have to get up off his arse, get a job, go on the dole, go for the charity at the St. Vincent de Paul Society or go on the relief.

The room had a fireplace where we could boil water for our tea or an egg in case we ever came into money. We had a table and three chairs and a bed, which Mam said was the biggest she had ever seen. We were glad of the bed that night, worn out after nights on floors in Dublin and in Grandma's. It didn't matter that there were six of us in the bed, we were together, away from grandmothers and guards, Malachy could say ye ye ye and we could laugh as much as we liked.

Dad and Mam lay at the head of the bed, Malachy and I at the bottom, the twins wherever they could find comfort. Malachy made us laugh again. Ye, ye, ye, he said, and oy oy oy, and then fell asleep. Mam made the little hink hink snore sound that told us she was sleeping. In the moonlight I could look up the length of the bed and see Dad still awake and when Oliver cried in his sleep Dad reached for him and held him. Whisht, he said. Whisht.

Then Eugene sat up, screaming, tearing at himself. Ah, ah, Mommy, Mommy. Dad sat up. What? What's up, son? Eugene went on crying and when Dad leaped from the bed and turned on the gaslight we saw the fleas, leaping, jumping, fastened to our flesh. We slapped at them and slapped but they hopped from body to body, hopping, biting. We tore at the bites till they bled. We jumped from the bed, the twins crying, Mam moaning, Oh, Jesus, will we have no rest! Dad poured water and salt into a jam jar and dabbed at our bites. The salt burned but he said we'd feel better soon.

Mam sat by the fireplace with the twins on her lap. Dad pulled on his trousers and dragged the mattress off the bed and out to the street. He filled the kettle and the pot with water, stood the mattress against the wall, pounded it with a shoe, told me to keep pouring water on the ground to drown the fleas dropping there. The Limerick moon was so bright I could see bits of it shimmering in the water and I wanted to scoop up moon bits but how could I with the fleas leaping on my legs. Dad kept pounding with the shoe and I had to run back through the house to the backyard tap for more water in the kettle and the pot. Mam said, Look at you. Your shoes are drenched and you'll catch your death and your father will surely get the pneumonia without a shoe to his foot.

A man on a bicycle stopped and wanted to know why Dad was beating that mattress. Mother o' God, he said, I never heard such a cure for fleas. Do you know that if a man could jump like a flea one lep would take him halfway to the moon? The thing to do is this, when you go back inside with that mattress stick it on the bed upside down and that will confuse the little buggers. They won't know where they are and they'll be biting the mattress or each other, which is the best cure of all. After they bite the human being they have the frenzy, you know, for there are other fleas around them that also bit the human being and the smell of the blood is too much for them and they go out of their minds. They're a right bloody torment an' I should know for didn't I grow up in Limerick, down in the Irishtown, an' the fleas there were so plentiful an' forward they'd sit on the toe of your boot an' discuss Ireland's woeful history with you. It is said there were no fleas in ancient Ireland, that they were brought in be the English to drive us out of our wits entirely, an' I wouldn't put it past the English. An' isn't it a very curious thing that St. Patrick drove the snakes out of Ireland an' the English brought in the fleas. For centuries Ireland was a lovely peaceful place, snakes gone, not a flea to be found. You could stroll the four green fields of Ireland without fear of snakes an' have a good night's sleep with no fleas to bother you. Them snakes were doin' no harm, they wouldn't bother you unless you cornered them an' they lived off other creatures that move under bushes an' such places, whereas the flea sucks the blood from you mornin' noon an' night for that's his nature an' he can't help

60

himself. I hear for a fact that places that have snakes galore have no fleas. Arizona, for instance. You're forever hearing about the snakes of Arizona but when did you ever hear of fleas in Arizona? Good luck to you. I have to be careful standin' here for if one of them gets on my clothes I might as well invite his whole family home. They multiply faster than Hindus.

Dad said, You wouldn't by any chance have a cigarette, would you?

A cigarette? Oh, sure, of course. Here you are. Aren't I nearly destroyed from the fags myself. The oul' hacking cough, you know. So powerful it nearly knocks me off the bicycle. I can feel that cough stirring in me solar plexus an' workin' its way up through me entrails till the next thing it takes off the top o' me head.

He struck a match on a box, lit a cigarette for himself and held out the match for Dad. Of course, he said, you're bound to have the cough when you live in Limerick because this is the capital city of the weak chest and the weak chest leads to the consumption. If all the people that has consumption in Limerick were to die this would be a ghost town, though I don't have consumption meself. No, this cough was a present from the Germans. He paused, puffed on his cigarette, and struggled with a cough. Bejesus, excuse the language, but the fags'll get me in the end. Well, I'll leave you now to the mattress an' remember what I told you, confuse the little buggers.

He wobbled away on his bicycle, the cigarette dangling from his mouth, the cough racking his body. Dad said, Limerickmen talk too much. Come on, we'll put this mattress back and see if there's any sleep in this night.

Mam sat by the fireplace with the twins asleep on her lap, and Malachy lay curled up on the floor by her feet. She said, Who was that you were talking to? It sounded very like Pa Keating, Aggie's husband. I could tell by the cough. He got that cough in France in the war when he swallowed the gas.

We slept the rest of that night, and in the morning we saw where the fleas had feasted, our flesh pink with flea welts and bright with the blood of our scratches.

Mam made tea and fried bread, and once more Dad dabbed at our bites with the salty water. He hauled the mattress outside again to the backyard. On a cold day like this the fleas would surely freeze to death and we'd all have a good night's sleep.

. . .

A few days later when we're settled into the room Dad is shaking me out of my dreams. Up, Francis, up. Put on your clothes and run over for your aunt Aggie. Your mother needs her. Hurry.

Mam is moaning in the bed, her face pure white. Dad has Malachy and the twins out of the bed and sitting on the floor by the dead fire. I run across the street and knock on Aunt Aggie's door till Uncle Pat Keating comes coughing and grumbling, What's up? What's up?

My mother is moaning in the bed. I think she's sick.

Now Aunt Aggie comes grumbling. Ye are nothing but trouble since ye came from America.

Leave him alone, Aggie, he's only a child that's doing what he's told.

She tells Uncle Pa go back to bed, that he has to go to work in the morning not like some from the North that she won't mention. He says, No, no, I'm coming. There's something wrong with Angela.

Dad tells me sit over there with my brothers. I don't know what's up with Mam because everyone is whispering and I can barely hear Aunt Aggie telling Uncle Pa the child is lost run for the ambulance and Uncle Pa is out the door, Aunt Aggie telling Mam you can say what you like about Limerick but the ambulance is fast. She doesn't talk to my father, never looks at him.

Malachy says, Dad, is Mammy sick?

Och, she'll be all right, son. She has to see the doctor.

I wonder what child is lost because we're all here, one two three four of us, not a lost child anywhere and why can't they tell me what's wrong with my mother. Uncle Pa comes back and the ambulance is right behind him. A man comes in with a stretcher and after they carry Mam away there are blood spots on the floor by the bed. Malachy bit his tongue and there was blood and the dog on the street had blood and he died. I want to ask Dad to tell me if Mam will be gone forever like my sister Margaret but he's going with Mam and there's no use asking Aunt Aggie anything for fear she'd bite your head off. She wipes away the blood spots and tells us get back into bed and stay there till Dad comes home.

It's the middle of the night and the four of us are warm in the bed and we fall asleep till Dad comes home and tells us Mam is nice and comfortable in the hospital and she'll be home in no time.

Later, Dad goes to the Labour Exchange for the dole. There is no hope of a laboring man with a North of Ireland accent getting a job in Limerick.

When he returns, he tells Mam we'll be getting nineteen shillings a week. She says that's just enough for all of us to starve on. Nineteen shillings for six of us? That's less than four dollars in American money and how are we supposed to live on that? What are we to do when we have to pay rent in a fortnight? If the rent for this room is five shillings a week we'll have fourteen shillings for food and clothes and coal to boil the water for the tea.

Dad shakes his head, sips his tea from a jam jar, stares out the window and whistles "The Boys of Wexford." Malachy and Oliver clap their hands and dance around the room and Dad doesn't know whether to whistle or smile because you can't do both and he can't help himself. He has to stop and smile and pat Oliver's head and then go back to the whistling. Mam smiles, too, but it's a very quick smile and when she looks into the ashes you can see the worry where the corners of her mouth turn down.

Next day she tells Dad to mind the twins and takes Malachy and me with her to the St. Vincent de Paul Society. We stand in a queue with women wearing black shawls. They ask our names and smile when we talk. They say, Lord above, would you listen to the little Yankees, and they wonder why Mam in her American coat would be looking for charity since there's hardly enough for the poor people of Limerick without Yanks coming over and taking the bread out of their mouths.

Mam tells them a cousin gave her that coat in Brooklyn, that her husband has no work, that she has other children at home, twin boys. The women sniff and pull their shawls about them, they have their own troubles. Mam tells them she had to leave America because she couldn't stand it after her baby girl died. The women sniff again but now it's because Mam is crying. Some say they lost little ones, too, and there's nothing worse in the world, you could live as long as Methuselem's wife but you never get over it. No man can ever know what it is to be a mother that has lost a child, not if the man lived longer than two Methuselems.

They all have a good cry till a red-haired woman passes a little box around. The women pick something from the box between their fingers and stuff it up their noses. A young woman sneezes and the red-haired woman laughs. Ah, sure, Biddy, you're not able for that snuff. Come here, little Yankee boys, have a pinch. She plants the brown stuff in our nostrils and we sneeze so hard the women stop crying and laugh till they have to wipe their eyes with their shawls. Mam tells us, That's good for ye, 'twill clear yeer heads.

The young woman, Biddy, tells Mam we're two lovely boys. She points at Malachy. That little fella with the goldy ringlet, isn't he gorgeous? He could be a film star with Shirley Temple. And Malachy smiles and warms up the queue.

The woman with the snuff says to Mam, Missus, I don't want to be forward but I think you should be sitting down for we heard about your loss.

Another woman worries, Ah, no, they don't like that.

Who don't like what?

Ah, sure, Nora Molloy, the Society don't like us sittin' on the steps. They want us to be standin' respectful against the wall.

They can kiss my arse, says Nora, the red-haired woman. Sit down there, missus, on that step an' I'll sit next to you an' if there's one word out of the St. Vincent de Paul Society I'll take the face off 'em, so I will. Do you smoke, missus?

I do, says Mam, but I don't have them.

Nora takes a cigarette from a pocket in her apron, breaks it, and offers half to Mam.

The worried woman says, They don't like that either. They say every fag you smoke is taking food from the mouth of your child. Mr. Quinlivan inside is dead against it. He says if you have money for the fags you have money for food.

Quinlivan can kiss my arse, too, the grinny oul' bastard. Is he going to begrudge us a puff of a fag, the only comfort we have in the world?

A door opens at the end of the hall and a man appears. Are any of ye waiting for children's boots?

Women raise their hands, I am. I am.

Well, the boots are all gone. Ye'll have to come back next month.

But my Mikey needs boots for school.

They're all gone, I told you.

But 'tis freezin' abroad, Mr. Quinlivan.

The boots are all gone. Nothing I can do. What's this? Who's smoking?

64

Nora waves her cigarette. I am, she says, and enjoying it down to the last ash.

Every puff you take, he starts.

I know, she says, I'm taking food out of the mouths of my children.

You're insolent, woman. You'll get no charity here.

Is that a fact? Well, Mr. Quinlivan, if I don't get it here I know where I will.

What are you talking about?

I'll go to the Quakers. They'll give me the charity.

Mr. Quinlivan steps toward Nora and points a finger. Do you know what we have here? We have a souper in our midst. We had the soupers in the Famine. The Protestants went round telling good Catholics that if they gave up their faith and turned Protestant they'd get more soup than their bellies could hold and, God help us, some Catholics took the soup, and were ever after known as soupers and lost their immortal souls doomed to the deepest part of hell. And you, woman, if you go to the Quakers you'll lose your immortal soul and the souls of your children.

Then, Mr. Quinlivan, you'll have to save us, won't you?

He stares at her and she stares back at him. His eyes wander to the other women. One puts her hand to her mouth to smother a laugh.

What are you tittering about? he barks.

Oh, nothing, Mr. Quinlivan. Honest to God.

I'm telling ye once more, no boots. And he slams the door behind him.

One by one the women are called into the room. When Nora comes out she's smiling and waving a piece of paper. Boots, she says. Three pairs I'm gettin' for my children. Threaten the men in there with the Quakers and they'll give you the drawers off their arses.

When Mam is called she brings Malachy and me in with her. We stand before a table where three men are sitting asking questions. Mr. Quinlivan starts to say something but the man in the middle says, Enough out of you, Quinlivan. If we left it up to you we'd have the poor people of Limerick jumping into the arms of the Protestants.

He turns to Mam, he wants to know where she got that fine red coat. She tells him what she told the women outside and when she comes to the death of Margaret she shakes and sobs. She tells the men she's very sorry for crying like that but it was only a few months ago and she's not over it yet, not even knowing where her baby was buried if she was buried at all, not knowing even if she was baptized itself because she was so weak from having the four boys she didn't have the energy to be going to the church for the baptism and it's a heart scald to think Margaret might be in Limbo forever with no hope of her ever seeing the rest of us whether we're in heaven, hell, or Purgatory itself.

Mr. Quinlivan brings her his chair. Ah, now, missus. Ah, now. Sit down, will you. Ah, now.

The other men look at the table, the ceiling. The man in the middle says he's giving Mam a docket to get a week's groceries at McGrath's shop on Parnell Street. There will be tea, sugar, flour, milk, butter and a separate docket for a bag of coal from Sutton's coal yard on the Dock Road.

The third man says, Of course you won't be getting this every week, missus. We will be visiting your house to see if there's a real need. We have to do that, missus, so we can review your claim.

Mam wipes her face on the back of her sleeve and takes the docket. She tells the men, God bless you for your kindness. They nod and look at the table, the ceiling, the walls and tell her send in the next woman.

The women outside tell Mam, When you go to McGrath's, keep an eye on the oul' bitch for she'll cheat you on the weight. She'll put stuff on a paper on the scale with the paper hanging down on her side behind the counter where she thinks you can't see it. She'll pull on that paper so that you're lucky if you get half of what you're supposed to get. And she has pictures of the Virgin Mary and the Sacred Heart of Jesus all over the shop, and she's forever on her knees abroad in St. Joseph's chapel clackin' her rosary beads an' breathing like a virgin martyr, the oul' bitch.

Nora says, I'll go with you, missus. I'm on to the same Mrs. McGrath and I'll know if she's cheating you.

She leads the way to the shop in Parnell Street. The woman behind the counter is pleasant to Mam in her American coat till Mam shows the St. Vincent de Paul docket. The woman says, I don't know what you're doing here at this hour of the day. I never serve the charity cases before six in the evening. But this is your first time and I'll make an exception.

She says to Nora, Do you have a docket, too?

No. I'm a friend helping this poor family with their first docket from the St. Vincent de Paul.

The woman lays a sheet of newspaper on the scale and pours on flour from a large bag. When she finishes pouring, she says, There's a pound of flour.

I don't think so, says Nora. That's a very small pound of flour.

The woman flushes and glares, Are you accusin' me?

Ah, no, Mrs. McGrath, says Nora. I think there was a little accident there the way your hip was pressed against that paper and you didn't even know the paper was pulled down a bit. Oh, God, no. A woman like you that's forever on her knees before the Virgin Mary is an inspiration to us all and is that your money I see on the floor there?

Mrs. McGrath steps back quickly and the needle on the scale jumps and quivers. What money? she says, till she looks at Nora, and knows. Nora smiles. Must be a trick of the shadows, she says, and smiles at the scale. There was a mistake right enough for that shows barely half a pound of flour.

That scale gives me more trouble, says Mrs. McGrath.

I'm sure it does, says Nora.

But my conscience is clear before God, says Mrs. McGrath.

I'm sure it is, says Nora, and you're admired by one and all at the St. Vincent de Paul Society and the Legion of Mary.

I try to be a good Catholic.

Try? God knows 'tis little trying you'd have for you're well known for having a kind heart and I was wondering if you could spare a couple of sweets for the little boys here.

Well, now, I'm not a millionaire, but here . . .

God bless you, Mrs. McGrath, and I know it's asking a lot but could you possibly lend me a couple of cigarettes?

Well, now, they're not on the docket. I'm not here to supply luxuries.

If you could see your way, missus, I'd be sure to mention your kindness to the St. Vincent de Paul.

All right, all right, says Mrs. McGrath. Here. One time for the cigarettes and one time only.

God bless you, says Nora, and I'm sorry you had so much trouble with that scale.

On the way home we stopped in the People's Park and sat on a bench while Malachy and I sucked on our sweets and Mam and Nora smoked their cigarettes. The smoking brought on Nora's cough and she told Mam the fags would kill her in the end, that there was a touch of consumption in her family and no one lived to a ripe old age, though who would want to in Limerick, a place where you could look around and the first thing you noticed was a scarcity of gray hairs, all the gray hairs either in the graveyard or across the Atlantic working on railroads or sauntering around in police uniforms.

You're lucky, missus, that you saw a bit of the world. Oh, God, I'd give anything to see New York, people dancing up and down Broadway without a care. No, I had to go and fall for a boozer with the charm, Peter Molloy, a champion pint drinker that had me up the pole and up the aisle when I was barely seventeen. I was ignorant, missus. We grew up ignorant in Limerick, so we did, knowing feck all about anything and signs on, we're mothers before we're women. And there's nothing here but rain and oul' biddies saying the rosary. I'd give me teeth to get out, go to America or even England itself. The champion pint drinker is always on the dole and sometimes he even drinks that and drives me so demented I wind up in the lunatic asylum.

She drew on her cigarette and gagged, coughing till her body rocked back and forth, and in between the coughs she whimpered, Jesus, Jesus. When the cough died away she said she had to go home and take her medicine. She said, I'll see you next week, missus, at the St. Vincent de Paul. If you're stuck for anything send a message to me at Vize's Field. Ask anyone for the wife of Peter Molloy, champion pint drinker.

Eugene is sleeping under a coat on the bed. Dad sits by the fireplace with Oliver on his lap. I wonder why Dad is telling Oliver a Cuchulain story. He knows the Cuchulain stories are mine, but when I look at Oliver I don't mind. His cheeks are bright red, he's staring into the dead fire, and you can see he has no interest in Cuchulain. Mam puts her hand on his forehead. I think he has a fever, she says. I wish I had an onion and I'd boil it in milk and pepper. That's good for the fever. But even if I had what would I boil the milk on? We need coal for that fire.

She gives Dad the docket for the coal down the Dock Road. He takes me with him but it's dark and all the coal yards are closed.

What are we going to do now, Dad?

I don't know, son.

Ahead of us women in shawls and small children are picking up coal along the road.

There, Dad, there's coal.

Och, no, son. We won't pick coal off the road. We're not beggars.

He tells Mam the coal yards are closed and we'll have to drink milk and eat bread tonight, but when I tell her about the women on the road she passes Eugene to him.

If you're too grand to pick coal off the road I'll put on my coat and go down the Dock Road.

She gets a bag and takes Malachy and me with her. Beyond the Dock Road there is something wide and dark with lights glinting in it. Mam says that's the River Shannon. She says that's what she missed most of all in America, the River Shannon. The Hudson was lovely but the Shannon sings. I can't hear the song but my mother does and that makes her happy. The other women are gone from the Dock Road and we search for the bits of coal that drop from lorries. Mam tells us gather anything that burns, coal, wood, cardboard, paper. She says, There are them that burn the horse droppings but we're not gone that low yet. When her bag is nearly full she says, Now we have to find an onion for Oliver. Malachy says he'll find one but she tells him, No, you don't find onions on the road, you get them in shops.

The minute he sees a shop he cries out, There's a shop, and runs in.

Oonyen, he says. Oonyen for Oliver.

Mam runs into the shop and tells the women behind the counter, I'm sorry. The woman says, Lord, he's a dote. Is he an American or what?

Mam says he is. The woman smiles and shows two teeth, one on each side of her upper gum. A dote, she says, and look at them gorgeous goldy curls. And what is it he wants now? A sweet?

Ah, no, says Mam. An onion.

The woman laughs, An onion? I never heard a child wanting an onion before. Is that what they like in America?

Mam says, I just mentioned I wanted to get an onion for my other child that's sick. Boil the onion in milk, you know.

True for you, missus. You can't beat the onion boiled in milk. And look, little boy, here's a sweet for yourself and one for the other little boy, the brother, I suppose.

Mam says, Ah, sure, you shouldn't. Say thank you, boys.

The woman says, Here's a nice onion for the sick child, missus.

Mam says, Oh, I can't buy the onion now, missus. I don't have a penny on me.

I'm giving you the onion, missus. Let it never be said a child went sick in Limerick for want of an onion. And don't forget to sprinkle in a little pepper. Do you have pepper, missus?

Ah, no, I don't but I should be getting it any day now.

Well, here, missus. Pepper and a little salt. Do the child all the good in the world.

Mam says, God bless you, ma'am, and her eyes are watery.

Dad is walking back and forth with Oliver in his arms and Eugene is playing on the floor with a pot and a spoon. Dad says, Did you get the onion?

I did, says Mam, and more. I got coal and the way of lighting it.

I knew you would. I said a prayer to St. Jude. He's my favorite saint, patron of desperate cases.

I got the coal. I got the onion, no help from St. Jude.

Dad says, You shouldn't be picking up coal off the road like a common beggar. It isn't right. Bad example for the boys.

Then you should have sent St. Jude down the Dock Road.

Malachy says, I'm hungry, and I'm hungry, too, but Mam says, Ye'll wait till Oliver has his onion boiled in milk.

She gets the fire going, cuts the onion in half, drops it in the boiling milk with a little butter and sprinkles the milk with pepper. She takes Oliver on her lap and tries to feed him but he turns away and looks into the fire.

Ah, come on, love, she says. Good for you. Make you big and strong.

He tightens his mouth against the spoon. She puts the pot down, rocks him till he's asleep, lays him on the bed and tells the rest of us be quiet or she'll demolish us. She slices the other half of the onion and fries it in butter with slices of bread. She lets us sit on the floor around the fire where we eat the fried bread and sip at the scalding sweet tea in jam jars. She says, That fire is good and bright so we can turn off that gaslight till we get money for the meter.

The fire makes the room warm and with the flames dancing in the coal you can see faces and mountains and valleys and animals leaping. Eugene falls asleep on the floor and Dad lifts him to the bed beside Oliver. Mam puts the boiled onion pot up on the mantelpiece for fear a mouse or rat might be at it. She says she's tired out from the day, the

Vincent de Paul Society, Mrs. McGrath's shop, the search for coal down the Dock Road, the worry over Oliver not wanting the boiled onion, and if he's like this tomorrow she's taking him to the doctor, and now she's going to bed.

Soon we're all in bed and if there's the odd flea I don't mind because it's warm in the bed with the six of us and I love the glow of the fire the way it dances on the walls and ceiling and makes the room go red and black, red and black, till it dims to white and black and all you can hear is a little cry from Oliver turning in my mother's arms.

In the morning Dad is lighting the fire, making tea, cutting the bread. He's already dressed and he's telling Mam hurry up and get dressed. He says to me, Francis, your little brother Oliver is sick and we're taking him to the hospital. You are to be a good boy and take care of your two brothers. We'll be back soon.

Mam says, When we're out go easy with that sugar. We're not millionaires.

When Mam picks up Oliver and wraps him in a coat Eugene stands on the bed. I want Ollie, he says. Ollie play.

Ollie will be back soon, she says, and you can play with him. Now you can play with Malachy and Frank.

Ollie, Ollie, I want Ollie.

He follows Oliver with his eyes and when they're gone he sits on the bed looking out the window. Malachy says, Genie, Genie, we have bread, we have tea. Sugar on your bread, Genie. He shakes his head and pushes away the bread Malachy is offering. He crawls to the place where Oliver slept with Mam, puts his head down and stares out the window.

Grandma is at the door. I heard your father and mother were running down Henry Street with the child in their arms. Now where are they gone to?

Oliver is sick, I said. He wouldn't eat the boiled onion in milk.

What are you blatherin' about?

Wouldn't eat the boiled onion and got sick.

And who's minding ye?

I am.

And what's up with the child in the bed? What's his name?

That's Eugene. He misses Oliver. They're twins.

71

I know they're twins. That child looks starved. Have ye any porridge here?

What's porridge? says Malachy.

Jesus, Mary and Holy St. Joseph! What's porridge! Porridge is porridge. That's what porridge is. Ye are the most ignorant bunch o' Yanks I ever seen. Come on, put on yeer clothes and we'll go across the street to your aunt Aggie. She's there with the husband, Pa Keating, and she'll give ye some porridge.

She picks up Eugene, wraps him in her shawl and we cross the street to Aunt Aggie's. She's living with Uncle Pa again because he said she wasn't a fat cow after all.

Do you have any porridge? Grandma says to Aunt Aggie.

Porridge? Am I supposed to be feeding porridge to a crowd of Yanks?

Pity about you, says Grandma. It won't kill you to give them a little porridge.

And I suppose they'll be wanting sugar and milk on top of everything or they might be banging on my door looking for an egg if you don't mind. I don't know why we have to pay for Angela's mistakes.

Jesus, says Grandma, 'tis a good thing you didn't own that stable in Bethlehem or the Holy Family would still be wanderin' the world crumblin' with the hunger.

Grandma pushes her way past Aunt Aggie, puts Eugene on a chair near the fire and makes the porridge. A man comes in from another room. He has black curly hair and his skin is black and I like his eyes because they're very blue and ready to smile. He's Aunt Aggie's husband, the man who stopped the night we were attacking the fleas and told us all about fleas and snakes, the man with the cough he got from swallowing gas in the war.

Malachy says, Why are you all black? and Uncle Pa Keating laughs and coughs so hard he has to ease himself with a cigarette. Oh, the little Yanks, he says. They're not a bit shy. I'm black because I work at the Limerick Gas Works shoveling coal and coke into the furnaces. Gassed in France and back to Limerick to work in the gas works. When you grow up you'll laugh.

Malachy and I have to leave the table so the big people can sit and have tea. They have their tea but Uncle Pa Keating, who is my uncle because he's married to my aunt Aggie, picks up Eugene and takes him on his lap. He says, This is a sad little fella, and makes funny faces and silly sounds. Malachy and I laugh but Eugene only reaches up to touch the blackness of Pa Keating's skin, and then when Pa pretends to bite his little hand, Eugene laughs and everyone in the room laughs. Malachy goes to Eugene and tries to make him laugh even more but Eugene turns away and hides his face in Pa Keating's shirt.

I think he likes me, says Pa, and that's when Aunt Aggie puts down her teacup and starts to bawl, Waah, waah, waah, big teardrops tumbling down her fat red face.

Aw, Jesus, says Grandma, there she is again. What's up with you this time?

And Aunt Aggie blubbers, To see Pa there with a child on his lap an' me with no hope of having my own.

Grandma barks at her, Stop talkin' like that in front of the children. Have you no shame? When God is good and ready He'll send you your family.

Aunt Aggie sobs, Angela with five born an' one just gone an' her so useless she couldn't scrub a floor an' me with none an' I can scrub an' clean with the best and make any class of a stew or a fry.

Pa Keating laughs, I think I'll keep this little fella.

Malachy runs to him. No, no, no. That's my brother, that's Eugene. And I say, No, no, no, that's our brother.

Aunt Aggie pats the tears on her cheeks. She says, I don't want nothing of Angela's. I don't want nothing that's half Limerick and half North of Ireland, so I don't, so ye can take him home. I'll have me own someday if I have to do a hundred novenas to the Virgin Mary and her mother, St. Ann, or if I have to crawl from here to Lourdes on me two bended knees.

Grandma says, That's enough. Ye have had yeer porridge and 'tis time to go home and see if yeer father and mother are back from the hospital.

She puts on her shawl and goes to pick up Eugene but he clutches so hard at Pa Keating's shirt she has to pull him away though he keeps looking back at Pa till we're out the door.

We followed Grandma back to our room. She put Eugene in the bed and gave him a drink of water. She told him to be a good boy and go to sleep for his little brother, Oliver, would be home soon and they'd be playing again there on the floor.

But he kept looking out the window.

She told Malachy and me we could sit on the floor and play but to be quiet because she was going to say her prayers. Malachy went to the bed and sat by Eugene and I sat on a chair at the table making out words on the newspaper that was our tablecloth. All you could hear in the room was Malachy whispering to make Eugene happy and Grandma mumbling to the click of her rosary beads. It was so quiet I put my head on the table and fell asleep.

Dad is touching my shoulder. Come on, Francis, you have to take care of your little brothers.

Mam is slumped on the edge of the bed, making small crying sounds like a bird. Grandma is pulling on her shawl. She says, I'll go down to Thompson the undertaker about the coffin and the carriage. The St. Vincent de Paul Society will surely pay for that, God knows.

She goes out the door. Dad stands facing the wall over the fire, beating on his thighs with his fists, sighing, Och, och, och.

Dad frightens me with his och, och, och, and Mam frightens me with her small bird sounds and I don't know what to do though I wonder if anyone will light the fire in the grate so that we can have tea and bread because it's a long time since we had the porridge. If Dad would move away from the fireplace I could light the fire myself. All you need is paper, a few bits of coal or turf, and a match. He won't move so I try to go around his legs while he's beating on his thighs but he notices me and wants to know why I'm trying to light the fire. I tell him we're all hungry and he lets out a crazy laugh. Hungry? he says. Och, Francis, your wee brother Oliver is dead. Your wee sister is dead and your wee brother is dead.

He picks me up and hugs me so hard I cry out. Then Malachy cries, my mother cries, Dad cries, I cry, but Eugene stays quiet. Then Dad sniffles, We'll have a feast. Come on, Francis.

He tells my mother we'll be back in awhile but she has Malachy and Eugene on her lap in the bed and she doesn't look up. He carries me through the streets of Limerick and we go from shop to shop with him asking for food or anything they can give to a family that has two children dead in a year, one in America, one in Limerick, and in danger of losing three more for the want of food and drink. Most shopkeepers shake their heads. Sorry for your troubles but you could go to the St. Vincent de Paul Society or get the public assistance.

Dad says he's glad to see the spirit of Christ alive in Limerick and they tell him they don't need the likes of him with his northern accent to be telling them about Christ and he should be ashamed of himself dragging a child around like that like a common beggar, a tinker, a knacker.

A few shopkeepers give bread, potatoes, tins of beans and Dad says, We'll go home now and you boys can eat something, but we meet Uncle Pa Keating and he tells Dad he's very sorry for his troubles and would Dad like to have a pint in this pub here?

There are men sitting in this pub with great glasses of black stuff before them. Uncle Pa Keating and Dad have the black stuff, too. They lift their glasses carefully and slowly drink. There is creamy white stuff on their lips, which they lick with little sighs. Uncle Pa gets me a bottle of lemonade and Dad gives me a piece of bread and I don't feel hungry anymore. Still, I wonder how long we'll sit here with Malachy and Eugene hungry at home, hours from the porridge, which Eugene didn't eat anyway.

Dad and Uncle Pa drink their glass of black stuff and have another. Uncle Pa says, Frankie, this is the pint. This is the staff of life. This is the best thing for nursing mothers and for those who are long weaned.

He laughs and Dad smiles and I laugh because I think that's what you're supposed to do when Uncle Pa says something. He doesn't laugh when he tells the other men about Oliver dying. The other men tip their hats to Dad. Sorry for your troubles, mister, and surely you'll have a pint.

Dad says yes to the pints and soon he's singing Roddy McCorley and Kevin Barry and song after song I never heard before and crying over his lovely little girl, Margaret, that died in America and his little boy, Oliver, dead beyond in the City Home Hospital. It frightens me the way he yells and cries and sings and I wish I could be at home with my three brothers, no, my two brothers, and my mother.

The man behind the bar says to Dad, I think now, mister, you've had enough. We're sorry for your troubles but you have to take that child home to his mother that must be heartbroken by the fire.

Dad says, One, one more pint, just one, eh? and the man says no. Dad shakes his fist. I did me bit for Ireland, and when the man comes out and takes Dad's arm, Dad tries to push him away.

Uncle Pa says, Come on now, Malachy, stop the blaguarding. You have to go home to Angela. You have a funeral tomorrow and the lovely children waiting for you.

But Dad struggles till a few men push him out into the darkness. Uncle Pa stumbles out with the bag of food. Come on, he says. We'll go back to your room.

Dad wants to go to another place for a pint but Uncle Pa says he has no more money. Dad says he'll tell everyone his sorrows and they'll give him pints. Uncle Pa says that's a disgraceful thing to do and Dad cries on his shoulder. You're a good friend, he tells Uncle Pa. He cries again till Uncle Pa pats him on the back. It's terrible, terrible, says Uncle Pa, but you'll get over this in time.

Dad straightens up and looks at him. Never, he says. Never.

Next day we rode to the hospital in a carriage with a horse. They put Oliver in a white box that came with us in the carriage and we took him to the graveyard. They put the white box into a hole in the ground and covered it with earth. My mother and Aunt Aggie cried, Grandma looked angry, Dad, Uncle Pa Keating, and Uncle Pat Sheehan looked sad but did not cry and I thought that if you're a man you can cry only when you have the black stuff that is called the pint.

I did not like the jackdaws that perched on trees and gravestones and I did not want to leave Oliver with them. I threw a rock at a jackdaw that waddled over toward Oliver's grave. Dad said I shouldn't throw rocks at jackdaws, they might be somebody's soul. I didn't know what a soul was but I didn't ask him because I didn't care. Oliver was dead and I hated jackdaws. I'd be a man someday and I'd come back with a bag of rocks and I'd leave the graveyard littered with dead jackdaws.

The morning after Oliver's burial Dad went to the Labour Exchange to sign and collect the week's dole, nineteen shillings and sixpence. He said he'd be home by noon, that he'd get coal and make a fire, that we'd have rashers and eggs and tea in honor of Oliver, that we might even have a sweet or two.

He wasn't home by noon, or one, or two, and we boiled and ate the few potatoes the shopkeepers had given the day before. He wasn't home anytime before the sun went down that day in May. There was no sign of him till we heard him, long after the pubs closed, rolling along Windmill Street, singing,

> When all around a vigil keep,
> The West's asleep, the West's alseep—
> Alas, and well may Erin weep
> When Connacht lies in slumber deep.
> There lake and plain smile fair and free,
> 'Mid rocks their guardian chivalry.
> Sing, Oh, let man learn liberty
> From crashing wind and lashing sea.

He stumbled into the room, hanging on to the wall. A snot oozed from his nose and he wiped it away with the back of his hand. He tried to speak. Zeeze shildren should be in bed. Lishen to me. Shildren go to bed.

Mam faced him. These children are hungry. Where's the dole money? We'll get fish and chips so they'll have something in their bellies when they go to sleep.

She tried to stick her hands into his pockets but he pushed her away. Have respheck, he said. Reshpeck in front of shildren.

She struggled to get at his pockets. Where's the money? The children are hungry. You mad oul' bastard, did you drink all the money again? Just what you did in Brooklyn.

He blubbered, Och, poor Angela. And poor wee Margaret and poor wee Oliver.

He staggered to me and hugged me and I smelled the drink I used to smell in America. My face was wet from his tears and his spit and his snot and I was hungry and I didn't know what to say when he cried all over my head.

Then he let me go and hugged Malachy, still going on about the wee sister and the wee brother cold in the ground, and how we all have to pray and be good, how we have to be obedient and do what our mother tells us. He said we have our troubles but it's time for Malachy and me to start school because there's nothing like an education, it will stand to you in the end, and you have to get ready to do your bit for Ireland.

Mam says she can't spend another minute in that room on Windmill Street. She can't sleep with the memory of Oliver in that room, Oliver in the bed, Oliver playing on the floor, Oliver sitting on Dad's lap by the fire. She says it's not good for Eugene to be in that place, that a twin will suffer more over the loss of his brother than even a mother can understand. There's a room going on Hartstonge Street with two beds instead of the one we have here for the six of us, no, the five of us. We're getting that room and to make sure she's going to the Labour Exchange on Thursday to stand in the queue to take the dole money the minute it's handed to Dad. He says she can't do that, he'd be disgraced with the other men. The Labour Exchange is a place for men not for women taking the money from under their noses. She says, Pity about you. If you didn't squander the money in the pubs I wouldn't have to follow you the way I did in Brooklyn.

He tells her he'll be shamed forever. She says she doesn't care. She wants that room on Hartstonge Street, a nice warm comfortable room with a lavatory down the hall like the one in Brooklyn, a room without fleas and the dampness that kills. She wants that room because it's on the same street as Leamy's National School and Malachy and I can come home at the dinner hour, which is noon, for a cup of tea and a cut of fried bread.

On Thursday Mam follows Dad to the Labour Exchange. She marches in behind him and when the man pushes the money toward Dad she takes it. The other men on the dole nudge each other and grin and Dad is disgraced because a woman is never supposed to interfere with a man's dole money. He might want to put sixpence on a horse or have a pint and if all the women start acting like Mam the horses will stop running and Guinness will go broke. But she has the money now and we move to Hartstonge Street. Then she carries Eugene in her arms and we go up the street to Leamy's National School. The headmaster, Mr. Scallan, says we are to return on Monday with a composition book, a pencil, and a pen with a good nib on it. We are not to come to school with ringworm or lice and our noses are to be blown at all times, not on the floor, that spreads the consumption, or on our sleeves, but in a handkerchief or a clean rag. He asks us if we are good boys and when we say we are, he says, Good Lord, what's this? Are they Yanks or what?

Mam tells him about Margaret and Oliver and he says, Lord above, Lord above, there's great suffering in the world. Anyway, we'll put the little fellow, Malachy, in the infants' class and his brother in first class. They're in the same room with one master. Monday morning, then, nine o'clock prompt.

The boys in Leamy's want to know why we talk like that. Are ye Yanks or what? And when we tell them we came from America they want to know, Are ye gangsters or cowboys?

A big boy sticks his face up to mine. I'm asking ye a question, he says. Are ye gangsters or cowboys?

I tell him I don't know and when he pokes his finger into my chest Malachy says, I'm a gangster, Frank's a cowboy. The big boy says, Your little brother is smart and you're a stupid Yank.

The boys around him are excited. Fight, they yell, fight, and he pushes me so hard I fall. I want to cry but the blackness comes over me the way it did with Freddie Leibowitz and I rush at him, kicking and punching. I knock him down and try to grab his hair to bang his head on the ground but there's a sharp sting across the backs of my legs and I'm pulled away from him.

Mr. Benson, the master, has me by the ear and he's whacking me across the legs. You little hooligan, he says. Is that the kind of behavior you brought from America? Well, by God, you'll behave yourself before I'm done with you.

He tells me hold out one hand and then the other and hits me with his stick once on each hand. Go home now, he says, and tell your mother what a bad boy you were. You're a bad Yank. Say after me, I'm a bad boy.

I'm a bad boy.

Now say, I'm a bad Yank.

I'm a bad Yank.

Malachy says, He's not a bad boy. It's that big boy. He said we were cowboys and gangsters.

Is that what you did, Heffernan?

I was only jokin', sir.

No more joking, Heffernan. It's not their fault that they're Yanks.

'Tisn't, sir.

And you, Heffernan, should get down on your two knees every night and thank God you're not a Yank for if you were, Heffernan, you'd be the greatest gangster on two sides of the Atlantic. Al Capone would be coming to you for lessons. You're not to be bothering these two Yanks anymore, Heffernan.

I won't, sir.

And if you do, Heffernan, I'll hang your pelt on the wall. Now go home, all of ye.

There are seven masters in Leamy's National School and they all have leather straps, canes, blackthorn sticks. They hit you with the sticks on the shoulders, the back, the legs, and, especially, the hands. If they hit you on the hands it's called a slap. They hit you if you're late, if you have a leaky nib on your pen, if you laugh, if you talk, and if you don't know things.

They hit you if you don't know why God made the world, if you don't know the patron saint of Limerick, if you can't recite the Apostles' Creed, if you can't add nineteen to forty-seven, if you can't subtract nineteen from forty-seven, if you don't know the chief towns and products of the thirty-two counties of Ireland, if you can't find Bulgaria on the wall map of the world that's blotted with spit, snot, and blobs of ink thrown by angry pupils expelled forever.

They hit you if you can't say your name in Irish, if you can't say the Hail Mary in Irish, if you can't ask for the lavatory pass in Irish.

It helps to listen to the big boys ahead of you. They can tell you about the master you have now, what he likes and what he hates.

One master will hit you if you don't know that Eamon De Valera is the greatest man that ever lived. Another master will hit you if you don't know that Michael Collins was the greatest man that ever lived.

Mr. Benson hates America and you have to remember to hate America or he'll hit you.

Mr. O'Dea hates England and you have to remember to hate England or he'll hit you.

If you ever say anything good about Oliver Cromwell they'll all hit you.

. . .

Even if they slap you six times on each hand with the ash plant or the blackthorn with the knobs you must not cry. You'll be a sissy. There are boys who might jeer at you and mock you on the street but even they have to be careful because the day will come when the master hits and slaps them and they have to keep the tears behind their eyes or be disgraced forever. Some boys say it is better to cry because that pleases the masters. If you don't cry the masters hate you because you've made them look weak before the class and they promise themselves the next time they have you up they'll draw tears or blood or both.

Big boys in fifth class tell us Mr. O'Dea likes to get you in front of the class so that he can stand behind you, pinch your sideburns, which are called cossicks, pull up on them. Up, up, he says, till you're on tiptoe and the tears are filling your eyes. You don't want the boys in the class to see you cry but pulling on the cossicks makes the tears come whether you like it or not and the master likes that. Mr. O'Dea is the one master who can always bring the tears and the shame.

It is better not to cry because you have to stick with the boys in the school and you never want to give the masters any satisfaction.

If the master hits you there's no use complaining to your father or mother. They always say, You deserve it. Don't be a baby.

I know Oliver is dead and Malachy knows Oliver is dead but Eugene is too small to know anything. When he wakes in the morning he says, Ollie, Ollie, and toddles around the room looking under the beds or he climbs up on the bed by the window and points to children on the street, especially children with fair hair like him and Oliver. Ollie, Ollie, he says, and Mam picks him up, sobs, hugs him. He struggles to get down because he doesn't want to be picked up and hugged. He wants to find Oliver.

Dad and Mam tell him Oliver is in heaven playing with angels and we'll all see him again someday but he doesn't understand because he's only two and doesn't have the words and that's the worst thing in the whole world.

Malachy and I play with him. We try to make him laugh. We make funny faces. We put pots on our heads and pretend to let them fall off. We run across the room and pretend to fall down. We take him to the People's Park to see the lovely flowers, play with dogs, roll in the grass.

He sees small children with fair hair like Oliver. He doesn't say Ollie anymore. He only points.

Dad says Eugene is lucky to have brothers like Malachy and me because we help him forget and soon, with God's help, he'll have no memory of Oliver at all.

He died anyway.

Six months after Oliver went, we woke on a mean November morning and there was Eugene, cold in the bed beside us. Dr. Troy came and said that child died of pneumonia and why wasn't he in the hospital long ago? Dad said he didn't know and Mam said she didn't know and Dr. Troy said that's why children die. People don't know. He said if Malachy or I showed the slightest sign of a cough or the faintest rattle in the throat we were to be brought to him no matter what time of day or night. We were to be kept dry at all times because there seemed to be a bit of a weakness in the chest in this family. He told Mam he was very sorry for her troubles and he'd give her a prescription for something to ease the pain of the days to come. He said God was asking too much, too damn much.

Grandma came over to our room with Aunt Aggie. She washed Eugene, and Aunt Aggie went to a shop for a little white gown and a set of rosary beads. They dressed him in a white gown and laid him on the bed by the window where he used to look out for Oliver. They placed his hands on his chest, one hand on top of the other, bound in the little white rosary beads. Grandma brushed the hair back from his eyes and forehead and she said, Doesn't he have lovely soft silky hair? Mam went to the bed and pulled a blanket over his legs to keep him warm. Grandma and Aunt Aggie looked at each other and said nothing. Dad stood at the end of the bed beating his fists against his thighs, talking to Eugene, telling him, Och, it was the River Shannon that harmed you, the dampness from that river that came and took you and Oliver. Grandma said, Will you stop that? You're making the whole house nervous. She took Dr. Troy's prescription and told me run over to O'Connor the chemist for the pills, that there would be no charge due to the kindness of Dr. Troy. Dad said he'd come with me, that we'd go to the Jesuit church and say a prayer for Margaret and Oliver and Eugene, all happy in heaven. The chemist gave us the pills, we stopped to say the prayers, and when we returned to the room, Grandma gave Dad money to bring a few bottles of stout from the pub. Mam said, No, no, but Grandma said, He doesn't have the pills to ease him, God help us, and a bottle of stout will be some small comfort. Then she told him he'd have to go to the undertaker tomorrow to bring the coffin back in a carriage. She told me to go with my father and make sure he didn't stay in the pub all night and drink all the money. Dad said, Och, Frankie shouldn't be in pubs, and she said, Then don't stay there. He put on his cap and we went to South's pub and he told me at the door I could go home now, that he'd be home after one pint. I said, No, and he said, Don't be disobedient. Go home to your poor mother. I said, No, and he said I was a bad boy and God would be displeased. I said I wasn't going home without him and he said, Och, what is the world coming to? He had one quick pint of porter in the pub and we went home with the bottles of stout. Pa Keating was in our room with a small bottle of whiskey and bottles of stout and Uncle Pat Sheehan brought two bottles of stout for himself. Uncle Pat sat on the floor with his arms around his bottles and he kept saying, They're mine, they're mine, for fear they'd be taken from him. People who were dropped on their heads always worry someone will steal their stout. Grandma said, All right, Pat, drink your stout yourself. No one will bother you. She and Aunt Aggie sat on the bed by Eugene. Pa Keating sat at the kitchen table drinking his stout and offering everyone a sip of his whiskey. Mam took her pills and sat by the fire with Malachy on her lap. She kept saying Malachy had hair like Eugene and Aunt Aggie said no he did not till Grandma drove her elbow into Aunt Aggie's chest and told her shut up. Dad stood against the wall drinking his stout between the fireplace and the bed with Eugene. Pa Keating told stories and the big people laughed even though they didn't want to laugh or they weren't supposed to laugh in the presence of a dead child. He said when he was in the English army in France the Germans sent gas over which made him so sick they had to take him to the hospital. They kept him in the hospital a while and then sent him back to the trenches. English soldiers were sent home but they didn't give a fiddler's fart about the Irish soldiers, whether they lived or died. Instead of dying Pa made a vast fortune. He said he solved one of the great problems of trench warfare. In the trenches it was so wet and muddy they had no way of boiling the water for the tea. He said to himself, Jasus, I have all this gas in my system and 'tis a great pity to waste it.

So he shoved a pipe up his arse, lit a match to it, and there in a second he had a fine flame ready to boil water in any billycan. Tommies came running from trenches all around when they heard the news and they gave him any amount of money if he'd let them boil water. He made so much money he was able to bribe the generals to let him out of the army and off he went to Paris where he had a fine time drinking wine with artists and models. He had such a high time of it he spent all his money and when he came back to Limerick the only job he could get was in the gas works shoveling coal into the furnaces. He said there was so much gas in his system now he could supply light to a small town for a year. Aunt Aggie sniffed and said that was not a proper story to be telling in the presence of a dead child and Grandma said it was better to have a story like that than to be sitting around with the long face. Uncle Pat Sheehan, sitting on the floor with his stout, said he was going to sing a song. More power to you, said Pa Keating, and Uncle Pat sang "The Road to Rasheen." He kept saying, Rasheen, Rasheen, mavourneen mean, and the song made no sense because his father dropped him on his head long ago and every time he sang that song he had different words. Grandma said that was a fine song and Pa Keating said Caruso better look over his shoulder. Dad went over to the bed in the corner where he slept with Mam. He sat on the edge, put his bottle on the floor, covered his face with his hands and cried. He said, Frank, Frank, come here, and I had to go to him so that he could hug me the way Mam was hugging Malachy. Grandma said, We better go now and sleep a bit before the funeral tomorrow. They each knelt by the bed and said a prayer and kissed Eugene's forehead. Dad put me down, stood up and nodded to them as they left. When they were gone he lifted each of the stout bottles to his mouth and drained it. He ran his finger inside the whiskey bottle and licked it. He turned down the flame in the paraffin oil lamp on the table and said it was time for Malachy and me to be in bed. We'd have to sleep with him and Mam that night as little Eugene would be needing the bed for himself. It was dark in the room now except for the sliver of streetlight that fell on Eugene's lovely soft silky hair.

Dad lights the fire in the morning, makes the tea, toasts the bread in the fire. He brings Mam's toast and tea but she waves it away and turns to the wall. He brings Malachy and me to Eugene to kneel and say a prayer. He says the prayers of one child like us are worth more in heaven than the prayers of ten cardinals and forty bishops. He shows us how to bless ourselves, In the name of the Father, and of the Son, and of the Holy Ghost. Amen, and he says, Dear God, this is what you want, isn't it? You want my son, Eugene. You took his brother, Oliver, You took his sister, Margaret. I'm not supposed to question that, am I? Dear God above, I don't know why children have to die but that is Your will. You told the river to kill and the Shannon killed. Could You at last be merciful? Could You leave us the children we have? That is all we ask. Amen.

He helps Malachy and me wash our heads and feet so that we'll be clean for Eugene's funeral. We have to be very quiet even when he hurts us cleaning our ears with the corner of the towel we brought from America. We have to be quiet because Eugene is there with his eyes closed and we don't want him to be waking up and looking out the window for Oliver.

Grandma comes and tells Mam she has to get up. There are children dead, she says, but there are children alive and they need their mother. She brings Mam a little tea in a mug to wash down the pills that ease the pain. Dad tells Grandma it's Thursday and he has to go to the Labour Exchange for the dole and then down to the undertaker to bring the mourning carriage and the coffin. Grandma tells him to take me with him but he says it's better for me to stay with Malachy so that I can pray for my little brother dead in the bed. Grandma says, Is it coddin' me you are? Pray for a little child that's barely two and already playing with his little brother in heaven? You'll take your son with you and he'll remind you this is no day for the pubs. She looks at him and he looks at her and he puts on his cap.

At the Labour Exchange we stand at the end of the queue till a man comes from behind the counter and tells Dad he's very sorry for his troubles and he should go ahead of everyone else on this sorrowful day. Men touch their caps and say they're sorry for his troubles and some pat my head and give me pennies, twenty-four pennies, two shillings. Dad tells me I'm rich now and I should buy myself a sweet while he goes into this place for a minute. I know this place is a pub and I know he wants to get the black stuff that is called a pint but I don't say anything because I want to go to the shop next door for a piece of toffee. I chew my toffee till it melts and leaves my mouth all sweet and sticky. Dad is still in the pub and I wonder if I should get another piece of toffee as long as he's in there with the pint. I'm about to give the money to the woman in the shop when my hand is slapped down and there's Aunt Aggie, raging. Is this what you do, she says, on the day of your brother's funeral? Gorgin' yourself on sweets. And where's that father of yours?

He's, he's, in the pub.

Of course he's in the pub. You out here stuffin' yourself with sweets and him in there gettin' himself into a staggerin' condition the day your poor little brother goes to the graveyard. She tells the shop woman, Just like his father, the same odd manner, the same oul' northern jaw.

She tells me get into that pub and tell my father to stop the drinking and get the coffin and the carriage. She will not set foot inside the pub for the drink is the curse of this poor godforsaken country.

Dad is sitting at the back of the pub with a man who has a dirty face and hair growing out of his nose. They're not talking but staring straight ahead and their black pints are resting on a small white coffin on the seat between them. I know that's Eugene's coffin because Oliver had one like it and I want to cry when I see the black pints on top of it. I'm sorry now I ever ate that toffee and I wish I could take it out of my stomach and give it back to the woman in the shop because it's not right to be eating toffee when Eugene is dead in the bed and I'm frightened by the two black pints on his white coffin. The man with Dad is saying, No, mister, you can't leave a child's coffin in a carriage no more. I did that once, went in for a pint and they robbed that little coffin out of the bloody carriage. Can you credit that? It was empty, thank God, but there you are. Desperate times we live in, desperate. The man with Dad lifts his pint and takes a long swallow and when he puts his glass down there's a hollow sound in the coffin. Dad nods at me. We'll be going in a minute, son, but when he goes to put his glass on the coffin after the long swallow I push it away.

That's Eugene's coffin. I'll tell Mam you put your glass on Eugene's coffin.

Now, son. Now, son.

Dad, that's Eugene's coffin.

The other man says, Will we have another pint, mister?

Dad says to me, Wait outside another few minutes, Francis.

No.

Don't be a bad boy.

No.

The other man says, By Jesus, if that was my son I'd kick his arse from here to the County Kerry. He have no right to be talkin' to his father in that manner on a sorrowful day. If a man can't have a pint the day of a funeral what's the use of livin' at all, at all.

Dad says, All right. We'll go.

They finish their pints and wipe the wet brown stains off the coffin with their sleeves. The man climbs up to the driver's seat of the carriage and Dad and I ride inside. He has the coffin on his lap and he presses it against his chest. At home our room is filled with big people, Mam, Grandma, Aunt Aggie, her husband, Pa Keating, Uncle Pat Sheehan, Uncle Tom Sheehan, who is Mam's oldest brother and who never came near us before because he hates people from the North of Ireland. Uncle Tom has his wife, Jane, with him. She's from Galway and people say she has the look of a Spaniard and that's why no one in the family talks to her.

The man takes the coffin from Dad and when he brings it into the room Mam moans, Oh, no, oh, God, no. The man tells Grandma he'll be back in awhile to take us to the graveyard. Grandma tells him he'd better not come back to this house in a drunken state because this child that's going to the graveyard suffered greatly and deserves a bit of dignity and she won't put up with a driver that's drunk and ready to fall out of the high seat.

The man says, Missus, I drove dozens o' children to the graveyard an' never once fell out of any seat, high or low.

The men are drinking stout from bottles again and the women are sipping sherry from jam jars. Uncle Pat Sheehan tells everyone, This is my stout, this is my stout, and Grandma says, 'Tis all right, Pat. No one will take your stout. Then he says he wants to sing "The Road to Rasheen" till Pa Keating says, No, Pat, you can't sing on the day of a funeral. You can sing the night before. But Uncle Pat keeps saying, This is my stout and I want to sing "The Road to Rasheen," and everyone knows he talks like that because he was dropped on his head. He starts to sing his song but stops when Grandma takes the lid off the coffin and Mam sobs, Oh, Jesus, oh, Jesus, will it ever stop? Will I be left with one child?

Mam is sitting on a chair at the head of the bed. She's stroking Eugene's hair and face and hands. She tells him that of all the children in the world he was the sweetest and the most delicate and loving. She tells him 'tis a terrible thing to lose him but isn't he in heaven now with his brother and his sister and isn't that a comfort to us, knowing Oliver is no longer lonesome for his twin. Still, she puts her head down next to Eugene and cries so hard all the women in the room cry with her. She cries till Pa Keating tells her we have to go before the darkness falls, that we can't be in graveyards in the dark.

Grandma whispers to Aunt Aggie, Who'll put the child in the coffin? and Aunt Aggie whispers, I won't. That's the job for the mother.

Uncle Pat hears them. I'll put the child in the coffin, he says. He limps to the bed and places his arms around Mam's shoulders. She looks up at him and her face is drenched. He says, I'll put the child in the coffin, Angela.

Oh, Pat, she says. Pat.

I can do it, he says. Sure he's only a small child an' I never lifted a small child before in my life. I never had a small child in me arms. I won't drop him, Angela. I won't. Honest to God, I won't.

I know you won't, Pat. I know you won't.

I'll lift him an' I won't be singin' "The Road to Rasheen."

I know you won't, Pat, Mam says.

Pat pulls down the blanket Mam put there to keep Eugene warm. Eugene's feet are white and bright with little blue veins. Pat bends over, picks up Eugene and holds him against his chest. He kisses Eugene's forehead and then everyone in the room kisses Eugene. He places Eugene in the coffin and steps back. We are all gathered around looking at Eugene for the last time.

Uncle Pat says, See, I didn't drop him, Angela, and she touches his face.

Aunt Aggie goes to the pub for the driver. He puts the lid on the coffin and screws it down. He says, Who's comin' in the carriage? and takes the coffin to the carriage. There's room only for Mam and Dad, Malachy and me. Grandma says, Ye go ahead to the graveyard and we'll wait here.

I don't know why we can't keep Eugene. I don't know why they have to send him away with that man who puts his pint on the white coffin. I don't know why they had to send Margaret away and Oliver. It is a bad thing to put my sister and my brothers in a box and I wish I could say something to someone.

The horse clop-clopped through the streets of Limerick. Malachy said, Are we going to see Oliver? and Dad said, No, Oliver is in heaven and don't ask me what heaven is because I don't know.

Mam said, Heaven is a place where Oliver and Eugene and Margaret are happy and warm and we'll see them there some day.

Malachy said, The horse did his doodoo on the street and there was a smell, and Mam and Dad had to smile.

At the graveyard the driver climbs down and opens the door of the carriage. Gimme that coffin, he says, an' I'll carry it up to the grave. He yanks at the coffin and stumbles. Mam says, You're not carrying my child in the condition you're in. She turns to Dad. You carry him, she says.

Do what you like, says the driver. Do what you bloody well like, and he climbs up to his seat.

It's getting dark now and the coffin seems whiter than ever in Dad's arms. Mam takes our hands and we follow Dad through the graves. The jackdaws are quiet in the trees because their day is nearly over and they have to rest so that they can get up early in the morning and feed their babies.

Two men with shovels are waiting by a small open grave. One man says, Ye are very late. Good thing this is a small job or we'd be gone. He climbs into the grave. Hand it to me, he says, and Dad hands him the coffin.

The man sprinkles some straw and grass on the coffin and as he climbs out the other man shovels in the earth. Mam lets out a long cry, Oh, Jesus, Jesus, and a jackdaw croaks in a tree. I wish I had a rock to hit that jackdaw. When the men finish shoveling in the earth they wipe their foreheads and wait. One says, Ah, well, now, there's usually a little something for the thirst that's in it.

Dad says, Oh, yes, yes, and gives them money. They say, Sorry for your troubles, and they leave.

We make our way back to the carriage at the graveyard gate but the carriage is gone. Dad looks around in the darkness and comes back shaking his head. Mam says, That driver is nothing but a dirty old drunkard, God forgive me.

It's a long walk from the graveyard to our room. Mam tells Dad, These children need some nourishment and you have money left from the dole this morning. If you're thinking of going to the pubs tonight you can forget it. We're taking them to Naughton's and they can have fish and chips and lemonade for 'tisn't every day they bury a brother.

The fish and chips are delicious with vinegar and salt and the lemonade is tart in our throats.

When we get home the room is empty. There are empty stout bottles on the table and the fire is out. Dad lights the paraffin oil lamp and you can see the hollow left in the pillow by Eugene's head. You expect to hear him and see him toddling across the room, climbing up on the bed to look out the window for Oliver.

Dad tells Mam he's going out for a walk. She says no. She knows what he's up to, that he can't wait to spend his last few shillings in the pubs. All right, he says. He lights the fire and Mam makes tea and soon we're in bed.

Malachy and I are back in the bed where Eugene died. I hope he's not cold in that white coffin in the graveyard though I know he's not there anymore because angels come to the graveyard and open the coffin and he's far from the Shannon dampness that kills, up in the sky in heaven with Oliver and Margaret where they have plenty of fish and chips and toffee and no aunts to bother you, where all the fathers bring home the money from the Labour Exchange and you don't have to be running around to pubs to find them.

III

Mam says she can't spend another minute in that room on Hartstonge Street. She sees Eugene morning, noon and night. She sees him climbing the bed to look out at the street for Oliver and sometimes she sees Oliver outside and Eugene inside, the two of them chatting away. She's happy they're chatting like that but she doesn't want to be seeing and hearing them the rest of her life. It's a shame to move when we're so near Leamy's National School but if she doesn't move soon she'll go out of her mind and wind up in the lunatic asylum.

We move to Roden Lane on top of a place called Barrack Hill. There are six houses on one side of the lane, one on the opposite side. The houses are called two up, two down, two rooms on top, two on the bottom. Our house is at the end of the lane, the last of the six. Next to our door is a small shed, a lavatory, and next to that a stable.

Mam goes to the St. Vincent de Paul Society to see if there's any chance of getting furniture. The man says he'll give us a docket for a table, two chairs, and two beds. He says we'll have to go to a secondhand furniture shop down in the Irishtown and haul the furniture home ourselves. Mam says we can use the pram she had for the twins and when she says that she cries. She wipes her eyes on her sleeves and asks the man if the beds we're getting are secondhand. He says of course they are, and she says she's very worried about sleeping in beds someone might have died in, especially if they had the consumption. The man says, I'm very sorry, but beggars can't be choosers.

It takes us all day to haul the furniture on the pram from one end of Limerick to the other. There are four wheels on the pram but one is bockety, it wants to go in a different direction. We have two beds, one sideboard with a mirror, a table and two chairs. We're happy with the house. We can walk from room to room and up and down the stairs. You feel very rich when you can go up and down the stairs all day as much as you please. Dad lights the fire and Mam makes the tea. He sits at the table on one chair, she sits on the other and Malachy and I sit on the trunk we brought from America. While we're drinking our tea an old man passes our door with a bucket in his hand. He empties the bucket into the lavatory and flushes and there's a powerful stink in our kitchen. Mam goes to the door and says, Why are you emptying your bucket in our lavatory? He raises his cap to her. Your lavatory, missus? Ah, no. You're making a bit of a mistake there, ha, ha. This is not your lavatory. Sure, isn't this the lavatory for the whole lane. You'll see passing your door here the buckets of eleven families and I can tell you it gets very powerful here in the warm weather, very powerful altogether. 'Tis December now, thank God, with a chill in the air and Christmas around the corner and the lavatory isn't that bad, but the day will come when you'll be calling for a gas mask. So, good night to you, missus, and I hope you'll be happy in your house.

Mam says, Wait a minute, sir. Could you tell me who cleans this lavatory?

Cleans? Ah, Jasus, that's a good one. Cleans, she says. Is it joking you are? These houses were built in the time of Queen Victoria herself and if this lavatory was ever cleaned it must have been done by someone in the middle of the night when no one was lookin'.

And he shuffles up the lane laughing away to himself.

Mam comes back to her chair and her tea. We can't stay here, she says. That lavatory will kill us with all diseases.

Dad says, We can't move again. Where will we get a house for six shillings a week? We'll keep the lavatory clean ourselves. We'll boil buckets of water and throw them in there.

Oh, will we? says Mam, and where will we get the coal or turf or blocks to be boiling water?

Dad says nothing. He finishes his tea and looks for a nail to hang our one picture. The man in the picture has a thin face. He wears a yellow skullcap and a black robe with a cross on his chest. Dad says he was a Pope, Leo the Thirteenth, a great friend of the workingman. He brought this picture all the way from America where he found it thrown out by someone who had no time for the workingman. Mam says he's talking a lot of bloody nonsense and he says she shouldn't say bloody in front of the children. Dad finds a nail but wonders how he's going to get it into the wall without a hammer. Mam says he could go borrow one from the people next door but he says you don't go around borrowing from people you don't know. He leans the picture against the wall and drives the nail with the bottom of a jam jar. The jam jar breaks and cuts his hand and a blob of blood falls on the Pope's head. He wraps his hand in the dish rag and tells Mam, Quick, quick, wipe the blood off the Pope before it dries. She tries to wipe the blood away with her sleeve but it's wool and spreads the blood till the whole side of the Pope's face is smeared. Dad says, Lord above, Angela, you've destroyed the Pope entirely, and she says, Arrah, stop your whining, we'll get some paint and go over his face some day, and Dad says, He's the only Pope that was ever a friend to the workingman and what are we to say if someone from the St. Vincent de Paul Society comes in and sees blood all over him? Mam says, I don't know. It's your blood and 'tis a sad thing when a man can't even drive a nail straight. It just goes to show how useless you are. You'd be better off digging fields and anyway I don't care. I have pain in my back and I'm going to bed.

Och, what am I going to do? Dad says.

Take down the Pope and hide him in the coal hole under the stairs where he won't be seen and he'll be out of harm's way.

I can't, says Dad. It would be bad luck. Coal hole is no place for a Pope. When the Pope is up, he's up.

Suit yourself, says Mam.

I will, says Dad.

This is our first Christmas in Limerick and the girls are out in the lane, skipping rope and singing,

> *Christmas is coming*
> *And the goose is getting fat,*
> *Please put a penny*
> *In the old man's hat.*

93

If you haven't a penny
A ha'penny will do
And if you haven't a ha'penny
God bless you.

Boys tease the girls and call out,

May your mother have an accident
Abroad in the loo.

Mam says she'd like to have a nice Christmas dinner but what can you do when the Labour Exchange reduces the dole to sixteen shillings after Oliver and Eugene died? You pay the rent of six shillings, you have ten shillings left, and what use is that to four people?

Dad can't get any work. He gets up early on weekdays, lights the fire, boils water for the tea and his shaving mug. He puts on a shirt and attaches a collar with studs. He puts on his tie and his cap and goes to the Labour Exchange to sign for the dole. He will never leave the house without collar and tie. A man without collar and tie is a man with no respect for himself. You never know when the clerk at the Labour Exchange might tell you there's a job going at Rank's Flour Mills or the Limerick Cement Company, and even if it's a laboring job what will they think if you appear without collar and tie?

Bosses and foremen always show him respect and say they're ready to hire him, but when he opens his mouth and they hear the North of Ireland accent, they take a Limerickman instead. That's what he tells Mam by the fire and when she says, Why don't you dress like a proper workingman? he says he'll never give an inch, never let them know, and when she says, Why can't you try to talk like a Limerickman? he says he'll never sink that low and the greatest sorrow of his life is that his sons are now afflicted with the Limerick accent. She says, Sorry for your troubles and I hope that's all you'll ever have, and he says that some day, with God's help, we'll get out of Limerick and far from the Shannon that kills.

I ask Dad what afflicted means and he says, Sickness, son, and things that don't fit.

When he's not looking for work Dad goes for long walks, miles into the country. He asks farmers if they need any help, that he grew up on a farm and can do anything. If they hire him he goes to work right away with his cap on and his collar and tie. He works so hard and long the farmers have to tell him to stop. They wonder how a man can work through a long hot day with no thought of food or drink. Dad smiles. He never brings home the money he earns on farms. That money seems to be different from the dole, which is supposed to be brought home. He takes the farm money to the pub and drinks it. If he's not home when the Angelus rings at six o'clock Mam knows he had a day of work. She hopes he might think of his family and pass the pub even once, but he never does. She hopes he might bring home something from the farm, potatoes, cabbage, turnips, carrots, but he'll never bring home anything because he'd never stoop so low as to ask a farmer for anything. Mam says 'tis all right for her to be begging at the St. Vincent de Paul Society for a docket for food but he can't stick a few spuds in his pocket. He says it's different for a man. You have to keep the dignity. Wear your collar and tie, keep up the appearance, and never ask for anything. Mam says, I hope it keeps fine for you.

When the farm money is gone he rolls home singing and crying over Ireland and his dead children, mostly about Ireland. If he sings Roddy McCorley, it means he had only the price of a pint or two. If he sings Kevin Barry, it means he had a good day, that he is now falling down drunk and ready to get us out of bed, line us up and make us promise to die for Ireland, unless Mam tells him leave us alone or she'll brain him with the poker.

You wouldn't do that, Angela.

I would and more. You better stop the nonsense and go to bed.

Bed, bed, bed. What's the use of going to bed? If I go to bed I'll only have to get up again and I can't sleep in a place where there's a river sending poison to us in mist and fog.

He goes to bed, pounds the wall with his fist, sings a woeful song, falls asleep. He's up at daylight because no one should sleep beyond the dawn. He wakes Malachy and me and we're tired from being kept up the night before with his talking and singing. We complain and say we're sick, we're tired, but he pulls back the overcoats that cover us and forces us out on the floor. It's December and it's freezing and we can see our breath. We pee into the bucket by the bedroom door and run down stairs for the warmth of the fire Dad has already started. We wash our faces and hands in a basin that sits under the water tap by the door. The pipe that leads to the tap has to be held to the wall by a piece of twine looped around a nail. Everything around the tap is damp, the floor, the wall, the chair the basin sits on. The water from the tap is icy and our fingers turn numb. Dad says this is good for us, it will make men of us. He throws the icy water on his face and neck and chest to show there's nothing to fear. We hold our hands to the fire for the heat that's in it but we can't stay there long because we have to drink our tea and eat our bread and go to school. Dad makes us say grace before meals and grace after meals and he tells us be good boys at school because God is watching every move and the slightest disobedience will send us straight to hell where we'll never have to worry about the cold again.

And he smiles.

Two weeks before Christmas Malachy and I come home from school in a heavy rain and when we push in the door we find the kitchen empty. The table and chairs and trunk are gone and the fire is dead in the grate. The Pope is still there and that means we haven't moved again. Dad would never move without the Pope. The kitchen floor is wet, little pools of water all around, and the walls are twinkling with the damp. There's a noise upstairs and when we go up we find Dad and Mam and the missing furniture. It's nice and warm there with a fire blazing in the grate, Mam sitting in the bed, and Dad reading *The Irish Press* and smoking a cigarette by the fire. Mam tells us there was a terrible flood, that the rain came down the lane and poured in under our door. They tried to stop it with rags but they only turned sopping wet and let the rain in. People emptying their buckets made it worse and there was a sickening stink in the kitchen. She thinks we should stay upstairs as long as there is rain. We'll be warm through the winter months and then we can go downstairs in the springtime if there is any sign of a dryness in the walls or the floor. Dad says it's like going away on our holidays to a warm foreign place like Italy. That's what we'll call the upstairs from now on, Italy. Malachy says the Pope is still on the wall downstairs and he's going to be all cold and couldn't we bring him up? but Mam says, No, he's going to stay where he is because I don't want him on the wall glaring at me in the bed. Isn't it enough that we dragged him all the way from Brooklyn to Belfast to Dublin to Limerick? All I want now is a little peace, ease and comfort.

. . . .

Mam takes Malachy and me to the St. Vincent de Paul Society to stand in the queue and see if there's any chance of getting something for the Christmas dinner—a goose or a ham, but the man says everyone in Limerick is desperate this Christmas. He gives her a docket for groceries at McGrath's shop and another one for the butcher.

No goose, says the butcher, no ham. No fancy items when you bring the docket from the St. Vincent de Paul. What you can have now, missus, is black pudding and tripe or a sheep's head or a nice pig's head. No harm in a pig's head, missus, plenty of meat and children love it, slice that cheek, slather it with mustard and you're in heaven, though I suppose they wouldn't have the likes of that in America where they're mad for the steak and all classes of poultry, flying, walking or swimming itself.

He tells Mam, no, she can't have boiled bacon or sausages and if she has any sense she'll take the pig's head before they're all gone the way the poor people of Limerick are clamoring for them.

Mam says the pig's head isn't right for Christmas and he says 'tis more than the Holy Family had in that cold stable in Bethlehem long ago. You wouldn't find them complaining if someone offered them a nice fat pig's head.

No, they wouldn't complain, says Mam, but they'd never eat the pig's head. They were Jewish.

And what does that have to do with it? A pig's head is a pig's head.

And a Jew is a Jew and 'tis against their religion and I don't blame them.

The butcher says, Are you a bit of an expert, missus, on the Jews and the pig.

I am not, says Mam, but there was a Jewish woman, Mrs. Leibowitz, in New York, and I don't know what we would have done without her.

The butcher takes the pig's head off a shelf and when Malachy says, Ooh, look at the dead dog, the butcher and Mam burst out laughing. He wraps the head in newspaper, hands it to Mam and says, Happy Christmas. Then he wraps up some sausages and tells her, Take these sausages for your breakfast on Christmas Day. Mam says, Oh, I can't afford sausages, and he says, Am I asking you for money? Am I? Take these sausages. They might help make up for the lack of a goose or a ham.

Sure, you don't have to do that, says Mam.

I know that, missus. If I had to do it, I wouldn't.

Mam says she has a pain in her back, that I'll have to carry the pig's head. I hold it against my chest but it's damp and when the newspaper begins to fall away everyone can see the head. Mam says, I'm ashamed of me life that the world should know we're having pig's head for Christmas. Boys from Leamy's National School see me and they point and laugh. Aw, Gawd, look at Frankie McCourt an' his pig's snout. Is that what the Yanks ate for Christmas dinner, Frankie?

One calls to another, Hey, Christy, do you know how to ate a pig's head?

No, I don't, Paddy.

Grab him by the ears an' chew the face offa him.

And Christy says, Hey, Paddy, do you know the only part of the pig the McCourts don't ate?

No, I don't, Christy.

The only part they don't ate is the oink.

After a few streets the newspaper is gone altogether and everyone can see the pig's head. His nose is flat against my chest and pointing up at my chin and I feel sorry for him because he's dead and the world is laughing at him. My sister and two brothers are dead, too, but if anyone laughed at them I'd hit them with a rock.

I wish Dad would come and help us because Mam has to stop every few steps and lean against a wall. She's holding her back and telling us she'll never be able to climb Barrack Hill. Even if Dad came he wouldn't be much use because he never carries anything, parcels, bags, packages. If you carry such things you lose your dignity. That's what he says. He carried the twins when they were tired and he carried the Pope, but that was not the same as carrying ordinary things like a pig's head. He tells Malachy and me that when you grow up you have to wear a collar and tie and never let people see you carry things.

He's upstairs sitting by the fire, smoking a cigarette, reading *The Irish Press,* which he loves because it's De Valera's paper and he thinks De Valera is the greatest man in the world. He looks at me and the pig's head and tells Mam it's a disgraceful thing to let a boy carry an object like that through the streets of Limerick. She takes off her coat and eases herself into the bed and tells him that next Christmas he can go out and find the dinner. She's worn out and gasping for a cup of tea so would he drop his grand airs, boil the water for the tea and fry some bread before his two small sons starve to death.

On Christmas morning he lights the fire early so that we can have sausages and bread and tea. Mam sends me to Grandma to see if we can borrow a pot for the pig's head. Grandma says, What are ye having for yeer dinner? Pig's head! Jesus, Mary an' Joseph, that's goin' beyond the beyonds. Couldn't your father get out and find a ham or a goose at least? What kind of man is he at all, at all?

Mam puts the head in the pot, just covered with water, and while the pig is boiling away Dad takes Malachy and me to Mass at the Redemptorist church. It's warm in the church and sweet with flowers and incense and candles. He takes us to see the Baby Jesus in the crib. He's a big fat baby with fair curls like Malachy. Dad tells us that's Jesus' mother there, Mary, in the blue dress, and his father, St. Joseph, the old man with the beard. He says they're sad because they know Jesus will grow up and be killed so that we can all go to heaven. I ask why the Baby Jesus has to die and Dad says you can't ask questions like that. Malachy says, Why? and Dad tells him be quiet.

Mam is in a terrible state at home. There isn't enough coal to cook the dinner, the water isn't boiling anymore and she says she's demented with worry. We'll have to go down the Dock Road again to see if there's any coal or turf lying around from the lorries. Surely we'll find something on the road this day of all days. Even the poorest of the poor don't go out on Christmas Day picking coal off the road. There's no use asking Dad to go because he will never stoop that low and even if he did he won't carry things through the streets. It's a rule he has. Mam can't go because of the pain in her back.

She says, You'll have to go, Frank, and take Malachy with you.

It's a long way to the Dock Road but we don't mind because our bellies are filled with sausages and bread and it's not raining. We carry a canvas bag Mam borrowed from Mrs. Hannon next door and Mam is right, there is no one on the Dock Road. The poor are all at home having pig's head or maybe a goose and we have the Dock Road to ourselves. We find bits of coal and turf stuck in cracks on the road and in the walls of the coal yards. We find bits of paper and cardboard that will be useful in starting the fire again. We're wandering around trying to fill the bag when Pa Keating comes along. He must have washed himself for Christmas because he's not as black as he was when Eugene died. He wants to know what we're doing with that bag and when Malachy tells him he says, Jesus, Mary and Holy St. Joseph! Christmas Day and ye don't have a fire for yeer pig's head. That's a bloody disgrace.

He takes us to South's pub, which is not supposed to be open, but he's a regular customer and there's a back door for men who want their pint to celebrate the birthday of the Baby Jesus above in the crib. He orders his pint and lemonade for us and asks the man if there's any chance of getting a few lumps of coal. The man says he's been serving drink for twenty-seven years and nobody ever asked him for coal before. Pa says it would be a favor and the man says if Pa asked for the moon he'd fly up and bring it back. The man leads us to the coal hole under the stairs and tells us take what we can carry. It's real coal and not bits from the Dock Road and if we can't carry it we can drag it along the ground.

It takes us a long time to go from South's pub to Barrack Hill because of a hole in the bag. I pull the bag and it's Malachy's job to pick up the lumps that fall through the hole and put them back again. Then it starts to rain and we can't stand in a doorway till it passes because we have that coal and it's leaving a black trail along the pavement and Malachy is turning black from picking up the lumps, pushing them into the bag and wiping the rain from his face with his wet black hands. I tell him he's black, he tells me I'm black, and a woman in a shop tells us get away from that door, 'tis Christmas Day and she doesn't want to be looking at Africa.

We have to keep dragging the bag or we'll never have our Christmas dinner. It will take ages to get a fire going and ages more to get our dinner because the water has to be boiling when Mam puts in the head of cabbage and the potatoes to keep the pig company in the pot. We drag the bag up O'Connell Avenue and we see people in their houses sitting around tables with all kinds of decorations and bright lights. At one house they push up the window and the children point and laugh and call to us, Look at the Zulus. Where are yeer spears?

Malachy makes faces at them and wants to throw coal at them but I tell him if he throws coal there's less for the pig and we'll never get our dinner.

The downstairs in our house is a lake again from the rain pouring under the door but it doesn't matter because we're drenched anyway and we can wade through the water. Dad comes down and drags the bag upstairs to Italy. He says we're good boys for getting so much coal, that the Dock Road must have been covered with it. When Mam sees us she starts to laugh, and then she cries. She's laughing because we're so black and crying because we're sopping wet. She tells us take off all our clothes and she washes the coal off our hands and faces. She tells Dad the pig's head can wait a while so that we can have a jam jar of hot tea.

It's raining outside and there's a lake downstairs in our kitchen but up here in Italy the fire is going again and the room is so dry and warm that, after our tea, Malachy and I doze off in the bed and we don't wake till Dad tells us the dinner is ready. Our clothes are still wet, so Malachy sits on the trunk at the table wrapped in Mam's red American overcoat and I'm wrapped in an old coat that Mam's father left behind when he went to Australia.

There are delicious smells in the room, cabbage, potatoes, and the pig's head, but when Dad lifts the head from the pot to a plate Malachy says, Oh, the poor pig. I don't want to eat the poor pig.

Mam says, If you were hungry you'd eat it. Now stop the nonsense and eat your dinner.

Dad says, Wait a minute. He takes slices from the two cheeks, places them on our plates and smears them with mustard. He takes the plate that holds the pig's head and puts it on the floor under the table. Now, he says to Malachy, that's ham, and Malachy eats it because he's not looking at what it came from and it isn't pig's head anymore. The cabbage is soft and hot and there are plenty of potatoes with butter and salt. Mam peels our potatoes but Dad eats his skin and all. He says all the nourishment of a potato is in the skin and Mam says it's a good thing he's not eating eggs, he'd be chewing the shells and all.

He says he would, and it's a disgrace that the Irish throw out millions of potato skins every day and that's why thousands are dying of consumption and surely there's nourishment in the shell of an egg since waste is the eighth deadly sin. If he had his way, and Mam says, Never mind your way. Eat your dinner.

He eats half a potato with its skin on and puts the other half back in the pot. He eats a small slice of the pig's cheek and a leaf of cabbage and leaves the rest on his plate for Malachy and me. He makes more tea and we have that with bread and jam so that no one can say we didn't have a sweet on Christmas Day.

It's dark now and still raining outside and the coal is glowing in the grate where Mam and Dad sit and smoke their cigarettes. There's nothing to do when your clothes are wet but get back into bed where it's cozy and your father can tell you a story about how Cuchulain became a Catholic and you fall asleep and dream about the pig standing in the crib at the Redemptorist church crying because he and the Baby Jesus and Cuchulain all have to grow up and die.

The angel that brought Margaret and the twins comes again and brings us another brother, Michael. Dad says he found Michael on the seventh step of the stairs to Italy. He says that's what you have to watch for when you ask for a new baby, the Angel on the Seventh Step.

Malachy wants to know how you can get a new brother from the Angel on the Seventh Step if you don't have any stairs in your house and Dad tells him that asking too many questions is an affliction.

Malachy wants to know what an affliction is.

Affliction. I'd like to know what that word means. Affliction, but Dad says, Och, child, the world is an affliction and everything in it, puts on his cap and goes to the Bedford Row Hospital to see Mam and Michael. She's in the hospital with the pain in her back and she has the baby with her to make sure he was healthy when he was left on the seventh step. I don't understand this because I'm sure angels would never leave a sick baby on the seventh step. There's no use asking Dad or Mam about this. They say, You're getting as bad as your brother for asking questions. Go play.

I know that big people don't like questions from children. They can ask all the questions they like, How's school? Are you a good boy? Did you say your prayers? but if you ask them did they say their prayers you might be hit on the head.

Dad brings Mam home with the new baby and she has to stay in bed for a few days with the pain in her back. She says this baby is the spitting image of our sister who died, with his wavy black hair, his lovely blue eyes, and the gorgeous eyebrows. That's what Mam says.

I want to know if the baby will be spitting. I also want to know which is the seventh step because there are nine steps on the stairs and I'd like to know if you count from the bottom or the top. Dad doesn't mind answering this question. Angels come down from above, he says, and not up from kitchens like ours which are lakes from October till April.

So I find the seventh step by counting from the top.

. . .

The baby Michael has a cold. His head is stuffed and he can barely breathe. Mam worries because it's Sunday and the Dispensary for the poor is closed. If you go to the doctor's house and the maid sees you're from the lower classes she tells you go to the Dispensary where you belong. If you tell her the child is dying in your arms she'll say the doctor is in the country riding his horse.

Mam cries because the baby is struggling to get air through his mouth. She tries to clear his nostrils with a bit of rolled-up paper but she's afraid to push it too far up. Dad says, There's no need for that. You're not supposed to be pushing things inside a child's head. It looks like he's going to kiss the baby. Instead, he has his mouth on the little nose and he's sucking sucking the bad stuff out of Michael's head. He spits it into the fire, Michael gives out a loud cry and you can see him drawing the air into his head and kicking his legs and laughing. Mam looks at Dad as if he just came down from heaven and Dad says, That's what we did in Antrim long before there were doctors riding their horses.

Michael entitles us to a few extra shillings on the dole but Mam says it isn't enough and now she has to go to the St. Vincent de Paul Society for food. One night there is a knock on the door and Mam sends me down to see who it is. There are two men from the St. Vincent de Paul and they want to see my mother and father. I tell them my parents are upstairs in Italy and they say, What?

Upstairs where 'tis dry. I'll tell them.

They want to know what that little shed is beside our front door. I tell them it's the lavatory. They want to know why it isn't in the back of the house and I tell them it's the lavatory for the whole lane and it's a good thing it's not in the back of our house or we'd have people traipsing through our kitchen with buckets that would make you sick.

They say, Are you sure there's one lavatory for the whole lane?

I am.

They say, Mother of God.

Mam calls down from Italy. Who's down there?

The men.

What men?

From the St. Vincent de Paul.

They're careful the way they step into the lake in the kitchen and they make tsk tsk and tut tut noises and they tell one another, Isn't this a disgrace? till they get upstairs to Italy. They tell Mam and Dad they're sorry to disturb them but the Society has to be sure they're helping deserving cases. Mam offers them a cup of tea but they look around and say, No, thank you. They want to know why we're living upstairs. They want to know about the lavatory. They ask questions because big people can ask all the questions they like and write in notebooks, especially when they're wearing collars and ties and suits. They ask how old Michael is, how much Dad gets at the Labour Exchange, when did he last have a job, why doesn't he have a job now and what class of an accent is that he has?

Dad tells them the lavatory could kill us with every class of disease, that the kitchen floods in the winter and we have to move upstairs to stay dry. He says the River Shannon is responsible for all the dampness in the world and killing us one by one.

Malachy tells them we're living in Italy and they smile.

Mam asks if there's any chance of getting boots for Malachy and me and they say she'll have to come down to Ozanam House and apply. She says she hasn't been feeling well since the baby came and she wouldn't be able to stand long in a queue, but they say everyone has to be treated the same, even a woman down in the Irishtown that had triplets and, thank you, we'll make our report to the Society.

When they're leaving Malachy wants to show them where the angel left Michael on the seventh step but Dad tells him, Not now, not now. Malachy cries and one of the men gives him a piece of toffee from his pocket and I wish I had something to cry about so that I'd get a piece, too.

I have to go downstairs again and show the men where to step to keep their feet dry. They keep shaking their heads and saying, God Almighty and Mother of God, this is desperate. That's not Italy they have upstairs, that's Calcutta.

Dad is telling Mam up in Italy she should never beg like that.

What do you mean, beg?

Don't you have any pride, begging for boots like that?

And what would you do, Mr. Grand Manner? Would you let them go barefoot?

I'd rather fix the shoes they have.

The shoes they have are falling to pieces.

I can fix them, he says.

You can't fix anything. You're useless, she says.

He comes home the next day with an old bicycle tire. He sends me to Mr. Hannon next door for the loan of a last and a hammer. He takes Mam's sharp knife and he hacks at the tire till he has pieces to fit on the soles and heels of our shoes. Mam tells him he's going to destroy the shoes altogether but he pounds away with the hammer, driving the nails through the rubber pieces and into the shoes. Mam says, God above, if you left the shoes alone they'd last till Easter, at least, and we might get the boots from the St. Vincent de Paul. But he won't stop till the soles and heels are covered with squares of rubber tire which stick out on each side of the shoe and flop before and behind. He makes us put on the shoes and tells us our feet will be good and warm but we don't want to wear them anymore because the tire pieces are so lumpy we stumble when we walk around Italy. He sends me back to Mr. Hannon with the last and hammer and Mrs. Hannon says, God above, what's up with your shoes? She laughs and Mr. Hannon shakes his head and I feel ashamed. I don't want to go to school next day and I pretend to be sick but Dad gets us up and gives us our fried bread and tea and tells us we should be grateful we have any shoes at all, that there are boys in Leamy's National School who go to school barefoot on bitter days. On our way to school Leamy's boys laugh at us because the tire pieces are so thick they add a few inches to our height and the boys say, How's the air up there? There are six or seven barefoot boys in my class and they don't say anything and I wonder if it's better to have shoes with rubber tires that make you trip and stumble or to go barefoot. If you have no shoes at all you'll have all the barefoot boys on your side. If you have rubber tires on your shoes you're all alone with your brother and you have to fight your own battles. I sit on a bench in the schoolyard shed and take off my shoes and stockings but when I go into the class the master wants to know where my shoes are. He knows I'm not one of the barefoot boys and he makes me go back to the yard, bring in the shoes and put them on. Then he says to the class, There is sneering here. There is jeering at the misfortunes of others. Is there anyone in this class that thinks he's perfect? Raise your hands.

There are no hands.

Is there anyone in this class that comes from a rich family with money galore to spend on shoes? Raise your hands.

There are no hands.

He says, There are boys here who have to mend their shoes whatever way they can. There are boys in this class with no shoes at all. It's not their fault and it's no shame. Our Lord had no shoes. He died shoeless. Do you see Him hanging on the cross sporting shoes? Do you, boys?

No, sir.

What is it you don't see Our Lord doing?

Hanging on the cross and sporting shoes, sir.

Now if I hear of one boy in this class jeering and sneering at McCourt or his brother over their shoes the stick will come out. What will come out, boys?

The stick, sir.

The stick will sting, boys. The ash plant will whistle through the air, it will land on the backside of the boy that jeers, the boy that sneers. Where will it land, boys?

On the boy that jeers, sir.

And?

The boy that sneers, sir.

The boys bother us no more and we wear our shoes with the rubber tires the few weeks to Easter when the St. Vincent de Paul Society gives us the gift of boots.

If I have to get up in the middle of the night to pee in the bucket I go to the top of the stairs and look down to see if the angel might be on the seventh step. Sometimes I'm sure there's a light there and if everyone's asleep I sit on the step in case the angel might be bringing another baby or just coming for a visit. I ask Mam if the angel just brings the babies and then forgets about them. She says, Of course not. The angel never forgets the babies and comes back to make sure the baby is happy.

I could ask the angel all kinds of questions and I'm sure he'd answer, unless it's a girl angel. But I'm sure a girl angel would answer questions, too. I never heard anyone say they didn't.

I sit on the seventh step a long time and I'm sure the angel is there. I tell him all the things you can't tell your mother or father for fear of being hit on the head or told go out and play. I tell him all about school and how I'm afraid of the master and his stick when he roars at us in Irish and I still don't know what he's talking about because I came from America and the other boys were learning Irish a year before me.

I stay on the seventh step till it gets too cold or Dad gets up and tells me go back to bed. He's the one who told me the angel comes to the seventh step in the first place and you'd think he'd know why I'm sitting there. I told him one night that I was waiting for the angel, and he said, Och, now, Francis, you're a bit of a dreamer.

I get back into bed but I can hear him whisper to my mother. The poor wee lad was sitting on the stairs talking away to an angel.

He laughs and my mother laughs and I think, Isn't it curious the way big people laugh over the angel who brought them a new child.

Before Easter we move back downstairs to Ireland. Easter is better than Christmas because the air is warmer, the walls are not dripping with the damp, and the kitchen isn't a lake anymore, and if we're up early we might catch the sun slanting for a minute through the kitchen window.

In fine weather men sit outside smoking their cigarettes if they have them, looking at the world and watching us play. Women stand with their arms folded, chatting. They don't sit because all they do is stay at home, take care of the children, clean the house and cook a bit and the men need the chairs. The men sit because they're worn out from walking to the Labour Exchange every morning to sign for the dole, discussing the world's problems and wondering what to do with the rest of the day. Some stop at the bookie to study the form and place a shilling or two on a sure thing. Some spend hours in the Carnegie Library reading English and Irish newspapers. A man on the dole needs to keep up with things because all the other men on the dole are experts on what's going on in the world. A man on the dole must be ready in case another man on the dole brings up Hitler or Mussolini or the terrible state of the Chinese millions. A man on the dole goes home after a day with the bookie or the newspaper and his wife will not begrudge him a few minutes with the ease and peace of his cigarette and his tea and time to sit in his chair and think of the world.

Easter is better than Christmas because Dad takes us to the Redemptorist church where all the priests wear white and sing. They're happy because Our Lord is in heaven. I ask Dad if the baby in the crib is dead and he says, No, He was thirty-three when He died and there He is, hanging on the cross. I don't understand how He grew up so fast that He's hanging there with a hat made of thorns and blood everywhere, dripping from His head, His hands, His feet, and a big hole near His belly.

Dad says I'll understand when I grow up. He tells me that all the time now and I want to be big like him so that I can understand everything. It must be lovely to wake up in the morning and understand everything. I wish I could be like all the big people in the church, standing and kneeling and praying and understanding everything.

At the Mass people go up to the altar and the priest puts something into their mouths. They come back to their seats with their heads down, their mouths moving. Malachy says he's hungry and he wants some, too. Dad says, Shush, that's Holy Communion, the body and blood of Our Lord.

But, Dad.

Shush, it's a mystery.

There's no use asking more questions. If you ask a question they tell you it's a mystery, you'll understand when you grow up, be a good boy, ask your mother, ask your father, for the love o' Jesus leave me alone, go out and play.

Dad gets his first job in Limerick at the cement factory and Mam is happy. She won't have to stand in the queue at the St. Vincent de Paul Society asking for clothes and boots for Malachy and me. She says it's not begging, it's charity, but Dad says it's begging and shameful. Mam says she can now pay off the few pounds she owes at Kathleen O'Connell's shop and she can pay back what she owes her own mother. She hates to be under obligation to anyone, especially her own mother.

The cement factory is miles outside Limerick and that means Dad has to be out of the house by six in the morning. He doesn't mind because he's used to the long walks. The night before Mam makes him a flask of tea, a sandwich, a hard-boiled egg. She feels sorry for him the way he has to walk three miles out and three miles back. A bicycle would be handy but you'd have to be working a year for the price of it.

Friday is payday and Mam is out of the bed early, cleaning the house and singing.

Anyone can see why I wanted your kiss,
It had to be and the reason is this . . .

There isn't much to clean in the house. She sweeps the kitchen floor and the floor of Italy upstairs. She washes the four jam jars we use for mugs. She says if Dad's job lasts we'll get proper cups and maybe saucers and some day, with the help of God and His Blessed Mother, we'll have sheets on the bed and if we save a long time a blanket or two instead of those old coats which people must have left behind during the Great Famine. She boils water and washes the rags that keep Michael from shitting all over the pram and the house itself. Oh, she says, we'll have a lovely tea when your Pop brings home the wages tonight.

Pop. She's in a good mood.

Sirens and whistles go off all over the city when the men finish work at half-past five. Malachy and I are excited because we know that when your father works and brings home the wages you get the Friday Penny. We know this from other boys whose fathers work and we know that after your tea you can go to Kathleen O'Connell's shop and buy sweets. If your mother is in a good mood she might even give you tuppence to go to the Lyric Cinema the next day to see a film with James Cagney.

The men who work in factories and shops in the city are coming into the lanes to have their supper, wash themselves and go to the pub. The women go to the films at the Coliseum or the Lyric Cinema. They buy sweets and Wild Woodbine cigarettes and if their husbands are working a long time they treat themselves to boxes of Black Magic chocolates. They love the romance films and they have a great time crying their eyes out when there's an unhappy ending or a handsome lover goes away to be shot by Hindus and other non-Catholics.

We have to wait a long time for Dad to walk the miles from the cement factory. We can't have our tea till he's home and that's very hard because you smell the cooking of other families in the lane. Mam says it's a good thing payday is Friday when you can't eat meat because the smell of bacon or sausages in other houses would drive her out of her mind. We can still have bread and cheese and a nice jam jar of tea with lashings of milk and sugar and what more do you want?

The women are gone to the cinemas, the men are in the pubs, and still Dad isn't home. Mam says it's a long way to the cement factory even if he's a fast walker. She says that but her eyes are watery and she's not singing anymore. She's sitting by the fire smoking a Wild Woodbine she got on credit from Kathleen O'Connell. The fag is the only luxury she has and she'll never forget Kathleen for her goodness. She doesn't know how long she can keep the water boiling in this kettle. There's no use making the tea till Dad gets home because it will be stewed, coddled, boiled and unfit to drink. Malachy says he's hungry and she gives him a piece of bread and cheese to keep him going. She says, This job could be the saving of us. 'Tis hard enough for him to get a job with his northern accent and if he loses this one I don't know what we're going to do.

The darkness is in the lane and we have to light a candle. She has to give us our tea and bread and cheese because we're so hungry we can't wait another minute. She sits at the table, eats a bit of bread and cheese, smokes her Wild Woodbine. She goes to the door to see if Dad is coming down the lane and she talks about the paydays when we searched for him all over Brooklyn. She says, Some day we'll all go back to America and we'll have a nice warm place to live and a lavatory down the hall like the one in Classon Avenue and not this filthy thing outside our door.

The women are coming home from the cinemas, laughing, and the men, singing, from the pubs. Mam says there's no use waiting up any longer. If Dad stays in the pubs till closing time there will be nothing left from his wages and we might as well go to bed. She lies in her bed with Michael in her arms. It's quiet in the lane and I can hear her crying even though she pulls an old coat over her face and I can hear in the distance, my father.

I know it's my father because he's the only one in Limerick who sings that song from the North, Roddy McCorley goes to die on the bridge of Toome today. He comes round the corner at the top of the lane and starts Kevin Barry. He sings a verse, stops, holds on to a wall, cries over Kevin Barry. People stick their heads out windows and doors and tell him, For Jasus' sake, put a sock in it. Some of us have to get up in the morning for work. Go home and sing your feckin' patriotic songs.

He stands in the middle of the lane and tells the world to step outside, he's ready to fight, ready to fight and die for Ireland, which is more than he can say for the men of Limerick, who are known the length and breadth of the world for collaborating with the perfidious Saxons.

He's pushing in our door and singing,

> *And if, when all a vigil keep,*
> *The West's asleep, the West's asleep!*
> *Alas! and well my Erin weep,*
> *That Connacht lies in slumber deep,*
> *But hark! a voice like thunder spake*
> *'The West's awake! the West's awake!*
> *Sing, Oh, hurrah, let England quake,*
> *We'll watch till death for Erin's sake!'*

He calls from the bottom of the stairs, Angela, Angela, is there a drop of tea in this house?

She doesn't answer and he calls again, Francis, Malachy, come down here, boys. I have the Friday Penny for you.

I want to go down and get the Friday Penny but Mam is sobbing with the coat over her mouth and Malachy says, I don't want his old Friday Penny. He can keep it.

Dad is stumbling up the stairs, making a speech about how we all have to die for Ireland. He lights a match and touches it to the candle by Mam's bed. He holds the candle over his head and marches around the room, singing,

> *See who comes over the red-blossomed heather,*
> *Their green banners kissing the pure mountain air,*
> *Heads erect, eyes to front, stepping proudly together,*
> *Sure freedom sits throned on each proud spirit there.*

Michael wakes and lets out a loud cry, the Hannons are banging on the wall next door, Mam is telling Dad he's a disgrace and why doesn't he get out of the house altogether.

He stands in the middle of the floor with the candle over his head. He pulls a penny from his pocket and waves it to Malachy and me. Your Friday Penny, boys, he says. I want you to jump out of that bed and line up here like two soldiers and promise to die for Ireland and I'll give the two of you the Friday Penny.

Malachy sits up in the bed. I don't want it, he says.

And I tell him I don't want it, either.

Dad stands for a minute, swaying, and puts the penny back in his pocket. He turns toward Mam and she says, You're not sleeping in this bed tonight. He makes his way downstairs with the candle, sleeps on a chair, misses work in the morning, loses the job at the cement factory, and we're back on the dole again.

IV

The master says it's time to prepare for First Confession and First Communion, to know and remember all the questions and answers in the catechism, to become good Catholics, to know the difference between right and wrong, to die for the Faith if called on.

The master says it's a glorious thing to die for the Faith and Dad says it's a glorious thing to die for Ireland and I wonder if there's anyone in the world who would like us to live. My brothers are dead and my sister is dead and I wonder if they died for Ireland or the Faith. Dad says they were too young to die for anything. Mam says it was disease and starvation and him never having a job. Dad says, Och, Angela, puts on his cap and goes for a long walk.

The master says we're each to bring threepence for the First Communion catechism with the green cover. The catechism has all the questions and answers we have to know by heart before we can receive First Communion. Older boys in the fifth class have the thick Confirmation catechism with the red cover and that costs sixpence. I'd love to be big and important and parade around with the red Confirmation catechism but I don't think I'll live that long the way I'm expected to die for this or that. I want to ask why there are so many big people who haven't died for Ireland or the Faith but I know if you ask a question like that you get you the thump on the head or you're told go out and play.

It's very handy to have Mikey Molloy living around the corner from me. He's eleven, he has fits and behind his back we call him Molloy the Fit. People in the lane say the fit is an affliction and now I know what affliction means. Mikey knows everything because he has visions in his fits and he reads books. He's the expert in the lane on Girls' Bodies and Dirty Things in General and he promises, I'll tell you everything, Frankie, when you're eleven like me and you're not so thick and ignorant.

It's a good thing he says Frankie so I'll know he's talking to me because he has crossed eyes and you never know who he's looking at. If he's talking to Malachy and I think he's talking to me he might go into a rage and have a fit that will carry him off. He says it's a gift to have crossed eyes because you're like a god looking two ways at once and if you had crossed eyes in the ancient Roman times you had no problem getting a good job. If you look at pictures of Roman emperors you'll see there's always a great hint of crossed eyes. When he's not having the fit he sits on the ground at the top of the lane reading the books his father brings home from the Carnegie Library. His mother says books books books, he's ruining his eyes with the reading, he needs an operation to straighten them but who'll pay for it. She tells him if he keeps on straining his eyes they'll float together till he has one eye in the middle of his head. Ever after his father calls him Cyclops, who is in a Greek story.

Nora Molloy knows my mother from the queues at the St. Vincent de Paul Society. She tells Mam that Mikey has more sense than twelve men drinking pints in a pub. He knows the names of all the Popes from St. Peter to Pius the Eleventh. He's only eleven but he's a man, oh, a man indeed. Many a week he saves the family from pure starvation. He borrows a handcart from Aidan Farrell and knocks on doors all over Limerick to see if there are people who want coal or turf delivered, and down the Dock Road he'll go to haul back great bags a hundredweight or more. He'll run messages for old people who can't walk and if they don't have a penny to give him a prayer will do.

If he earns a little money he hands it over to his mother, who loves her Mikey. He is her world, her heart's blood, her pulse, and if anything ever happened to him they might as well stick her in the lunatic asylum and throw away the key.

Mikey's father, Peter, is a great champion. He wins bets in the pubs by drinking more pints than anyone. All he has to do is go out to the jakes, stick his finger down his throat and bring it all up so that he can start another round. Peter is such a champion he can stand in the jakes and throw up without using his finger. He's such a champion they could chop off his fingers and he'd carry on regardless. He wins all that money but doesn't bring it home. Sometimes he's like my father and drinks the dole itself and that's why Nora Molloy is often carted off to the lunatic asylum demented with worry over her hungry famishing family. She knows as long as you're in the asylum you're safe from the world and its torments, there's nothing you can do, you're protected, and what's the use of worrying. It's well known that all the lunatics in the asylum have to be dragged in but she's the only one that has to be dragged out, back to her five children and the champion of all pint drinkers.

You can tell when Nora Molloy is ready for the asylum when you see her children running around white with flour from poll to toe. That happens when Peter drinks the dole money and leaves her desperate and she knows the men will come to take her away. You know she's inside frantic with the baking. She wants to make sure the children won't starve while she's gone and she roams Limerick begging for flour. She goes to priests, nuns, Protestants, Quakers. She goes to Rank's Flour Mills and begs for the sweepings from the floor. She bakes day and night. Peter begs her to stop but she screams, This is what comes of drinking the dole. He tells her the bread will only go stale. There's no use talking to her. Bake bake bake. If she had the money she'd bake all the flour in Limerick and regions beyond. If the men didn't come from the lunatic asylum to take her away she'd bake till she fell to the floor.

The children stuff themselves with so much bread people in the lane say they're looking like loaves. Still the bread goes stale and Mikey is so bothered by the waste he talks to a rich woman with a cookbook and she tells him make bread pudding. He boils the hard bread in water and sour milk and throws in a cup of sugar and his brother loves it even if that's all they have the fortnight their mother is in the lunatic asylum.

My father says, Do they take her away because she's gone mad baking bread or does she go mad baking bread because they're taking her away?

Nora comes home calm as if she had been at the seaside. She always says, Where's Mikey? Is he alive? She worries over Mikey because he's not a proper Catholic and if he had a fit and died who knows where he might wind up in the next life. He's not a proper Catholic because he could never receive his First Communion for fear of getting anything on his tongue that might cause a fit and choke him. The master tried over and over with bits of the *Limerick Leader* but Mikey kept spitting them out till the master got into a state and sent him to the priest, who wrote to the bishop, who said, Don't bother me, handle it yourself. The master sent a note home saying Mikey was to practice receiving Communion with his father or mother but even they couldn't get him to swallow a piece of the *Limerick Leader* in the shape of a wafer. They even tried a piece of bread shaped like the wafer with bread and jam and it was no use. The priest tells Mrs. Molloy not to worry. God moves in mysterious ways His wonders to perform and surely He has a special purpose for Mikey, fits and all. She says, Isn't it remarkable he can swally all kinds of sweets and buns but if he has to swally the body of Our Lord he goes into a fit? Isn't that remarkable? She worries Mikey might have the fit and die and go to hell if he has any class of a sin on his soul though everyone knows he's an angel out of heaven. Mikey tells her God is not going to afflict you with the fit and then boot you into hell on top of it. What kind of a God would do a thing like that?

Are you sure, Mikey?

I am. I read it in a book.

He sits under the lamppost at the top of the lane and laughs over his First Communion day, which was all a cod. He couldn't swallow the wafer but did that stop his mother from parading him around Limerick in his little black suit for The Collection? She said to Mikey, Well, I'm not lying so I'm not. I'm only saying to the neighbors, Here's Mikey in his First Communion suit. That's all I'm saying, mind you. Here's Mikey. If they think you swallied your First Communion who am I to contradict them and disappoint them? Mikey's father said, Don't worry, Cyclops. You have loads of time. Jesus didn't become a proper Catholic till he took the bread and wine at the Last Supper and He was thirty-three years of age. Nora Molloy said, Will you stop calling him Cyclops? He has two eyes in his head and he's not a Greek. But Mikey's father, champion of all pint drinkers, is like my uncle Pa Keating, he doesn't give a fiddler's fart what the world says and that's the way I'd like to be myself.

Mikey tells me the best thing about First Communion is The Collection. Your mother has to get you a new suit somehow so she can show you off to the neighbors and relations and they give you sweets and money and you can go to the Lyric Cinema to see Charlie Chaplin.

What about James Cagney?

Never mind James Cagney. Lots of blather. Charlie Chaplin is your only man. But you have to be with your mother on The Collection. The grown-up people of Limerick are not going to be handing out money to every little Tom Dick and Mick with a First Communion suit that doesn't have his mother with him.

Mikey got over five shillings on his First Communion day and ate so many sweets and buns he threw up in the Lyric Cinema and Frank Goggin, the ticket man, kicked him out. He says he didn't care because he had money left over and went to the Savoy Cinema the same day for a pirate film and ate Cadbury chocolate and drank lemonade till his stomach stuck out a mile. He can't wait for Confirmation day because you're older, there's another collection and that brings more money than First Communion. He'll go to the cinema the rest of his life, sit next to girls from lanes and do dirty things like an expert. He loves his mother but he'll never get married for fear he might have a wife in and out of the lunatic asylum. What's the use of getting married when you can sit in cinemas and do dirty things with girls from lanes who don't care what they do because they already did it with their brothers. If you don't get married you won't have any children at home bawling for tea and bread and gasping with the fit and looking in every direction with their eyes. When he's older he'll go to the pub like his father, drink pints galore, stick the finger down the throat to bring it all up, drink more pints, win the bets and bring the money home to his mother to keep her from going demented. He says he's not a proper Catholic which means he's doomed so he can do anything he bloody well likes.

He says, I'll tell you more when you grow up, Frankie. You're too young now and you don't know your arse from your elbow.

The master, Mr. Benson, is very old. He roars and spits all over us every day. The boys in the front row hope he has no diseases for it's the spit that carries all the diseases and he might be spreading consumption right and left. He tells us we have to know the catechism backwards, forwards and sideways. We have to know the Ten Commandments, the

Seven Virtues, Divine and Moral, the Seven Sacraments, the Seven Deadly Sins. We have to know by heart all the prayers, the Hail Mary, the Our Father, the Confiteor, the Apostles' Creed, the Act of Contrition, the Litany of the Blessed Virgin Mary. We have to know them in Irish and English and if we forget an Irish word and use English he goes into a rage and goes at us with the stick. If he had his way we'd be learning our religion in Latin, the language of the saints who communed intimately with God and His Holy Mother, the language of the early Christians, who huddled in the catacombs and went forth to die on rack and sword, who expired in the foaming jaws of the ravenous lion. Irish is fine for patriots, English for traitors and informers, but it's the Latin that gains us entrance to heaven itself. It's the Latin the martyrs prayed in when the barbarians pulled out their nails and cut their skin off inch by inch. He tells us we're a disgrace to Ireland and her long sad history, that we'd be better off in Africa praying to bush or tree. He tells us we're hopeless, the worst class he ever had for First Communion but as sure as God made little apples he'll make Catholics of us, he'll beat the idler out of us and the Sanctifying Grace into us.

Brendan Quigley raises his hand. We call him Question Quigley because he's always asking questions. He can't help himself. Sir, he says, what's Sanctifying Grace?

The master rolls his eyes to heaven. He's going to kill Quigley. Instead he barks at him, Never mind what's Sanctifying Grace, Quigley. That's none of your business. You're here to learn the catechism and do what you're told. You're not here to be asking questions. There are too many people wandering the world asking questions and that's what has us in the state we're in and if I find any boy in this class asking questions I won't be responsible for what happens. Do you hear me, Quigley?

I do.

I do what?

I do, sir.

He goes on with his speech, There are boys in this class who will never know the Sanctifying Grace. And why? Because of the greed. I have heard them abroad in the schoolyard talking about First Communion day, the happiest day of your life. Are they talking about receiving the body and blood of Our Lord? Oh, no. Those greedy little blaguards are talking about the money they'll get, The Collection. They'll go from house to house in their little suits like beggars for The Collection. And will they take any of that money and send it to the little black babies in Africa? Will they think of those little pagans doomed forever for lack of baptism and knowledge of the True Faith? Little black babies denied knowledge of the Mystical Body of Christ? Limbo is packed with little black babies flying around and crying for their mothers because they'll never be admitted to the ineffable presence of Our Lord and the glorious company of saints, martyrs, virgins. Oh, no. It's off to the cinemas, our First Communion boys run to wallow in the filth spewed across the world by the devil's henchmen in Hollywood. Isn't that right, McCourt?

'Tis, sir.

Question Quigley raises his hand again. There are looks around the room and we wonder if it's suicide he's after.

What's henchmen, sir?

The master's face goes white, then red. His mouth tightens and opens and spit flies everywhere. He walks to Question and drags him from his seat. He snorts and stutters and his spit flies around the room. He flogs Question across the shoulders, the bottom, the legs. He grabs him by the collar and drags him to the front of the room.

Look at this specimen, he roars.

Question is shaking and crying. I'm sorry, sir.

The master mocks him. I'm sorry, sir. What are you sorry for?

I'm sorry I asked the question. I'll never ask a question again, sir.

The day you do, Quigley, will be the day you wish God would take you to His bosom. What will you wish, Quigley?

That God will take me to His bosom, sir.

Go back to your seat, you omadhaun, you poltroon, you thing from the far dark corner of a bog.

He sits down with the stick before him on the desk. He tells Question to stop the whimpering and be a man. If he hears a single boy in this class asking foolish questions or talking about The Collection again he'll flog that boy till the blood spurts.

What will I do, boys?

Flog the boy, sir.

Till?

Till the blood spurts, sir.

Now, Clohessy, what is the Sixth Commandment?

Thou shalt not commit adultery.

Thou shalt not commit adultery what?

Thou shalt not commit adultery, sir.

And what is adultery, Clohessy?

Impure thoughts, impure words, impure deeds, sir.

Good, Clohessy. You're a good boy. You may be slow and forgetful in the sir department and you may not have a shoe to your foot but you're powerful with the Sixth Commandment and that will keep you pure.

Paddy Clohessy has no shoe to his foot, his mother shaves his head to keep the lice away, his eyes are red, his nose always snotty. The sores on his kneecaps never heal because he picks at the scabs and puts them in his·mouth. His clothes are rags he has to share with his six brothers and a sister and when he comes to school with a bloody nose or a black eye you know he had a fight over the clothes that morning. He hates school. He's seven going on eight, the biggest and oldest boy in the class, and he can't wait to grow up and be fourteen so that he can run away and pass for seventeen and join the English army and go to India where it's nice and warm and he'll live in a tent with a dark girl with the red dot on her forehead and he'll be lying there eating figs, that's what they eat in India, figs, and she'll cook the curry day and night and plonk on a ukelele and when he has enough money he'll send for the whole family and they'll all live in the tent especially his poor father who's at home coughing up great gobs of blood because of the consumption. When my mother sees Paddy on the street she says, Wisha, look at that poor child. He's a skeleton with rags and if they were making a film about the famine he'd surely be put in the middle of it.

I think Paddy likes me because of the raisin and I feel a bit guilty because I wasn't that generous in the first place. The master, Mr. Benson, said the government was going to give us the free lunch so we wouldn't have to be going home in the freezing weather. He led us down to a cold room in the dungeons of Leamy's School where the charwoman, Nellie Ahearn, was handing out the half pint of milk and the raisin bun. The milk was frozen in the bottles and we had to melt it between our thighs. The boys joked and said the bottles would freeze our things off and the master roared, Any more of that talk and I'll warm the bottles on the backs of yeer heads. We all searched our raisin buns for a raisin but Nellie said they must have forgotten to put them in and she'd inquire from the man who delivered. We searched again every day till at last I found a raisin in my bun and held it up. The boys started grousing and said they wanted a raisin and Nellie said it wasn't her fault. She'd ask the man again. Now the boys were begging me for the raisin and offering me everything, a slug of their milk, a pencil, a comic book. Toby Mackey said I could have his sister and Mr. Benson heard him and took him out to the hallway and knocked him around till he howled. I wanted the raisin for myself but I saw Paddy Clohessy standing in the corner with no shoes and the room was freezing and he was shivering like a dog that had been kicked and I always felt sad over kicked dogs so I walked over and gave Paddy the raisin because I didn't know what else to do and all the boys yelled that I was a fool and a feckin' eejit and I'd regret the day and after I handed the raisin to Paddy I longed for it but it was too late now because he pushed it right into his mouth and gulped it and looked at me and said nothing and I said in my head what kind of an eejit are you to be giving away your raisin.

Mr. Benson gave me a look and said nothing and Nellie Ahearn said, You're a great oul' Yankee, Frankie.

The priest will come soon to examine us on the catechism and everything else. The master himself has to show us how to receive Holy Communion. He tells us gather round him. He fills his hat with the *Limerick Leader* torn into little bits. He gives Paddy Clohessy the hat, kneels on the floor, tells Paddy to take one bit of paper and place it on his tongue. He shows us how to stick out the tongue, receive the bit of paper, hold it a moment, draw in the tongue, fold your hands in prayer, look toward heaven, close your eyes in adoration, wait for the paper to melt in your mouth, swallow it, and thank God for the gift, the Sanctifying Grace wafting in on the odor of sanctity. When he sticks out his tongue we have to hold in the laugh because we never saw a big purple tongue before. He opens his eyes to catch the boys who are giggling but he can't say anything because he still has God on his tongue and it's a holy moment. He gets off his knees and tells us kneel around the classroom for the Holy Communion practice. He goes around the room placing bits of paper on our tongues and mumbling in Latin. Some boys giggle and he roars at them that if the giggling doesn't stop it's not Holy Communion they'll be getting but the Last Rites and what is that sacrament called, McCourt?

Extreme Unction, sir.

That's right, McCourt. Not bad for a Yank from the sinful shores of Amerikay.

He tells us we have to be careful to stick out our tongues far enough so that the Communion wafer won't fall to the floor. He says, That's the worst thing that can happen to a priest. If the wafer slides off your tongue that poor priest has to get down on his two knees, pick it up with his own tongue and lick the floor around it in case it bounced from one spot to another. The priest could get a splinter that would make his tongue swell to the size of a turnip and that's enough to choke you and kill you entirely.

He tells us that next to a relic of the True Cross the Communion wafer is the holiest thing in the world and our First Communion is the holiest moment in our lives. Talking about First Communion makes the master all excited. He paces back and forth, waves his stick, tells us we must never forget that the moment the Holy Communion is placed on our tongues we become members of that most glorious congregation, the One, Holy, Roman, Catholic and Apostolic Church, that for two thousand years men, women and children have died for the Faith, that the Irish have nothing to be ashamed of in the martyr department. Haven't we provided martyrs galore? Haven't we bared our necks to the Protestant ax? Haven't we mounted the scaffold, singing, as if embarking on a picnic, haven't we, boys?

We have, sir.

What have we done, boys?

Bared our necks to the Protestant ax, sir.

And?

Mounted the scaffold singing, sir.

As if?

Embarking on a picnic, sir.

He says that, perhaps, in this class there is a future priest or a martyr for the Faith, though he doubts it very much for we are the laziest gang of ignoramuses it has ever been his misfortune to teach.

But it takes all kinds, he says, and surely God had some purpose when He sent the likes of ye to infest this earth. Surely God had a purpose when among us He sent Clohessy with no shoes, Quigley with his damnable questions and McCourt heavy with sin from America. And remember this, boys, God did not send His only begotten Son to hang on the cross so that ye can go around on yeer First Communion day with the paws clutching for The Collection. Our Lord died so that ye might be redeemed. It is enough to receive the gift of Faith. Are ye listening to me?

We are, sir.

And what's enough?

The gift of Faith, sir.

Good. Go home.

At night three of us sit under the light pole at the top of the lane reading, Mikey, Malachy and I. The Molloys are like us with their father drinking the dole money or the wages and leaving no money for candles or paraffin oil for the lamp. Mikey reads books and the rest of us read comic books. His father, Peter, brings books from the Carnegie Library so that he'll have something to do when he's not drinking pints or when he's looking after the family anytime Mrs. Molloy is in the lunatic asylum. He lets Mikey read any book he likes and now Mikey is reading this book about Cuchulain and talking as if he knows everything about him. I want to tell him I knew all about Cuchulain when I was three going on four, that I saw Cuchulain in Dublin, that Cuchulain thinks nothing of dropping into my dreams. I want to tell him stop talking about Cuchulain, he's mine, he was mine years ago when I was young, but I can't because Mikey reads us a story I never heard of before, a dirty story about Cuchulain which I can never tell my father or mother, the story of how Emer became Cuchulain's wife.

Cuchulain was getting to be an old man of twenty-one. He was lonely and wanted to get married, which made him weak, says Mikey, and got him killed in the end. All the women in Ireland were mad about Cuchulain and they wanted to marry him. He said that would be grand, he wouldn't mind marrying all the women of Ireland. If he could fight all the men of Ireland why couldn't he marry all the women? But the King, Conor MacNessa, said, That's all very well for you, Cu, but the men of Ireland don't want to be lonely in the far reaches of the night. The King decided there would have to be a contest to see who would marry Cuchulain and it would be a pissing contest. All the women of Ireland assembled on the plains of Muirthemne to see who could piss the longest and it was Emer. She was the champion woman pisser of

Ireland and married Cuchulain and that's why to this day she is called Great Bladdered Emer.

Mikey and Malachy laugh over this story though I don't think Malachy understands it. He's young and far from his First Communion and he's only laughing over the piss word. Then Mikey tells me I've committed a sin by listening to a story that has that word in it and when I go to my First Confession I'll have to tell the priest. Malachy says, That's right. Piss is a bad word and you have to tell the priest because 'tis a sin word.

I don't know what to do. How can I go to the priest and tell him this terrible thing in my First Confession? All the boys know what sins they're going to tell so that they'll get the First Communion and make The Collection and go to see James Cagney and eat sweets and cakes at the Lyric Cinema. The master helped us with our sins and everyone has the same sins. I hit my brother. I told a lie. I stole a penny from my mother's purse. I disobeyed my parents, I ate a sausage on Friday.

But now I have a sin no one else has and the priest is going to be shocked and drag me out of the confession box into the aisle and out into the street where everyone will know I listened to a story about Cuchulain's wife being the champion woman pisser in all Ireland. I'll never be able to make my First Communion and mothers will hold their small children up and point at me and say, Look at him. He's like Mikey Molloy, never made his First Communion, wandering around in a state of sin, never made The Collection, never saw James Cagney.

I'm sorry I ever heard of First Communion and The Collection. I'm sick and I don't want any tea or bread or anything. Mam tells Dad it's a strange thing when a child won't have his bread and tea and Dad says, Och, he's just nervous over the First Communion. I want to go over to him and sit on his lap and tell him what Mikey Molloy did to me but I'm too big to be sitting on laps and if I did Malachy would go out in the lane and tell everyone I was a big baby. I'd like to tell my troubles to the Angel on the Seventh Step but he's busy bringing babies to mothers all over the world. Still, I'll ask Dad.

Dad, does the Angel on the Seventh Step have other jobs besides bringing babies?

He does.

Would the Angel on the Seventh Step tell you what to do if you didn't know what to do?

Och, he would, son, he would. That's the job of an angel, even the one on the seventh step.

Dad goes for a long walk, Mam takes Michael and goes to see Grandma, Malachy plays in the lane, and I have the house to myself so that I can sit on the seventh step and talk to the angel. I know he's there because the seventh step feels warmer than the other steps and there's a light in my head. I tell him my troubles and I hear a voice. Fear not, says the voice.

He's talking backward and I tell him I don't know what he's talking about.

Do not fear, says the voice. Tell the priest your sin and you'll be forgiven.

Next morning I'm up early and drinking tea with Dad and telling him about the Angel on the Seventh Step. He places his hand on my forehead to see if I'm feeling all right. He asks if I'm sure I had a light in my head and heard a voice and what did the voice say?

I tell him the voice said Fear not and that means Do not fear.

Dad tells me the angel is right, I shouldn't be afraid, and I tell him what Mikey Molloy did to me. I tell him all about Great Bladdered Emer and I even use the piss word because the angel said, Fear not. Dad puts down his jam jar of tea and pats the back of my hand. Och, och, och, he says, and I wonder if he's going demented like Mrs. Molloy, in and out of the lunatic asylum, but he says, Is that what you were worried about last night?

I tell him it is and he says it's not a sin and I don't have to tell the priest.

But the Angel on the Seventh Step said I should.

All right. Tell the priest if you like but the Angel on the Seventh Step said that only because you didn't tell me first. Isn't it better to be able to tell your father your troubles rather than an angel who is a light and a voice in your head?

'Tis, Dad.

The day before First Communion the master leads us to St. Joseph's Church for First Confession. We march in pairs and if we so much as move a lip on the streets of Limerick he'll kill us on the spot and send us to hell bloated with sin. That doesn't stop the bragging about the big sins. Willie Harold is whispering about his big sin, that he looked at his sister's naked body. Paddy Hartigan says he stole ten shillings from his aunt's purse and made himself sick with ice cream and chips. Question Quigley says he ran away from home and spent half the night in a ditch with four goats. I try to tell them about Cuchulain and Emer but the master catches me talking and gives me a thump on the head.

We kneel in the pews by the confession box and I wonder if my Emer sin is as bad as looking at your sister's naked body because I know now that some things in the world are worse than others. That's why they have different sins, the sacrilege, the mortal sin, the venial sin. Then the masters and grown-up people in general talk about the unforgivable sin, which is a great mystery. No one knows what it is and you wonder how you can know if you've committed it if you don't know what it is. If I tell a priest about Great Bladdered Emer and the pissing contest he might say that's the unforgivable sin and kick me out of the confession box and I'll be disgraced all over Limerick and doomed to hell tormented forever by devils who have nothing else to do but stab me with hot pitchforks till I'm worn out.

I try to listen to Willie's confession when he goes in but all I can hear is a hissing from the priest and when Willie comes out he's crying.

It's my turn. The confession box is dark and there's a big crucifix hanging over my head. I can hear a boy mumbling his confession on the other side. I wonder if there's any use trying to talk to the Angel on the Seventh Step. I know he's not supposed to be hanging around confession boxes but I feel the light in my head and the voice is telling me, Fear not.

The panel slides back before my face and the priest says, Yes, my child?

Bless me, Father, for I have sinned. This is my First Confession.

Yes, my child, and what sins have you committed?

I told a lie. I hit my brother. I took a penny from my mother's purse. I said a curse.

Yes, my child. Anything else?

I, I listened to a story about Cuchulain and Emer.

Surely that's not a sin, my child. After all we are assured by certain writers that Cuchulain turned Catholic in his last moments as did his King, Conor MacNessa.

'Tis about Emer, Father, and how she married him.

How was that, my child?

She won him in a pissing contest.

There is heavy breathing. The priest has his hand over his mouth and he's making choking sounds and talking to himself, Mother o' God.

Who, who told you that story, my child?

Mikey Molloy, Father.

And where did he hear it?

He read it in a book, Father.

Ah, a book. Books can be dangerous for children, my child. Turn your mind from those silly stories and think of the lives of the saints. Think of St. Joseph, the Little Flower, the sweet and gentle St. Francis of Assisi, who loved the birds of the air and the beasts of the field. Will you do that, my child?

I will, Father.

Are there any other sins, my child?

No, Father.

For your penance say three Hail Marys, three Our Fathers, and say a special prayer for me.

I will. Father, was that the worst sin?

What do you mean?

Am I the worst of all the boys, Father?

No, my child, you have a long way to go. Now say an Act of Contrition and remember Our Lord watches you every minute. God bless you, my child.

First Communion day is the happiest day of your life because of The Collection and James Cagney at the Lyric Cinema. The night before I was so excited I couldn't sleep till dawn. I'd still be sleeping if my grandmother hadn't come banging at the door.

Get up! Get up! Get that child outa the bed. Happiest day of his life an' him snorin' above in the bed.

I ran to the kitchen. Take off that shirt, she said. I took off the shirt and she pushed me into a tin tub of icy cold water. My mother scrubbed me, my grandmother scrubbed me. I was raw, I was red.

They dried me. They dressed me in my black velvet First Communion suit with the white frilly shirt, the short pants, the white stockings, the black patent leather shoes. Around my arm they tied a white satin bow and on my lapel they pinned the Sacred Heart of Jesus, a picture of the Sacred Heart, with blood dripping from it, flames erupting all around it and on top a nasty-looking crown of thorns.

Come here till I comb your hair, said Grandma. Look at that mop, it won't lie down. You didn't get that hair from my side of the family. That's that North of Ireland hair you got from your father. That's the kind of hair you see on Presbyterians. If your mother had married a proper decent Limerickman you wouldn't have this standing up, North of Ireland, Presbyterian hair.

She spat twice on my head.

Grandma, will you please stop spitting on my head.

If you have anything to say, shut up. A little spit won't kill you. Come on, we'll be late for the Mass.

We ran to the church. My mother panted along behind with Michael in her arms. We arrived at the church just in time to see the last of the boys leaving the altar rail where the priest stood with the chalice and the host, glaring at me. Then he placed on my tongue the wafer, the body and blood of Jesus. At last, at last.

It's on my tongue. I draw it back.

It stuck.

I had God glued to the roof of my mouth. I could hear the master's voice, Don't let that host touch your teeth for if you bite God in two you'll roast in hell for eternity.

I tried to get God down with my tongue but the priest hissed at me, Stop that clucking and get back to your seat.

God was good. He melted and I swallowed Him and now, at last, I was a member of the True Church, an official sinner.

When the Mass ended there they were at the door of the church, my mother with Michael in her arms, my grandmother. They each hugged me to their bosoms. They each told me it was the happiest day of my life. They each cried all over my head and after my grandmother's contribution that morning my head was a swamp.

Mam, can I go now and make The Collection?

She said, After you have a little breakfast.

No, said Grandma. You're not making no collection till you've had a proper First Communion breakfast at my house. Come on.

We followed her. She banged pots and rattled pans and complained that the whole world expected her to be at their beck and call. I ate the egg, I ate the sausage, and when I reached for more sugar for my tea she slapped my hand away.

Go aisy with that sugar. Is it a millionaire you think I am? An American? Is it bedecked in glitterin' jewelry you think I am? Smothered in fancy furs?

The food churned in my stomach. I gagged. I ran to her backyard and threw it all up. Out she came.

Look at what he did. Thrun up his First Communion breakfast. Thrun up the body and blood of Jesus. I have God in me backyard. What am I goin' to do? I'll take him to the Jesuits for they know the sins of the Pope himself.

She dragged me through the streets of Limerick. She told the neighbors and passing strangers about God in her backyard. She pushed me into the confession box.

In the name of the Father, the Son, the Holy Ghost. Bless me, Father, for I have sinned. It's a day since my last confession.

A day? And what sins have you committed in a day, my child?

I overslept. I nearly missed my First Communion. My grandmother said I have standing up, North of Ireland, Presbyterian hair. I threw up my First Communion breakfast. Now Grandma says she has God in her backyard and what should she do.

The priest is like the First Confession priest. He has the heavy breathing and the choking sounds.

Ah . . . ah . . . tell your grandmother to wash God away with a little water and for your penance say one Hail Mary and one Our Father. Say a prayer for me and God bless you, my child.

Grandma and Mam were waiting close to the confession box. Grandma said, Were you telling jokes to that priest in the confession box? If 'tis a thing I ever find out you were telling jokes to Jesuits I'll tear the bloody kidneys outa you. Now what did he say about God in me backyard?

He said wash Him away with a little water, Grandma.

Holy water or ordinary water?

He didn't say, Grandma.

Well, go back and ask him.

But, Grandma . . .

She pushed me back into the confessional.

Bless me, Father, for I have sinned, it's a minute since my last confession.

A minute! Are you the boy that was just here?

I am, Father.

What is it now?

My grandma says, Holy water or ordinary water?

Ordinary water, and tell your grandmother not to be bothering me again.

I told her, Ordinary water, Grandma, and he said don't be bothering him again.

Don't be bothering him again. That bloody ignorant bogtrotter.

I asked Mam, Can I go now and make The Collection? I want to see James Cagney.

Grandma said, You can forget about The Collection and James Cagney because you're not a proper Catholic the way you left God on the ground. Come on, go home.

Mam said, Wait a minute. That's my son. That's my son on his First Communion day. He's going to see James Cagney.

No he's not.

Yes he is.

Grandma said, Take him then to James Cagney and see if that will save his Presbyterian North of Ireland American soul. Go ahead.

She pulled her shawl around her and walked away.

Mam said, God, it's getting very late for The Collection and you'll never see James Cagney. We'll go to the Lyric Cinema and see if they'll let you in anyway in your First Communion suit.

We met Mikey Molloy on Barrington Street. He asked if I was going to the Lyric and I said I was trying. Trying? he said. You don't have money?

I was ashamed to say no but I had to and he said, That's all right. I'll get you in. I'll create a diversion.

What's a diversion?

I have the money to go and when I get in I'll pretend to have the fit and the ticket man will be out of his mind and you can slip in when I let out the big scream. I'll be watching the door and when I see you in I'll have a miraculous recovery. That's a diversion. That's what I do to get my brothers in all the time.

Mam said, Oh, I don't know about that, Mikey. Wouldn't that be a sin and surely you wouldn't want Frank to commit a sin on his First Communion day.

Mikey said if there was a sin it would be on his soul and he wasn't a proper Catholic anyway so it didn't matter. He let out his scream and

I slipped in and sat next to Question Quigley and the ticket man, Frank Goggin, was so worried over Mikey he never noticed. It was a thrilling film but sad in the end because James Cagney was a public enemy and when they shot him they wrapped him in bandages and threw him in the door, shocking his poor old Irish mother, and that was the end of my First Communion day.

V

Grandma won't talk to Mam anymore because of what I did with God in her backyard. Mam doesn't talk to her sister, Aunt Aggie, or her brother Uncle Tom. Dad doesn't talk to anyone in Mam's family and they don't talk to him because he's from the North and he has the odd manner. No one talks to Uncle Tom's wife, Jane, because she's from Galway and she has the look of a Spaniard. Everyone talks to Mam's brother Uncle Pat, because he was dropped on his head, he's simple, and he sells newspapers. Everyone calls him The Abbot or Ab Sheehan and no one knows why. Everyone talks to Uncle Pa Keating because he was gassed in the war and married Aunt Aggie and if they didn't talk to him he wouldn't give a fiddler's fart anyway and that's why the men in South's pub call him a gas man.

That's the way I'd like to be in the world, a gas man, not giving a fiddler's fart, and that's what I tell the Angel on the Seventh Step till I remember you're not supposed to say fart in the presence of an angel.

Uncle Tom and Galway Jane have children but we're not supposed to talk to them because our parents are not talking. They have a son and daughter, Gerry and Peggy, and Mam will yell at us for talking to them but we don't know how not to talk to our cousins.

People in families in the lanes of Limerick have their ways of not talking to each other and it takes years of practice. There are people who don't talk to each other because their fathers were on opposite sides in the Civil War in 1922. If a man goes off and joins the English army his family might as well move to another part of Limerick where there are families with men in the English army. If anyone in your family was the least way friendly to the English in the last eight hundred years it will be brought up and thrown in your face and you might as well move to Dublin where no one cares. There are families that are ashamed of themselves because their forefathers gave up their religion for the sake of a bowl of Protestant soup during the Famine and those families are known ever after as soupers. It's a terrible thing to be a souper because you're doomed forever to the souper part of hell. It's even worse to be an informer. The master at school said that everytime the Irish were about to demolish the English in a fair fight a filthy informer betrayed them. A man who's discovered to be an informer deserves to be hanged or, even worse, to have no one talk to him for if no one talks to you you're better off hanging at the end of a rope.

In every lane there's always someone not talking to someone or everyone not talking to someone or someone not talking to everyone. You can always tell when people are not talking by the way they pass each other. The women hoist their noses, tighten their mouths and turn their faces away. If the woman is wearing a shawl she takes a corner and flings it over her shoulder as if to say, One word or look from you, you ma-faced bitch, and I'll tear the countenance from the front of your head.

It's bad when Grandma won't talk to us because we can't run to her when we need to borrow sugar or tea or milk. There's no use going to Aunt Aggie. She'll only bite your head off. Go home, she'll say, and tell your father to get off his northern arse and get a job like the decent men of Limerick.

They say she's always angry because she has red hair or she has red hair because she's always angry.

Mam is friendly with Bridey Hannon, who lives next door with her mother and father. Mam and Bridey talk all the time. When my father goes for his long walk Bridey comes in and she and Mam sit by the fire drinking tea and smoking cigarettes. If Mam has nothing in the house Bridey brings tea, sugar and milk. Sometimes they use the same tea leaves over and over and Mam says the tea is stewed, coddled and boiled.

Mam and Bridey sit so close to the fire their shins turn red and purple and blue. They talk for hours and they whisper and laugh over secret things. We're not supposed to hear the secret things so we're told go out and play. I often sit on the seventh step listening and they have no notion I'm there. It might be lashing rain out but Mam says, Rain or no, out you go, and she'll tell us, If you see your father coming, run in and tell me. Mam says to Bridey, Did you ever hear that poem that someone must have made up about me and him?

What poem, Angela?

'Tis called "The Man from the North." I got this poem from Minnie MacAdorey in America.

I never heard that poem. Say it for me.

Mam says the poem but she laughs all through it and I don't know why,

> *He came from the North so his words were few*
> *But his voice was kind and his heart was true.*
> *And I knew by his eyes that no guile had he,*
> *So I married my man from the North Country.*
>
> *Oh, Garryowen may be more gay*
> *Than this quiet man from beside Lough Neagh*
> *And I know that the sun shines softly down*
> *On the river that runs through my native town.*
>
> *But there's not—and I say it with joy and with pride*
> *A better man in all Munster wide*
> *And Limerick town has no happier hearth*
> *Than mine has been with my man from the North.*
>
> *I wish that in Limerick they only knew*
> *The kind kind neighbors I came unto.*
> *Small hate or scorn would there ever be*
> *Between the South and the North Country.*

She always repeats the third verse and laughs so hard she's crying and I don't know why. She goes into hysterics when she says,

And Limerick town has no happier hearth
Than mine has been with my man from the North.

If he comes back early and sees Bridey in the kitchen the man from the North says, Gossip, gossip, gossip, and stands there with his cap on till she leaves.

Bridey's mother and other people in our lane and lanes beyond will come to the door to ask Dad if he'll write a letter to the government or a relation in a distant place. He sits at the table with his pen and bottle of ink and when the people tell him what to write he says, Och, no, that's not what you want to say, and he writes what he feels like writing. The people tell him that's what they wanted to say in the first place, that he has a lovely way with the English language and a fine fist for the writing. They offer him sixpence for his trouble but he waves it away and they hand it to Mam because he's too grand to be taking sixpence. When the people leave he takes the sixpence and sends me to Kathleen O'Connell's shop for cigarettes.

Grandma sleeps in a big bed upstairs with a picture of the Sacred Heart of Jesus over her head and a statue of the Sacred Heart on the mantelpiece. She wants to switch from gaslight to electric light someday so that she'll have a little red light under the statue forever. Her devotion to the Sacred Heart is known up and down the lane and in lanes beyond.

Uncle Pat sleeps in a small bed in a corner of the same room where Grandma can make sure he comes in at a proper hour and kneels by the bed to say his prayers. He might have been dropped on his head, he may not know how to read and write, he may drink one pint too many, but there's no excuse for not saying his prayers before he goes to sleep.

Uncle Pat tells Grandma he met a man who is looking for a place to stay that will let him wash himself morning and night and give him two meals a day, dinner and tea. His name is Bill Galvin and he has a good job down at the lime kiln. He's covered all the time with white lime dust but surely that's better than coal dust.

Grandma will have to give up her bed and move into the small room. She'll take the Sacred Heart picture and leave the statue to watch over the two men. Besides, she has no place for a statue in her little room.

Bill Galvin comes after work to see the place. He's small, all white, and he snuffles like a dog. He asks Grandma if she'd mind taking down that statue because he's a Protestant and he wouldn't be able to sleep. Grandma barks at Uncle Pat for not telling her he was dragging a Protestant into the house. Jesus, she says, there will be gossip up and down the lane and beyond.

Uncle Pat says he didn't know Bill Galvin was a Protestant. You could never tell by looking at him especially the way he's covered with lime. He looks like an ordinary Catholic and you'd never imagine a Protestant would be shoveling lime.

Bill Galvin says his poor wife that just died was a Catholic and she had the walls covered with pictures of the Sacred Heart and the Virgin Mary showing their hearts. He's not against the Sacred Heart himself, it's just that seeing the statue will remind him of his poor wife and give him the heartache.

Grandma says, Ah, God help us, why didn't you tell me that in the first place? Sure I can put the statue on the windowsill in my room and your heart won't be tormented at the sight of it.

Every morning Grandma cooks Bill's dinner and takes it to him at the lime kiln. Mam wonders why he can't take it with him in the morning and Grandma says, Do you expect me to get up at dawn and boil cabbage and pig's toes for his lordship to take in his dinner can?

Mam tells her, In another week school will be over and if you give Frank sixpence a week he'll surely be glad to take Bill Galvin his dinner.

I don't want to go to Grandma's every day. I don't want to take Bill Galvin his dinner all the way down the Dock Road, but Mam says that's sixpence we could use and if I don't do it I'm going nowhere else.

You're staying in the house, she says. You're not playing with your pals.

Grandma warns me to take the dinner can directly and not be meandering, looking this way and that, kicking canisters and ruining the toes of my shoes. This dinner is hot and that's the way Bill Galvin wants it.

There's a lovely smell from the dinner can, boiled bacon and cabbage and two big floury white potatoes. Surely he won't notice if I try

136

half a potato. He won't complain to Grandma because he hardly ever talks outside of a snuffle or two.

It's better if I eat the other half potato so that he won't be asking why he got a half. I might as well try the bacon and cabbage too and if I eat the other potato he'll surely think she didn't send one at all.

The second potato melts in my mouth and I'll have to try another bit of cabbage, another morsel of bacon. There isn't much left now and he'll be very suspicious so I might as well finish off the rest.

What am I going to do now? Grandma will destroy me, Mam will keep me in for a year. Bill Galvin will bury me in lime. I'll tell him I was attacked by a dog on the Dock Road and he ate the whole dinner and I'm lucky I escaped without being eaten myself.

Oh, is that so? says Bill Galvin. And what's that bit of cabbage hanging on your gansey? Did the dog lick you wit his cabbagey gob? Go home and tell your grandmother you ate me whole dinner and I'm falling down with the hunger here in this lime kiln.

She'll kill me.

Tell her don't kill you till she sends me some class of a dinner and if you don't go to her now and get me a dinner I'll kill you and throw your body into the lime there and there won't be much left for your mother to moan over.

Grandma says, What are you doin' back with that can? He could bring that back by himself.

He wants more dinner.

What do you mean more dinner? Jesus above, is it a hole he has in his leg?

He's falling down with the hunger below in the lime kiln.

Is it coddin' me you are?

He says send him any class of a dinner.

I will not. I sent him his dinner.

He didn't get it.

He didn't? Why not?

I ate it.

What?

I was hungry and I tasted it and I couldn't stop.

Jesus, Mary and holy St. Joseph.

She gives me a clout on the head that brings tears to my eyes. She screams at me like a banshee and jumps around the kitchen and threatens to drag me to the priest, the bishop, the Pope himself if he lived around the corner. She cuts bread and waves the knife at me and makes sandwiches of brawn and cold potatoes.

Take these sandwiches to Bill Galvin and if you even look cross-eyed at them I'll skin your hide.

Of course she runs to Mam and they agree the only way I can make up for my terrible sin is to deliver Bill Galvin's dinner for a fortnight without pay. I'm to bring back the can every day and that means I have to sit watching him stuff the food into his gob and he's not one that would ever ask you if you had a mouth in your head.

Every day I take the can back Grandma makes me kneel to the statue of the Sacred Heart and tell Him I'm sorry and all this over Bill Galvin, a Protestant.

Mam says, I'm a martyr for the fags and so is your father.

There may be a lack of tea or bread in the house but Mam and Dad always manage to get the fags, the Wild Woodbines. They have to have the Woodbines in the morning and anytime they drink tea. They tell us every day we should never smoke, it's bad for your lungs, it's bad for your chest, it stunts your growth, and they sit by the fire puffing away. Mam says, If 'tis a thing I ever see you with a fag in your gob I'll break your face. They tell us the cigarettes rot your teeth and you can see they're not lying. The teeth turn brown and black in their heads and fall out one by one. Dad says he has holes in his teeth big enough for a sparrow to raise a family. He has a few left but he gets them pulled at the clinic and applies for a false set. When he comes home with the new teeth he shows his big new white smile that makes him look like an American and whenever he tells us a ghost story by the fire he pushes the lower teeth up beyond his lip to his nose and frightens the life out of us. Mam's teeth are so bad she has to go to Barrington's Hospital to have them all pulled at the same time and when she comes home she's holding at her mouth a rag bright with blood. She has to sit up all night by the fire because you can't lie down when your gums are pumping blood or you'll choke in your sleep. She says she'll give up smoking entirely when this bleeding stops but she needs one puff of a fag this minute for the comfort that's in it. She tells Malachy go to Kathleen O'Connell's shop and ask her would she ever let her have five Woodbines till Dad collects the dole on Thursday. If anyone can get the fags out of Kathleen, Malachy can. Mam says he has the charm, and she tells me, There's no use sending you with your long puss and your father's odd manner.

When the bleeding stops and Mam's gums heal she goes to the clinic for her false teeth. She says she'll give up the smoking when her new teeth are in but she never does. The new teeth rub on her gums and make them sore and the smoke of the Woodbines eases them. She and Dad sit by the fire when we have one and smoke their cigarettes and when they talk their teeth clack. They try to stop the clacking by moving their jaws back and forth but that only makes it worse and they curse the dentists and the people above in Dublin who made the teeth and while they curse they clack. Dad claims these teeth were made for rich people in Dublin and didn't fit so they were passed on to the poor of Limerick who don't care because you don't have much to chew when you're poor anyway and you're grateful you have any class of a tooth in your head. If they talk too long their gums get sore and the teeth have to come out. Then they sit talking by the fire with their faces collapsed. Every night they leave the teeth in the kitchen in jam jars filled with water. Malachy wants to know why and Dad tells him it cleans them. Mam says, No, you can't have teeth in your head while you're sleeping for they'll slip and choke you to death entirely.

The teeth are the cause of Malachy going to Barrington's Hospital and me having an operation. Malachy whispers to me in the middle of the night, Do you want to go downstairs and see if we can wear the teeth?

The teeth are so big we have trouble getting them into our mouths but Malachy won't give up. He forces Dad's upper teeth into his mouth and can't get them out again. His lips are drawn back and the teeth make a big grin. He looks like a monster in a film and it makes me laugh but he pulls at them and grunts, Uck, uck, and tears come to his eyes. The more he goes Uck, uck, the harder I laugh till Dad calls from upstairs, What are you boys doing? Malachy runs from me, up the stairs, and now I hear Dad and Mam laughing till they see he can choke on the teeth. They both stick their fingers in to pull out the teeth but Malachy gets frightened and makes desperate uck uck sounds. Mam says, We'll have to take him to the hospital, and Dad says he'll take him. He makes me go in case the doctor has questions because I'm older than Malachy and that means I must have started all the trouble. Dad rushes through the streets with Malachy in his arms and I try to keep up. I feel sorry for

Malachy up there on Dad's shoulder, looking back at me, tears on his cheeks and Dad's teeth bulging in his mouth. The doctor at Barrington's Hospital says, No bother. He pours oil into Malachy's mouth and has the teeth out in a minute. Then he looks at me and says to Dad, Why is that child standing there with his mouth hanging open?

Dad says, That's a habit he has, standing with his mouth open.

The doctor says, Come here to me. He looks up my nose, in my ears, down my throat, and feels my neck.

The tonsils, he says. The adenoids. They have to come out. The sooner the better or he'll look like an idiot when he grows up with that gob wide as a boot.

Next day Malachy gets a big piece of toffee as a reward for sticking in teeth he can't get out and I have to go to the hospital to have an operation that will close my mouth.

On a Saturday morning Mam finishes her tea and says, You're going to dance.

Dance? Why?

You're seven years old, you made your First Communion, and now 'tis time for the dancing. I'm taking you down to Catherine Street to Mrs. O'Connor's Irish dancing classes. You'll go there every Saturday morning and that'll keep you off the streets. That'll keep you from wandering around Limerick with hooligans.

She tells me wash my face not forgetting ears and neck, comb my hair, blow my nose, take the look off my face, what look? never mind, just take it off, put on my stockings and my First Communion shoes which, she says, are destroyed because I can't pass a canister or a rock without kicking it. She's worn out standing in the queue at the St. Vincent de Paul Society begging for boots for me and Malachy so that we can wear out the toes with the kicking. Your father says it's never too early to learn the songs and dances of your ancestors.

What's ancestors?

Never mind, she says, you're going to dance.

I wonder how I can die for Ireland if I have to sing and dance for Ireland, too. I wonder why they never say, You can eat sweets and stay home from school and go swimming for Ireland.

Mam says, Don't get smart or I'll warm your ear.

Cyril Benson dances. He has medals hanging from his shoulders to his kneecaps. He wins contests all over Ireland and he looks lovely in his saffron kilt. He's a credit to his mother and he gets his name in the paper all the time and you can be sure he brings home the odd few pounds. You don't see him roaming the streets kicking everything in sight till the toes hang out of his boots, oh, no, he's a good boy, dancing for his poor mother.

Mam wets an old towel and scrubs my face till it stings, she wraps the towel around her finger and sticks it in my ears and claims there's enough wax there to grow potatoes, she wets my hair to make it lie down, she tells me shut up and stop the whinging, that these dancing lessons will cost her sixpence every Saturday, which I could have earned bringing Bill Galvin his dinner and God knows she can barely afford it. I try to tell her, Ah, Mam, sure you don't have to send me to dancing school when you could be smoking a nice Woodbine and having a cup of tea, but she says, Oh, aren't you clever. You're going to dance if I have to give up the fags forever.

If my pals see my mother dragging me through the streets to an Irish dancing class I'll be disgraced entirely. They think it's all right to dance and pretend you're Fred Astaire because you can jump all over the screen with Ginger Rogers. There is no Ginger Rogers in Irish dancing and you can't jump all over. You stand straight up and down and keep your arms against yourself and kick your legs up and around and never smile. My uncle Pa Keating said Irish dancers look like they have steel rods up their arses, but I can't say that to Mam, she'd kill me.

There's a gramophone in Mrs. O'Connor's playing an Irish jig or a reel and boys and girls are dancing around kicking their legs out and keeping their hands to their sides. Mrs. O'Connor is a great fat woman and when she stops the record to show the steps all the fat from her chin to her ankles jiggles and I wonder how she can teach the dancing. She comes over to my mother and says, So, this is little Frankie? I think we have the makings of a dancer here. Boys and girls, do we have the makings of a dancer here?

We do, Mrs. O'Connor.

Mam says, I have the sixpence, Mrs. O'Connor.

Ah, yes, Mrs. McCourt, hold on a minute.

She waddles to a table and brings back the head of a black boy with kinky hair, big eyes, huge red lips and an open mouth. She tells me put the sixpence in the mouth and take my hand out before the black boy bites me. All the boys and girls watch and they have little smiles. I drop in the sixpence and pull my hand back before the mouth snaps shut. Everyone laughs and I know they wanted to see my hand caught in the mouth. Mrs. O'Connor gasps and laughs and says to my mother, Isn't that a howl, now? Mam says it's a howl. She tells me behave myself and come home dancing.

I don't want to stay in this place where Mrs. O'Connor can't take the sixpence herself instead of letting me nearly lose my hand in the black boy's mouth. I don't want to stay in this place where you have to stand in line with boys and girls, straighten your back, hands by your sides, look ahead, don't look down, move your feet, move your feet, look at Cyril, look at Cyril, and there goes Cyril, all dressed up in his saffron kilt and the medals jingling, medals for this and medals for that and the girls love Cyril and Mrs. O'Connor loves Cyril for didn't he bring her fame and didn't she teach him every step he knows, oh, dance, Cyril, dance, oh, Jesus, he floats around the room, he's an angel out of heaven and stop the frowning, Frankie McCourt, or you'll have a puss on you like a pound of tripe, dance, Frankie, dance, pick up your feet for the love o' Jesus, onetwothreefourfivesixseven onetwothree and a onetwothree, Maura, will you help that Frankie McCourt before he ties his two feet around his poll entirely, help him, Maura.

Maura is a big girl about ten. She dances up to me with her white teeth and her dancer's dress with all the gold and yellow and green figures that are supposed to come from olden times and she says, Give me your hand, little boy, and she wheels me around the room till I'm dizzy and making a pure eejit of myself and blushing and foolish till I want to cry but I'm saved when the record stops and the gramophone goes hoosh hoosh.

Mrs. O'Connor says, Oh, thank you, Maura, and next week, Cyril, you can show Frankie a few of the steps that made you famous. Next week, boys and girls, and don't forget the sixpence for the little black boy.

Boys and girls leave together. I make my own way down the stairs and out the door hoping my pals won't see me with boys who wear kilts and girls with white teeth and fancy dresses from olden times.

Mam is having tea with Bridey Hannon, her friend from next door. Mam says, What did you learn? and makes me dance around the kitchen, onetwothreefourfivesixseven onetwothree and a onetwothree. She has a good laugh with Bridey. That's not too bad for your first time. In a month you'll be like a regular Cyril Benson.

I don't want to be Cyril Benson. I want to be Fred Astaire.

They turn hysterical, laughing and squirting tea out of their mouths, Jesus love him, says Bridey. Doesn't he have a great notion of himself. Fred Astaire how are you.

Mam says Fred Astaire went to his lessons every Saturday and didn't go around kicking the toes out of his boots and if I wanted to be like him I'd have to go to Mrs. O'Connor's every week.

The fourth Saturday morning Billy Campbell knocks at our door. Mrs. McCourt, can Frankie come out and play? Mam tells him, No, Billy. Frankie is going to his dancing lesson.

He waits for me at the bottom of Barrack Hill. He wants to know why I'm dancing, that everyone knows dancing is a sissy thing and I'll wind up like Cyril Benson wearing a kilt and medals and dancing all over with girls. He says next thing I'll be sitting in the kitchen knitting socks. He says dancing will destroy me and I won't be fit to play any kind of football, soccer, rugby or Gaelic football itself because the dancing teaches you to run like a sissy and everyone will laugh.

I tell him I'm finished with the dancing, that I have sixpence in my pocket for Mrs. O'Connor that's supposed to go into the black boy's mouth, that I'm going to the Lyric Cinema instead. Sixpence will get the two of us in with tuppence left over for two squares of Cleeves' toffee, and we have a great time looking at *Riders of the Purple Sage*.

Dad is sitting by the fire with Mam and they want to know what steps I learned today and what they're called. I already did "The Siege of Ennis" and "The Walls of Limerick," which are real dances. Now I have to make up names and dances. Mam says she never heard of a dance called "The Siege of Dingle" but if that's what I learned go ahead, dance it, and I dance around the kitchen with my hands down by my sides making my own music, diddley eye di eye di eye diddley eye do you do you, Dad and Mam clapping in time with my feet. Dad says, Och, that's a fine dance and you'll be a powerful Irish dancer and a credit to the men who died for their country. Mam says, That wasn't much for a sixpence.

Next week it's a George Raft film and the week after that a cowboy film with George O'Brien. Then it's James Cagney and I can't take

Billy because I want to get a bar of chocolate to go with my Cleeves' toffee and I'm having a great time till there's a terrible pain in my jaw and it's a tooth out of my gum stuck in my toffee and the pain is killing me. Still, I can't waste the toffee so I pull out the tooth and put it in my pocket and chew the toffee on the other side of my mouth blood and all. There's pain on one side and delicious toffee on the other and I remember what my uncle Pa Keating would say, There are times when you wouldn't know whether to shit or go blind.

I have to go home now and worry because you can't go through the world short a tooth without your mother knowing. Mothers know everything and she's always looking into our mouths to see if there's any class of disease. She's there by the fire and Dad is there and they're asking me the same old questions, the dance and the name of the dance. I tell them I learned "The Walls of Cork" and I dance around the kitchen trying to hum a made-up tune and dying with the pain of my tooth. Mam says, "Walls o' Cork," my eye, there's no such dance, and Dad says, Come over here. Stand there before me. Tell us the truth, Did you go to your dancing classes today?

I can't tell a lie anymore because my gum is killing me and there's blood in my mouth. Besides, I know they know everything and that's what they're telling me now. Some snake of a boy from the dancing school saw me going to the Lyric Cinema and told and Mrs. O'Connor sent a note to say she hadn't seen me in ages and was I all right because I had great promise and could follow in the footsteps of the great Cyril Benson.

Dad doesn't care about my tooth or anything. He says I'm going to confession and drags me over to the Redemptorist church because it's Saturday and confessions go on all day. He tells me I'm a bad boy, he's ashamed of me that I went to the pictures instead of learning Ireland's national dances, the jig, the reel, the dances that men and women fought and died for down those sad centuries. He says there's many a young man that was hanged and now moldering in a lime pit that would be glad to rise up and dance the Irish dance.

The priest is old and I have to yell my sins at him and he tells me I'm a hooligan for going to the pictures instead of my dancing lessons although he thinks himself that dancing is a dangerous thing almost as bad as the films, that it stirs up thoughts sinful in themselves, but even if dancing is an abomination I sinned by taking my mother's sixpence and lying and there's a hot place in hell for the likes of me, say a decade of the rosary and ask God's forgiveness for you're dancing at the gates of hell itself, child.

I'm seven, eight, nine going on ten and still Dad has no work. He drinks his tea in the morning, signs for the dole at the Labour Exchange, reads the papers at the Carnegie Library, goes for his long walks far into the country. If he gets a job at the Limerick Cement Company or Rank's Flour Mills he loses it in the third week. He loses it because he goes to the pubs on the third Friday of the job, drinks all his wages and misses the half day of work on Saturday morning.

Mam says, Why can't he be like the other men from the lanes of Limerick? They're home before the Angelus rings at six o'clock, they hand over their wages, change their shirts, have their tea, get a few shillings from the wife and they're off to the pub for a pint or two.

Mam tells Bridey Hannon that Dad can't be like that and won't be like that. She says he's a right bloody fool the way he goes to pubs and stands pints to other men while his own children are home with their bellies stuck to their backbones for the want of a decent dinner. He'll brag to the world he did his bit for Ireland when it was neither popular nor profitable, that he'll gladly die for Ireland when the call comes, that he regrets he has only one life to give for his poor misfortunate country and if anyone disagrees they're invited to step outside and settle this for once and for all.

Oh, no, says Mam, they won't disagree and they won't step outside, that bunch of tinkers and knackers and begrudgers that hang around the pubs. They tell him he's a grand man, even if he's from the North, and 'twould be an honor to accept a pint from such a patriot.

Mam tells Bridey, I don't know under God what I'm going to do. The dole is nineteen shillings and sixpence a week, the rent is six and six, and that leaves thirteen shillings to feed and clothe five people and keep us warm in the winter.

Bridey drags on her Woodbine, drinks her tea and declares that God is good. Mam says she's sure God is good for someone somewhere but He hasn't been seen lately in the lanes of Limerick.

Bridey laughs. Oh, Angela, you could go to hell for that, and Mam says, Aren't I there already, Bridey?

And they laugh and drink their tea and smoke their Woodbines and tell one another the fag is the only comfort they have.

'Tis.

Question Quigley tells me I have to go to the Redemptorist church on Friday and join the boys' division of the Arch Confraternity. You have to join. You can't say no. All the boys in the lanes and back streets that have fathers on the dole or working in laboring jobs have to join.

Question says, Your father is a foreigner from the North and he don't matter but you still have to join.

Everyone knows Limerick is the holiest city in Ireland because it has the Arch Confraternity of the Holy Family, the biggest sodality in the world. Any city can have a Confraternity, only Limerick has the Arch.

Our Confraternity fills the Redemptorist church five nights a week, three for the men, one for the women, one for the boys. There is Benediction and hymn singing in English, Irish and Latin and best of all the big powerful sermon Redemptorist priests are famous for. It's the sermon that saves millions of Chinese and other heathens from winding up in hell with the Protestants.

The Question says you have to join the Confraternity so that your mother can tell the St. Vincent de Paul Society and they'll know you're a good Catholic. He says his father is a loyal member and that's how he got a good pensionable job cleaning lavatories at the railway station and when he grows up himself he'll get a good job too unless he runs away and joins the Royal Canadian Mounted Police so that he can sing "I'll Be Calling You Ooo Ooo Ooo," like Nelson Eddy singing to Jeanette MacDonald expiring with consumption there on the sofa. If he brings me to the Confraternity the man in the office will write his name in a big book and some day he might be promoted to prefect of a section, which is all he wants in life next to wearing the Mountie uniform.

The prefect is head of a section which is thirty boys from the same lanes and streets. Every section has the name of a saint whose picture is painted on a shield stuck on top of a pole by the prefect's seat. The prefect and his assistant take the attendance and keep an eye on us so that they can give us a thump on the head in case we laugh during Benediction or commit any other sacrileges. If you miss one night the man in the office wants to know why, wants to know if you're slipping away from the Confraternity or he might say to the other man in the office, I think our little friend here has taken the soup. That's the worst thing you can say to any Catholic in Limerick or Ireland itself because of what happened in the Great Famine. If you're absent twice the man in the office sends you a yellow summons to appear and explain yourself and if you're absent three times he sends The Posse, which is five or six big boys from your section who search the streets to make sure you're not out enjoying yourself when you should be on your knees at the Confraternity praying for the Chinese and other lost souls. The Posse will go to your house and tell your mother your immortal soul is in danger. Some mothers worry but others will say, Get away from my door or I'll come out and give every one o' ye a good fong in the hole of yeer arse. These are not good Confraternity mothers and the director will say we should pray for them that they'll see the error of their ways.

The worst thing of all is a visit from the director of the Confraternity himself, Father Gorey. He'll stand at the top of the lane and roar in the voice that converted the Chinese millions, Where is the house of Frank McCourt? He roars even though he has your address in his pocket and knows very well where you live. He roars because he wants the world to know you're slipping away from the Confraternity and putting your immortal soul in danger. The mothers are terrified and the fathers will whisper, I'm not here, I'm not here, and they'll make sure you go to the Confraternity from this on out so they won't be disgraced and shamed entirely with the neighbors muttering behind their hands.

The Question takes me to the section St. Finbar's, and the prefect tells me sit over there and shut up. His name is Declan Collopy, he's fourteen and he has lumps on his forehead that look like horns. He has thick ginger eyebrows that meet in the middle and hang over his eyes and his arms hang down to his kneecaps. He tells me he's making this the best section in the Confraternity and if I'm ever absent he'll break my arse and send the bits to my mother. There's no excuse for absence because there was a boy in another section that was dying and still they brought him in on a stretcher. He says, If you're ever absent it better be a death, not a death in the family but your own death. Do you hear me?

I do, Declan.

Boys in my section tell me that prefects get rewards if there is perfect attendance. Declan wants to get out of school as soon as he can and get a job selling linoleum at Cannock's big shop on Patrick Street. His uncle, Foncey, sold linoleum there for years and made enough money to start his own shop in Dublin, where he has his three sons selling linoleum. Father Gorey, the director, can easily get Declan the reward of a job at Cannock's if he's a good prefect and has perfect attendance in his section and that's why Declan will destroy us if we're absent. He tells us, No one will stand between me and the linoleum.

Declan likes Question Quigley and lets him miss an occasional Friday night because the Question said, Declan, when I grow up and get married I'm going to cover my house in linoleum and I'll buy it all from you.

Other boys in the section try this trick with Declan but he says, Bugger off, ye'll be lucky enough to have a pot to piss in never mind yards of linoleum.

Dad says when he was my age in Toome he served Mass for years and it's time for me to be an altar boy. Mam says, What's the use? The child doesn't have proper clothes for school never mind the altar. Dad says the altar boy robes will cover the clothes and she says we don't have the money for robes and the wash they need every week.

He says God will provide and makes me kneel on the kitchen floor. He takes the part of the priest for he has the whole Mass in his head and I have to know the responses. He says, *Introibo ad altare Dei,* and I have to say, *Ad Deum qui laetificat juventutem meam.*

Every evening after tea I kneel for the Latin and he won't let me move till I'm perfect. Mam says he could at least let me sit but he says Latin is sacred and it is to be learned and recited on the knees. You won't find the Pope sitting around drinking tea while he speaks the Latin.

The Latin is hard and my knees are sore and scabby and I'd like to be out in the lane playing though still I'd like to be an altar boy helping the priest vest in the sacristy, up there on the altar all decked out in my red and white robes like my pal Jimmy Clark, answering the priest in Latin, moving the big book from one side of the tabernacle to the other, pouring water and wine into the chalice, pouring water over the priest's hands, ringing the bell at Consecration, kneeling, bowing, swinging the censer at Benediction, sitting off to the side with the palms of my hands on my knees all serious while he gives his sermon, everyone in St. Joseph's looking at me and admiring my ways.

In a fortnight I have the Mass in my head and it's time to go to St. Joseph's to see the sacristan, Stephen Carey, who is in charge of altar boys. Dad polishes my boots. Mam darns my socks and throws an extra coal on the fire to heat up the iron to press my shirt. She boils water to scrub my head, neck, hands and knees and any inch of skin that shows. She scrubs till my skin burns and tells Dad she wouldn't give it to the world to say her son went on the altar dirty. She wishes I didn't have scabby knees from running around kicking canisters and falling down pretending I was the greatest footballer in the world. She wishes we had a drop of hair oil in the house but water and spit will keep my hair from sticking up like black straw in a mattress. She warns me speak up when I go to St. Joseph's and don't be mumbling in English or Latin. She says, 'Tis a great pity you grew out of your First Communion suit but you have nothing to be ashamed of, you come from good blood, McCourts, Sheehans, or my mother's family the Guilfoyles that owned acre after acre in County Limerick before the English took it away and gave it to footpads from London.

Dad holds my hand going through the streets and people look at us because of the way we're saying Latin back and forth. He knocks at the sacristy door and tells Stephen Carey, This is my son, Frank, who knows the Latin and is ready to be an altar boy.

Stephen Carey looks at him, then me. He says, We don't have room for him, and closes the door.

Dad is still holding my hand and squeezes till it hurts and I want to cry out. He says nothing on the way home. He takes off his cap, sits by the fire and lights a Woodbine. Mam is smoking, too. Well, she says, is he going to be an altar boy?

There's no room for him.

Oh. She puffs on her Woodbine. I'll tell you what it is, she says. 'Tis class distinction. They don't want boys from lanes on the altar. They don't want the ones with scabby knees and hair sticking up. Oh, no, they want the nice boys with hair oil and new shoes that have fathers with suits and ties and steady jobs. That's what it is and 'tis hard to hold on to the Faith with the snobbery that's in it.

Och, aye.

Oh, och aye my arse. That's all you ever say. You could go to the priest and tell him you have a son that has a head stuffed with Latin and why can't he be an altar boy and what is he going to do with all that Latin?

Och, he might grow up to be a priest.

I ask him if I can go out and play. Yes, he says, go out and play.

Mam says, You might as well.

VI

Mr. O'Neill is the master in the fourth class at school. We call him Dotty because he's small like a dot. He teaches in the one classroom with a platform so that he can stand above us and threaten us with his ash plant and peel his apple for all to see. The first day of school in September he writes on the blackboard three words which are to stay there the rest of the year, Euclid, geometry, idiot. He says if he catches any boy interfering with these words that boy will go through the rest of his life with one hand. He says anyone who doesn't understand the theorems of Euclid is an idiot. Now, repeat after me, Anyone who doesn't understand the theorems of Euclid is an idiot. Of course we all know what an idiot is because that's what the masters keep telling us we are.

Brendan Quigley raises his hand. Sir, what's a theorem and what's a Euclid?

We expect Dotty to lash at Brendan the way all the masters do when you ask them a question but he looks at Brendan with a little smile. Ah, now, here's a boy with not one but two questions. What is your name, boy?

Brendan Quigley, sir.

This is a boy who will go far. Where will he go, boys?

Far, sir.

Indeed and he will. The boy who wants to know something about the grace, elegance and beauty of Euclid can go nowhere but up. In what direction and no other can this boy go, boys?

Up, sir.

Without Euclid, boys, mathematics would be a poor doddering thing. Without Euclid we wouldn't be able to go from here to there. Without Euclid the bicycle would have no wheel. Without Euclid St. Joseph could not have been a carpenter for carpentry is geometry and geometry is carpentry. Without Euclid this very school could never have been built.

Paddy Clohessy mutters behind me, Feckin' Euclid.

Dotty barks at him. You, boy, what is your name?

Clohessy, sir.

Ah, the boy flies on one wing. What is your Christian name?

Paddy.

Paddy what?

Paddy, sir.

And what, Paddy, were you saying to McCourt?

I said we should get down on our two knees and thank God for Euclid.

I'm sure you did, Clohessy. I see the lie festering in your teeth. What do I see, boys?

The lie, sir.

And what is the lie doing, boys?

Festering, sir.

Where, boys, where?

In his teeth, sir.

Euclid, boys, was a Greek. What, Clohessy, is a Greek?

Some class of a foreigner, sir.

Clohessy, you are a half-wit. Now, Brendan, surely you know what a Greek is?

Yes, sir. Euclid was a Greek.

Dotty gives him the little smile. He tells Clohessy he should model himself on Quigley, who knows what a Greek is. He draws two lines side by side and tells us these are parallel lines and the magical and mysterious thing is that they never meet, not if they were to be extended to infinity, not if they were extended to God's shoulders and that, boys, is a long way though there is a German Jew who is upsetting the whole world with his ideas on parallel lines.

We listen to Dotty and wonder what all this has to do with the state of the world with the Germans marching everywhere and bombing everything that stands. We can't ask him ourselves but we can get Brendan Quigley to do it. Anyone can see Brendan is the master's pet and that means he can ask any question he likes. After school we tell Brendan he has to ask the question tomorrow, What use is Euclid and all those lines that go on forever when the Germans are bombing everything? Brendan says he doesn't want to be the master's pet, he didn't ask for it, and he doesn't want to ask the question. He's afraid if he asks that question Dotty will attack him. We tell him if he doesn't ask the question we'll attack him.

Next day Brendan raises his hand. Dotty gives him the little smile. Sir, what use is Euclid and all the lines when the Germans are bombing everything that stands?

The little smile is gone. Ah, Brendan. Ah, Quigley. Oh, boys, oh, boys.

He lays his stick on the desk and stands on the platform with his eyes closed. What use is Euclid? he says. Use? Without Euclid the Messerschmitt could never have taken to the sky. Without Euclid the Spitfire could not dart from cloud to cloud. Euclid brings us grace and beauty and elegance. What does he bring us, boys?

Grace, sir.

And?

Beauty, sir.

And?

Elegance, sir.

Euclid is complete in himself and divine in application. Do you understand that, boys?

We do, sir.

I doubt it, boys, I doubt it. To love Euclid is to be alone in this world.

He opens his eyes and sighs and you can see the eyes are a little watery.

Paddy Clohessy is leaving the school that day and he's stopped by Mr. O'Dea, who teaches the fifth class. Mr. O'Dea says, You, what's your name?

Clohessy, sir.

What class are you in?

Fourth class, sir.

Now tell me, Clohessy, is that master of yours talking to you about Euclid?

He is, sir.

And what is he saying?

He's saying he's a Greek.

Of course he is, you diddering omadhaun. What else is he saying?

He's saying there would be no school without Euclid.

Ah. Now is he drawing anything on the board?

He's drawing lines side by side that will never meet even if they land on God's shoulders.

Mother o' God.

No, sir. God's shoulders.

I know, you idiot. Go home.

The next day there's a great noise at our classroom door and Mr. O'Dea is yelling, Come out, O'Neill, you chancer, you poltroon. We can hear everything he's saying because of the broken glass over the door.

The new headmaster, Mr. O'Halloran, is saying, Now, now, Mr. O'Dea. Control yourself. No quarreling in front of our pupils.

Well, then, Mr. O'Halloran, tell him stop teaching the geometry. The geometry is for the fifth form and not the fourth. The geometry is mine. Tell him to teach the long division and leave Euclid to me. Long division will stretch his intellect such as it is, God help us. I don't want the minds of these boys destroyed by that chancer up there on the platform, him handing out apple skins and causing diarrhea right and left. Tell him Euclid is mine, Mr. O'Halloran, or I'll put a stop to his gallop.

Mr. O'Halloran tells Mr. O'Dea to return to his classroom and asks Mr. O'Neill to step into the hall. Mr. O'Halloran says, Now, Mr. O'Neill, I have asked you before to stay away from Euclid.

You have, Mr. O'Halloran, but you might as well ask me to stop eating my daily apple.

I'll have to insist, Mr. O'Neill. No more Euclid.

Mr. O'Neill comes back to the room and his eyes are watery again. He says little has changed since the time of the Greeks for the barbarians are within the gates and their names are legion. What has changed since the time of the Greeks, boys?

It is torture to watch Mr. O'Neill peel the apple every day, to see the length of it, red or green, and if you're up near him to catch the freshness of it in your nose. If you're the good boy for that day and you answer the questions he gives it to you and lets you eat it there at your desk so that you can eat it in peace with no one to bother you the way they would if you took it into the yard. Then they'd torment you, Gimme a piece, gimme a piece, and you'd be lucky to have an inch left for yourself.

There are days when the questions are too hard and he torments us by dropping the apple peel into the wastebasket. Then he borrows a boy from another class to take the wastebasket down to the furnace to burn papers and apple peel or he'll leave it for the charwoman, Nellie Ahearn, to take it all away in her big canvas sack. We'd like to ask Nellie to keep the peel for us before the rats get it but she's weary from cleaning the whole school by herself and she snaps at us, I have other things to be doin' with me life besides watchin' a scabby bunch rootin' around for the skin of an apple. Go 'way.

He peels the apple slowly. He looks around the room with the little smile. He teases us, Do you think, boys, I should give this to the pigeons on the windowsill? We say, No, sir, pigeons don't eat apples. Paddy Clohessy calls out, 'Twill give them the runs, sir, and we'll have it on our heads abroad in the yard.

Clohessy, you are an omadhaun. Do you know what an omadhaun is?

I don't, sir.

It's the Irish, Clohessy, your native tongue, Clohessy. An omadhaun is a fool, Clohessy. You are an omadhaun. What is he, boys?

An omadhaun, sir.

Clohessy says, That's what Mr. O'Dea called me, sir, a diddering omadhaun.

He pauses in his peeling to ask us questions about everything in the world and the boy with the best answers wins. Hands up, he says, who is the President of the United States of America?

Every hand in the class goes up and we're all disgusted when he asks a question that any omadhaun would know. We call out, Roosevelt.

Then he says, You, Mulcahy, who stood at the foot of the cross when Our Lord was crucified?

Mulcahy is slow. The Twelve Apostles, sir.

Mulcahy, what is the Irish word for fool?

Omadhaun, sir.

And what are you, Mulcahy?

An omadhaun, sir.

Fintan Slattery raises his hand. I know who stood at the foot of the cross, sir.

Of course Fintan knows who stood at the foot of the cross. Why wouldn't he? He's always running off to Mass with his mother, who is known for her holiness. She's so holy her husband ran off to Canada to cut down trees, glad to be gone and never to be heard from again. She and Fintan say the rosary every night on their knees in the kitchen and read all kinds of religious magazines: *The Little Messenger of the Sacred Heart, The Lantern, The Far East,* as well as every little book printed by the Catholic Truth Society. They go to Mass and Communion rain or shine and every Saturday they confess to the Jesuits who are known for their interest in intelligent sins not the usual sins you hear from people in lanes who are known for getting drunk and sometimes eating meat on Fridays before it goes bad and cursing on top of it. Fintan and his mother live on Catherine Street and Mrs. Slattery's neighbors call her Mrs. Offer-It-Up because no matter what happens, a broken leg, a spilled cup of tea, a disappeared husband, she says, Well, now, I'll offer that up and I'll have no end of Indulgences to get me into heaven. Fintan is just as bad. If you push him in the schoolyard or call him names he'll smile and tell you he'll pray for you and he'll offer it up for his soul and yours. The boys in Leamy's don't want Fintan praying for them and they threaten to give him a good fong in the arse if they catch him praying for them. He says he wants to be a saint when he grows up, which is ridiculous because you can't be a saint till you're dead. He says our grandchildren will be praying to his picture. One big boy says, My grandchildren will piss on your picture, and Fintan just smiles. His sister ran away to England when she was seventeen and everyone knows he wears her blouse at home and curls his hair with hot iron tongs every Saturday night so that he'll look gorgeous at Mass on Sunday. If he meets you going to Mass he'll say, Isn't my hair gorgeous, Frankie? He loves that word, gorgeous, and no other boy will ever use it.

Of course he knows who stood at the foot of the cross. He probably knows what they were wearing and what they had for breakfast and now he's telling Dotty O'Neill it was the three Marys.

Dotty says, Come up here, Fintan, and take your reward.

He takes his time going to the platform and we can't believe our eyes when he takes out a pocketknife to cut the apple peel into little bits so that he can eat them one by one and not be stuffing the whole thing into his mouth like the rest of us when we win. He raises his hand, Sir, I'd like to give some of my apple away.

The apple, Fintan? No, indeed. You do not have the apple, Fintan. You have the peel, the mere skin. You have not nor will you ever achieve heights so dizzy you'll be feasting on the apple itself. Not my apple, Fintan. Now did I hear you say you want to give away your reward?

You did, sir. I'd like to give three pieces, to Quigley, Clohessy and McCourt.

Why, Fintan?

They're my friends, sir.

The boys around the room are sneering and nudging each other and I feel ashamed because they'll say I curl my hair and I'll be tormented in the schoolyard and why does he think I'm his friend? If they say I wear my sister's blouse there's no use telling them I don't have a sister because they'll say, You'd wear it if you had a sister. There's no use saying anything in the schoolyard because there's always someone with an answer and there's nothing you can do but punch them in the nose and if you were to punch everyone who has an answer you'd be punching morning noon and night.

Quigley takes the bit of peel from Fintan. Thanks, Fintan.

The whole class is looking at Clohessy because he's the biggest and the toughest and if he says thanks I'll say thanks. He says, Thanks very much, Fintan, and blushes and I say, Thanks very much, Fintan, and I try to stop myself from blushing but I can't and all the boys sneer again and I'd like to hit them.

After school the boys call to Fintan, Hoi, Fintan, are you goin' home to curl your gorgeous hair? Fintan smiles and climbs the steps of the schoolyard. A big boy from seventh class says to Paddy Clohessy, I suppose you'd be curlin' your hair too if you wasn't a baldy with a shaved head.

Paddy says, Shurrup, and the boy says, Oh, an' who's goin' to make me? Paddy tries a punch but the big boy hits his nose and knocks him down and there's blood. I try to hit the big boy but he grabs me by the throat and bangs my head against the wall till I see lights and black dots. Paddy walks away holding his nose and crying and the big boy pushes me after him. Fintan is outside on the street and he says, Oh, Francis, Francis, oh, Patrick, Patrick, what's up? Why are you crying, Patrick? and Paddy says, I'm hungry. I can't fight nobody because I'm starving with the hunger an' fallin' down an' I'm ashamed of meself.

Fintan says, Come with me, Patrick. My mother will give us something, and Paddy says, Ah, no, me nose is bleedin'.

Don't worry. She'll put something on your nose or a key on the back of your neck. Francis, you must come, too. You always look hungry.

Ah, no, Fintan.

Ah, do, Francis.

All right, Fintan.

Fintan's flat is like a chapel. There are two pictures, the Sacred Heart of Jesus and the Immaculate Heart of Mary. Jesus is showing His heart with the crown of thorns, the fire, the blood. His head is tilted to the left to show His great sorrow. The Virgin Mary is showing her heart and it would be a pleasant heart if it didn't have that crown of thorns. Her head is tilted to the right to show her sorrow because she knows her Son will come to a sad end.

There's a picture on another wall of a man with a brown robe and birds sitting all over him. Fintan says, Do you know who that is, Francis? No? That's your patron, St. Francis of Assisi, and do you know what today is?

The fourth of October.

That's right and it's his feast day and special for you because you can ask St. Francis for anything and he'll surely give it to you. That's why I wanted you to come here today. Sit down, Patrick, sit down, Francis.

Mrs. Slattery comes in with her rosary beads in her hand. She's happy to meet Fintan's new friends and would we like a cheese sandwich? And look at your poor nose, Patrick. She touches his nose with the cross on her rosary beads and says a little prayer. She tells us these rosary beads were blessed by the Pope himself and would stop the flow of a river if requested never mind Patrick's poor nose.

Fintan says he won't have a sandwich because he's fasting and praying for the boy who hit Paddy and me. Mrs. Slattery gives him a kiss on the head and tells him he's a saint out of heaven and asks if we'd like mustard on our sandwiches and I tell her I never heard of mustard on cheese and I'd love it. Paddy says, I dunno. I never had a sangwidge in me life, and we all laugh and I wonder how you could live ten years like Paddy and never have a sandwich. Paddy laughs, too, and you can see his teeth are white and black and green.

We eat the sandwich and drink tea and Paddy wants to know where the lavatory is. Fintan takes him through the bedroom to the backyard and when they come back Paddy says, I have to go home. Me mother'll kill me. I'll wait for you outside, Frankie.

Now I have to go to the lavatory and Fintan leads me to the backyard. He says, I have to go, too, and when I unbutton my fly I can't pee because he's looking at me and he says, You were fooling. You don't have to go at all. I like to look at you, Francis. That's all. I wouldn't want to commit any class of a sin with our Confirmation coming next year.

Paddy and I leave together. I'm bursting and run behind a garage to pee. Paddy is waiting for me and as we walk along Hartstonge Street he says, That was a powerful sangwidge, Frankie, an' him an' his mother is very holy but I wouldn't want to go to Fintan's flat anymore because he's very odd, isn't he, Frankie?

He is, Paddy.

The way he looks at it when you take it out, that's odd, isn't it, Frankie?

'Tis, Paddy.

A few days later Paddy whispers, Fintan Slattery said we could come to his flat at lunchtime. His mother won't be there and she leaves his lunch for him. He might give us some too and he has lovely milk. Will we go?

Fintan sits two rows from us. He knows what Paddy is saying to me and he moves his eyebrows up and down as if to say, Will you come? I whisper yes to Paddy and he nods to Fintan and the master barks at us to stop waggling our eyebrows and our lips or the ash plant will sing across our backsides.

Boys in the schoolyard see the three of us walk out and they pass remarks. Oh, Gawd, look at Fintan and his ingles. Paddy says, Fintan, what's an ingle? and Fintan says it's just a boy from olden times who sits in a corner, that's all. He tells us sit at the table in his kitchen and we can read his comic books if we like, *Film Fun,* the *Beano,* the *Dandy,* or the religious magazines or his mother's romance magazines, the *Miracle* and the *Oracle,* which always have stories about factory girls who are poor but beautiful in love with sons of earls and vice versa and the factory girl ends up throwing herself into the Thames with the hopelessness only to be rescued by a passing carpenter who is poor but honest and will love the factory girl for her own humble self though it turns out the passing carpenter is really the son of a duke, which is much higher than an earl, so that now the poor factory girl is a duchess and can look down her nose at the earl who spurned her because she's happy tending her roses on her twelve-thousand-acre estate in Shropshire and being kind to her poor old mother, who refuses to leave her humble little cottage for all the money in the world.

Paddy says, I don't want to read nothing, it's all a cod, all them stories. Fintan removes the cloth covering his sandwich and glass of milk. The milk looks creamy and cool and delicious and the sandwich bread is almost as white. Paddy says, Is that a ham sangwidge? and Fintan says, 'Tis. Paddy says, That's a lovely looking sangwidge and is there mustard on it? Fintan nods and slices the sandwich in two. Mustard seeps out. He licks it off his fingers and takes a nice mouthful of milk. He cuts the sandwich again into quarters, eighths, sixteenths, takes *The Little Messenger of the Sacred Heart* from the pile of magazines and reads while he eats his sandwich bits and drinks his milk and Paddy and I look at him and I know Paddy is wondering what we're doing here at all, at all, because that's what I'm wondering myself hoping Fintan will pass over the plate to us but he doesn't, he finishes the milk, leaves bits of sandwich on the plate, covers it with the cloth and wipes his lips in his dainty way, lowers his head, blesses himself and says grace after meals and, God, we'll be late for school, and blesses himself again on the way out with holy water from the little china font hanging by the door with the little image of the Virgin Mary showing her heart and pointing at it with two fingers as if we couldn't make it out for ourselves.

It's too late for Paddy and me to run and get the bun and milk from Nellie Ahearn and I don't know how I'm going to last from now till I can run home after school and get a piece of bread. Paddy stops at the school gate. He says, I can't go in there starving with the hunger. I'd fall asleep and Dotty'd kill me.

Fintan is anxious. Come on, come on, we'll be late. Come on, Francis, hurry up.

I'm not going in, Fintan. You had your lunch. We had nothing.

Paddy explodes. You're a feckin' chancer, Fintan. That's what you are an' a feckin' begrudger too with your feckin' sangwidge an' your feckin' Sacred Heart of Jesus on the wall an' your feckin' holy water. You can kiss my arse, Fintan.

Oh, Patrick.

Oh, Patrick my feckin' arse, Fintan. Come on, Frankie.

Fintan runs into school and Paddy and I make our way to an orchard in Ballinacurra. We climb a wall and a fierce dog comes at us till

Paddy talks to him and tells him he's a good dog and we're hungry and go home to your mother. The dog licks Paddy's face and trots away waving his tail and Paddy is delighted with himself. We stuff apples into our shirts till we can barely get back over the wall to run into a long field and sit under a hedge eating the apples till we can't swallow another bit and we stick our faces into a stream for the lovely cool water. Then we run to opposite ends of a ditch to shit and wipe ourselves with grass and thick leaves. Paddy is squatting and saying, There's nothing in the world like a good feed of apples, a drink of water and a good shit, better than any sangwidge of cheese and mustard and Dotty O'Neill can shove his apple up his arse.

There are three cows in a field with their heads over a stone wall and they say moo to us. Paddy says, Bejasus, 'tis milkin' time, and he's over the wall, stretched on his back under a cow with her big udder hanging into his face. He pulls on a teat and squirts milk into his mouth. He stops squirting and says, Come on, Frankie, fresh milk. 'Tis lovely. Get that other cow, they're all ready for the milkin'.

I get under the cow and pull on a teat but she kicks and moves and I'm sure she's going to kill me. Paddy comes over and shows me how to do it, pull hard and straight and the milk comes out in a powerful stream. The two of us lie under the one cow and we're having a great time filling ourselves with milk when there's a roar and there's a man with a stick charging across the field. We're over the wall in a minute and he can't follow us because of his rubber boots. He stands at the wall and shakes his stick and shouts that if he ever catches us we'll have the length of his boot up our arses and we laugh because we're out of harm's way and I'm wondering why anyone should be hungry in a world full of milk and apples.

It's all right for Paddy to say Dotty can shove the apple up his arse but I don't want to rob orchards and milk cows forever and I'll always try to win Dotty's apple peel so that I can go home and tell Dad how I answered the hard questions.

We're walking back through Ballinacurra. There's rain and lightning and we run but it's hard for me with the sole of my shoe flapping and threatening to trip me. Paddy can run all he wants in his long bare feet and you hear them slapping on the pavement. My shoes and stockings are soaked and they make their own sound, squish, squish. Paddy notices that and we make a song from our two sounds, slap slap, squish, squish, slap squish, squish slap. We laugh so hard over our song we have to hold on to one another. The rain gets heavier and we know we can't stand under a tree or we'll be fried entirely so we stand by a door which is opened in a minute by a big fat maid in a little white hat and a black dress with a little white apron who tells us get away from this door we're a disgrace. We run from the door and Paddy calls back, Mullingar heifer, beef to the heels, and he laughs till he chokes and has to lean against a wall with the weakness. There's no sense in standing in from the rain anymore, we're soaked to the skin, so we take our time down O'Connell Avenue. Paddy says he learned that Mullingar heifer thing from his uncle Peter, the one that was in India in the English army and they have a photo of him standing with a group of soldiers with their helmets and guns and bandoliers around their chests and there are dark men in uniform who are Indians and loyal to the King. Uncle Peter had a great time for himself in a place called Kashmir, which is lovelier than Killarney that they're always bragging about and singing. Paddy goes on again about running away and winding up in India in a silken tent with the girl with the red dot and the curry and the figs and he's making me hungry even if I'm stuffed with apples and milk.

The rain is clearing and there are birds honking over our heads. Paddy says they're ducks or geese or something on their way to Africa where it's nice and warm. The birds have more sense than the Irish. They come to the Shannon for their holidays and then they go back to the warm places, maybe even India. He says he'll write me a letter when he's over there and I can come to India and have my own girl with a red dot.

What's that dot for, Paddy?

It shows they're high class, the quality.

But, Paddy, would the quality in India talk to you if they knew you were from a lane in Limerick and had no shoes?

Course they would, but the English quality wouldn't. The English quality wouldn't give you the steam of their piss.

Steam of their piss? God, Paddy, did you think of that yourself?

Naw, naw, that's what my father says below in the bed when he's coughin' up the gobs and blamin' the English for everything.

And I think, Steam of their piss. I'll keep that for myself. I'll go around Limerick saying it, Steam of their piss, Steam of their piss, and when I go to America some day I'll be the only one who knows it.

Question Quigley is wobbling toward us on a big woman's bicycle and calls to me, Hoi, Frankie McCourt, you're going to be killed. Dotty O'Neill sent a note to your house and said you didn't come back to school after lunch, that you went on the mooch with Paddy Clohessy. Your mother is going to kill you. Your father is out looking for you and he's going to kill you, too.

Oh, God, I feel cold and empty and I wish I could be in India where it's nice and warm and there's no school and my father could never find me to kill me. Paddy tells the Question, He didn't go on the mooch and I didn't either. Fintan Slattery starved us to death and we were too late for the bun and the milk. Then Paddy says to me, Don't mind 'em, Frankie, 'tis all a cod. They're always sendin' notes to our house and we wipe our arses with them.

My mother and father would never wipe their arses with a note from the master and I'm afraid now to go home. The Question rides off on the bicycle, laughing, and I don't know why because he once ran away from home and slept in a ditch with four goats and that's worse than mooching from school half a day anytime.

I could turn up the Barrack Road now and go home and tell my parents I'm sorry I went on the mooch and I did it because of the hunger but Paddy says, Come on, we'll go down the Dock Road and throw rocks in the Shannon.

We throw rocks in the river and we swing on the iron chains along the bank. It's getting dark and I don't know where I'm going to sleep. I might have to stay there by the Shannon or find a door or I might have to go back out the country and find a ditch like Brendan Quigley with four goats. Paddy says I can go home with him, I can sleep on the floor and I'll dry out.

Paddy lives in one of the tall houses on Arthur's Quay looking at the river. Everyone in Limerick knows these houses are old and might fall down at any minute. Mam often says, I don't want any of ye going down to Arthur's Quay and if I find ye there I'll break yeer faces. The people down there are wild and ye could get robbed and killed.

It's raining again and small children are playing in the hallway and up the stairs. Paddy says, Mind yourself, because some of the steps are missing and there is shit on the ones that are still there. He says that's because there's only one privy and it's in the backyard and children don't get down the stairs in time to put their little arses on the bowl, God help us.

There's a woman with a shawl sitting on the fourth flight smoking a cigarette. She says, Is that you, Paddy?

'Tis, Mammy.

I'm fagged out, Paddy. Them steps is killin' me. Did you have your tea?

I didn't.

Well, I don't know if there's any bread left. Go up an' see.

Paddy's family live in one big room with a high ceiling and a small fireplace. There are two tall windows and you can see out to the Shannon. His father is in a bed in the corner, groaning and spitting into a bucket. Paddy's brothers and sisters are on mattresses on the floor, sleeping, talking, looking at the ceiling. There's a baby with no clothes crawling over to Paddy's father's bucket and Paddy pulls him away. His mother comes in, gasping, from the stairs. Jesus, I'm dead, she says.

She finds some bread and makes weak tea for Paddy and me. I don't know what I'm supposed to do. They don't say anything. They don't say what are you doing here or go home or anything till Mr. Clohessy says, Who's that? and Paddy tells him, 'Tis Frankie McCourt.

Mr. Clohessy says, McCourt? What class of a name is that?

My father is from the North, Mr. Clohessy.

And what's your mother's name?

Angela, Mr. Clohessy.

Ah, Jaysus, 'twouldn't be Angela Sheehan, would it?

'Twould, Mr. Clohessy.

Ah, Jaysus, he says, and he has a coughing fit which brings up all kinds of stuff from his insides and has him hanging over the bucket. When the cough passes he falls back on the pillow. Ah, Frankie, I knew your mother well. Danced with her, Mother o' Christ, I'm dying inside, danced with her I did below in the Wembley Hall and a champion dancer she was too.

He hangs over the bucket again. He gasps for air and reaches his arms out to get it. He suffers but he won't stop talking.

Champion dancer she was, Frankie. Not skinny mind you but a feather in my arms and there was many a sorry man when she left Limerick. Can you dance, Frankie?

Ah, no, Mr. Clohessy.

Paddy says, He can, Dada. He had the lessons from Mrs. O'Connor and Cyril Benson.

Well, dance, Frankie. Round the house an' mind the dresser, Frankie. Lift the foot, lad.

I can't, Mr. Clohessy. I'm no good.

No good? Angela's Sheehan's son? Dance, Frankie, or I'll get outa this bed an' wheel you round the house.

My shoe is broken, Mr. Clohessy.

Frankie, Frankie, you're bringin' the cough on me. Will you dance for the love o' Jesus so I can remember me youth with your mother in the Wembley Hall. Take off the feckin' shoe, Frankie, an' dance.

I have to make up dances and tunes to go with them the way I did a long time ago when I was young. I dance around the room with one shoe because I forgot to take it off. I try to make up words, Oh, The Walls of Limerick are falling down, falling down, falling down, The Walls of Limerick falling down and the River Shannon kills us.

Mr. Clohessy is laughing in the bed. Oh, Jaysus, I never heard likes o' that on land or sea. That's a great leg for the dancing you have there, Frankie. Oh, Jaysus. He coughs and brings up ropes of green and yellow stuff. It makes me sick to look at it and I wonder if I should go home from all this sickness and this bucket and let my parents kill me if they want to.

Paddy lies down on a mattress by the window and I lie beside him. I keep my clothes on like everybody else and I even forget to take off my other shoe, which is wet and squishy and stinks. Paddy falls asleep right away and I look at his mother sitting by the bit of a fire smoking another cigarette. Paddy's father groans and coughs and spits into the bucket. He says, Feckin' blood, and she says, You'll have to go into the sanatorium sooner or later.

I will not. The day they put you in there is the end of you.

You could be givin' the consumption to the children. I could get the guards to take you away you're that much of a danger to the children.

If they were to get it they'd have it be now.

The fire dies and Mrs. Clohessy climbs over him into the bed. In a minute she's snoring even if he's still coughing and laughing about the days of his youth when he danced with Angela Sheehan light as a feather in the Wembley Hall.

It's cold in the room and I'm shivering in my wet clothes. Paddy is shivering too but he's asleep and he doesn't know he's cold. I don't know if I should stay here or get up and go home but who wants to be wandering the streets when a guard might ask you what you're doing out. It's my first time away from my family and I know I'd rather be in my own house with the smelly lavatory and stable next door. It's bad when our kitchen is a lake and we have to go up to Italy but it's worse in the Clohessys' when you have to go down four flights to the lavatory and slip on shit all the way down. I'd be better off with four goats in a ditch.

I drift in and out of sleep but I have to wake up for good when Mrs. Clohessy goes around pulling at her family to get them up. They all went to bed with their clothes on so they don't have to get dressed and there's no fighting. They grumble and run out the door to get downstairs to the backyard lavatory. I have to go too and I run down with Paddy but his sister Peggy is on the bowl and we have to piss against a wall. She says, I'll tell Ma what ye did, and Paddy says, Shurrup or I'll push you down into that feckin' lavatory. She jumps off the lavatory, pulls her drawers up and runs up the stairs crying, I'll tell, I'll tell, and when we get back to the room Mrs. Clohessy gives Paddy a belt on the head for what he did to his poor little sister. Paddy says nothing because Mrs. Clohessy is spooning porridge into mugs and jam jars and one bowl and telling us to eat up and go to school. She sits at the table eating her porridge. Her hair is gray black and dirty. It dangles in the bowl and picks up bits of porridge and drops of milk. The children slurp the porridge and complain they didn't get enough, they're starving with the hunger. They have snotty noses and sore eyes and scabby knees. Mr. Clohessy coughs and squirms on the bed and brings up the great gobs of blood and I run out of the room and puke on the stairs where there's a step missing and there's a shower of porridge and bits of apple to the floor below where people go back and forth to the lavatory in the yard. Paddy comes down and says, Sure that's all right. Everywan gets sick an' shits on them stairs an' the whole feckin' place is falling down anyway.

I don't know what I'm supposed to do now. If I go back to school I'll be killed and why should I go back to school or go home to get killed when I can go out the road and live on milk and apples the rest of my life till I go to America. Paddy says, Come on. School is all a cod anyway an' the masters is all madmen.

There's a knock at the Clohessys' door and it's Mam holding my little brother, Michael, by the hand, and Guard Dennehy, who is in charge of school attendance. Mam sees me and says, What are you doing with one shoe on? and Guard Dennehy says, Ah, now, missus, I think a more important question would be, What are you doing with one shoe off, ha, ha.

Michael runs to me. Mammy was crying. Mammy was crying for you, Frankie.

She says, Where were you all night?

I was here.

You had me demented. Your father walked every street in Limerick looking for you.

Mr. Clohessy says, Who's at the door?

It's my mother, Mr. Clohessy.

God above, is that Angela?

'Tis, Mr. Clohessy.

He struggles up on his elbows. Well, for the love of God, will you come in, Angela. Don't you know me?

Mam looks puzzled. It's dark in the room and she tries to make out who is in the bed. He says, 'Tis me, Dennis Clohessy, Angela.

Ah, no.

'Tis, Angela.

Ah, no.

I know, Angela. I'm changed. The cough is killin' me. But I remember the nights at the Wembley Hall. Aw, Jaysus, you were a great dancer. Nights at the Wembley Hall, Angela, and the fish and chips after. Oh, boys, oh, boys, Angela.

My mother has tears running down her face. She says, You were a great dancer yourself, Dennis Clohessy.

We could have won competitions, Angela. Fred and Ginger would have been lookin' over their shoulders but you had to run off to America. Aw, Jaysus.

He has another coughing fit and we have to stand and watch him hang over the bucket again and bring up the bad stuff from his insides. Guard Dennehy says, I think, missus, we found the by an' I'll be going. He says to me, If you ever go on the mooch again, by, we'll have you in the jail above. Are you listenin' to me, by?

I am, Guard.

Don't be tormentin' your mother, by. That's wan thing the guards won't put up with, the tormentin' of mothers.

I won't, Guard. I won't torment her.

He leaves and Mam goes to the bed to take Mr. Clohessy's hand. His face is caved in all around his eyes and his hair is shiny black with the sweat running from the top of his head. His children stand around the bed looking at him and looking at Mam. Mrs. Clohessy sits by the fire rattling the poker in the grate and pushing the baby away from the fire. She says, 'Tis his own bloody fault for not goin' into hospital, so 'tis.

Mr. Clohessy gasps, I'd be all right if I could live in a dry place. Angela, is America a dry place?

'Tis, Dennis.

The doctor told me go to Arizona. A funny man that doctor. Arizona how are you. I don't have the money to go around the corner for a pint.

Mam says, You'll be all right, Dennis. I'll light a candle for you.

Save your money, Angela. My dancin' days are done.

I have to go now, Dennis. My son has to go to school.

Before you go, Angela, will you do one thing for me?

I will, Dennis, if 'tis in my power.

Would you ever give us a verse of that song you sang the night before you went to America?

That's a hard song, Dennis. I wouldn't have the wind for it.

Ah, come on, Angela. I never hear a song anymore. There isn't a song in this house. The wife there doesn't have a note in her head an' no step in her foot.

Mam says, All right. I'll try.

Oh, the nights of the Kerry dancing, Oh, the ring of the piper's tune,
Oh, for one of those hours of gladness, gone, alas, like our youth too soon.
When the boys began to gather in the glen of a Summer night,
And the Kerry piper's tuning made us long with wild delight.

She stops and presses her hand to her chest, Oh, God, my wind is gone. Help me, Frank, with the song, and I sing along,

Oh, to think of it, Oh, to dream of it, fills my heart with tears.
Oh, the nights of the Kerry dancing, Oh, the ring of the piper's tune
Oh, for one of those hours of gladness, gone, alas, like our youth too soon.

Mr. Clohessy tries to sing with us, gone, alas, like our youth too soon, but it brings on the cough. He shakes his head and cries, I wouldn't doubt you, Angela. It takes me back. God bless you.

God bless you, too, Dennis, and thanks, Mrs. Clohessy, for having Frankie here off the streets.

'Twas no trouble, Mrs. McCourt. He's quiet enough.

Quiet enough, says Mr. Clohessy, but he's not the dancer his mother was.

Mam says, 'Tis hard to dance with one shoe, Dennis.

I know, Angela, but you'd wonder why he didn't take it off. Is he a bit strange?

Ah, sometimes he has the odd manner like his father.

Oh, yes. The father is from the North, Angela, and that would account for it. They'd think nothing of dancing with one shoe in the North.

We walk up Patrick Street and O'Connell Street, Paddy Clohessy and Mam and Michael and myself, and Mam sobs all the way. Michael says, Don't cry, Mammy. Frankie won't run away.

She lifts him up and hugs him. Oh, no, Michael, 'tisn't Frankie I'm crying about. 'Tis Dennis Clohessy and the dancing nights at the Wembley Hall and the fish and chips after.

She comes into the school with us. Mr. O'Neill looks cross and tells us sit down he'll be with us in a minute. He talks a long time at the door with my mother and when she leaves he walks between the seats and pats Paddy Clohessy on the head.

I'm very sorry for the Clohessys and all their troubles but I think they saved me from getting into trouble with my mother.

VII

There are Thursdays when Dad gets his dole money at the Labour Exchange and a man might say, Will we go for a pint, Malachy? and Dad will say, One, only one, and the man will say, Oh, God, yes, one, and before the night is over all the money is gone and Dad comes home singing and getting us out of bed to line up and promise to die for Ireland when the call comes. He even gets Michael up and he's only three but there he is singing and promising to die for Ireland at the first opportunity. That's what Dad calls it, the first opportunity. I'm nine and Malachy is eight and we know all the songs. We sing all the verses of Kevin Barry and Roddy McCorley, "The West's Asleep," "O'Donnell Abu," "The Boys of Wexford." We sing and promise to die because you never know when Dad might have a penny or two left over from the drinking and if he gives it to us we can run to Kathleen O'Connell's next day for toffee. Some nights he says Michael is the best singer of all and he gives him the penny. Malachy and I wonder what's the use of being eight and nine and knowing all the songs and ready to die when Michael gets the penny so that he can go to the shop next day and stuff his gob with toffee galore. No one can ask him to die for Ireland at the age of three, not even Padraig Pearse, who was shot by the English in Dublin in 1916 and expected the whole world to die with him. Besides, Mikey Molloy's father said anyone who wants to die for Ireland is a donkey's arse. Men have been dying for Ireland since the beginning of time and look at the state of the country.

It's bad enough that Dad loses jobs in the third week but now he drinks all the dole money once a month. Mam gets desperate and in the morning she has the bitter face and she won't talk to him. He has his tea and leaves the house early for the long walk into the country. When he returns in the evening she still won't talk to him and she won't make his tea. If the fire is dead for the want of coal or turf and there's no way of boiling water for the tea, he says, Och, aye, and drinks water out of a jam jar and smacks his lips the way he would with a pint of porter. He says good water is all a man needs and Mam makes a snorting sound. When she's not talking to him the house is heavy and cold and we know we're not supposed to talk to him either for fear she'll give us the bitter look. We know Dad has done the bad thing and we know you can make anyone suffer by not talking to him. Even little Michael knows that when Dad does the bad thing you don't talk to him from Friday to Monday and when he tries to lift you to his lap you run to Mam.

I'm nine years old and I have a pal, Mickey Spellacy, whose relations are dropping one by one of the galloping consumption. I envy Mickey because every time someone dies in his family he gets a week off from school and his mother stitches a black diamond patch on his sleeve so that he can wander from lane to lane and street to street and people will know he has the grief and pat his head and give him money and sweets for his sorrow.

But this summer Mickey is worried. His sister, Brenda, is wasting away with the consumption and it's only August and if she dies before September he won't get his week off from school because you can't get a week off from school when there's no school. He comes to Billy Campbell and me to ask if we'll go around the corner to St. Joseph's Church and pray for Brenda to hang on till September.

What's in it for us, Mickey, if we go around the corner praying?

Well, if Brenda hangs on and I get me week off ye can come to the wake and have ham and cheese and cake and sherry and lemonade and everything and ye can listen to the songs and stories all night.

Who could say no to that? There's nothing like a wake for having a good time. We trot around to the church where they have statues of St. Joseph himself as well as the Sacred Heart of Jesus, the Virgin Mary and St. Thérèse of Lisieux, the Little Flower. I pray to the Little Flower because she died of the consumption herself and she'd understand.

One of our prayers must have been powerful because Brenda stays alive and doesn't die till the second day of school. We tell Mickey we're sorry for his troubles but he's delighted with his week off and he gets the black diamond patch which will bring the money and sweets.

My mouth is watering at the thought of the feast at Brenda's wake. Billy knocks on the door and there's Mickey's aunt. Well?

We came to say a prayer for Brenda and Mickey said we could come to the wake.

She yells, Mickey!

What?

Come here. Did you tell this gang they could come to your sister's wake?

No.

But, Mickey, you promised . . .

She slams the door in our faces. We don't know what to do till Billy Campbell says, We'll go back to St. Joseph's and pray that from now on everyone in Mickey Spellacy's family will die in the middle of the summer and he'll never get a day off from school for the rest of his life.

One of our prayers is surely powerful because next summer Mickey himself is carried off by the galloping consumption and he doesn't get a day off from school and that will surely teach him a lesson.

Proddy Woddy ring the bell,
Not for heaven but for hell.

On Sunday mornings in Limerick I watch them go to church, the Protestants, and I feel sorry for them, especially the girls, who are so lovely, they have such beautiful white teeth. I feel sorry for the beautiful Protestant girls, they're doomed. That's what the priests tell us. Outside the Catholic Church there is no salvation. Outside the Catholic Church there is nothing but doom. And I want to save them. Protestant girl, come with me to the True Church. You'll be saved and you won't have the doom. After Mass on Sunday I go with my friend Billy

Campbell to watch them play croquet on the lovely lawn beside their church on Barrington Street. Croquet is a Protestant game. They hit the ball with the mallet, pock and pock again, and laugh. I wonder how they can laugh or don't they even know they're doomed? I feel sorry for them and I say, Billy, what's the use of playing croquet when you're doomed?

He says, Frankie, what's the use of not playing croquet when you're doomed?

Grandma says to Mam, Your brother Pat, bad leg an' all, was selling papers all over Limerick by the time he was eight and that Frank of yours is big and ugly enough to work.

But he's only nine and still in school.

School. 'Tis school that has him the way he is talkin' back an' goin' around with the sour puss an' the odd manner like his father. He could get out an' help poor Pat of a Friday night when the *Limerick Leader* is a ton weight. He could run up the long garden paths of the quality an' save Pat's poor legs an' earn a few pennies into the bargain.

He has to go to the Confraternity on Friday nights.

Never mind the Confraternity. There's nothin' in the catechism about confraternities.

I meet Uncle Pat at the *Limerick Leader* on Friday evening at five. The man handing out the papers says my arms are that skinny I'd be lucky to carry two stamps but Uncle Pat sticks eight papers under each arm. He tells me, I'll kill you if you drop 'em for 'tis raining abroad, pelting out of the heavens. He tells me hug the walls going up O'Connell Street to keep the papers dry. I'm to run in where there's a delivery, climb the outside steps, in the door, up the stairs, yell Paper, get the money they owe him for the week, down the stairs, give him the money and on to the next stop. Customers give him tips for his troubles and he keeps them for himself.

We make our way up O'Connell Avenue, out Ballinacurra, in by the South Circular Road, down Henry Street and back to the office for more papers. Uncle Pat wears a cap and a thing like a cowboy poncho to keep his papers dry but he complains his feet are killing him and we stop in a pub for a pint for his poor feet. Uncle Pa Keating is there all black and having a pint and he says to Uncle Pat, Ab, are you going

173

to let that boy stand there with his face hanging out for the want of a lemonade?

Uncle Pat says, Wha? and Uncle Pa Keating gets impatient. Christ, he's dragging your feckin' papers all over Limerick and you can't—Oh, never mind. Timmy, give the child a lemonade. Frankie, don't you have a raincoat at home?

No, Uncle Pa.

You're not supposed to be out in this weather. You're drenched entirely. Who sent you out in this muck?

Grandma said I had to help Uncle Pat because of his bad leg.

Course she did, the oul' bitch, but don't tell them I said that.

Uncle Pat is struggling off the seat and gathering up his papers. Come on, 'tis gettin' dark.

He hobbles along the streets calling, Anna Lie Sweets Lie, which doesn't sound a bit like *Limerick Leader* and it doesn't matter because everyone knows this is Ab Sheehan that was dropped on his head. Here, Ab, give us a *Leader*, how's your poor leg, keep the change an' get yourself a fag for 'tis an awful feckin' night to be out sellin' the feckin' papers.

Tanks, says Ab, my uncle. Tanks, tanks, tanks, and it's hard to keep up with him on the streets bad as his leg is. He says, How many *Leaders* have you under your oxter?

One, Uncle Pat.

Take that *Leader* in to Mr. Timoney. He owes me for a fortnight now. Get that money an' there's a tip. He's a good man for the tip an' don't be shovin' it in your pocket like your cousin Gerry. Shoved it in his pocket, the little bugger.

I bang on the door with the knocker and there's a great howl from a dog so big he makes the door shake. A man's voice says, Macushla, quit the bloody racket or I'll give you a good fong in the arse for yourself. The racket stops, the door opens and the man is there, white hair, thick glasses, white sweater, a stick in his hand. He says, Who is it? Who do we have?

The paper, Mr. Timoney.

We don't have Ab Sheehan here, do we?

I'm his nephew, sir.

Is it Gerry Sheehan we have here?

No, sir. I'm Frank McCourt.

Another nephew? Does he make them? Is there a little nephew factory in the backyard? Here's the money for the fortnight and give me the paper or keep it. What's the use? I can't read anymore and Mrs. Minihan that's supposed to read to me didn't come. Legless with the sherry, that's what she is. What's your name?

Frank, sir.

Can you read?

I can, sir.

Do you want to earn a sixpence?

I do, sir.

Come here tomorrow. Your name is Francis, isn't it?

Frank, sir.

Your name is Francis. There was never a St. Frank. That's a name for gangsters and politicians. Come here tomorrow at eleven and read to me.

I will, sir.

Are you sure you can read?

I am, sir.

You can call me Mr. Timoney.

I will, Mr. Timoney.

Uncle Pat is mumbling at the gate, rubbing his leg. Where's me money an' you're not supposed to be chattin' with the customers an' me here with the leg destroyed be the rain. He has to stop at the pub at Punch's Cross to have a pint for the destroyed leg. After the pint he says he can't walk another inch and we get on a bus. The conductor says, Fares, please, fares, but Uncle Pat says, Go 'way an' don't be botherin' me, can't you see the state o' me leg?

Oh, all right, Ab, all right.

The bus stops at the O'Connell Monument and Uncle Pat goes to the Monument Fish and Chip Café where the smells are so delicious my stomach beats with the hunger. He gets a shilling's worth of fish and chips and my mouth is watering but when we get to Grandma's door he gives me a threepenny bit, tells me meet him again next Friday and go home now to my mother.

The dog Macushla is lying outside Mr. Timoney's door and when I open the little garden gate to go up the path she rushes at me and knocks me back out on the pavement and she'd eat my face if Mr. Timoney didn't come out and flail at her with his stick and yell, Come in out of it, ye hoor, ye overgrown man-eatin' bitch. Didn't you have your breakfast, you hoor? Are you all right, Francis? Come in. That dog is a right Hindu, so she is, and that's where I found her mother wandering around Bangalore. If ever you're getting a dog, Francis, make sure it's a Buddhist. Good-natured dogs, the Buddhists. Never, never get a Mahommedan. They'll eat you sleeping. Never a Catholic dog. They'll eat you every day including Fridays. Sit down and read to me.

The *Limerick Leader*, Mr. Timoney?

No, not the bloody *Limerick Leader*. I wouldn't wipe the hole of my arse with the *Limerick Leader*. There's a book over there on the table, *Gulliver's Travels*. That's not what I want you to read. Look in the back for another thing, *A Modest Proposal*. Read that to me. It begins, It is a melancholy object to those who walk . . . Do you have that? I have the whole bloody thing in my head but I still want you to read to me.

He stops me after two or three pages. You're a good reader. And what do you think of that, Francis, that a young healthy child well nursed is at a year old a most delicious, nourishing, and wholesome food, whether stewed, roasted, baked, or boiled, eh? Macushla would love a dinner of a nice plump Irish infant, wouldn't you, you oul' hoor?

He gives me sixpence, and tells me return next Saturday.

Mam is delighted I earned sixpence for reading to Mr. Timoney and what was it he wanted read, the *Limerick Leader*? I tell her I had to read *A Modest Proposal* from the back of *Gulliver's Travels* and she says, That's all right, 'tis only a children's book. You'd expect him to want something strange for he's a little off in the head after years in the sun in the English army in India and they say he was married to one of them Indian women and she was accidentally shot by a soldier during some class of a disturbance. That's the kind of thing that would drive you to children's books. She knows this Mrs. Minihan who lives next door to Mr. Timoney and used to clean house but couldn't stand it anymore the way he laughed at the Catholic Church and said one man's sin was another man's romp. Mrs. Minihan didn't mind the odd drop of sherry of a Saturday morning but then he tried to turn her into a Buddhist, which he said he was himself and the Irish would be much better off in general if they sat under a tree and watched the Ten Commandments and the Seven Deadly Sins float down the Shannon and far out to sea.

The next Friday Declan Collopy from the Confraternity sees me on the street delivering the papers with my uncle Pat Sheehan. Hoi, Frankie McCourt, what are you doin' with Ab Sheehan?

He's my uncle.

You're supposed to be at the Confraternity.

I'm working, Declan.

You're not supposed to be working. You're not even ten and you're destroyin' the perfect attendance in our section. If you're not there next Friday I'll give you a good thump in the gob, do you hear me?

Uncle Pat says, Go 'way, go 'way, or I'll walk on you.

Ah, shut up, Mr. Stupid that was dropped on your head. He pushes Uncle Pat on the shoulder and knocks him back against the wall. I drop the papers and run at him but he steps aside and punches me on the back of the neck and my forehead is rammed into the wall and it puts me in such a rage I can't see him anymore. I go at him with arms and legs and if I could tear his face off with my teeth I would but he has long arms like a gorilla and he just keeps pushing me away so that I can't touch him. He says, You mad feckin' eejit. I'll destroy you in the Confraternity, and he runs away.

Uncle Pat says, You shouldn't be fightin' like that an' you dropped all me papers an' some o' them is wet an' how am I supposed to sell wet papers, and I wanted to jump on him too and hit him for talking about papers after I stood up to Declan Collopy.

At the end of the night he gives me three chips from his bag and sixpence instead of threepence. He complains it's too much money and it's all my mother's fault for going on to Grandma about the low pay.

Mam is delighted I'm getting sixpence on Fridays from Uncle Pat and sixpence on Saturdays from Mr. Timoney. A shilling a week makes a big difference and she gives me tuppence to see the Dead End Kids at the Lyric after I'm finished the reading.

Next morning Mr. Timoney says, Wait till we get to *Gulliver*, Francis. You'll know Jonathan Swift is the greatest Irish writer that ever lived, no, the greatest man to put pen to parchment. A giant of a man, Francis. He laughs all through *A Modest Proposal* and you'd wonder what he's laughing at when it's all about cooking Irish babies. He says, You'll laugh when you grow up, Francis.

You're not supposed to talk back to grown-ups but Mr. Timoney is different and he doesn't mind when I say, Mr. Timoney, big people are always telling us that. Oh, you'll laugh when you grow up.

You'll understand when you grow up. Everything will come when you grow up.

He lets out such a roar of a laugh I think he's going to collapse. Oh, Mother o' God, Francis. You're a treasure. What's up with you? Do you have a bee up your arse? Tell me what's up.

Nothing, Mr. Timoney.

I think you have the long puss, Francis, and I wish I could see it. Go over to the mirror on the wall, Snow White, and tell me if you have the long puss. Never mind. Just tell me what's up.

Declan Collopy was at me last night and I got into a fight.

He makes me tell him about the Confraternity and Declan and my uncle Pat Sheehan, who was dropped on his head, and then he tells me he knows my uncle Pa Keating, who was gassed in the war and works in the gas works. He says, Pa Keating is a jewel of a man. And I'll tell you what I'll do, Francis. I'll talk to Pa Keating and we'll go to the crawthumpers at the Confraternity. I'm a Buddhist myself and I don't hold with fighting but I haven't lost it. They're not going to interfere with my little reader, oh, by Jesus, no.

Mr. Timoney is an old man but he talks like a friend and I can say what I feel. Dad would never talk to me like Mr. Timoney. He'd say, Och, aye, and go for a long walk.

Uncle Pat Sheehan tells Grandma he doesn't want me to help with the papers anymore, he can get another boy much cheaper and he thinks I should be giving him some of my Saturday morning sixpence anyway since I'd never have the reading job without him.

A woman next door to Mr. Timoney tells me I'm wasting my time knocking on the door, Macushla bit the postman, the milkman and a passing nun on the same day and Mr. Timoney couldn't stop laughing though he cried when the dog was taken away to be put down. You can bite postmen and milkmen all you like but the case of the passing nun goes all the way to the bishop and he takes steps especially if the owner of the dog is a known Buddhist and a danger to good Catholics around him. Mr. Timoney was told this and cried and laughed so hard the doctor came and said he was gone beyond recall so they carted him off to the City Home, where they keep old people who are helpless or demented.

That's the end of my Saturday sixpence but I'll read to Mr. Timoney money or no money. I wait down the street till the woman next door goes in, I climb in Mr. Timoney's window for *Gulliver's Travels* and walk miles to the City Home so that he won't miss his reading. The man at the gate says, What? You want to come in an' read to an oul' man? Is it coddin' me you are? Get outa here before I call the guards.

Could I leave the book for someone else to read to Mr. Timoney?

Leave it. Leave it for Jaysus sake an' don't be botherin' me. I'll send it up to him.

And he laughs.

Mam says, What's up with you? Why are you moping? And I tell her how Uncle Pat doesn't want me anymore and how they put Mr. Timoney in the City Home for laughing just because Macushla bit the postman, the milkman and a passing nun. She laughs too and I'm sure the world is gone mad. Then she says, Ah, I'm sorry and it's a pity you lost two jobs. You might as well start going to the Confraternity again to keep The Posse away and, worse, the director, Father Gorey.

Declan tells me sit in front of him and if there's any blaguarding he'll break my feckin' neck for he'll be watching me as long as he's prefect and no little shit like me is going to keep him from a life in linoleum.

Mam says she has trouble climbing the stairs and she's moving her bed to the kitchen. She laughs, I'll come back up to Sorrento when the walls are damp and the rain runs under the door. School is over and she can stay in bed in the kitchen as long as she likes because she doesn't have to get up for us. Dad lights the fire, makes the tea, cuts the bread, makes sure we wash our faces and tells us go out and play. He lets us stay in bed if we like but you never want to stay in bed when there's no school. We're ready to run out and play in the lane the minute we wake.

Then one day in July he says we can't go downstairs. We have to stay up here and play.

Why, Dad?

Never mind. Play here with Malachy and Michael and you can go down later when I tell you.

He stands at the door in case we might get a notion to wander down the stairs. We push our blanket up in the air with our feet and pretend we're in a tent, Robin Hood and his Merry Men. We hunt fleas and squash them between our thumbnails.

Then there's a baby's cry and Malachy says, Dad, did Mam get a new baby?

Och, aye, son.

I'm older so I tell Malachy the bed is in the kitchen so that the angel can fly down and leave the baby on the seventh step but Malachy doesn't understand because he's only eight going on nine and I'll be ten next month.

Mam is in the bed with the new baby. He has a big fat face and he's red all over. There's a woman in the kitchen in a nurse's uniform and we know she's there to wash new babies who are always dirty from the long journey with the angel. We want to tickle the baby but she says, No, no, ye can look at him but don't lay a finger.

Don't lay a finger. That's the way nurses talk.

We sit at the table with our tea and bread looking at our new brother but he won't even open his eyes to look back at us so we go out and play.

In a few days Mam is out of the bed holding the baby on her lap by the fire. His eyes are open and when we tickle him he makes a gurgling sound, his belly shakes and that makes us laugh. Dad tickles him and sings a Scottish song,

> *Oh, oh, stop your ticklin', Jock,*
> *Stop your ticklin', Jock.*
> *Stop your ticklin',*
> *Ickle ickle icklin*
> *Stop your ticklin', Jock.*

Dad has a job so Bridey Hannon is able to visit Mam and the baby any time she likes and for once Mam doesn't tell us go out and play so they can talk about secret things. They sit by the fire smoking and talking about names. Mam says she likes the names Kevin and Sean but Bridey says, Ah, no, there's too many of them in Limerick. Jesus, Angela, if you stuck your head out the door and called, Kevin or Sean, come in for your tea, you'd have half o' Limerick running to your door.

Bridey says if she had a son which please God she will some day she'll call him Ronald because she's mad about Ronald Colman that you see in the Coliseum Cinema. Or Errol, now that's another lovely name, Errol Flynn.

Mam says, Will you go way outa that, Bridey. I'd never be able to stick my head out the door and say, Errol, Errol, come in for your tea. Sure the poor child would be a laughingstock.

Ronald, says Bridey, Ronald. He's gorgeous.

No, says Mam, it has to be Irish. Isn't that what we fought for all these years? What's the use of fighting the English for centuries if we're going to call our children Ronald?

Jesus, Angela, you're starting to talk like himself with his Irish this and his English that.

Still an' all, Bridey, he's right.

Suddenly Bridey is gasping, Jesus, Angela, there's something wrong with that child.

Mam is out of the chair, hugging the child, moaning. Oh, Jesus, Bridey, he's choking.

Bridey says, I'll run for my mother, and she's back in a minute with Mrs. Hannon. Castor oil, says Mrs. Hannon. Do you have it? Any oil. Cod liver oil? That'll do.

She pours the oil into the baby's mouth, turns him over, presses on his back, turns him back over, sticks a spoon down his throat and brings up a white ball. That's it now, she says. The milk. It collects and gets hard in their little throats so you have to ease it with any class of an oil.

Mam is crying, Jesus, I nearly lost him. Oh, I'd die so I would.

She's clutching the baby and crying and trying to thank Mrs. Hannon.

Yerra, don't mention it, missus. Take the child and get back into that bed for the two o' ye had a great shock.

While Bridey and Mrs. Hannon are helping Mam to the bed I notice spots of blood on her chair. Is my mother bleeding to death? Is it all right to say, Look, there's blood on Mam's chair? No, you can't say anything because they always have secrets. I know if you say anything the grown-up people will tell you, Never mind, you're always gawking, none of your business, go out and play.

I have to keep it inside or I can talk to the angel. Mrs. Hannon and Bridey leave and I sit on the seventh step. I try to tell the angel Mam is bleeding to death. I want him to tell me, Fear not, but the step is cold and there's no light, no voice. I'm sure he's gone forever and I wonder if that happens when you go from nine to ten.

Mam doesn't bleed to death. She's out of the bed next day getting the baby ready for baptism, telling Bridey she could never forgive herself if the baby died and went to Limbo, a place for unbaptized babies, where it may be nice and warm but, still, dark forever and no hope of escape even on the Judgment Day.

Grandma is there to help and she says, That's right, no hope in heaven for the infant that's not baptized.

Bridey says it would be a hard God that would do the likes of that.

He has to be hard, says Grandma, otherwise you'd have all kinds of babies clamorin' to get into heaven, Protestants an' everything, an' why should they get in after what they did to us for eight hundred years?

The babies didn't do it, says Bridey. They're too small.

They would if they got the chance, says Grandma. They're trained for it.

They dress the baby in the Limerick lace dress we were all baptized in. Mam says we can all go to St. Joseph's and we're excited because there will be lemonade and buns after.

Malachy says, Mam, what's the baby's name?

Alphonsus Joseph.

The words fly out of my mouth, That's a stupid name. It's not even Irish.

Grandma glares at me with her old red eyes. She says, That fella needs a good clitther on the gob. Mam slaps me across the face and sends me flying across the kitchen. My heart is pounding and I want to cry but I can't because my father isn't there and I'm the man of the family. Mam says, You go upstairs with your big mouth and don't move from that room.

I stop at the seventh step but it's still cold, no light, no voice.

The house is quiet with everyone gone to the chapel. I sit and wait upstairs, knocking the fleas off my arms and legs, wishing I had Dad here, thinking of my little brother and his foreign name, Alphonsus, an affliction of a name.

In awhile there are voices downstairs and there is talk of tea, sherry, lemonade, buns, and isn't that child the loveliest little fella in the world, little Alphie, foreign name but still an' all still an' all not a sound outa him the whole time he's that good-natured God bless him sure he'll live forever with the sweetness that's in him the little dote spittin' image of his mother his father his grandma his little brothers dead an' gone.

Mam calls from the bottom of the stairs, Frank, come down and have lemonade and a bun.

I don't want it. You can keep it.

I said come down this minute for if I have to climb these stairs I'll warm your behind and you'll rue the day.

Rue? What's rue?

Never mind what's rue. Come down here at once.

Her voice is sharp and rue sounds dangerous. I'll go down.

In the kitchen Grandma says, Look at the long puss on him. You'd think he'd be happy for his little brother except that a boy that's going from nine to ten is always a right pain in the arse an' I know for didn't I have two of 'em.

The lemonade and bun are delicious and Alphie the new baby is chirping away enjoying his baptism day too innocent to know his name is an affliction.

Grandpa in the North sends a telegram money order for five pounds for the baby Alphie. Mam wants to cash it but she can't go far from the bed. Dad says he'll cash it at the post office. She tells Malachy and me to go with him. He cashes it and tells us, All right, boys, go home and tell your mother I'll be home in a few minutes.

Malachy says, Dad, you're not to go to the pub. Mam said you're to bring home the money. You're not to drink the pint.

Now, now, son. Go home to your mother.

Dad, give us the money. That money is for the baby.

Now, Francis, don't be a bad boy. Do what your father tells you.

He walks away from us and into South's pub.

Mam is sitting by the fireplace with Alphie in her arms. She shakes her head. He went to the pub, didn't he?

He did.

I want ye to go back down to that pub and read him out of it. I want ye to stand in the middle of the pub and tell every man your father is drinking the money for the baby. Ye are to tell the world there isn't a scrap of food in this house, not a lump of coal to start the fire, not a drop of milk for the baby's bottle.

We walk through the streets and Malachy practices his speech at the top of his voice, Dad, Dad, that five pounds is for the new baby. That's not for the drink. The child is above in the bed bawling and roaring for his milk and you're drinking the pint.

He's gone from South's pub. Malachy still wants to stand and make his speech but I tell him we have to hurry and look in other pubs before Dad drinks the whole five pounds. We can't find him in other pubs either. He knows Mam would come for him or send us and there are so many pubs at this end of Limerick and beyond we could be looking for a month. We have to tell Mam there's no sign of him and she tells us we're pure useless. Oh, Jesus, I wish I had my strength and I'd search every pub in Limerick. I'd tear the mouth out of his head, so I would. Go on, go back down and try all the pubs around the railway station and try Naughton's fish and chip shop.

I have to go by myself because Malachy has the runs and can't stray far from the bucket. I search all the pubs on Parnell Street and around. I look into the snugs where the women drink and in all the men's lavatories. I'm hungry but I'm afraid to go home till I find my father. He's not in Naughton's fish and chip shop but there's a drunken man asleep at a table in the corner and his fish and chips are on the floor in their *Limerick Leader* wrapping and if I don't get them the cat will so I shove them under my jersey and I'm out the door and up the street to sit on the steps at the railway station eat my fish and chips watch the drunken soldiers pass by with the girls that giggle thank the drunken man in my mind for drowning the fish and chips in vinegar and smothering them in salt and then remember that if I die tonight I'm in a state of sin for stealing and I could go straight to hell stuffed with fish and chips but it's Saturday and if the priests are still in the confession boxes I can clear my soul after my feed.

The Dominican church is just up Glentworth Street.

Bless me, Father, for I have sinned, it's a fortnight since my last confession. I tell him the usual sins and then, I stole fish and chips from a drunken man.

Why, my child?

I was hungry, Father.

And why were you hungry?

There was nothing in my belly, Father.

He says nothing and even though it's dark I know he's shaking his head. My dear child, why can't you go home and ask your mother for something?

Because she sent me out looking for my father in the pubs, Father, and I couldn't find him and she hasn't a scrap in the house because he's drinking the five pounds Grandpa sent from the North for the new baby and she's raging by the fire because I can't find my father.

I wonder if this priest is asleep because he's very quiet till he says, My child, I sit here. I hear the sins of the poor. I assign the penance. I bestow absolution. I should be on my knees washing their feet. Do you understand me, my child?

I tell him I do but I don't.

Go home, child. Pray for me.

No penance, Father?

No, my child.

I stole the fish and chips. I'm doomed.

You're forgiven. Go. Pray for me.

He blesses me in Latin, talks to himself in English and I wonder what I did to him.

I wish I could find my father so I could say to Mam, Here he is and he has three pounds left in his pocket. I'm not hungry now so I can go up one side of O'Connell Street and down the other and search pubs on the side streets and there he is in Gleeson's, how could I miss him with his singing,

> 'Tis alone my concern if the grandest surprise
> Would be shining at me out of somebody's eyes.
> 'Tis my private affair what my feelings would be
> While the Green Glens of Antrim were welcoming me.

My heart is banging away in my chest and I don't know what to do because I know I'm raging inside like my mother by the fire and all I can think of doing is running in and giving him a good kick in the leg and running out again but I don't because we have the mornings by the fire when he tells me about Cuchulain and De Valera and Roosevelt and if he's there drunk and buying pints with the baby's money he has that look in his eyes Eugene had when he searched for Oliver and I might as well go home and tell my mother a lie that I never saw him couldn't find him.

She's in the bed with the baby. Malachy and Michael are up in Italy asleep. I know I don't have to tell Mam anything, that soon when the pubs close he'll be home singing and offering us a penny to die for Ireland and it will be different now because it's bad enough to drink the dole or the wages but a man that drinks the money for a new baby is gone beyond the beyonds as my mother would say.

VIII

I'm ten years old and ready to go to St. Joseph's Church for my Confirmation. In school the master, Mr. O'Dea, prepares us. We have to know all about Sanctifying Grace, a pearl of great price, bought for us by Jesus in His dying. Mr. O'Dea's eyes roll in his head when he tells us that with Confirmation we will become part of Divinity. We will have the Gifts of the Holy Ghost: Wisdom, Understanding, Counsel, Fortitude, Knowledge, Piety, the Fear of the Lord. Priests and masters tell us Confirmation means you're a true soldier of the Church and that entitles you to die and be a martyr in case we're invaded by Protestants or Mahommedans or any other class of a heathen. More dying. I want to tell them I won't be able to die for the Faith because I'm already booked to die for Ireland.

Mikey Molloy says, Is it jokin' you are? That thing about dying for the Faith is all a cod. 'Tis only a saying they made up to frighten you. Ireland too. No one dies for anything anymore. All the dying is done. I wouldn't die for Ireland or the Faith. I might die for my mother but that's all.

Mikey knows everything. He's going on fourteen. He gets the fits. He has visions.

The grown-ups tell us it's a glorious thing to die for the Faith, only we're not ready for that yet because Confirmation day is like First

Communion day, you make the rounds of lanes and back streets and you get cakes and sweets and money, The Collection.

That's where poor Peter Dooley comes in. We call him Quasimodo because he has a hump on his back like the one on the hunchback of Notre Dame, whose real name we know is Charles Laughton.

Quasimodo has nine sisters and it is said his mother never wanted him but that was what the angel brought her and it's a sin to question what's sent. Quasimodo is old, he's fifteen. His red hair sticks up in all directions. He has green eyes and one rolls around in his head so much he's constantly tapping his temple to keep it where it's supposed to be. His right leg is short and twisted and when he walks he does a little twirly dance and you never know when he'll fall. That's when you're surprised. He curses his leg, he curses the world, but he curses in a lovely English accent which he got from the radio, the BBC. Before he leaves his house he always sticks his head out the door and tells the lane, Here's me head, me arse is coming. When he was twelve Quasimodo decided that with the way he looked and the way the world looked at him the best thing would be to prepare for a job where he could be heard and not seen and what better than sitting behind a microphone at the BBC in London reading the news?

But you can't get to London without money and that's why he hobbles up to us that Friday, the day before Confirmation. He has an idea for Billy and me. He knows the next day we'll be getting Confirmation money and if we promise to pay him a shilling each he'll let us climb up the rainspout behind his house this very night to look in the window and see his sisters' naked bodies when they take their weekly wash. I sign right away. Billy says, I have my own sister. Why should I pay to see your naked sisters?

Quasimodo says that looking at your own sister's naked body is the worst sin of all and he's not sure if there's a priest in the world can forgive you, that you might have to go to the bishop, who everyone knows is a holy terror.

Billy signs.

Friday night we climb the wall of Quasimodo's backyard. It's a lovely night with the June moon floating high over Limerick and you can feel a warm breeze off the Shannon River. Quasimodo is about to let Billy up the spout and who comes clambering over the wall but Mikey Molloy the Fit himself hissing at Quasimodo, Here's a shilling,

Quasimodo. Let me up the spout. Mikey is fourteen now, bigger than any of us and strong from his job delivering coal. He's black from the coal like Uncle Pa Keating and all you can see are the whites of his eyes and the white froth on his lower lip, which means he could have the fit anytime.

Quasimodo says, Wait, Mikey. They're first. Wait, my arse, says Mikey, and he's away up the spout. Billy complains but Quasimodo shakes his head, I can't help it. He comes every week with the shilling. I have to let him up the spout or he'll beat me up and tell my mother and the next thing she locks me in the coal hole all day with the rats. The Fit is up hanging on to the spout with one hand. The other hand is in his pocket moving, moving and when the spout itself starts to move and creak Quasimodo hisses, Molloy, there's to be no whankin' up the spout. He hops around the yard cackling. His BBC accent is gone and he's pure Limerick. Jaysus, Molloy, come down off that spout or I'll tell me mother. Mikey's hand goes faster in his pocket, so fast the spout gives a lurch and collapses and Mikey is rolling on the ground yelping, I'm dead. I'm destroyed. Oh, God. You can see the froth on his lips and the blood that comes from biting his tongue.

Quasimodo's mother comes screaming through the door, What in the name of Jesus! and the kitchen light fills the yard. The sisters are squawking from the window above. Billy tries to escape and she drags him off the wall. She tells him run to O'Connor the chemist around the corner to ring up an ambulance or a doctor or something for Mikey. She screams at us to get into the kitchen. She kicks Quasimodo into the hall. He's on his hands and knees and she drags him to the coal hole under the stairs and locks him in. Stay there till you come to your senses.

He's crying and calling to her in a pure Limerick accent. Ah, Mamma, Mamma, let me out. The rats is here. I only want to go to the BBC, Mamma. Aw, Jasus, Mamma, Jasus. I'll never let anyone up the spout again. I'll send money from London, Mamma. Mamma!

Mikey is still on his back, jerking and twisting around the yard. The ambulance takes him off to the hospital with a broken shoulder and his tongue in ribbons.

Our mothers are there in no time. Mrs. Dooley says, I'm disgraced, so I am, disgraced. My daughters can't wash theirselves of a Friday night without the whole world gawking in the window and them boys there are in a state of sin and should be taken to the priest for confession before their Confirmation tomorrow.

But Mam says, I don't know about the rest of the world but I saved a whole year for Frank's Confirmation suit and I'm not going to the priest to have him tell me my son is not fit for Confirmation so that I'll have to wait another year when he grows out of this suit and all because he climbed a spout for an innocent gawk at the scrawny arse of Mona Dooley.

She drags me home by the ear and makes me kneel before the Pope. Swear, she says, swear to that Pope that you didn't look at Mona Dooley in her pelt.

I swear.

If you're lying you won't be in a state of grace for Confirmation tomorrow and that's the worst kind of sacrilege.

I swear.

Only the bishop himself could forgive a sacrilege like that.

I swear.

All right. Go to bed and from this day out stay far away from that misfortunate Quasimodo Dooley.

We are all confirmed the next day. The bishop asks me a catechism question, What is the Fourth Commandment? and I tell him, Honor thy father and thy mother. He pats my cheek and that makes me a soldier of the True Church. I kneel in the pew and think of Quasimodo locked in the coal hole under the stairs and I wonder, Should I give him the shilling anyway for his career at the BBC?

But I forget all about Quasimodo because my nose starts bleeding and I feel dizzy. Confirmation boys and girls are outside St. Joseph's with their parents and there is hugging and kissing in the bright sun and I don't care. My father is working and I don't care. My mother kisses me and I don't care. The boys talk about The Collection and I don't care. My nose won't stop and Mam is worried I'll ruin my suit. She runs into the church to see if Stephen Carey, the sacristan, would spare her a rag and he gives her some kind of canvas cloth that makes my nose sore. She says, Do you want to make your collection? and I tell her I don't care. Malachy says, Do, do, Frankie, and he's sad because I promised I'd take him to the Lyric Cinema to see the film and stuff ourselves with sweets. I want to lie down. I could lie down there on the steps of St. Joseph's and sleep forever. Mam says, Grandma is making a nice breakfast, and the mention of food makes me so sick I run to the edge of the pavement to throw up and the whole world is looking at me and I don't care. Mam says she'd better take me home and put me to bed and my pals look surprised that anyone can go to bed when there's a collection to be made.

She helps me take off my Confirmation suit and puts me to bed. She wets a rag and places it under my neck and after awhile the bleeding stops. She brings tea but the look of it makes me sick and I have to throw up in the bucket. Mrs. Hannon comes in from next door and I can hear her say that's a very sick child and he should have a doctor. Mam says it's Saturday, the Dispensary is closed and where would you get a doctor?

Dad comes home from his job at Rank's Flour Mills and tells Mam I'm going through a stage, growing pains. Grandma comes up and says the same thing. She says when boys go from the one number year, which is nine, to the two number year, which is ten, they're changing and prone to the nosebleed. She says I might have too much blood in me anyway and a good cleaning out wouldn't do me one bit of harm.

The day passes and I'm in and out of sleep. Malachy and Michael come into the bed at night and I can hear Malachy say, Frankie is very hot. Michael says, He's bleeding on my leg. Mam puts the wet rag on my nose and a key on my neck but it won't stop the bleeding. On Sunday morning there's blood on my chest and all around me. Mam tells Dad I'm bleeding through my bottom and he says I might have a case of the runs, which is common with the growing pains.

Dr. Troy is our doctor but he's away on holiday and the man that comes to see me on Monday has a smell of whiskey on him. He examines me and tells my mother I have a bad cold and keep me in bed. Days pass and I sleep and bleed. Mam makes tea and beef tea and I don't want it. She even brings ice cream and the look of it makes me sick. Mrs. Hannon comes in again and says that doctor doesn't know what he's talking about, see if Dr. Troy is back.

Mam comes with Dr. Troy. He feels my forehead, rolls up my eyelids, turns me over to see my back, picks me up and runs to his motor car. Mam runs after him and he tells her I have typhoid fever. Mam cries, Oh, God, oh, God, am I to lose the whole family? Will it ever end? She gets into the car, holds me in her lap and moans all the way to the Fever Hospital at the City Home.

The bed has cool white sheets. The nurses have clean white uniforms and the nun, Sister Rita, is all in white. Dr. Humphrey and Dr. Campbell have white coats and things hanging from their necks which they stick against my chest and all over. I sleep and sleep but I'm awake when they bring in jars of bright red stuff that hang from tall poles above my bed and they stick tubes into my ankles and the back of my right hand. Sister Rita says, You're getting blood, Francis. Soldier's blood from the Sarsfield Barracks.

Mam is sitting by the bed and the nurse is saying, You know, missus, this is very unusual. No one is ever allowed into the Fever Hospital for fear they'd catch something but they made an exception for you with his crisis coming. If he gets over this he'll surely recover.

I fall asleep. Mam is gone when I wake but there's movement in the room and it's the priest, Father Gorey, from the Confraternity saying Mass at a table in the corner. I drift off again and now they're waking me and pulling down the bedclothes. Father Gorey is touching me with oil and praying in Latin. I know it's Extreme Unction and that means I'm going to die and I don't care. They wake me again to receive Communion. I don't want it, I'm afraid I might get sick. I keep the wafer on my tongue and fall asleep and when I wake up again it's gone.

It's dark and Dr. Campbell is sitting by my bed. He's holding my wrist and looking at his watch. He has red hair and glasses and he always smiles when he talks to me. He sits now and hums and looks out the window. His eyes close and he snores a little. He tilts over on the chair and farts and smiles to himself and I know now I'm going to get better because a doctor would never fart in the presence of a dying boy.

Sister Rita's white habit is bright in the sun that comes in the window. She's holding my wrist, looking at her watch, smiling. Oh, she says, we're awake, are we? Well, Francis, I think we've come through the worst. Our prayers are answered and all the prayers of those hundreds of little boys at the Confraternity. Can you imagine that? Hundreds of boys saying the rosary for you and offering up their communion.

My ankles and the back of my hand are throbbing from the tubes bringing in the blood and I don't care about boys praying for me. I can hear the swish of Sister Rita's habit and the click of her rosary beads when she leaves the room. I fall asleep and when I wake it's dark and Dad is sitting by the bed with his hand on mine.

Son, are you awake?

I try to talk but I'm dry, nothing will come out and I point to my mouth. He holds a glass of water to my lips and it's sweet and cool. He presses my hand and says I'm a great old soldier and why wouldn't I? Don't I have the soldier's blood in me?

The tubes are not in me anymore and the glass jars are gone.

Sister Rita comes in and tells Dad he has to go. I don't want him to go because he looks sad. He's like Paddy Clohessy the day I gave him the raisin. When he looks sad it's the worst thing in the world and I start crying. Now what's this? says Sister Rita. Crying with all that soldier blood in you? There's a big surprise for you tomorrow, Francis. You'll never guess. Well, I'll tell you, we're bringing you a nice biscuit with your tea in the morning. Isn't that a treat? And your father will be back in a day or two, won't you, Mr. McCourt?

Dad nods and puts his hand on mine again. He looks at me, steps away, stops, comes back, kisses me on the forehead for the first time in my life and I'm so happy I feel like floating out of the bed.

The other two beds in my room are empty. The nurse says I'm the only typhoid patient and I'm a miracle for getting over the crisis.

The room next to me is empty till one morning a girl's voice says, Yoo hoo, who's there?

I'm not sure if she's talking to me or someone in the room beyond.

Yoo hoo, boy with the typhoid, are you awake?

I am.

Are you better?

I am.

Well, why are you here?

I don't know. I'm still in the bed. They stick needles in me and give me medicine.

What do you look like?

I wonder, What kind of a question is that? I don't know what to tell her.

Yoo hoo, are you there, typhoid boy?

I am.

What's your name?

Frank.

That's a good name. My name is Patricia Madigan. How old are you?

Ten.

Oh. She sounds disappointed.

But I'll be eleven in August, next month.

Well, that's better than ten. I'll be fourteen in September. Do you want to know why I'm in the Fever Hospital?

I do.

I have diphtheria and something else.

What's something else?

They don't know. They think I have a disease from foreign parts because my father used to be in Africa. I nearly died. Are you going to tell me what you look like?

I have black hair.

You and millions.

I have brown eyes with bits of green that's called hazel.

You and thousands.

I have stitches on the back of my right hand and my two feet where they put in the soldier's blood.

Oh, God, did they?

They did.

You won't be able to stop marching and saluting.

There's a swish of habit and click of beads and then Sister Rita's voice. Now, now, what's this? There's to be no talking between two rooms especially when it's a boy and a girl. Do you hear me, Patricia?

I do, Sister.

Do you hear me, Francis?

I do, Sister.

You could be giving thanks for your two remarkable recoveries. You could be saying the rosary. You could be reading *The Little Messenger of the Sacred Heart* that's beside your beds. Don't let me come back and find you talking.

She comes into my room and wags her finger at me. Especially you, Francis, after thousands of boys prayed for you at the Confraternity. Give thanks, Francis, give thanks.

She leaves and there's silence for awhile. Then Patricia whispers, Give thanks, Francis, give thanks, and say your rosary, Francis, and I laugh so hard a nurse runs in to see if I'm all right. She's a very stern nurse from the County Kerry and she frightens me. What's this, Francis? Laughing? What is there to laugh about? Are you and that Madigan girl talking? I'll report you to Sister Rita. There's to be no laughing for you could be doing serious damage to your internal apparatus.

She plods out and Patricia whispers again in a heavy Kerry accent, No laughing, Francis, you could be doin' serious damage to your internal apparatus. Say your rosary, Francis, and pray for your internal apparatus.

Mam visits me on Thursdays. I'd like to see my father, too, but I'm out of danger, crisis time is over, and I'm allowed only one visitor. Besides, she says, he's back at work at Rank's Flour Mills and please God this job will last a while with the war on and the English desperate for flour. She brings me a chocolate bar and that proves Dad is working. She could never afford it on the dole. He sends me notes. He tells me my brothers are all praying for me, that I should be a good boy, obey the doctors, the nuns, the nurses, and don't forget to say my prayers. He's sure St. Jude pulled me through the crisis because he's the patron saint of desperate cases and I was indeed a desperate case.

Patricia says she has two books by her bed. One is a poetry book and that's the one she loves. The other is a short history of England and do I want it? She gives it to Seamus, the man who mops the floors every day, and he brings it to me. He says, I'm not supposed to be bringing anything from a dipteria room to a typhoid room with all the germs flying around and hiding between the pages and if you ever catch dipteria on top of the typhoid they'll know and I'll lose my good job and be out on the street singing patriotic songs with a tin cup in my hand, which I could easily do because there isn't a song ever written about Ireland's sufferings I don't know and a few songs about the joy of whiskey too.

Oh, yes, he knows Roddy McCorley. He'll sing it for me right enough but he's barely into the first verse when the Kerry nurse rushes in. What's this, Seamus? Singing? Of all the people in this hospital you should know the rules against singing. I have a good mind to report you to Sister Rita.

Ah, God, don't do that, nurse.

Very well, Seamus. I'll let it go this one time. You know the singing could lead to a relapse in these patients.

When she leaves he whispers he'll teach me a few songs because singing is good for passing the time when you're by yourself in a typhoid room. He says Patricia is a lovely girl the way she often gives him sweets from the parcel her mother sends every fortnight. He stops mopping the floor and calls to Patricia in the next room, I was telling Frankie you're a lovely girl, Patricia, and she says, You're a lovely man, Seamus. He smiles because he's an old man of forty and he never had children but the ones he can talk to here in the Fever Hospital. He says, Here's the book, Frankie. Isn't it a great pity you have to be reading all about England after all they did to us, that there isn't a history of Ireland to be had in this hospital.

The book tells me all about King Alfred and William the Conqueror and all the kings and queens down to Edward, who had to wait forever for his mother, Victoria, to die before he could be king. The book has the first bit of Shakespeare I ever read.

> *I do believe, induced by potent circumstances*
> *That thou art mine enemy.*

The history writer says this is what Catherine, who is a wife of Henry the Eighth, says to Cardinal Wolsey, who is trying to have her head cut off. I don't know what it means and I don't care because it's Shakespeare and it's like having jewels in my mouth when I say the words. If I had a whole book of Shakespeare they could keep me in the hospital for a year.

Patricia says she doesn't know what induced means or potent circumstances and she doesn't care about Shakespeare, she has her poetry book and she reads to me from beyond the wall a poem about an owl and a pussycat that went to sea in a green boat with honey and money and it makes no sense and when I say that Patricia gets huffy and says that's the last poem she'll ever read to me. She says I'm always reciting the lines from Shakespeare and they make no sense either. Seamus stops mopping again and tells us we shouldn't be fighting over poetry because we'll have enough to fight about when we grow up and get married. Patricia says she's sorry and I'm sorry too so she reads me part of another poem which I have to remember so I can say it back to her early in the morning or late at night when there are no nuns or nurses about,

> *The wind was a torrent of darkness among the gusty trees,*
> *The moon was a ghostly galleon tossed upon cloudy seas,*
> *The road was a ribbon of moonlight over the purple moor,*
> *And the highwayman came riding*
> > *Riding riding*
> *The highwayman came riding, up to the old inn-door.*

He'd a French cocked-hat on his forehead, a bunch of lace at his chin,
A coat of the claret velvet, and breeches of brown doe-skin,
They fitted with never a wrinkle, his boots were up to the thigh.
And he rode with a jewelled twinkle,
    His pistol butts a-twinkle,
His rapier hilt a-twinkle, under the jewelled sky.

Every day I can't wait for the doctors and nurses to leave me alone so I can learn a new verse from Patricia and find out what's happening to the highwayman and the landlord's red-lipped daughter. I love the poem because it's exciting and almost as good as my two lines of Shakespeare. The redcoats are after the highwayman because they know he told her, I'll come to thee by moonlight, though hell should bar the way.

I'd love to do that myself, come by moonlight for Patricia in the next room not giving a fiddler's fart though hell should bar the way. She's ready to read the last few verses when in comes the nurse from Kerry shouting at her, shouting at me, I told ye there was to be no talking between rooms. Dipthteria is never allowed to talk to typhoid and visa versa. I warned ye. And she calls out, Seamus, take this one. Take the by. Sister Rita said one more word out of him and upstairs with him. We gave ye a warning to stop the blathering but ye wouldn't. Take the by, Seamus, take him.

Ah, now, nurse, sure isn't he harmless. 'Tis only a bit o' poetry.

Take that by, Seamus, take him at once.

He bends over me and whispers, Ah, God, I'm sorry, Frankie. Here's your English history book. He slips the book under my shirt and lifts me from the bed. He whispers that I'm a feather. I try to see Patricia when we pass through her room but all I can make out is a blur of dark head on a pillow.

Sister Rita stops us in the hall to tell me I'm a great disappointment to her, that she expected me to be a good boy after what God had done for me, after all the prayers said by hundreds of boys at the Confraternity, after all the care from the nuns and nurses of the Fever Hospital, after the way they let my mother and father in to see me, a thing rarely allowed, and this is how I repaid them lying in the bed reciting silly poetry back and forth with Patricia Madigan knowing very well there was a ban on all talk between typhoid and diphtheria. She says I'll have plenty of time to reflect on my sins in the big ward upstairs and I should beg God's forgiveness for my disobedience reciting a pagan English poem about a thief on a horse and a maiden with red lips who commits a terrible sin when I could have been praying or reading the life of a saint. She made it her business to read that poem so she did and I'd be well advised to tell the priest in confession.

The Kerry nurse follows us upstairs gasping and holding on to the banister. She tells me I better not get the notion she'll be running up to this part of the world every time I have a little pain or a twinge.

There are twenty beds in the ward, all white, all empty. The nurse tells Seamus put me at the far end of the ward against the wall to make sure I don't talk to anyone who might be passing the door, which is very unlikely since there isn't another soul on this whole floor. She tells Seamus this was the fever ward during the Great Famine long ago and only God knows how many died here brought in too late for anything but a wash before they were buried and there are stories of cries and moans in the far reaches of the night. She says 'twould break your heart to think of what the English did to us, that if they didn't put the blight on the potato they didn't do much to take it off. No pity. No feeling at all for the people that died in this very ward, children suffering and dying here while the English feasted on roast beef and guzzled the best of wine in their big houses, little children with their mouths all green from trying to eat the grass in the fields beyond, God bless us and save us and guard us from future famines.

Seamus says 'twas a terrible thing indeed and he wouldn't want to be walking these halls in the dark with all the little green mouths gaping at him. The nurse takes my temperature, 'Tis up a bit, have a good sleep for yourself now that you're away from the chatter with Patricia Madigan below who will never know a gray hair.

She shakes her head at Seamus and he gives her a sad shake back.

Nurses and nuns never think you know what they're talking about. If you're ten going on eleven you're supposed to be simple like my uncle Pat Sheehan who was dropped on his head. You can't ask questions. You can't show you understand what the nurse said about Patricia Madigan, that she's going to die, and you can't show you want to cry over this girl who taught you a lovely poem which the nun says is bad.

The nurse tells Seamus she has to go and he's to sweep the lint from under my bed and mop up a bit around the ward. Seamus tells me she's a right oul' bitch for running to Sister Rita and complaining about the poem going between the two rooms, that you can't catch a disease from a poem unless it's love ha ha and that's not bloody likely when you're what? ten going on eleven? He never heard the likes of it, a little fella shifted upstairs for saying a poem and he has a good mind to go to the *Limerick Leader* and tell them print the whole thing except he has this job and he'd lose it if ever Sister Rita found out. Anyway, Frankie, you'll be outa here one of these fine days and you can read all the poetry you want though I don't know about Patricia below, I don't know about Patricia, God help us.

He knows about Patricia in two days because she got out of the bed to go to the lavatory when she was supposed to use a bedpan and collapsed and died in the lavatory. Seamus is mopping the floor and there are tears on his cheeks and he's saying, 'Tis a dirty rotten thing to die in a lavatory when you're lovely in yourself. She told me she was sorry she had you reciting that poem and getting you shifted from the room, Frankie. She said 'twas all her fault.

It wasn't, Seamus.

I know and didn't I tell her that.

Patricia is gone and I'll never know what happened to the highwayman and Bess, the landlord's daughter. I ask Seamus but he doesn't know any poetry at all especially English poetry. He knew an Irish poem once but it was about fairies and had no sign of a highwayman in it. Still he'll ask the men in his local pub where there's always someone reciting something and he'll bring it back to me. Won't I be busy meanwhile reading my short history of England and finding out all about their perfidy. That's what Seamus says, perfidy, and I don't know what it means and he doesn't know what it means but if it's something the English do it must be terrible.

He comes three times a week to mop the floor and the nurse is there every morning to take my temperature and pulse. The doctor listens to my chest with the thing hanging from his neck. They all say, And how's our little soldier today? A girl with a blue dress brings meals three times a day and never talks to me. Seamus says she's not right in the head so don't say a word to her.

The July days are long and I fear the dark. There are only two ceiling lights in the ward and they're switched off when the tea tray is taken away and the nurse gives me pills. The nurse tells me go to sleep but I can't because I see people in the nineteen beds in the ward all dying and green around their mouths where they tried to eat grass and moaning for soup Protestant soup any soup and I cover my face with the pillow hoping they won't come and stand around the bed clawing at me and howling for bits of the chocolate bar my mother brought last week.

No, she didn't bring it. She had to send it in because I can't have any more visitors. Sister Rita tells me a visit to the Fever Hospital is a privilege and after my bad behavior with Patricia Madigan and that poem I can't have the privilege anymore. She says I'll be going home in a few weeks and my job is to concentrate on getting better and learn to walk again after being in bed for six weeks and I can get out of bed tomorrow after breakfast. I don't know why she says I have to learn how to walk when I've been walking since I was a baby but when the nurse stands me by the side of the bed I fall to the floor and the nurse laughs, See, you're a baby again.

I practice walking from bed to bed back and forth back and forth. I don't want to be a baby. I don't want to be in this empty ward with no Patricia and no highwayman and no red-lipped landlord's daughter. I don't want the ghosts of children with green mouths pointing bony fingers at me and clamoring for bits of my chocolate bar.

Seamus says a man in his pub knew all the verses of the highwayman poem and it has a very sad end. Would I like him to say it because he never learned how to read and he had to carry the poem in his head? He stands in the middle of the ward leaning on his mop and recites,

Tlot-tlot, in the frosty silence! Tlot-tlot in the echoing night!
Nearer he came and nearer! Her face was like a light!
Her eyes grew wide for a moment, she drew one last deep breath,
Then her finger moved in the moonlight,
    Her musket shattered the moonlight,
Shattered her breast in the moonlight and warned him—with her death.

He hears the shot and escapes but when he learns at dawn how Bess died he goes into a rage and returns for revenge only to be shot down by the redcoats.

Blood-red were his spurs in the golden noon; wine-red was his velvet coat,
When they shot him down on the highway,
    Down like a dog on the highway,
And he lay in his blood on the highway, with a bunch of lace at his throat.

Seamus wipes his sleeve across his face and sniffles. He says, There was no call at all to shift you up here away from Patricia when you didn't even know what happened to the highwayman and Bess. 'Tis a very sad story and when I said it to my wife she wouldn't stop crying the whole night till we went to bed. She said there was no call for them redcoats to shoot that highwayman, they are responsible for half the troubles of the world and they never had any pity on the Irish, either. Now if you want to know any more poems, Frankie, tell me and I'll get them from the pub and bring 'em back in my head.

The girl with the blue dress who's not right in the head suddenly says one day, Would you like a book for to read? and she brings me *The Amazing Quest of Mr. Ernest Bliss* by E. Phillips Oppenheim, which is all about an Englishman who is fed up and doesn't know what to do with himself every day even though he's so rich he can't count his money. His manservant brings him the morning paper the tea the egg the toast and marmalade and he says, Take it away, life is empty. He can't read his paper, he can't eat his egg, and he pines away. His doctor tells him go and live among the poor in the East End of London and he'll learn to love life, which he does and falls in love with a girl who is poor but honest and very intelligent and they get married and move into his house in the West End which is the rich part because it's easier to help the poor and not be fed up when you're nice and comfortable.

Seamus likes me to tell him what I'm reading. He says that story about Mr. Ernest Bliss is a made-up story because no one in his right mind would have to go to a doctor over having too much money and not eating his egg though you never know. It might be like that in England. You'd never find the likes of that in Ireland. If you didn't eat your egg here you'd be carted off to the lunatic asylum or reported to the bishop.

I can't wait to go home and tell Malachy about this man who won't eat his egg. Malachy will fall down on the floor laughing because such a thing could never happen. He'll say I'm making it up but when I tell him this story is about an Englishman he'll understand.

I can't tell the girl in the blue dress that this story was silly because she might have a fit. She says if you're finished with that book I'll bring you another one because there's a whole box of books left behind by patients from the old days. She brings me a book called *Tom Brown's School-Days,* which is hard to read, and no end of books by P. G. Wodehouse, who makes me laugh over Ukridge and Bertie Wooster and Jeeves and all the Mulliners. Bertie Wooster is rich but he eats his egg every morning for fear of what Jeeves might say. I wish I could talk to the girl in the blue dress or anyone about the books but I'm afraid the Kerry nurse or Sister Rita might find out and they'd move me to a bigger ward upstairs with fifty empty beds and Famine ghosts galore with green mouths and bony fingers pointing. At night I lie in bed thinking about Tom Brown and his adventures at Rugby School and all the characters in P. G. Wodehouse. I can dream about the red-lipped landlord's daughter and the highwayman, and the nurses and nuns can do nothing about it. It's lovely to know the world can't interfere with the inside of your head.

It's August and I'm eleven. I've been in this hospital for two months and I wonder if they'll let me out for Christmas. The Kerry nurse tells me I should get down on my two knees and thank God I'm alive at all at all and not be complaining.

I'm not complaining, nurse, I'm only wondering if I'll be home for Christmas.

She won't answer me. She tells me behave myself or she'll send Sister Rita up to me and then I'll behave myself.

Mam comes to the hospital on my birthday and sends up a package with two chocolate bars and a note with names of people in the lane telling me get better and come home and you're a great soldier, Frankie. The nurse lets me talk to her through the window and it's hard because the windows are high and I have to stand on Seamus's shoulders. I tell Mam I want to go home but she says I'm a bit too weak and surely I'll be out in no time. Seamus says, 'Tis a grand thing to be eleven because any day now you'll be a man shaving and all and ready to get out and get a job and drink your pint good as any man.

After fourteen weeks Sister Rita tells me I can go home and aren't I a lucky boy that the day will be the feast of St. Francis of Assisi. She tells me I was a very good patient, except for that little problem with the poem and Patricia Madigan, God rest her, and I'm invited to come back and have a big Christmas dinner in the hospital. Mam comes for me and with my weak legs it takes us a long time to walk to the bus at Union Cross. She says, Take your time. After three and a half months we can spare an hour.

People are at their doors on Barrack Road and Roden Lane telling me it's grand to see me back, that I'm a great soldier, a credit to my father and mother. Malachy and Michael run up to me in the lane and say, God, you're walking very slow. Can't you run anymore?

It's a bright day and I'm happy till I see Dad sitting in the kitchen with Alphie on his lap and there's an empty feeling in my heart because I know he's out of work again. All along I was sure he had a job, Mam told me he did, and I thought there would be no shortage of food and shoes. He smiles at me and tells Alphie, Och, there's your big brother home from the hospital.

Mam tells him what the doctor said, that I'm to have plenty of nourishing food and rest. The doctor said beef would be the right thing for building me up again. Dad nods. Mam makes beef tea from a cube and Malachy and Mike watch me drink it. They say they'd like some too but Mam says go away, ye didn't have the typhoid. She says the doctor wants me to go to bed early. She tried to get rid of the fleas but they're worse than ever with the warm weather we're having. Besides, she says, they won't get much out of you all bones and little skin.

I lie in bed and think of the hospital where the white sheets were changed every day and there wasn't a sign of a flea. There was a lavatory where you could sit and read your book till someone asked if you were dead. There was a bath where you could sit in hot water as long as you liked and say,

> *I do believe,*
> *Induced by potent circumstances*
> *That thou art mine enemy,*

And saying that helps me fall asleep.

When Malachy and Michael get up for school in the morning Mam tells me I can stay in bed. Malachy is in fifth class now with Mr. O'Dea and he likes to tell everyone he's learning the big red catechism for Confirmation and Mr. O'Dea is telling them all about state of grace and Euclid and how the English tormented the Irish for eight hundred long years.

I don't want to stay in bed anymore. The October days are lovely and I want to sit outside looking up the lane at the way the sun slants along the wall opposite our house. Mikey Moloney brings me P. G. Wodehouse books his father gets from the library and I have great days with Ukridge and Bertie Wooster and all the Mulliners. Dad lets me read his favorite book, John Mitchel's *Jail Journal,* which is all about a great Irish rebel the English condemned to exile in Van Diemen's land in Australia. The English tell John Mitchel he's free to come and go as he pleases all over Van Diemen's land if he gives his word of honor as a gentleman he won't try to escape. He gives his word till a ship comes to help him escape and he goes to the office of the English magistrate and says, I'm escaping, jumps on his horse and winds up in New York. Dad says he doesn't mind if I read silly English books by P. G. Wodehouse as long as I don't forget the men who did their bit and gave their lives for Ireland.

I can't stay at home forever and Mam takes me back to Leamy's School in November. The new headmaster, Mr. O'Halloran, says he's sorry, I've missed over two months of school and I have to be put back in fifth class. Mam says surely I'm ready for sixth class. After all, she says, he's missed only a few weeks. Mr. O'Halloran says he's sorry, take the boy next door to Mr. O'Dea.

We walk along the hallway and I tell Mam I don't want to be in fifth class. Malachy is in that class and I don't want to be in a class with my brother who is a year younger. I made my Confirmation last year. He didn't. I'm older. I'm not bigger anymore because of the typhoid but I'm older.

Mam says, It won't kill you.

She doesn't care and I'm put into that class with Malachy and I know all his friends are there sneering at me because I was put back. Mr. O'Dea makes me sit in the front and tells me get that sour look off my puss or I'll feel the end of his ash plant.

Then a miracle happens and it's all because of St. Francis of Assisi, my favorite saint, and Our Lord Himself. I find a penny in the street that first day back at school and I want to run to Kathleen O'Connell's for a big square of Cleeves' toffee but I can't run because my legs are still weak from the typhoid and sometimes I have to hold on to a wall. I'm desperate for the Cleeves' toffee but I'm also desperate to get out of fifth class.

I know I have to go to the statue of St. Francis of Assisi. He's the only one who will listen but he's at the other end of Limerick and it takes me an hour to walk there, sitting on steps, holding on to walls. It's a penny to light a candle and I wonder if I should just light the candle and keep the penny. No, St. Francis would know. He loves the bird in the air and the fish in the stream but he's not a fool. I light the candle, I kneel at his statue and beg him to get me out of fifth class where I'm stuck with my brother, who is probably going around the lane now bragging that his big brother was kept back. St. Francis doesn't say a word but I know he's listening and I know he'll get me out of that class. It's the least he could do after all my trouble coming to his statue, sitting on steps, holding on to walls, when I could have gone to St. Joseph's Church and lit a candle to the Little Flower or the Sacred Heart of Jesus Himself. What's the use of being named after him if he's going to desert me in my hour of need?

I have to sit in Mr. O'Dea's class listening to the catechism and all the other stuff he taught last year. I'd like to raise my hand and give the answers but he says, Be quiet, let your brother answer. He gives them tests in arithmetic and makes me sit there and correct them. He dictates to them in Irish and makes me correct what they've written. Then he gives me special compositions to write and makes me read them to the class because of all I learned from him last year. He tells the class, Frank McCourt is going to show you how well he learned to write in this class last year. He's going to write a composition on Our Lord, aren't you, McCourt? He's going to tell us what it would be like if Our Lord had grown up in Limerick which has the Arch Confraternity of the Holy Family and is the holiest city in Ireland. We know that if Our Lord had grown up in Limerick He would never have been crucified because the people of Limerick were always good Catholics and not given to crucifixion. So, McCourt, you are to go home and write that composition and bring it in tomorrow.

Dad says Mr. O'Dea has a great imagination but didn't Our Lord suffer enough on the cross without sticking Him in Limerick on top of it with the damp from the River Shannon. He puts on his cap and goes for a long walk and I have to think about Our Lord by myself and wonder what I'm going to write tomorrow.

The next day Mr. O'Dea says, All right, McCourt, read your composition to the class.

The name of my composition is—

The title, McCourt, the title.

The title of my composition is, "Jesus and the Weather."

What?

"Jesus and the Weather."

All right, read it.

This is my composition. I don't think Jesus Who is Our Lord would have liked the weather in Limerick because it's always raining and the Shannon keeps the whole city damp. My father says the Shannon is a killer river because it killed my two brothers. When you look at pictures of Jesus He's always wandering around ancient Israel in a sheet. It never rains there and you never hear of anyone coughing or getting consumption or anything like that and no one has a job there because all they do is stand around and eat manna and shake their fists and go to crucifixions.

Anytime Jesus got hungry all He had to do was walk up the road to a fig tree or an orange tree and have His fill. If He wanted a pint He could wave His hand over a big glass and there was the pint. Or He could visit Mary Magdalene and her sister, Martha, and they'd give Him His dinner no questions asked and He'd get his feet washed and dried with Mary Magdalene's hair while Martha washed the dishes, which I don't think is fair. Why should she have to wash the dishes while her sister sits out there chatting away with Our Lord? It's a good thing Jesus decided to be born Jewish in that warm place because if he was born in Limerick he'd catch the consumption and be dead in a month and there wouldn't be any Catholic Church and there wouldn't be any Communion or Confirmation and we wouldn't have to learn the catechism and write compositions about Him. The End.

Mr. O'Dea is quiet and gives me a strange look and I'm worried because when he's quiet like that it means someone is going to suffer. He says, McCourt, who wrote that composition?

I did, sir.

Did your father write that composition?

He didn't, sir.

Come here, McCourt.

I follow him out the door, along the hall to the headmaster's room. Mr. O'Dea shows him my composition and Mr. O'Halloran gives me the strange look, too. Did you write this composition?

I did, sir.

I'm taken out of the fifth class and put into Mr. O'Halloran's sixth class with all the boys I know, Paddy Clohessy, Fintan Slattery, The Question Quigley, and when school is over that day I have to go back down to the statue of St. Francis of Assisi to thank him even if my legs are still weak from the typhoid and I have to sit on steps and hold on to walls and I wonder was it something good I said in that composition or something bad.

Mr. Thomas L. O'Halloran teaches three classes in one room, sixth, seventh, eighth. He has a head like President Roosevelt and he wears gold glasses. He wears suits, navy blue or gray, and there's a gold watch chain that hangs across his belly from pocket to pocket in his waistcoat. We call him Hoppy because he has a short leg and hops when he walks. He knows what we call him and he says, Yes, I'm Hoppy and I'll hop on you. He carries a long stick, a pointer, and if you don't pay attention or give a stupid answer he gives you three slaps on each hand or whacks you across the backs of your legs. He makes you learn everything by heart, everything, and that makes him the hardest master in the school. He loves America and makes us know all the American states in alphabetical order. He makes charts of Irish grammar, Irish history and algebra at home, hangs them on an easel and we have to chant our way through the cases, conjugations and declensions of Irish, famous names and battles, proportions, ratios, equations. We have to know all the important dates in Irish history. He tells us what is important and why. No master ever told us why before. If you asked why you'd be hit on the head. Hoppy doesn't call us idiots and if you ask a question he doesn't go into a rage. He's the only master who stops and says, Do ye understand what I'm talking about? Do ye want to ask a question?

It's a shock to everyone when he says, the Battle of Kinsale in sixteen nought one was the saddest moment in Irish history, a close battle with cruelty and atrocities on both sides.

Cruelty on both sides? The Irish side? How could that be? All the other masters told us the Irish always fought nobly, they always fought the fair fight. He recites and makes us remember,

> *They went forth to battle, but they always fell,*
> *Their eyes were fixed above the sullen shields.*
> *Nobly they fought and bravely, but not well,*
> *And sank heart-wounded by a subtle spell.*

If they lost it was because of traitors and informers. But I want to know about these Irish atrocities.

Sir, did the Irish commit atrocities at the Battle of Kinsale?

They did, indeed. It is recorded that they killed prisoners but they were no better nor worse than the English.

Mr. O'Halloran can't lie. He's the headmaster. All these years we were told the Irish were always noble and they made brave speeches before the English hanged them. Now Hoppy O'Halloran is saying the Irish did bad things. Next thing he'll be saying the English did good things. He says, You have to study and learn so that you can make up your own mind about history and everything else but you can't make up an empty mind. Stock your mind, stock your mind. It is your house of treasure and no one in the world can interfere with it. If you won the Irish Sweepstakes and bought a house that needed furniture would you fill it with bits and pieces of rubbish? Your mind is your house and if you fill it with rubbish from the cinemas it will rot in your head. You might be poor, your shoes might be broken, but your mind is a palace.

He calls us one by one to the front of the room and looks at our shoes. He wants to know why they're broken or why we have no shoes at all. He tells us this is a disgrace and he's going to have a raffle to raise money so that we can have strong warm boots for the winter. He gives us books of tickets and we swarm all over Limerick for Leamy's School boot fund, first prize five pounds, five prizes of a pound each. Eleven boys with no boots get new boots. Malachy and I don't get any because we have shoes on our feet even if the soles are worn away and we wonder why we ran all over Limerick selling tickets so that other boys could get boots. Fintan Slattery says we gain plenary Indulgences for works of charity and Paddy Clohessy says, Fintan, would you ever go and have a good shit for yourself.

I know when Dad does the bad thing. I know when he drinks the dole money and Mam is desperate and has to beg at the St. Vincent de Paul Society and ask for credit at Kathleen O'Connell's shop but I don't want to back away from him and run to Mam. How can I do that when I'm up with him early every morning with the whole world asleep? He lights the fire and makes the tea and sings to himself or reads the paper to me in a whisper that won't wake up the rest of the family. Mikey Molloy stole Cuchulain, the Angel on the Seventh Step is gone someplace else, but my father in the morning is still mine. He gets the *Irish Press* early and tells me about the world, Hitler, Mussolini, Franco. He says this war is none of our business because the English are up to their tricks again. He tells me about the great Roosevelt in Washington and the great De Valera in Dublin. In the morning we have the world to ourselves and he never tells me I should die for Ireland. He tells me about the old days in Ireland when the English wouldn't let the Catholics have schools because they wanted to keep the people ignorant, that the Catholic children met in hedge schools in the depths of the country and learned English, Irish, Latin and Greek. The people loved learning. They loved stories and poetry even if none of this was any good for getting a job. Men, women and children would gather in ditches to hear those great masters and everyone wondered at how much a man could carry in his head. The masters risked their lives going from ditch to ditch and hedge to hedge because if the English caught them teaching they might be transported to foreign parts or worse. He tells me school is easy now, you don't have to sit in a ditch learning your sums or the glorious history of Ireland. I should be good in school and some day I'll go back to America and get an inside job where I'll be sitting at a desk with two fountain pens in my pocket, one red and one blue, making decisions. I'll be in out of the rain and I'll have a suit and shoes and a warm place to live and what more could a man want? He says you can do anything in America, it's the land of opportunity. You can be a fisherman in Maine or a farmer in California. America is not like Limerick, a gray place with a river that kills.

When you have your father to yourself by the fire in the morning you don't need Cuchulain or the Angel on the Seventh Step or anything.

At night he helps us with our exercises. Mam says they call it homework in America but here it's exercises, the sums, the English, the Irish, the history. He can't help us with Irish because he's from the North and lacking in the native tongue. Malachy offers to teach him all the Irish words he knows but Dad says it's too late, you can't teach an old dog a new bark. Before bed we sit around the fire and if we say, Dad, tell us a story, he makes up one about someone in the lane and the story will take us all over the world, up in the air, under the sea and back to the lane. Everyone in the story is a different color and everything is upside down and backward. Motor cars and planes go under water and submarines fly through the air. Sharks sit in trees and giant salmon sport with kangaroos on the moon. Polar bears wrestle with elephants in Australia and penguins teach Zulus how to play bagpipes. After the story he takes us upstairs and kneels with us while we say our prayers. We say the Our Father, three Hail Marys, God bless the Pope. God bless Mam, God bless our dead sister and brothers, God bless Ireland, God bless De Valera, and God bless anyone who gives Dad a job. He says, Go to sleep, boys, because holy God is watching you and He always knows if you're not good.

I think my father is like the Holy Trinity with three people in him, the one in the morning with the paper, the one at night with the stories and the prayers, and then the one who does the bad thing and comes home with the smell of whiskey and wants us to die for Ireland.

I feel sad over the bad thing but I can't back away from him because the one in the morning is my real father and if I were in America I could say, I love you, Dad, the way they do in the films, but you can't say that in Limerick for fear you might be laughed at. You're allowed to say you love God and babies and horses that win but anything else is a softness in the head.

Day and night we're tormented in that kitchen with people emptying their buckets. Mam says it's not the River Shannon that will kill us but the stink from that lavatory outside our door. It's bad enough in the winter when everything flows over and seeps under our door but worse in the warm weather when there are flies and bluebottles and rats.

There is a stable next to the lavatory where they keep the big horse from Gabbett's coal yard. His name is Finn the Horse and we all love him but the stable man from the coal yard doesn't take proper care of the stable and the stink travels to our house. The stink from the lavatory and the stable attracts rats and we have to chase them with our new dog, Lucky. He loves to corner the rats and then we smash them to bits with rocks or sticks or stab them with the hay fork in the stable. The horse himself is frightened by the rats and we have to be careful when he rears up. He knows we're not rats because we bring him apples when we rob an orchard out the country.

Sometimes the rats escape and run into our house and into the coal hole under the stairs where it's pitch dark and you can't see them. Even when we bring in a candle we can't find them because they dig holes everywhere and we don't know where to look. If we have a fire we can boil water and pour it slowly in from the kettle spot and that will drive them out of the hole between our legs and out the door again unless

Lucky is there to catch them in his teeth and shake the life out of them. We expect him to eat the rats but he'll leave them in the lane with their guts hanging out and run to my father for a piece of bread dipped in tea. People in the lane say that's a peculiar way for a dog to behave but then what would you expect from a dog of the McCourts.

The minute there's a sign of a rat or a mention of one Mam is out the door and up the lane. She'd rather walk the streets of Limerick forever than stay one minute in a house that has a rat in it and she can never rest because she knows that with the stable and the lavatory there's always a rat nearby with his family waiting for their dinner.

We fight the rats and we fight the stink from that lavatory. We'd like to keep our door open in the warm weather but you can't when people are trotting down the lane to empty their brimming buckets. Some families are worse than others and Dad hates all of them even though Mam tells him it's not their fault if the builders a hundred years ago put up houses with no lavatories but this one outside our door. Dad says the people should empty their buckets in the middle of the night when we are asleep so that we won't be disturbed by the stink.

The flies are nearly as bad as the rats. On warm days they swarm to the stable and when a bucket is emptied they swarm to the lavatory. If Mam cooks anything they swarm into the kitchen and Dad says it's disgusting to think the fly sitting there on the sugar bowl was on the toilet bowl, or what's left of it, a minute ago. If you have an open sore they find it and torment you. By day you have the flies, by night you have the fleas. Mam says there's one good thing about fleas, they're clean, but flies are filthy, you never know where they came from and they carry diseases galore.

We can chase the rats and kill them. We can slap at the flies and the fleas and kill them but there's nothing we can do about the neighbors and their buckets. If we're out in the lane playing and we see someone with a bucket we call to our own house, Bucket coming, close the door, close the door, and whoever is inside runs to the door. In warm weather we run to close the door all day because we know which families have the worst buckets. There are families whose fathers have jobs and if they get into the habit of cooking with curry we know their buckets will stink to the heavens and make us sick. Now with the war on and men sending money from England more and more families are cooking with curry and our house is filled with the stink day and night. We know the families with the curry, we know the ones with the cabbage. Mam is sick all the time, Dad takes longer and longer walks into the country, and we play outside as much as we can and far from the lavatory. Dad doesn't complain about the River Shannon anymore. He knows now the lavatory is worse and he takes me with him to the Town Hall to complain. The man there says, Mister, all I can tell you is you can move. Dad says we can't afford to move and the man says there's nothing he can do. Dad says, This is not India. This is a Christian country. The lane needs more lavatories. The man says, Do you expect Limerick to start building lavatories in houses that are falling down anyway, that will be demolished after the war? Dad says that lavatory could kill us all. The man says we live in dangerous times.

Mam says it's hard enough keeping a fire going to cook the Christmas dinner but if I'm going to Christmas dinner at the hospital I'll have to wash myself from top to bottom. She wouldn't give it to Sister Rita to say I was neglected or ripe for another disease. She boils a pot of water early in the morning before Mass and nearly scalds the scalp off me. She scours my ears and scrubs my skin so hard it tingles. She can afford tuppence for the bus out to the hospital but I'll have to walk back and that will be good for me because I'll be stuffed with food and now she has to get the fire going again for the pig's head and cabbage and floury white potatoes which she got once again through the kindness of the St. Vincent de Paul Society and she's determined this will be the last time we celebrate the birth of Our Lord with pig's head. Next year we'll have a goose or a nice ham and why wouldn't we, isn't Limerick famous the world over for the ham?

Sister Rita says, Now would you look at this, our little soldier looking so healthy. No meat on the bones but still. Now tell me, did you go to Mass this morning?

I did, Sister.

And did you receive?

I did, Sister.

She takes me into an empty ward and tells me sit there on that chair it won't be long now till I get my dinner. She leaves and I wonder if I'll be eating with nuns and nurses or will I be in a ward with children having their Christmas dinner. In awhile my dinner is brought in by the girl in the blue dress who brought me the books. She places the tray on the side of a bed and I pull up a chair. She frowns at me and screws up her face. You, she says, that's your dinner an' I'm not bringin' you any books.

The dinner is delicious, turkey, mashed potatoes, peas, jelly and custard, and a pot of tea. The jelly and custard dish looks delicious and I can't resist it so I'll have it first there's no one there to notice but when I'm eating it the girl in the blue dress comes in with bread and says, What are you doin'?

Nothing.

Yes, you are. You're atin' the sweet before the dinner, and she runs out calling, Sister Rita, Sister Rita, come in quick, and the nun rushes in, Francis, are you all right?

I am, Sister.

He's not all right, Sister. He do be atin' his jelly an custard before his dinner. That's a sin, Sister.

Ah, now, dear, you run along and I'll talk to Francis about that.

Do, Sister, talk to him or all the childer in the hospital will be atin' their sweet before their dinner an' then where will we be?

Indeed, indeed, where will we be? Run along now.

The girl leaves and Sister Rita smiles at me. God love her, she doesn't miss a thing even in her confusion. We have to be patient with her, Francis, the way she's touched.

She leaves and it's quiet in that empty ward and when I'm finished I don't know what to do because you're not supposed to do anything till they tell you. Hospitals and schools always tell you what to do. I wait a long time till the girl in the blue dress comes in for the tray. Are you finished? she says.

I am.

Well, that's all you're gettin' an' now you can go home.

Surely girls who are not right in the head can't tell you go home and I wonder if I should wait for Sister Rita. A nurse in the hallway tells me Sister Rita is having her dinner and is not to be bothered.

It's a long walk from Union Cross to Barrack Hill and when I get home my family are up in Italy and well into their pig's head and cabbage and floury white potatoes. I tell them about my Christmas dinner. Mam wants to know if I had it with the nurses and nuns and she gets a bit angry when I tell her I ate alone in a ward and that's no way to treat a child. She tells me sit down and have some pig's head and I force it into my mouth and I'm so stuffed I have to lie on the bed with my belly sticking out a mile.

It's early in the morning and there's a motor car outside our door, the first one we've ever seen in the lane. There are men in suits looking in the door of the stable of Finn the Horse and there must be something wrong because you never see men with suits in the lane.

It's Finn the Horse. He's lying on the floor of the stable looking up the lane and there's white stuff like milk around his mouth. The stable man who takes care of Finn the Horse says he found him like that this morning and it's strange because he's always up and ready for his feed. The men are shaking their heads. My brother Michael says to one of the men, Mister, what's up with Finn?

Sick horse, son. Go home.

The stable man who takes care of Finn has the whiskey smell on him. He says to Michael, That horse is a goner. We have to shoot him.

Michael pulls at my hand. Frank, they're not to shoot him. Tell them. You're big.

The stable man says, Go home, boy. Go home.

Michael attacks him, kicks him, scrawbs the back of his hand, and the man sends Michael flying. Hould that brother of yours, he tells me, hould him.

One of the other men takes something yellow and brown from a bag, goes to Finn, puts it to his head and there's a sharp crack. Finn shivers. Michael screams at the man and attacks him too but the man says, The horse was sick, son. He's better off.

The men in suits drive away and the stable man says he has to wait for the lorry to take Finn away, he can't leave him alone or the rats will be at him. He wants to know if we'd keep an eye on the horse with our dog Lucky while he goes to the pub, he's blue mouldy for a pint.

No rat has a chance to get near Finn the Horse the way Michael is there with a stick small as he is. The man comes back smelling of porter and then there's the big lorry to take the horse away, a big lorry with three men and two great planks that slope from the back of the lorry to Finn's head. The three men and the stable man tie ropes around Finn and pull him up the planks and the people in the lane yell at the men because of the nails and broken wood in the planks that catch at Finn and tear out bits of his hide and streak the planks with bright pink horse blood.

Ye are destroyin' that horse.

Can't ye have respect for the dead?

Go easy with that poor horse.

The stable man says, For the love o' Jaysus what are ye squawkin' about? 'Tis only a dead horse, and Michael runs at him again with his head down and his small fists flying till the stable man gives him a shove that sends him on his back and Mam goes at the stable man in such a rage he runs up the planks and over Finn's body to escape. He comes back drunk in the evening to sleep it off and after he leaves there's a smoldering in the hay and the stable burns down the rats running up the lane with every boy and dog chasing them till they escape into the streets of respectable people.

IX

Mam says, Alphie is enough. I'm worn out. That's the end of it. No more children.

Dad says, The good Catholic woman must perform her wifely duties and submit to her husband or face eternal damnation.

Mam says, As long as there are no more children eternal damnation sounds attractive enough to me.

What is Dad to do? There's a war on. English agents are recruiting Irishmen to work in their munitions factories, the pay is good, there are no jobs in Ireland, and if the wife turns her back to you there's no shortage of women in England where the able men are off fighting Hitler and Mussolini and you can do anything you like as long as you remember you're Irish and lower class and don't try to rise above your station.

Families up and down the lane are getting telegram money orders from their fathers in England. They rush to the post office to cash the money orders so they can shop and show the world their good fortune on Saturday night and Sunday morning. The boys get their hair cut on Saturdays, the women curl their hair with iron tongs hot from the fire. They're very grand now the way they pay sixpence or even a shilling for seats at the Savoy Cinema where you'll meet a better class of people than the lower classes who fill the tuppenny seats in the gods at the Lyric Cinema and are never done shouting at the screen, the kind of people if you don't mind who are liable to cheer on the Africans when they throw spears at Tarzan or the Indians when they're scalping the United States Cavalry. The new rich people go home after Mass on Sundays all airs and stuff themselves with meat and potatoes, sweets and cakes galore, and they think nothing of drinking their tea from delicate little cups which stand in saucers to catch the tea that overflows and when they lift the cups they stick out their little fingers to show how refined they are. Some stop going to fish and chip shops altogether because you see nothing in those places but drunken soldiers and night girls and men that drank their dole and their wives screeching at them to come home. The brave new rich will be seen at the Savoy Restaurant or the Stella drinking tea, eating little buns, patting their lips with serviettes if you don't mind, coming home on the bus and complaining the service is not what it used to be. They have electricity now so they can see things they never saw before and when darkness falls they turn on the new wireless to hear how the war is going. They thank God for Hitler because if he hadn't marched all over Europe the men of Ireland would still be at home scratching their arses on the queue at the Labour Exchange.

Some families sing,

> Yip aye aidy aye ay aye oh
> Yip aye aidy aye ay,
> We don't care about England or France,
> All we want is the German advance.

If there's a chill in the air they'll turn on the electric fire for the comfort that's in it and sit in their kitchens listening to the news declaring how sorry they are for the English women and children dying under the German bombs but look what England did to us for eight hundred years.

The families with fathers in England are able to lord it over the families that don't. At dinnertime and teatime the new rich mothers stand at their doors and call to their children, Mikey, Kathleen, Paddy, come in for yeer dinner. Come in for the lovely leg o' lamb and the gorgeous green peas and the floury white potatoes.

Sean, Josie, Peggy, come in for yeer tea, come in at wanst for the fresh bread and butter and the gorgeous blue duck egg what no one else in the lane have.

Brendan, Annie, Patsy, come in for the fried black puddin', the sizzlin' sausages and the lovely trifle soaked in the best of Spanish sherry.

At times like this Mam tells us to stay inside. We have nothing but bread and tea and she doesn't want the tormenting neighbors to see us with our tongues hanging out, suffering over the lovely smells floating up and down the lane. She says 'tis easy to see they're not used to having anything the way they brag about everything. 'Tis a real low-class mind that will call out the door and tell the world what they're having for the supper. She says 'tis their way of getting a rise out of us because Dad is a foreigner from the North and he won't have anything to do with any of them. Dad says all that food comes from English money and no luck will come to those who took it but what could you expect from Limerick anyway, people who profit from Hitler's war, people who will work and fight for the English. He says he'll never go over there and help England win a war. Mam says, No, you'll stay here where there's no work and hardly a lump of coal to boil water for the tea. No, you'll stay here and drink the dole when the humor is on you. You'll watch your sons going around with broken shoes and their arses hanging out of their trousers. Every house in the lane has electricity and we're lucky if we have a candle. God above, if I had the fare I'd be off to England myself for I'm sure they need women in the factories.

Dad says a factory is no place for a woman.

Mam says, Sitting on your arse by the fire is no place for a man.

I say to him, Why can't you go to England, Dad, so we can have electricity and a wireless and Mam can stand at the door and tell the world what we're having at dinnertime?

He says, Don't you want to have your father here at home with you?

I do but you can come back at the end of the war and we can all go to America.

He sighs, Och, aye, och, aye. All right he'll go to England after Christmas because America is in the war now and the cause must be just. He'd never go if the Americans hadn't gone in. He tells me I'll have to be the man of the house, and he signs up with an agent to work in a factory in Coventry which, everyone says, is the most bombed city in England. The agent says, There's plenty of work for willing men. You can work overtime till you drop and if you save it up, mate, you'll be Rockefeller at the end of the war.

We're up early to see Dad off at the railway station. Kathleen O'Connell at the shop knows Dad is off to England and money will be flowing back so she's happy to let Mam have credit for tea, milk, sugar, bread, butter and an egg.

An egg.

Mam says, This egg is for your father. He needs the nourishment for the long journey before him.

It's a hard-boiled egg and Dad peels off the shell. He slices the egg five ways and gives each of us a bit to put on our bread. Mam says, Don't be such a fool. Dad says, What would a man be doing with a whole egg to himself? Mam has tears on her eyelashes. She pulls her chair over to the fireplace. We all eat our bread and egg and watch her cry till she says, What are ye gawkin' at? and turns away to look into the ashes. Her bread and egg are still on the table and I wonder if she has any plans for them. They look delicious and I'm still hungry but Dad gets up and brings them to her with the tea. She shakes her head but he presses them on her and she eats and drinks, snuffling and crying. He sits opposite her a while, silent, till she looks up at the clock and says, 'Tis time to go. He puts on his cap and picks up his bag. Mam wraps Alphie in an old blanket and we set off through the streets of Limerick.

There are other families in the streets. The going-away fathers walk ahead, the mothers carry babies or push prams. A mother with a pram will say to other mothers, God above, missus, you must be fagged out carrying that child. Sure, why don't you stick him into the pram here and rest your poor arms.

Prams might be packed with four or five babies squalling away because the prams are old and the wheels bockety and the babies are rocked till they get sick and throw up their goody.

The men call to each other. Grand day, Mick. Lovely day for the journey, Joe. 'Tis, indeed, Mick. Arrah, we might as well have a pint before we go, Joe. We might as well, Mick. Might as well be drunk as the way we are, Joe.

They laugh and the women behind them are teary-eyed and red-nosed.

In the pubs around the railway station the men are packed in drinking the money the agents gave them for travel food. They're having the last pint, the last drop of whiskey on Irish soil, For God knows it might be the last we'll ever have, Mick, the way the Jerries are bombing the bejesus outa England and not a minute too soon after what they did to us and isn't it a tragic thing entirely the way we have to go over there and save the arse of the ancient foe.

The women stay outside the pubs talking. Mam tells Mrs. Meehan, The first telegram money order I get I'll be in the shop buying a big breakfast so that we can all have our own egg of a Sunday morning.

I look at my brother Malachy. Did you hear that? Our own egg of a Sunday morning. Oh, God, I already had plans for my egg. Tap it around the top, gently crack the shell, lift with a spoon, a dab of butter down into the yolk, salt, take my time, a dip of the spoon, scoop, more salt, more butter, into the mouth, oh, God above, if heaven has a taste it must be an egg with butter and salt, and after the egg is there anything in the world lovelier than fresh warm bread and a mug of sweet golden tea?

Some men are already too drunk to walk and the English agents are paying sober men to drag them out of the pubs and throw them on a great horse-drawn float to be hauled to the station and dumped into the train. The agents are desperate to get everyone out of the pubs. Come on, men. Miss this train and you'll miss a good job. Come on, men, we have the Guinness in England. We have the Jameson. Now, men, please, men. You're drinking your food money and you'll get no more.

The men tell the agents to kiss their Irish arses, that the agents are lucky they're alive, lucky they're not hanging from the nearest lamppost after what they did to Ireland. And the men sing,

> On Mountjoy one Monday morning
> High upon the gallows tree,
> Kevin Barry gave his young life
> For the cause of liberty.

The train wails in the station and the agents beg the women to get their men out of the pubs and the men stumble out singing and crying and hugging their wives and children and promising to send so much money Limerick will be turned into another New York. The men climb the station steps and the women and children call after them,

Kevin, love, mind yourself and don't be wearing damp shirts.

Dry your socks, Michael, or the bunions will destroy you entirely.

Paddy, go easy on the drink, are you listenin', Paddy?

Dad, Dad, don't go, Dad.

Tommy, don't forget to send the money. The children are skin and bones.

Peter, don't forget to be takin' the medicine for your weak chest, God help us.

Larry, mind them bloody bombs.

Christy, don't be talkin' to them Englishwomen. They're full of diseases.

Jackie, come back. Sure we'll manage somehow. Don't go, Jack-e-e, Jack-e-e, oh, Jesus, don't go.

Dad pats our heads. He tells us remember our religious duties but, above all, obey our mother. He stands before her. She has the baby Alphie in her arms. She says, Mind yourself. He drops the bag and puts his arms around her. They stay that way a moment till the baby yelps between them. He nods, picks up his bag, climbs the steps to the station, turns to wave and he's gone.

Back at home Mam says, I don't care. I know it sounds extravagant but I'm going to light the fire and make more tea for it isn't every day your father goes to England.

We sit around the fire and drink our tea and cry because we have no father, till Mam says, Don't cry, don't cry. Now that your father is gone to England surely our troubles will be over.

Surely.

Mam and Bridey Hannon sit by the fire upstairs in Italy smoking Woodbines, drinking tea, and I sit on the stairs listening. We have a father in England so that we can get all we want from Kathleen O'Connell's shop and pay when he starts sending the money in a fortnight. Mam tells Bridey she can't wait to get out of this bloody lane to a place with a decent lavatory that we don't have to share with half the world. We'll all have new boots and coats to keep off the rain so we won't be coming home from school famished. We'll have eggs and rashers on Sunday for breakfast and ham and cabbage and potatoes for dinner. We'll have electric light and why shouldn't we? Weren't Frank and Malachy born to it in America where everyone has it?

All we have to do now is wait for two weeks till the telegram boy knocks at the door. Dad will have to settle into his job in England, buy work clothes and get a place to stay, so the first money order won't be big, three pounds or three pounds ten, but soon we'll be like other families in the lane, five pounds a week, paying off debts, buying new clothes, putting something in the savings against the time we'll pack up and move to England entirely and save there to go to America. Mam herself could get a job in an English factory making bombs or something and God knows we wouldn't know ourselves with the money pouring in. She wouldn't be happy if we grew up with English accents but better an English accent than an empty belly.

Bridey says it doesn't matter what class of an accent an Irishman has for he'll never forget what the English did to us for eight hundred long years.

We know what Saturdays are in the lane. We know some families like the Downeses across from us get their telegram early because Mr. Downes is a steady man who knows how to have a pint or two on a Friday and go home to his bed. We know men like him run to the post office the minute they're paid so their families won't know a minute of waiting or worry. Men like Mr. Downes send their sons RAF wings to wear on their coats. That's what we want and that's what we told Dad before he left, Don't forget the RAF badges, Dad.

We see the telegram boys on their bicycles swing into the lane. They're happy telegram boys because the tips they get in the lanes are bigger than anything they get in the grand streets and avenues where rich people will begrudge you the steam of their piss.

The families that get the early telegrams have that contented look. They'll have all day Saturday to enjoy the money. They'll shop, they'll eat, they'll have all day to think about what they'll do that night and that's almost as good as the thing itself because Saturday night when you have a few shillings in your pocket is the most delicious night of the week.

There are families don't get the telegram every week and you know them by the anxious look. Mrs. Meagher has waited at her door every Saturday for two months. My mother says she'd be ashamed of her life to wait at the door like that. All the children play in the lane and keep an eye out for the telegram boy. Hoi, telegram boy, do you have anything for Meagher? and when he says no they say, Are you sure? and he'll say, Course I'm sure. I know what I have in my feckin' pouch.

Everyone knows the telegram boys stop coming when the Angelus rings at six and darkness brings desperation to the women and children.

Telegram boy, will you look in your pouch again? Please. Aw, God.
I did. I have nothing for ye.

Aw, God, please look. Our name is Meagher. Will you look?

I know bloody well yeer name is Meagher and I looked.

The children claw at him up on his bicycle and he kicks at them, Jesus, will ye get away from me.

Once the Angelus rings at six in the evening the day is over. The ones with the telegrams are having their supper with the electric light blazing away and the ones that didn't get the telegrams have to light candles and see if Kathleen O'Connell might let them have tea and bread till this time next week when surely with the help of God and His Blessed Mother the telegram will come.

Mr. Meehan at the top of the lane went to England with Dad and when the telegram boy stops at Meehan's we know we'll be next. Mam has her coat ready to go to the post office but she won't leave the chair by the fire in Italy till she has the telegram in her hand. The telegram boy rides down the lane and swings over to Downeses'. He hands them their telegram, takes the tip and turns his bicycle around to head back up the lane. Malachy calls, Telegram boy, do you have something for McCourt? Ours is coming today. The telegram boy shakes his head and rides away.

Mam puffs on her Woodbine. Well, we have all day though I'd like to do a bit of shopping early before the best hams are gone at Barry the butcher. She can't leave the fire and we can't leave the lane for fear the telegram boy might come and find no one at home. Then we'd have to wait till Monday to cash the money order and that would destroy the weekend entirely. We'd have to watch the Meehans and everyone else parading around in their new clothes and staggering home with eggs and potatoes and sausages for Sunday and sailing off to the films on Saturday night. No, we can't move an inch till that telegram boy comes. Mam says don't be too worried between noon and two because so many telegram boys go for their dinner and there will surely be a big rush between two and the Angelus. We don't have a thing to worry about till six. We stop every telegram boy. We tell them our name is McCourt, that this is our first telegram, it should be three pounds or more, they might have forgotten to put our name on it or our address, is he sure? is he sure? One boy tells us he'll inquire at the post office. He says he knows what 'tis like to wait for the telegram because his own father is a drunken oul' shit over in England that never sent a penny. Mam hears him inside and tells us you should never talk about your father like that. The same telegram boy comes back just before the

Angelus at six and tells us he asked Mrs. O'Connell at the post office if they had anything for McCourt all day and they didn't. Mam turns toward the dead ashes in the fire and sucks at the last bit of goodness in the Woodbine butt caught between the brown thumb and the burnt middle finger. Michael who is only five and won't understand anything till he's eleven like me wants to know if we're having fish and chips tonight because he's hungry. Mam says, Next week, love, and he goes back out to play in the lane.

You don't know what to do with yourself when the first telegram doesn't come. You can't stay out in the lane playing with your brothers all night because everyone else is gone in and you'd be ashamed to stay out in the lane to be tormented with smells of sausages and rashers and fried bread. You don't want to look at electric light coming through the windows after dark and you don't want to hear the news from the BBC or Radio Eireann from other people's wirelesses. Mrs. Meagher and her children are gone in and there's only the dim light of a candle from their kitchen. They're ashamed too. They stay inside on Saturday nights and they don't even go to Mass on Sunday mornings. Bridey Hannon told Mam that Mrs. Meagher is in a constant state of shame over the rags they wear and so desperate she goes down to the Dispensary for the public assistance. Mam says that's the worst thing that could happen to any family. It's worse than going on the dole, it's worse than going to the St. Vincent de Paul Society, it's worse than begging on the streets with the tinkers and the knackers. It's the last thing you'd do to keep yourself out of the poor house and the children from the orphanage.

There's a sore at the top of my nose between my eyebrows, gray and red and itching. Grandma says, Don't touch that sore and don't put water near it or it'll spread. If you broke your arm she'd say don't touch that with water it'll spread. The sore spreads into my eyes anyway and now they're red and yellow from the stuff that oozes and makes them stick in the morning. They stick so hard I have to force my eyelids open with my fingers and Mam has to scrub off that yellow stuff with a damp rag and boric powder. The eyelashes fall off and every bit of dust in Limerick blows into my eyes on windy days. Grandma tells me I have naked eyes and she says it's my own fault, all that eye trouble comes from sitting up there at the top of the lane under the light pole in all kinds of weather with my nose stuck in books and the same thing will happen to Malachy if he doesn't give over with the reading. You can see little Michael is getting just as bad sticking his nose in books when he should be out playing like a healthy child. Books, books, books, says Grandma, ye will ruin yeer eyes entirely.

She's having tea with Mam and I hear her whisper, The thing to do is give him St. Anthony's spit.

What's that? says Mam.

Your fasting spit in the morning. Go to him before he wakes and spit on his eyes for the spit of a fasting mother has powerful cures in it.

But I'm always awake before Mam. I force my eyes open long before she stirs. I can hear her coming across the floor and when she stands over me for the spit I open my eyes. God, she says, your eyes are open.

I think they're getting better.

That's good, and she goes back to bed.

The eyes don't heal and she takes me to the Dispensary where the poor people see doctors and get their medicines. It's the place to apply for public assistance when a father is dead or disappeared and there's no dole money, no wages.

There are benches along the walls by the doctors' offices. The benches are always packed with people talking about their ailments. Old men and women sit and groan and babies scream and mothers say hush, love, hush. There's a high platform in the middle of the Dispensary with a counter circling it chest-high. When you want anything you stand in a queue before that platform to see Mr. Coffey or Mr. Kane. The women in the queue are like the women at the St. Vincent de Paul Society. They wear shawls and they're respectful to Mr. Coffey and Mr. Kane because if they're not they might be told go away and come back next week when it's this minute you need the public assistance or a docket to see the doctor. Mr. Coffee and Mr. Kane love to have a good laugh with the women. They'll decide if you're desperate enough for the public assistance or if you're sick enough to see a doctor. You have to tell them in front of everyone what's wrong with you and they often have a good laugh with that. They'll say, And what is it you want, Mrs. O'Shea? A docket for the doctor, is it? And what is your trouble, Mrs. O'Shea? A pain, is it? A touch of the wind, maybe. Or maybe too much cabbage. Oh, the cabbage will do it right enough. They laugh and Mrs. O'Shea laughs and all the women laugh and say Mr. Coffee and Mr. Kane are funny men, they'd give Laurel and Hardy a run for their money.

Mr. Coffee says, Now, woman, what's your name?

Angela McCourt, sir.

And what's up with you?

'Tis my son, sir. He has two bad eyes.

Oh, by God, he does, woman. They're desperate-looking eyes altogether. They look like two rising suns. The Japs could use him on their flag, ha ha ha. Did he pour acid on his face or what?

'Tis some class of infection, sir. He had the typhoid last year and then this came.

All right, all right, we don't need the life story. Here's your docket to Dr. Troy.

Two long benches are filled with patients for Dr. Troy. Mam sits next to a woman who has a big sore on her nose that won't go away. I tried everything, missus, every known cure on God's lovely earth. I'm eighty-three years of age and I'd like to go to my grave healthy. Is it too much to ask that I meet my Redeemer with a healthy nose? And what's up with yourself, missus?

My son. The eyes.

Ah, God bless us and save us, look at them eyes. They're the sorest two eyes I ever seen in me life. I never seen that color red before.

'Tis an infection, missus.

Sure there's a cure for that. You need the caul.

What's that now?

Babies are born with this thing on their heads, a class of a hood, rare and magical. Get a caul and put that on his head any day that has a three in it, make him hold his breath for three minutes even if you have to clap your hand over his face, sprinkle him with holy water three times head to toenail and his two eyes will shine in the dawn.

And where would I get a caul?

Don't all the midwives have cauls, missus. What's a midwife without a caul? It cures all classes of disease and keeps off more.

Mam says she'll talk to Nurse O'Halloran and see if she has a spare caul.

Dr. Troy looks at my eyes. Into the hospital with this boy at once. Take him to the eye ward at the City Home. Here's the docket to get him in.

What does he have, Doctor?

The worst case of conjunctivitis I've ever seen in my life and something else in there I can't make out. He needs the eye man.

How long will he be in, Doctor?

Only God knows that. I should have seen this child weeks ago.

There are twenty beds in the ward and there are men and boys with bandages around their heads, black patches on their eyes, thick glasses. Some walk around tapping at beds with sticks. A man cries all the time that he'll never see again, he's too young, his children are babies, he'll never see them again. Jesus Christ, oh, Jesus Christ, and the nuns are shocked at the way he takes the name of the Lord in vain. Stop that, Maurice, stop the blasphemy. You have your health. You're alive. We all have our problems. Offer it up and think of the sufferings of Our Lord on the cross, the crown of thorns, the nails in His poor hands and feet, the wound in His side. Maurice says, Oh, Jesus, look down and have pity on me. Sister Bernadette warns him if he doesn't mind his language they'll put him in a ward alone and he says, Heavenly God, and that isn't as bad as Jesus Christ so she's satisfied.

In the morning I have to go downstairs for drops. The nurse says, Sit in this high chair and here's a nice sweet. The doctor has a bottle with brown stuff in it. He tells me put my head back, that's right, now open up, open your eyes and he pours the stuff into my right eye and it's a flame going through my skull. The nurse says, Open the other eye, come on be a good boy, and she has to force the eyelids open so the doctor can set fire to the other side of my skull. She wipes my cheeks and tells me run along upstairs but I can barely see and I want to stick my face into an icy stream. The doctor says, Run along, be a man, be a good trooper.

The whole world is brown and blurry on the stairs. The other patients are sitting by their beds with dinner trays and mine is there too but I don't want it with the way my skull is raging. I sit by my bed and a boy across the way says, Hoi, don't you want your dinner? I'll take it, and he comes for it.

I try to lie on the bed but a nurse says, Now, now, no lying on the bed in the middle of the day. Your case isn't that serious.

I have to sit with my eyes closed and everything going brown and black, black and brown and I'm sure I must be having a dream because Lord God above, is that the little fella with the typhoid, little Frankie, the moon was a ghostly galleon tossed upon cloudy seas, is that yourself, Frankie, for wasn't I promoted out of the Fever Hospital, thank God, where there's every class of disease and you never know what germs you might be bringing home to the wife in your clothes and what's up with you, Frankie, and the two eyes in your head all gone brown?

I have an infection, Seamus.

Yerra, you'll be over that before you're married, Frankie. The eyes need exercise. The blink is great value for the eyes. I had an uncle with bad eyes and the blink saved him. He sat an hour ever day and blinked and it stood to him in the end. Wound up with powerful eyes, so he did.

I want to ask him more about the blink and the powerful eyes but he says, Now do you remember the poem, Frankie, the lovely poem of Patricia?

He stands in the aisle between the beds with his mop and his bucket and says the highwayman poem and all the patients stop their moaning and the nuns and nurses stand and listen and on and on goes Seamus till he comes to the end and everyone goes mad clapping and cheering him and he tells the world he loves that poem he'll have it in his head forever no matter where he goes and if it wasn't for Frankie McCourt and his typhoid there and poor Patricia Madigan with the dipteria that's gone God rest her he'd never know the poem and there I am famous in the eye ward of the City Home Hospital and all because of Seamus.

Mam can't come to visit every day, it's a long way out, she doesn't always have the money for the bus and the walk is hard on her corns. She thinks my eyes look better though you can't tell with all that brown stuff, which looks and smells like iodine and if it's anything like iodine it must burn. Still, they say the bitterer the medicine the quicker the cure. She gets permission to take me for a walk around the grounds when the weather clears and there's a strange sight, Mr. Timoney standing against the wall where the old people are with his eyes raised to the sky. I want to talk to him and I have to ask Mam because you never know what's right or wrong in a hospital.

Mr. Timoney.

Who is it? Who do we have?

Frank McCourt, sir.

Francis, ah, Francis.

Mam says, I'm his mother, Mr. Timoney.

Well, then, the two of ye are blessed. I have neither kith nor kin nor Macushla my dog. And what are you doing in this place, Francis?

I have an infection in my eyes.

Ah, Jesus, Francis, not the eyes, not the eyes. Mother of Christ, you're too young for that.

Mr. Timoney, would you like me to read to you?

With them eyes, Francis? Ah, no, son, Save the eyes. I'm beyond reading. In my head I have everything I need. I was smart enough to put things in my head in my youth and now I have a library in my head. The English shot my wife. The Irish put down my poor innocent Macushla. Isn't it a joke of a world?

Mam says, Terrible world but God is good.

Indeed, missus. God made the world, it's a terrible world, but God is good. Good-bye, Francis. Rest your eyes and then read till they fall out of your head. We had good times with old Jonathan Swift, didn't we, Francis?

We did, Mr. Timoney.

Mam takes me back to the eye ward. She tells me, Don't be crying over Mr. Timoney, he's not even your father. Besides you'll be ruining your eyes.

Seamus comes to the ward three times a week and brings new poems in his head. He says, You made Patricia sad, Frankie, when you didn't like the one about the owl and the pussycat.

I'm sorry, Seamus.

I have it in my head, Frankie, and I'll say it for you if you don't say 'tis foolish.

I won't, Seamus.

He says the poem and everyone in the ward loves it. They want the words and he says it three more times till the whole ward is saying,

The Owl and the Pussy-cat went to sea
In a beautiful pea-green boat.
They took some honey, and plenty of money
Wrapped up in a five-pound note.
The Owl looked up to the stars above,
And sang to a small guitar,
O lovely Pussy, O Pussy, my love,
What a beautiful Pussy you are,
You are,
You are.
What a beautiful Pussy you are.

They say it along with Seamus now and when it's finished they cheer and clap and Seamus laughs, delighted with himself. When he's gone with his mop and bucket you can hear them at all hours of the day and night

O lovely Pussy, O Pussy, my love,
What a beautiful Pussy you are,
You are,
You are.
What a beautiful Pussy you are.

Then Seamus comes with no mop and no bucket and I'm afraid he's sacked over the poetry but he's smiling and telling me he's off to England to work in a factory and earn decent wages for a change. He'll work for two months and bring the wife over and God might be pleased to send them children for he has to do something with all the poems in his head and what better than saying them to small ones in memory of that sweet Patricia Madigan dead of the dipteria.

Good-bye, Francis. If I had the right fist I'd write to you but I'll get the wife to write when she comes over. I might even learn to read and write myself so that the child that comes won't have a fool for a father.

I want to cry but you can't cry in the eye ward with brown stuff in your eyes and nurses saying, What's this what's this be a man, and nuns going on, Offer it up, think of the sufferings of Our Lord on the cross, the crown of thorns, the lance in the side, the hands and feet torn to bits with nails.

I'm a month in the hospital and the doctor says I can go home even if there's still a bit of infection but if I keep the eyes clean with soap and clean towels and build up my health with nourishing food plenty of beef and eggs I'll have a pair of sparkling eyes in no time ha ha.

Mr. Downes across the way comes back from England for his mother's funeral. He tells Mrs. Downes about my father. She tells Bridey Hannon and Bridey tells my mother. Mr. Downes says that Malachy McCourt is gone pure mad with the drink, that he squanders his wages in pubs all over Coventry, that he sings Irish rebel songs which the English don't mind because they're used to the way the Irish carry on about the hundreds of years of suffering, but they won't put up with any man that stands up in a pub and insults the King and Queen of England, their two lovely daughters and the Queen Mother herself. Insulting the Queen Mother is going beyond the beyonds. What did she ever do to anyone, that poor old lady? Time after time Malachy drinks away his rent money and winds up sleeping in parks when the landlord throws him out. He's a regular disgrace, so he is, and Mr. Downes is glad McCourt is not a Limerickman bringing shame to this ancient city. The magistrates in Coventry are losing their patience and if Malachy McCourt doesn't stop the bloody nonsense he'll be kicked out of the country entirely.

Mam tells Bridey she doesn't know what she's going to do with these stories from England, she never felt so desperate in her life. She can see Kathleen O'Connell doesn't want to give any more credit at the shop and her own mother barks at her if she asks for the loan of a shilling and the St. Vincent de Paul Society want to know when she'll stop asking for charity especially with a husband in England. She's ashamed of the way we look with the dirty old torn shirts, raggedy ganseys, broken shoes, holes in our stockings. She lies awake at night thinking the most merciful thing of all would be to put the four boys in an orphanage so that she could go to England herself and find some type of work where she could bring us all over in a year for the better life. There might be bombs but she'd prefer bombs anytime to the shame of begging from this one and that one.

No, no matter what she can't bear the thought of putting us in the orphanage. That might be all right if you had the likes of Boys' Town in America with a nice priest like Spencer Tracy but you could never trust the Christian Brothers out in Glin who get their exercise beating boys and starving the life out of them.

Mam says there's nothing left but the Dispensary and the public assistance, the relief, and she's ashamed of her life to go and ask for it. It means you're at the end of your rope and maybe one level above tinkers, knackers and street beggars in general. It means you have to crawl before Mr. Coffey and Mr. Kane and thank God the Dispensary is at the other end of Limerick so that people in our lane won't know we're getting the relief.

She knows from other women it's wise to be there early in the morning when Mr. Coffey and Mr. Kane might be in a good mood. If you go late in the morning they're liable to be cranky after seeing hundreds of men women and children sick and asking for help. She will take us with her to prove she has four children to feed. She gets us up early

231

and tells us for once in our lives don't wash our faces, don't comb our hair, dress in any old rag. She tells me give my sore eyes a good rub and make them as red as I can for the worse you look at the Dispensary the more pity you get and the better your chances of getting the public assistance. She complains that Malachy Michael and Alphie look too healthy and you'd wonder why on this day of days they couldn't have their usual scabby knees or the odd cut bruise or black eye. If we meet anyone in the lane or the streets of Limerick we are not to tell them where we're going. She feels ashamed enough without telling the whole world and wait till her own mother hears.

There is a queue already outside the Dispensary. There are women like Mam with children in their arms, babies like Alphie, and children playing on the pavement. The women comfort the babies against the cold and scream at the ones playing in case they run into the street and get hit by a motor car or a bicycle. There are old men and women huddled against the wall talking to themselves or not talking at all. Mam warns us not to wander from her and we wait half an hour for the big door to open. A man tells us move inside in proper order and queue up before the platform, that Mr. Coffey and Mr. Kane will be there in a minute when they finish their tea in the room beyond. A woman complains her children are freezing with the cold and couldn't Coffey and Kane bloody well hurry up with their tea. The man says she's a troublemaker but he won't take her name this time with the cold that's in the morning but if there's another word she'll be a sorry woman.

Mr. Coffey and Mr. Kane get up on the platform and pay no attention to the people. Mr. Kane puts on his glasses, takes them off, polishes them, puts them on, looks at the ceiling. Mr. Coffey reads papers, writes something, passes papers to Mr. Kane. They whisper to each other. They take their time. They don't look at us.

Then Mr. Kane calls the first old man to the platform. What's your name?

Timothy Creagh, sir.

Creagh, hah? A fine old Limerick name you have there.

I do, sir. Indeed I do.

And what do you want, Creagh?

Ah, sure, I do be havin' them pains in me stomach again an' I'd like to see Dr. Feeley.

Well, now, Creagh, are you sure it's not the pints of porter that are going against your stomach.

Ah, no, indeed, sir. Sure I hardly touch the pint at all with the pains. My wife is home in the bed and I have to take care of her too.

There's great laziness in the world, Creagh. And Mr. Kane says to the people on the queue, Did ye hear that, ladies? Great laziness, isn't there?

And the women say, Oh, there is, indeed, Mr. Kane, great laziness.

Mr. Creagh gets his docket to see the doctor, the queue moves ahead and Mr. Kane is ready for Mam.

The public assistance, is that what you want, woman, the relief?

'Tis, Mr. Kane.

And where's your husband?

Oh, he's in England, but—

England, is it? And where is the weekly telegram, the big five pounds?

He didn't send us a penny in months, Mr. Kane.

Is that a fact? Well, we know why, don't we? We know what the men of Ireland are up to in England. We know there's the occasional Limerickman seen trotting around with a Piccadilly tart, don't we?

He looks out at the people on the queue and they know they're supposed to say, We do, Mr. Kane, and they know they're supposed to smile and laugh or things will go hard with them when they reach the platform. They know he might turn them over to Mr. Coffey and he's notorious for saying no to everything.

Mam tells Mr. Kane that Dad is in Coventry and nowhere near Piccadilly and Mr. Kane takes off his glasses and stares at her. What's this? Are we having a little contradiction here?

Oh, no, Mr. Kane, God no.

I want you to know, woman, that it is the policy here to give no relief to women with husbands in England. I want you to know you're taking the bread from the mouths of more deserving people who stayed in this country to do their bit.

Oh, yes, Mr. Kane.

And what's your name?

McCourt, sir.

That's not a Limerick name. Where did you get a name like that?

My husband, sir. He's from the North.

He's from the North and he leaves you here to get the relief from the Irish Free State. Is this what we fought for, is it?

I don't know, sir.

Why don't you go up to Belfast and see what the Orangemen will do for you, ah?

I don't know, sir.

You don't know. Of course you don't know. There's great ignorance in the world.

He looks out at the people, I said there's great ignorance in the world, and the people nod their heads and agree there's great ignorance in the world.

He whispers to Mr. Coffey and they look at Mam, they look at us. He tells Mam at last that she can have the public assistance but if she gets a single penny from her husband she's to drop all claims and give the money back to the Dispensary. She promises she will and we leave.

We follow her to Kathleen O'Connell's shop to get tea and bread and a few sods of turf for the fire. We climb the stairs to Italy and get the fire going and it's cozy when we have our tea. We're all very quiet, even the baby Alphie, because we know what Mr. Kane did to our mother.

X

It's cold and wet down in Ireland but we're up in Italy. Mam says we should bring the poor Pope up to hang on the wall opposite the window. After all he's a friend of the workingman, he's Italian, and they're a warm weather people. Mam sits by the fire, shivering, and we know something is wrong when she makes no move for a cigarette. She says she feels a cold coming and she'd love to have a tarty drink, a lemonade. But there's no money in the house, not even for bread in the morning. She drinks tea and goes to bed.

The bed creaks all night with her twistings and turnings and she keeps us awake with her moaning for water. In the morning, she stays in bed, still shivering, and we keep quiet. If she sleeps long enough Malachy and I will be too late for school. Hours pass and still she makes no move and when I know it's well past school time I start the fire for the kettle. She stirs and calls for lemonade but I give her a jam jar of water. I ask her if she'd like some tea and she acts like a woman gone deaf. She looks flushed and it's odd she doesn't even mention cigarettes.

We sit quietly by the fire, Malachy, Michael, Alphie, myself. We drink our tea while Alphie chews the last bit of bread covered with sugar. He makes us laugh the way he smears the sugar all over his face and grins at us with his fat sticky cheeks. But we can't laugh too much or Mam will jump out of the bed and order Malachy and me off to school where we'll be killed for being late. We don't laugh long, there is no more bread and we're hungry, the four of us. We can get no more credit at O'Connell's shop. We can't go near Grandma, either. She yells at us all the time because Dad is from the North and he never sends money home from England where he is working in a munitions factory. Grandma says we could starve to death for all he cares. That would teach Mam a lesson for marrying a man from the North with sallow skin, an odd manner and a look of the Presbyterian about him.

Still, I'll have to try Kathleen O'Connell once more. I'll tell her my mother is sick above in the bed, my brothers are starving and we'll all be dead for the want of bread.

I put on my shoes and run quickly through the streets of Limerick to keep myself warm against the February frost. You can look in people's windows and see how cozy it is in their kitchens with fires glowing or ranges black and hot everything bright in the electric light cups and saucers on the tables with plates of sliced bread pounds of butter jars of jam smells of fried eggs and rashers coming through the windows enough to make the water run in your mouth and families sitting there digging in all smiling the mother crisp and clean in her apron everyone washed and the Sacred Heart of Jesus looking down on them from the wall suffering and sad but still happy with all that food and light and good Catholics at their breakfast.

I try to find music in my own head but all I can find is my mother moaning for lemonade.

Lemonade. There's a van pulling away from South's pub leaving crates of beer and lemonade outside and there isn't a soul on the street. In a second I have two bottles of lemonade up under my jersey and I saunter away trying to look innocent.

There's a bread van outside Kathleen O'Connell's shop. The back door is open on shelves of steaming newly baked bread. The van driver is inside the shop having tea and a bun with Kathleen and it's no trouble for me to help myself to a loaf of bread. It's wrong to steal from Kathleen with the way she's always good to us but if I go in and ask her for bread she'll be annoyed and tell me I'm ruining her morning cup of tea, which she'd like to have in peace ease and comfort thank you. It's easier to stick the bread up under my jersey with the lemonade and promise to tell everything in confession.

My brothers are back in bed playing games under the overcoats but they jump when they see the bread. We tear at the loaf because we're too hungry to slice it and we make tea from this morning's leaves. When my mother stirs Malachy holds the lemonade bottle to her lips and she gasps till she finishes it. If she likes it that much I'll have to find more lemonade.

We put the last of the coal on the fire and sit around telling stories which we make up the way Dad did. I tell my brothers about my adventures with the lemonade and bread and I make up stories about how I was chased by pub owners and shopkeepers and how I ran into St. Joseph's Church where no one can follow you if you're a criminal, not even if you killed your own mother. Malachy and Michael look shocked over the way I got the bread and lemonade but then Malachy says it was only what Robin Hood would have done, rob the rich and give to the poor. Michael says I'm an outlaw and if they catch me they'll hang me from the highest tree in the People's Park the way outlaws are hanged in films at the Lyric Cinema. Malachy says I should make sure I'm in a state of grace because it might be hard to find a priest to come to my hanging. I tell him a priest would have to come to the hanging. That's what priests are for. Roddy McCorley had a priest and so did Kevin Barry. Malachy says there were no priests at the hanging of Roddy McCorley and Kevin Barry because they're not mentioned in the songs and he starts singing the songs to prove it till my mother groans in the bed and says shut up.

Alphie the baby is asleep on the floor by the fire. We put him into the bed with Mam so that he'll be warm though we don't want him to catch her disease and die. If she wakes up and finds him dead in the bed beside her there will be no end to the lamentations and she'll blame me on top of it.

The three of us get back into our own bed, huddling under the overcoats and trying not to roll into the hole in the mattress. It's pleasant there till Michael starts to worry over Alphie getting Mam's disease and me getting hanged for an outlaw. He says it isn't fair because that would leave him with only one brother and everyone in the world has brothers galore. He falls asleep from the worry and soon Malachy drifts off and I lie there thinking of jam. Wouldn't it be lovely to have another loaf of bread and a jar of strawberry jam or any kind of jam. I can't remember ever seeing a jam van making a delivery and I wouldn't want to be like Jesse James blasting my way into a shop demanding jam. That would surely lead to a hanging.

There's a cold sun coming through the window and I'm sure it must be warmer outside and wouldn't my brothers be surprised if they woke and found me there with more bread and jam. They'd gobble everything and then go on about my sins and the hanging.

Mam is still asleep though her face is red and there's a strangling sound when she snores.

I have to be careful going through the street because it's a school day and if Guard Dennehy sees me he'll drag me off to school and Mr. O'Halloran will knock me all over the classroom. The guard is in charge of school attendance and he loves chasing you on his bicycle and dragging you off to school by the ear.

There's a box sitting outside the door of one of the big houses on Barrington Street. I pretend to knock on the door so that I can see what's in the box, a bottle of milk, a loaf of bread, cheese, tomatoes and, oh, God, a jar of marmalade. I can't shove all that under my jersey. Oh, God. Should I take the whole box? The people passing by pay me no attention. I might as well take the whole box. My mother would say you might as well be hung for a sheep as a lamb. I lift the box and try to look like a messenger boy making a delivery and no one says a word.

Malachy and Michael are beside themselves when they see what's in the box and they're soon gobbling thick cuts of bread slathered with golden marmalade. Alphie has the marmalade all over his face and hair and a good bit on his legs and belly. We wash down the food with cold tea because we have no fire to heat it.

Mam mumbles again for lemonade and I give her half the second bottle to keep her quiet. She calls for more and I mix it with water to stretch it because I can't be spending my life running around lifting lemonade from pubs. We're having a fine time of it till Mam begins to rave in the bed about her lovely little daughter taken from her and her twin boys gone before they were three and why couldn't God take the rich for a change and is there any lemonade in the house? Michael wants to know if Mam will die and Malachy tells him you can't die till a priest comes. Then Michael wonders if we'll ever have a fire and hot tea again because he's freezing in the bed even with the overcoats left over from olden times. Malachy says we should go from house to house asking for turf and coal and wood and we could use Alphie's pram to carry the load. We should take Alphie with us because he's small and he smiles and people will see him and feel sorry for him and us. We try to wash all the dirt and lint and feathers and sticky marmalade but when we touch him with water he howls. Michael says he'll only get dirty again in the pram so what's the use of washing him. Michael is small but he's always saying remarkable things like that.

We push the pram out to the rich avenues and roads but when we knock on the doors the maids tell us go away or they'll call the proper authorities and it's a disgrace to be dragging a baby around in a wreck of a pram that smells to the heavens a filthy contraption that you wouldn't use to haul a pig to the slaughterhouse and this is a Catholic country where babies should be cherished and kept alive to hand down the faith from generation to generation. Malachy tells one maid to kiss his arse and she gives him such a clout the tears leap to his eyes and he says he'll never in his life ask the rich for anything again. He says there's no use asking anymore, that we should go around the backs of the houses and climb over the walls and take what we want. Michael can ring the front doorbells to keep the maids busy and Malachy and I can throw coal and turf over the walls and fill the pram all around Alphie.

We collect that way from three houses but then Malachy throws a piece of coal over a wall and hits Alphie and he starts screaming and we have to run forgetting Michael, still ringing doorbells and getting abuse from maids. Malachy says we should take the pram home first and then go back for Michael. We can't stop now with Alphie bawling and people giving us dirty looks and telling us we're a disgrace to our mother and Ireland in general.

When we're back home it takes a while to dig Alphie out from under the load of coal and turf and he won't stop screaming till I give him bread and marmalade. I'm afraid Mam will leap from her bed but she only mumbles on about Dad and drink and babies dead.

Malachy is back with Michael, with stories of his adventures ringing doorbells. One rich woman answered the door herself and invited him into the kitchen for cake and milk and bread and jam. She asked him all about his family and he told her his father had a big job in England but his mother is in the bed with a desperate disease and calling for lemonade morning noon and night. The rich woman wanted to know who was taking care of us and Michael bragged we were taking care of ourselves, that there was no shortage of bread and marmalade. The rich woman wrote down Michael's name and address and told him be a good boy and go home to his brothers and his mother in the bed.

Malachy barks at Michael for being such a fool as to tell a rich woman anything. She'll go now and tell on us and before we know it we'll have the priests of the world banging on the door and disturbing us.

There's the banging on the door already. But it isn't a priest, it's Guard Dennehy. He calls up, Hello, hello, is anybody home? Are you there, Mrs. McCourt?

Michael knocks on the window and waves at the guard. I give him a good kick for himself and Malachy thumps him on the head and he yells, I'll tell the guard. I'll tell the guard. They're killing me, guard. They're thumping and kicking.

He won't shut up and Guard Dennehy shouts at us to open the door. I call out the window and tell him I can't open the door because my mother is in bed with a terrible disease.

Where's your father?

He's in England.

Well, I'm coming in to talk to your mother.

You can't. You can't. She has the disease. We all have the disease. It might be the typhoid. It might be the galloping consumption. We're getting spots already. The baby has a lump. It could kill.

He pushes in the door and climbs the stairs to Italy just as Alphie crawls out from under the bed covered with marmalade and dirt. He looks at him and my mother and us, takes off his cap and scratches his head. He says, Jesus, Mary and Joseph, this is a desperate situation. How did your mother get sick like that?

I tell him he shouldn't go near her and when Malachy says we might not be able to go to school for ages the guard says we'll go to school no matter what, that we're on the earth to go to school the way he's on the earth to make sure we go to school. He wants to know if we have any relations and he sends me off to tell Grandma and Aunt Aggie to come to our house.

They scream at me and tell me I'm filthy. I try to explain that Mam has the disease and I'm worn out trying to make ends meet, keeping the home fires burning, getting lemonade for Mam and bread for my brothers. There's no use telling them about the marmalade for they'll only scream again. There's no use telling them about the nastiness of rich people and their maids.

They push me all the way back to the lane, barking at me and disgracing me on the streets of Limerick. Guard Dennehy is still scratching his poll. He says, Look at this, a disgrace. You wouldn't see the likes of this in Bombay or the Bowery of New York itself.

Grandma is wailing at my mother, Mother o' God, Angela, what's up with you in the bed? What did they do to you?

My mother runs her tongue over her dry lips and gasps for more lemonade.

She wants lemonade, says Michael, and we got it for her and bread and marmalade and we're all outlaws now. Frankie was the first outlaw till we went raiding for coal all over Limerick.

Guard Dennehy looks interested and takes Michael downstairs by the hand and in a few minutes we hear him laughing. Aunt Aggie says that's a disgraceful way to behave with my mother sick in the bed. The guard comes back and tells her go for a doctor. He keeps covering his face with his cap whenever he looks at me or my brothers. Desperadoes, he says, desperadoes.

The doctor comes with Aunt Aggie in his motor car and he has to rush my mother to the hospital with her pneumonia. We'd all like to go riding in the doctor's car but Aunt Aggie says, No, ye are all coming to my house till yeer mother comes home from the hospital.

I tell her not to bother. I'm eleven and I can easily look after my brothers. I'd be glad to stay at home from school and make sure everyone is fed and washed. But Grandma screams I will do no such a thing and Aunt Aggie gives me a thump for myself. Guard Dennehy says I'm too young yet to be an outlaw and a father but I have a promising future in both departments.

Get your clothes, says Aunt Aggie, ye are coming to my house till yeer mother is out of the hospital. Jesus above, that baby is a disgrace.

She finds a rag and ties it around Alphie's bottom for fear he might shit all over the pram. Then she looks at us and wants to know why we're standing there with our faces hanging out after she told us get our clothes. I'm afraid she'll hit me or yell at me when I tell her it's all right, we have our clothes, they're on us. She stares at me and shakes her head. Here, she says, put some sugar and water in the child's bottle. She tells me I have to push Alphie through the streets, she can't manage the pram with that bockety wheel that makes it rock back and forth and besides 'tis a disgraceful-looking object she'd be ashamed to put a mangy dog in. She takes the three old coats from our bed and piles them on the pram till you can hardly see Alphie at all.

Grandma comes with us and barks at me all the way from Roden Lane to Aunt Aggie's flat in Windmill Street. Can't you push that pram properly? Jesus, you're going to kill that child. Stop goin' from side to side or I'll give you a good clitther on the gob. She won't come into Aunt Aggie's flat. She can't stand the sight of us one more minute. She's fed up with the whole McCourt clan from the days when she had to send six fares to bring us all back from America, dishing out more money for funerals for dead children, giving us food every time our father drank the dole or the wages, helping Angela carry on while that blaguard from the North drinks his wages all over England. Oh, she's fed up, so she is, and off she goes across Henry Street with her black shawl pulled up around her white head, limping along in her black high-laced boots.

When you're eleven and your brothers are ten, five and one, you don't know what to do when you go to someone's house even if she's your mother's sister. You're told to leave the pram in the hall and bring the baby into the kitchen but if it's not your house you don't know what to do once you get into the kitchen for fear the aunt will yell at you or hit you on the skull. She takes off her coat and takes it to the bedroom and you stand with the baby in your arms waiting to be told. If you take one step forward or one step to the side she might come out and say where are you going and you don't know what to answer because you don't know yourself. If you say anything to your brothers she might say who do you think you're talking to in my kitchen? We have to stand and be quiet and that's hard when there's a tinkling sound from the bedroom and we know she's on the chamber pot peeing away. I don't want to look at Malachy. If I do I'll smile and he'll smile and Michael will smile and there's danger we'll start laughing and if we do we won't be able to stop for days at the picture in our heads of Aunt Aggie's big white bum perched on a flowery little chamber pot. I'm able to control myself. I won't laugh. Malachy and Michael won't laugh and it's easy to see we're all proud of ourselves for not laughing and getting into trouble with Aunt Aggie till Alphie in my arms smiles and says Goo goo and that sets us off. The three of us burst out laughing and Alphie grins with his dirty face and says Goo goo again till we're helpless and Aunt Aggie roars out of the room pulling her dress down and gives me a thump on the head that sends me against the wall baby and all. She hits Malachy too and she tries to hit Michael but he runs to the other side of her round table and she can't get at him. Come over here, she says, and I'll wipe that grin off your puss, but Michael keeps running around the table and she's too fat to catch him. I'll get you later, she says, I'll warm your arse, and you, Lord Muck, she says to me, put that child down on the floor over there by the range. She puts the old coats from the pram on the floor and Alphie lies there with his sugary water and says Goo goo and smiles. She tells us take off every scrap of our clothes, get out to the tap in the backyard and scrub every inch of our bodies. We are not to come back into this house till we're spotless. I want to tell her it's the middle of February, it's freezing outside, we could all die, but I know if I open my mouth I might die right here on the kitchen floor.

We're out in the yard naked dousing ourselves with icy water from the tap. She opens the kitchen window and throws out a scrub brush and a big bar of brown soap like the one they used on Finn the Horse. She orders us to scrub each other's backs and don't stop till she tells us. Michael says his hands and feet are falling off with the cold but she doesn't care. She keeps telling us we're still dirty and if she has to come out to scrub us we'll rue the day. Another rue. I scrub myself harder. We all scrub till we're pink and our jaws chatter. It's not enough for Aunt Aggie. She comes out with a bucket and sloshes cold water all over us. Now, she says, get inside and dry yeerselves. We stand in the little shed next to her kitchen drying ourselves with one towel. We stand and shiver and wait because you can't go marching into her kitchen till she tells you. We hear her inside starting the fire, rattling the poker in the range, then yelling at us, Are ye goin' to stand in there all day? Come in here and put on yeer clothes.

She gives us mugs of tea and cuts of fried bread and we sit at the table eating quietly because you're not supposed to say a word unless she tells you. Michael asks her for a second cut of fried bread and we expect her to knock him off the chair for his cheek but she just grumbles, 'Tis far from two cuts of fried bread ye were brought up, and gives each of us another cut. She tries to feed Alphie bread soaked in tea but he won't eat it till she sprinkles it with sugar and when he's finished he smiles and pees all over her lap and we're delighted. She runs out to the shed to dab at herself with a towel and we're able to grin at each other at the table and tell Alphie he's the champion baby in the world. Uncle Pa Keating comes in the door all black from his job at the gas works. Oh, bejay, he says, what's this?

Michael says, My mother is in the hospital, Uncle Pa.

Is that so? What's up with her?

Pneumonia, says Malachy.

Well, now, that's better than oldmonia.

We don't know what he's laughing at and Aunt Aggie comes in

from the shed and tells him how Mam is in the hospital and we're to stay with them till she gets out. He says, Grand, grand, and goes to the shed to wash himself though when he comes back you'd never know he touched himself with water at all he's that black.

He sits at the table and Aunt Aggie gives him his supper, which is fried bread and ham and sliced tomatoes. She tells us get away from the table and stop gawking at him having his tea and tells him to stop giving us bits of ham and tomato. He says, Arrah, for Jaysus sake, Aggie, the children are hungry, and she says, 'Tis none of your business. They're not yours. She tells us go out and play and be home for bed by half-past eight. We know it's freezing outside and we'd like to stay in by that warm range but it's easier to be in the streets playing than inside with Aunt Aggie and her nagging.

She calls me in later and sends me upstairs to borrow a rubber sheet from a woman who had a child that died. The woman says tell your aunt I'd like that rubber sheet back for the next child. Aunt Aggie says, Twelve years ago that child died and she still keeps the rubber sheet. Forty-five she is now and if there's another child we'll have to look for a star in the East. Malachy says, What's that? and she tells him mind his own business, he's too young.

Aunt Aggie places the rubber sheet on her bed and puts Alphie on it between herself and Uncle Pa. She sleeps inside against the wall and Uncle Pa outside because he has to get up in the morning for work. We are to sleep on the floor against the opposite wall with one coat under us and two over. She says if she hears a word out of us during the night she'll warm our arses and we're to be up early in the morning because it's Ash Wednesday and it wouldn't do us any harm to go to Mass and pray for our poor mother and her pneumonia.

The alarm clock shocks us out of our sleep. Aunt Aggie calls from her bed, The three of ye are to get up and go to Mass. Do ye hear me? Up. Wash yeer faces and go to the Jesuits.

Her backyard is all frost and ice and our hands sting from the tap water. We throw a little on our faces and dry with the towel that's still damp from yesterday. Malachy whispers our wash was a lick and a promise, that's what Mam would say.

The streets are frosty and icy, too, but the Jesuit church is warm. It must be grand to be a Jesuit, sleeping in a bed with sheets blankets pillows and getting up to a nice warm house and a warm church with nothing to do but say Mass hear confessions and yell at people for their

244

sins have your meals served up to you and read your Latin office before you go to sleep. I'd like to be a Jesuit some day but there's no hope of that when you grow up in a lane. Jesuits are very particular. They don't like poor people. They like people with motor cars who stick out their little fingers when they pick up their teacups.

The church is crowded with people at seven o'clock Mass getting the ashes on their foreheads. Malachy whispers that Michael shouldn't get the ashes because he won't be making his First Communion till May and it would be a sin. Michael starts to cry, I want the ashes, I want the ashes. An old woman behind us says, What are ye doin' to that lovely child? Malachy explains the lovely child never made his First Communion and he's not in a state of grace. Malachy is getting ready for Confirmation himself, always showing off his knowledge of the catechism, always going on about state of grace. He won't admit I knew all about the state of grace a year ago, so long ago I'm starting to forget it. The old woman says you don't have to be in a state of grace to get a few ashes on your forehead and tells Malachy stop tormenting his poor little brother. She pats Michael on the head and tells him he's a lovely child and go up there and get your ashes. He runs to the altar and when he comes back the woman gives him a penny to go with his ashes.

Aunt Aggie is still in the bed with Alphie. She tells Malachy to fill Alphie's bottle with milk and bring it to him. She tells me to start the fire in the range, that there's paper and wood in a box and coal in the coal scuttle. If the fire won't start sprinkle it with a little paraffin oil. The fire is slow and smoky and I sprinkle it with the paraffin oil, it flares up, whoosh, and nearly takes my eyebrows off. There is smoke everywhere and Aunt Aggie rushes into the kitchen. She shoves me away from the range. Jesus above, can't you do anything right? You're supposed to open the damper, you eejit.

I don't know anything about dampers. In our house we have a fireplace in Ireland downstairs and a fireplace in Italy upstairs and no sign of a damper. Then you go to your aunt's house and you're supposed to know all about dampers. There's no use telling her this is the first time you ever lit a fire in a range. She'll just give you another thump on the skull and send you flying. It's hard to know why grown people get so angry over little things like dampers. When I'm a man I won't go around thumping small children over dampers or anything else. Now she yells at me, Look at Lord Muck standing there. Would you ever think of opening the window and letting out the smoke? Of course you wouldn't.

You have a puss on you like your father from the North. Do you think now you can boil the water for the tea without burning the house down?

She cuts three slices from a loaf, smears them with margarine for us and goes back to bed. We have the tea and bread and it's one morning we're glad to go to school where it's warm and there are no yelling aunts.

After school she tells me sit at the table and write my father a letter about Mam in the hospital and how we're all at Aunt Aggie's till Mam comes home. I'm to tell him we're all happy and in the best of health, send money, food is very dear, growing boys eat a lot, ha ha, Alphie the baby needs clothes and nappies.

I don't know why she's always angry. Her flat is warm and dry. She has electric light in the house and her own lavatory in the backyard. Uncle Pa has a steady job and he brings home his wages every Friday. He drinks his pints at South's pub but never comes home singing songs of Ireland's long woeful history. He says, A pox on all their houses, and he says the funniest thing in the world is that we all have arses that have to be wiped and no man escapes that. The minute a politician or a Pope starts his blather Uncle Pa thinks of him wiping his arse. Hitler and Roosevelt and Churchill all wipe their arses. De Valera, too. He says the only people you can trust in that department are the Mahommedans for they eat with one hand and wipe with the other. The human hand itself is a sneaky bugger and you never know what it's been up to.

There are good times with Uncle Pa when Aunt Aggie goes to the Mechanics' Institute to play cards, forty-five. He says, To hell with the begrudgers. He gets himself two bottles of stout from South's, six buns and a half pound of ham from the shop on the corner. He makes tea and we sit by the range drinking it, eating our ham sandwiches and buns and laughing over Uncle Pa and the way he goes on about the world. He says, I swallowed the gas, I drink the pint, I don't give a fiddler's fart about the world and its cousin. If little Alphie gets tired and cranky and cries Uncle Pa pulls his shirt back from his chest and tells him, Here, have a suck of diddy momma. The sight of that flat chest and the nipple shocks Alphie and makes him good again.

Before Aunt Aggie comes home we have to wash the mugs and clean up so she won't know we were stuffing ourselves with buns and ham sandwiches. She'd nag Uncle Pa for a month if she ever found out and that's what I don't understand. Why does he let her nag him like that? He went to the Great War, he was gassed, he's big, he has a job, he makes the world laugh. It's a mystery. That's what the priests and the masters tell you, everything is a mystery and you have to believe what you're told.

I could easily have Uncle Pa for a father. We'd have great times sitting by the fire in the range drinking tea and laughing over the way he farts and says, Light a match. That's a present from the Germans.

Aunt Aggie torments me all the time. She calls me scabby eyes. She says I'm the spitting image of my father, I have the odd manner, I have the sneaky air of a northern Presbyterian, I'll probably grow up and build an altar to Oliver Cromwell himself, I'll run off and marry an English tart and cover my house with pictures of the royal family.

I want to get away from her and I can think of only one way, to make myself sick and go to the hospital. I get up in the middle of the night and go to her backyard. I can pretend I'm going to the lavatory. I stand out in the open in the freezing weather and hope I'll catch pneumonia or the galloping consumption so that I'll go to the hospital with the nice clean sheets and the meals in the bed and books brought by the girl in the blue dress. I might meet another Patricia Madigan and learn a long poem. I stand in the backyard for ages in my shirt and bare feet looking up at the moon which is a ghostly galleon riding upon cloudy seas and go back to bed shivering hoping I'll wake up in the morning with a terrible cough and flushed cheeks. But I don't. I feel fresh and lively and I'd be in great form if I could be at home with my mother and brothers.

There are days when Aunt Aggie tells us she can't stand the sight of us another minute, Get away from me. Here, scabby eyes, take Alphie out in his pram, take your brothers, go to the park and play, do anything ye like and don't come back till teatime when the Angelus is ringing, not a minute later, do ye hear me, not a minute later. It's cold but we don't care. We push the pram up O'Connell Avenue out to Ballinacurra or the Rosbrien Road. We let Alphie crawl around in fields to look at cows and sheep and we laugh when the cows nuzzle him. I get under the cows and squirt the milk into Alphie's mouth till he's full and throws it up. Farmers chase us till they see how small Michael and Alphie are. Malachy laughs at the farmers. He says, Hit me now with the child in me arms. Then he has a great notion, Why can't we go to our own house and play a while? We find twigs and bits of wood in the fields and rush to Roden Lane. There are matches by the fireplace in Italy and we have a good fire going in no time. Alphie falls asleep and soon the rest of us drift off till the Angelus booms out of the Redemptorist church and we know we're in trouble with Aunt Aggie for being late.

We don't care. She can yell at us all she wants but we had a grand time out the country with the cows and the sheep and then the lovely fire above in Italy.

You can tell she never has grand times like that. Electric light and a lavatory but no grand times.

Grandma comes for her on Thursdays and Sundays and they take the bus to the hospital to see Mam. We can't go because children are not allowed and if we say, How's Mam? they look cranky and tell us she's all right, she'll live. We'd like to know when she's getting out of hospital so that we can all go back home but we're afraid to open our mouths.

Malachy tells Aunt Aggie one day he's hungry and could he have a piece of bread. She hits him with a rolled-up *Little Messenger of the Sacred Heart* and there are tears on his eyelashes. He doesn't come home from school the next day and he's still gone at bedtime. Aunt Aggie says, Well, I suppose he ran away. Good riddance. If he was hungry he'd be here. Let him find comfort in a ditch.

Next day Michael runs in from the street, Dad's here, Dad's here, and runs back out and there's Dad sitting on the hall floor hugging Michael, crying, Your poor mother, your poor mother, and there's a smell of drink on him. Aunt Aggie is smiling, Oh, you're here, and she makes tea and eggs and sausages. She sends me out for a bottle of stout for Dad and I wonder why she's so pleasant and generous all of a sudden. Michael says, Are we going to our own house, Dad?

We are, son.

Alphie is back in the pram with the three old coats and coal and wood for the fire. Aunt Aggie stands at her door and tells us be good boys, come back for tea anytime, and there's a bad word for her in my head, Oul' bitch. It's in my head and I can't help it and I'll have to tell the priest in confession.

Malachy isn't in a ditch, he's there in our own house eating fish and chips a drunken soldier dropped at the gate of the Sarsfield Barracks.

Mam comes home in two days. She's weak and white and walks slowly. She says, The doctor told me keep warm, have plenty of rest and nourishing food, meat and eggs three times a week. God help us, those poor doctors don't have a notion of not having. Dad makes tea and toasts bread for her on the fire. He fries bread for the rest of us and we have a lovely night up in Italy where it's warm. He says he can't stay forever, he has to go back to work in Coventry. Mam wonders how he'll get to Coventry without a penny in his pocket. He's up early on Holy Saturday and I have tea with him by the fire. He fries four cuts of bread and wraps them in pages of the *Limerick Chronicle*, two cuts in each coat pocket. Mam is still in bed and he calls to her from the bottom of the stairs, I'm going now. She says, All right. Write when you land. My father is going to England and she won't even get out of the bed. I ask if I can go with him to the railway station. No, he's not going there. He's going to the Dublin road to see if he can get a lift. He pats my head, tells me take care of my mother and brothers and goes out the door. I watch him go up the lane till he turns the corner. I run up the lane to see him go down Barrack Hill and down St. Joseph's Street. I run down the hill and follow him as far as I can. He must know I'm following him because he turns and calls to me, Go home, Francis. Go home to your mother.

In a week there's a letter to say he arrived safely, that we are to be good boys, attend to our religious duties and above all obey our mother. In another week there's a telegram money order for three pounds and we're in heaven. We'll be rich, there will be fish and chips, jelly and custard, films every Saturday at the Lyric, the Coliseum, the Carlton, the Atheneum, the Central and the fanciest of all, the Savoy. We might even wind up having tea and cakes at the Savoy Café with the nobs and toffs of Limerick. We'll be sure to hold our teacups with our little fingers sticking out.

The next Saturday there's no telegram nor the Saturday after nor any Saturday forever. Mam begs again at the St. Vincent de Paul Society and smiles at the Dispensary when Mr. Coffey and Mr. Kane have their bit of a joke about Dad having a tart in Piccadilly. Michael wants to know what a tart is and she tells him it's something you have with tea. She spends most of the day by the fire with Bridey Hannon puffing on her Woodlbines, drinking weak tea. The bread crumbs from the morning are always on the table when we come home from school. She never washes the jam jars or mugs and there are flies in the sugar and wherever there is sweetness.

She says Malachy and I have to take turns looking after Alphie, taking him out in the pram for a bit of fresh air. The child can't be kept in Italy from October to April. If we tell her we want to play with our pals she might let fly with a right cross to the head that stings the ears.

We play games with Alphie and the pram. I stand at the top of Barrack Hill and Malachy is at the bottom. When I give the pram a push down the hill Malachy is supposed to stop it but he's looking at a pal on roller skates and it speeds by him across the street and through the doors of Leniston's pub where men are having a peaceful pint and not expecting a pram with a dirty-faced child saying Goo goo goo goo. The barman shouts this is a disgrace, there must be a law against this class of behavior, babies roaring through the door in bockety prams, he'll call the guards on us, and Alphie waves at him and smiles and he says, all right, all right, the child can have a sweet and a lemonade, the brothers can have lemonade too, that raggedy pair, and God above, 'tis a hard world, the minute you think you're getting ahead a pram comes crashing through the door and you're dishing out sweets and lemonade right and left, the two of ye take that child and go home to yeer mother.

Malachy has another powerful idea, that we could go around Limerick like tinkers pushing Alphie in his pram into pubs for the sweets and lemonade, but I don't want Mam finding out and hitting me with her right cross. Malachy says I'm not a sport and runs off. I push the pram over to Henry Street and up by the Redemptorist church. It's a gray day, the church is gray and the small crowd of people outside the door of the priests' house is gray. They're waiting to beg for any food left over from the priests' dinner.

There in the middle of the crowd in her dirty gray coat is my mother.

This is my own mother, begging. This is worse than the dole, the St. Vincent de Paul Society, the Dispensary. It's the worst kind of shame, almost as bad as begging on the streets where the tinkers hold up their scabby children, Give us a penny for the poor child, mister, the poor child is hungry, missus.

My mother is a beggar now and if anyone from the lane or my school sees her the family will be disgraced entirely. My pals will make up new names and torment me in the schoolyard and I know what they'll say,

> Frankie McCourt
> *beggar woman's boy*
> *scabby-eyed*
> *dancing*
> *blubber-gob*
> *Jap*

The door of the priests' house swings open and the people rush with their hands out. I can hear them, Brother, brother, here, brother, ah, for the love o' God, brother. Five children at home, brother. I can see my own mother pushed along. I can see the tightness of her mouth when she snatches at a bag and turns from the door and I push the pram up the street before she can see me.

I don't want to go home anymore. I push the pram down to the Dock Road, out to Corkanree where all the dust and garbage of Limerick is dumped and burned. I stand a while and look at boys chase rats. I don't know why they have to torture rats that are not in their houses. I'd keep going on into the country forever if I didn't have Alphie bawling with the hunger, kicking his chubby legs, waving his empty bottle.

Mam has the fire going and something boiling in a pot. Malachy smiles and says she brought home corned beef and a few spuds from Kathleen O'Connell's shop. He wouldn't be so happy if he knew he was the son of a beggar. She calls us in from the lane and when we sit at the table it's hard for me to look at my mother the beggar. She lifts the pot to the table, spoons out the potatoes one each and uses a fork to lift out the corned beef.

It isn't corned beef at all. It's a great lump of quivering gray fat and the only sign of corned beef is a little nipple of red meat on top. We stare at that bit of meat and wonder who will get it. Mam says, That's for Alphie. He's a baby, he's growing fast, he needs it. She puts it on a saucer in front of him. He pushes it away with his finger, then pulls it back. He lifts it to his mouth, looks around the kitchen, sees Lucky the dog and throws it to him.

There's no use saying anything. The meat is gone. We eat our potatoes with plenty of salt and I eat my fat and pretend it's that nipple of red meat.

XI

Mam warns us, Ye are to keep yeer paws out of that trunk for there's nothing in there that's of the slightest interest or any of yeer business.

All she has in that trunk is a lot of papers, certificates of birth and baptism, her Irish passport, Dad's English passport from Belfast, our American passports and her bright red flapper dress with spangles and black frills she brought all the way from America. She wants to keep that dress forever to remind herself she was young and dancing.

I don't care what she has in the trunk till I start a football team with Billy Campbell and Malachy. We can't afford uniforms or boots and Billy says, How will the world know who we are? We don't even have a name.

I remember the red dress and a name comes to me, The Red Hearts of Limerick. Mam never opens the trunk so what does it matter if I cut off a piece of the dress to make seven red hearts we can stick on our chests? What you don't know won't bother you, she always says herself.

The dress is buried under the papers. I look at my passport picture when I was small and I can see why they call me Jap. There's a paper that says Marriage Certificate, that Malachy McCourt and Angela Sheehan were joined in Holy Matrimony on the twenty-eighth of March, 1930. How could that be? I was born on the nineteenth of August and Billy Campbell told me the father and mother have to be married nine months before there's a sign of a child. Here I am born into the world in half the time. That means I must be a miracle and I might grow up to be a saint with people celebrating the feast of St. Francis of Limerick.

I'll have to ask Mikey Molloy, still the expert on Girls' Bodies and Dirty Things in General.

Billy says if we're to be great soccer players we have to practice and we're to meet over in the park. The boys complain when I hand out the hearts and I tell them if they don't like it they can go home and cut up their own mother's dresses and blouses.

We have no money for a proper ball so one of the boys brings a sheep's bladder stuffed with rags. We kick the bladder up and down the meadow till there are holes and rags start falling out and we get fed up kicking a bladder that's hardly there anymore. Billy says we're to meet tomorrow morning which is Saturday and go out Ballinacurra to see if we can challenge rich Crescent College boys to a proper game, seven a side. He says we're to pin our red hearts to our shirts even if they're red rags.

Malachy is going home for tea but I can't go because I have to see Mikey Molloy and find out why I was born in half the time. Mikey is coming out of his house with his father, Peter. It's Mikey's sixteenth birthday and his father is taking him to Bowles's pub for his first pint. Nora Molloy is inside screeching after Peter that if they go they can stay gone, she's done baking bread, she's never going to the lunatic asylum again, if he brings that child home drunk she'll go to Scotland and disappear from the face of the earth.

Peter tells Mikey, Pay no attention to her, Cyclops. The mothers of Ireland are always enemies of the first pint. My own mother tried to kill my father with a frying pan when he took me for the first pint.

Mikey asks Peter if I can come with them and have a lemonade.

Peter tells everyone in the pub that Mikey is there for his first pint and when all the men want to stand Mikey a pint Peter says, Ah, no, 'twould be a terrible thing if he had too much and turned against it entirely.

The pints are drawn and we sit against the wall, the Molloys with their pints and I with my lemonade. The men wish Mikey all the best in the life to come and wasn't it a gift from God that he fell off that spout years ago and never had the fit since and wasn't it a great pity about that poor little bugger, Quasimodo Dooley, carried off with the consumption after all his trouble talking for years like an Englishman so he could be on the BBC which is no fit place for an Irishman anyway.

Peter is talking to the men and Mikey, sipping his first pint, whispers to me, I don't think I like it, but don't tell my father. Then he tells me how he practices the English accent in secret so that he can be a BBC announcer, Quasimodo's dream. He tells me I can have Cuchulain back, that he's no use to you when you're reading the news on the BBC. Now that he's sixteen he wants to go to England and if ever I get a wireless that will be him on the BBC Home Service.

I tell him about the marriage certificate, how Billy Campbell said it has to be nine months but I was born in half the time and would he know if I was some class of a miracle.

Naw, he says, naw. You're a bastard. You're doomed.

You don't have to be cursing me, Mikey.

I'm not. That's what they call people who aren't born inside the nine months of the marriage, people conceived beyond the blanket.

What's that?

What's what?

Conceived.

That's when the sperm hits the egg and it grows and there you are nine months later.

I don't know what you're talking about.

He whispers, The thing between your legs is the excitement. I don't like the other names, the dong, the prick, the dick, the langer. So your father shoves his excitement into your mother and there's a spurt and these little germs go up into your mother where there's an egg and that grows into you.

I'm not an egg.

You are an egg. Everyone was an egg once.

Why am I doomed? 'Tisn't my fault I'm a bastard.

All bastards are doomed. They're like babies that weren't baptized. They're sent to Limbo for eternity and there's no way out and it's not their fault. It makes you wonder about God up there on His throne with no mercy for the little unbaptized babies. That's why I don't go near the chapel anymore. Anyway, you're doomed. Your father and mother had the excitement and they weren't married so you're not in a state of grace.

What am I going to do?

Nothing. You're doomed.

Can't I light a candle or something.

You could try the Blessed Virgin. She's in charge of the doom.

But I don't have a penny for the candle.

All right, all right, here's a penny. You can give it back when you get a job a million years from now. 'Tis costing me a fortune to be the expert on Girls' Bodies and Dirty Things in General.

The barman is doing a crossword puzzle and he says to Peter, What's the opposite of advance?

Retreat, says Peter.

That's it, says the barman. Everything has an opposite.

Mother o' God, says Peter.

What's up with you, Peter? says the barman.

What was that you said before, Tommy?

Everything has an opposite.

Mother o' God.

Are you all right, Peter? Is the pint all right?

The pint is grand, Tommy, and I'm the champion of all pint drinkers, amn't I?

Begod an' you are, Peter. No denyin' that to you.

That means I could be the champion in the opposite department.

What are you talking about, Peter?

I could be the champion of no pints at all.

Ah, now, Peter, I think you're going a bit far. Is the wife all right at home?

Tommy, take this pint away from me. I'm the champion of no pints at all.

Peter turns and takes the glass from Mikey. We're going home to your mother, Mikey.

You didn't call me Cyclops, Dad.

You're Mikey. You're Michael. We're going to England. No more pints for me, no pints for you, no more bread baking for your mother. Come on.

We're leaving the pub and Tommy the barman calls after us, You know what 'tis, Peter. 'Tis all them bloody books you're reading. They have your head destroyed.

Peter and Mikey turn to go home. I have to go to St. Joseph's to light the candle that will save me from the doom but I look in the window of Counihan's shop and there in the middle is a great slab of

Cleeves' toffee and a sign, TWO PIECES FOR A PENNY. I know I'm doomed but the water is running along the sides of my tongue and when I put my penny on the counter for Miss Counihan I promise the Virgin Mary the next penny I get I'll be lighting a candle and would she please talk to her Son and delay the doom for awhile.

A penn'orth of Cleeves' toffee doesn't last forever and when it's gone I have to think of going home to a mother who let my father push his excitement into her so that I could be born in half the time and grow up to be a bastard. If she ever says a word about the red dress or anything I'll tell her I know all about the excitement and she'll be shocked.

Saturday morning I meet The Red Hearts of Limerick and we wander out the road looking for a football challenge. The boys are still grousing that the bits of red dress don't look like hearts till Billy tells them if they don't want to play football go home and play with their sisters' dolls.

There are boys playing football in a field in Ballinacurra and Billy challenges them. They have eight players and we have only seven but we don't mind because one of them has one eye and Billy tells us stay on his blind side. Besides, he says, Frankie McCourt is nearly blind with his two bad eyes and that's worse. They're all togged out in blue and white jerseys and white shorts and proper football boots. One of them says we look like something the cat brought in and Malachy has to be held back from fighting them. We agree to play half an hour because the Ballinacurra boys say they have to go to lunch. Lunch. The whole world has dinner in the middle of the day but they have lunch. If no one scores in half an hour it's a draw. We play back and forth till Billy gets the ball and goes speeding and dancing up the sideline so fast no one can catch him and in goes the ball for a goal. The half hour is nearly up but the Ballinacurra boys want another half hour and they manage to score well into the second half hour. Then the ball goes over the line for touch. It's our ball. Billy stands on the touch line with the ball over his head. He pretends to look at Malachy but throws the ball to me. It comes to me as if it's the only thing that exists in the whole world. It comes straight to my foot and all I have to do is swivel to the left and swing that ball straight into the goal. There's a whiteness in my head and I feel like a boy in heaven. I'm floating over the whole field till The Red Hearts of Limerick clap me on the back and tell me that was a great goal, Frankie, you too, Billy.

We walk back along O'Connell Avenue and I keep thinking of the way the ball came to my foot and surely it was sent by God or the Blessed Virgin Mary who would never send such a blessing to one doomed for being born in half the time and I know as long as I live I'll never forget that ball coming from Billy Campbell, that goal.

Mam meets Bridey Hannon and her mother going up the lane and they tell her about Mr. Hannon's poor legs. Poor John, it's a trial for him to cycle home every night after delivering coal and turf all day on the great float for the coal merchants on the Dock Road. He's paid from eight in the morning till half five in the evening though he has to get the horse ready well before eight and settle him for the night well after half five. He's up and down on that float all day hoisting bags of coal and turf, desperate to keep the bandages in place on his legs so the dirt won't get into the open sores. The bandages are forever sticking and have to be ripped away and when he comes home she washes the sores with warm water and soap, covers them with ointment and wraps them in clean bandages. They can't afford new bandages every day so she keeps washing the old ones over and over till they're gray.

Mam says Mr. Hannon should see the doctor and Mrs. Hannon says, Sure, he seen the doctor a dozen times and the doctor says he has to stay off them legs. That's all. Stay off them legs. Sure how can he stay off them legs? He has to work. What would we live on if he didn't work?

Mam says maybe Bridey could get some kind of a job herself and Bridey is offended. Don't you know I have a weak chest, Angela? Don't you know I had rheumatic fever an' I could go at any time? I have to be careful.

Mam often talks about Bridey and her rheumatic fever and weak chest. She says, That one is able to sit here by the hour and complain about her ailments but it doesn't stop her from puffing away on the Woodbines.

Mam tells Bridey she's very sorry over the weak chest and it's terrible the way her father suffers. Mrs. Hannon tells my mother that John is getting worse every day, And what would you think, Mrs. McCourt, if your boy Frankie went on the float with him a few hours a week and helped him with the bags? We can barely afford it but Frankie could earn a shilling or two and John could rest his poor legs.

Mam says, I don't know, he's only eleven and he had that typhoid and the coal dust wouldn't be good for his eyes.

Bridey says, He'd be out in the air and there's nothing like fresh air for someone with bad eyes or getting over the typhoid, isn't that right, Frankie?

'Tis, Bridey.

I'm dying to go around with Mr. Hannon on the great float like a real workingman. If I'm good at it they might let me stay at home from school forever but Mam says, He can do it as long as it doesn't interfere with school and he can start on a Saturday morning.

I'm a man now so I light the fire early on Saturday morning and make my own tea and fried bread. I wait next door for Mr. Hannon to come out with his bicycle and there's a lovely smell of rashers and eggs coming through the window. Mam says Mr. Hannon gets the best of food because Mrs. Hannon is as mad about him as she was the day she married him. They're like two lovers out of an American film the way they go on. Here he is pushing the bicycle and puffing away on the pipe in his mouth. He tells me climb up on the bar of his bike and off we go to my first job as a man. His head is over mine on the bike and the smell of the pipe is lovely. There's a coal smell on his clothes and that makes me sneeze.

Men are walking or cycling toward the coal yards and Rank's Flour Mills and the Limerick Steamship Company on the Dock Road. Mr. Hannon takes his pipe from his mouth and tells me this is the best morning of all, Saturday, half day. We'll start at eight and be finished by the time the Angelus rings at twelve.

First we get the horse ready, give him a bit of a rub, fill the wooden tub with oats and the bucket with water. Mr. Hannon shows me how to put on the harness and lets me back the horse into the shafts of the float. He says, Jaysus, Frankie, you have the knack of it.

That makes me so happy I want to jump up and down and drive a float the rest of my life.

There are two men filling bags with coal and turf and weighing them on the great iron scale, a hundredweight in each bag. It's their job to stack the bags on the float while Mr. Hannon goes to the office for the delivery dockets. The bag men are fast and we're ready for our rounds. Mr. Hannon sits up on the left side of the float and flicks the whip to show where I'm to sit on the right side. It's hard to climb up the way the float is so high and packed with bags and I try to get up by climbing the wheel. Mr. Hannon says I should never do the likes of that again. Never put your leg or hand near a wheel when the horse is harnessed in the shafts. A horse might take a notion to go for a walk for himself and there you are with the leg or the arm caught in the wheel and twisted off your body and you looking at it. He says to the horse, G'up ower that, and the horse shakes his head and rattles the harness and Mr. Hannon laughs. That fool of a horse loves to work, he says. He won't be rattling his harness in a few hours.

When the rain starts we cover ourselves with old coal bags and Mr. Hannon turns his pipe upside down in his mouth to keep the tobacco dry. He says the rain makes everything heavier but what's the use of complaining. You might as well complain about the sun in Africa.

We cross the Sarsfield Bridge for deliveries to the Ennis Road and the North Circular Road. Rich people, says Mr. Hannon, and very slow to put their hands in their pockets for a tip.

We have sixteen bags to deliver. Mr. Hannon says we're lucky today because some houses get more than one and he doesn't have to be climbing on and off that float destroying his legs. When we stop he gets down and I pull the bag to the edge and lay it on his shoulders. Some houses have areas outside where you pull up a trap door and tip the bag till it empties and that's easy. There are other houses with long backyards and you can see Mr. Hannon suffering with his legs when he has to carry the bags from the float to the sheds near the back doors. Ah, Jaysus, Frankie, ah, Jaysus, is the only complaint out of him and he asks me to give him a hand to climb back on the float. He says if he had a handcart he could wheel the bags from float to house and that would be a blessing but a handcart would cost two weeks' wages and who could afford that?

The bags are delivered and the sun is out, the float is empty, and the horse knows his workday is over. It's lovely to sit on the float looking along the length of the horse from his tail to his head rocking along the Ennis Road over the Shannon and up the Dock Road. Mr. Hannon says the man who delivered sixteen hundredweights of coal and turf deserves a pint and the boy who helped him deserves a lemonade. He tells me I should go to school and not be like him working away with the two legs rotting under him. Go to school, Frankie, and get out of Limerick and Ireland itself. This war will be over some day and you can go to America or Australia or any big open country where you can look up and see no end to the land. The world is wide and you can have great adventures. If I didn't have these two legs I'd be over in England making a fortune in the factories like the rest of the Irishmen, like your father. No, not like your father. I hear he left you high and dry, eh? I don't know how a man in his right mind can go off and leave a wife and family to starve and shiver in a Limerick winter. School, Frankie, school. The books, the books, the books. Get out of Limerick before your legs rot and your mind collapses entirely.

The horse clops along and when we get to the coal yard we feed and water him and give him a rubdown. Mr. Hannon talks to him all the time and calls him Me oul' segosha, and the horse snuffles and pushes his nose against Mr. Hannon's chest. I'd love to bring this horse home and let him stay downstairs when we're up in Italy but even if I could get him in the door my mother would yell at me that the last thing we need in this house is a horse.

The streets going up from the Dock Road are too hilly for Mr. Hannon to ride the bicycle and carry me, so we walk. His legs are sore from the day and it takes a long time to get up to Henry Street. He leans on the bicycle or sits on the steps outside houses, grinding down on the pipe in his mouth.

I'm wondering when I'll get the money for the day's work because Mam might let me go to the Lyric Cinema if I get home in time with my shilling or whatever Mr. Hannon gives me. Now we're at the door of South's pub and he tells me come in, didn't he promise me a lemonade?

Uncle Pa Keating is sitting in the pub. He's all black as usual and he's sitting next to Bill Galvin, all white as usual, snuffling and taking great slugs out of his black pint. Mr. Hannon says, How're you? and sits on the other side of Bill Galvin and everyone in the pub laughs. Jaysus, says the barman, look at that, two lumps of coal and a snowball. Men come in from other parts of the pub to see the two coal-black men with the lime-white man in the middle and they want to send down to the *Limerick Leader* for a man with a camera.

Uncle Pa says, What are you doing all black yourself, Frankie? Did you fall down a coal mine?

I was helping Mr. Hannon on the float.

Your eyes look atrocious, Frankie. Piss holes in the snow.

'Tis the coal dust, Uncle Pa.

Wash them when you go home.

I will, Uncle Pa.

Mr. Hannon buys me a lemonade, gives me the shilling for my morning's work and tells me I can go home now, I'm a great worker and I can help him again next week after school.

On the way home I see myself in the glass of a shop window all black from the coal, and I feel like a man, a man with a shilling in his pocket, a man who had a lemonade in a pub with two coal men and a lime man. I'm not a child anymore and I could easily leave Leamy's School forever. I could work with Mr. Hannon every day and when his legs got too bad I could take over the float and deliver coal to the rich people the rest of my life and my mother wouldn't have to be a beggar at the Redemptorist priests' house.

People on the streets and lanes give me curious looks. Boys and girls laugh and call out, Here's the chimney sweep. How much do you want for cleaning our chimney? Did you fall into a coal hole? Were you burned by the darkness?

They're ignorant. They don't know I spent the day delivering hundredweights of coal and turf. They don't know I'm a man.

Mam is sleeping up in Italy with Alphie and there's a coat over the window to keep the room dark. I tell her I earned a shilling and she says I can go to the Lyric, I deserve it. Take tuppence and leave the rest of the shilling on the mantelpiece downstairs so that she can send out for a loaf of bread for the tea. The coat suddenly drops from the window and the room is bright. Mam looks at me, God above, look at your eyes. Go downstairs and I'll be down in a minute to wash them.

She heats water in the kettle and dabs at my eyes with boric acid powder and tells me I can't go to the Lyric Cinema today or any day till my eyes clear up though God knows when that will be. She says, You can't be delivering coal with the state of your eyes. The dust will surely destroy them.

I want the job. I want to bring home the shilling. I want to be a man.

You can be a man without bringing home a shilling. Go upstairs and lie down and rest your two eyes or it's a blind man you'll be.

I want that job. I wash my eyes three times a day with the boric acid powder. I remember Seamus in the hospital and how his uncle's eyes were cured with the blink exercise and I make sure to sit and blink for an hour every day. You can't beat the blink for the strong eye, he said.

And now I blink and blink till Malachy runs to my mother, talking out in the lane with Mrs. Hannon, Mam, something is up with Frankie, he's upstairs blinking and blinking.

She comes running up. What's wrong with you?

I'm making my eyes strong with the exercise.

What exercise?

The blinking.

Blinking is not exercise.

Seamus in the hospital says you can't beat the blink for the strong eye. His uncle had powerful eyes from the blinking.

She says I'm getting odd and goes back to the lane and her chat with Mrs. Hannon and I blink and bathe my eyes with the boric acid powder in warm water. I can hear Mrs. Hannon through the window, Your little Frankie is a godsend to John for 'tis the climbing up and down on that float that was ruining his legs entirely.

Mam doesn't say anything and that means she feels so sorry for Mr. Hannon she'll let me help him again on his heavy delivery day, Thursday. I wash my eyes three times a day and I blink till I get a pain in my eyebrows. I blink in school when the master isn't looking and all the boys in my class are calling me Blinky and adding that to the list of names.

> Blinky McCourt
> beggar woman's son
> scabby-eyed
> blubber gob
> dancing
> Jap.

I don't care what they call me anymore as long as my eyes are clearing up and I have a regular job lifting hundredweights of coal on a float. I wish they could see me on Thursday after school when I'm on the float and Mr. Hannon hands me the reins so that he can smoke his pipe in comfort. Here you are, Frankie, nice and gentle for this is a good horse and he doesn't need to be pulled at.

He hands me the whip too but you never need the whip with this horse. It's all for show and I just flick it at the air like Mr. Hannon or I might knock a fly off the horse's great golden rump swinging between the shafts.

Surely the world is looking at me and admiring the way I rock with the float, the cool way I have with the reins and the whip. I wish I had a pipe like Mr. Hannon and a tweed cap. I wish I could be a real coal man with black skin like Mr. Hannon and Uncle Pa Keating so that people would say, There goes Frankie McCourt that delivers all the coal in Limerick and drinks his pint in South's pub. I'd never wash my face. I'd be black every day of the year even Christmas when you're supposed to give yourself a good wash for the coming of the Infant Jesus. I know He wouldn't mind because I saw the Three Wise Men in the Christmas crib at the Redemptorist church and one of them was blacker than Uncle Pa Keating, the blackest man in Limerick, and if a Wise Man is black it means that everywhere you go in the world someone is delivering coal.

The horse lifts his tail and great lumps of steaming yellow shit drop from his behind. I start to pull on the reins so that he can stop and have a bit of comfort for himself but Mr. Hannon says, No, Frankie, let him trot. They always shit on the trot. That's one of the blessings horses have, they shit on the trot, and they're not dirty and stinking like the human race, not at all, Frankie. The worst thing in the world is to go into a lavatory after a man that had a feed of pig's feet and a night of pints. The stink from that could twist the nostrils of a strong man. Horses are different. All they have is oats and hay and what they drop is clean and natural.

I work with Mr. Hannon after school on Tuesdays and Thursdays and the half day on Saturday morning and that means three shillings for my mother though she worries all the time over my eyes. The minute I get home she washes them and makes me rest them for half an hour.

Mr. Hannon says he'll wait near Leamy's School for me on Thursdays after his deliveries on Barrington Street. Now the boys will see me. Now they'll know I'm a workingman and more than a scabby-eyed blubber gob dancing Jap. Mr. Hannon says, Up you get, and I climb up on the float like any workingman. I look at the boys gawking at me. Gawking. I tell Mr. Hannon if he wants to smoke his pipe in comfort I'll take the reins and when he hands them over I'm sure I hear the boys gasping. I tell the horse, G'up ower that, like Mr. Hannon. We trot away and I know dozens of Leamy's boys are committing the deadly sin of envy. I tell the horse again, G'up ower that, to make sure everyone heard, to make sure they know I'm driving that float and no one else, to make sure they'll never forget it was me they saw on that float with the reins and the whip. It's the best day of my life, better than my First Communion day, which Grandma ruined, better than my Confirmation day when I had the typhoid.

They don't call me names anymore. They don't laugh at my scabby eyes. They want to know how I got such a good job at eleven years of age and what I'm paid and if I'll have that job forever. They want to know if there are any other good jobs going in the coal yards and would I put in a good word for them.

Then there are big boys of thirteen who stick their faces in mine and say they should have that job because they're bigger and I'm nothing but a scrawny little runt with no shoulders. They can talk as much as they like. I have the job and Mr. Hannon tells me I'm powerful.

There are days his legs are so bad he can hardly walk at all and you can see Mrs. Hannon worries. She gives me a mug of tea and I watch her roll up his trouser legs and peel away the dirty bandages. The sores are red and yellow and clogged with coal dust. She washes them with soapy water and smears them with a yellow ointment. She props the legs up on a chair and that's where he stays the rest of the night reading the paper or a book from the shelf above his head.

The legs are getting so bad he has to get up an hour earlier in the morning to get the stiffness out, to put on another dressing. It's still dark one Saturday morning when Mrs. Hannon knocks at our door and asks me if I'd go to a neighbor and borrow their handcart to take on the float for Mr. Hannon will never be able to carry the bags today and maybe I'd just roll them on the handcart for him. He won't be able to carry me on his bicycle so I can meet him at the yard with the handcart.

The neighbor says, Anything for Mr. Hannon, God bless him.

I wait at the gate of the coal yard and watch him cycle toward me, slower than ever. He's so stiff he can hardly get off the bike and he says, You're a great man, Frankie. He lets me get the horse ready though I still have trouble getting on the harness. He lets me handle the float out of the yard and into the frosty streets and I wish I could drive forever and never go home. Mr. Hannon shows me how to pull the bags to the edge of the float and drop them on the ground so that I can pull them on to the handcart and push them to the houses. He tells me how to lift and push the bags without straining myself and we have the sixteen bags delivered by noon.

I wish the boys at Leamy's could see me now, the way I drive the horse and handle the bags, the way I do everything while Mr. Hannon rests his legs. I wish they could see me pushing the handcart to South's pub and having my lemonade with Mr. Hannon and Uncle Pa and me all black and Bill Galvin all white. I'd like to show the world the tips Mr. Hannon lets me keep, four shillings, and the shilling he gives me for the morning's work, five shillings altogether.

Mam is sitting by the fire and when I hand her the money she looks at me, drops it in her lap and cries. I'm puzzled because money is supposed to make you happy. Look at your eyes, she says. Go to that glass and look at your eyes.

My face is black and the eyes are worse than ever. The whites and the eyelids are red, and the yellow stuff oozes to the corners and out over the lower lids. If the ooze sits a while it forms a crust that has to be picked off or washed away.

Mam says that's the end of it. No more Mr. Hannon. I try to explain that Mr. Hannon needs me. He can barely walk anymore. I had to do everything this morning, drive the float, wheel the handcart with the bags, sit in the pub, drink lemonade, listen to the men discussing who is the best, Rommel or Montgomery.

She says she's sorry for Mr. Hannon's troubles but we have troubles of our own and the last thing she needs now is a blind son stumbling through the streets of Limerick. Bad enough you nearly died of typhoid, now you want to go blind on top of it.

And I can't stop crying now because this was my one chance to be a man and bring home the money the telegram boy never brought from my father. I can't stop crying because I don't know what Mr. Hannon is going to do on Monday morning when he has no one to help him pull the bags to the edge of the float, to push the bags into the houses. I can't stop crying because of the way he is with that horse he calls sweet because he's so gentle himself and what will the horse do if Mr. Hannon isn't there to take him out, if I'm not there to take him out? Will that horse fall down hungry for the want of oats and hay and the odd apple?

Mam says I shouldn't be crying, it's bad for the eyes. She says, We'll see. That's all I can tell you now. We'll see.

She washes my eyes and gives me sixpence to take Malachy to the Lyric to see Boris Karloff in *The Man They Could Not Hang* and have two pieces of Cleeves' toffee. It's hard to see the screen with the yellow stuff oozing from my eyes and Malachy has to tell me what's happening. People around us tell him shut up, they'd like to hear what Boris

Karloff is saying, and when Malachy talks back to them and tells them he's only helping his blind brother they call the man in charge, Frank Goggin, and he says if he hears another word out of Malachy he'll throw the two of us out.

I don't mind. I have a way of squeezing the stuff out of one eye and clearing it so that I can see the screen while the other eye fills up and I go back and forth, squeeze, look, squeeze, look, and everything I see is yellow.

Monday morning Mrs. Hannon is knocking on our door again. She asks Mam if Frank would ever go down to the coal yard and tell the man in the office that Mr. Hannon can't come in today, that he has to see a doctor about his legs, that he'll surely be in tomorrow and what he can't deliver today he will tomorrow. Mrs. Hannon always calls me Frank now. Anyone that delivers hundredweights of coal is not a Frankie.

The man in the office says, Humph. I think we're very tolerant with Hannon. You, what's your name?

McCourt, sir.

Tell Hannon we'll need a note from the doctor. Do you understand that?

I do, sir.

The doctor tells Mr. Hannon he has to go to the hospital or it's a case of gangrene he'll have and the doctor won't be responsible. The ambulance takes Mr. Hannon away and my big job is gone. Now I'll be white like everyone else in Leamy's, no float, no horse, no shillings to bring home to my mother.

In a few days Bridey Hannon comes to our door. She says her mother would like me to come and see her, have a cup of tea with her. Mrs. Hannon is sitting by the fire with her hand on the seat of Mr. Hannon's chair. Sit down, Frank, she says, and when I go to sit on one of the ordinary kitchen chairs she says, No, sit here. Sit here on the chair of himself. Do you know how old he is, Frank?

Oh, he must be very old, Mrs. Hannon. He must be thirty-five.

She smiles. She has lovely teeth. He's forty-nine, Frank, and a man that age shouldn't have legs like that.

He shouldn't, Mrs. Hannon.

Did you know you were a joy to him going around on that float?

I didn't, Mrs. Hannon.

You were. We had two daughters, Bridey that you know, and Kathleen, the nurse above in Dublin. But no son and he said you gave him the feeling of a son.

I feel my eyes burning and I don't want her to see me crying especially when I don't know why I'm crying. That's all I do lately. Is it the job? Is it Mr. Hannon? My mother says, Oh, your bladder is near your eye.

I think I'm crying because of the quiet way Mrs. Hannon is talking and she's talking like that because of Mr. Hannon.

Like a son, she says, and I'm glad he had that feeling. His working days are over, you know. He has to stay at home from this out. There might be a cure and if there is sure he might be able to get a job as a watchman where he doesn't have to be lifting and hauling.

I won't have a job anymore, Mrs. Hannon.

You have a job, Frank. School. That's your job.

That's not a job, Mrs. Hannon.

You'll never have another job like it, Frank. It breaks Mr. Hannon's heart to think of you dragging bags of coal off a float and it breaks your mother's heart and 'twill destroy your eyes. God knows I'm sorry I ever got you into this for it had your poor mother caught between your eyes and Mr. Hannon's legs.

Can I go to the hospital to see Mr. Hannon?

They might not let you in but surely you can come here to see him. God knows he won't be doing much but reading and looking out the window.

Mam tells me at home, You shouldn't cry but then again tears are salty and they'll wash the bad stuff from your eyes.

XII

_____

There's a letter from Dad. He's coming home two days before Christmas. He says everything will be different, he's a new man, he hopes we're good boys, obeying our mother, attending to our religious duties, and he's bringing us all something for Christmas.

Mam takes me to the railway station to meet him. The station is always exciting with all the coming and going, people leaning from carriages, crying, smiling, waving good-bye, the train hooting and calling, chugging away in clouds of steam, people sniffling on the platform, the railway tracks silvering into the distance, on to Dublin and the world beyond.

Now it's near midnight and cold on the empty platform. A man in a railway cap asks us if we'd like to wait in a warm place. Mam says, Thank you very much, and laughs when he leads us to the end of the platform where we have to climb a ladder to the signal tower. It takes her a while because she's heavy and she keeps saying, Oh, God, oh, God.

We're above the world and it's dark in the signal tower except for the lights that blink red and green and yellow when the man bends over the board. He says, I'm just having a bit of supper and you're welcome.

Mam says, Ah, no, thanks, we couldn't take your supper from you.

He says, The wife always makes too much for me and if I was up in this tower for a week I wouldn't be able to eat it. Sure it's not hard work looking at lights and pulling on the odd lever.

He takes the top off a flask and pours cocoa into a mug. Here, he says to me, put yourself outside that cocoa.

He hands Mam half a sandwich. Ah, no, she says, surely you could take that home to your children.

I have two sons, missus, and they're off there fighting in the forces of His Majesty, the King of England. One did his bit with Montgomery in Africa and the other is over in Burma or some other bloody place, excuse the language. We get our freedom from England and then we fight her wars. So here, missus, take the bit of sandwich.

Lights on the board are clicking and the man says, Your train is coming, missus.

Thank you very much and Happy Christmas.

Happy Christmas to yourself, missus, and a Happy New Year, too. Mind yourself on that ladder, young fella. Help your mother.

Thank you very much, sir.

We wait again on the platform while the train rumbles into the station. Carriage doors open and a few men with suitcases step to the platform and hurry toward the gate. There is a clanking of milk cans dropped to the platform. A man and two boys are unloading newspapers and magazines.

There is no sign of my father. Mam says he might be asleep in one of the carriages but we know he hardly sleeps even in his own bed. She says the boat from Holyhead might have been late and that would make him miss the train. The Irish Sea is desperate at this time of the year.

He's not coming, Mam. He doesn't care about us. He's just drunk over there in England.

Don't talk about your father like that.

I say no more to her. I don't tell her I wish I had a father like the man in the signal tower who gives you sandwiches and cocoa.

Next day Dad walks in the door. His top teeth are missing and there's a bruise under his left eye. He says the Irish Sea was rough and when he leaned over the side his teeth dropped out. Mam says, It wouldn't be the drink, would it? It wouldn't be a fight?

Och, no, Angela.

Michael says, You said you'd have something for us, Dad.

Oh, I do.

He takes a box of chocolates from his suitcase and hands it to Mam.

She opens the box and shows us the inside where half the chocolates are gone.

Could you spare it? she says.

She shuts the box and puts it on the mantelpiece. We'll have chocolates after our Christmas dinner tomorrow.

Mam asks him if he brought any money. He tells her times are hard, jobs are scarce, and she says, Is it coddin' me you are? There's a war on and there's nothing but jobs in England. You drank the money, didn't you?

You drank the money, Dad.

You drank the money, Dad.

You drank the money, Dad.

We're shouting so loud Alphie begins to cry. Dad says, Och, boys, now boys. Respect for your father.

He puts on his cap. He has to see a man. Mam says, Go see your man but don't come drunk to this house tonight singing Roddy McCorley or anything else.

He comes home drunk but he's quiet and passes out on the floor next to Mam's bed.

We have a Christmas dinner next day because of the food voucher Mam got from the St. Vincent de Paul Society. We have sheep's head, cabbage, floury white potatoes, and a bottle of cider because it's Christmas. Dad says he's not hungry, he'll have tea, borrows a cigarette from Mam. She says, Eat something. It's Christmas.

He tells her again he's not hungry but if no one else wants them he'll eat the sheep's eyes. He says there's great nourishment in the eye and we all make sounds of disgust. He washes them down with his tea and smokes the rest of his Woodbine. He puts on his cap and goes upstairs for his suitcase.

Mam says, Where are you going?

London.

On this day of Our Lord? Christmas Day?

It's the best day for travel. People in motor cars will always give the workingman a lift to Dublin. They think of the hard times of the Holy Family.

And how will you get on the boat to Holyhead without a penny in your pocket?

The way I came. There's always a time when they're not looking.

He kisses each of us on the forehead, tells us be good boys, obey

Mam, say our prayers. He tells Mam he'll write and she says, Oh, yes, the way you always did. He stands before her with his suitcase. She gets up, takes down the box of chocolates and hands them around. She puts a chocolate in her mouth and takes it out again because it's too hard and she can't chew it. I have a soft one and I offer it for the hard one, which will last longer. It's creamy and rich and there's a nut in the middle. Malachy and Michael complain they didn't get a nut and why is it Frank always gets the nut? Mam says, What do you mean, always? This is the first time we ever had a box of chocolates.

Malachy says, He got the raisin in the bun at school and all the boys said he gave it to Paddy Clohessy, so why couldn't he give us the nut?

Mam says, Because 'tis Christmas and he has sore eyes and the nut is good for the sore eyes.

Michael says, Will the nut make his eyes better?

'Twill.

Will it make one eye better or will it make two eyes better?

The two eyes, I think.

Malachy says, If I had another nut I'd give it to him for his eyes.

Mam says, I know you would.

Dad watches us a moment eating our chocolates. He lifts the latch, goes out the door and pulls it shut.

Mam tells Bridey Hannon, Days are bad but nights are worse and will this rain ever stop? She tries to ease the bad days by staying in bed and letting Malachy and me light the fire in the morning while she sits up in the bed passing Alphie bits of bread and holding the mug to his mouth for the tea that's in it. We have to go downstairs to Ireland to wash our faces in the basin under the tap and try to dry ourselves in the old damp shirt that hangs over the back of a chair. She makes us stand by the bed to see if we left rings of dirt around our necks and if we did it's back down to the tap and the damp shirt. When there's a hole in a pair of pants she sits up and patches it with any rag she can find. We wear short pants till we're thirteen or fourteen and our long stockings always have holes to be darned. If she has no wool for the darning and the stockings are dark we can blacken our ankles with shoe polish for the respectability that's in it. It's a terrible thing to walk the world with skin showing through the holes of our stockings. When we wear them week after week the holes grow so big we have to pull the stocking forward

271

under the toes so that the hole in the back is hidden in the shoe. On rainy days the stockings are soggy and we have to hang them before the fire at night and hope they'll dry by morning. Then they're hard with dirt cake and we're afraid to pull them on our feet for fear they'll fall on the floor in bits before our eyes. We might be lucky enough to get our stockings on but then we have to block the holes in our shoes and I fight with my brother, Malachy, over any scrap of cardboard or paper in the house. Michael is only six and he has to wait for anything left over unless Mam threatens us from the bed that we're to help our small brother. She says, If ye don't fix yeer brother's shoes an' I have to get out of this bed there will be wigs on the green. You'd have to feel sorry for Michael because he's too old to play with Alphie and too young to play with us and he can't fight with anyone for the same reasons.

The rest of the dressing is easy, the shirt I wore to bed is the shirt I wear to school. I wear it day in day out. It's the shirt for football, for climbing walls, for robbings orchards. I go to Mass and the Confraternity in that shirt and people sniff the air and move away. If Mam gets a docket for a new one at the St. Vincent de Paul the old shirt is promoted to towel and hangs damp on the chair for months or Mam might use bits of it to patch other shirts. She might even cut it up and let Alphie wear it a while before it winds up on the floor pushed against the bottom of the door to block the rain from the lane.

We go to school through lanes and back streets so that we won't meet the respectable boys who go to the Christian Brothers' School or the rich ones who go to the Jesuit school, Crescent College. The Christian Brothers' boys wear tweed jackets, warm woolen sweaters, shirts, ties and shiny new boots. We know they're the ones who will get jobs in the civil service and help the people who run the world. The Crescent College boys wear blazers and school scarves tossed around their necks and over their shoulders to show they're cock o' the walk. They have long hair which falls across their foreheads and over their eyes so that they can toss their quiffs like Englishmen. We know they're the ones who will go to university, take over the family business, run the government, run the world. We'll be the messenger boys on bicycles who deliver their groceries or we'll go to England to work on the building sites. Our sisters will mind their children and scrub their floors unless they go off to England, too. We know that. We're ashamed of the way we look and if boys from the rich schools pass remarks we'll get into a fight and wind up with bloody noses or torn clothes. Our masters will have no patience with us and our fights because their sons go to the rich schools and, Ye have no right to raise your hands to a better class of people so ye don't.

You never know when you might come home and find Mam sitting by the fire chatting with a woman and a child, strangers. Always a woman and child. Mam finds them wandering the streets and if they ask, Could you spare a few pennies, miss? her heart breaks. She never has money so she invites them home for tea and a bit of fried bread and if it's a bad night she'll let them sleep by the fire on a pile of rags in the corner. The bread she gives them always means less for us and if we complain she says there are always people worse off and we can surely spare a little from what we have.

Michael is just as bad. He brings home stray dogs and old men. You never know when you'll find a dog in the bed with him. There are dogs with sores, dogs with no ears, no tails. There's a blind greyhound he found in the park tormented by children. Michael fought off the children, picked up the greyhound that was bigger than himself and told Mam the dog could have his supper. Mam says, What supper? We're lucky if there's a cut of bread in the house. Michael tells her the dog can have his bread. Mam says that dog has to go tomorrow and Michael cries all night and cries worse in the morning when he finds the dog dead in the bed beside him. He won't go to school because he has to dig a grave outside where the stable was and he wants all of us to dig with him and say the rosary. Malachy says it's useless saying prayers for a dog, how do you know he was even a Catholic? Michael says, Of course he was a Catholic dog. Didn't I have him in my arms? He cries so hard over the dog Mam lets us all stay at home from school. We're so delighted we don't mind helping Michael with the grave and we say three Hail Marys. We're not going to stand there wasting a good day off from school saying the rosary for a dead greyhound. Michael is only six but when he brings old men home he manages to get the fire going and give them tea. Mam says it's driving her crazy to come home and find these old men drinking out of her favorite mug and mumbling and scratching by the fire. She tells Bridey Hannon that Michael has a habit of bringing home old men all a bit gone in the head and if he doesn't have a bit of bread for them he knocks on neighbors' doors and has no shame begging for it. In the end she tells Michael, No more old men. One of them left us with lice and we're plagued.

The lice are disgusting, worse than rats. They're in our heads and ears and they sit in the hollows of our collarbones. They dig into our skin. They get into the seams of our clothes and they're everywhere in the coats we use as blankets. We have to search every inch of Alphie's body because he's a baby and helpless.

The lice are worse than the fleas. Lice squat and suck and we can see our blood through their skins. Fleas jump and bite and they're clean and we prefer them. Things that jump are cleaner than things that squat.

We all agree there will be no more stray women and children, dogs and old men. We don't want any more diseases and infections.

Michael cries.

Grandma's next door neighbor, Mrs. Purcell, has the only wireless in her lane. The government gave it to her because she's old and blind. I want a radio. My grandmother is old but she's not blind and what's the use of having a grandmother who won't go blind and get a government radio?

Sunday nights I sit outside on the pavement under Mrs. Purcell's window listening to plays on the BBC and Radio Eireann, the Irish station. You can hear plays by O'Casey, Shaw, Ibsen and Shakespeare himself, the best of all, even if he is English. Shakespeare is like mashed potatoes, you can never get enough of him. And you can hear strange plays about Greeks plucking out their eyes because they married their mothers by mistake.

One night I'm sitting under Mrs. Purcell's window listening to *Macbeth*. Her daughter, Kathleen, sticks her head out the door. Come in, Frankie. My mother says you'll catch the consumption sitting on the ground in this weather.

Ah, no, Kathleen. It's all right.

No. Come in.

They give me tea and a grand cut of bread slathered with blackberry jam. Mrs. Purcell says, Do you like the Shakespeare, Frankie?

I love the Shakespeare, Mrs. Purcell.

Oh, he's music, Frankie, and he has the best stories in the world. I don't know what I'd do with meself of a Sunday night if I didn't have the Shakespeare.

When the play finishes she lets me fiddle with the knob on the radio and I roam the dial for distant sounds on the shortwave band, strange whispering and hissing, the whoosh of the ocean coming and going and the Morse Code dit dit dit dot. I hear mandolins, guitars, Spanish bagpipes, the drums of Africa, boatmen wailing on the Nile. I see sailors on watch sipping mugs of hot cocoa. I see cathedrals, skyscrapers, cottages. I see Bedouins in the Sahara and the French Foreign Legion, cowboys on the American prairie. I see goats skipping along the rocky coast of Greece where the shepherds are blind because they married their mothers by mistake. I see people chatting in cafés, sipping wine, strolling on boulevards and avenues. I see night women in doorways, monks chanting vespers, and here is the great boom of Big Ben, This is the BBC Overseas Service and here is the news.

Mrs. Purcell says, Leave that on, Frankie, so we'll know the state of the world.

After the news there is the American Armed Forces Network and it's lovely to hear the American voices easy and cool and here is the music, oh, man, the music of Duke Ellington himself telling me take the A train to where Billie Holiday sings only to me,

I can't give you anything but love, baby.
That's the only thing I've plenty of, baby.

Oh, Billie, Billie, I want to be in America with you and all that music, where no one has bad teeth, people leave food on their plates, every family has a lavatory, and everyone lives happily ever after.

And Mrs. Purcell says, Do you know what, Frankie?

What, Mrs. Purcell?

That Shakespeare is that good he must have been an Irishman.

The rent man is losing his patience. He tells Mam, Four weeks behind you are, missus. That's one pound two shillings. This has to stop for I have to go back to the office and report to Sir Vincent Nash that the McCourts are a month behind. Where am I then, missus? Out on my arse jobless and a mother to support that's ninety-two and a daily communicant in the Franciscan church. The rent man collects the rents, missus, or he loses the job. I'll be back next week and if you don't have the money, one pound eight shillings and sixpence total, 'tis out on the pavement you'll be with the skies dripping on your furniture.

Mam comes back up to Italy and sits by the fire wondering where in God's name she'll get the money for a week's rent never mind the arrears.

She'd love a cup of tea but there's no way of boiling the water till Malachy pulls a loose board off the wall between the two upstairs rooms. Mam says, Well, 'tis off now and we might as well chop it up for the fire. We boil the water and use the rest of the wood for the morning tea but what about tonight and tomorrow and ever after? Mam says, One more board from that wall, one more and not another one. She says that for two weeks till there's nothing left but the beam frame. She warns us we are not to touch the beams for they hold up the ceiling and the house itself.

Oh, we'd never touch the beams.

She goes to see Grandma and it's so cold in the house I take the hatchet to one of the beams. Malachy cheers me on and Michael claps his hands with excitement. I pull on the beam, the ceiling groans and down on Mam's bed there's a shower of plaster, slates, rain. Malachy says, Oh, God, we'll all be killed, and Michael dances around singing, Frankie broke the house, Frankie broke the house.

We run through the rain to tell Mam the news. She looks puzzled with Michael chanting, Frankie broke the house, till I explain there's a hole in the house and it's falling down. She says, Jesus, and runs through the streets with Grandma trying to keep up.

Mam sees her bed buried under plaster and slates and pulls at her hair, What'll we do at all, at all? and screams at me for interfering with the beams. Grandma says, I'll go to the landlord's office and tell them fix this before ye are all drowned entirely.

She's back in no time with the rent man. He says, Great God in heaven, where's the other room?

Grandma says, What room?

I rented ye two rooms up here and one is gone. Where is that room?

Mam says, What room?

There were two rooms up here and now there's one. And what happened to the wall? There was a wall. Now there's no wall. I distinctly remember a wall because I distinctly remember a room. Now where is that wall? Where is that room?

Grandma says, I don't remember a wall and if I don't remember a wall how can I remember a room?

Ye don't remember? Well, I remember. Forty years a landlord's agent and I never seen the likes of this. By God, 'tis a desperate situation altogether when you can't turn your back but tenants are not paying their rent and making walls and rooms disappear on top of it. I want to know where that wall is and what ye did with the room, so I do.

Mam turns to us. Do any of ye remember a wall?

Michael pulls at her hand. Is that the wall we burned in the fire?

The rent man says, Dear God in heaven, this beats Banagher, this takes the bloody biscuit, this is goin' beyond the beyonds. No rent and what am I to tell Sir Vincent below in the office? Out, missus, I'm puttin' ye out. One week from today I'll knock on this door and I want to find nobody at home, everybody out never to return. Do you have me, missus?

Mam's face is tight. 'Tis a pity you weren't alive in the times when the English were evicting us and leaving us on the side of the road.

No lip, missus, or I'll send the men to put ye out tomorrow.

He goes out the door and leaves it open to show what he thinks of us. Mam says, I don't know in God's name what I'm going to do. Grandma says, Well, I don't have room for ye but your cousin, Gerard Griffin, is living out the Rosbrien Road in that little house of his mother's and he'd surely be able to take ye in till better times come. 'Tis all hours of the night but I'll go up and see what he says and Frank can come with me.

She tells me put on a coat but I don't have one and she says, I suppose there's no use in asking if ye have an umbrella either. Come on.

She pulls the shawl over her head and I follow her out the door, up the lane, through the rain to Rosbrien Road nearly two miles away. She knocks on the door of a little cottage in a long row of little cottages. Are you there, Laman? I know you're in there. Open the door.

Grandma, why are you calling him Laman? Isn't his name Gerard?

How would I know? Do I know why the world calls your uncle Pat Ab? Everyone calls this fella Laman. Open the door. We'll go in. He might be working overtime.

She pushes the door. It's dark and there's a damp sweet smell in the room. This room looks like the kitchen and there's a smaller room next to it. There's a little loft above the bedroom with a skylight where the rain is beating. There are boxes everywhere, newspapers, magazines, bits of food, mugs, empty tins. We can see two beds taking up all the space in the bedroom, a great acre of a bed and a smaller one near the window. Grandma pokes at a lump in the big bed. Laman, is that you? Get up, will you, get up.

What? What? What? What?

There's trouble. Angela is gettin' evicted with the children an' 'tis delvin' out of the heavens. They need a bit of shelter till they get on their feet an' I have no room for them. You can put them up in the loft if you like but that wouldn't do because the small ones wouldn't be able to climb and they'd fall down an' get killed so you go up there an' they can move in here.

All right, all right, all right, all right.

He hoists himself from the bed and there's a whiskey smell. He goes to the kitchen and pulls the table to the wall for his climb to the loft. Grandma says, That's fine now. Ye can move up here tonight an' ye won't have the eviction men coming after ye.

Grandma tells Mam she's going home. She's tired and drenched and she's not twenty-five anymore. She says there's no need to be taking beds or furniture with all the stuff that's up in Laman Griffin's. We put Alphie in the pram and pile around him the pot, the pan, the kettle, the jam jars and mugs, the Pope, two bolsters and the coats from the beds. We drape the coats over our heads and push the pram through the streets. Mam tells us be quiet going up the lane or the neighbors will know we got the eviction and there will be shame. The pram has a bockety wheel which tilts it and makes it go in different directions. We try to keep it straight and we're having a great time because it must be after midnight and surely Mam won't make us go to school tomorrow. We're moving so far from Leamy's School now maybe we'll never have to go again. Once we get away from the lane Alphie bangs on the pot with the spoon and Michael sings a song he heard in a film with Al Jolson, Swanee, how I love ya, how I love ya, my dear ol' Swanee. He makes us laugh the way he tries to sing in a deep voice like Al Jolson.

Mam says she's glad it's late and there's no one on the streets to see our shame.

Once we get to the house we take Alphie and everything else from the pram so that Malachy and I can run back down to Roden Lane for the trunk. Mam says she'd die if she lost that trunk and everything in it.

Malachy and I sleep at opposite ends of the small bed. Mam takes the big bed with Alphie beside her and Michael at the bottom. Everything is damp and musty and Laman Griffin snores over our heads. There are no stairs in this house and that means no angel ever on the seventh step.

But I'm twelve going on thirteen and I might be too old for angels.

It's still dark when the alarm goes off in the morning and Laman Griffin snorts and blows his nose and hawks the stuff from his chest.

The floor creaks under him and when he pisses for ages into the chamber pot we have to stuff our mouths with coats to stop the laughing and Mam hisses at us to be quiet. He grumbles away above us before he climbs down to get his bicycle and bang his way out the door. Mam whispers, The coast is clear, go back to sleep. Ye can stay at home today.

We can't sleep. We're in a new house, we have to pee and we want to explore. The lavatory is outside, about ten steps from the back door, our own lavatory, with a door you can close and a proper seat where you can sit and read squares of the *Limerick Leader* Laman Griffin left behind for wiping himself. There is a long backyard, a garden with tall grass and weeds, an old bicycle that must have belonged to a giant, tin cans galore, old papers and magazines rotting into the earth, a rusted sewing machine, a dead cat with a rope around his neck that somebody must have thrown over the fence.

Michael gets a notion in his head that this is Africa and keeps asking, Where's Tarzan? Where's Tarzan? He runs up and down the backyard with no pants on trying to imitate Tarzan yodeling from tree to tree. Malachy looks over the fences into the other yards and tells us, They have gardens. They're growing things. We can grow things. We can have our own spuds and everything.

Mam calls from the back door, See if ye can find anything to start the fire in here.

There's a wooden shed built against the back of the house. It's collapsing and surely we could use some of the wood for the fire. Mam is disgusted with the wood we bring in. She says it's rotten and full of white maggots but beggars can't be choosers. The wood sizzles above the burning paper and we watch the white maggots try to escape. Michael says he feels sorry for the white maggots but we know he's sorry for everything in the world.

Mam tells us this house used to be a shop, that Laman Griffin's mother sold groceries through the little window and that's how she was able to send Laman away to Rockwell College so that he could wind up as an officer in the Royal Navy. Oh, he was, indeed. An officer in the Royal Navy, and here's a picture of him with other officers all having dinner with a famous American film star Jean Harlow. He was never the same after he met Jean Harlow. He fell madly in love with her but what was the use? She was Jean Harlow and he was nothing but an officer in the Royal Navy and it drove him to drink and they threw him out of the Navy. Now look at him, a common laborer for the Electricity Supply Board and a house that's a disgrace. You'd look at this house and never know there was a human being living in it. You can see Laman never moved a thing since his mother died and now we have to clean up so that we can live in this place.

There are boxes packed with bottles of purple hair oil. While Mam is out in the lavatory we open a bottle and smear it on our heads. Malachy says the smell is gorgeous but when Mam comes back she says, What's that horrible stink? and wants to know why our heads are suddenly greasy. She makes us stick our heads under the tap outside and dry ourselves with an old towel pulled out from under a pile of magazines called *The Illustrated London News* so old they have pictures of Queen Victoria and Prince Edward waving. There are bars of Pear's soap and a thick book called *Pear's Encyclopedia,* which keeps me up day and night because it tells you everything about everything and that's all I want to know.

There are bottles of Sloan's Liniment, which Mam says will come in handy when we get cramps and pains from the damp. The bottles say, Here's the pain, Where's the Sloan's? There are boxes of safety pins and bags packed with women's hats that crumble when you touch them. There are bags with corsets, garters, women's high button shoes and different laxatives that promise glowing cheeks, bright eyes and a curl in your hair. There are letters from General Eoin O'Duffy to Gerard Griffin, Esq., saying welcome to the ranks of the National Front, the Irish Blueshirts, that it is a privilege to know a man like Gerard Griffin is interested in the movement with his excellent education, his Royal Navy training, his reputation as a great rugby player on the Young Munster team that won the national championship, the Bateman Cup. General O'Duffy is forming an Irish Brigade that will soon sail off to Spain to fight with that great Catholic Generalissimo Franco himself, and Mr. Griffin would be a powerful addition to the Brigade.

Mam says Laman's mother wouldn't let him go. She didn't spend all those years slaving away in a little shop to send him to college so that he could go gallivanting off to Spain for Franco so he stayed at home and got that job digging holes for the poles of the Electricity Supply Board along country roads and his mother was happy to have him home to herself every night but Friday when he drank his pint and moaned over Jean Harlow.

Mam is happy we'll have loads of paper for lighting the fire though the wood we burn from that collapsing shed leaves a sickening smell and she worries the white maggots will escape and breed.

We work all day moving boxes and bags to the shed outside. Mam opens all the windows to air the house and let out the smell of the hair oil and the years of no air. She says it's a relief to be able to see the floor again and now we can sit down and have a nice cup of tea in peace, ease and comfort, and won't it be lovely when the warm weather comes and we might be able to have a garden and sit outside with our tea the way the English do.

Laman Griffin comes home at six every night but Friday, has his tea and goes to bed till next morning. Saturdays he goes to bed at one in the afternoon and stays there till Monday morning. He pulls the kitchen table over to the wall under the loft, climbs up on a chair, pulls the chair up to the table, climbs up on the chair again, catches a leg of the bed, pulls himself up. If he's too drunk on Fridays he makes me climb up for his pillow and blankets and sleeps on the kitchen floor by the fire or falls into bed with me and my brothers and snores and farts all night.

When we first moved in he complained over how he gave up his room downstairs for the loft and he's worn out climbing up and down to go to the lavatory in the backyard. He calls down, Bring the table, the chair, I'm coming down, and we have to clear off the table and pull it to the wall. He's fed up, he's finished with the climbing, he's going to use his mother's lovely chamber pot. He lies in bed all day reading books from the library, smoking Gold Flake cigarettes and throwing Mam a few shillings to send one of us to the shop so that he can have scones with his tea or a nice bit of ham and sliced tomato. Then he calls to Mam, Angela, this chamber pot is full, and she drags chair and table to climb for the chamber pot, empty it in the lavatory outside, rinse it and climb back to the loft. Her face gets tight and she says, Is there anything else your lordship would like this day? and he laughs, Woman's work, Angela, woman's work and free rent.

Laman throws down his library card from the loft and tells me get him two books, one on angling, one on gardening. He writes a note to the librarian to say his legs are killing him from digging holes for the Electricity Supply Board and from now on Frank McCourt will be getting his books. He knows the boy is only thirteen going on fourteen and he knows the rules are strict about allowing children into the adult part of the library but the boy will wash his hands and behave himself and do what he's told, thank you.

The librarian reads the note and says 'tis an awful pity about Mr. Griffin, he's a true gentleman and a man of great learning, you wouldn't believe the books he reads, sometimes four a week, that one day he took home a book in French, French, if you don't mind, on the history of the rudder, the rudder, if you don't mind, she'd give anything for a look inside his head for it must be packed with all sorts of learning, packed, if you don't mind.

She picks out a gorgeous book with colored pictures about English gardens. She says, I know what he likes in the fishing department, and chooses a book called *In Search of the Irish Salmon* by Brigadier General Hugh Colton. Oh, says the librarian, he reads hundreds of books about English officers fishing in Ireland. I've read some myself out of pure curiosity and you can see why those officers are glad to be in Ireland after all they put up with in India and Africa and other desperate places. At least the people here are polite. We're known for that, the politeness, not running around throwing spears at people.

Laman lies in the bed, reads his books, talks down from the loft about the day his legs will heal and he'll be out there in the back planting a garden which will be famous far and wide for color and beauty and when he's not gardening he'll be roaming the rivers around Limerick and bringing home salmon that will make your mouth water. His mother left a recipe for salmon that's a family secret and if he had the time and his legs weren't killing him he'd find it someplace in this house. He says now that I'm reliable I can get a book for myself every week but don't be bringing home filth. I want to know what the filth is but he won't tell me so I'll have to find out for myself.

Mam says she wants to join the library too but it's a long walk from Laman's house, two miles, and would I mind getting her a book every week, a romance by Charlotte M. Brame or any other nice writer. She doesn't want any books about English officers looking for salmon or books about people shooting each other. There's enough trouble in the world without reading about people bothering fish and each other.

Grandma caught a chill the night we had the trouble in the house in Roden Lane and the chill turned into pneumonia. They shifted her to the City Home Hospital and now she's dead.

Her oldest son, my uncle Tom, thought he'd go to England to work like other men in the lanes of Limerick but his consumption got worse and he came back to Limerick and now he's dead.

His wife, Galway Jane, followed him, and four of their six children had to be put into orphanages. The oldest boy, Gerry, ran away and joined the Irish army, deserted and crossed to the English army. The oldest girl, Peggy, went to Aunt Aggie and lives in misery.

The Irish army is looking for boys who are musical and would like to train in the Army School of Music. They accept my brother, Malachy, and he goes off to Dublin to be a soldier and play the trumpet.

Now I have only two brothers at home and Mam says her family is disappearing before her very eyes.

XIII

Boys from my class at Leamy's School are going on a weekend cycling trip to Killaloe. They tell me I should borrow a bicycle and come. All I need is a blanket, a few spoons of tea and sugar and a few cuts of bread to keep me going. I'll learn to cycle on Laman Griffin's bicycle every night after he goes to bed and he'll surely let me borrow it for the two days in Killaloe.

The best time to ask him for anything is Friday night when he's in a good mood after his night of drinking and his dinner. He brings home the same dinner in his overcoat pockets, a big steak dripping blood, four potatoes, an onion, a bottle of stout. Mam boils the potatoes and fries the steak with sliced onion. He keeps his overcoat on, sits at the table and eats the steak out of his hands. The grease and blood roll down his chin and on to the overcoat where he wipes his hands. He drinks his stout and laughs that there's nothing like a great bloody steak of a Friday night and if that's the worst sin he ever commits he'll float to heaven body and soul, ha ha ha.

Of course you can have my bike, he says. Boy should be able to get out and see the countryside. Of course. But you have to earn it. You can't be getting something for nothing, isn't that right?

'Tis.

And I have a job for you. You don't mind doing a bit of a job, do you?

I don't.

And you'd like to help your mother?

I would.

Well, now, that very chamber pot is full since this morning. I want you to climb up and get it and take it to the lavatory and rinse it under the tap abroad and climb back up with it.

I don't want to empty his chamber pot but I dream of cycling miles on the road to Killaloe, fields and sky far from this house, a swim in the Shannon, a night sleeping in a barn. I pull the table and chair to the wall. I climb up and under the bed there's the plain white chamber pot streaked brown and yellow, brimming with piss and shit. I lay it gently at the edge of the loft so that it won't spill, climb down to the chair, reach for the chamber pot, bring it down, turn my face away, hold it while I step down to the table, place it on the chair, step to the floor, take the chamber pot to the lavatory, empty it, and get sick behind the lavatory till I get used to this job.

Laman says I'm a good boy and the bike is mine anytime I want it as long as the chamber pot is empty and I'm there to run to the shop for his cigarettes, go to the library for books and do whatever else he wants. He says, You have a great way with a chamber pot. He laughs and Mam stares into the dead ashes in the fireplace.

It's raining so hard one day, Miss O'Riordan the librarian says, Don't go out in that or you'll ruin the books you're carrying. Sit down over there and behave yourself. You can read all about the saints while you're waiting.

There are four big books, *Butler's Lives of the Saints.* I don't want to spend my life reading about saints but when I start I wish the rain would last forever. Whenever you see pictures of saints, men or women, they're always looking up to heaven where there are clouds filled with little fat angels carrying flowers or harps giving praise. Uncle Pa Keating says he can't think of a single saint in heaven he'd want to sit down and have a pint with. The saints in these books are different. There are stories about virgins, martyrs, virgin martyrs and they're worse than any horror film at the Lyric Cinema.

I have to look in the dictionary to find out what a virgin is. I know the Mother of God is the Virgin Mary and they call her that because she didn't have a proper husband, only poor old St. Joseph. In the *Lives of the Saints* the virgins are always getting into trouble and I don't know why. The dictionary says, Virgin, woman (usually a young woman) who is and remains in a state of inviolate chastity.

Now I have to look up inviolate and chastity and all I can find here is that inviolate means not violated and chastity means chaste and that means pure from unlawful sexual intercourse. Now I have to look up intercourse and that leads to intromission, which leads to intromittent, the copulatory organ of any male animal. Copulatory leads to copulation, the union of the sexes in the art of generation and I don't know what that means and I'm too weary going from one word to another in this heavy dictionary which leads me on a wild goose chase from this word to that word and all because the people who wrote the dictionary don't want the likes of me to know anything.

All I want to know is where I came from but if you ask anyone they tell you ask someone else or send you from word to word.

All these virgin martyrs are told by Roman judges they have to give up their faith and accept the Roman gods but they say, Nay, and the judges have them tortured and killed. My favorite is St. Christina the Astonishing who takes ages to die. The judge says, Cut off her breast, and when they do she throws it at him and he goes deaf dumb and blind. Another judge is brought on the case and he says, Cut off the other breast, and the same thing happens. They try to kill her with arrows but they just bounce off her and kill the soldiers who shot them. They try to boil her in oil but she rocks in the vat and takes a nap for herself. Then the judges get fed up and have her head cut off and that does the job. The feast of St. Christina the Astonishing is the twenty-fourth of July and I think I'll keep that for myself along with the feast of St. Francis of Assisi on the fourth of October.

The librarian says, You have to go home now, the rain is stopped, and when I'm going out the door she calls me back. She wants to write a note to my mother and she doesn't mind one bit if I read it. The note says, Dear Mrs. McCourt, Just when you think Ireland is gone to the dogs altogether you find a boy sitting in the library so absorbed in the *Lives of the Saints* he doesn't realize the rain has stopped and you have to drag him away from the aforesaid *Lives*. I think, Mrs. McCourt, you might have a future priest on your hands and I will light a candle in hopes it comes true. I remain, Yours truly, Catherine O'Riordan, Asst. Librarian.

· · ·

Hoppy O'Halloran is the only master in Leamy's National School who ever sits. That's because he's the headmaster or because he has to rest himself from the twisting walk that comes from the short leg. The other masters walk back and forth in the front of the room or up and down the aisles and you never know when you'll get a whack of a cane or a slap of a strap for giving the wrong answer or writing something sloppy. If Hoppy wants to do anything to you he calls you to the front of the room to punish you before three classes.

There are good days when he sits at the desk and talks about America. He says, My boys, from the frozen wastes of North Dakota to the fragrant orange groves of Florida, Americans enjoy all climates. He talks about American history, If the American farmer, with flintlock and musket, could wrest from the English a continent, surely we, warriors ever, can recover our island.

If we don't want him tormenting us with algebra or Irish grammar all we have to do is ask him a question about America and that gets him so excited he might go on for the whole day.

He sits at his desk and recites the tribes and chiefs he loves. Arapaho, Cheyenne, Chippewa, Sioux, Apache, Iroquois. Poetry, my boys, poetry. And listen to the chiefs, Kicking Bear, Rain-in-the-Face, Sitting Bull, Crazy Horse, and the genius, Geronimo.

In seventh class he hands out a small book, a poem that goes on for pages and pages, *The Deserted Village*, by Oliver Goldsmith. He says that this seems to be a poem about England but it is a lament for the poet's native land, our own native land, Ireland. We are to get this poem by heart, twenty lines a night to be recited every morning. Six boys are called to the front of the room for reciting and if you miss a line you are slapped twice on each hand. He tells us put the books under the desks and the whole class chants the passage on the schoolmaster in the village.

> *Beside yon straggling fence that skirts the way,*
> *With blossomed furze unprofitably gay,*
> *There, in his noisy mansion, skilled to rule*
> *The village master taught his little school.*
> *A man severe he was and stern to view,*
> *I knew him well, and every truant knew.*
> *Full well the boding tremblers learned to trace*
> *The day's disaster in his morning face.*

> *Full well they laughed with counterfeited glee*
> *At all his jokes for many a joke had he.*
> *Full well the busy whisper circling round*
> *Conveyed the dismal tidings when he frowned.*

He always closes his eyes and smiles when we reach the last lines of the passage,

> *Yet he was kind, or, if severe in aught,*
> *The love he bore to learning was in fault.*
> *The village all declared how much he knew.*
> *'Twas certain he could write, and cipher too.*
> *Lands he could measure, terms and tides presage,*
> *And even the story ran that he could gauge.*
> *In arguing, too, the parson owned his skill,*
> *For, even though vanquished, he could argue still,*
> *While words of learned length and thundering sound*
> *Amazed the gazing rustics ranged around.*
> *And still they gazed, and still the wonder grew,*
> *That one small head could carry all he knew.*

We know he loves these lines because they're about a schoolmaster, about him, and he's right because we wonder how one small head could carry all he knows and we will remember him in these lines. He says, Ah, boys, boys, You can make up your own minds but first stock them. Are you listening to me? Stock your minds and you can move through the world resplendent. Clarke, define resplendent.

I think it's shining, sir.

Pithy, Clarke, but adequate. McCourt, give us a sentence with pithy.

Clarke is pithy but adequate, sir.

Adroit, McCourt. You have a mind for the priesthood, my boy, or politics. Think of that.

I will, sir.

Tell your mother come and see me.

I will, sir.

Mam says, No, I could never go near Mr. O'Halloran. I don't have a decent dress or a proper coat. What does he want to see me for?

I don't know.

Well, ask him.

I can't. He'll kill me. If he says bring your mother you have to bring your mother or out comes the stick.

She comes to see him and he talks to her in the hallway. He tells her that her son Frank must continue school. He must not fall into the messenger boy trap. That leads nowhere. Take him up to the Christian Brothers, tell them I sent you, tell them he is a bright boy and ought to be going to secondary school and beyond that, university.

He tells her he did not become headmaster of Leamy's National School to preside over an academy of messenger boys.

Mam says, Thank you, Mr. O'Halloran.

I wish Mr. O'Halloran would mind his own business. I don't want to go to the Christian Brothers. I want to quit school forever and get a job, get my wages every Friday, go to the pictures on Saturday nights like everyone.

A few days later Mam tells me give my face and hands a good wash, we're going to the Christian Brothers. I tell her I don't want to go, I want to work, I want to be a man. She tells me stop the whining, I'm going to secondary school and we'll all manage somehow. I'm going to school if she has to scrub floors and she'll practice on my face.

She knocks on the door at the Christian Brothers and says she wants to see the superior, Brother Murray. He comes to the door, looks at my mother and me and says, What?

Mam says, This is my son, Frank. Mr. O'Halloran at Leamy's says he's bright and would there be any chance of getting him in here for secondary school?

We don't have room for him, says Brother Murray and closes the door in our faces.

Mam turns away from the door and it's a long silent walk home. She takes off her coat, makes tea, sits by the fire. Listen to me, she says. Are you listening?

I am.

That's the second time a door was slammed in your face by the Church.

Is it? I don't remember.

Stephen Carey told you and your father you couldn't be an altar boy and closed the door in your face. Do you remember that?

I do.

And now Brother Murray slams the door in your face.

I don't mind. I want to get a job.

Her face tightens and she's angry. You are never to let anybody slam the door in your face again. Do you hear me?

She starts to cry by the fire, Oh, God, I didn't bring ye into the world to be a family of messenger boys.

I don't know what to do or say, I'm so relieved I don't have to stay in school for five or six more years.

I'm free.

I'm thirteen going on fourteen and it's June, the last month of school forever. Mam takes me to see the priest, Dr. Cowpar, about getting a job as telegram boy. The supervisor in the post office, Mrs. O'Connell, says, Do you know how to cycle, and I lie that I do. She says I can't start till I'm fourteen so come back in August.

Mr. O'Halloran tells the class it's a disgrace that boys like McCourt, Clarke, Kennedy, have to hew wood and draw water. He is disgusted by this free and independent Ireland that keeps a class system foisted on us by the English, that we are throwing our talented children on the dungheap.

You must get out of this country, boys. Go to America, McCourt. Do you hear me?

I do, sir.

Priests come to the school to recruit us for the foreign missions, Redemptorists, Franciscans, Holy Ghost Fathers, all converting the distant heathen. I ignore them. I'm going to America till one priest catches my attention. He says he comes from the order of the White Fathers, missionaries to the nomadic Bedouin tribes and chaplains to the French Foreign Legion.

I ask for the application.

I will need a letter from the parish priest and a physical examination by my family doctor. The parish priest writes the letter on the spot. He would have been glad to see me go last year. The doctor says, What's this?

That's an application to join the White Fathers, missionaries to the nomadic tribes of the Sahara and chaplains to the French Foreign Legion.

Oh, yeh? French Foreign Legion, is it? Do you know the preferred form of transportation in the Sahara Desert?

Trains?

No. It's the camel. Do you know what a camel is?

It has a hump.

It has more than a hump. It has a nasty, mean disposition and its teeth are green with gangrene and it bites. Do you know where it bites?

In the Sahara?

No, you omadhaun. It bites your shoulder, rips it right off. Leaves you standing there tilted in the Sahara. How would you like that, eh? And what class of a spectacle you'd be strolling down the street, lopsided in Limerick. What girl in her right mind will look at an ex-White Father with one miserable scrawny shoulder? And look at your eyes. They're bad enough here in Limerick. In the Sahara they'll fester and rot and fall out of your head. How old are you?

Thirteen.

Go home to your mother.

It's not our house and we don't feel free in it the way we did in Roden Lane, up in Italy or down in Ireland. When Laman comes home he wants to read in his bed or sleep and we have to be quiet. We stay in the streets till after dark and when we come inside there's nothing to do but go to bed and read a book if we have a candle or paraffin oil for the lamp.

Mam tells us go to bed, she'll be after us in a minute as soon as she climbs to the loft with Laman's last mug of tea. We often fall asleep before she goes up but there are nights we hear them talking, grunting, moaning. There are nights when she never comes down and Michael and Alphie have the big bed to themselves. Malachy says she stays up there because it's too hard for her to climb down in the dark.

He's only twelve and he doesn't understand.

I'm thirteen and I think they're at the excitement up there.

I know about the excitement and I know it's a sin but how can it be a sin if it comes to me in a dream where American girls pose in swimming suits on the screen at the Lyric Cinema and I wake up pushing and pumping? It's a sin when you're wide awake and going at yourself the way the boys talked about it in Leamy's schoolyard after Mr. O'Dea roared the Sixth Commandment at us, Thou Shalt Not Commit Adultery, which means impure thoughts, impure words, impure deeds, and that's what adultery is, Dirty Things in General.

One Redemptorist priest barks at us all the time about the Sixth Commandment. He says impurity is so grave a sin the Virgin Mary turns her face away and weeps.

And why does she weep, boys? She weeps because of you and what you are doing to her Beloved Son. She weeps when she looks down the long dreary vista of time and beholds in horror the spectacle of Limerick boys defiling themselves, polluting themselves, interfering with themselves, abusing themselves, soiling their young bodies, which are the temples of the Holy Ghost. Our Lady weeps over these abominations knowing that every time you interfere with yourself you nail to the cross her Beloved Son, that once more you hammer into His dear head the crown of thorns, that you reopen those ghastly wounds. In an agony of thirst He hangs on the cross and what is He offered by those perfidious Romans? A lavatory sponge plunged into vinegar and gall and thrust into His poor mouth, a mouth that moves rarely except to pray, to pray even for you, boys, even for you who nailed Him to that cross. Consider Our Lord's suffering. Consider the crown of thorns. Consider a small pin driven into your skull, the agony of the piercing. Consider then twenty thorns driven into your head. Reflect, meditate on the nails tearing His hands, His feet. Could you endure a fraction of that agony? Take that pin again, that mere pin. Force it into your side. Enlarge that sensation a hundredfold and you are penetrated by that awful lance. Oh, boys, the devil wants your souls. He wants you with him in hell and know this, that every time you interfere with yourself, every time you succumb to the vile sin of self-abuse you not only nail Christ to the cross you take another step closer to hell itself. Retreat from the abyss, boys. Resist the devil and keep your hands to yourself.

I can't stop interfering with myself. I pray to the Virgin Mary and tell her I'm sorry I put her Son back on the cross and I'll never do it again but I can't help myself and swear I'll go to confession and after that, surely after that, I'll never never do it again. I don't want to go to hell with devils chasing me for eternity jabbing me with hot pitchforks.

The priests of Limerick have no patience with the likes of me. I go to confession and they hiss that I'm not in a proper spirit of repentance, that if I were I'd give up this hideous sin. I go from church to church looking for an easy priest till Paddy Clohessy tells me there's one in the Dominican church who's ninety years old and deaf as a turnip. Every few weeks the old priest hears my confession and mumbles that I should pray for him. Sometimes he falls asleep and I don't have the heart to wake him up so I go to Communion the next day without penance or absolution. It's not my fault if priests fall asleep on me and surely I'm in a state of grace just for going to confession. Then one day the little panel in the confession box slides back and it's not my man at all, it's a young priest with a big ear like a seashell. He'll surely hear everything.

Bless me, Father, for I have sinned, it's a fortnight since my last confession.

And what have you done since then, my child?

I hit my brother, I went on the mooch from school, I lied to my mother.

Yes, my child, and what else?

I— I— I did dirty things, Father.

Ah, my child, was that with yourself or with another or with some class of beast?

Some class of beast. I never heard of a sin like that before. This priest must be from the country and if he is he's opening up new worlds to me.

The night before I'm to go to Killaloe Laman Griffin comes home drunk and eats a great bag of fish and chips at the table. He tells Mam boil water for tea and when she says she has no coal or turf he yells at her and calls her a great lump living free under his roof with her pack of brats. He throws money at me to go to the shop for a few sods of turf and wood for kindling. I don't want to go. I want to hit him for the way he treats my mother but if I say anything he won't let me have the bicycle tomorrow after I've waited three weeks.

When Mam gets the fire going and boils the water I remind him of his promise to loan me the bike.

Did you empty the chamber pot today?

Oh, I forgot. I'll do it this minute.

He shouts, You didn't empty my damn chamber pot. I promise you the bike. I give you tuppence a week to run messages for me and empty the chamber pot and you stand there with your thick gob hanging out and tell me you didn't do it.

I'm sorry. I forgot. I'll do it now.

You will, will you? And how do you think you'll get up to the loft? Are you going to pull the table out from under my fish and chips?

Mam says, Sure, he was at school all day and he had to go to the doctor for his eyes.

Well, you can bloody well forget about the bicycle. You didn't live up to the bargain.

But he couldn't do it, says Mam.

He tells her shut up and mind her own business and she goes quiet by the fire. He goes back to his fish and chips but I tell him again, You promised me. I emptied that chamber pot and did your messages for three weeks.

Shut up and go to bed.

You can't tell me go to bed. You're not my father, and you promised me.

I'm telling you, as sure as God made little apples, that if I get up from this table you'll be calling for your patron saint.

You promised me.

He pushes the chair back from the table. He stumbles toward me and sticks his finger between my eyes. I'm telling you shut your gob, scabby eyes.

I won't. You promised me.

He punches my shoulders and when I won't stop moves to my head. My mother jumps up, crying, and tries to pull him away. He punches and kicks me into the bedroom but I keep saying, You promised me. He knocks me to my mother's bed and punches till I cover my face and head with my arms.

I'll kill you, you little shit.

Mam is screaming and pulling at him till he falls backward into the kitchen. She says, Come on, oh, come on. Eat your fish and chips. He's only a child. He'll get over it.

I hear him go back to his chair and pull it to the table. I hear him snuffle and slurp when he eats and drinks. Hand me the matches, he says. By Jesus, I need a fag after that. There's a put-put sound when he puffs on the cigarette and a whimper from my mother.

He says, I'm going to bed, and with the drink in him it takes him a while to climb the chair to the table, pull up the chair, climb to the loft. The bed squeaks under him and he grunts when he pulls off his boots and drops them to the floor.

I can hear Mam crying when she blows into the globe of the paraffin oil lamp and everything goes dark. After what happened she'll surely want to get into her own bed and I'm ready to go to the small one against the wall. Instead, there's the sound of her climbing the chair, the table, the chair, crying up into the loft and telling Laman Griffin, He's only a boy, tormented with his eyes, and when Laman says, He's a little shit and I want him out of the house, she cries and begs till there's whispering and grunting and moaning and nothing.

In awhile they're snoring in the loft and my brothers are asleep around me. I can't stay in this house for if Laman Griffin comes at me again I'll take a knife to his neck. I don't know what to do or where to go.

I leave the house and follow the streets from the Sarsfield Barracks to the Monument Café. I dream of how I'll get back at Laman some day. I'll go to America and see Joe Louis. I'll tell him my troubles and he'll understand because he comes from a poor family. He'll show me how to build up my muscles, how to hold my hands and use my feet. He'll show me how to dig my chin into my shoulder the way he does and how to let go with a right uppercut that will send Laman flying. I'll drag Laman to the graveyard at Mungret where his family and Mam's family are buried and I'll cover him with earth all the way to his chin so that he won't be able to move and he'll beg for his life and I'll say, End of the road, Laman, you're going to meet your Maker, and he'll beg and beg while I trickle dirt on his face till it's covered completely and he's gasping and asking God for forgiveness for not giving me the bike and punching me all over the house and doing the excitement with my mother and I'll be laughing away because he's not in a state of grace after the excitement and he's going to hell as sure as God made little apples as he used to say himself.

The streets are dark and I have to keep an eye out in case I might be lucky like Malachy long ago and find fish and chips dropped by drunken soldiers. There's nothing on the ground. If I find my uncle, Ab Sheehan, he might give me some of his Friday night fish and chips, but they tell me in the café he came and went already. I'm thirteen now so I don't call him Uncle Pat anymore. I call him Ab or The Abbot like everybody else. Surely if I go to Grandma's house he'll give me a piece of bread or something and maybe he'll let me stay the night. I can tell him I'll be working in a few weeks delivering telegrams and getting big tips at the post office and ready to pay my own way.

He's sitting up in bed finishing his fish and chips, dropping to the floor the *Limerick Leader* they were wrapped in, wiping his mouth and hands with the blanket. He looks at me, That face is all swole. Did you fall on that face?

I tell him I did because there's no use telling him anything else. He wouldn't understand. He says, You can stay in me mother's bed tonight. You can't walk the streets with that face and them two red eyes in your head.

He says there's no food in the house, not a scrap of bread, and when he falls asleep I take the greasy newspaper from the floor. I lick the front page, which is all advertisements for films and dances in the city. I lick the headlines. I lick the great attacks of Patton and Montgomery in France and Germany. I lick the war in the Pacific. I lick the obituaries and the sad memorial poems, the sports pages, the market prices of eggs butter and bacon. I suck the paper till there isn't a smidgen of grease.

I wonder what I'll do tomorrow.

XIV

In the morning The Abbot gives me the money to go to Kathleen O'Connell's for bread, margarine, tea, milk. He boils water on the gas ring and tells me I can have a mug of tea and, Go aisy with the sugar, I'm not a millionaire. You can have a cut o' bread but don't make it too thick.

It's July and school is over forever. In a few weeks I'll be delivering telegrams at the post office, working like a man. In the weeks I'm idle I can do anything I like, get up in the morning, stay in bed, take long walks out the country like my father, wander around Limerick. If I had the money I'd go over to the Lyric Cinema, eat sweets, see Errol Flynn conquering everyone in sight. I can read the English and Irish papers The Abbot brings home or I can use the library cards of Laman Griffin and my mother till I'm found out.

Mam sends Michael with a milk bottle of warm tea, a few cuts of bread smeared with dripping, a note to say Laman Griffin isn't angry anymore and I can come back. Michael says, Are you coming home, Frankie?

No.

Ah, do, Frankie. Come on.

I live here now. I'm never going back.

But Malachy is gone to the army and you're here and I have no big brother. All the boys have big brothers and I only have Alphie. He's not even four and can't talk right.

I can't go back. I'm never going back. You can come here any time you like.

His eyes glint with tears and that gives me such a pain in my heart I want to say, All right, I'll come with you. I'm only saying that. I know I'll never be able to face Laman Griffin again and I don't know if I can look at my mother. I watch Michael go up the lane with the sole of his shoe broken and clacking along the pavement. When I start that job at the post office I'll buy him shoes so I will. I'll give him an egg and take him to the Lyric Cinema for the film and the sweets and then we'll go to Naughton's and eat fish and chips till our bellies are sticking out a mile. I'll get money some day for a house or a flat with electric light and a lavatory and beds with sheets blankets pillows like the rest of the world. We'll have breakfast in a bright kitchen with flowers dancing in a garden beyond, delicate cups and saucers, eggcups, eggs soft in the yolk and ready to melt the rich creamery butter, a teapot with a cozy on it, toast with butter and marmalade galore. We'll take our time and listen to music from the BBC or the American Armed Forces Network. I'll buy proper clothes for the whole family so our arses won't be hanging out of our pants and we won't have the shame. The thought of the shame brings a pain in my heart and starts me sniffling. The Abbot says, What's up with you? Didn't you have your bread? Didn't you have your tay? What more do you want? 'Tis an egg you'll be lookin' for next.

There's no use talking to someone who was dropped on his head and sells papers for a living.

He complains he can't be feeding me forever and I'll have to get my own bread and tea. He doesn't want to come home and find me reading in the kitchen with the electric lightbulb blazing away. He can read numbers so he can and when he goes out to sell papers he reads the electric meter so he'll know how much I used and if I don't stop turning on that light he'll take the fuse out and carry it in his pocket and if I put another fuse in he'll have the electricity pulled out altogether and go back to gas, which was good enough for his poor dead mother and will surely suit him for all he does is sit up in the bed to eat his fish and chips and count his money before he goes to sleep.

I get up early like Dad and go on long walks into the country. I walk around the graveyard in the old abbey at Mungret where my mother's relations are buried and I go up the boreen to the Norman castle at Carrigogunnell where Dad brought me twice. I climb to the top and Ireland is spread out before me, the Shannon shining its way to the

Atlantic. Dad told me this castle was built hundreds of years ago and if you wait for the larks to stop their singing over there you can hear the Normans below hammering and talking and getting ready for battle. Once he brought me here in the dark so that we could hear Norman and Irish voices down through the centuries and I heard them. I did.

Sometimes I'm up there alone on the heights of Carrigogunnell and there are voices of Norman girls from olden times laughing and singing in French and when I see them in my mind I'm tempted and I climb to the very top of the castle where once there was a tower and there in full view of Ireland I interfere with myself and spurt all over Carrigogunnell and fields beyond.

That's a sin I could never tell a priest. Climbing to great heights and going at yourself before all of Ireland is surely worse than doing it in a private place with yourself or with another or with some class of a beast. Somewhere down there in the fields or along the banks of the Shannon a boy or a milkmaid might have looked up and seen me in my sin and if they did I'm doomed because the priests are always saying that anyone who exposes a child to sin will have a millstone tied around his neck and be cast into the sea.

Still, the thought of someone watching me brings on the excitement again. I wouldn't want a small boy to be watching me. No, no, that would surely lead to the millstone, but if there was a milkmaid gawking up she'd surely get excited and go at herself though I don't know if girls can go at themselves when they don't have anything to go at. No equipment, as Mikey Molloy used to say.

I wish that old deaf Dominican priest would come back so that I could tell him my troubles with the excitement but he's dead now and I'll have to face a priest who'll go on about the millstone and the doom.

Doom. That's the favorite word of every priest in Limerick.

I walk back along O'Connell Avenue and Ballinacurra where people have their bread and milk delivered early to their doorsteps and surely there's no harm if I borrow a loaf or a bottle with every intention of giving it back when I get my job at the post office. I'm not stealing, I'm borrowing, and that's not a mortal sin. Besides, I stood on top of a castle this morning and committed a sin far worse than stealing bread and milk and if you commit one sin you might as well commit a few more because you get the same sentence in hell. One sin, eternity. A dozen sins, eternity.

Might as well be hung for a sheep as a lamb, as my mother would say. I drink the odd pint of milk and leave the bottle so that the milk-man won't be blamed for not delivering. I like milkmen because one of them gave me two broken eggs which I swallowed raw with bits of shells and all. He said I'd grow up powerful if I had nothing else but two eggs in a pint of porter every day. Everything you need is in the egg and everything you want is in the pint.

Some houses get better bread than others. It costs more and that's what I take. I feel sorry for the rich people who will get up in the morning and go to the door and find their bread missing but I can't let myself starve to death. If I starve I'll never have the strength for my telegram boy job at the post office, which means I'll have no money to put back all that bread and milk and no way of saving to go to America and if I can't go to America I might as well jump into the River Shannon. It's only a few weeks till I get my first wages in the post office and surely these rich people won't collapse with the hunger till then. They can always send the maid out for more. That's the difference between the poor and the rich. The poor can't send out for more because there's no money to send out for more and if there was they wouldn't have a maid to send. It's the maids I have to worry about. I have to be careful when I borrow the milk and the bread and they're at the front doors polishing knobs, knockers and letter boxes. If they see me they'll be running to the woman of the house, Oh, madam, madam, there's an urchin beyant that's makin' off with all the milk and bread.

Beyant. Maids talk like that because they're all from the country, Mullingar heifers, says Paddy Clohessy's uncle, beef to the heels, and they wouldn't give you the steam of their piss.

I bring home the bread and even if The Abbot is surprised he doesn't say, Where did you get it? because he was dropped on his head and that knocks the curiosity out of you. He just looks at me with his big eyes that are blue in the middle and yellow all around and slurps his tea from the great cracked mug his mother left behind. He tells me, That's me mug and don't be drinkin' your tay oush of ish.

Oush of ish. That's the Limerick slum talk that always worried Dad. He said, I don't want my sons growing up in a Limerick lane saying, Oush of ish. It's common and low class. Say out of it properly.

And Mam said, I hope it keeps fine for you but you're not doing much to get us oush of ish.

· · · ·

Out beyond Ballinacurra I climb orchard walls for apples. If there's a dog I move on because I don't have Paddy Clohessy's way of talking to them. Farmers come at me but they're always slow in their rubber boots and even if they jump on a bicycle to chase me I jump over walls where they can't take a bike.

The Abbot knows where I got the apples. If you grow up in the lanes of Limerick you're bound to rob the odd orchard sooner or later. Even if you hate apples you have to rob orchards or your pals will say you're a sissy.

I always offer The Abbot an apple but he won't eat it because of the scarcity of teeth in his head. He has five left and he won't risk leaving them in an apple. If I cut the apple into slices he still won't eat it because that's not the proper way to eat an apple. That's what he says and if I say, You slice bread before you eat it, don't you? he says, Apples is apples and bread is bread.

That's how you talk when you're dropped on your head.

Michael comes again with warm tea in a milk bottle and two cuts of fried bread. I tell him I don't need it anymore. Tell Mam I'm taking care of myself and I don't need her tea and fried bread, thank you very much. Michael is delighted when I give him an apple and I tell him come every second day and he can have more. That stops him from asking me to go back to Laman Griffin's and I'm glad it stops his tears.

There's a market down in Irishtown where the farmers come on Saturdays with their vegetables, hens, eggs, butter. If I'm there early they'll give me a few pennies for helping unload their carts or motor cars. At the end of the day they'll give me vegetables they can't sell, anything crushed, bruised or rotten in parts. One farmer's wife always gives me cracked eggs and tells me, Fry them eggs tomorrow when you come back from Mass in a state of grace for if you ate them eggs with a sin on your sowl they'll stick in your gullet, so they will.

She's a farmer's wife and that's how they talk.

I'm not much better than a beggar now myself the way I stand at the doors of fish and chip shops when they're closing in hopes they might have burnt chips left over or bits of fish floating around in the grease. If they're in a hurry the shop owners will give me the chips and a sheet of paper for wrapping.

The paper I like is the *News of the World*. It's banned in Ireland but people sneak it in from England for the shocking pictures of girls in swimming suits that are almost not there. Then there are stories of people committing all kinds of sins you wouldn't find in Limerick, getting divorces, committing adultery.

Adultery. I still have to find out what that word means, look it up in the library. I'm sure it's worse than what the masters taught us, bad thoughts, bad words, bad deeds.

I take my chips home and get into bed like The Abbot. If he has a few pints taken he sits up eating his chips from the *Limerick Leader* and singing "The Road to Rasheen." I eat my chips. I lick the *News of the World*. I lick the stories about people doing shocking things. I lick the girls in their bathing suits and when there's nothing left to lick I look at the girls till The Abbot blows out the light and I'm committing a mortal sin under the blanket.

I can go to the library any time with Mam's card or Laman Griffin's. I'll never be caught because Laman is too lazy to get out of bed on a Saturday and Mam will never go near a library with the shame of her clothes.

Miss O'Riordan smiles. The *Lives of the Saints* are waiting for you, Frank. Volumes and volumes. Butler, O'Hanlon, Baring-Gould. I've told the head librarian all about you and she's so pleased she's ready to give you your own grown-up card. Isn't that wonderful?

Thanks, Miss O'Riordan.

I'm reading all about St. Brigid, virgin, February first. She was so beautiful that men from all over Ireland panted to marry her and her father wanted her to marry someone important. She didn't want to marry anyone so she prayed to God for help and He caused her eye to melt in her head so that it dribbled down her cheek and left such a great welt the men of Ireland lost interest.

Then there's St. Wilgefortis, virgin martyr, July twentieth. Her mother had nine children, all at the same time, four sets of twins and Wilgefortis the odd one, all winding up martyrs for the faith. Wilgefortis was beautiful and her father wanted to marry her off to the King of Sicily. Wilgefortis was desperate and God helped her by allowing a beard and a mustache to grow on her face, which made the King of Sicily think twice but sent her father into such a rage he had her crucified beard and all.

St. Wilgefortis is the one you pray to if you're an Englishwoman with a troublesome husband.

The priests never tell us about virgin martyrs like St. Agatha, February fifth. February is a powerful month for virgin martyrs. Sicilian pagans ordered Agatha to give up her faith in Jesus and like all the virgin martyrs she said, Nay. They tortured her, stretched her on the rack, tore her sides with iron hooks, burned her with blazing torches, and she said, Nay, I will not deny Our Lord. They crushed her breasts and cut them off but when they rolled her over hot coals it was more than she could bear so she expired, giving praise.

Virgin martyrs always died singing hymns and giving praise not minding one bit if lions tore big chunks from their sides and gobbled them on the spot.

How is it the priests never told us about St. Ursula and her eleven thousand maiden martyrs, October twenty-first? Her father wanted her to marry a pagan king but she said, I'll go away for awhile, three years, and think about it. So off she goes with her thousand noble ladies-in-waiting and their companions, ten thousand. They sailed around for awhile and traipsed through various countries till they stopped in Cologne where the chief of the Huns asked Ursula to marry him. Nay, she said, and the Huns killed her and the maidens with her. Why couldn't she say yes and save the lives of eleven thousand virgins? Why did virgin martyrs have to be so stubborn?

I like St. Moling, an Irish bishop. He didn't live in a palace like the bishop of Limerick. He lived in a tree and when other saints visited him for dinner they would sit around on branches like birds having a grand time with their water and dry bread. He was walking along one day and a leper said, Hoy, St. Moling, where are you going? I'm going to Mass, says St. Moling. Well, I'd like to go to Mass too, so why don't you hoist me up on your back and carry me? St. Moling did but he no sooner had the leper up on his back than the leper started to complain. Your hair shirt, he said, is hard on my sores, take it off. St. Moling took off the shirt and off they went again. Then the leper says, I need to blow my nose. St. Moling says, I don't have any class of a handkerchief, use your hand. The leper says, I can't hold on to you and blow my nose at the same time. All right, says St. Moling, you can blow into my hand. That won't do, says the leper, I barely have a hand left with the leprosy and I can't hold on and blow into your hand. If you were a proper saint you'd twist around here and suck the stuff out of my head. St. Moling didn't want to suck the leper's snot but he did and offered it up and praised God for the privilege.

I could understand my father sucking the bad stuff out of Michael's head when he was a baby and desperate but I don't understand why God wanted St. Moling to go around sucking the snot out of leper's heads. I don't understand God at all and even if I'd like to be a saint and have everyone adore me I'd never suck the snot of a leper. I'd like to be a saint but if that's what you have to do I think I'll stay the way I am.

Still, I'm ready to spend my life in this library reading about virgins and virgin martyrs till I get into trouble with Miss O'Riordan over a book someone left on the table. The author is Lin Yütang. Anyone can tell this is a Chinese name and I'm curious to know what the Chinese talk about. It's a book of essays about love and the body and one of his words sends me to the dictionary. Turgid. He says, The male organ of copulation becomes turgid and is inserted into the receptive female orifice.

Turgid. The dictionary says swollen and that's what I am, standing there looking at the dictionary because I know now what Mikey Molloy was talking about all along, that we're no different from the dogs that get stuck in each other in the streets and it's shocking to think of all the mothers and fathers doing the likes of this.

My father lied to me for years about the Angel on the Seventh Step.

Miss O'Riordan wants to know what word I'm looking for. She always looks worried when I'm at the dictionary so I tell her I'm looking for canonize or beatific or any class of a religious word.

And what's this? she says. This is not the *Lives of the Saints*.

She picks up Lin Yütang and starts reading the page where I left the book face down on the table.

Mother o' God. Is this what you were reading? I saw this in your hand.

Well, I—I—only wanted to see if the Chinese, if the Chinese, ah, had any saints.

Oh, indeed, you did. This is disgraceful. Filth. No wonder the Chinese are the way they are. But what could you expect of slanty eyes and yellow skin and you, now that I look at you, have a bit of the slanty eye yourself. You are to leave this library at once.

But I'm reading the *Lives of the Saints*.

Out or I'll call the head librarian and she'll have the guards on you. Out. You should be running to the priest and confessing your sins. Out, and before you go hand me the library cards of your poor mother and Mr. Griffin. I have a good mind to write to your poor mother and I would if I thought it wouldn't destroy her entirely. Lin Yütang, indeed. Out.

There's no use trying to talk to librarians when they're in that state. You could stand there for an hour telling them all you've read about Brigid and Wilgefortis and Agatha and Ursula and the maiden martyrs but all they think about is one word on one page of Lin Yütang.

The People's Park is behind the library. It's a sunny day, the grass is dry, and I'm worn out begging for chips and putting up with librarians who get into a state over turgid and I'm looking at the clouds drifting above the monument and drifting off myself all turgid till I'm having a dream about virgin martyrs in bathing suits in the *News of the World* pelting Chinese writers with sheeps' bladders and I wake up in a state of excitement with something hot and sticky pumping out of me oh God my male organ of copulation sticking out a mile people in the park giving me curious looks and mothers telling their children come over here love come away from that fella someone should call the guards on him.

The day before my fourteenth birthday I see myself in the glass in Grandma's sideboard. The way I look how can I ever start my job at the post office. Everything is torn, shirt, gansey, short pants, stockings, and my shoes are ready to fall off my feet entirely. Relics of oul' decency, my mother would call them. If my clothes are bad I'm worse. No matter how I drench my hair under the tap it sticks out in all directions. The best cure for standing up hair is spit, only it's hard to spit on your own head. You have to let go with a good one up in the air and duck to catch it on your poll. My eyes are red and oozing yellow, there are matching red and yellow pimples all over my face and my front teeth are so black with rot I'll never be able to smile in my life.

I have no shoulders and I know the whole world admires shoulders. When a man dies in Limerick the women always say, Grand man he was, shoulders that big and wide he wouldn't come in the door for you, had to come in sideways. When I die they'll say, Poor little divil, died without a sign of a shoulder. I wish I had some sign of a shoulder so that people would know I was at least fourteen years of age. All the boys in Leamy's had shoulders except for Fintan Slattery and I don't want to be like him with no shoulders and knees worn away from prayer. If I had any money left I'd light a candle to St. Francis and ask him if there's any chance God could be persuaded to perform a miracle on my shoulders.

Or if I had a stamp I could write to Joe Louis and say, Dear Joe, Is there any chance you could tell me where you got your powerful shoulders even though you were poor?

I have to look decent for my job so I take off all my clothes and stand naked in the backyard washing them under the tap with a bar of carbolic soap. I hang them on Grandma's clothesline, shirt, gansey, pants, stockings, and pray to God it won't rain, pray they'll be dry for tomorrow, which is the start of my life.

I can't go anywhere in my pelt so I stay in bed all day reading old newspapers, getting excited with the girls in the *News of the World* and thanking God for the drying sun. The Abbot comes home at five and makes tea downstairs and even though I'm hungry I know he'll grumble if I ask him for anything. He knows the one thing that worries me is he might go to Aunt Aggie and complain I'm staying in Grandma's house and sleeping in her bed and if Aunt Aggie hears that she'll come over and throw me into the street.

He hides the bread when he's finished and I can never find it. You would think that one who was never dropped on his head would be able to find the hidden bread of one who was dropped on his head. Then I realize if the bread is not in the house he must take it with him in the pocket of the overcoat he wears winter and summer. The minute I hear him clumping from the kitchen to the backyard lavatory I run downstairs, pull the loaf from the pocket, cut off a thick slice, back into the pocket, up the stairs and into bed. He can never say a word, never accuse me. You'd have to be a thief of the worst class to steal one slice of bread and no one would ever believe him, not even Aunt Aggie. Besides, she'd bark at him and say, What are you doing anyway going around with a loaf of bread in your pocket? That's no place for a loaf of bread.

I chew the bread slowly. One mouthful every fifteen minutes will make it last and if I wash it down with water the bread will swell in my belly and give me the full feeling.

I look out the back window to make sure the evening sun is drying my clothes. Other backyards have lines with clothes that are bright and colorful and dance in the wind. Mine hang from the line like dead dogs.

The sun is bright but it's cold and damp in the house and I wish I had something to wear in the bed. I have no other clothes and if I touch anything of The Abbot's he'll surely run to Aunt Aggie. All I can find in the wardrobe is Grandma's old black woolen dress. You're not supposed to wear your Grandmother's old dress when she's dead and you're a boy but what does it matter if it keeps you warm and you're in bed under the blankets where no one will ever know. The dress has the smell of old dead grandmother and I worry she might rise from the grave and curse me before the whole family and all assembled. I pray to St. Francis, ask him to keep her in the grave where she belongs, promise him a candle when I start my job, remind him the robe he wore himself wasn't too far from a dress and no one ever tormented him over it and fall asleep with the image of his face in my dream.

The worst thing in the world is to be sleeping in your dead grandmother's bed wearing her black dress when your uncle The Abbot falls on his arse outside South's pub after a night of drinking pints and people who can't mind their own business rush to Aunt Aggie's house to tell her so that she gets Uncle Pa Keating to help her carry The Abbot home and upstairs to where you're sleeping and she barks at you, What are you doin' in this house, in that bed? Get up and put on the kettle for tea for your poor uncle Pat that fell down, and when you don't move she pulls the blankets and falls backward like one seeing a ghost and yelling Mother o' God what are you doin' in me dead mother's dress?

That's the worst thing of all because it's hard to explain that you're getting ready for the big job in your life, that you washed your clothes, they're drying abroad on the line, and it was so cold you had to wear the only thing you could find in the house, and it's even harder to talk to Aunt Aggie when The Abbot is groaning in the bed, Me feet is like a fire, put water on me feet, and Uncle Pa Keating is covering his mouth with his hand and collapsing against the wall laughing and telling you that you look gorgeous and black suits you and would you ever straighten your hem. You don't know what to do when Aunt Aggie tells you, Get out of that bed and put the kettle on downstairs for tea for your poor uncle. Should you take off the dress and put on a blanket or should you go as you are? One minute she's screaming, What are you doin' in me poor mother's dress? the next she's telling you put on that bloody kettle. I tell her I washed my clothes for the big job.

What big job?

Telegram boy at the post office.

She says if the post office is hiring the likes of you they must be in a desperate way altogether, go down and put on that kettle.

The next worse thing is to be out in the backyard filling the kettle from the tap with the moon beaming away and Kathleen Purcell from next door perched up on the wall looking for her cat. God, Frankie McCourt, what are you doin' in your grandmother's dress? and you have to stand there in the dress with the kettle in your hand and explain how you washed your clothes which are hanging there on the line for all to see and you were so cold in the bed you put on your grandmother's dress and your uncle Pat, The Abbot, fell down and was brought home by Aunt Aggie and her husband, Pa Keating, and she drove you into the backyard to fill this kettle and you'll take off this dress as soon as ever your clothes are dry because you never had any desire to go through life in your dead grandmother's dress.

Now Kathleen Purcell lets out a scream, falls off the wall, forgets the cat, and you can hear her giggling into her blind mother, Mammy, Mammy, wait till I tell you about Frankie McCourt abroad in the backyard in his dead grandmother's dress. You know that once Kathleen Purcell gets a bit of scandal the whole lane will know it before morning and you might as well stick your head out the window and make a general announcement about yourself and the dress problem.

By the time the kettle boils The Abbot is asleep from the drink and Aunt Aggie says she and Uncle Pa will have a drop of tea themselves and she doesn't mind if I have a drop myself. Uncle Pa says on second thought the black dress could be the cassock of a Dominican priest and he goes down on his knees and says, Bless me, Father, for I have sinned. Aunt Aggie says, Get up, you oul' eejit, and stop makin' a feck of religion. Then she says, And you what are you doin' in this house?

I can't tell her about Mam and Laman Griffin and the excitement in the loft. I tell her I was thinking of staying here a while because of the great distance from Laman Griffin's house to the post office and as soon as I get on my feet we'll surely find a decent place and we'll all move on, my mother and brothers and all.

Well, she says, that's more than your father would do.

XV

It's hard to sleep when you know the next day you're fourteen and starting your first job as a man. The Abbot wakes at dawn moaning. Would I ever make him some tay and if I do I can have a big cut of bread from the half loaf in his pocket which he was keeping there out of the way of the odd rat and if I look in Grandma's gramophone where she used to keep the records I'll find a jar of jam.

He can't read, he can't write, but he knows where to hide the jam.

I bring The Abbot his tea and bread and make some for myself. I put on my damp clothes and get into the bed hoping that if I stay there the clothes will dry from my own heat before I go to work. Mam always says it's the damp clothes that give you the consumption and an early grave. The Abbot is sitting up telling me he has a terrible pain in his head from a dream where I was wearing his poor mother's black dress and she flying around screaming, Sin, sin, 'tis a sin. He finishes his tea and falls into a snore sleep and I wait for his clock to say half-past eight, time to get up and be at the post office at nine even if the clothes are still damp on my skin.

On my way out I wonder why Aunt Aggie is coming down the lane. She must be coming to see if The Abbot is dead or needing a doctor. She says, What time do you have to be at that job?

Nine.

All right.

She turns and walks with me to the post office on Henry Street. She doesn't say a word and I wonder if she's going to the post office to denounce me for sleeping in my grandmother's bed and wearing her black dress. She says, Go up and tell them your aunt is down here waiting for you and you'll be an hour late. If they want to argue I'll go up and argue.

Why do I have to be an hour late?

Do what you're bloody well told.

There are telegram boys sitting on a bench along a wall. There are two women at a desk, one fat, one thin. The thin one says, Yes?

My name is Frank McCourt, miss, and I'm here to start work.

What kind of work would that be now?

Telegram boy, miss.

The thin one cackles, Oh, God, I thought you were here to clean the lavatories.

No, miss. My mother brought a note from the priest, Dr. Cowpar, and there's supposed to be a job.

Oh, there is, is there? And do you know what day this is?

I do, miss. 'Tis my birthday. I'm fourteen.

Isn't that grand, says the fat woman.

Today is Thursday, says the thin woman. Your job starts on Monday. Go away and wash yourself and come back then.

The telegram boys along the wall are laughing. I don't know why but I feel my face turning hot. I tell the women, Thank you, and on the way out I hear the thin one, Jesus above, Maureen, who dragged in that specimen? and they laugh along with the telegram boys.

Aunt Aggie says, Well? and I tell her I don't start till Monday. She says my clothes are a disgrace and what did I wash them in.

Carbolic soap.

They smell like dead pigeons and you're making a laughingstock of the whole family.

She takes me to Roche's Stores and buys me a shirt, a gansey, a pair of short pants, two pairs of stockings and a pair of summer shoes on sale. She gives me two shillings to have tea and a bun for my birthday. She gets on the bus to go back up O'Connell Street too fat and lazy to walk. Fat and lazy, no son of her own, and still she buys me the clothes for my new job.

I turn toward Arthur's Quay with the package of new clothes under my arm and I have to stand at the edge of the River Shannon so that the whole world won't see the tears of a man the day he's fourteen.

Monday morning I'm up early to wash my face and flatten my hair with water and spit. The Abbot sees me in my new clothes. Jaysus, he says, is it gettin' married you are? and goes back to sleep.

Mrs. O'Connell, the fat woman, says, Well, well, aren't we the height of fashion, and the thin one, Miss Barry, says, Did you rob a bank on the weekend? and there's a great laugh from the telegram boys sitting on the bench along the wall.

I'm told to sit at the end of the bench and wait for my turn to go out with telegrams. Some telegram boys in uniforms are the permanent ones who took the exam. They can stay in the post office forever if they like, take the next exam for postman and then the one for clerk that lets them work inside selling stamps and money orders behind the counter downstairs. The post office gives permanent boys big waterproof capes for the bad weather and they get two weeks holiday every year. Everyone says these are good jobs, steady and pensionable and respectable, and if you get a job like this you never have to worry again in your whole life, so you don't.

Temporary telegram boys are not allowed to stay in the job beyond the age of sixteen. There are no uniforms, no holidays, the pay is less, and if you stay out sick a day you can be fired. No excuses. There are no waterproof capes. Bring your own raincoat or dodge the raindrops.

Mrs. O'Connell calls me to her desk to give me a black leather belt and pouch. She says there's a great shortage of bicycles so I'll have to walk my first batch of telegrams. I'm to go to the farthest address first, work my way back, and don't take all day. She's long enough in the post office to know how long it takes to deliver six telegrams even by foot. I'm not to be stopping in pubs or bookies or even home for a cup of tea and if I do I'll be found out. I'm not to be stopping in chapels to say a prayer. If I have to pray do it on the hoof or on the bicycle. If it rains pay no attention. Deliver the telegrams and don't be a sissy.

One telegram is addressed to Mrs. Clohessy of Arthur's Quay and that couldn't be anyone but Paddy's mother.

Is that you, Frankie McCourt? she says. God, I wouldn't know you you're that big. Come in, will you.

She's wearing a bright frock with flowers all over and shiny new shoes. There are two children on the floor playing with a toy train. On the table there is a teapot, cups with saucers, a bottle of milk, a loaf of bread, butter, jam. There are two beds over by the window where there were none before. The big bed in the corner is empty and she must know what I'm wondering. He's gone, she says, but he's not dead. Gone t' England with Paddy. Have a cup o' tay an' a bit o' bread. You need it, God help us. You look like one left over from the Famine itself. Ate that bread an' jam an' build yourself up. Paddy always talked about you and Dennis, my poor husband that was in the bed, never got over the day your mother came an' sang the song about the Kerry dancing. He's over in England now making sandwiches in a canteen and sending me a few bob every week. You'd wonder what the English are thinking about when they take a man that has the consumption and give him a job making sandwiches. Paddy has a grand job in a pub in Cricklewood, which is in England. Dennis would still be here if it wasn't for Paddy climbin' the wall for the tongue.

Tongue?

Dennis had the craving, so he did, for a nice sheep's head with a bit of cabbage and a spud so up with me to Barry the butcher with the last few shillings I had. I boiled that head an' sick an' all as he was Dennis couldn't wait for it to be done. He was a demon there in the bed callin' for the head an' when I gave it to him on the plate he was delighted with himself suckin' the marrow outa every inch of that head. Then he finishes an' he says, Mary, where is the tongue?

What tongue? says I.

The tongue of this sheep. Every sheep is born with a tongue that lets him go ba ba ba and there's a great lack of tongue in this head. Go up to Barry the butcher and demand it.

So up with me to Barry the butcher and he said, That bloody sheep came in here bleatin' an' cryin' so much we cut the tongue from her and thrun it to the dog who gobbled it up and ever since ba bas like a sheep and if he doesn't quit I'll cut his tongue and throw it to the cat.

Back I go to Dennis and he gets frantic in the bed. I want that tongue, he says. All the nourishment is in the tongue. And what do you think happens next but my Paddy, that was your friend, goes up to Barry the butcher after dark, climbs the wall, cuts the tongue of a sheep's head that's on a hook on the wall and brings it back to his poor father in the bed. Of course I have to boil that tongue with salt galore and Dennis, God love him, ates it, lies back in the bed a minute, throws back the blanket and stands out on his two feet announcing to the world that consumption or no consumption, he's not going to die in that bed, if he's going to die at all it might as well be under a German bomb with him making a few pounds for his family instead of whining in the bed there beyond.

She shows me a letter from Paddy. He's working in his uncle Anthony's pub twelve hours a day, twenty-five shillings a week and every day soup and a sandwich. He's delighted when the Germans come over with the bombs so that he can sleep while the pub is closed. At night he sleeps on the floor of the hallway upstairs. He will send his mother two pounds every month and he's saving the rest to bring her and the family to England where they'll be much better off in one room in Cricklewood than ten rooms in Arthur's Quay. She'll be able to get a job no bother. You'd have to be a sad case not to be able to get a job in a country that's at war especially with Yanks pouring in and spending money right and left. Paddy himself is planning to get a job in the middle of London where Yanks leave tips big enough to feed an Irish family of six for a week.

Mrs. Clohessy says, We have enough money for food and shoes at last, thanks be to God and His Blessed Mother. You'll never guess who Paddy met over there in England fourteen years of age an' workin' like a man. Brendan Kiely, the one ye used to call Question. Workin' he is an' savin' so he can go an' join the Mounties an' ride all over Canada like Nelson Eddy singin' I'll be callin' you ooh ooh ooh ooh ooh ooh. If it wasn't for Hitler we'd all be dead an' isn't that a terrible thing to say. And how's your poor mother, Frankie?

She's grand, Mrs. Clohessy.

No, she's not. I seen her in the Dispensary and she looks worse than my Dennis did in the bed. You have to mind your poor mother. You look desperate too, Frankie, with them two red eyes starin' outa your head. Here's a little tip for you. Thruppence. Buy yourself a sweet.

I will, Mrs. Clohessy.

Do.

At the end of the week Mrs. O'Connell hands me the first wages of my life, a pound, my first pound. I run down the stairs and up to O'Connell Street, the main street, where the lights are on and people are going home from work, people like me with wages in their pockets. I want them to know I'm like them, I'm a man, I have a pound. I walk up one side of O'Connell Street and down the other and hope they'll notice me. They don't. I want to wave my pound note at the world so they'll say, There he goes, Frankie McCourt the workingman, with a pound in his pocket.

It's Friday night and I can do anything I like. I can have fish and chips and go to the Lyric Cinema. No, no more Lyric. I don't have to sit up in the gods anymore with people all around me cheering on the Indians killing General Custer and the Africans chasing Tarzan all over the jungle. I can go to the Savoy Cinema now, pay sixpence for a seat down front where there's a better class of people eating boxes of chocolates and covering their mouths when they laugh. After the film I can have tea and buns in the restaurant upstairs.

Michael is across the street calling me. He's hungry and wonders if there's any chance he could go to The Abbot's for a bit of bread and stay there for the night instead of going all the way to Laman Griffin's. I tell him he doesn't have to worry about a bit of bread. We'll go to the Coliseum Café and have fish and chips, all he wants, lemonade galore, and then we'll go to see *Yankee Doodle Dandy* with James Cagney and eat two big bars of chocolate. After the film we have tea and buns and we sing and dance like Cagney all the way to The Abbot's. Michael says it must be great to be in America where people have nothing else to do but sing and dance. He's half asleep but he says he's going there some day to sing and dance and would I help him go and when he's asleep I start thinking about America and how I have to save money for my fare instead of squandering it on fish and chips and tea and buns. I'll have to save a few shillings from my pound because if I don't I'll be in Limerick forever. I'm fourteen now and if I save something every week surely I should be able to go to America by the time I'm twenty.

There are telegrams for offices, shops, factories where there's no hope of a tip. Clerks take the telegrams without a look at you or a thank you. There are telegrams for the respectable people with maids along the Ennis Road and the North Circular Road where there's no hope of a tip. Maids are like clerks, they don't look at you or say thank you. There are telegrams for the houses of priests and nuns and they have maids, too, even if they say poverty is noble. If you waited for tips from priests or nuns you'd die on their doorstep. There are telegrams for people miles outside the city, farmers with muddy yards and dogs who want to eat your legs. There are telegrams for rich people in big houses with gate lodges and miles of land surrounded by walls. The gatekeeper waves you in and you have to cycle for miles up long drives past lawns, flower beds, fountains to reach the big house. If the weather is fine people are playing croquet, the Protestant game, or strolling around, talking and laughing, all decked out in flowery dresses and blazers with crests and golden buttons and you'd never know there was a war on. There are Bentleys and Rolls-Royces parked outside the great front door where a maid tells you go around to the servants' entrance don't you know any better.

People in the big houses have English accents and they don't tip telegram boys.

The best people for tips are widows, Protestant ministers' wives and the poor in general. Widows know when the telegram money order is due from the English government and they wait by the window. You have to be careful if they ask you in for a cup of tea because one of the temporary boys, Scrawby Luby, said an old widow of thirty-five had him in for tea and tried to take down his pants and he had to run out of the house though he was really tempted and had to go to confession the next Saturday. He said it was very awkward hopping up on the bike with his thing sticking out but if you cycle very fast and think of the sufferings of the Virgin Mary you'll go soft in no time.

Protestant ministers' wives would never carry on like Scrawby Luby's old widow unless they're widows themselves. Christy Wallace, who is a permanent telegram boy and ready to be a postman any day, says Protestants don't care what they do even if they're ministers' wives. They're doomed anyway, so what does it matter if they have a bit of a romp with a telegram boy. All the telegram boys like Protestant ministers' wives. They might have maids but they answer doors themselves and say, One moment, please, and give you sixpence. I'd like to talk to them and ask them how it feels to be doomed but they might get offended and take back the sixpence.

The Irishmen working in England send their telegram money

orders on Friday nights and all day Saturday and that's when we get the good tips. The minute we deliver one batch we're out with another.

The worst lanes are in the Irishtown, off High Street or Mungret Street, worse than Roden Lane or O'Keeffe's Lane or any lane I lived in. There are lanes with channels running down the middle. Mothers stand at doors and yell gardyloo when they empty their slop buckets. Children make paper boats or float matchboxes with little sails on the greasy water.

When you ride into a lane the children call out, Here's the telegram boy, here's the telegram boy. They run to you and the women wait at the door. If you give a small child a telegram for his mother he's the hero of the family. Little girls know they're supposed to wait till the boys get their chance though they can get the telegram if they have no brothers. Women at the door will call to you that they have no money now but if you're in this lane tomorrow knock on the door for your tip, God bless you an' all belongin' to you.

Mrs. O'Connell and Miss Barry at the post office tell us every day our job is to deliver telegrams and nothing else. We are not to be doing things for people, going to the shop for groceries or any other kind of message. They don't care if people are dying in the bed. They don't care if people are legless, lunatic or crawling on the floor. We are to deliver the telegram and that's all. Mrs. O'Connell says, I know everything ye do, everything, for the people of Limerick have their eye on ye and there are reports which I have here in my drawers.

A fine place to keep reports, says Toby Mackey under his breath.

But Mrs. O'Connell and Miss Barry don't know what it's like in the lane when you knock on a door and someone says come in and you go in and there's no light and there's a pile of rags on a bed in a corner the pile saying who is it and you say telegram and the pile of rags tells you would you ever go to the shop for me I'm starving with the hunger and I'd give me two eyes for a cup of tea and what are you going to do say I'm busy and ride off on your bike and leave the pile of rags there with a telegram money order that's pure useless because the pile of rags is helpless to get out of the bed to go to the post office to cash the bloody money order.

What are you supposed to do?

You're told never never go to the post office to cash one of those money orders for anyone or you'll lose your job forever. But what are you supposed to do when an old man that was in the Boer War hundreds of years ago says his legs are gone and he'd be forever grateful if you'd go to Paddy Considine in the post office and tell him the situation and Paddy will surely cash the money order and keep two shillings for yourself grand boy that you are. Paddy Considine says no bother but don't tell anyone or I'd be out on my arse and so would you, son. The old man from the Boer War says he knows you have telegrams to deliver now but would you ever come back tonight and maybe go to the shop for him for he doesn't have a thing in the house and he's freezing on top of it. He sits in an old armchair in the corner covered with bits of blankets and a bucket behind the chair that stinks enough to make you sick and when you look at that old man in the dark corner you want to get a hose with hot water and strip him and wash him down and give him a big feed of rashers and eggs and mashed potatoes with loads of butter salt and onions.

I want to take the man from the Boer War and the pile of rags in the bed and put them in a big sunny house in the country with birds chirping away outside the window and a stream gurgling.

Mrs. Spillane in Pump Lane off Carey's Road has two crippled twin children with big blond heads, small bodies, and bits of legs that dangle over the edges of the chairs. They look into the fire all day and say, Where's Daddy? They speak English like everybody else but they babble away to one another in a language they made up, Hung sup tea tea sup hung. Mrs. Spillane says that means, When are we getting our supper? She tells me she's lucky if her husband sends four pounds a month and she's beside herself with the abuse she gets from the Dispensary over him being in England. The children are only four and they're very bright even if they can't walk or take care of themselves. If they could walk, if they were any way normal, she'd pack up and move to England out of this godforsaken country that fought so long for freedom and look at the state of us, De Valera in his mansion above in Dublin the dirty oul' bastard and the rest of the politicians that can all go to hell, God forgive me. The priests can go to hell too and I won't ask God to forgive me for saying the likes of that. There they are, the priests and the nuns telling us Jesus was poor and 'tis no shame, lorries driving up to their houses with crates and barrels of whiskey and wine, eggs galore and legs of ham and they telling us what we should give up for Lent. Lent, my arse. What are we to give up when we have Lent all year long?

I want to take Mrs. Spillane and her two blond crippled children and put them in that house in the country with the pile of rags and the man from the Boer War and wash everyone and let them all sit in the sun with the birds singing and the streams gurgling.

I can't leave the pile of rags alone with a useless money order because the pile is an old woman, Mrs. Gertrude Daly, all twisted with every class of disease you can get in a Limerick lane, arthritis, rheumatism, falling hair, a nostril half gone from her jabbing at it with her finger, and you wonder what kind of a world is it when this old woman sits up from the rags and smiles at you with teeth that gleam white in the dark, her own teeth and perfect.

That's right, she says, me own teeth, and when I rot in the grave they'll find me teeth a hundred years from now all white an' shiny an' I'll be declared a saint.

The telegram money order, three pounds, is from her son. It has a message, Happy Birthday, Mammy, Your fond son, Teddy. She says, A wonder he can spare it, the little shit, trottin' around with every tart in Piccadilly. She asks if I'd ever do her a favor and cash the money order and get her a little Baby Powers whiskey at the pub, a loaf of bread, a pound of lard, seven potatoes, one for each day of the week. Would I boil a potato for her, mash it up with a lump of lard, give her a cut of bread, bring her a drop of water to go with the whiskey? Would I go to O'Connor the chemist for ointment for her sores and while I'm at it bring some soap so she can give her body a good scrub and she'll be forever grateful and say a prayer for me and here's a couple of shillings for all my troubles.

Ah, no thanks, ma'am.

Take the money. Little tip. You did me great favors.

I couldn't, ma'am, the way you are.

Take the money or I'll tell the post office you're not to deliver my telegram anymore.

Oh, all right, ma'am. Thanks very much.

Good night, son. Be good to your mother.

Good night, Mrs. Daly.

School starts in September and some days Michael stops at The Abbot's before the walk home to Laman Griffin's. On rainy days he says, Can I stay here tonight? and soon he doesn't want to go back to Laman Griffin's at all. He's worn out and hungry with two miles out and two miles back.

When Mam comes looking for him I don't know what to say to her. I don't know how to look at her and I keep my eyes off to one side. She says, How's the job? as if nothing ever happened in Laman Griffin's and I say, Grand, as if nothing ever happened in Laman Griffin's. If the rain is too heavy for her to go home she stays in the small room upstairs with Alphie. She goes back to Laman's the next day but Michael stays and soon she's moving in herself bit by bit till she stops going to Laman's altogether.

The Abbot pays the rent every week. Mam gets the relief and the food dockets till someone informs on her and she's cut off from the Dispensary. She's told that if her son is bringing in a pound a week that's more than some families get on the dole and she should be grateful he has a job. Now I have to hand over my wages. Mam says, A pound? Is that all you get for riding around in all kinds of weather? This would be four dollars in America. Four dollars. And you couldn't feed a cat for four dollars in New York. If you were delivering telegrams for Western Union in New York you'd be earning twenty-five dollars a week and living in luxury. She always translates Irish money into American so that she won't forget and tries to convince everyone times were better over there. Some weeks she lets me keep two shillings but if I go to a film or buy a secondhand book there's nothing left, I won't be able to save for my fare, and I'll be stuck in Limerick till I'm an old man of twenty-five.

Malachy writes from Dublin to say he's fed up and doesn't want to spend the rest of his life blowing a trumpet in the army band. He's home in a week and complains when he has to share the big bed with Michael, Alphie and me. He had his own army cot up there in Dublin with sheets and blankets and a pillow. Now he's back to overcoats and a bolster that sends up a cloud of feathers when you touch it. Mam says, Pity about you. I'm sorry for your troubles. The Abbot has his own bed, and my mother has the small room. We're all together again, no Laman tormenting us. We make tea and fried bread and sit on the kitchen floor. The Abbot says you're not supposed to be sitting on kitchen floors, what are tables and chairs for? He tells Mam that Frankie is not right in the head and Mam says we'll all catch our death from the damp of the floor. We sit on the floor and sing and Mam and The Abbot sit on chairs. She sings "Are You Lonesome Tonight?" and the Abbot sings "The Road to Rasheen" and we still don't know what his song is about. We sit on the floor and tell stories about things that happened, things that never happened and things that will happen when we all go to America.

There are slow days at the post office and we sit on the bench and talk. We can talk but we are not to laugh. Miss Barry says we should be grateful we're getting paid to sit there, bunch of idlers and streetboys that we are, and that there is to be no laughing. Getting paid for sitting and chatting is no laughing matter and the first titter out of any of us and out we go till we come to our senses and if the tittering continues we'll be reported to the proper authorities.

The boys talk about her under their breath. Toby Mackey says, What that oul' bitch needs is a good rub o' the relic, a good rub o' the brush. Her mother was a streetwalking flaghopper and her father escaped from a lunatic asylum with bunions on his balls and warts on his wank.

There laughing along the bench and Miss Barry calls to us, I warned ye against the laughing. Mackey, what is it you're prattling about over there?

I said we'd all be better off out in the fresh air on this fine day delivering telegrams, Miss Barry.

I'm sure you did, Mackey. Your mouth is a lavatory. Did you hear me?

I did, Miss Barry.

You have been heard on the stairs, Mackey.

Yes, Miss Barry.

Shut up, Mackey.

I will, Miss Barry.

Not another word, Mackey.

No, Miss Barry.

I said shut up, Mackey.

All right, Miss Barry.

That's the end of it, Mackey. Don't try me.

I won't, Miss Barry.

Mother o' God give me patience.

Yes, Miss Barry.

Take the last word, Mackey. Take it, take it, take it.

I will, Miss Barry.

Toby Mackey is a temporary telegram boy like me. He saw a film called *The Front Page* and now he wants to go to America some day and be a tough newspaper reporter with a hat and a cigarette. He keeps a notebook in his pocket because a good reporter has to write down what happens. Facts. He has to write down facts not a lot of bloody poetry, which is all you hear in Limerick with men in pubs going on about our great sufferings under the English. Facts, Frankie. He writes down the number of telegrams he delivers and how far he travels. We sit on the bench making sure we don't laugh and he tells me that if we deliver forty telegrams a day that's two hundred a week and that's ten thousand a year and twenty thousand in our two years at the job. If we cycle one hundred and twenty-five miles in a week that's thirteen thousand miles in two years and that's halfway around the world, Frankie, and no wonder there isn't a scrap of flesh on our arses.

Toby says nobody knows Limerick like the telegram boy. We know every avenue, road, street, terrace, mews, place, close, lane. Jasus, says Toby, there isn't a door in Limerick we don't know. We knock on all kinds of doors, iron, oak, plywood. Twenty thousand doors, Frankie. We rap, kick, push. We ring and buzz bells. We shout and whistle, Telegram boy, telegram boy. We drop telegrams in letter boxes, shove them under doors, throw them over the transom. We climb in windows where people are bedridden. We fight off every dog who wants to turn us into dinner. You never know what's going to happen when you hand people their telegrams. They laugh and sing and dance and cry and scream and fall down in a weakness and you wonder if they'll wake up at all and give you the tip. It's not a bit like delivering telegrams in America where Mickey Rooney rides around in a film called *The Human Comedy* and people are pleasant and falling over themselves to give you a tip, inviting you in, giving you a cup of tea and a bun.

Toby Mackey says he has facts galore in his notebook and he doesn't give a fiddler's fart about anything and that's the way I'd like to be myself.

Mrs. O'Connell knows I like the country telegrams and if a day is sunny she gives me a batch of ten that will keep me away all morning and I don't have to return till after the dinner hour at noon. There are fine autumn days when the Shannon sparkles and the fields are green and glinting with silver morning dew. Smoke blows across fields and there's the sweet smell of turf fires. Cows and sheep graze in the fields and I wonder if these are the beasts the priest was talking about. I wouldn't be surprised because there's no end to the bulls climbing on cows, rams on sheep, stallions on mares, and they all have such big things it makes me break out in a sweat to look at them and I feel sorry for all the female creatures in the world who have to suffer like that though I wouldn't mind being a bull myself because they can do what they like and it's never a sin for an animal. I wouldn't mind going at myself here but you never know when a farmer might come along the road driving cows and sheep to a fair or to another field raising his stick and bidding you, Good day, young fella, grand morning, thank God and His Blessed Mother. A farmer that religious might be offended if he saw you breaking the Sixth Commandment forninst his field. Horses like to stick their heads over fences and hedges to see what's passing by and I stop and talk to them because they have big eyes and long noses that show how intelligent they are. Sometimes two birds will be singing to each other across a field and I have to stop and listen to them and if I stay long enough more birds will join till every tree and bush is alive with birdsong. If there's a stream gurgling under a bridge on the road, birds singing and cows mooing and lambs baaing, that's better than any band in a film. The smell of dinner bacon and cabbage wafting from a farmhouse makes me so weak with the hunger I climb into a field and stuff myself with blackberries for half an hour. I stick my face into the stream and drink icy water that's better than the lemonade in any fish and chip shop.

When I'm finished delivering the telegrams there's enough time to go to the ancient monastery graveyard where my mother's relations are buried, the Guilfoyles and the Sheehans, where my mother wants to be buried. I can see from here the high ruins of Carrigogunnell Castle and there's plenty of time to cycle there, sit up on the highest wall, look at the Shannon flowing out to the Atlantic on its way to America and dream of the day I'll be sailing off myself.

The boys at the post office tell me I'm lucky to get the Carmody family telegram, a shilling tip, one of the biggest tips you'll ever get in Limerick. So why am I getting it? I'm the junior boy. They say, Well, sometimes Theresa Carmody answers the door. She has the consumption and they're afraid of catching it from her. She's seventeen, in and out of the sanatorium, and she'll never see eighteen. The boys at the post office say sick people like Theresa know there's little time left and that makes them mad for love and romance and everything. Everything. That's what the consumption does to you, say the boys at the post office.

I cycle through wet November streets thinking of that shilling tip, and as I turn into the Carmody street the bicycle slides out from under me and I skid along the ground scraping my face and tearing open the back of my hand. Theresa Carmody opens the door. She has red hair. She had green eyes like the fields beyond Limerick. Her cheeks are bright pink and her skin is a fierce white. She says, Oh, you're all wet and bleeding.

I skidded on my bike.

Come in and I'll put something on your cuts.

I wonder, Should I go in? I might get the consumption and that will be the end of me. I want to be alive when I'm fifteen and I want the shilling tip.

Come in. You'll perish standing there.

She puts on the kettle for the tea. Then she dabs iodine on my cuts and I try to be a man and not whimper. She says, Oh, you're a great bit of a man. Go into the parlor and dry yourself before the fire. Look, why don't you take off your pants and dry them on the screen of the fire?

Ah, no.

Ah, do.

I will.

I drape my pants over the screen. I sit there watching the steam rise and I watch myself rise and I worry she might come in and see me in my excitement.

There she is with a plate of bread and jam and two cups of tea. Lord, she says, you might be a scrawny bit of a fellow but that's a fine boyo you have there.

She puts the plate and the cups on a table by the fire and there they stay. With her thumb and forefinger she takes the tip of my excitement and leads me across the room to a green sofa against the wall and all the time my head is filled with sin and iodine and fear of consumption and the shilling tip and her green eyes and she's on the sofa don't stop or I'll die and she's crying and I'm crying for I don't know what's happening to me if I'm killing myself catching consumption from her mouth I'm riding to heaven I'm falling off a cliff and if this is a sin I don't give a fiddler's fart.

We take our ease on the sofa a while till she says, Don't you have more telegrams to deliver? and when we sit up she gives a little cry, Oh, I'm bleeding.

What's up with you?

I think it's because it's the first time.

I tell her, Wait a minute. I bring the bottle from the kitchen and splash the iodine on her injury. She leaps from the sofa, dances around the parlor like a wild one and runs into the kitchen to douse herself with water. After she dries herself she says, Lord, you're very innocent. You're not supposed to be pouring iodine on girls like that.

I thought you were cut.

For weeks after that I deliver the telegram. Sometimes we have the excitement on the sofa but there are other days she has the cough and you can see the weakness on her. She never tells me she has the weakness. She never tells me she has the consumption. The boys at the post office say I must have been having a great time with the shilling tip and Theresa Carmody. I never tell them I stopped taking the shilling tip. I never tell them about the green sofa and the excitement. I never tell them of the pain that comes when she opens the door and I can see the weakness on her and all I want to do then is make tea for her and sit with my arms around her on the green sofa.

One Saturday I'm told to deliver the telegram to Theresa's mother at her job in Woolworth's. I try to be casual. Mrs. Carmody, I always deliver the telegram to your, I think your daughter, Theresa?

Yes, she's in the hospital.

Is she in the sanatorium?

I said she's in the hospital.

She's like everyone else in Limerick, ashamed of the TB, and she doesn't give me a shilling or any kind of tip. I cycle out to the sanatorium to see Theresa. They say you have to be a relation and you have to be adult. I tell them I'm her cousin and I'll be fifteen in August. They tell me go away. I cycle to the Franciscan church to pray for Theresa. St. Francis, would you please talk to God. Tell Him it wasn't Theresa's fault. I could have refused that telegram Saturday after Saturday. Tell God Theresa was not responsible for the excitement on the sofa because that's what the consumption does to you. It doesn't matter anyway, St. Francis, because I love Theresa. I love her as much as you love any bird or beast or fish and will you tell God take the consumption away and I promise I'll never go near her again.

The next Saturday they give me the Carmody telegram. From halfway up the street I can see the blinds are drawn. I can see the black crepe wreath on the door. I can see the white purple-lined mourning card. I can see beyond the door and walls where Theresa and I tumbled naked and wild on the green sofa and I know now she is in hell and all because of me.

I slip the telegram under the door and cycle back down to the Franciscan church to beg for the repose of Theresa's soul. I pray to every statue, to the stained glass windows, the Stations of the Cross. I swear I'll lead a life of faith, hope and charity, poverty, chastity and obedience.

Next day, Sunday, I go to four Masses. I do the Stations of the Cross three times. I say rosaries all day. I go without food and drink and wherever I find a quiet place I cry and beg God and the Virgin Mary to have mercy on the soul of Theresa Carmody.

On Monday I follow the funeral to the graveyard on my post office bicycle. I stand behind a tree a distance from the grave. Mrs. Carmody weeps and moans. Mr. Carmody snuffles and looks puzzled. The priest recites the Latin prayers and sprinkles the coffin with holy water.

I want to go to the priest, to Mr. and Mrs. Carmody. I want to tell them how I'm the one who sent Theresa to hell. They can do whatever they like with me. Abuse me. Revile me. Throw grave dirt at me. But I stay behind the tree till the mourners leave and the grave diggers fill in the grave.

Frost is already whitening the fresh earth on the grave and I think of Theresa cold in the coffin, the red hair, the green eyes. I can't understand the feelings going through me but I know that with all the people who died in my family and all the people who died in the lanes around me and all the people who left I never had a pain like this in my heart and I hope I never will again.

It's getting dark. I walk my bicycle out of the graveyard. I have telegrams to deliver.

XVI

Mrs. O'Connell gives me telegrams to deliver to Mr. Harrington, the Englishman with the dead wife that was born and bred in Limerick. The boys at the post office say sympathy telegrams are a waste of time. People just cry and moan with the grief and they think they're excused from the tip. They'll ask you if you'd like to come in for a look at the departed and a prayer by the bed. That wouldn't be so bad if they offered you a drop of sherry and a ham sandwich. Oh, no, they're happy to get your prayer but you're only a telegram boy and you're lucky if you get a dry biscuit. Older boys at the post office say you have to play your cards right to get the grief tip. If you're asked in to say a prayer you have to kneel by the corpse, give a powerful sigh, bless yourself, drop your forehead to the bedclothes so they won't see your face, let your shoulders shake like one collapsing with sorrow, hold on to the bed with your two hands as if they're going to have to tear you away to deliver the rest of your telegrams, make sure your cheeks are glinting with tears or the spit you dabbed on, and if you don't get a tip after all that push the next batch of telegrams under the door or fire them over the transom and leave them to their grief.

This isn't my first time delivering telegrams to the Harrington house. Mr. Harrington is always away on business for the insurance company and Mrs. Harrington is generous with the tip. But she's gone and Mr. Harrington answers the doorbell. His eyes are red and he sniffles. He says, Are you Irish?

Irish? What else would I be standing there on his doorstep in Limerick with a batch of telegrams in my hand? I am, sir. He says, Come in. Put the telegrams on the hall stand. He shuts the hall door, locks it, puts the key in his pocket and I think, Aren't Englishmen very peculiar.

You'll want to see her, of course. You'll want to see what you people have done to her with your damn tuberculosis. Race of ghouls. Follow me.

He leads me first to the kitchen where he picks up a plate of ham sandwiches and two bottles, and then upstairs. Mrs. Harrington looks lovely in the bed, blond, pink, peaceful.

This is my wife. She may be Irish but she doesn't look it, thank God. Like you. Irish. You'll need a drink, of course. You Irish quaff at every turn. Barely weaned before you clamor for the whiskey bottle, the pint of stout. You'll have what, whiskey, sherry?

Ah, a lemonade will be lovely.

I am mourning my wife not celebrating the bloody citrus. You'll have a sherry. Swill from bloody Catholic fascist Spain.

I gulp the sherry. He refills my glass and goes to refill his own with whiskey. Damn. Whiskey all gone. Stay here. Do you hear me? I'm going to the pub for another bottle of whiskey. Stay till I come back. Don't move.

I'm confused, dizzy from the sherry. I don't know what you're supposed to do with grieving Englishmen. Mrs. Harrington, you look lovely in the bed. But you're a Protestant, already doomed, in hell, like Theresa. Priest said, Outside the Church there is no salvation. Wait, I might be able to save your soul. Baptize you Catholic. Make up for what I did to Theresa. I'll get some water. Oh, God, the door is locked. Why? Maybe you're not dead at all? Watching me. Are you dead, Mrs. Harrington? I'm not afraid. Your face is icy. Oh, you're dead all right. I'll baptize you with sherry from bloody Catholic fascist Spain. I baptize thee in the name of the Father, the Son, the—

What the bloody hell are you doing? Get off my wife, you wretched Papist twit. What primitive Paddy ritual is this? Did you touch her? Did you? I'll wring your scrawny neck.

I— I,—

Oi, Oi, speak English, you scrap.

I was just, a little sherry to get her into heaven.

Heaven? We had heaven, Ann, I, our daughter, Emily. You'll never lay your pink piggy eyes on her. Oh, Christ, I can't stand it. Here, more sherry.

Ah, no, thanks.

Ah, no thanks. That puny Celtic whine. You people love your alcohol. Helps you crawl and whine better. Of course you want food. You have the collapsed look of a starving Paddy. Here. Ham. Eat.

Ah, no thanks.

Ah, no thanks. Say that again and I'll ram the ham up your arse.

He waves a ham sandwich at me, with the heel of his hand pushes it into my mouth.

He collapses into a chair. Oh, God, God, what am I to do? Must rest a moment.

My stomach heaves. I rush to the window, stick my head out and throw up. He leaps from the chair and charges me.

You, you, God blast you to hell, you vomited on my wife's rosebush.

He lunges at me, misses, falls to the floor. I climb out the window, hang on to the ledge. He's at the window, grabbing at my hands. I let go, drop to the rosebush, into the ham sandwich and sherry I've just thrown up. I'm pricked by rose thorns, stung, my ankle is twisted. He's at the window, barking, Come back here, you Irish runt. He'll report me to the post office. He hits me in the back with the whiskey bottle, pleads, Will you not watch one hour with me?

He pelts me with sherry glasses, whiskey glasses, assorted ham sandwiches, items from his wife's dressing table, powders, creams, brushes.

I climb on my bike and wobble through the streets of Limerick, dizzy with sherry and pain. Mrs. O'Connell attacks me, Seven telegrams, one address, and you're gone all day.

I was, I was,

You was. You was. Drunk is what you was. Drunk is what you are. Reeking. Oh, we heard. That nice man rang, Mr. Harrington, lovely Englishman that sounds like James Mason. Lets you in to say a prayer for his poor wife and next thing you're out the window with the sherry and the ham. Your poor mother. What she brought into the world.

He made me eat the ham, drink the sherry.

Made you? Jesus, that's a good one. Made you. Mr. Harrington is a refined Englishman and there is no reason for him to lie and we don't want your kind in this post office, people that can't keep their hands off the ham and sherry, so hand in your telegram pouch and bicycle for your days are done in this post office.

But I need the job. I have to save and go to America.

America. Sad day when America lets in the likes of you.

I hobble through the streets of Limerick. I'd like to go back and throw a brick through Mr. Harrington's window. No. Respect for the dead. I'll go across the Sarsfield Bridge and out the riverbank where I can lie down somewhere in the bushes. I don't know how I can go home and tell my mother I lost my job. Have to go home. Have to tell her. Can't stay out the riverbank all night. She'd be frantic.

Mam begs the post office to take me back. They say no. They never heard the likes. Telegram boy mauling corpse. Telegram boy fleeing scene with ham and sherry. He will never set foot in the post office again. No.

She gets a letter from the parish priest. Take the boy back, says the parish priest. Oh, yes, Father, indeed, says the post office. They'll let me stay till my sixteenth birthday, not a minute longer. Besides, says Mrs. O'Connell, when you think of what the English did to us for eight hundred years that man had no right to complain over a little ham and sherry. Compare a little ham and sherry to the Great Famine and where are you? If my poor husband was alive and I told him what you did he'd say you struck a blow, Frank McCourt, struck a blow.

Every Saturday morning I swear I'll go to confession and tell the priest of my impure acts at home, on lonely boreens around Limerick with cows and sheep gawking, on the heights of Carrigogunnell with the world looking up.

I'll tell him about Theresa Carmody and how I sent her to hell, and that will be the end of me, driven from the Church.

Theresa is a torment to me. Every time I deliver a telegram to her street, every time I pass the graveyard I feel the sin growing in me like an abscess and if I don't go to confession soon I'll be nothing but an abscess riding around on a bicycle with people pointing and telling each other, There he is, there's Frankie McCourt, the dirty thing that sent Theresa Carmody to hell.

I look at people going to Communion on Sundays, everyone in a state of grace, returning to their seats with God in their mouths, peaceful, easy, ready to die at any moment and go straight to heaven or go home to their rashers and eggs without a worry in the world.

I'm worn out from being the worst sinner in Limerick. I want to get rid of this sin and have rashers and eggs and no guilt, no torment. I want to be ordinary.

The priests tell us all the time that God's mercy is infinite but how can any priest give absolution to someone like me who delivers telegrams and winds up in a state of excitement on a green sofa with a girl dying of the galloping consumption.

I cycle all around Limerick with telegrams and stop at every church. I ride from Redemptorists to Jesuits to Augustinians to Dominicans to Franciscans. I kneel before the statue of St. Francis of Assisi and beg him to help me but I think he's too disgusted with me. I kneel with people in the pews next to confessionals but when my turn comes I can't breathe, my heart pounds, my forehead turns cold and clammy and I run from the church.

I swear I'll go to confession at Christmas. I can't. Easter. I can't. Weeks and months pass and it's a year since Theresa died. I'll go on her anniversary but I can't. I'm fifteen now and I pass churches without stopping. I'll have to wait till I go to America where there are priests like Bing Crosby in *Going My Way* who won't kick me out of the confessional like Limerick priests.

I still have the sin in me, the abscess, and I hope it doesn't kill me entirely before I see the American priest.

There's a telegram for an old woman, Mrs. Brigid Finucane. She says, How old are you, by?

Fifteen and a half, Mrs. Finucane.

Young enough to make a fool of yourself and ould enough to know better. Are you shmart, by? Are you anyway intelligent?

I can read and write, Mrs. Finucane.

Arrah, there are people above in the lunatic asylum can read and write. Can you write a letter?

I can.

She wants me to write letters to her customers. If you need a suit or dress for your child you can go to her. She gives you a ticket to a shop and they give you the clothes. She gets a discount and charges you the full price and interest on top. You pay her back weekly. Some of her customers fall behind in their payments and they need threatening letters. She says, I'll give you threepence for every letter you write and another threepence if it brings a payment. If you want the job come here on Thursday and Friday nights, and bring your own paper and envelopes.

I'm desperate for that job. I want to go to America. But I have no money for paper and envelopes. Next day I'm delivering a telegram to Woolworth's and there is the answer, a whole section packed with paper and envelopes. I have no money so I have to help myself. But how? Two dogs save the day for me, two dogs at the door of Woolworth's stuck together after the excitement. They yelp and run in circles. Customers and sales clerks giggle and pretend to be looking someplace else and while they're busy pretending I slip paper and envelopes under my sweater, out the door and off on my bike far from stuck dogs.

Mrs. Finucane looks suspicious. That's very fancy stationery you have there, by. Is that your mother's? You'll give that back when you get the money, won't you, by?

Oh, I will.

From now on I'm never to come to her front door. There's a lane behind her house and I'm to come in the back door for fear someone might see me.

In a large ledger she gives me the names and addresses of six customers behind in their payments. Threaten 'em, by. Frighten the life out of 'em.

My first letter,

Dear Mrs. O'Brien,
    Inasmuch as you have not seen fit to pay me what you
owe me I may be forced to resort to legal action. There's your
son, Michael, parading around the world in his new suit
which I paid for while I myself have barely a crust to keep
body and soul together. I am sure you don't want to languish
in the dungeons of Limerick jail far from friends and family.
                    I remain, yours in litigious anticipation,
                                        Mrs. Brigid Finucane

She tells me, That's a powerful letter, by, better than anything you'd read in the *Limerick Leader*. That word, inasmuch, that's a holy terror of a word. What does it mean?

I think it means this is your last chance.

I write five more letters and she gives me money for stamps. On my way to the post office I think, Why should I squander money on stamps when I have two legs to deliver the letters myself in the dead of night? When you're poor a threatening letter is a threatening letter no matter how it comes in the door.

I run through the lanes of Limerick shoving letters under doors, praying no one will see me.

The next week Mrs. Finucane is squealing with joy. Four of 'em paid. Oh, sit down now and write more, by. Put the fear of God in 'em.

Week after week my threatening letters grow sharper and sharper. I begin to throw in words I hardly understand myself.

Dear Mrs. O'Brien,

Inasmuch as you have not succumbed to the imminence of litigation in our previous epistle be advised that we are in consultation with our barrister above in Dublin.

Next week Mrs. O'Brien pays. She came in tremblin' with tears in her eyes, by, and she promised she'd never miss another payment.

On Friday nights Mrs. Finucane sends me to a pub for a bottle of sherry. You're too young for sherry, by. You can make yourself a nice cup of tea but you have to use the tea leaves left over from this morning. No, you can't have a piece of bread with the prices they're charging. Bread is it? Next thing you'll be asking for an egg.

She rocks by the fire, sipping her sherry, counting the money in the purse on her lap, entering payments in her ledger before she locks everything in the trunk under her bed upstairs. After a few sherries she tells me what a lovely thing it is to have a little money so you can leave it to the Church for Masses to be said for the repose of your soul. It makes her so happy to think of priests saying Masses for her years and years after she's dead and buried.

Sometimes she falls asleep and if the purse drops to the floor I help myself to an extra few shillings for the overtime and the use of all the big new words. There will be less money for the priests and their Masses but how many Masses does a soul need and surely I'm entitled to a few pounds after the way the Church slammed doors in my face? They wouldn't let me be an altar boy, a secondary school pupil, a missionary with the White Fathers. I don't care. I have a post office savings account and if I keep writing successful threatening letters, helping myself to the odd few shillings from her purse and keeping the stamp money, I'll have my escape money to America. If my whole family dropped from the hunger I wouldn't touch this money in the post office.

Often I have to write threatening letters to neighbors and friends of my mother and I worry they might discover me. They complain to Mam, That oul' bitch, Finucane, below in Irishtown, sent me a threatening letter. What kind of a demon outa hell would torment her own kind with a class of a letter that I can't make head nor tail of anyway with words never heard on land or sea. The person that would write that letter is worse than Judas or any informer for the English.

My mother says anyone that writes such letters should be boiled in oil and have his fingernails pulled out by blind people.

I'm sorry for their troubles but there's no other way for me to save the money for America. I know that someday I'll be a rich Yank and send home hundreds of dollars and my family will never have to worry about threatening letters again.

Some of the temporary telegram boys are taking the permanent exam in August. Mrs. O'Connell says, You should take that exam, Frank McCourt. You have a bit of a brain in your head and you'd pass it no bother. You'd be a postman in no time and a great help to your poor mother.

Mam says I should take it, too, become a postman, save up, go to America and be a postman over there and wouldn't that be a lovely life.

I'm delivering a telegram to South's pub on a Saturday and Uncle Pa Keating is sitting there, all black as usual. He says, Have a lemonade there, Frankie, or is it a pint you want now that you're near sixteen?

Lemonade, Uncle Pa, thanks.

You'll want your first pint the day you're sixteen, won't you?

I will but my father won't be here to get it for me.

Don't worry about that. I know 'tis not the same without your father but I'll get you the first pint. 'Tis what I'd do if I had a son. Come here the night before you're sixteen.

I will, Uncle Pa.

I hear you're taking that exam for the post office?

I am.

Why would you do a thing like that?

'Tis a good job and I'd be a postman in no time and it has the pension.

Ah, pension my arse. Sixteen years of age an' talking about the pension. Is it coddin' me you are? Do you hear what I said, Frankie? Pension my arse. If you pass the exam you'll stay in the post office nice and secure the rest of your life. You'll marry a Brigid and have five little Catholics and grow little roses in your garden. You'll be dead in your head before you're thirty and dried in your ballocks the year before. Make up your own bloody mind and to hell with the safeshots and the begrudgers. Do you hear me, Frankie McCourt?

I do, Uncle Pa. That's what Mr. O'Halloran said.

What did he say?

Make up your own mind.

True for Mr. O'Halloran. 'Tis your life, make your own decisions and to hell with the begrudgers, Frankie. In the heel o' the hunt you'll be going to America anyway, won't you?

I will, Uncle Pa.

The day of the exam I'm excused from work. There's a sign in an office window on O'Connell Street, SMART BOY WANTED, NEAT HANDWRITING, GOOD AT SUMS, APPLY HERE TO MANAGER, MR. MCCAFFREY, EASONS LTD.

I stand outside the place of the exam, the house of the Limerick Protestant Young Men's Association. There are boys from all over Limerick climbing the steps to take the exam and a man at the door is handing them sheets of paper and pencils and barking at them to hurry up, hurry up. I look at the man at the door, I think of Uncle Pa Keating and what he said, I think of the sign in Easons' office, SMART BOY WANTED. I don't want to go in that door and pass that exam for if I do I'll be a permanent telegram boy with a uniform, then a postman, then a clerk selling stamps for the rest of my life. I'll be in Limerick forever, growing roses with my head dead and my ballocks all dried up.

The man at the door says, You, are you coming in here or are you goin' to stand there with your face hanging out?

I want to say to the man, Kiss my arse, but I still have a few weeks left in the post office and he might report me. I shake my head and walk up the street where a smart boy is wanted.

The manager, Mr. McCaffrey, says, I would like to see a specimen of your handwriting, to see, in short, if you have a decent fist. Sit down there at that table. Write your name and address and write me a paragraph explaining why you came here for this job and how you propose to rise in the ranks of Eason and Son, Ltd., by dint of perseverance and assiduity where there is great opportunity in this company for a boy that will keep his eye on the guidon ahead and guard his flanks from the siren call of sin.

I write,

> Frank McCourt,
> 4, Little Barrington Street,
> Limerick City,
> County Limerick,
> Ireland

> I am applying for this job so that I can rise to the highest ranks of Easons Ltd., by dint of perseverance and assadooty knowing that if I keep my eyes ahead and protect my flanks I'll be safe from all temptation and a credit to Easons and Ireland in general.

What's this? says Mr. McCaffrey. Do we have here a twisting of the truth?

I don't know, Mr. McCaffrey.

Little Barrington Street. That's a lane. Why are you calling it a street? You live in a lane, not a street.

They call it a street, Mr. McCaffrey.

Don't be getting above yourself, boy.

Oh, I wouldn't, Mr. McCaffrey.

You live in a lane and that means you have nowhere to go but up. Do you understand that, McCourt?

I do, sir.

You have to work your way out of the lane, McCourt.

I do, Mr. McCaffrey.

You have the cut and jib of a lane boy, McCourt.

Yes, Mr. McCaffrey.

You have the look of the lane all over you. All over you from poll to toe cap. Don't try to fool the populace, McCourt. You'd have to rise early in the morning to fool the likes of me.

Oh, I wouldn't, Mr. McCaffrey.

Then there's the eyes. Very sore eyes you have there. Can you see?

I can, Mr. McCaffrey.

You can read and write but can you do addition and subtraction?

I can, Mr. McCaffrey.

Well, I don't know what the policy is on sore eyes. I would have to ring Dublin and see where they stand on sore eyes. But your writing is clear, McCourt. A good fist. We'll take you on pending the decision on the sore eyes. Monday morning. Half six at the railway station.

In the morning?

In the morning. We don't give out the bloody morning papers at night, do we?

No, Mr. McCaffrey.

Another thing. We distribute *The Irish Times*, a Protestant paper, run by the freemasons in Dublin. We pick it up at the railway station. We count it. We take it to the newsagents. But we don't read it. I don't want to see you reading it. You could lose the Faith and by the look of those eyes you could lose your sight. Do you hear me, McCourt?

I do, Mr. McCaffrey.

No *Irish Times,* and when you come in next week I'll tell you about all the English filth you're not to read in this office. Do you hear me?

I do, Mr. McCaffrey

Mrs. O'Connell has the tight mouth and she won't look at me. She says to Miss Barry, I hear a certain upstart from the lanes walked away from the post office exam. Too good for it, I suppose.

True for you, says Miss Barry.

Too good for us, I suppose.

True for you.

Do you think he'd ever tell us why he didn't take the exam?

Oh, he might, says Miss Barry, if we went down on our two knees.

I tell her, I want to go to America, Mrs. O'Connell.

Did you hear that, Miss Barry?

I did, indeed, Mrs. O'Connell.

He spoke.

He did, indeed.

He will rue the day, Miss Barry.

Rue he will, Mrs. O'Connell.

Mrs. O'Connell talks past me to the boys waiting on the bench for their telegrams, This is Frankie McCourt who thinks he's too good for the post office.

I don't think that, Mrs. O'Connell.

And who asked you to open your gob, Mr. High and Mighty? Too grand for us, isn't he, boys?

He is, Mrs. O'Connell.

And after all we did for him, giving him the telegrams with the good tips, sending him to the country on fine days, taking him back after his disgraceful behavior with Mr. Harrington, the Englishman, disrespecting the body of poor Mrs. Harrington, stuffing himself with ham sandwiches, getting fluthered drunk on sherry, jumping out the window and destroying every rosebush in sight, coming in here three sheets to the wind, and who knows what else he did delivering telegrams for two years, who knows indeed, though we have a good idea, don't we, Miss Barry?

We do, Mrs. O'Connell, though 'twouldn't be a fit subject to be talking about.

She whispers to Miss Barry and they look at me and shake their heads.

A disgrace he is to Ireland and his poor mother. I hope she never finds out. But what would you expect of one born in America and his father from the North. We put up with all that and still took him back.

She keeps talking past me again to the boys on the bench.

Going to work for Easons he is, working for that pack of freemasons and Protestants above in Dublin. Too good for the post office but ready and willing to deliver all kinds of filthy English magazines all over Limerick. Every magazine he touches will be a mortal sin. But he's leaving now, so he is, and a sorry day it is for his poor mother that prayed for a son with a pension to take care of her in her latter days. So here, take your wages and go from the sight of us.

Miss Barry says, He's a bad boy, isn't he, boys?

He is, Miss Barry.

I don't know what to say. I don't know what I did wrong. Should I say I'm sorry? Good-bye?

I lay my belt and pouch on Mrs. O'Connell's desk. She glares at me, Go on. Go to your job at Easons. Go from us. Next boy, come up for your telegrams.

They're back at work and I'm down the stairs to the next part of my life.

XVII

I don't know why Mrs. O'Connell had to shame me before the whole world, and I don't think I'm too good for the post office or anything else. How could I with my hair sticking up, pimples dotting my face, my eyes red and oozing yellow, my teeth crumbling with the rot, no shoulders, no flesh on my arse after cycling thirteen thousand miles to deliver twenty thousand telegrams to every door in Limerick and regions beyond?

Mrs. O'Connell said a long time ago she knew everything about every telegram boy. She must know about the times I went at myself on top of Carrigogunnell, milkmaids gawking, little boys looking up.

She must know about Theresa Carmody and the green sofa, how I got her into a state of sin and sent her to hell, the worst sin of all, worse than Carrigogunnell a thousand times. She must know I never went to confession after Theresa, that I'm doomed to hell myself.

A person that commits a sin like that is never too good for the post office or anything else.

The barman at South's remembers me from the time I sat with Mr. Hannon, Bill Galvin, Uncle Pa Keating, black white black. He remembers my father, how he spent his wages and his dole while singing patriotic songs and making speeches from the dock like a condemned rebel.

And what is it you'd like? says the barman.

I'm here to meet Uncle Pa Keating and have my first pint.

Oh, begod, is that a fact? He'll be here in a minute and sure there's no reason why I shouldn't draw his pint and maybe draw your first pint, is there now?

There isn't, sir.

Uncle Pa comes in and tells me sit next to him against the wall. The barman brings the pints, Uncle Pa pays, lifts his glass, tells the men in the pub, This is my nephew, Frankie McCourt, son of Angela Sheehan, the sister of my wife, having his first pint, here's to your health and long life, Frankie, may you live to enjoy the pint but not too much.

The men lift their pints, nod, drink, and there are creamy lines on their lips and mustaches. I take a great gulp of my pint and Uncle Pa tells me, Slow down for the love o' Jasus, don't drink it all, there's more where that came from as long as the Guinness family stays strong and healthy.

I tell him I want to stand him a pint with my last wages from the post office but he says, No, take the money home to your mother and you can stand me a pint when you come home from America flushed with success and the heat from a blonde hanging on your arm.

The men in the pub are talking about the terrible state of the world and how in God's name Hermann Goering escaped the hangman an hour before the hanging. The Yanks are over there in Nuremberg declaring they don't know how the Nazi bastard hid that pill. Was it in his ear? Up his nostril? Up his arse? Surely the Yanks looked in every hole and cranny of every Nazi they captured and still Hermann wiped their eye. There you are. It shows you can sail across the Atlantic, land in Normandy, bomb Germany off the face of the earth, but when all's said and done they can't find a little pill planted in the far reaches of Goering's fat arse.

Uncle Pa buys me another pint. It's harder to drink because it fills me and makes my belly bulge. The men are talking about concentration camps and the poor Jews that never harmed a soul, men, women, children crammed into ovens, children, mind you, what harm could they do, little shoes scattered everywhere, crammed in, and the pub is misty and the voices fading in and out. Uncle Pa says, Are you all right? You're as white as a sheet. He takes me to the lavatory and the two of us have a good long piss against the wall which keeps moving back and forth. I can't go into the pub again, cigarette smoke, stale Guinness, Goering's fat arse, small shoes scattered, can't go in again, good night, Uncle Pa, thanks, and he tells me go straight home to my mother, straight home, oh, he doesn't know about the excitement in the loft or the excitement on the green sofa or me in such a state of doom that if I died now I'd be in hell in a wink.

Uncle Pa goes back to his pint. I'm out on O'Connell Street and why shouldn't I take the few steps to the Jesuits and tell all my sins this last night I'll be fifteen. I ring the bell at the priests' house and a big man answers, Yes? I tell him, I want to go to confession, Father. He says, I'm not a priest. Don't call me father. I'm a brother.

All right, Brother. I want to go to confession before I'm sixteen tomorrow. State o' grace on my birthday.

He says, Go away. You're drunk. Child like you drunk as a lord ringing for a priest at this hour. Go away or I'll call the guards.

Ah, don't. Ah, don't. I only want to go to confession. I'm doomed.

You're drunk and you're not in a proper spirit of repentance.

He closes the door in my face. Another door closed in the face, but I'm sixteen tomorrow and I ring again. The brother opens the door, swings me around, kicks my arse and sends me tripping down the steps.

He says, Ring this bell again and I'll break your hand.

Jesuit brothers are not supposed to talk like that. They're supposed to be like Our Lord, not walking the world threatening people's hands.

I'm dizzy. I'll go home to bed. I hold on to railings along Barrington Street and keep to the wall going down the lane. Mam is by the fire smoking a Woodbine, my brothers upstairs in the bed. She says, That's a nice state to come home in.

It's hard to talk but I tell her I had my first pint with Uncle Pa. No father to get me the first pint.

Your Uncle Pa should know better.

I stagger to a chair and she says, Just like your father.

I try to control the way my tongue moves in my mouth. I'd rather be, I'd rather, rather be like my father than Laman Griffin.

She turns away from me and looks into the ashes in the range but I won't leave her alone because I had my pint, two pints, and I'm sixteen tomorrow, a man.

Did you hear me? I'd rather be like my father than Laman Griffin.

She stands up and faces me. Mind your tongue, she says.

Mind your own bloody tongue.

Don't talk to me like that. I'm your mother.

I'll talk to you any bloody way I like.

You have a mouth like a messenger boy.

Do I? Do I? Well, I'd rather be a messenger boy than the likes of Laman Griffin oul' drunkard with the snotty nose and his loft and people climbing up there with him.

She walks away from me and I follow her upstairs to the small room. She turns, Leave me alone, leave me alone, and I keep barking at her, Laman Griffin, Laman Griffin, till she pushes me, Get out of this room, and I slap her on the cheek so that tears jump in her eyes and there's a small whimpering sound from her, You'll never have the chance to do that again, and I back away from her because there's another sin on my long list and I'm ashamed of myself.

I fall into my bed, clothes and all, and wake up in the middle of the night puking on my pillow, my brothers complaining of the stink, telling me clean up, I'm a disgrace. I hear my mother crying and I want to tell her I'm sorry but why should I after what she did with Laman Griffin.

In the morning my small brothers are gone to school, Malachy is out looking for a job, Mam is at the fire drinking tea. I place my wages on the table by her elbow and turn to go. She says, Do you want a cup of tea?

No.

'Tis your birthday.

I don't care.

She calls up the lane after me, You should have something in your stomach, but I give her my back and turn the corner without answering. I still want to tell her I'm sorry but if I do I'll want to tell her she's the cause of it all, that she should not have climbed to the loft that night and I don't give a fiddler's fart anyway because I'm still writing threatening letters for Mrs. Finucane and saving to go to America.

I have the whole day before I go to Mrs. Finucane to write the threatening letters and I wander down Henry Street till the rain drives me into the Franciscan church where St. Francis stands with his birds and lambs. I look at him and wonder why I ever prayed to him. No, I didn't pray, I begged.

I begged him to intercede for Theresa Carmody but he never did a thing, stood up there on his pedestal with the little smile, the birds, the lambs, and didn't give a fiddler's fart about Theresa or me.

I'm finished with you, St. Francis. Moving on. Francis. I don't know why they ever gave me that name. I'd be better off if they called me Malachy, one a king, the other a great saint. Why didn't you heal

Theresa? Why did you let her go to hell? You let my mother climb to the loft. You let me get into a state of doom. Little children's shoes scattered in concentration camps. I have the abscess again. It's in my chest and I'm hungry.

St. Francis is no help, he won't stop the tears bursting out of my two eyes, the sniffling and choking and the God oh Gods that have me on my knees with my head on the back of the pew before me and I'm so weak with the hunger and the crying I could fall on the floor and would you please help me God or St. Francis because I'm sixteen today and I hit my mother and sent Theresa to hell and wanked all over Limerick and the county beyond and I dread the millstone around my neck.

There is an arm around my shoulders, a brown robe, click of black rosary beads, a Franciscan priest.

My child, my child, my child.

I'm a child and I lean against him, little Frankie on his father's lap, tell me all about Cuchulain, Dad, my story that Malachy can't have or Freddie Leibowitz on the swings.

My child, sit here with me. Tell me what troubles you. Only if you want to. I am Father Gregory.

I'm sixteen today, Father.

Oh, lovely, lovely, and why should that be a trouble to you?

I drank my first pint last night.

Yes?

I hit my mother.

God help us, my child. But He will forgive you. Is there anything else?

I can't tell you, Father.

Would you like to go to confession?

I can't, Father. I did terrible things.

God forgives all who repent. He sent His only Beloved Son to die for us.

I can't tell, Father. I can't.

But you could tell St. Francis, couldn't you?

He doesn't help me anymore.

But you love him, don't you?

I do. My name is Francis.

Then tell him. We'll sit here and you'll tell him the things that trouble you. If I sit and listen it will only be a pair of ears for St. Francis and Our Lord. Won't that help?

I talk to St. Francis and tell him about Margaret, Oliver, Eugene, my father singing Roddy McCorley and bringing home no money, my father sending no money from England, Theresa and the green sofa, my terrible sins on Carrigogunnell, why couldn't they hang Hermann Goering for what he did to the little children with shoes scattered around concentration camps, the Christian Brother who closed the door in my face, the time they wouldn't let me be an altar boy, my small brother Michael walking up the lane with the broken shoe clacking, my bad eyes that I'm ashamed of, the Jesuit brother who closed the door in my face, the tears in Mam's eyes when I slapped her.

Father Gregory says, Would you like to sit and be silent, perhaps pray a few minutes?

His brown robe is rough against my cheek and there's a smell of soap. He looks at St. Francis and the tabernacle and nods and I suppose he's talking to God. Then he tells me kneel, gives me absolution, tells me say three Hail Marys, three Our Fathers, three Glory Bes. He tells me God forgives me and I must forgive myself, that God loves me and I must love myself for only when you love God in yourself can you love all God's creatures.

But I want to know about Theresa Carmody in hell, Father.

No, my child. She is surely in heaven. She suffered like the martyrs in olden times and God knows that's penance enough. You can be sure the sisters in the hospital didn't let her die without a priest.

Are you sure, Father?

I am, my child.

He blesses me again, asks me to pray for him, and I'm happy trotting through the rainy streets of Limerick knowing Theresa is in heaven with the cough gone.

Monday morning and it's dawn in the railway station. Newspapers and magazines are piled in bundles along the platform wall. Mr. McCaffrey is there with another boy, Willie Harold, cutting the twine on the bundles, counting, entering the count in a ledger. English newspapers and *The Irish Times* have to be delivered early, magazines later in the morning. We count out the papers and label them for delivery to shops around the city.

Mr. McCaffrey drives the van and stays at the wheel while Willie and I run into shops with bundles and take orders for the next day, add or drop in the ledger. After the papers are delivered we unload the magazines at the office and go home to breakfast for fifty minutes.

When I return to the office there are two other boys, Eamon and Peter, already sorting magazines, counting and stuffing them into newsagents' boxes along the wall. Small orders are delivered by Gerry Halvey on his messenger bicycle, big orders in the van. Mr. McCaffrey tells me stay in the office so that I can learn to count magazines and enter them in the ledger. The minute Mr. McCaffrey leaves Eamon and Peter pull out a drawer where they hide cigarette butts and light up. They can't believe I don't smoke. They want to know if there's something wrong with me, the bad eyes or the consumption maybe. How can you go out with a girl if you don't smoke? Peter says, Wouldn't you be a right eejit if you were going out the road with the girl and she asked you for a fag and you said you didn't smoke, wouldn't you be a right eejit then? How would you ever get her into a field for a bit of a feel? Eamon says, 'Tis what my father says about men who don't drink, they're not to be trusted. Peter says if you find a man that won't drink or smoke that's a man that's not even interested in girls and you'd want to keep your hand over the hole of your arse, that's what you'd want to be doing.

They laugh and that brings on the cough and the more they laugh the more they cough till they're holding on to one another banging one another between the shoulder blades and wiping tears from their cheeks. When the fit passes we pick out English and American magazines and look at the advertisements for women's underwear, brassieres and panties and long nylon stockings. Eamon is looking at an American magazine called *See* with pictures of Japanese girls who keep the soldiers happy so far away from home and Eamon says he has to go to the lavatory and when he does Peter gives me a wink, You know what he's up to in there, don't you? and sometimes Mr. McCaffrey gets into a state when boys linger in the lavatory interfering with themselves and wasting the valuable time for which Easons is paying them and on top of it putting their immortal souls in danger. Mr. McCaffrey won't come right out and say, Stop that wanking, because you can't accuse someone of a mortal sin unless you have proof. Sometimes he goes snooping in the lavatory when a boy comes out. He comes back himself with the threatening look and tells the boys, Ye are not to be looking at those dirty magazines from foreign parts. Ye are to count them and put them in the boxes and that's all.

Eamon comes back from the lavatory and Peter goes in with an American magazine, *Collier's*, that has pictures of girls in a beauty contest. Eamon says, Do you know what he's doing in there? At himself. Five times a day he goes in. Every time a new American magazine comes in with the women's underwear he goes in. Never done going at himself. Borrows magazines to take home unbeknownst to Mr. McCaffrey and God knows what he does with himself and the magazines all night. If he fell dead in there the jaws of hell would open wide.

I'd like to get into the lavatory myself when Peter comes out but I don't want them saying, There he goes, new boy, first day on the job, already at himself. Won't light up a fag oh no but wanks away like an oul' billygoat.

Mr. McCaffrey returns from van delivery and wants to know why all the magazines aren't counted out, bundled and ready to go. Peter tells him, We were busy teaching the new boy, McCourt. God help us, he was a bit slow with the bad eyes you know but we kept at him and now he's getting faster.

Gerry Halvey, the messenger boy, won't be in for a week because he's entitled to his holidays and he wants to spend the time with his girlfriend, Rose, who's coming back from England. I'm the new boy and I have to be messenger boy while he's gone, cycling around Limerick on the bicycle with the big metal basket in front. He shows me how to balance papers and magazines so that the bicycle won't tip over with me in the saddle and a lorry passing by that will run over me and leave me like a piece of salmon in the road. He saw a soldier once that was run over by an army lorry and that's what he looked like, salmon.

Gerry is making a last delivery at Easons kiosk at the railway station at noon on Saturday and that's handy because I can meet him there to get the bicycle and he can meet Rose off the train. We stand at the gate waiting and he tells me he hasn't seen Rose in a year. She's over there working in a pub in Bristol and he doesn't like that one bit because the English are forever pawing the Irish girls, hands up under the skirts and worse, and the Irish girls are afraid to say anything for fear of losing their jobs. Everyone knows Irish girls keep themselves pure especially Limerick girls known the world over for their purity who have a man to come back to like Gerry Halvey himself. He'll be able to tell if she was true to him by her walk. If a girl comes back after a year with a certain class of a walk that's different from the one she went away with then you know she was up to no good with the Englishmen dirty horny bastards that they are.

The train hoots into the station and Gerry waves and points to Rose coming toward us from the far end of the train, Rose smiling away with her white teeth and lovely in a green dress. Gerry stops waving and mutters under his breath, Look at the walk on her, bitch, hoor, street-walker, flaghopper, trollop, and runs from the station. Rose walks up to me, Was that Gerry Halvey you were standing with?

'Twas.

Where is he?

Oh, he went out.

I know he went out. Where did he go?

I don't know. He didn't tell me. He just ran out.

Didn't say anything?

I didn't hear him say anything.

Do you work with him?

I do. I'm taking over the bike.

What bike?

The messenger bike.

Is he on a messenger bike?

He is.

He told me he worked in Easons office, clerk, inside job?

I feel desperate. I don't want to make a liar of Gerry Halvey, to get him into trouble with the lovely Rose. Oh, we all take turns on the messenger bike. An hour in the office, an hour on the bike. The manager says 'tis good to get out in the fresh air.

Well, I'll just go home and put my suitcase down and go to his house. I thought he'd carry this for me.

I have the bike here and you can stick the case in the basket and I'll walk you home.

We walk up to her house in Carey's Road and she tells me she's so excited about Gerry. She saved her money in England and now she wants to go back with him and get married even if he's only nineteen and she's only seventeen. What matter when you're in love. I lived like a nun in England and dreamt of him every night and thank you very much for carrying my case.

I turn away to jump on the bike and cycle back to Easons when Gerry comes at me from behind. His face is red and he's snorting like a bull. What were you doing with my girl, you little shite? Eh?

What? If 'tis a thing I ever find out you did anything with my girl I'll kill you.

I didn't do anything. Carried her case because 'twas heavy.

Don't look at her again or you're dead.

I won't, Gerry. I don't want to look at her.

Oh, is that a fact? Is she ugly or what?

No, no, Gerry, she's yours and she loves you.

How do you know?

She told me.

She did?

She did, honest to God.

Jasus.

He bangs on her door, Rose, Rose, are you there? and she comes out, Of course, I'm here, and I ride away on the messenger bicycle with the sign on the basket that says Easons wondering about the way he's kissing her now and the terrible things he said about her in the station and wondering how Peter in the office could tell Mr. McCaffrey a barefaced lie about me and my eyes when all the time he and Eamon were looking at girls in their underwear and then going at themselves in the lavatory.

Mr. McCaffrey is in a terrible state in the office. Where were you? Great God above in heaven, does it take you all day to cycle from the railway station? We have an emergency here and we should have Halvey but he's gone off on his friggin' holidays, God forgive the language, and you'll have to cycle around as fast as you can, good thing you were a telegram boy that knows every inch of Limerick, and go to every bloody shop that's a customer and walk right in grab whatever copies you see of *John O'London's Weekly* tear out page sixteen and if anyone bothers you tell them 'tis government orders and they're not to interfere in government business and if they lay a finger on you they're liable to arrest, imprisonment and a large fine now go for God's sake and bring back every page sixteen you tear out so that we can burn them here in the fire.

Every shop, Mr. McCaffrey?

I'll do the big ones, you do the small ones all the way to Ballinacurra and out the Ennis Road and beyond, God help us. Go on, go.

I'm jumping on the bike and Eamon runs down the steps. Hey, McCourt, wait. Listen. Don't give him all the page sixteens when you come back.

Why?

We can sell 'em, me an' Peter.

Why?

'Tis all about birth control and that's banned in Ireland.

What's birth control?

Aw, Christ above, don't you know anything? 'Tis condoms, you know, rubbers, French letters, things like that to stop the girls from getting up the pole.

Up the pole?

Pregnant. Sixteen years of age an' you're pure ignorant. Hurry up an' get the pages before everybody starts runnin' to the shop for *John O'London's Weekly*.

I'm about to push away on the bike when Mr. McCaffrey runs down the steps. Hold on, McCourt, we'll go in the van. Eamon, you come with us.

What about Peter?

Leave him. He'll wind up with a magazine in the lavatory anyway.

Mr. McCaffrey talks to himself in the van. Nice bloody how do you do ringing down here from Dublin on a fine Saturday to send us tearing around Limerick ripping pages out of an English magazine when I could be at home with a cup of tea and a nice bun and a read of *The Irish Press* with my feet up on a box under the picture of the Sacred Heart nice bloody how do you do entirely.

Mr. McCaffrey runs into every shop with us behind him. He grabs the magazines, hands each of us a pile and tells us start tearing. Shop owners scream at him, What are ye doing? Jesus, Mary and Holy St. Joseph, is it pure mad ye are? Put back them magazines or I'll call the guards.

Mr. McCaffrey tells them, Government orders, ma'am. There is filth in *John O'London* this week that's not fit for any Irish eyes and we are here to do God's work.

What filth? What filth? Show me the filth before ye go mutilatin' the magazines. I won't pay Easons for these magazines, so I won't.

Ma'am, we don't care at Easons. We'd rather lose large amounts than have the people of Limerick and Ireland corrupted by this filth.

What filth?

Can't tell you. Come on, boys.

We throw the pages on the floor of the van and when Mr. McCaffrey is in a shop arguing we stuff some into our shirts. There are old magazines in the van and we tear and scatter them so that Mr. McCaffrey will think they're all page sixteen from *John O'London.*

The biggest customer for the magazine, Mr. Hutchinson, tells Mr. McCaffrey get to hell out of his shop or he'll brain him, get away from them magazines, and when Mr. McCaffrey keeps on tearing out pages Mr. Hutchinson throws him into the street, Mr. McCaffrey yelling that this is a Catholic country and just because Hutchinson is a Protestant that doesn't give him the right to sell filth in the holiest city in Ireland. Mr. Hutchinson says, Ah, kiss my arse, and Mr. McCaffrey says, See, boys? See what happens when you're not a member of the True Church?

Some shops says they've already sold all their copies of *John O'London* and Mr. McCaffrey says, Oh, Mother o' God, what's going to become of us all? Who did ye sell them to?

He demands the names and address of the customers who are in danger of losing their immortal souls from reading articles on birth control. He will go to their houses and rip out that filthy page but the shopkeepers say, 'Tis Saturday night, McCaffrey, and getting dark and would you ever take a good running jump for yourself.

On the way back to the office Eamon whispers to me in the back of the van, I have twenty-one pages. How many do you have? I tell him fourteen but I have over forty and I'm not telling him because you never have to tell the truth to people who lie about your bad eyes. Mr. McCaffrey tells us bring in the pages from the van. We scoop up everything on the floor and he's happy sitting at his desk at the other end of the office ringing Dublin to tell them how he stormed through shops like God's avenger and saved Limerick from the horrors of birth control while he watches a dancing fire of pages that have nothing to do with *John O'London's Weekly.*

Monday morning I cycle through the streets delivering magazines and people see the Easons sign on the bike and stop me to see if there's any chance they could get their hands on a copy of *John O'London's Weekly.* They're all rich-looking people, some in motor cars, men with hats, collars and ties, and two fountain pens in their pockets, women with hats and little bits of fur dangling from their shoulders, people who have tea at the Savoy or the Stella and stick out their little fingers to show how well bred they are and now want to read this page about birth control.

Eamon told me early in the day, Don't sell the bloody page for less than five shillings. I asked him if he was joking. No, he wasn't. Everyone in Limerick is talking about this page and they're dying to get their hands on it.

Five shillings or nothing, Frankie. If they're rich charge more but that's what I'm charging so don't be going around on your bicycle and puttin' me out of business with low prices. We have to give Peter something or he'll be running to McCaffrey and spilling the beans.

Some people are willing to pay seven shillings and sixpence and I'm rich in two days with over ten pounds in my pocket minus one for Peter the snake, who would betray us to McCaffrey. I put eight pounds in the post office for my fare to America and that night we have a big supper of ham, tomatoes, bread, butter, jam. Mam wants to know if I won the sweepstakes and I tell her people give me tips. She's not happy I'm a messenger boy because that's the lowest you can drop in Limerick but if it brings in ham like this we should light a candle in gratitude. She doesn't know the money for my fare is growing in the post office and she'd die if she knew what I was earning from writing threatening letters.

Malachy has a new job in the stockroom of a garage handing out parts to mechanics and Mam herself is taking care of an old man, Mr. Sliney, out in the South Circular Road while his two daughters go off to work every day. She tells me if I'm delivering papers out there to come to the house for tea and a sandwich. The daughters will never know and the old man won't mind because he's only half conscious most of the time worn out from all his years in the English army in India.

She looks peaceful in the kitchen of this house in her spotless apron, everything clean and polished around her, flowers bobbing in the garden beyond, birds chirping away, music from Radio Eireann on the wireless. She sits at the table with a pot of tea, cups and saucers, plenty of bread, butter, cold meats of all kinds. I can have any class of a sandwich but all I know is ham and brawn. She doesn't have any brawn because that's the kind of thing you'd find people eating in lanes not in a house on the South Circular Road. She says the rich won't eat brawn because it's what they scoop off floors and counters in bacon factories and you never know what you're getting. The rich are very particular about what they stick between two slices of bread. Over in America brawn is called head cheese and she doesn't know why.

She gives me a ham sandwich with juicy slices of tomato and tea in a cup with little pink angels flying around shooting arrows at other little flying angels who are blue and I wonder why they can't make teacups and chamber pots without all kinds of angels and maidens cavorting in the glen. Mam says that's the way the rich are, they love the bit of decoration and wouldn't we if we had the money. She'd give her two eyes to have a house like this with flowers and birds abroad in the garden and the wireless playing that lovely *Warsaw Concerto* or the *Dream of Olwyn* and no end of cups and saucers with angels shooting arrows.

She says she has to look in on Mr. Sliney he's so old and feeble he forgets to call for the chamber pot.

Chamber pot? You have to empty his chamber pot?

Of course I do.

There's a silence here because I think we're remembering the cause of all our troubles, Laman Griffin's chamber pot. But that was a long time ago and now it's Mr. Sliney's chamber pot, which is no harm because she's paid for this and he's harmless. When she comes back she tells me Mr. Sliney would like to see me, so come in while he's awake.

He's lying in a bed in the front parlor, the window blocked with a black sheet, no sign of light. He tells my mother, Lift me up a bit, missus, and pull back that bloody thing off the window so I can see the boy.

He has long white hair down to his shoulders. Mam whispers he won't let anyone cut it. He says, I have me own teeth, son. Would you credit that? Do you have your own teeth, son?

I do, Mr. Sliney.

Ah. I was in India you know. Me and Timoney up the road. Bunch of Limerick men in India. Do you know Timoney, son?

I did, Mr. Sliney.

He's dead, you know. Poor bugger went blind. I have me sight. I have me teeth. Keep your teeth, son.

I will, Mr. Sliney.

I'm getting tired, son, but there's one thing I want to tell you. Are you listening to me?

I am, Mr. Sliney.

Is he listening to me, missus?

Oh, he is, Mr. Sliney.

Good. Now here's what I want to tell you. Lean over here so I can whisper in your ear. What I want to tell you is, Never smoke another man's pipe.

Halvey goes off to England with Rose and I have to stay on the messenger bike all through the winter. It's a bitter winter, ice everywhere, and I never know when the bike will go out from under me and send me flying into the street or onto the pavement, magazines and papers scattered. Shops complain to Mr. McCaffrey that *The Irish Times* is coming in decorated with bits of ice and dog shit and he mutters to us that's the way that paper should be delivered, Protestant rag that it is.

Every day after my deliveries I take *The Irish Times* home and read it to see where the danger is. Mam says it's a good thing Dad isn't here. He'd say, Is this what the men of Ireland fought and died for that my own son is sitting there at the kitchen table reading the freemason paper?

There are letters to the editor from people all over Ireland claiming they heard the first cuckoo of the year and you can read between the lines that people are calling each other liars. There are reports about Protestant weddings and pictures and the women always look lovelier than the ones we know in the lanes. You can see Protestant women have perfect teeth although Halvey's Rose had lovely teeth.

I keep reading *The Irish Times* and wondering if it's an occasion of sin though I don't care. As long as Theresa Carmody is in heaven not coughing I don't go to confession anymore. I read *The Irish Times* and *The Times* of London because that tells me what the King is up to every day and what Elizabeth and Margaret are doing.

I read English women's magazines for all the food articles and the answers to women's questions. Peter and Eamon put on English accents and pretend they're reading from English women's magazines.

Peter says, Dear Miss Hope, I'm going out with a fellow from Ireland named McCaffrey and he has his hands all over me and his thing pushing against my belly button and I'm demented not knowing what to do. I remain, yours anxiously, Miss Lulu Smith, Yorkshire.

Eamon says, Dear Lulu, If this McCaffrey is that tall that he's pushing his yoke against your belly button I suggest you find a smaller man who will slip it between your thighs. Surely you can find a decent short man in Yorkshire.

Dear Miss Hope, I am thirteen years old with black hair and something terrible is happening and I can't tell anyone not even my mother. I'm bleeding every few weeks you know where and I'm afraid I'll be found out. Miss Agnes Tripple, Little Biddle-on-the-Twiddle, Devon.

Dear Agnes, You are to be congratulated. You are now a woman and you can get your hair permed because you are having your monthlies. Do not fear your monthlies for all Englishwomen have them. They are a gift of God to purify us so that we can have stronger children for the empire, soldiers to keep the Irish in their place. In some parts of the world a woman with a monthly is unclean but we British cherish our women with the monthlies, oh we do indeed.

In the springtime there's a new messenger boy and I'm back in the office. Peter and Eamon drift off to England. Peter is fed up with Limerick, no girls, and you're driven to yourself, wank wank wank, that's all we ever do in Limerick. There are new boys. I'm senior boy and the job is easier because I'm fast and when Mr. McCaffrey is out in the van and my work is done I read the English, Irish, American magazines and papers. Day and night I dream of America.

Malachy goes to England to work in a rich Catholic boys' boarding school and he walks around cheerful and smiling as if he's the equal of any boy in the school and everyone knows when you work in an English boarding school you're supposed to hang your head and shuffle like a proper Irish servant. They fire him for his ways and Malachy tells them they can kiss his royal Irish arse and they say that's the kind of foul language and behavior you'd expect. He gets a job in the gas works in Coventry shoveling coal into the furnaces like Uncle Pa Keating, shoveling coal and waiting for the day he can go to America after me.

XVIII

I'm seventeen, eighteen, going on nineteen, working away at Easons, writing threatening letters for Mrs. Finucane, who says she's not long for this world and the more Masses said for her soul the better she'll feel. She puts money in envelopes and sends me to churches around the city to knock on priests' doors, hand in the envelopes with the request for Masses. She wants prayers from all the priests but the Jesuits. She says, They're useless, all head and no heart. That's what they should have over their door in Latin and I won't give them a penny because every penny you give a Jesuit goes to a fancy book or a bottle of wine.

She sends the money, she hopes the Masses are said, but she's never sure and if she's not sure why should I be handing out all that money to priests when I need the money to go to America and if I keep back a few pounds for myself and put it in the post office who will ever know the difference and if I say a prayer for Mrs. Finucane and light candles for her soul when she dies won't God listen even if I'm a sinner long past my last confession.

I'll be nineteen in a month. All I need is a few pounds to make up the fare and a few pounds in my pocket when I land in America.

The Friday night before my nineteenth birthday Mrs. Finucane sends me for the sherry. When I return she is dead in the chair, her eyes wide open, and her purse on the floor wide open. I can't look at her but I help myself to a roll of money. Seventeen pounds. I take the key to the trunk upstairs. I take forty of the hundred pounds in the trunk and the ledger. I'll add this to what I have in the post office and I have enough to go to America. On my way out I take the sherry bottle to save it from being wasted.

I sit by the River Shannon near the dry docks sipping Mrs. Finucane's sherry. Aunt Aggie's name is in the ledger. She owes nine pounds. It might have been the money she spent on my clothes a long time ago but now she'll never have to pay it because I heave the ledger into the river. I'm sorry I'll never be able to tell Aunt Aggie I saved her nine pounds. I'm sorry I wrote threatening letters to the poor people in the lanes of Limerick, my own people, but the ledger is gone, no one will ever know what they owe and they won't have to pay their balances. I wish I could tell them, I'm your Robin Hood.

Another sip of the sherry. I'll spare a pound or two for a Mass for Mrs. Finucane's soul. Her ledger is well on its way down the Shannon and out to the Atlantic and I know I'll follow it someday soon.

The man at O'Riordan's Travel Agency says he can't get me to America by air unless I travel to London first, which would cost a fortune. He can put me on a ship called the *Irish Oak,* which will be leaving Cork in a few weeks. He says, Nine days at sea, September October, best time of the year, your own cabin, thirteen passengers, best of food, bit of a holiday for yourself and that will cost fifty-five pounds, do you have it?

I do.

I tell Mam I'm going in a few weeks and she cries. Michael says, Will we all go some day?

We will.

Alphie says, Will you send me a cowboy hat and a thing you throw that comes back to you?

Michael tells him that's a boomerang and you'd have to go all the way to Australia to get the likes of that, you can't get it in America.

Alphie says you can get it in America yes you can and they argue about America and Australia and boomerangs till Mam says, For the love o' Jesus, yeer brother is leaving us and the two of ye are there squabbling over boomerangs. Will ye give over?

Mam says we'll have to have a bit of party the night before I go. They used to have parties in the old days when anyone would go to America, which was so far away the parties were called American wakes because the family never expected to see the departing one again in this life. She says 'tis a great pity Malachy can't come back from England but we'll be together in America someday with the help of God and His Blessed Mother.

On my days off from work I walk around Limerick and look at all the places we lived, the Windmill Street, Hartstonge Street, Roden Lane, Rosbrien Road, Little Barrington Street, which is really a lane. I stand looking at Theresa Carmody's house till her mother comes out and says, What do you want? I sit at the graves of Oliver and Eugene in the old St. Patrick's Burying Ground and cross the road to St. Lawrence's Cemetery where Theresa is buried. Wherever I go I hear voices of the dead and I wonder if they can follow you across the Atlantic Ocean.

I want to get pictures of Limerick stuck in my head in case I never come back. I sit in St. Joseph's Church and the Redemptorist church and tell myself take a good look because I might never see this again. I walk down Henry Street to say good-bye to St. Francis though I'm sure I'll be able to talk to him in America.

Now there are days I don't want to go to America. I'd like to go to O'Riordan's Travel Agency and get back my fifty-five pounds. I could wait till I'm twenty-one and Malachy can go with me so that I'll know at least one person in New York. I have strange feelings and sometimes when I'm sitting by the fire with Mam and my brothers I feel tears coming and I'm ashamed of myself for being weak. At first Mam laughs and tells me, Your bladder must be near your eye, but then Michael says, We'll all go to America, Dad will be there, Malachy will be there and we'll all be together, and she gets the tears herself and we sit there, the four of us, like weeping eejits.

Mam says this is the first time we ever had a party and isn't it a sad thing altogether that you have it when your children are slipping away one by one, Malachy to England, Frank to America. She saves a few shillings from her wages taking care of Mr. Sliney to buy bread, ham, brawn, cheese, lemonade and a few bottles of stout. Uncle Pa Keating brings stout, whiskey and a little sherry for Aunt Aggie's delicate stomach and she brings a cake loaded with currants and raisins she baked herself. The Abbot brings six bottles of stout and says, That's all right, Frankie, ye can all drink it as long as I have a bottle or two for meself to help me sing me song.

He sings "The Road to Rasheen." He holds his stout, closes his eyes, and song comes out in a high whine. The words make no sense and everyone wonders why tears are seeping from his shut eyes. Alphie whispers to me, Why is he crying over a song that makes no sense?

I don't know.

The Abbot ends his song, opens his eyes, wipes his cheeks and tells us that was a sad song about an Irish boy that went to America and got shot by gangsters and died before a priest could reach his side and he tells me don't be gettin' shot if you're not near a priest.

Uncle Pa says that's the saddest song he ever heard and is there any chance we could have something lively. He calls on Mam and she says, Ah, no, Pa, sure I don't have the wind.

Come on, Angela, come on. One voice now, one voice and one voice only.

All right. I'll try.

We all join in the chorus of her sad song,

> *A mother's love is a blessing*
> *No matter where you roam.*
> *Keep her while you have her,*
> *You'll miss her when she's gone.*

Uncle Pa says one song is worse than the one before and are we turning this night into a wake altogether, is there any chance someone would sing a song to liven up the proceedings or will he be driven to drink with the sadness.

Oh, God, says Aunt Aggie, I forgot. The moon is having an eclipse abroad this minute.

We stand out in the lane watching the moon disappear behind a round black shadow. Uncle Pa says, That's a very good sign for you going to America, Frankie.

No, says Aunt Aggie, 'tis a bad sign. I read in the paper that the moon is practicing for the end of the world.

Oh, end of the world my arse, says Uncle Pa. 'Tis the beginning for Frankie McCourt. He'll come back in a few years with a new suit and fat on his bones like any Yank and a lovely girl with white teeth hangin' from his arm.

Mam says, Ah, no, Pa, ah, no, and they take her inside and comfort her with a drop of sherry from Spain.

It's late in the day when the *Irish Oak* sails from Cork, past Kinsale and Cape Clear, and dark when lights twinkle on Mizen Head, the last of Ireland I'll see for God knows how long.

Surely I should have stayed, taken the post office examination, climbed in the world. I could have brought in enough money for Michael and Alphie to go to school with proper shoes and bellies well filled. We could have moved from the lane to a street or even an avenue where houses have gardens. I should have taken that examination and Mam would never again have to empty the chamber pots of Mr. Sliney or anyone else.

It's too late now. I'm on the ship and there goes Ireland into the night and it's foolish to be standing on this deck looking back and thinking of my family and Limerick and Malachy and my father in England and even more foolish that songs are going through my head Roddy McCorley goes to die and Mam gasping Oh the days of the Kerry dancing with poor Mr. Clohessy hacking away in the bed and now I want Ireland back at least I had Mam and my brothers and Aunt Aggie bad as she was and Uncle Pa, standing me my first pint, and my bladder is near my eye and here's a priest standing by me on the deck and you can see he's curious.

He's a Limerickman but he has an American accent from his years in Los Angeles. He knows how it is to leave Ireland, did it himself and never got over it. You live in Los Angeles with sun and palm trees day in day out and you ask God if there's any chance He could give you one soft rainy Limerick day.

The priest sits beside me at the table of the First Officer, who tells us ship's orders have been changed and instead of sailing to New York we're bound for Montreal.

Three days out and orders are changed again. We are going to New York after all.

Three American passengers complain, Goddam Irish. Can't they get it straight?

359

The day before we sail into New York orders are changed again. We are going to a place up the Hudson River called Albany.

The Americans say, Albany? Goddam Albany? Why the hell did we have to sail on a goddam Irish tub? Goddam.

The priest tells me pay no attention. All Americans are not like that.

I'm on deck the dawn we sail into New York. I'm sure I'm in a film, that it will end and lights will come up in the Lyric Cinema. The priest wants to point out things but he doesn't have to. I can pick out the Statue of Liberty, Ellis Island, the Empire State Building, the Chrysler Building, the Brooklyn Bridge. There are thousands of cars speeding along the roads and the sun turns everything to gold. Rich Americans in top hats white ties and tails must be going home to bed with the gorgeous women with white teeth. The rest are going to work in warm comfortable offices and no one has a care in the world.

The Americans are arguing with the captain and a man who climbed aboard from a tugboat. Why can't we get off here? Why do we have to sail all the goddam way to goddam Albany?

The man says, Because you're passengers on the vessel and the captain is the captain and we have no procedures for taking you ashore.

Oh, yeah. Well, this is a free country and we're American citizens.

Is that a fact? Well, you're on an Irish ship with an Irish captain and you'll do what he goddam tells you or swim ashore.

He climbs down the ladder, tugboat chugs away, and we sail up the Hudson past Manhattan, under the George Washington Bridge, past hundreds of Liberty ships that did their bit in the war, moored now and ready to rot.

The captain announces the tide will force us to drop anchor overnight opposite a place called, the priest spells it for me, Poughkeepsie. The priest says that's an Indian name and the Americans say goddam Poughkeepsie.

After dark a small boat put-puts to the ship and an Irish voice calls up, Hello, there. Bejasus, I saw the Irish flag, so I did. Couldn't believe me two eyes. Hello, there.

He invites the First Officer to go ashore for a drink and bring a friend and, You, too, Father. Bring a friend.

The priest invites me and we climb down a ladder to the small boat with the First Officer and the Wireless Officer. The man in the boat says his name is Tim Boyle from Mayo God help us and we docked there at the right time because there's a bit of a party and we're all invited. He takes us to a house with a lawn, a fountain and three pink birds standing on one leg. There are five women in a room called a living room. The women have stiff hair, spotless frocks. They have glasses in their hands and they're friendly and smile with perfect teeth. One says, Come right in. Just in time for the pawty.

Pawty. That's the way they talk and I suppose I'll be talking like that in a few years.

Tim Boyle tells us the girls are having a bit of a time while their husbands are away overnight hunting deer, and one woman, Betty, says, Yeah. Buddies from the war. That war is over nearly five years and they can't get over it so they shoot animals every weekend and drink Rheingold till they can't see. Goddam war, excuse the language, Fawder.

The priest whispers to me, These are bad women. We won't stay here long.

The bad women say, Whatcha like to drink? We got everything. What's your name, honey?

Frank McCourt.

Nice name. So you take a little drink. All the Irish take a little drink. You like a beer?

Yes, please.

Gee, so polite. I like the Irish. My grandmother was half Irish so that makes me half, quarter? I dunno. My name is Frieda. So here's your beer, honey.

The priest sits at the end of a sofa which they call a couch and two women talk to him. Betty asks the First Officer if he'd like to see the house and he says, Oh, I would, because we don't have houses like this in Ireland. Another woman tells the Wireless Officer he should see what they have growing in the garden, you wouldn't believe the flowers. Frieda asks me if I'm okay and I tell her yes but would she mind telling me where the lavatory is.

The what?

Lavatory.

Oh, you mean the bathroom. Right this way, honey, down the hall.

Thanks.

She pushes in the door, turns on the light, kisses my cheek and whispers she'll be right outside if I need anything.

I stand at the toilet bowl firing away and wonder what I'd need at a time like this and if this is a common thing in America, women waiting outside while you take a splash.

I finish, flush and go outside. She takes my hand and leads me into a bedroom, puts down her glass, locks the door, pushes me down on the bed. She's fumbling at my fly. Damn buttons. Don't you have zippers in Ireland? She pulls out my excitement climbs up on me slides up and down up and down Jesus I'm in heaven and there's a knock on the door the priest Frank are you in there Frieda putting her finger to her lips and her eyes rolling to heaven Frank are you in there Father would you ever take a good running jump for yourself and oh God oh Theresa do you see what's happening to me at long last I don't give a fiddler's fart if the Pope himself knocked on this door and the College of Cardinals gathered gawking at the windows oh God the whole inside of me is gone into her and she collapses on me and tells me I'm wonderful and would I ever consider settling in Poughkeepsie.

Frieda tells the priest I had a bit of a dizziness after going to the bathroom, that's what happens when you travel and you're drinking a strange beer like Rheingold, which she believes they don't have in Ireland. I can see the priest doesn't believe her and I can't stop the way the heat is coming and going in my face. He already wrote down my mother's name and address and now I'm afraid he'll write and say your fine son spent his first night in America in a bedroom in Poughkeepsie romping with a woman whose husband was away shooting deer for a bit of relaxation after doing his bit for America in the war and isn't this a fine way to treat the men who fought for their country.

The First Officer and the Wireless Officer return from their tours of the house and the garden and they don't look at the priest. The women tell us we must be starving and they go into the kitchen. We sit in the living room saying nothing to each other and listening to the women whispering and laughing in the kitchen. The priest whispers to me again, Bad women, bad women, occasion of sin, and I don't know what to say to him.

The bad women bring out sandwiches and pour more beer and when we finish eating they put on Frank Sinatra records and ask if anyone would like to dance. No one says yes because you'd never get up and dance with bad women in the presence of a priest, so the women dance with each other and laugh as if they all had little secrets. Tim Boyle drinks whiskey and falls asleep in a corner till Frieda wakes him and tells him take us back to the ship. When we're leaving Frieda leans toward me as if she might kiss my cheek but the priest says good night in a very sharp way and no one shakes hands. As we walk down the street to the river we hear the women laughing, tinkling and bright in the night air.

We climb the ladder and Tim calls to us from his little boat, Mind yourselves going up that ladder. Oh, boys, oh, boys, wasn't that a grand night? Good night, boys, and good night, Father.

We watch his little boat till it disappears into the dark of the Poughkeepsie riverbank. The priest says good night and goes below and the First Officer follows him.

I stand on the deck with the Wireless Officer looking at the lights of America twinkling. He says, My God, that was a lovely night, Frank. Isn't this a great country altogether?

XIX

'T is.

Frank McCourt

'Tis

A MEMOIR

Flamingo
An Imprint of HarperCollinsPublishers

ACKNOWLEDGEMENTS

Friends and family members have smiled and bestowed on me various graces: Nan Graham, Susan Moldow and Pat Eisemann at Scribner; Sarah Mosher, formerly at Scribner; Molly Friedrich, Aaron Priest, Paul Cirone and Lucy Childs of the Aaron Priest Literary Agency; the late Tommy Butler, Mike Reardon and Nick Browne, high priests of the long bar at the Lion's Head; Paul Schiffman, poet and mariner, who served at that same bar but rocked with the sea; Sheila McKenna, Dennis Duggan, Dennis Smith, Mary Breasted Smyth and Ted Smyth, Jack Deacy, Pete Hamill, Bill Flanagan, Marcia Rock, Peter Quinn, Brian Brown, Terry Moran, Isaiah Sheffer, Pat Mulligan, Brian Kelly, Mary Tierney, Gene Secunda, the late Paddy Clancy, the late Kevin Sullivan, friends all from the Lion's Head and the First Friday Club; my brothers, of course, Alphonsus, Michael, Malachy, and their wives Lynn, Joan, Diana; Robert and Cathy Frey, parents of Ellen.

My thanks, my love.

This book is dedicated to
My daughter, Maggie, for her warm, searching heart
and to
My wife, Ellen, for joining her side to mine

'TIS

PROLOGUE

That's your dream out now.

That's what my mother would say when we were children in Ireland and a dream we had came true. The one I had over and over was where I sailed into New York Harbor awed by the skyscrapers before me. I'd tell my brothers and they'd envy me for having spent a night in America till they began to claim they'd had that dream, too. They knew it was a sure way to get attention even though I'd argue with them, tell them I was the oldest, that it was my dream and they'd better stay out of it or there would be trouble. They told me I had no right to that dream for myself, that anyone could dream about America in the far reaches of the night and there was nothing I could do about it. I told them I could stop them. I'd keep them awake all night and they'd have no dreams at all. Michael was only six and here he was laughing at the picture of me going from one of them to the other trying to stop their dreams of the New York skyscrapers. Malachy said I could do nothing about his dreams because he was born in Brooklyn and could dream about America all night and well into the day if he liked. I appealed to my mother. I told her it wasn't fair the way the whole family was invading my dreams and she said, Arrah, for the love o' God, drink your tea and go to school and stop tormenting us with your dreams. My brother, Alphie, was only two and learning words and he banged a spoon on the table and chanted, Tomentin' dreams, tomentin' dreams, till everyone laughed and I knew I could share my dreams with him anytime, so why not with Michael, why not Malachy?

★

1

When the MS *Irish Oak* sailed from Cork in October, 1949, we expected to be in New York City in a week. Instead, after two days at sea, we were told we were going to Montreal in Canada. I told the First Officer all I had was forty dollars and would Irish Shipping pay my train fare from Montreal to New York. He said, No, the company wasn't responsible. He said freighters are the whores of the high seas, they'll do anything for anyone. You could say a freighter is like Murphy's oul' dog, he'll go part of the road with any wanderer.

Two days later Irish Shipping changed its mind and gave us the happy news, Sail for New York City, but two days after that the Captain was told, Sail for Albany.

The First Officer told me Albany was a city far up the Hudson River, capital of New York State. He said Albany had all the charm of Limerick, ha ha ha, a great place to die but not a place where you'd want to get married or rear children. He was from Dublin and knew I was from Limerick and when he sneered at Limerick I didn't know what to do. I'd like to destroy him with a smart remark but then I'd look at myself in the mirror, pimply face, sore eyes, and bad teeth and know I could never stand up to anyone, especially a First Officer with a uniform and a promising future as master of his own ship. Then I'd say to myself, Why should I care what anyone says about Limerick anyway? All I had there was misery.

Then the peculiar thing would happen. I'd sit on a deck chair in the lovely October sun with the gorgeous blue Atlantic all around me and try to imagine what New York would be like. I'd try to see Fifth Avenue or Central Park or Greenwich Village where everyone looked like movie stars, powerful tans, gleaming white teeth. But Limerick would push me into the past. Instead of me sauntering up Fifth Avenue with the tan, the teeth, I'd be back in the lanes of Limerick, women standing at doors chatting away and pulling their shawls around their shoulders, children with faces dirty from bread and jam, playing and laughing and crying to their mothers. I'd see people at Mass on Sunday morning where a whisper would run through the church when someone with a hunger weakness would collapse in the pew and have to be carried outside by men from the back of the church who'd tell everyone, Stand back, stand back, for the lovea Jaysus, can't you see she's gasping for the air, and I wanted to be a man like that telling people stand back because that gave you the right to stay outside till the Mass was over and you could go off to the pub which is why you were standing in the back with all the other men in the first place. Men who didn't drink always knelt right up there by the altar to show how good they were and how they didn't care if the pubs stayed closed till Doomsday. They knew the responses to the Mass better than anyone and they'd be blessing themselves and standing and kneeling and sighing over their prayers as if they felt the pain of Our Lord more than the rest of the congregation. Some had given up the pint entirely and they were the worst, always preaching the evil of the pint and looking down on the ones still in the grip as if they were on the right track to heaven. They acted as if God Himself would turn His back on a man drinking the pint when everyone knew you'd rarely hear a priest up in the pulpit denounce the pint or the men who drank it. Men with the thirst stayed in the back ready to streak out the door the minute the priest said, Ite, missa est, Go, you are dismissed. They stayed in the back because their mouths were dry and they felt too humble to be up there with the sober ones. I stayed near the door so that I could hear the men whispering about the slow Mass. They went to Mass because it's a mortal sin if you don't though you'd wonder if it wasn't a worse sin to be joking to the man next to you that if this priest didn't hurry up you'd expire of the thirst on the spot. If Father White came out to give the sermon they'd shuffle and groan over his sermons, the slowest in the world, with him rolling

4

his eyes to heaven and declaring we were all doomed unless we mended our ways and devoted ourselves to the Virgin Mary entirely. My Uncle Pa Keating would have the men laughing behind their hands with his, I would devote myself to the Virgin Mary if she handed me a lovely creamy black pint of porter. I wanted to be there with my Uncle Pa Keating all grown up with long trousers and stand with the men in the back with the great thirst and laugh behind my hand.

I'd sit on that deck chair and look into my head to see myself cycling around Limerick City and out into the country delivering telegrams. I'd see myself early in the morning riding along country roads with the mist rising in the fields and cows giving me the odd moo and dogs coming at me till I drove them away with rocks. I'd hear babies in farmhouses crying for their mothers and farmers whacking cows back to the fields after the milking.

And I'd start crying to myself on that deck chair with the gorgeous Atlantic all around me, New York ahead, city of my dreams where I'd have the golden tan, the dazzling white teeth. I'd wonder what in God's name was wrong with me that I should be missing Limerick already, city of grey miseries, the place where I dreamed of escape to New York. I'd hear my mother's warning, The devil you know is better than the devil you don't know.

There were to be fourteen passengers on the ship but one cancelled and we had to sail with an unlucky number. The first night out the Captain stood up at dinner and welcomed us. He laughed and said he wasn't superstitious over the number of passengers but since there was a priest among us wouldn't it be lovely if His Reverence would say a prayer to come between us and all harm. The priest was a plump little man, born in Ireland, but so long in his Los Angeles parish he had no trace of an Irish accent. When he got up to say a prayer and blessed himself four passengers kept their hands in their laps and that told me they were Protestants. My mother used to say you could spot Protestants a mile away by their reserved manner. The priest asked Our Lord to look down on us with pity and love, that whatever happened on these stormy seas we were ready to be enfolded forever in His Divine Bosom. An old Protestant reached for his wife's hand. She smiled and shook her head back at him and he smiled, too, as if to say, Don't worry.

The priest sat next to me at the dinner table. He whispered that those two old Protestants were very rich from raising thoroughbred racehorses in Kentucky and if I had any sense I'd be nice to them, you never know.

I wanted to ask what was the proper way to be nice to rich Protestants who raise racehorses but I couldn't for fear the priest might think I was a fool. I heard the Protestants say the Irish people were so charming and their children so adorable you hardly noticed how poor they were. I knew that if I ever talked to the rich Protestants I'd have to smile and show my destroyed teeth and that would be the end of it. The minute I made some money in America I'd have to rush to a dentist to have my smile mended. You could see from the magazines and the films how the smile opened doors and brought girls running and if I didn't have the smile I might as well go back to Limerick and get a job sorting letters in a dark back room at the post office where they wouldn't care if you hadn't a tooth in your head.

Before bedtime the steward served tea and biscuits in the lounge. The priest said, I'll have a double Scotch, forget the tea, Michael, the whiskey helps me sleep. He drank his whiskey and whispered to me again, Did you talk to the rich people from Kentucky?

I didn't.

Dammit. What's the matter with you? Don't you want to get ahead in the world?

I do.

Well, why don't you talk to the rich people from Kentucky? They might take a fancy to you and give you a job as stable boy or something and you could rise in the ranks instead of going to New York which is one big occasion of sin, a sink of depravity where a Catholic has to fight day and night to keep the faith. So, why can't you talk to the nice people from Kentucky and make something of yourself?

Whenever he brought up the rich people from Kentucky he whispered and I didn't know what to say. If my brother Malachy were here he'd march right up to the rich people and charm them and they'd probably adopt him and leave him their millions along with stables, racehorses, a big house, and maids to clean it. I never talked to rich people in my life except to say, Telegram, ma'am, and then I'd be told go round to the servants' entrance, this is the front door and don't you know any better.

That is what I wanted to tell the priest but I didn't know how to

6

talk to him either. All I knew about priests was that they said Mass and everything else in Latin, that they heard my sins in English and forgave me in Latin on behalf of Our Lord Himself who is God anyway. It must be a strange thing to be a priest and wake up in the morning lying there in the bed knowing you have the power to forgive people or not forgive them depending on your mood. When you know Latin and forgive sins it makes you powerful and hard to talk to because you know the dark secrets of the world. Talking to a priest is like talking to God Himself and if you say the wrong thing you're doomed.

There wasn't a soul on that ship who could tell me how to talk to rich Protestants and demanding priests. My uncle by marriage, Pa Keating, could have told me but he was back in Limerick where he didn't give a fiddler's fart about anything. I knew if he were here he'd refuse to talk to the rich people entirely and then he'd tell the priest to kiss his royal Irish arse. That's how I'd like to be myself but when your teeth and eyes are destroyed you never know what to say or what to do with yourself.

There was a book in the ship's library, *Crime and Punishment*, and I thought it might be a good murder mystery even if it was filled with confusing Russian names. I tried to read it in a deck chair but the story made me feel strange, a story about a Russian student, Raskolnikov, who kills an old woman, a moneylender, and then tries to convince himself he's entitled to the money because she's useless to the world and her money would pay for his university expenses so that he could become a lawyer and go round defending people like himself who kill old women for their money. It made me feel strange because of the time in Limerick when I had a job writing threatening letters for an old woman moneylender, Mrs Finucane, and when she died in a chair I took some of her money to help me pay my fare to America. I knew I didn't kill Mrs Finucane but I took her money and that made me almost as bad as Raskolnikov and if I died this minute he'd be the first one I'd run into in hell. I could save my soul by confessing to the priest and even though he's supposed to forget your sins the minute he gives you absolution he'd have power over me and he'd give me strange looks and tell me go charm the rich Protestants from Kentucky.

I fell asleep reading the book and a sailor, a deckhand, woke me to tell me, Your book is getting wet in the rain, sir.

Sir. Here I was from a lane in Limerick and there's a man with grey hair calling me sir even though he's not supposed to say a word to me in the first place because of the rules. The First Officer told me an ordinary sailor was never allowed to speak to passengers except for a Good Day or Good Night. He told me this particular sailor with the grey hair was once an officer on the *Queen Elizabeth* but he was fired because he was caught with a first-class passenger in her cabin and what they were doing was a cause of confession. This man's name was Owen and he was peculiar the way he spent all his time reading below and when the ship docked he'd go ashore with a book and read in a cafe while the rest of the crew got roaring drunk and had to be hauled back to the ship in taxis. Our own captain had such respect for him he'd have him up to his cabin and they'd have tea and talk of the days they served together on an English destroyer that was torpedoed, the two of them hanging on to a raft in the Atlantic drifting and freezing and chatting about the time they'd get back to Ireland and have a nice pint and a mountain of bacon and cabbage.

Owen spoke to me next day. He said he knew he was breaking the rules but he couldn't help talking to anyone on this ship who was reading *Crime and Punishment*. There were great readers in the crew right enough but they wouldn't move beyond Edgar Wallace or Zane Grey and he'd give anything to be able to chat about Dostoyevsky. He wanted to know if I'd read *The Possessed* or *The Brothers Karamazov* and he looked sad when I said I'd never heard of them. He told me the minute I got to New York I should rush to a bookshop and get Dostoyevsky books and I'd never be lonely again. He said no matter what Dostoyevsky book you read he always gave you something to chew on and you can't beat that for a bargain. That's what Owen said though I had no notion of what he was talking about.

Then the priest came along the deck and Owen moved away. The priest said, Were you talking to that man? I could see you were. Well, I'm telling you he's not good company. You can see that, can't you? I heard all about him. Him with his grey hair swabbing decks at his age. It's a strange thing you can talk to deckhands with no morals but if I ask you to talk to the rich Protestants from Kentucky you can't find a minute.

We were only talking about Dostoyevsky.

Dostoyevsky, indeed. Lotta good that'll do you in New York. You won't see many Help Wanted signs requiring a knowledge of

Dostoyevsky. Can't get you to talk to the rich people from Kentucky but you sit here for hours yacking with sailors. Stay away from old sailors. You know what they are. Talk to people who'll do you some good. Read the *Lives of the Saints*.

Along the New Jersey side of the Hudson River there were hundreds of ships docked tightly together. Owen the sailor said they were the Liberty ships that brought supplies to Europe during the war and after and it's sad to think they'll be hauled away any day to be broken up in shipyards. But that's the way the world is, he said, and a ship lasts no longer than a whore's moan.

2

The priest asks if I have anyone meeting me and when I tell him there's no one he says I can travel with him on the train to New York City. He'll keep an eye on me. When the ship docks we take a taxi to the big Union Station in Albany and while we wait for the train we have coffee in great thick cups and pie on thick plates. It's the first time I ever had lemon meringue pie and I'm thinking if this is the way they eat all the time in America I won't be a bit hungry and I'll be fine and fat, as they say in Limerick. I'll have Dostoyevsky for the loneliness and pie for the hunger.

The train isn't like the one in Ireland where you share a carriage with five other people. This train has long cars where there are dozens of people and is so crowded some have to stand. The minute we get on people give up their seats to the priest. He says, Thank you, and points to the seat beside him and I feel the people who offered up their seats are not happy when I take one because it's easy to see I'm nobody.

Farther up the car people are singing and laughing and calling for the church key. The priest says they're college kids going home for the weekend and the church key is the can opener for the beer. He says they're probably nice kids but they shouldn't drink so much and he hopes I won't turn out like that when I live in New York. He says I should put myself under the protection of the Virgin Mary and ask her to intercede with her Son to keep me pure and sober and out of harm's way. He'll pray for me all the way out there in Los Angeles and he'll say a special Mass for me on the eighth of December, the Feast of the Immaculate Conception. I want to ask him why he'd choose that feast day but I keep silent because he might start bothering me again about the rich Protestants from Kentucky.

He's telling me this but I'm dreaming of what it would be like to be a student somewhere in America, in a college like the ones in the films where there's always a white church spire with no cross to show it's Protestant and there are boys and girls strolling the campus carrying great books and smiling at each other with teeth like snow drops.

When we arrive at Grand Central Station I don't know where to go. My mother said I could try to see an old friend, Dan MacAdorey. The priest shows me how to use the telephone but there's no answer from Dan. Well, says the priest, I can't leave you on your own in Grand Central Station. He tells the taxi driver we're going to the Hotel New Yorker.

We take our bags to a room where there's one bed. The priest says, Leave the bags. We'll get something to eat in the coffee shop downstairs. Do you like hamburgers?

I don't know. I never had one in my life.

He rolls his eyes and tells the waitress bring me a hamburger with french fries and make sure the burger is well done because I'm Irish and we overcook everything. What the Irish do to vegetables is a crying shame. He says if you can guess what the vegetable is in an Irish restaurant you get the door prize. The waitress laughs and says she understands. She's half-Irish on her mother's side and her mother is the worst cook in the world. Her husband was Italian and he really knew how to cook but she lost him in the war.

Waw. That's what she says. She really means war but she's like all Americans who don't like to say 'r' at the end of a word. They say caw instead of car and you wonder why they can't pronounce words the way God made them.

I like the lemon meringue pie but I don't like the way Americans leave out the 'r' at the end of a word.

While we're eating our hamburgers the priest says I'll have to stay the night with him and tomorrow we'll see. It's strange taking off my clothes in front of a priest and I wonder if I should get down on my two knees and pretend to say my prayers. He tells me I can take a shower if I like and it's the first time in my life I ever had a shower with plenty of hot water and no shortage of soap, a bar for your body and a bottle for your head.

When I'm finished I dry myself with the thick towel draped on the bathtub and I put on my underwear before going back into the room. The priest is sitting in the bed with a towel wrapped around his fat belly, talking to someone on the phone. He puts down the phone and stares at me. My God, where did you get those drawers?

In Roche's Stores in Limerick.

If you hung those drawers out the window of this hotel people would surrender. Piece of advice, don't ever let Americans see you in those drawers. They'll think you just got off Ellis Island. Get briefs. You know what briefs are?

I don't.

Get 'em anyway. Kid like you should be wearing briefs. You're in the USA now. OK, hop in the bed, and that puzzles me because there's no sign of a prayer and that's the first thing you'd expect of a priest. He goes off to the bathroom but he's no sooner in there than he sticks his head out and asks me if I dried myself.

I did.

Well, your towel isn't touched so what did you dry yourself with?

The towel that's on the side of the bathtub.

What? That's not a towel. That's the bathmat. That's what you stand on when you get out of the shower.

I can see myself in a mirror over the desk and I'm turning red and wondering if I should tell the priest I'm sorry for what I did or if I should stay quiet. It's hard to know what to do when you make a mistake your first night in America but I'm sure in no time I'll be a regular Yank doing everything right. I'll order my own hamburger, learn to call chips french fries, joke with waitresses, and never again dry myself with the bathmat. Some day I'll say war and car with no 'r' at the end but not if I ever go back to Limerick. If I ever went back to Limerick with an American accent they'd say I was putting on airs and tell me I had a fat arse like all the Yanks.

The priest comes out of the bathroom, wrapped in a towel, patting his face with his hands, and there's a lovely smell of perfume in the air. He says there's nothing as refreshing as after-shave lotion and I can put on some if I like. It's right there in the bathroom. I don't know what to say or do. Should I say, No, thanks, or should I get out of the bed and go all the way to the bathroom and slather myself with after-shave lotion? I never heard of anyone in Limerick putting stuff on their faces after they shaved but I suppose it's different in America. I'm sorry I didn't look for a book that tells you what to do on your first night in New York in a hotel with a priest where you're liable to make a fool of yourself right and left. He says, Well? and I tell him, Ah, no, thanks. He says, Suit yourself, and I can tell he's a bit impatient the way he was when I didn't talk to the rich Protestants from Kentucky. He could easily tell me leave and there I'd be out on the street with my brown suitcase and nowhere to go in New York. I don't want to chance that so I tell him I'd like to put on the after-shave lotion after all. He shakes his head and tells me go ahead.

I can see myself in the bathroom mirror putting on the after-shave lotion and I'm shaking my head at myself feeling if this is the way it's going to be in America I'm sorry I ever left Ireland. It's hard enough coming here in the first place without priests criticizing you over your failure to hit it off with rich Kentucky Protestants, your ignorance of bathmats, the state of your underwear and your doubts about after-shave lotion.

The priest is in the bed and when I come out of the bathroom he tells me, OK, into the bed. We've got a long day tomorrow.

He lifts the bedclothes to let me in and it's a shock to see he's wearing nothing. He says, Good night, turns off the light and starts snoring without even saying a Hail Mary or a prayer before sleep. I always thought priests spent hours on their knees before sleeping but this man must be in a great state of grace and not a bit afraid of dying. I wonder if all priests are like that, naked in the bed. It's hard to fall asleep in a bed with a naked priest snoring beside you. Then I wonder if the Pope himself goes to bed in that condition or if he has a nun bring in pajamas with the Papal colors and the Papal coat of arms. I wonder how he gets out of that long white robe he wears, if he pulls it over his head or lets it drop to the floor and steps out of it. An old Pope would never be able to pull it over his head and he'd probably have to call a passing cardinal to give him a hand unless the cardinal himself was too old and he might have to call a nun unless the Pope was wearing nothing under the white robe which the cardinal would know about anyway because there isn't a cardinal in the world that doesn't know what the Pope wears since they all want to be Pope themselves and can't wait for this one to die. If a nun is called in she has to take the white robe to be washed down in the steaming depths of the Vatican laundry room by other nuns and novices who sing hymns and praise the Lord for the privilege of washing all the clothes of the Pope and the College of Cardinals except for the underwear which is washed in another room by old nuns who are blind and not liable to think sinful thoughts because of what they have in their hands and what I have in my own hand is what I shouldn't have in the presence of a priest in the bed and for once in my life I resist the sin and turn on my side and go to sleep.

Next day the priest finds a furnished room in the paper for six dollars a week and he wants to know if I can afford it till I get a job. We go to East Sixty-Eighth Street and the landlady, Mrs Austin, takes me upstairs to see the room. It's the end of a hallway blocked off with a partition and a door with a window looking out on the street. There's barely space for the bed and a small chest of drawers with a mirror and a table and if I stretch my arms I can touch the walls on both sides. Mrs Austin says this is a very nice room and I'm lucky it wasn't snapped up. She's Swedish and she can tell I'm Irish. She hopes I don't drink and if I do I'm not to bring girls into this room under any circumstances, drunk or sober. No girls, no food, no drink. Cockroaches smell food a mile away and once they're in you have them forever. She says, Of course you never saw a cockroach in Ireland. There's no food there. All you people do is drink. Cockroaches would starve to death or turn into drunks. Don't tell me, I know. My sister is married to an Irishman, worst thing she ever did. Irishmen great to go out with but don't marry them.

She takes the six dollars and tells me she needs another six for security, gives me a receipt and tells me I can move in anytime that day and she trusts me because I came with that nice priest even if she's not Catholic herself, that it's enough her sister married one, an Irishman, God help her, and she's suffering for it.

The priest calls another taxi to take us to the Biltmore Hotel across the street from where we came out at Grand Central Station. He says it's a famous hotel and we're going to the headquarters of the

Democratic Party and if they can't find a job for an Irish kid no one can.

A man passes us in the hallway and the priest whispers, Do you know who that is?

I don't.

Of course you don't. If you don't know the difference between a towel and a bathmat how could you know that's the great Boss Flynn from the Bronx, the most powerful man in America next to President Truman.

The great Boss presses the button for the elevator and while he's waiting he shoves a finger up his nose, looks at what he has on his fingertip and flicks it away on the carpet. My mother would call that digging for gold. This is the way it is in America. I'd like to tell the priest I'm sure De Valera would never pick his nose like that and you'd never find the Bishop of Limerick going to bed in a naked state. I'd like to tell the priest what I think of the world in general where God torments you with bad eyes and bad teeth but I can't for fear he might go on about the rich Protestants from Kentucky and how I missed the opportunity of a lifetime.

The priest talks to a woman at a desk in the Democratic Party and she picks up the telephone. She says to the telephone, Got a kid here . . . just off the boat . . . you got a high school diploma? . . . na, no diploma . . . well, whaddya expect . . . Old Country still a poor country . . . yeah, I'll send him up.

I'm to report on Monday morning to Mr Carey on the twenty-second floor and he'll put me to work right here in the Biltmore Hotel and aren't I a lucky kid walking into a job right off the boat. That's what she says and the priest tells her, This is a great country and the Irish owe everything to the Democratic Party, Maureen, and you just clinched another vote for the party if the kid here ever votes, ha ha ha.

The priest tells me go back to the hotel and he'll come for me later to go to dinner. He says I can walk, that the streets run east and west, the avenues north and south, and I'll have no trouble. Just walk across Forty-Second to Eighth Avenue and south till I come to the New Yorker Hotel. I can read a paper or a book or take a shower if I promise to stay away from the bathmat, ha ha. He says, If we're lucky we might meet the great Jack Dempsey himself. I tell him I'd rather meet Joe Louis if that's possible and he snaps at me, You better learn to stick with your own kind.

At night the waiter at Dempsey's smiles at the priest. Jack's not here, Fawdah. He's over to the Gawden checkin' out a middleweight from New Joisey.

Gawden. Joisey. My first day in New York and already people are talking like gangsters from the films I saw in Limerick.

The priest says, My young friend here is from the Old Country and he'd prefer to meet Joe Louis. He laughs and the waiter laughs and says, Well, that's a greenhorn talkin', Fawdah. He'll loin. Give him six months in this country and he'll run like hell when he sees a darky. An' what would you like to order, Fawdah? Little something before dinner?

I'll have a double martini dry and I mean dry straight up with a twist.

And the greenhorn?

He'll have a . . . well, what'll you have?

A beer, please.

You eighteen, kid?

Nineteen.

You don't look it though it don't matter nohow long as you with the fawdah. Right, Fawdah?

Right. I'll keep an eye on him. He doesn't know a soul in New York and I'm going to settle him in before I leave.

The priest drinks his double martini and orders another with his steak. He tells me I should think of becoming a priest. He could get me a job in Los Angeles and I'd live the life of Riley with widows dying and leaving me everything including their daughters, ha ha, this is one hell of a martini excuse the language. He eats most of his steak and tells the waiter bring two apple pies with ice cream and he'll have a double Hennessy to wash it down. He eats only the ice cream, drinks half the Hennessy and falls asleep with his chin on his chest moving up and down.

The waiter loses his smile. Goddam, he's gotta pay his check. Where's his goddam wallet? Back pocket, kid. Hand it to me.

I can't rob a priest.

You're not robbing. He's paying his goddam check and you're gonna need a taxi to take him home.

Two waiters help him to a taxi and two bellhops at the New Yorker Hotel haul him through the lobby, up the elevator, and dump him on the bed. The bellhops tell me, A buck tip would be nice, a buck each, kid.

They leave and I wonder what I'm supposed to do with a drunken priest. I remove his shoes the way they do when someone passes out in the films but he sits up and runs to the bathroom where he's sick a long time and when he comes out he's pulling at his clothes, throwing them on the floor, collar, shirt, trousers, underwear. He collapses on the bed on his back and I can see he's in a state of excitement with his hand on himself. Come here to me, he says, and I back away. Ah, no, Father, and he rolls out of the bed, slobbering and stinking of drink and puke and tries to grab my hand to put it on him but I back away even faster till I'm out the door to the hallway with him standing in the door, a little fat priest crying to me, Ah, come back, son, come back, it was the drink. Mother o' God, I'm sorry.

But the elevator is open and I can't tell the respectable people already in it and looking at me that I changed my mind, that I'm running back to this priest who, in the first place, wanted me to be polite to rich Kentucky Protestants so that I could get a job cleaning stables and now waggles his thing at me in a way that's surely a mortal sin. Not that I'm in a state of grace myself, no, I'm not, but you'd expect a priest to set a good example and not make a holy show of himself my second night in America. I have to step into the elevator and pretend I don't hear the priest slobbering and crying, naked at the door of his room.

There's a man at the front door of the hotel dressed up like an admiral and he says, Taxi, sir. I tell him, No, thanks, and he says, Where you from? Oh, Limerick. I'm from Roscommon myself, over here four years.

I have to ask the man from Roscommon how to get to East Sixty-Eighth Street and he tells me walk east on Thirty-Fourth Street which is wide and well lit till I come to Third Avenue and I can get the El or if I'm anyway lively I can walk straight up till I come to my street. He tells me, Good luck, stick with your own kind and watch out for the Puerto Ricans, they all carry knives and that's a known fact, they got that hot blood. Walk in the light along the edge of the sidewalk or they'll be leppin' at you from dark doorways.

★   ★   ★

Next morning the priest calls Mrs Austin and tells her I should come get my suitcase. He tells me, Come in, the door is open. He's in his black suit sitting on the far side of the bed with his back to me and my suitcase is just inside the door. Take it, he says. I'm going to a retreat house in Virginia for a few months. I don't want to look at you and I don't want to see you ever again because what happened was terrible and it wouldn't have happened if you'd used your head and gone off with the rich Protestants from Kentucky. Goodbye.

It's hard to know what to say to a priest in a bad mood with his back to you who's blaming you for everything so all I can do is go down in the elevator with my suitcase wondering how a man like that who forgives sins can sin himself and then blame me. I know if I did something like that, getting drunk and bothering people to put their hands on me, I'd say I did it. That's all, I did it. And how can he blame me just because I refused to talk to rich Protestants from Kentucky? Maybe that's the way priests are trained. Maybe it's hard listening to people's sins day in day out when there's a few you'd like to commit yourself and then when you have a drink all the sins you've heard explode inside you and you're like everyone else. I know I could never be a priest listening to those sins all the time. I'd be in a constant state of excitement and the Bishop would be worn out shipping me off to the retreat house in Virginia.

3

When you're Irish and you don't know a soul in New York and you're walking along Third Avenue with trains rattling along on the El above there's great comfort in discovering there's hardly a block without an Irish bar: Costello's, the Blarney Stone, the Blarney Rose, P. J. Clarke's, the Breffni, the Leitrim House, the Sligo House, Shannon's, Ireland's Thirty-Two, the All Ireland. I had my first pint in Limerick the day before I turned sixteen and it made me sick and my father nearly destroyed the family and himself with the drink but I'm lonely in New York and I'm lured in by Bing Crosby on jukeboxes singing "Galway Bay" and blinking green shamrocks the likes of which you'd never see in Ireland.

There's an angry-looking man behind the end of the bar in Costello's and he's saying to a customer, I don't give a tinker's damn if you have ten pee haitch dees. I know more about Samuel Johnson than you know about your hand and if you don't comport yourself properly you'll be out on the sidewalk. I'll say no more.

The customer says, But.

Out, says the angry man. Out. You'll get no more drink in this house.

The customer claps on his hat and stalks out and the angry man turns to me. And you, he says, are you eighteen?

I am, sir. I'm nineteen.

How do I know?

I have my passport, sir.

And what is an Irishman doing with an American passport?

I was born here, sir.

He allows me to have two fifteen-cent beers and tells me I'd be better off spending my time in the library than in bars like the rest of our miserable race. He tells me Dr Johnson drank forty cups of tea a day and his mind was clear to the end. I ask him who Dr Johnson was and he glares at me, takes my glass away, and tells me, Leave this bar. Walk west on Forty-Second till you come to Fifth. You'll see two great stone lions. Walk up the steps between those two lions, get yourself a library card and don't be an idiot like the rest of the bogtrotters getting off the boat and stupefying themselves with drink. Read your Johnson, read your Pope and avoid the dreamy micks. I want to ask him where he stands on Dostoyevsky till he points at the door, Don't come back here till you've read *The Lives of the Poets*. Go on. Get out.

It's a warm October day and I have nothing else to do but what I'm told and what harm is there in wandering up to Fifth Avenue where the lions are. The librarians are friendly. Of course I can have a library card and it's so nice to see young immigrants using the library. I can borrow four books if I like as long as they're back on the due date. I ask if they have a book called *The Lives of the Poets* by Samuel Johnson and they say, My, my, my, you're reading Johnson. I want to tell them I never read Johnson before but I don't want them to stop admiring me. They tell me feel free to walk around, take a look at the Main Reading Room on the third floor. They're not a bit like the librarians in Ireland who stood guard and protected the books against the likes of me.

The sight of the Main Reading Room, North and South, makes me go weak at the knees. I don't know if it's the two beers I had or the excitement of my second day in New York but I'm near tears when I look at the miles of shelves and know I'll never be able to read all those books if I live till the end of the century. There are acres of shiny tables where all sorts of people sit and read as long as they like seven days a week and no one bothers them unless they fall asleep and snore. There are sections with English, Irish, American books, literature, history, religion, and it makes me shiver to think I can come here anytime I like and read anything as long as I like if I don't snore.

I stroll back to Costello's with four books under my arm. I want to show the angry man I have *The Lives of the Poets* but he's not there. The barman says that would be Mr Tim Costello himself that was going on about Johnson and as he's talking the angry man comes out of the kitchen. He says, Are you back already?

I have *The Lives of the Poets*, Mr Costello.

You may have *The Lives of the Poets* under your oxter, young fellow, but you don't have them in your head so go home and read.

It's Thursday and I have nothing to do till the job starts on Monday. For lack of a chair I sit up in the bed in my furnished room and read till Mrs Austin knocks on my door at eleven and tells me she's not a millionaire and it's house policy that lights be turned off at eleven to keep down her electricity bill. I turn off the light and lie on the bed listening to New York, people talking and laughing, and I wonder if I'll ever be part of the city, out there talking and laughing.

There's another knock at the door and this young man with red hair and an Irish accent tells me his name is Tom Clifford and would I like a fast beer because he works in an East Side building and he has to be there in an hour. No, he won't go to an Irish bar. He wants nothing to do with the Irish so we walk to the Rhinelander on Eighty-Sixth Street where Tom tells me how he was born in America but was taken to Cork and got out as fast as he could by joining the American Army for three good years in Germany when you could get laid ten times over for a carton of cigarettes or a pound of coffee. There's a dance floor and a band in the back of the Rhinelander and Tom asks a girl from one of the tables to dance. He tells me, Come on. Ask her friend to dance.

But I don't know how to dance and I don't know how to ask a girl to dance. I know nothing about girls. How could I after growing up in Limerick? Tom asks the other girl to dance with me and she leads me out on the floor. I don't know what to do. Tom is stepping and twirling and I don't know whether to go backwards or forwards with this girl in my arms. She tells me I'm stepping on her shoes and when I tell her I'm sorry she says, Oh, forget it. I don't feel like clumping around. She goes back to her table and I follow her with my face on fire. I don't know whether to sit at her table or go back to the bar till she says, You left your beer on the bar. I'm glad I have an excuse to leave her because I wouldn't know what to say if I sat. I'm sure she wouldn't be interested if I told her I spent hours reading Johnson's *The Lives of the Poets* or if I told her how excited I was at the Forty-Second Street Library. I might have to find a book in the library on how to talk to girls or I might have to ask Tom who dances and laughs and has no trouble with the talk. He comes back to the bar and says he's going to call in sick which means he's not going to work. The girl likes him and says she'll let him take her home. He whispers to me he might get laid which means he might go to bed with her. The only problem is the other girl. He calls her my girl. Go ahead, he says. Ask her if you can take her home. Let's sit at their table and you can ask her.

The beer is working on me and I'm feeling braver and I don't feel shy about sitting at the girls' table and telling them about Tim Costello and Dr Samuel Johnson. Tom nudges me and whispers, For Christ's sake, stop the Samuel Johnson stuff, ask her home. When I look at her I see two and I wonder which I should ask home but if I look between the two I see one and that's the one I ask.

Home? she says. You kiddin' me. That's a laugh. I'm a secretary, a private secretary, and you don't even have a high school diploma. I mean, did you look in the mirror lately? She laughs and my face is on fire again. Tom takes a long drink of beer and I know I'm useless with these girls so I leave and walk down Third Avenue taking the odd look at my reflection in shop windows and giving up hope.

4

Monday morning my boss, Mr Carey, tells me I'll be a houseman, a very important job where I'll be out front in the lobby dusting, sweeping, emptying ashtrays and it's important because a hotel is judged by its lobby. He says we have the best lobby in the country. It's the Palm Court and known the world over. Anyone who's anyone knows about the Palm Court and the Biltmore clock. Chrissakes, it's right there in books and short stories, Scott Fitzgerald, people like that. Important people say, Let's meet under the clock at the Biltmore, and what happens if they come in and the place is covered with dust and buried in garbage. That's my job, to keep the Biltmore famous. I'm to clean and I'm not to talk to guests, not even look at them. If they talk to me I'm to say, Yes, sir or ma'am, or No, sir or ma'am, and keep working. He says I'm to be invisible, and that makes him laugh. Imagine that, eh, you're the invisible man cleaning the lobby. He says this is a big job and I'd never have it if I hadn't been sent by the Democratic Party at the request of the priest from California. Mr Carey says the last guy on this job was fired for talking to college girls under the clock but he was Italian so whaddya expect. He tells me keep my eye on the ball, don't forget to take a shower every day, this is America, stay sober, stick with your own kind of people, you can't go wrong with the Irish, go easy with the drink, and in a year I might rise to the rank of porter or busboy and make tips and, who knows, rise up to be a waiter and wouldn't that be the end of all my worries. He says anything is possible in America, Look at me, I have four suits.

The head waiter in the lobby is called maitre d'. He tells me I'm to sweep up only what falls to the floor and I'm not to touch anything on the tables. If money falls to the floor or jewelry or anything like that I'm to hand it to him, the maitre d' himself, and he'll decide what to do with it. If an ashtray is full I'm to wait for a busboy or a waiter to tell me empty it. Sometimes there are things in ashtrays that need to be taken care of. A woman might remove an earring because of the soreness and forget she left it in the ashtray and there are earrings worth thousands of dollars, not that I'd know anything about that just off the boat. It's the job of the maitre d' to hold on to all earrings and return them to the women with the sore ears.

There are two waiters working in the lobby and they rush back and forth, running into each other and barking in Greek. They tell me, You, Irish, come 'ere, clean up, clean up, empty goddam ashtray, take garbage, come on, come on, less go, you drunk or sompin'? They yell at me in front of the college students who swarm in on Thursdays and Fridays. I wouldn't mind Greeks yelling at me if they'd didn't do it in front of the college girls who are golden. They toss their hair and smile with teeth you see only in America, white, perfect, and everyone has tanned movie star legs. The boys sport crewcuts, the teeth, football shoulders, and they're easy with the girls. They talk and laugh and the girls lift their glasses and smile at the boys with shining eyes. They might be my age but I move among them ashamed of my uniform and my dustpan and broom. I wish I could be invisible but I can't when the waiters yell at me in Greek and English and something in between or a busboy might accuse me of interfering with an ashtray that had something on it.

There are times when I don't know what to do or say. A college boy with a crewcut says, Do you mind not cleaning around here just now? I'm talking to the lady. If the girl looks at me and then looks away I feel my face getting hot and I don't know why. Sometimes a college girl will smile at me and say, Hi, and I don't know what to say. I'm told by the hotel people above me I'm not to say a word to the guests though I wouldn't know how to say Hi anyway because we never said it in Limerick and if I said it I might be fired from my new job and be out on the street with no priest to get me another one. I'd like to say Hi and be part of that lovely world for a minute except that a crewcut boy might think I was gawking at his girl and report me to the maitre d'. I could go home tonight and sit up in the bed and practice smiling and saying Hi. If I kept at it I'd surely be able to handle the Hi but I'd have to say it without the smile for if I drew my lips back at all I'd frighten the wits out of the golden girls under the Biltmore clock.

There are days when the girls take off their coats and the way they look in sweaters and blouses is such an occasion of sin I have to lock myself in a toilet cubicle and interfere with myself and I have to be quiet for fear of being discovered by someone, a Puerto Rican busboy or a Greek waiter, who will run to the maitre d' and report that the lobby houseman is wankin' away in the bathroom.

5

There's a poster outside the Sixty-Eighth Street Playhouse that says *Hamlet* with Laurence Olivier: Coming Next Week. I'm already planning to treat myself to a night out with a bottle of ginger ale and a lemon meringue pie from the bakery like the one I had with the priest in Albany, the loveliest taste I ever had in my life. There I'll be watching Hamlet on the screen tormenting himself and everybody else, and I'll have tartness of ginger ale and sweetness of pie clashing away in my mouth. Before I go to the cinema I can sit in my room and read *Hamlet* to make sure I know what they're all saying in that Old English. The only book I brought from Ireland is the *Complete Works of Shakespeare* which I bought in O'Mahony's Bookshop for thirteen shillings and sixpence, half my wages when I worked at the post office delivering telegrams. The play I like best is *Hamlet* because of what he had to put up with when his mother carried on with her husband's brother, Claudius, and the way my own mother in Limerick carried on with her cousin, Laman Griffin. I could understand Hamlet raging at his mother the way I did with my mother the night I had my first pint and went home drunk and slapped her face. I'll be sorry for that till the day I die though I'd still like to go back to Limerick some day and find Laman Griffin in a pub and tell him step outside and I'd wipe the floor with him till he begged for mercy. I know it's useless talking like that because Laman Griffin will surely be dead of the drink and the consumption by the time I return to Limerick and he'll be a long time in hell before I ever say a prayer or light a candle for him even if Our Lord says we should forgive our enemies and turn the other cheek. No, even if Our Lord came back on earth and ordered me to forgive Laman Griffin on pain of being cast into the sea with a millstone around my neck, the thing I fear most in the world, I'd have to say, Sorry, Our Lord, I can never forgive that man for what he did to my mother and my family. Hamlet didn't wander around Elsinore forgiving people in a made-up story, so why should I in real life.

The last time I went to the Sixty-Eighth Street Playhouse the usher wouldn't let me in with a bar of Hershey's chocolate in my hand. He said I couldn't bring in food or drink and I'd have to consume it outside. Consume. He couldn't say eat, and that's one of the things that bothers me in the world the way ushers and people in uniforms in general always like to use big words. The Sixty-Eighth Street Playhouse isn't a bit like the Lyric Cinema in Limerick where you could bring in fish and chips or a good feed of pig's feet and a bottle of stout if the humor was on you. The night they wouldn't let me in with the chocolate bar I had to stand outside and gobble it with the usher glaring at me and he didn't care that I was missing funny parts of the Marx Brothers. Now I have to carry my black raincoat from Ireland over my arm so that the usher won't spot the bag with the lemon meringue pie or the ginger ale bottle stuck in a pocket.

The minute the film starts I try to go at my pie but the box crackles and people say, Shush, we're trying to watch this film. I know they're not the ordinary type of people who go to gangster films or musicals. These are people who probably graduated from college and live on Park Avenue and know every line of *Hamlet*. They'll never say they go to movies, only films. I'll never be able to open the box silently and my mouth is watering with the hunger and I don't know what to do till a man sitting next to me says, Hi, slips part of his raincoat over my lap and lets his hand wander under it. He says, Am I disturbing you? and I don't know what to say though something tells me take my pie and move away. I tell him, Excuse me, and go by him up the aisle and out to the men's lavatory where I'm able to open my pie box in comfort without Park Avenue shushing me. I feel sorry over missing part of *Hamlet* but all they were doing up there on the screen was jumping around and shouting about a ghost.

Even though the men's lavatory is empty I don't want to be seen opening my box and eating my pie, so I sit on the toilet in the cubicle eating quickly so that I can get back to *Hamlet* as long as I don't have to sit beside the man with the coat on his lap and the wandering hand. The pie makes my mouth dry and I think I'll have a nice drink of ginger ale till I realize you have to have some class of a church key to lift off the cap. There's no use going to an usher because they're always barking and telling people they're not supposed to be bringing in food or drink from the outside even if they're from Park Avenue. I lay the pie box on the floor and decide the only way to knock the cap off the ginger ale bottle is to place it against the sink and give it a good rap with the back of my hand and when I do the neck of the bottle breaks and the ginger ale gushes up in my face and there's blood on the sink where I cut my hand on the bottle and I feel sad with all the things happening to me that my pie is being drowned on the floor with blood and ginger ale and wondering at the same time will I ever be able to see *Hamlet* with all the troubles I'm having when a desperate-looking grey-haired man rushes in nearly knocking me over and steps on my pie box destroying it entirely. He stands at the urinal firing away, trying to shake the box off his shoe, and barking at me, Goddam, goddam, what the hell, what the hell. He stands away and swings his leg so that the pie box flies off his shoe and hits the wall all squashed and beyond eating. The man says, What the hell is going on here? and I don't know what to tell him because it seems like a long story going all the way back to how excited I was weeks ago about coming to see *Hamlet* and how I didn't eat all day because I had a delicious feeling about doing everything at the same time, eating my pie, drinking ginger ale, seeing *Hamlet* and hearing all the glorious speeches. I don't think the man is in the mood from the way he dances from one foot to the other telling me the toilet is not a goddam restaurant, that I have no goddam business hanging around public bathrooms eating and drinking and I'd better get my ass outa there. I tell him I had an accident trying to open the ginger ale bottle and he says, Didn't you ever hear of an opener or are you just off the goddam boat? He leaves the lavatory and just as I'm wrapping toilet paper around my cut the usher comes in and says there's a customer complaint about my behavior in here. He's like the grey-haired man with his goddam and what the hell and when I try to explain what happened he says, Get your ass outa here. I tell him I paid to see

28

Hamlet and I came in here so that I wouldn't be disturbing all the Park Avenue people around me who know *Hamlet* backwards and forwards but he says, I don't give a shit, get out before I call the manager or the cops who will surely be interested in the blood all over the place.

Then he points to my black raincoat draped on the sink. Take that goddam raincoat outa here. Whaddya doin' with a raincoat on a day there ain't a cloud in the sky? We know the raincoat trick and we're watching. We know the whole raincoat brigade. We're on to your little queer games. You sit there lookin' innocent and the next thing the hand is wandering over to innocent kids. So get your raincoat outa here, buddy, before I call the cops, you goddam pervert.

I take the broken ginger ale bottle with the drop left and walk down Sixty-Eighth Street and sit on the steps of my rooming house till Mrs Austin calls through the basement window there is to be no eating or drinking on the steps, cockroaches will come running from all over and people will say we're a bunch of Puerto Ricans who don't care where they eat or drink or sleep.

There is no place to sit anywhere along the street with landladies peering and watching and there's nothing to do but to wander over to a park by the East River and wonder why America is so hard and complicated that I have trouble going to see *Hamlet* with a lemon meringue pie and a bottle of ginger ale.

6

The worst part of getting up and going to work in New York is the way my eyes are so infected I have to pull the lids apart with thumb and forefinger. I'm tempted to pick at the hard yellow crust but if I do the eyelashes will come away with it and leave my eyelids red and sore, worse than they were before. I can stand in the shower and let hot water run on my eyes till they feel warm and clean even if they're still blazing red in my head. I try to freeze the red away with icy cold water but it never works. It just makes my eyeballs ache and things are bad enough without me going to the Biltmore lobby with an ache in the eyeball.

I could put up with the aching eyeballs if I didn't have the soreness and the redness and the yellow ooze. At least people wouldn't be staring at me as if I were some class of a leper.

It's shameful enough going around the Palm Court in the black houseman's uniform which means I'm just above the Puerto Rican dishwashers in the eyes of the world. Even the porters have a touch of gold on their uniforms and the doormen themselves look like admirals of the fleet. Eddie Gilligan, the union shop steward, says it's a good thing I'm Irish or it's down in the kitchen I'd be with the spics. That's a new word, spics, and I know from the way he says it that he doesn't like Puerto Ricans. He tells me Mr Carey takes good care of his own people and that's why I'm a houseman with a uniform instead of an apron down there with the PRs singing and yelling Mira mira all day. I'd like to ask him what's wrong with singing when you're washing dishes and yelling Mira mira when the humor is on you but I'm wary of asking questions for fear of being foolish. At least the Puerto Ricans are together down there singing and banging away on pots and pans, carried away with their own music and dancing around the kitchen till the bosses tell them cut it out. Sometimes I go down to the kitchen and they give me bits of leftover food and call me Frankie, Frankie, Irish boy, we teach you Sponish. Eddie Gilligan says I'm paid two dollars and fifty cents a week more than the dishwashers and I have opportunities for advancement they'll never have because all they want to do is not learn English and make enough money to go back to Puerto Rico and sit under trees drinking beer and having big families because that's all they're good for, drinking and screwing till their wives are worn out and die before their time and their kids run the streets ready to come to New York and wash dishes and start the whole goddam thing over again and if they can't get jobs we have to support them, you an' me, so they can sit on their stoops up in East Harlem playing their goddam guitars and drinking beer outa paper bags. That's the spics, kid, and don't you forget it. Stay away from that kitchen because they wouldn't think twice about pissing in your coffee. He says he saw them pissing in the coffee urn that was being sent to a big lunch for the Daughters of the British Empire and the Daughters never guessed for one second they were drinking Puerto Rican piss.

Then Eddie smiles and laughs and chokes on his cigarette because he's Irish-American and he thinks the PRs are great for what they did to the Daughters of the British Empire. He calls them PRs now instead of spics because they did something patriotic the Irish should have thought of in the first place. Next year he'll piss in the coffee urns himself and laugh himself to death watching the Daughters drink coffee that's Puerto Rican and Irish piss. He says it's a great pity the Daughters will never know. He'd like to get up there on the balcony of the nineteenth-floor ballroom and make a general announcement, Daughters of the British Empire, you have just drunk coffee filled with spick-mick piss and how does that feel after what you did to the Irish for eight hundred years? Oh, that'd be a sight, the Daughters clutching each other and throwing up all over the ballroom and Irish patriots dancing jigs in their graves. That'd be something, says Eddie, that'd be really something.

Now Eddie says maybe the PRs aren't that bad at all. He wouldn't want them marrying his daughter or moving into his neighborhood but you have to admit they're musical and they send up some pretty good baseball players, you have to admit that. You go down to that kitchen and they're always happy like kids. He says, They're like the Negroes, they don't take nothin' serious. Not like the Irish. We take everything serious.

The bad days in the lobby are Thursday and Friday when the boys and girls meet and sit and drink and laugh, nothing on their minds but college and romance, sailing around in the summer, skiing in the winter, and marrying each other so that they'll have children who will come to the Biltmore and do the same. I know they don't even see me in my houseman's uniform with my dustpan and broom and I'm glad because there are days my eyes are so red they look bloody and I dread it when a girl might say, Excuse me where is the rest room? It's hard to point with your dustpan and say, Over there beyond the elevators, and keep your face turned away at the same time. I tried that with one girl but she went to the maître d' and complained I was rude and now I have to look at everyone who asks a question and when they stare at me I blush so hard I'm sure my skin matches my eyes in the redness department. Sometimes I blush out of pure anger and I want to snarl at the people who stare but if I did I'd be fired on the spot.

They shouldn't stare. They should know better the way their mothers and fathers are spending fortunes to make them educated and what's the use of all that education if you're so ignorant you stare at people just off the boat with red eyes? You'd think the professors would be standing in front of their classes telling them that if you go to the Biltmore Hotel lobby or any lobby you're not to be staring at people with red eyes or one leg or any class of a disfigurement.

The girls stare anyway and the boys are worse the way they look at me and smile and nudge and pass remarks that make everyone laugh and I'd like to break my dustpan and broom over their heads till blood spurted and they begged me to stop and promise they'll never again pass remarks on anyone's sore eyes.

One day there's a yelp from a college girl and the maître d' rushes over. She's crying and he's moving things around on the table before her and looking under it, shaking his head. He calls across the lobby, McCourt, get over here right now. Did you clean up around this table?

I think I did.

You think you did? Godammit, excuse me, miss, don't you know?

I did, sir.

Did you remove a paper napkin?

I cleaned up. I emptied the ash trays.

Paper napkin that was here. Did you take it?

I don't know.

Well, lemme tell you something, McCourt. This young lady here is the daughter of the President of the Traffic Club that rents a huge space in this hotel and she had a paper napkin with a phone number from a Princeton boy and if you don't find that piece of paper your ass is in hot water, excuse me, miss. Now what did you do with the trash you took away?

It's gone down to the big garbage bins near the kitchen.

All right. Go down there and search for that paper napkin and don't come back without it.

The girl who lost the napkin sobs and tells me her father has a lotta influence here and she wouldn't want to be me if I don't find that piece of paper. Her friends are looking at me and I feel my face is on fire with my eyes.

The maitre d' snaps at me again. Go get it, McCourt, and report back here.

The garbage bins by the kitchen are overflowing and I don't know how I'm going to find a small piece of paper lost in all that waste, coffee grounds, bits of toast, fishbones, eggshells, grapefruit skins. I'm on my knees poking and separating with a fork from the kitchen where the Puerto Ricans are singing and laughing and banging on pots and that makes me wonder what I'm doing on my knees.

So I get up and go into the kitchen saying nothing to the Puerto Ricans calling to me, Frankie, Frankie, Irish boy, we teach you Sponish. I find a clean paper napkin, write a made-up phone number on it, stain it with coffee, hand it to the maitre d' who hands it to the girl with her friends cheering on all sides. She thanks the maitre d' and passes him a tip, a whole dollar, and my only sorrow is that I won't be there when she calls that number.

7

There's a letter from my mother to say times are hard at home. She knows my wages aren't great and she's grateful for the ten dollars every week but could I spare an extra few dollars for shoes for Michael and Alphie? She had a job taking care of an old man but he was a great disappointment the way he died unexpected when she thought he'd hang on till the New Year so that she'd have a few shillings for shoes and a Christmas dinner, ham or something with a bit of dignity in it. She says sick people shouldn't hire people to take care of them and give them false hope of a job when they know very well they're in the throes. There's nothing coming in now but the money I'm sending and it looks as if poor Michael will have to leave school and get a job the minute he turns fourteen next year and that's a shame and she'd like to know, Is this what we fought the English for that half the children of Ireland should be wandering street, field and boreen with nothing between them and their feet but the skin?

I'm already sending her the ten dollars out of the thirty-two I get at the Biltmore Hotel though it's more like twenty-six when they deduct the Social Security and the income tax. After the rent I have twenty dollars and my mother gets ten of that and I have ten for food and the subway when it rains. The rest of the time I walk to save the nickel. Now and then I go mad with myself and go to a film at the Sixty-Eighth Street Playhouse and I know enough to sneak in a Hershey bar or two bananas which is the cheapest food on earth. Sometimes when I peel my banana people from Park Avenue with sensitive noses will sniff and whisper to each other, Is that a banana I'm smelling? and the next thing is they're threatening to complain to the management.

But I don't care anymore. If they go to the usher to complain I'm not going to skulk in the men's room eating my banana. I'll go to the Democratic Party in the Biltmore Hotel and tell them I'm an American citizen with an Irish accent and why am I being tormented over eating a banana during a Gary Cooper film?

The winter might be coming in Ireland but it's colder here and the clothes I brought from Ireland are useless for a New York winter. Eddie Gilligan says if that's all I'm going to wear on the streets I'll be dead before I'm twenty. He says if I'm not too proud I can go to that big Salvation Army place on the West Side and get all the winter clothes I need for a few dollars. He says make sure I get clothes that make me look like an American and not the Paddy-from-the-bog stuff that makes me look like a turnip farmer.

But I can't go to the Salvation Army now because of the fifteen-dollar international money order for my mother and I can't get left-overs from the Puerto Ricans in the Biltmore kitchen anymore for fear they might catch my eye disease.

Eddie Gilligan says there's talk about my eyes. He was called in by personnel because he's the shop steward and they told him I'm never to go near the kitchen again in case I might touch a towel or something and leave all the Puerto Rican dishwashers and Italian cooks half blind with conjunctivitis or whatever I have. The only reason I'm kept on the job at all is that I was sent by the Democratic Party and they pay plenty for the big offices they rent in the hotel. Eddie says Mr Carey might be a tough boss but he stands up for his own kind and tells personnel where to get off, tells them the minute they try to lay off a kid with bad eyes the Democratic Party will know about it and that will be the end of the Biltmore Hotel. They'll see a strike that'll bring out the whole goddam Hotel Workers' Union. No more room service. No elevators. Eddie says, Fat bastards will have to walk and the chambermaids won't be putting toilet paper in the bathrooms. Imagine that: fat old bastards stuck with nothing to wipe their asses and all because of your bad eyes, kid.

We'll walk, says Eddie, the whole goddam union. We'll close down every hotel in the city. But I gotta tell you they gave me the name of this eye doctor on Lexington Avenue. You gotta see him and report back in a week.

The doctor's office is in an old building, up four flights of stairs. Babies are crying and a radio is playing

> *Boys and girls together*
> *Me and Mamie O'Rourke*
> *We'll trip the light fantastic*
> *On the sidewalks of New York.*

The doctor tells me, Come in, sit in this chair, whassa matter with your eyes? You here for glasses?

I have some kind of infection, doctor.

Jesus, yeah. That's some infection all right. How long you had this?

Nine years, doctor. I was in the eye hospital in Ireland when I was eleven.

He pokes at my eyes with a little piece of wood and pats them with cotton swabs which stick to the lids and make me blink. He tells me stop blinking, how the hell do I expect him to examine my eyes if I sit there blinking like a maniac? But I can't help it. The more he pokes and swabs the more I blink till he's so irritated he throws the stick with the swab stuck to it out the window. He pulls out drawers in his desk and curses and slams them in again till he finds a small bottle of whiskey and a cigar and that puts him in such a good humor he sits at his desk and laughs.

Still blinking, eh? Well, kid, I've been looking at eyes for thirty-seven years and I never saw anything like that. What are you, Mexican or something?

No, I'm Irish, doctor.

What you have there they don't have that in Ireland. And that's not conjunctivitis. I know conjunctivitis. That's something else and I can tell you you're lucky you have eyes at all. What you have I saw in guys coming back from the Pacific, New Guinea and places like that. You ever in New Guinea?

No, doctor.

Now what you have to do is shave that head completely. You've got some kind of infectious dandruff like the guys from New Guinea and it's falling into your eyes. That hair will have to come off and you'll have to scrub that scalp every day with a prescription soap. Scrub that scalp till it tingles. Scrub that scalp till it shines and come back to see me. That'll be ten dollars, kid.

The prescription soap is two dollars and the Italian barber on Third Avenue charges me another two dollars plus tip for cutting my hair and shaving my scalp. He tells me it's a crying shame shaving off a nice head of hair, if he had a head of hair like that they'd have to cut off his head to get it, that most of these doctors don't know shit from Shinola anyway but if that's what I want who is he to object.

He holds up a mirror to show how bald I look in the back and I feel weak with the shame of it, the bald head, the red eyes, the pimples, the bad teeth, and if anyone looks at me on Lexington Avenue I'll push him into traffic because I'm sorry I ever came to America which threatens to fire me over my eyes and makes me go bald through the streets of New York.

Of course they stare at me on the streets and I want to stare back in a threatening way but I can't with the yellow ooze in my eyes mixing with strands of cotton and blinding me entirely. I look up and down side streets for the ones least crowded and I zigzag across town and up. The best street is Third Avenue with the El rattling overhead and shadows everywhere and people in bars with their own troubles minding their own business and not staring at every pair of sore eyes that passes by. People coming out of banks and dress shops always stare but people in bars brood over their drinks and wouldn't care if you went eyeless on the avenue.

Of course Mrs Austin is gawking out the basement window. No sooner am I in the front door than she's up the stairs asking what happened to my head, did I have an accident, was I in a fire or something, and I want to snap at her and say, Does this look like a damn fire? But I tell her my hair was only singed in the hotel kitchen and the barber said it would be better to cut it off at the roots and start all over again. I have to be polite to Mrs Austin for fear she might tell me pack up and leave and there I'd be out on the street on a Saturday with a brown suitcase and a bald head and three dollars to my name. She says, Well, you're young, and goes back downstairs and all I can do is lie on my bed listening to people on the street talking and laughing, wondering how I can go to work on Monday morning in my baldy condition even if I am obeying the hotel and the doctor's orders.

I keep going to the mirror in my room, shocking myself with the whiteness of my scalp, and wishing I could stay here till the hair comes back but I'm hungry. Mrs Austin forbids food and drink in the room but once the darkness falls I go up the street for the big *Sunday Times* that will shield the bag with a sweet bun and a pint of milk from Mrs Austin's gawk. Now I have less than two dollars to last me till Friday and here it is only Saturday. If she stops me I'll say, Why shouldn't I have a sweet bun and a pint of milk after the way the doctor told me I had a New Guinea disease and a barber shaved my head to the bone? I wonder about all those films where they're waving the Stars and Stripes and placing their hands on their chests and declaring to the world this is the land of the free and the home of the brave and you know yourself you can't even go to see *Hamlet* with your lemon meringue pie and your ginger ale or a banana and you can't go into Mrs Austin's with any food or drink.

But Mrs Austin doesn't appear. Landladies never appear when you don't care.

I can't read the *Times* unless I wash out my eyes in the bathroom with warm water and toilet paper and it's lovely to lie in the bed with the paper and the bun and milk till Mrs Austin calls up the stairs complaining her electric bills are sky high and would I kindly put out the light, she's not a millionaire.

Once I switch off the light I remember it's time to smear my scalp with ointment but then I realize if I lie down the ointment will be all over the pillow and Mrs Austin will be at me again. The only thing to do is sit up with my head resting against the iron bedstead where I can wipe off any stray ointment. The iron is made up of little scrolls and flowers with petals that stick out and make it impossible to get a decent sleep and the only thing I can do is get out and sleep on the floor where Mrs Austin will have nothing to complain about.

Monday morning there's a note on my time card telling me report to the nineteenth floor. Eddie Gilligan says it's nothing personal but they don't want me in the lobby anymore with the bad eyes and now the bald head. It's a well-known fact that people who lose their hair suddenly are not long for this world even if you were to stand up in the middle of the lobby and announce it was the barber who did it. People want to believe the worst and they're in the personnel office saying, Bad eyes, bald head, put the two together and you have big problems with the guests in the lobby. When the hair grows back and the eyes clear up I might be returned to the lobby, maybe as busboy some day, and I'd be making tips so big I'd be able to support my family in Limerick in high style but not now, not with with this head, these eyes.

8

Eddie Gilligan works on the nineteenth floor with his brother, Joe. Our job is to set up for functions, meetings in rooms and banquets and weddings in the ballroom, and Joe isn't much use the way his hands and fingers are like roots. He walks around with a long-handled broom in one hand and a cigarette in the other pretending to look busy but he spends most of his time in the lavatory or smoking with Digger Moon the carpetman who claims he's a Blackfoot Indian and can lay carpet faster and tighter than anyone in the US of A unless he's had a few and then watch out because he remembers the sufferings of his people. When Digger remembers the sufferings of his people the only man he can talk to is Joe Gilligan because Joe himself is suffering with arthritis and Digger says Joe understands. When you have arthritis so bad you can barely wipe your ass you understand all kinds of suffering. That's what Digger says and when Digger isn't going from floor to floor laying carpet or pulling up carpet he sits cross-legged on the floor of the carpet room suffering with Joe, one with the past, the other with the arthritis. No one is going to bother Digger or Joe because everyone in the Biltmore Hotel knows of their suffering and they can spend days in the carpet room or stepping across the street to McAnn's Bar for relief. Mr Carey himself suffers with a bad stomach. He makes his inspection rounds in the morning suffering from the breakfast his wife cooks and on the afternoon inspection he's suffering from the lunch his wife packs. He tells Eddie his wife is a beautiful woman, the only one he ever loved, but she's killing him slowly and she's not in such good shape herself with her legs all swollen with rheumatism. Eddie tells Mr Carey his wife is in bad shape, too, after four miscarriages and now some kind of blood infection that has the doctor worried. The morning we set up for the annual banquet of the American-Irish Historical Society, Eddie and Mr Carey stand at the entrance to the nineteenth-floor ballroom, Eddie smoking a cigarette and Mr Carey in his double-breasted suit draped nicely to make you think he doesn't have that much of a belly, stroking it to ease the pain. Eddie tells Mr Carey he never smoked till he was hit on Omaha Beach and some asshole, excuse the language, Mr Carey, shoved a cigarette in his mouth while he was lying there waiting for the medics. He took a drag on that cigarette and it gave him such relief lying there with his gut hanging out on Omaha Beach he's been smoking ever since, can't give 'em up, tried, Christ knows, but can't. Now Digger Moon strolls up with a huge carpet on his shoulder and tells Eddie something has to be done about his brother, Joe, that that poor son-of-a-bitch is suffering more than seven Indian tribes and Digger knows something about suffering after his stint with the infantry all over the goddam Pacific when he was hit with everything the Japs could throw at him, malaria, everything. Eddie says, Yeah, yeah, he knows about Joe and he's sorry, after all it's his brother, but he has his own troubles with his wife and her miscarriages and blood infection and his own gut messed up from not being put back right and he worries about Joe the way he mixes alcohol and all kinds of pain-killers. Mr Carey belches and groans and Digger says, You still eating shit? because Digger isn't afraid of Mr Carey or anyone else. That's how it is when you're a great carpetman, you can say what you like to anyone and if they fire you there's always a job in the Hotel Commodore or the Hotel Roosevelt or even, Jesus, yeah, the Waldorf-Astoria, where they're always trying to steal Digger away. Some days Digger is so overcome by the sufferings of his people he refuses to lay any carpet and when Mr Carey won't fire him Digger says, That's right. White man can't get along without us Indians. White man gotta have Iroquois sixty floors up the skyscrapers to dance along steel beams. White man gotta have Blackfoot to lay good carpet. Every time Digger hears Mr Carey belch he tells him stop eating shit and have a nice beer because beer never bothered nobody and it's Mrs

41

Carey's sandwiches that are killing Mr Carey. Digger tells Mr Carey he has a theory about women, that they're like black widow spiders who kill the males after they screw, bite their goddam heads off, that women don't care about men, once they're past the age of having kids men are really useless unless they're up on the horse attacking another tribe. Eddie Gilligan says you'd look pretty fuckin' silly riding your horse up Madison Avenue to attack another tribe and Digger says that's exactly what he means. He says a man is put on this earth to paint his face, ride the horse, throw the spear, kill the other tribe and when Eddie says, Aw, bullshit, Digger says, Aw, bullshit, my ass, what are you doin', Eddie? spending your life here setting up for dinners and weddings? Is that a way for a man to live? Eddie shrugs and puffs on his cigarette and when Digger suddenly swings around to walk away he catches Mr Carey and Eddie with the end of the carpet and knocks them five feet into the ballroom.

It's an accident and no one says anything but still I admire the way Digger goes through the world not giving a fiddler's fart like my Uncle Pa in Limerick just because no one can lay carpet like him. I wish I could be like Digger but not with carpets. I hate carpets.

If I had the money I could buy a torch and read till dawn. In America a torch is called a flashlight. A biscuit is called a cookie, a bun is a roll. Confectionery is pastry and minced meat is ground. Men wear pants instead of trousers and they'll even say this pant leg is shorter than the other which is silly. When I hear them saying pant leg I feel like breathing faster. The lift is an elevator and if you want a WC or a lavatory you have to say bathroom even if there isn't a sign of a bath there. And no one dies in America, they pass away or they're deceased and when they die the body, which is called the remains, is taken to a funeral home where people just stand around and look at it and no one sings or tells a story or takes a drink and then it's taken away in a casket to be interred. They don't like saying coffin and they don't like saying buried. They never say graveyard. Cemetery sounds nicer.

If I had the money I could buy a hat and go out but I can't wander the streets of Manhattan in my bald state for fear people might think they were looking at a snowball on a pair of scrawny shoulders. In a week when the hair darkens my scalp I'll be able to go out again and there's nothing Mrs Austin can do about that. That's what gives me such pleasure, lying on the bed and thinking of the things you can do that nobody else can interfere with. That's what Mr O'Halloran, the headmaster, used to tell us in school in Limerick, Your mind is a treasure house that you should stock well and it's the one part of you the world can't interfere with.

New York was the city of my dreams but now I'm here the dreams are gone and it's not what I expected at all. I never thought I'd be going around a hotel lobby cleaning up after people and scouring toilet bowls in the lavatories. How could I ever write my mother or anyone in Limerick and tell them the way I'm living in this rich land with two dollars to last me for a week, a bald head and sore eyes, and a landlady who won't let me turn on the light? How could I ever tell them I have to eat bananas every day, the cheapest food in the world, because the hotel won't let me near the kitchen for leftovers for fear the Puerto Ricans might catch my New Guinea infection? They'd never believe me. They'd say, Go away ower that, and they'd laugh because all you have to do is look at the films to see how well off Americans are, the way they fiddle with their food and leave something on their plate and then push the plate away. It's hard even to feel sorry for Americans who are supposed to be poor in a film like *The Grapes of Wrath* when everything dries up and they have to move to California. At least they're dry and warm. My Uncle Pa Keating used to say if we had a California in Ireland the whole country would flock there, eat oranges galore and spend the whole day swimming. When you're in Ireland it's hard to believe there are poor people in America because you see the Irish coming back, Returned Yanks they're called, and you can spot them a mile away with their fat arses waggling along O'Connell Street in trousers too tight and colors you'd never see in Ireland, blues, pinks, light greens, and even flashes of puce. They always act rich and talk through their noses about their refrigerators and automobiles and if they go into a pub they want American drinks no one ever heard of, cocktails if you don't mind, though if you act like that in a Limerick pub the barman will put you in your place and remind you how you went to America with your arse hanging out of your trousers and don't be putting on airs here, Mick, I knew you when the snot hung from your nose to your kneecaps. You can always spot the Real Yanks, too, with their light colors and fat arses and the way they look around and smile and give pennies to raggedy children. Real Yanks don't put on airs. They don't have to after coming from a country where everyone has everything.

If Mrs Austin won't let me have a light I can still sit up in the bed or lie down or I can decide to stay in or go out. I won't go out tonight because of my bald head and I don't mind because I can stay here and turn my mind into a film about Limerick. This is the greatest discovery I've made from lying in the room, that if I can't read because of my eyes or Mrs Austin complaining about the light I can start any kind of a film in my head. If it's midnight here it's five in the morning in Limerick and I can picture my mother and brothers asleep with the dog, Lucky, growling at the world and my uncle, Ab Sheehan, snorting away in his bed from all the pints he had the night before and farting from his great feed of fish and chips.

I can float through Limerick and see people shuffling through the streets for the first Sunday Mass. I can go in and out of churches, shops, pubs, graveyards and see people asleep or groaning with pain in the hospital at the City Home. It's magic to go back to Limerick in my mind even when it brings the tears. It's hard to pass through the lanes of the poor and look into their houses and hear babies crying and women trying to start fires to boil water in kettles for the breakfast of tea and bread. It's hard to see children shivering when they have to leave their beds for school or Mass and there's no heat in the house like the heat we have here in New York with radiators singing away at six in the morning. I'd like to empty out the lanes of Limerick and bring all the poor people to America and put them in houses with heat and give them warm clothes and shoes and let them stuff themselves with porridge and sausages. Some day I'll make millions and I'll bring the poor people to America and send them back to Limerick fat arsed and waddling up and down O'Connell Street in light colors.

I can do anything I like in this bed, anything. I can dream about Limerick or I can interfere with myself even if it's a sin, and Mrs Austin will never know. No one will ever know unless I go to confession and I'm too doomed for that.

Other nights when I have hair on my head and no money I can walk around Manhattan. I don't mind that one bit because the streets are as lively as any film at the Sixty-Eighth Street Playhouse. There's always a fire engine screaming around a corner or an ambulance or a police car and sometimes they come screaming together and you know there's a fire. People always watch for the fire engine to slow down and that tells you what block to go to and where to look for smoke and flames. If someone is at a window ready to jump that makes it more exciting. The ambulance will wait with flashing lights and cops will tell everyone move back. That's the main job of cops in New York, telling everyone move back. They're powerful with their guns and sticks but the real hero is the fireman especially if he climbs a ladder and plucks a child from a window. He could save an old man with crutches and nothing on but a nightshirt but it's different when it's a child sucking her thumb and resting her curly head on the fireman's broad shoulder. That's when we all cheer and look at each other and know we're all happy about the same thing.

And that's what makes us look in the *Daily News* the next day to see if there's any chance we might be in the picture with the brave fireman and the curly-haired child.

9

Mrs Austin tells me her sister, Hannah, that's married to the Irishman, is coming for a little visit on Christmas before they go out to her house in Brooklyn and she'd like to meet me. We'll have a sandwich and a Christmas drink and that will get Hannah's mind off her troubles with that crazy Irishman. Mrs Austin doesn't understand herself why Hannah would want to spend Christmas Eve with the likes of me, another Irishman, but she was always a bit strange and maybe she likes the Irish after all. Their mother warned them a long time ago back in Sweden, over twenty years, would you believe it, to stay away from Irishmen and Jews, to marry their own kind and Mrs Austin doesn't mind telling me her husband, Eugene, was half Swedish, half Hungarian, that never drank a drop in his life though he loved to eat and that's what killed him in the end. She doesn't mind telling me he was big as a house when he died, that when she wasn't cooking he was raiding the refrigerator and when they got a TV set that was really the end of him. He'd sit there eating and drinking and worrying about the state of the world so much his heart just stopped, just like that. She misses him and it's hard after twenty-three years especially when they had no kids. Her sister, Hannah, has five kids and that's because the Irishman won't ever leave her alone, a couple of drinks and he's jumping on her, just like a typical Irish Catholic. Eugene wasn't like that, he had respect.

In any case she'll expect to see me after work on Christmas Eve.

On the day itself Mr Carey invites the housemen of the hotel and four chambermaid supervisors to his office for a little Christmas drink. There's a bottle of Paddy's Irish whiskey and a bottle of Four Roses which Digger Moon won't touch. He wants to know why anyone would drink piss like Four Roses when they can have the best thing that ever came out of Ireland, the whiskey. Mr Carey strokes his belly along the double-breasted suit and says it's all the same to him, he can't drink anything. It would kill him. But drink anyway, here's to a Merry Christmas and who knows what the next year will bring.

Joe Gilligan is already smiling from whatever he's been swigging all day from the flask in his back pocket and between that and the arthritis there's the odd stumble. Mr Carey tells him, Here, Joe, sit in my chair, and when Joe tries to sit he lets out a great groan and there are tears on his cheeks. Mrs Hynes, the head of all the chambermaids, goes over to him and holds his head against her chest and pats him and rocks him. She says, Ah, poor Joe, poor Joe, I don't know how the good Lord could twist your bones after what you did for America in the war. Digger Moon says that's where Joe got the arthritis, in the goddam Pacific, where they have every goddam disease known to man. Remember this, Joe, it was the goddam Japs gave you that arthritis the way they gave me malaria. We haven't been the same since, Joe, you an' me.

Mr Carey tells him take it easy, take it easy with the language, there are ladies present, and Digger says, okay, Mr Carey, I respect you for that and it's Christmas so what the hell. Mrs Hynes says, That's right, it's Christmas and we must love each other and forgive our enemies. Digger says, Forgive my ass. I don't forgive the white man and I don't forgive the Japs. But I forgive you, Joe. You suffered more than ten Indian tribes with that goddam arthritis. When he grabs Joe's hand to shake it Joe howls with pain and Mr Carey says, Digger, Digger. Mrs Hynes says, Will you, for the love o' Jesus, have respect for Joe's arthritis. Digger says, Sorry, ma'am, I have the greatest respect for Joe's arthritis, and to prove it he holds a large glass of Paddy's to Joe's lips.

Eddie Gilligan stands over in a corner with his glass and I wonder why he looks and says nothing when the world is worried about his brother. I know he has his own troubles with his wife's blood infection but I can't understand why he won't at least stand closer to his brother.

47

Jerry Kerrisk whispers we should get away from this crazy crowd and have a beer. I don't like spending money in bars with the trouble my mother is in but it's Christmas and the whiskey I had already makes me feel better about myself and the world in general and why shouldn't I be good to myself. It's the first time in my life I ever drank whiskey like a man and now that I'm in a bar with Jerry I can talk and not worry about my eyes or anything. Now I can ask Jerry why Eddie Gilligan is so cold to his brother.

Women, says Jerry. Eddie was engaged to this girl when he was drafted but when he went away she and Joe fell in love and when she sent Eddie back the engagement ring he went crazy and said he'd kill Joe the minute he saw him. But Eddie was sent to Europe and Joe to the Pacific and they were busy killing other people and while they were away Joe's wife, the one Eddie was supposed to marry, got the drinking habit and now makes Joe's life hell. Eddie said that was punishment for the son of a bitch for stealing his girl. He met a nice Italian girl himself in the army, a W A C, but she has the blood infection and you'd think there's a curse on the whole Gilligan family.

Jerry says he thinks the Irish mothers are right after all. You should marry your own kind, Irish Catholics, and make sure they're not alcoholics or Italians with blood infections.

He laughs when he says that but there's something serious in his eyes and I don't say anything because I know I don't want to marry an Irish Catholic myself and spend the rest of my life dragging the kids to confession and communion and saying, Yes, Father, oh, indeed, Father, every time I see a priest.

Jerry wants to stay in the bar and drink more beer and he turns peevish when I tell him I have to visit Mrs Austin and her sister, Hannah. Why would I want to spend Christmas Eve with two old Swedish women, forty years old at least, when I could be having a grand time for myself with girls from Mayo and Kerry up at Ireland's Thirty-Two? Why?

I can't answer him because I don't know where I want to be or what I'm supposed to do. That's what you're faced with when you come to America, one decision after another. I knew what to do in Limerick and I had answers for questions but this is my first Christmas Eve in New York and here I am pulled one way by Jerry Kerrisk, Ireland's Thirty-Two, the promise of girls from Mayo and Kerry, and the other way by two old Swedish women, one always gawking out the window in case I might smuggle in food or drink, the other unhappy with her Irish husband and who knows what way she'll jump. I'm afraid if I don't go to Mrs Austin she might turn savage on me and tell me leave and there I'll be out on the street on Christmas Eve with my brown suitcase and only a few dollars left after sending money home, paying my rent, and now buying beer right and left in this bar. After all this I can't afford to spend the night doling out beer money for the women of Ireland and that's the part Jerry understands, the part that takes away his peevishness. He knows money has to be sent home. He says, Happy Christmas, and laughs, I know you'll have a wild night with the old Swedish girls. The barman has his ear cocked and he says, Mind yourself at them Swedish parties. They'll be giving you their native drink, the glug, and if you drink that stuff you won't know Christmas Eve from the Feast of the Immaculate Conception. It's black and thick and you'd need a strong constitution for it, and then they make you eat all kinds of fish with it, raw fish, salty fish, smoked fish, all kinds of fish you wouldn't give a cat. The Swedes drink that glug and it makes them so crazy they think they're Vikings all over again.

Jerry says he didn't know the Swedes were Vikings. He thought you had to be a Dane.

Nodatall, says the barman. All them people in northern places were Vikings. Whenever you saw ice you were sure to see a Viking.

Jerry says it's remarkable the things people know and the barman says, I could tell you a story or two.

Jerry orders one more beer for the road and I drink it though I don't know what's going to become of me after my two large whiskeys in Mr Carey's office and four beers here with Jerry. I don't know how I'm going to face a night of glug and all kinds of fish if the barman is right in his prophecy.

We walk up Third Avenue singing "Don't Fence Me In" with people rushing past us frantic over Christmas, giving us nothing but hard stares. There are dancing Christmas lights everywhere, but up around Bloomingdale's the lights dance too much and I have to hold on to a Third Avenue El pillar and throw up. Jerry pushes in my stomach with his fist. Get it all up, he says, and you'll have plenty of room for the glug and you'll be a new man tomorrow. Then he says glug glug glug and laughs so hard over the sound of the word he's nearly hit by a car and a cop tells us move on, that we should be ashamed of ourselves, Irish kids that should respect the birthday of the Savior, goddamit.

There's a diner at Sixty-Seventh Street and Jerry says I should have coffee to straighten me out before I see the Swedes, he'll pay for it. We sit at the counter and he tells me he's not going to spend the rest of his life working like a slave at the Biltmore Hotel. He's not going to wind up like the Gilligans who fought for the USA and what the hell did they get for it? Arthritis and wives with blood infections and drinking problems, that's what they got. Oh, no, Jerry is heading for the Catskill Mountains on Memorial Day, the end of May, the Irish Alps. Plenty of work up there waiting on tables, cleaning up, anything, and the tips are good. There are Jewish places up there, too, but they're not too active in the tipping department because they pay for everything in advance and don't have to carry cash. The Irish drink and leave money on tables or the floor and when you clean up it's all yours. Sometimes they come back squawking but you didn't see a thing. You don't know nothing. You just sweep up the way you're paid to. Of course they don't believe you and they call you a liar and say things about your mother but there's nothing they can do except take their business elsewhere. There are plenty of girls up in the Catskills. Some places have outdoor dances and all you have to do is waltz your Mary into the woods and before you know it you're in a state of mortal sin. The Irish girls are mad for it once they get to the Catskills. They're hopeless in the city they way they all work in fancy places like Schrafft's with their little black dresses and little white aprons, Ah, yes, ma'am, ah, indeed, ma'am, are the mashed potatoes a little too lumpy, ma'am? but get them up in the mountains and they're like cats, up the pole, getting pregnant, and before they know what hit them, dozens of Seans and Kevins are dragging their arses up the aisle with the priests glaring at them and the girls' big brothers threatening them.

I want to sit in the diner all night listening to Jerry talking about Irish girls in the Catskills but the man says it's Christmas Eve and he's closing out of respect to his Christian customers even though he's Greek and it's not really his Christmas. Jerry wants to know how it could not be his Christmas since all you have to do is look out the window for proof but the Greek says, We're different.

That's enough for Jerry who doesn't argue about such things and that's what I like about him, the way he goes through life having another beer and dreaming of grand times in the Catskills and not arguing with Greeks about Christmas. I wish I could be like him but there's always some dark cloud at the back of my head, Swedish women waiting for me with glug, or a letter from my mother saying thanks for the few dollars, Michael and Alphie will have shoes and we'll have a nice goose for Christmas with the help of God and His Blessed Mother. She never mentions she needs shoes for herself and once I think of that I know I'll have another dark cloud at the back of my head. I wish there was a little panel I could slide back to release the clouds but there isn't and I'll have to find another way or stop collecting dark clouds.

The Greek says, Goodnight, gen'men, and would we like to take some day-old doughnuts. Take 'em, he says, or I trow out. Jerry says he'll have one to keep him going to Ireland's Thirty-Two where he'll have a feed of corned beef and cabbage and floury white potatoes. The Greek fills a bag with doughnuts and confectionery and tells me I look like I could use a decent meal, so take the bag.

Jerry says goodnight at Sixty-Eighth Street and I wish I could go with him. The whole day has me dizzy and it's still not over with the Swedes there waiting, stirring the glug, slicing the raw fish. The thought of it makes me puke all over again there on the street and people passing by, frantic with Christmas, make sounds of disgust and step away from me, telling their little children, Don't look at that disgusting man. He's drunk. I want to tell them, please don't turn the little children against me. I want to tell them this is not a habit I have. There are clouds at the back of my head, my mother has a goose, at least, but she needs shoes.

But there's no use trying to talk to people with parcels and children by the hand and their heads ringing with Christmas carols because they're going home to bright apartments and they know God's in His heaven, all's right with the world, as the poet said.

Mrs Austin opens the door. Oh, look, Hannah, Mr McCourt brought us a whole bag of doughnuts and pastries. Hannah gives a little wave from the couch and says, That's nice, you never know when you might need a bag of doughnuts. I always thought the Irish brought a bottle but you're different. Give the boy a drink, Stephanie.

Hannah is drinking red wine but Mrs Austin goes to a bowl on the table and ladles out the black stuff into a glass, the glug. My stomach turns again and I have to control it.

Siddown, says Hannah. Lemme tell you something, Irish boy. I don't give a shit about your people. You may be nice, my sister says you're nice, you bring nice doughnuts, but right under your skin you're nothing but shit.

Please, Hannah, says Mrs Austin.

Please Hannah, my ass. What did you people ever do for the world besides drink? Stephanie, give him some fish, decent Swedish food. Moon-faced mick. You make me sick, you little mick. Ah, ha, didja hear the poetry in that?

She cackles away over her poetry and I don't know what to do with my glug in one hand and Mrs Austin pushing fish at me with the other. Mrs Austin is drinking the glug, too, and she staggers from me to the bowl to the couch where Hannah is holding out her glass for more wine. She slurps her wine and glares at me. She says, A kid I was when I married that mick. Nineteen. How many years ago? Jesus, twenty-one. Whadda you, Stephanie? Forty-something? Wasted my life on that mick. And what are you doin' here? Who sent you?

Mrs Austin.

Mrs Austin. Mrs Austin. Speak up, you little spud-shitter. Drink your glug and speak up.

Mrs Austin sways before me with her glug glass. Come on, Eugene, less go to bed.

Oh, I'm not Eugene, Mrs Austin.

Oh.

She turns and wobbles away into another room and Hannah cackles again, See that. She still doesn't know she's a widow. Wish I was a goddam widow.

The glug I drank is making my stomach turn and I try to rush to the street but the door has three locks and I'm throwing up in the basement vestibule before I can get out. Hannah lurches from the couch and tells me get into the kitchen, get a mop and soap and clean up this goddam mess, don't you know it's Christmas Eve for Chrissakes and is this how you treat your gracious host.

From kitchen to door I go with dripping mop, swabbing, squeezing, rinsing in the kitchen sink and back again. Hannah pats my shoulder and kisses my ear and tells me I'm not such a bad mick after all, that I must have been well brought up the way I clean my mess. She tells me help myself to anything, glug, fish, even one of my own doughnuts, but I place the mop back where I found it and walk past

Hannah, with the idea in my head that once I cleaned up I don't have to listen to her anymore or anyone like her. She calls to me, Where you going? Where the hell do you think you're going? but I'm up the stairs to my room, my bed, so that I can lie there listening to Christmas carols on the radio with the world spinning around me and a great wonder in my head about the rest of my life in America. If I wrote to anyone in Limerick and told them about my Christmas Eve in New York they'd say I was making it up. They'd say New York must be a lunatic asylum.

In the morning there's a knock at my door and it's Mrs Austin in dark glasses. Hannah is farther down the stairs and she's in dark glasses, too. Mrs Austin says she heard I had an accident in her apartment but no one can blame her or her sister since they were prepared to offer the finest of Swedish hospitality and if I chose to arrive at their little party in a certain state they couldn't be blamed and it's too bad because they wanted nothing but a truly Christian Christmas Eve and I just wanted to tell you, Mr McCourt, we don't appreciate your behavior one bit, isn't that right, Hannah?

There's a croak from Hannah as she coughs and puffs on a cigarette.

They go back down the stairs and I want to call after Mrs Austin to see if there's any chance she could spare me a doughnut from the Greek's bag since I'm so empty from all the throwing up last night but they're out the door and from my window I can see them loading Christmas parcels into a car and driving off.

I can stand at the window all day looking at the happy people with children by the hand going off to church, as they say in America, or I can sit up in the bed with *Crime and Punishment* and see what Raskolnikov is up to but that will stir up all kinds of guilt and I don't have the strength for it and it's not the right kind of reading for a Christmas Day anyway. I'd like to go up the street for Communion at St Vincent Ferrer's but it's years since I went to confession and my soul is as black as Mrs Austin's glug. The happy Catholic people with children by the hand are surely going to St Vincent's and if I follow them I'm bound to have a Christmas feeling.

It's lovely to go into a church like St Vincent's where you know the Mass will be just like the Mass in Limerick or anywhere in the world. You could go to Samoa or Kabul and they'd have the same Mass and even if they wouldn't let me be an altar boy in Limerick I still have the Latin my father taught me and no matter where I go I can respond to the priest. No one can scoop out the contents of my head, all the saints' feast days I know by heart, the Mass Latin, the chief towns and products of the thirty-two counties of Ireland, songs galore of Ireland's sufferings, and Oliver Goldsmith's lovely poem, "The Deserted Village". They could put me in jail and throw away the key but they could never stop me from dreaming my way around Limerick and out along the banks of the Shannon or thinking about Raskolnikov and his troubles.

The people who go to St Vincent's are like the ones who go to the Sixty-Eighth Street Playhouse for *Hamlet* and they know the Latin responses the way they know the play. They share prayer books and sing hymns together and smile at each other because they know Brigid the maid is back there in the Park Avenue kitchen keeping an eye on the turkey. Their sons and daughters have the look of coming home from school and college and they smile at other people in the pews also home from school and college. They can afford to smile because they all have teeth so dazzling if they dropped them in snow they'd be lost forever.

The church is so crowded there are people standing in the back but I'm so weak with the hunger and the long Christmas Eve of whiskey, glug and throwing up I want to find a seat. There's an empty spot at the end of a pew far up the center aisle but as soon as I slip into it a man comes running at me. He's all dressed up in striped trousers, a coat with tails, and a frown over his face and he whispers to me, You must leave this pew at once. This is for regular pew holders, come on, come on. I feel my face turning red and that means my eyes are worse and when I go down the aisle I know the whole world is looking at me, the one who sneaked into the pew of a happy family with children home from school and college.

There's no use even standing at the back of the church. They all know and they'll be giving me looks, so I might as well leave and add another sin to the hundreds already on my soul, the mortal sin of not going to Mass on Christmas Day. At least God will know I tried and it's not my fault if I wandered into a happy family from Park Avenue pew.

I'm so empty now and hungry I want to go mad with myself and have a feast at the Horn and Hardart Automat but I don't want to be seen there for fear people might think I'm like the ones who sit there half the day with a cup of coffee, an old newspaper and nowhere to go. There's a Chock Full o'Nuts a few blocks away and that's where I have a bowl of pea soup, a nutted cheese on raisin bread, a cup of coffee, a doughnut with white sugar and a read of the *Journal-American* that someone left behind.

It's only two in the afternoon and I don't know what to do with myself when all the libraries are closed. People walking by with children by the hand might think I have nowhere to go so I keep my head up and walk up one street and down the other as if I were rushing for a turkey dinner. I wish I could open a door somewhere and have people say, Oh, hi, Frank, you're just in time. The people walking here and there on the streets of New York take it all for granted. They bring presents and get presents and have their big Christmas dinners and they never know there are people walking up one street and down the other on the holiest day of the year. I wish I could be an ordinary New Yorker stuffed after my dinner, talking to my family with Christmas carols on the radio in the background. Or I wouldn't mind being back in Limerick with my mother and brothers and the nice goose but here I am in the place I always dreamed about, New York, and I'm worn out with all these streets where there isn't even a bird to be seen.

There's nothing to do but go back to my room, listen to the radio, read *Crime and Punishment* and fall asleep wondering why Russians have to drag things out. You'd never find a New York detective wandering around with the likes of Raskolnikov talking about everything but the murder of the old woman. The New York detective would nab him, book him and the next thing is the electric chair in Sing Sing, and that's because Americans are busy people with no time for detectives to be chatting with people they already know committed the murder.

There's a knock on the door and it's Mrs Austin. Mr McCourt, she says, would you come downstairs a minute?

I don't know what to say. I'd like to tell her kiss my arse after the way her sister talked to me and the way she talked to me herself this morning but I follow her down and there she has all kinds of food laid out on the table. She says she brought it from her sister's, that they were worried I might have no place to go or nothing to eat on this beautiful day. She's sorry about the way she talked to me this morning and hopes I'm in a forgiving mood.

There's turkey and stuffing and all kinds of potatoes, white and yellow, with cranberry sauce to make everything sweet and all this

55

puts me in a forgiving mood. She'd give me some glug but her sister threw it out and it's just as well. It made everyone sick.

When I'm finished she invites me to sit and watch her new television set where there's a program about Jesus that's so holy I fall asleep in the armchair. When I awake the clock on her mantelpiece says twenty past four in the morning and Mrs Austin is in the other room letting out little cries, Eugene, Eugene, and that proves you can have a sister and go to her house for Christmas dinner but if you don't have your Eugene you're as lonely as anyone sitting in the Automat and it's a great comfort to know my mother and brothers in Limerick have a goose and next year when I'm promoted to busboy at the Biltmore I'll send them the money that will let them stroll around Limerick dazzling the world with their new shoes.

10

Eddie Gilligan tells me go to the lockers and get into my street clothes because there's a priest in Mr Carey's office who met me coming over on the ship and now wants to take me to lunch. Then he says, What are you blushing for? It's only a priest and you're getting the free lunch.

I wish I could say I don't want to meet the priest for lunch but Eddie and Mr Carey might ask questions. If a priest says come to lunch you have to go and it doesn't matter what happened in the hotel room even if it wasn't my fault. I could never tell Eddie or Mr Gilligan how the priest came at me. They'd never believe me. People sometimes say things about priests, that they're fat or pompous or mean, but no one would ever believe a priest would interfere with you in a hotel room especially people like Eddie or Mr Carey with sick wives always running to confession in case they die in their sleep. People like that wouldn't be surprised if priests walked on water.

Why can't this priest go back to Los Angeles and leave me alone? Why is he taking me to lunch when he should be out there visiting the sick and the dying? That's what priests are for. It's four months since he went off to that retreat house in Virginia to beg forgiveness and here he is still on this side of the continent with nothing on his mind but lunch.

Now Eddie comes to me in the locker room and tells me the

priest had another idea, meet him across the street in McAnn's.

It's hard to walk into a restaurant and sit down opposite a priest who came at you in a hotel room four months ago. It's hard to know what to do when he looks at you directly, shakes your hand, holds your elbow, eases you into your seat. He tells me I'm looking good, that I filled out a bit in the face and I must be eating right. He says America is a great country if you give it a chance but I could tell him how they won't let the Puerto Ricans give me leftovers anymore and how I'm weary of bananas but I don't want to say much in case he might think I've forgotten the New Yorker Hotel. I don't have any grudge against him. He didn't hit anyone or starve anyone and what he did came from the drink. What he did was not as bad as running off to England and leaving your wife and children to starve the way my father did but what he did was bad because he's a priest and they're not supposed to murder people or interfere with them in any way.

And what he did makes me wonder if there are any other priests wandering the world going at people in hotel rooms.

There he is gazing at me with his big grey eyes, his face all scrubbed and shiny, with his black suit and his gleaming white collar, telling me he wanted to make this one stop before returning to Los Angeles forever. It's easy to see how pleased he is to be in a state of grace after his four months in the retreat house and I know now it's hard for me to eat a hamburger with someone in such a state of grace. It's hard to know what to do with my own eyes when he gazes at me as if I were the one who went at someone in a hotel room. I'd like to be able to look right back at him but all I know of priests is what I've seen of them on altars, pulpits, and in the darkness of confessionals. He's probably thinking I've been up to all kinds of sin and he's right but at least I'm not a priest and I never bothered anyone else.

He tells the waiter, Yes, a hamburger is fine and no, no, Lord no, he won't have a beer, water is fine, nothing alcoholic will ever cross his lips again, and he smiles at me as if I should understand what he's talking about and the waiter smiles, too, as if to say isn't this a saintly priest.

He tells me he went to confession to a bishop in Virginia and even though he received absolution and spent four months in work and prayer he feels it wasn't enough. He has given up his parish and he'll spend the rest of his days with the poor Mexicans and Negroes in Los Angeles. He calls for the bill, tells me he never wants to see me again, it's too painful, but he'll remember me in his Masses. He says I should be careful of the Irish curse, the drink, and whenever I'm tempted to sin I should meditate like him on the purity of the Virgin Mary, good luck, God bless, go to night school, and he's into a taxi to Idlewild Airport.

There are days the rain is so heavy I have to spend a dime on the subway and I see people my own age with books and bags that say Columbia, Fordham, NYU, City College, and I know I want to be one of them, a student.

I know I don't want to spend years in the Biltmore Hotel setting up banquets and meetings and I don't want to be the houseman cleaning up in the Palm Court. I don't even want to be a busboy getting a share of the waiters' tips which they get from the rich students who drink their gin and tonic, talk about Hemingway and where should they have dinner and should they go to Vanessa's party on Sutton Place, it was such a bore last year.

I don't want to be houseman where people look at me as if I were part of a wall.

I see the college students in the subway and I dream that some day I'll be like them, carrying my books, listening to professors, graduating with a cap and gown, going on to a job where I'll wear a suit and tie and carry a briefcase, go home on the train every night, kiss the wife, eat my dinner, play with the kids, read a book, have the excitement with the wife, go to sleep so that I'll be rested and fresh the next day.

I'd like to be a college student in the subway because you can see from the books they're carrying their heads must be stuffed with all kinds of knowledge, that they could sit down with you and chat forever about Shakespeare and Samuel Johnson and Dostoyevsky. If I could go to college I'd make sure to ride the subways and let people see my books so that they could admire me and wish they could go to college, too. I'd hold up the books to let people see I was reading *Crime and Punishment* by Fyodor Dostoyevsky. It must be grand to be a student with nothing to do but listen to professors, read in libraries, sit under campus trees and discuss what you're learning. It must be grand to know you'll be getting a degree that puts you ahead of the rest of the world, that you'll marry a girl with a degree and you'll be sitting up in bed the rest of your life having great chats about the important matters.

But I don't know how I'll ever get a college degree and rise in the world with no high school diploma and two eyes like piss holes in the snow, as everyone tells me. Some old Irishmen tell me there's nothing wrong with hard work. Many a man made his way in America by the sweat of his brow and his strong back and it's a good thing to learn your station in life and not be getting above yourself. They tell me that's why God put pride at the top of the Seven Deadly Sins so that young fellas like me won't be getting off the boat with big notions. There's plenty of work in this country for anyone who wants to earn an honest dollar with his two hands and the sweat of his brow and no getting above himself.

The Greek in the diner on Third Avenue tells me his cleaning-up Puerto Rican quit on him and would I like to work an hour every morning, come in at six, sweep out the place, mop it, clean out the toilets. I could have an egg, a roll, a cup of coffee and two dollars and, who knows, it might lead to something permanent. He says he likes the Irish, they're like the Greeks, and that's because they came from Greece a long time ago. That's what a professor at Hunter College told him though when I said this to Eddie Gilligan at the hotel he said the Greek and the professor were full of shit, that the Irish were always there on their little island since the beginning of time and what the hell do Greeks know anyway? If they knew anything they wouldn't be slinging hash in restaurants and babbling in their own language that no one understands.

I don't care where the Irish came from with the Greek feeding me every morning and paying me two dollars adding up to ten for the week, five for my mother and her shoes and five for me so that I can get proper clothes for myself and not look like Paddy-off-the-boat.

I'm lucky to have an extra few dollars a week especially after Tom Clifford knocked on my door at Mrs Austin's and said, Let's get the hell outa here. He says there's a huge room the size of an apartment for rent up on Third Avenue and Eighty-Sixth Street over a shop called Harry's Hats and if we shared the rent we'd still be paying six dollars a week and we wouldn't have Mrs Austin watching every move. We could bring in anything we liked, food, drink, girls.

Yeah, says Tom, girls.

The new room has a front and a back and looks out on Third Avenue where we can watch the El pass right before us. We wave at the passengers and discover they don't mind waving back in the evening on the way home from work though very few wave in the morning because of the bad mood they're in going to work.

Tom works on the night shift at an apartment building and that leaves me on my own in the room. It's the first time in my life I ever had the feeling of freedom, no bosses, no Mrs Austin telling me put out the light. I can walk around the neighborhood and look at the German shops, bars, cafes and all the Irish bars on Third Avenue. There are Irish dances at the Caravan, the Tuxedo, the Leitrim House, the Sligo House. Tom won't go to the Irish dances. He wants to meet German girls because of his three happy years in Germany and because he's able to speak German. He says the Irish can kiss his ass and I don't understand that because every time I hear Irish music I feel tears coming and I want to be standing on the banks of the Shannon looking at swans. It's easy for Tom to talk to German girls or Irish girls when he's in the mood but it's never easy for me to talk to anyone because I know they're looking at my eyes.

Tom had a better education in Ireland than I did and he could go to college if he liked. He says he'd rather make money, that's what America is there for. He tells me I'm a fool for breaking my ass working at the Biltmore Hotel when I could look around and find a job with a decent wage.

He's right. I hate working at the Biltmore Hotel and cleaning up for the Greek every morning. When I clean the toilet bowls I feel angry with myself because it reminds me of the time I had to empty the chamber pot of my mother's cousin, Laman Griffin, for a few pennies and the loan of his bike. And I wonder why I'm so particular about the toilet bowls, why I want them to be spotless when I could give them a swish of the mop and let them be. No, I have to use plenty of detergent and make them sparkle as if people were going to have their dinners out of them. The Greek is pleased though he gives me strange looks that say, Very nice but why? I could tell him this extra ten dollars a week and the morning food is a gift and I don't want to lose it. Then he wants to know what I'm doing here in the first place. I'm a nice Irish boy, I know English, I'm intelligent, and why am I cleaning toilet bowls and working in hotels when I could be getting an education. If he knew English he'd be in a university studying the wonderful history of Greece and Plato and Socrates and all the great Greek writers. He wouldn't be cleaning toilet bowls. Anyone who knows English should not be cleaning toilet bowls.

11

Tom dances with Emer, a girl at the Tuxedo Ballroom, who is there with her brother, Liam, and when Tom and Liam go for a drink she dances with me even though I don't know how. I like her because she's kind even when I step on her feet and when she presses my arm or my back to go in the right direction for fear of colliding with the men and women of Kerry, Cork, Mayo and other counties. I like her because she laughs easily even though I feel sometimes she's laughing at my awkward ways. I'm twenty years of age and I never in my life took a girl to a dance or a film or even a cup of tea and now I have to learn how to do it. I don't even know how to talk to girls because we never had one in the house except my mother. I don't know anything after growing up in Limerick and listening to priests on Sundays thundering against dancing and walking out the road with girls.

The music ends and Tom and Liam are over there at the bar laughing over something and I don't know what to say or do with Emer. Should I stand in the middle of the ballroom and wait for the next dance or should I lead her over to Liam and Tom? If I stand here I'll have to talk to her and I don't know what to talk about and if I start walking her towards Tom and Liam she'll think I don't want to be with her and that would be the worst thing in the world because I do want to be with her and I'm so nervous over the state I'm in my heart is going like a machine gun and I can barely breathe and I wish Tom would come and cut in so that I could laugh with Liam though I don't want Tom to cut in since I want to be with Emer but he doesn't anyway and there I am with the music starting again, a jitterbug or something, where men throw girls around the room and up in the air, the kind of dancing I could never dream of doing when I'm so ignorant I can barely put one foot before the other and now I have to put my hands somewhere on Emer for the jitterbug and I don't know where till she takes my hand and leads me to where Tom and Liam are laughing with Liam telling me a few more nights in the Tuxedo and I'll be a regular Fred Astaire and they all laugh because they know that could never be true and when they laugh I blush because Emer is looking at me in a way that shows she knows more than what Liam is talking about or that she even knows about my heart beating and making me short of breath.

I don't know what to do without the high school diploma. I drag on from day to day not knowing how to escape till a small war breaks out in Korea and I'm told if it gets any bigger I'll be drafted into the US Army. Eddie Gilligan says, Not a chance. Army's gonna take a look at your scabby eyes and send you home to your momma.

But the Chinese jump into the war and there's a letter from the government that says, Greetings. I'm to report to Whitehall Street to see if I'm fit to fight the Chinese and the Koreans. Tom Clifford says if I don't want to go I should rub salt on my eyes to make them raw and I should moan when the doctor examines them. Eddie Gilligan says I should complain of headaches and pain and if they have me read from a chart to give them all the wrong letters. He says I shouldn't be a fool. Why should I get my ass shot off by a bunch of gooks when I could stay here at the Biltmore and rise in the ranks. I could go to night school, get my eyes and teeth fixed, put on a little weight and in a few years I'd be like Mr Carey, all togged out in double-breasted suits.

I can't tell Eddie or Tom or anyone else how I'd like to get down on my two knees and thank Mao Tse-tung for sending his troops into Korea and liberating me from the Biltmore Hotel.

The army doctors at Whitehall Street don't look at my eyes at all. They tell me read that chart on the wall. They say OK. They look in my ears. Beep. Can you hear that? Fine. They look in my mouth. Jesus, they say. First thing you do is see the dentist. No one was ever rejected from this man's army for teeth and a good thing because most of the men who come in here have teeth like garbage dumps.

We're told to line up in a room and a sergeant comes in with a doctor and tells us, Awright, you guys, drop your socks and grab your cocks. Now milk 'em. And the doctor looks at us one by one to see if there's any discharge from our dongs. The sergeant barks at one man, You, what's your name?

Maldonado, sergeant.

Is that a hard-on I see there, Maldonado?

Ah, no, sergeant. I . . . a . . . I . . . a . . .

You gettin' excited, Maldonado?

I want to look at Maldonado but if you look anywhere but straight ahead the sergeant barks at you and wants to know what the hell you're looking at, who told you to look, buncha goddam fairies. Then he tells us turn around, bend over, spread 'em, I mean spread your cheeks. And the doctor sits on a chair and we have to back up with our arses open for inspection.

We're lined up outside the cubicle of a psychiatrist. He asks me if I like girls and I blush because that's a silly question and I say, I do, sir.

Then why are you blushing?

I don't know, sir.

But you prefer girls to boys?

Yes, sir.

OK, move on.

We're sent to Camp Kilmer, New Jersey, for orientation and indoctrination, uniforms and equipment, and haircuts that leave us bald. We're told we're no-good sorry pieces of shit, the worst set of recruits and draftees ever to come into this camp, a disgrace to Uncle Sam, lumps of meat for Chinese bayonets, nothing but cannon fodder and don't you forget it for one minute you lazy ass-dragging gang of dropouts. We're told straighten up and fly right, chin in, chest out, shoulders back, suck in that belly, goddamit, boy, this is the army not a goddam beauty parlor, oh girls, you step so pretty, whaddya doin' Sattaday night?

I'm sent to Fort Dix, New Jersey, for sixteen weeks of basic infantry training and we're told once again and every day we're no good hup ho hup ho hup hup hup ho, get in line there, soldier, goddamit, kills me to call you soldier, goddam pimple on the ass of the army, get in line or you'll get a corporal's boot up your fat ass, hup ho, hup ho, come on come on sing it sound off.

> *I got a gal in Jersey City*
> *She got gumboils on her titty.*
> *Sound off, cadence count,*
> *Sound off, cadence count,*
> *One two three four*
> *One two three four.*

This is your rifle, ya listenin' to me, your rifle, not your goddam gun, call this a gun and I'll ram it up your ass, your rifle, soldier, your piece, got that? This is your rifle, your M1, your piece, your girlfriend the rest of your army life. This is what you sleep with. This is what comes between you and the goddam gooks and goddam Chinks. Got that? You hold this goddam piece the way you hold a woman, no, tighter'n a woman. Drop this and your ass is in a sling. Drop this piece and you're in the goddam stockade. A dropped rifle is a rifle that can go off, blow off somebody's ass. That happens, girls, and you're dead, you're fuckin' dead.

The men who drill and train us are draftees and recruits themselves, a few months ahead of us. They're known as training cadre and we have to call them corporals even if they're privates like us. They yell at us as if they hate us and if you ever talk back you're in trouble. They tell us, Your ass is in a sling, soldier. We got your balls and we're ready to squeeze.

There are men in my platoon who had fathers and brothers in World War Two and know everything about the army. They say you can't be a good soldier till the army breaks you down and builds you up again. You come into this man's army with all kinds of smartass ideas, think you're big shit, but the army's been around a long time, all the way back to Julius fuckin' Caesar and knows how to deal with shitass recruits with attitude. Even if you come in all gung-ho the army will knock that outa you. Gung-ho or negative all means shit to the army because the army will tell you what to think, army will tell you what to feel, army will tell you what to do, army will tell you when to shit, piss, fart, squeeze your fuckin' pimples and if you don't like it write to your Congressman, go ahead, and when we hear about that we will kick your little white ass from one end of Fort Dix to the fuckin' other so that you'll be cryin' for your momma, your sister, your girlfriend and the whore on the next street.

Before lights out I lie on my bunk and listen to the talk about girls, families, Mom's home cooking, what Dad did in the war, high school proms where everyone got laid, what we're gonna do when we get out of the goddam army, how we can't wait till we get to Debbie or Sue or Cathy and how we're gonna screw ourselves blue, shit, man, I won't wear my goddam clothes for a month, get into that goddam bed with my girl, my brother's girl, any girl, and I won't come up for air, and when I get discharged, get me a job, start a business, live out on Long Island, come home every night an' tell the wife, drop them panties, babe, I'm ready for action, have kids, yeah.

Awright, you guys, shut your miserable asses, lights out, not a goddam sound or I'll have you on KP quicker'n a whore's fart.

And when the corporal leaves it starts again, the talk, oh, that first weekend pass after five weeks of basic training, into the city, into Debbie, Sue, Cathy, anyone.

I wish I could say something like I'm going into New York on my first weekend pass to get laid. I wish I could say something that would make everyone smile, even nod their heads to show I'm one of them. But I know if I open my mouth they'll say, Yeah, get a load of the Irishman talking about girls, or one of them, Thompson, will start singing, "When Irish Eyes are Smiling", and they'll all laugh because they know my eyes.

In a way I don't mind because I can lie here on the bunk all clean and comfortable after the evening shower, tired from the day of marching and running with my sixty-pound backpack the corporals say is heavier than the packs carried in the French Foreign Legion, a day of training in weapons, taking them apart, reassembling, firing on ranges, crawling under barbed wire with machine guns clattering over my head, climbing ropes, trees, walls, charging at bags with fixed bayonets and screaming, fuckin' gook, the way the corporals tell me, wrestling in woods with men from other companies wearing blue helmets to show they're the enemy, running up hills with fifty-caliber machine gun barrels over my shoulder, scrambling through mud, swimming with my sixty-pound backpack, sleeping all night in the woods with backpack for pillow and mosquitoes feasting on my face.

When we're not out in the field we're in large rooms listening to lectures on how dangerous and sneaky the Koreans are, the North Koreans, and the Chinese who are even worse. The whole world knows what sneaky bastards the Chinks are and if there's anyone in this outfit who's Chinese tough shit but that's the way it is, my father was German, men, and he had to put up with a lotta shit during World War Two when sauerkraut was liberty cabbage, that's the way it was. This is war, men, and when I look at you specimens my heart sinks thinking of the future of America.

There are films about what a glorious army this is, the US Army, that fought the English, the French, the Indians, the Mexicans, the Spanish, the Germans, the Japs, and now the goddam gooks and Chinks, and never lost a war, never. Remember that, men, never lost a goddam war.

There are films about weapons and tactics and syphilis. The one about syphilis is called *The Silver Bullet* and shows men losing their voices and dying and telling the world how sorry they are, how foolish they were to go with diseased women in foreign places and now their penises are falling off and there's nothing they can do about it but ask God's forgiveness and the forgiveness of their families back home, Mom and Dad sipping lemonade on the porch, Sis laughing on a backyard swing pushed by Chuck the quarterback home from college.

The men in my platoon lie on their bunks and talk about *The Silver Bullet*. Thompson says that was a stupid fuckin' movie, you'd have to be a real horse's ass to get syphed up like that and what the hell do we have rubbers for, right, Di Angelo, you went to college?

Di Angelo says you have to be careful.

Thompson says, What the hell do you know, goddam spaghetti-eating guinea?

Di Angelo says, Say that again, Thompson, and I'll have to ask you to step outside.

Thompson laughs, Yeah, yeah.

Go ahead, Thompson, say it again.

Nah, you probably got a knife there. All you guineas got knives.

No knife, Thompson, just me.

Don't trust you, Di Angelo.

No knife, Thompson.

Yeah.

The whole platoon is quiet and I wonder why people like

Thompson have to talk to other people like that. It shows you're always something else in this country. You can't just be an American.

There's an old regular army corporal, Dunphy, who works in weapons, issuing and repairing, and smelling always of whiskey. Everyone knows he should have been kicked out of the army long ago but Master Sergeant Tole takes care of him. Tole is a huge black man with a belly so great it takes two cartridge belts to go around him. He's so fat he can't go anywhere without a jeep and he roars at us all the time that he can't stand the sight of us, we're the laziest lumps it has ever been his misfortune to see. He tells us and the whole regiment that if anyone bothers Corporal Dunphy he'll break their backs with his bare hands, that the corporal was killing Krauts at Monte Cassino when we were just starting to beat our meat.

The corporal sees me one night pushing a cleaning rod up and down in my rifle barrel. He snatches the rifle from me and tells me follow him to the latrine. He breaks down the rifle and plunges the barrel into hot soapy water and I want to tell him how we were warned by all the cadre corporals never never use water on your piece, use linseed oil, because water causes rust and the next thing is your piece is rotting and jamming in your hands and how the hell are you gonna defend yourself against a million Chinks swarming over a mountain.

The corporal says, Bullshit, dries the barrel with a rag on the end of the cleaning rod and peers down the barrel to the reflection of his thumbnail. He hands the barrel to me and I'm dazzled by the shine inside and I don't know what to say to him. I don't know why he's helping me and all I can say is, Thanks, corporal. He tells me I'm a nice kid and not only that he's going to let me read his favorite book.

It's *The Young Manhood of Studs Lonigan* by James T. Farrell, a paperback, falling apart. The corporal tells me I'm to guard this book with my life, that he reads it all the time, that James T. Farrell is the greatest writer that ever lived in the USA, a writer that understands you an' me, kid, not like those blue-ass bullshit artists they have in New England. He says I can have this book till I finish basic training and then I have to get my own copy.

Next day is colonel's inspection and we're confined to barracks after chow time to clean and scrub and shine. Before lights out we have to stand by our bunks for closer inspection by Master Sergeant Tole and two regular army sergeants who stick their noses into everything. If they find anything wrong we have to do fifty push-ups with Tole resting his foot on our backs and humming "Swing Low, Sweet Chariot, comin' for to carry me home".

The colonel doesn't check every rifle but when he looks down my barrel he steps back, stares at me, and says to Sergeant Tole, This is a hell of a clean rifle, sergeant and asks me, Who's the Vice-President of the United States, soldier?

Alben Barkley, sir.

Good. Name the city where the second atomic bomb was dropped.

Nagasaki, sir.

OK, sergeant, this is our man. And that's a hell of a clean rifle, soldier.

After formation a corporal tells me I'm to be colonel's orderly next day, all day, riding in his car with the driver, opening his door, saluting, closing the door, waiting, saluting, opening the door again, saluting, closing the door.

And if I'm a good colonel's orderly and don't fuck up I'll get a three-day pass next week, Friday night to Monday night, and I can go to New York and get laid. The corporal says there's isn't a man in Fort Dix who wouldn't pay fifty dollars to be colonel's orderly and they don't know why the hell I got it just for having a clean rifle barrel. Where the hell did I learn to clean a rifle like that?

In the morning the colonel has two long meetings and I have nothing to do but sit with and listen to his driver, Corporal Wade Hansen, complaining about the way the Vatican is taking over the world and if there's ever a Catholic President in this country he'll emigrate to Finland where they keep Catholics in their place. He's from Maine and he's a Congregationalist and proud of it and doesn't hold with foreign religions. His second cousin married a Catholic and she had to move out of the state to Boston which is crawling with Catholics all leaving their money to the Pope and those cardinals who like little boys.

It's a short day with the colonel because he gets drunk at lunch and dismisses us. Hansen drives him to his quarters and then tells me get out of the car, he wants no fish heads in his car. He's a corporal and I don't know what to say to him but even if he were a private I wouldn't know what to say because it's hard to understand people when they talk like that.

It's only two o'clock and I'm free till chow time at five so I can go to the PX and read magazines, listen to Tony Bennett on the juke box singing "Because of you there's a song in my heart", and I can dream about my three-day pass and seeing Emer, the girl in New York, and how we'll go out to dinner and a movie and maybe an Irish dance where she'll have to teach me the steps and it's a lovely dream because the weekend of my three-day pass is my birthday and I'll be twenty-one.

12

The Friday of my three-day pass I have to stand on line outside the orderly room with men waiting for ordinary weekend passes. A cadre corporal, Sneed, whose real name is a Polish name no one can pronounce, tells me, Hey, soldier, pick up that butt.

Oh, I don't smoke, Corporal.

I didn't ask you if you fuckin' smoked. Pick up that butt.

Howie Abramowitz nudges me and whispers, Don't be an asshole. Pick up the fuckin' butt.

Sneed has his hands on his hips. Well?

I didn't drop the butt, Corporal. I don't smoke.

OK, soldier, come with me.

I follow him into the orderly room and he picks up my pass. Now, he says, we're going to your barracks and you're changing into fatigues.

But, Corporal, I have a three-day pass. I was colonel's orderly.

I don't give a shit if you wiped the colonel's ass. Get into your fatigues and on the double and get your entrenching tool.

It's my birthday, Corporal.

On the double, soldier, or I'll have you in the fuckin' stockade.

He marches me past the men waiting on line. He waves my pass at them and tells them say bye bye to my pass and they laugh and wave because there's nothing else to do and they don't want to get into trouble. Only Howie Abramowitz shakes his head as if to say he's sorry over what's happening.

Sneed marches me across the parade ground and into a clearing in the woods beyond. OK, asshole, dig.

Dig?

Yeah, dig me a nice hole three feet deep, two feet wide, and the faster you do it the better for you.

That must mean the sooner I finish this the sooner I can take my pass and go. Or is it something else? Everyone in the company knows Sneed is bitter because he was a big football star at Bucknell University and wanted to play for the Philadelphia Eagles only the Eagles wouldn't have him and now he goes around making people dig holes. It's unfair. I know men have been forced to dig holes and bury their passes and dig them up again and I don't know why I should have to do that. I keep telling myself I wouldn't mind if this were an ordinary weekend pass but this is a three-day pass and it's my birthday and why do I have to do this? But there's nothing I can do about it. I might as well dig as fast as I can and bury the pass and dig it up again.

And while I'm digging I'm dreaming that what I'd really like to do is wrap my little shovel around Sneed's head and smash him till his head is raw and bloody and I wouldn't mind one bit digging a hole for his big fat football body. That's what I'd like to do.

He hands me the pass to bury and when I finish shoveling in the earth he tells me pat it with my entrenching tool. Make it nice, he says.

I don't know why he wants me to make it nice when I'll be digging it up in a minute but now he tells me, 'Bout face, forrard harch, and he marches me back the way we came, past the orderly room where the line of men waiting for passes is gone, and I'm wondering if he's had enough satisfaction for the day so that he might march inside for a replacement pass but, no, he keeps me going right to the mess hall and tells the sergeant there I'm a candidate for KP, that I need a little lesson in obeying orders. They have a good laugh over that and the sergeant says they must have a drink together sometime and talk about the Philadelphia Eagles, isn't that some goddam team. The sergeant calls over another man, Henderson, to show me my job, the worst job you can get in any mess hall, pots and pans.

Henderson tells me scrub those mothers till they shine because there's constant inspection and one spot of grease on any utensil will get me another hour of KP and at that rate I could be here till the gooks and Chinese are long gone home to their families.

It's dinner time and the pots and pans are piled high around the sinks. Garbage cans lined up against the wall behind me are alive with the feasting flies of New Jersey. Mosquitoes buzz in through open windows and feast on me. Everywhere there is steam and smoke from gas burners and ovens and running hot water and I'm sodden with sweat and grease in no time. Corporals and sergeants pass through and run their fingers around the pots and pans and tell me do them over and I know that's because Sneed is out in the mess hall telling football stories and telling them how they can have a little fun with the draftee on pots and pans.

When it grows quieter in the mess hall and the work slows the sergeant tells me I'm free for the night but I'm to report back here tomorrow morning, Saturday, 0600 hours and he means 0600. I want to tell him I'm supposed to have a three-day pass for being colonel's orderly, that tomorrow is my birthday, that there's a girl waiting for me in New York, but I know now it's better to say nothing because every time I open my mouth things get worse. I know what the army means: Tell 'em nothing but your name, rank and serial number.

Emer cries on the phone, Oh, Frank, where are you now?

I'm in the PX.

What is the PX?

Post Exchange. It's where we buy things and make phone calls.

And why aren't you here? We have a little cake and everything.

I'm on KP, pots, pans, tonight, tomorrow, maybe Sunday.

What is that? What are you talking about? Are you all right?

I'm worn out from digging holes and washing pots and pans.

Why?

I didn't pick up a butt.

Why didn't you pick up a butt?

Because I don't smoke. You know I don't smoke.

But why would you have to pick up a butt?

Because a fucking corporal, excuse me, a cadre corporal who was rejected by the Philadelphia Eagles told me pick up the butt and I told him I didn't smoke and that's why I'm here when I should be with you on my fucking, excuse me, birthday.

Frank, I know it's your birthday. Are you drinking?

No, I'm not drinking. How could I be drinking and digging holes and doing KP all at the same time?

But why were you digging holes?

Because they made me bury my damn pass.

Oh, Frank. When will I see you?

I don't know. You may never see me. They say every grease spot I leave on a pot gets me another hour of KP and I could be here till I'm discharged washing pots and pans.

My mother is saying couldn't you see a priest or something, a chaplain?

I don't want to see a priest. They're worse than corporals the way they . . .

The way they what?

Oh, nothing.

Oh, Frank.

Oh, Emer.

Saturday dinner is cold cuts and potato salad and the cooks are easy on the pots and pans. At six the sergeant tells me I'm finished and I don't have to report on Sunday morning. He shouldn't be saying this, he says, but that Sneed is a goddam Polack prick that no one likes and you can see why the Philadelphia Eagles didn't want him. The sergeant says he's sorry but there was nothing he could do about putting me on KP when I disobeyed a direct order. Yeah, he knew I was colonel's orderly and all but this is the army and the best policy for a draftee like me is a shut mouth. Tell them nothing but your name, rank and serial number. Do what you're told, keep your mouth shut especially when you have a brogue that stands out, and if you do that you'll see your girlfriend again with your balls intact.

Thank you, sergeant.

OK, kid.

The company area is deserted except for men in the orderly room and men confined to barracks.

Di Angelo is lying on his bunk confined to barracks because of the way he spoke up after they showed a film on how poor everyone is in China. He said Mao Tse-tung and the Communists would save China and the lieutenant showing the film said communism is evil, godless, unAmerican, and Di Angelo said capitalism was evil, godless

75

and unAmerican and he wouldn't give two cents for isms anyway because people with isms cause all the troubles in the world and you may have noticed there is no ism in democracy. The lieutenant told him he was out of order and Di Angelo said this is a free country and that got him confined to barracks and no weekend pass for three weeks.

He's on his bunk reading the copy of *The Young Manhood of Studs Lonigan* Corporal Dunphy loaned me and when he sees me he says he borrowed it from top of my locker and who, for God's sakes, dipped me in a grease pit. He says he did KP like that one weekend and Dunphy told him how to get the grease off the fatigues. What I should do now is stand in a hot shower in my fatigues, hot as I can bear it, and scrub off the grease with a scrubbing brush and a bar of the carbolic soap they use for cleaning lavatories.

While I'm in the shower scrubbing Dunphy sticks his head in and wants to know what I'm doing and when I tell him he says he used to do that, too, only he'd bring in his rifle and do everything at one time. When he was a kid first time in the army he had the cleanest fatigues and rifle in his outfit and if it wasn't for the goddam booze he'd be Top Sergeant by now and ready to retire. Speaking of booze, he's heading to the PX for a beer and would I like to come along after getting out of my soapy fatigues, of course.

I'd like to ask Di Angelo along but he's confined to barracks for praising the Chinese Communists. While I'm changing into khakis I tell him how much I owe Mao Tse-tung for attacking Korea and liberating me from the Palm Court at the Biltmore Hotel and he says I'd better be careful what I say or I'll wind up like him, confined to barracks.

Dunphy calls from the end of the barracks, Come on, kid, come on, I'm gasping for a beer. In a way I'd rather stay and talk to Di Angelo, he has such a gentle way about him, but Dunphy helped me become colonel's orderly, for all the good it did me, and he might need the company. If I were a regular army corporal I wouldn't be hanging around the base on a Saturday night but I know there are people like Dunphy who drink and have no one, no home to go to. Now he drinks beer so fast I could never keep up with him. I'd be sick if I tried. He drinks and smokes and points at the sky all the time with the middle finger of his right hand. He tells me the army is a great life especially in peacetime. You're never lonely unless you're some kind of asshole like Sneed, the goddam football player, and if you get married and have kids the army will take care of everything. All you have to do is keep yourself fit to fight. Yeah, yeah, he knows he's not keeping himself fit but he carries so much Kraut shrapnel in his body he could be sold for scrap metal and the drink is the only pleasure he has. He had a wife, two kids, all gone. Indiana, that's where they went, back to his wife's daddy and mom, and who the hell wants to go to Indiana. He takes pictures from his wallet, the wife, the two girls, and holds them up for me to see. I'm ready to tell him how lovely they are but he starts to cry so hard it brings on a cough and I have to clap him on the back to save him from choking. OK, he says, OK. Goddam, it gets to me every time I look at them. Look what I lost, kid. I could have them waiting for me in a little house near Fort Dix. I could be home with Monica making dinner, me with my feet up, taking a little nap in my Top Sergeant's uniform. OK, kid, let's go. Let's get outa here and see if I can straighten out my shit and go to Indiana.

Halfway to the barracks he changes his mind and goes back for more beer and I know from this he'll never get to Indiana. He's like my father and when I'm in my bunk I wonder if my father remembered the twenty-first birthday of his oldest son, if he raised his glass to me in a pub in Coventry.

I doubt it. My father is like Dunphy who will never see Indiana.

13

It's a surprise on Sunday morning when Di Angelo asks me if I'd like to go to Mass with him, a surprise because you'd think that people who sing the praises of Chinese Communists would never step into church, chapel, nor synagogue. On the way to the base chapel he explains the way he feels, that the Church belongs to him, he doesn't belong to the Church, and he doesn't agree with the way the Church acts like a big corporation declaring they own God and it's their right to dole Him out in little bits and pieces as long as people do what they're told by Rome. He sins every week himself by receiving Communion without first confessing his sins to a priest. He says his sins are nobody's business but his and God's and that's who he confesses to every Saturday night before he falls asleep.

He talks about God as if He were in the next room having a pint and smoking a cigarette. I know if I went back to Limerick and talked like that I'd be hit on the head and thrown on the next train to Dublin.

We might be on an army base with barracks all around us but inside the chapel it's pure America. There are officers with their wives and children and they have the clean scrubbed look that comes from shower and shampoo and a constant state of grace. They have the look of people from Maine or California, small towns, church on Sundays, leg of lamb afterwards, peas, mashed potatoes, apple pie, iced tea, Dad snoozing with the big Sunday paper dropped to the floor, kids reading comics, Mom in the kitchen washing dishes and humming "Oh, what a beautiful morning". They have the look of people who brush their teeth after every meal and fly the flag on the Fourth. They might be Catholics but I don't think they'd feel comfortable in Irish or Italian churches where there might be old men and women mumbling and snuffling, a suspicion of whiskey or wine in the air, a whiff of bodies untouched for weeks by soap and water.

I'd like to be part of an American family, to sidle up to a blonde blue-eyed teenage daughter of an officer and whisper I'm not what I seem. I might have pimples and bad teeth and fire alarm eyes but, underneath, I'm just like them, a well-scrubbed soul dreaming of a house in a suburb with a tidy lawn where our child, little Frank, pushes his tricycle and all I want is a read of the Sunday paper like a real American dad and maybe I'd wash and clean our spanking new Buick before we drive over to visit Mom's grandpa and grandma and rock on their porch with glasses of iced tea.

The priest is mumbling away on the altar and when I whisper the Latin responses Di Angelo nudges me and wants to know if I'm all right, if I'm hung over from my beer night with Dunphy. I wish I could be like Di Angelo, making up my own mind about everything, not giving a fiddler's fart like my Uncle Pa Keating back in Limerick. I know Di Angelo would laugh if I told him I'm so steeped in sin I'm afraid to go to confession for fear of being told I'm so far gone that only a bishop or a cardinal could give me absolution. He'd laugh if I told him that some nights I'm afraid to fall asleep in case I die and go to hell. How could hell be invented by a God who's in the next room with a beer and a cigarette?

This is when the dark clouds flutter like bats in my head and I wish I could open a window and release them.

Now the priest is asking for volunteers to pick up baskets from the back of the chapel and make the collection. Di Angelo gives me a little push and we're out in the aisle genuflecting and sending the baskets along the pews. Officers and non-coms with families always hand their contributions to their children to drop in the basket and that makes everyone smile, the little one is so proud and the parents are so proud of the little one. Officers' wives and non-coms' wives smile at each other as if to say, We're all one under the roof of the Catholic Church, though you know once they're outside they know they're different.

The basket goes from pew to pew till it's taken by a sergeant who will count the money and pass it on to the chaplain. Di Angelo whispers he knows this sergeant and when the money is counted it's two for you and one for me.

I tell Di Angelo I'm not going to Mass anymore. What's the use when I'm in such a state of sin for impurity and everything else? I can't be in the chapel with all those clean American families and their state of grace. I'll wait till I get the courage to go to confession and Communion and if I keep committing mortal sins by not going to Mass it won't matter since I'm doomed anyway. One mortal sin will get you into hell just as easily as ten mortal sins.

Di Angelo tells me I'm full of shit. He says I should go to Mass if I want to, that the priests don't own the Church.

I can't think like Di Angelo, not yet. I'm afraid of the priests and the nuns and the bishops and the cardinals and the Pope. I'm afraid of God.

Monday morning I'm told report to Master Sergeant Tole in his room at Company B. He's sitting in an armchair and sweating so much his khaki uniform is dark. I want to ask him about the book on the table next to him, *Notes from the Underground* by Dostoyevsky, and I'd like to tell him about Raskolnikov but you have to be careful what you say to master sergeants and the army in general. Say the wrong thing and you're back with the pots and pans.

He tells me stand easy and wants to know why I disobeyed a direct order and who the hell do I think I am defying a superior non-com even if he is training cadre, eh?

I don't know what to say because he knows everything and I'm afraid if I open my mouth I might be shipped to Korea tomorrow. He says Corporal Sneed or whatever the hell his Polish name is had every right to discipline me but he went too far especially when it was a three-day pass for the colonel's orderly. I'm entitled to that pass and if I still want it he'll arrange it for the coming weekend.

Thanks, sergeant.

OK. Dismissed.

Sergeant?

Yeah?

I read *Crime and Punishment*.

Oh, yeah? Well, I could have guessed you're not as dumb as you look. Dismissed.

In our fourteenth week of basic training there are rumors we're being shipped to Europe. In the fifteenth week the rumors say we're going to Korea. In the sixteenth week we're told we're definitely going to Europe.

14

We're shipped to Hamburg and from there to Sonthofen, a replacement depot in Bavaria. My outfit from Fort Dix is broken up and sent all over the European Command. I'm hoping they'll send me to England so that I can travel easily to Ireland. Instead they send me to a caserne in Lenggries, a small Bavarian village, where I'm assigned to dog training, the canine corps. I tell the captain I don't like dogs, they chewed my ankles to bits when I delivered telegrams in Limerick, but the captain says, Who asked you? He turns me over to a corporal chopping up great slabs of bloody red meat who tells me, Stop whining, fill that goddam tin plate with meat, get in that cage and feed your animal. Put the plate down and get your hand outa the way case your animal thinks it's his dinner.

I have to stay in the cage and watch my dog eating. The corporal calls this familiarization. He says, This animal will be your wife while you're on this base, well, not your wife exactly, because it's not a bitch, you know what I mean. Your M1 rifle and your animal will be all you'll have for a family.

My dog is a black German shepherd and I don't like him. His name is Ivan and he's not like the other dogs, the shepherds and Dobermans, who howl at anything that moves. When he's finished eating he looks at me, licks his lips and backs away, baring his teeth. The corporal is outside the cage telling me that's a hell of a goddam dog I have there, doesn't howl and make a lotta bullshit noise, the kinda dog you want in combat when one bark will get you killed. He tells me bend slowly, pick up the plate, tell my dog he's a good dog, good Ivan, nice Ivan, see you in the morning, honey, back out nice and easy, close the gate, drop that lock, get your hand outa the way. He tells me I did OK. He can see Ivan and I are already asshole buddies.

Every morning at eight I turn out with a platoon of dog handlers from all over Europe. We march in a circle with the corporal in the middle calling hup ho hup ho hup hup hup ho heel, and when we yank on the dogs' leashes we're glad they're growling behind muzzles.

For six weeks we march and run with the dogs. We climb the mountains behind Lenggries and race along the banks of rivers. We feed and groom them till we're ready to remove their muzzles. We're told this is the big day, like graduation or marriage.

And then the company commander sends for me. His company clerk, Corporal George Shemanski, is going stateside on furlough in three months and they're sending me to company clerk school for six weeks so that I can replace him. Dismissed.

I don't want to go to company clerk school. I want to stay with Ivan. Six weeks together and we're pals. I know when he growls at me he's just telling me he loves me though he still has a head of teeth in case I displease him. I love Ivan and I'm ready to remove his muzzle. No one else can remove his muzzle without losing a hand. I want to take him on maneuvers with the Seventh Army in Stuttgart where I'll dig a hole in the snow and we'll be warm and comfortable. I want to see what it would be like to turn him loose on a soldier pretending to be Russian and watch Ivan tear his protective clothing to bits before I bring him to heel. Or watch him lunge for the crotch and not the throat when I swing a dummy Russian at him. They can't send me to company clerk school for six weeks and let someone else handle Ivan. Everyone knows it's one man, one dog, and it takes months to break in another handler.

I don't know why they have to pick me for company clerk school when I never even went to high school and the base is filled with high school graduates. It makes me wonder if company clerk school is punishment for never going to high school.

My head is filled with dark clouds and I wish I could bang it against the wall. The only word in my head is fuck and that's a word

I hate because it means hate. I'd like to kill the company commander, and now here's this second lieutenant barking at me because I passed him without saluting.

Soldier, get over here. What do you do when you see an officer?

Salute him, sir.

And?

I'm sorry, sir. I didn't see you.

Didn't see me? Didn't see me? You'd go to Korea and claim you didn't see the gooks coming over the hill? Right, soldier?

I don't know what to say to this lieutenant who's my age and trying to grow a moustache with sad ginger hair. I want to tell him they're sending me to company clerk school and isn't that enough punishment for not saluting a thousand second lieutenants? I want to tell him about my six weeks with Ivan and my troubles back in Fort Dix when I had to bury my pass but there are dark clouds and I know I should be quiet, tell 'em nothing but your name, rank, serial number. I know I should be quiet but I'd like to tell this second lieutenant fuck off, kiss my ass with your miserable ginger mustache.

He tells me report to him in fatigues at twenty-one hundred hours sharp and he makes me pull weeds on the parade ground while other dog handlers pass by on their way to a beer in Lenggries.

When I'm finished I go to Ivan's cage and remove his muzzle. I sit on the ground and talk to him and if he chews me to pieces I won't have to go to company clerk school. But he growls a bit and licks my face and I'm glad there's no one here to see how I feel.

Company clerk school is in the Lenggries caserne. We sit at desks while instructors come and go. We're told the company clerk is the single most important soldier in an outfit. Officers get killed or move on, non-coms too, but an outfit without a clerk is doomed. The company clerk is the one in combat who knows when the outfit is under strength, who's dead, who's wounded, who's missing, the one who takes over when the supply clerk gets his fuckin' head blown off. The company clerk, men, is the one who delivers your mail when the mail clerk gets a bullet up his ass, the one who keeps you in touch with the folks back home.

After we've learned how important we are we learn to type. We have to type up a model of a daily attendance report with five carbon copies and if one mistake is made, one little stroke too much, an error in addition, a strikeover, the whole thing is to be retyped.

No erasures, goddamit. This is the United States Army and we don't allow erasures. Allow erasures on a report and you invite sloppiness all along the front. We're holding the line against the goddam Reds here, men. Can't have sloppiness. Perfection, men, perfection. Now type, goddamit.

The clatter and rattle of thirty typewriters makes the room sound like a combat zone with howls from soldier/typists hitting wrong keys and having to tear reports from machines and start all over. We punch our heads and shake our fists at heaven and tell the instructors we were almost finished, couldn't we please, please erase this one little goddam mark.

No erasures, soldier, and watch your language. I have my mother's picture in my pocket.

At the end of the course they give me a certificate with a rating of Excellent. The captain handing out the certificates says he's proud of us and they're proud of us all the way up to the Supreme Commander in Europe, Dwight D. Eisenhower himself. The Captain is proud to say that only nine men washed out in the course and the twenty-one of us who passed are a credit to the folks back home. He hands us our certificates and chocolate chip cookies baked by his wife and two small daughters and we have permission to eat our cookies right here and now this being a special occasion. Behind me men are cursing and mumbling these cookies taste like cat shit and the Captain smiles and gets ready to make another speech till a major whispers to him and what I hear later is that the major told him, Shaddap, you been drinking, and that's true because the Captain has the kind of face that never turned away from a whiskey bottle.

If Shemanski hadn't been granted a furlough I'd still be up in the kennels with Ivan or down in a *bierstube* in Lenggries with the other dog handlers. Now I have to spend a week watching him by his desk in the orderly room typing reports and letters and telling me I should be thanking him for getting me away from dogs and into a good job that might be useful in civilian life. He says I should be happy I learned to type, I might write another *Gone With the Wind* some day, ha ha ha.

The night before his furlough there's a party in a Lenggries beer hall. It's Friday night and I have a weekend pass. Shemanski has to return to the caserne because his furlough doesn't start till tomorrow and when he leaves his girlfriend, Ruth, asks me where I'm staying on my weekend pass. She tells me come to her place for a beer, Shemanski won't be there, but the minute we're in the door we're in the bed going wild with ourselves. Oh, Mac, she says, oh, Mac, you're so young. She's old herself, thirty-one, but you'd never know it the way she carries on depriving me of any sleep and if this is the way she is with Shemanski all the time it's no wonder he needs a long furlough in the USA. Then it's dawn and there's a knock on the door downstairs and when she peeks out the window she lets out a little squeal, Oh, *mein Gott*, it's Shemanski, go, go, go. I jump up and dress as fast as I can but there's a problem when I put on my boots and then try to pull my pants over them and the legs are stuck and entangled and Ruth is hissing and squealing, Out ze window, oh, pliss, oh, pliss. I can't leave by the front door with Shemanski standing there banging away, he'd surely kill me, so it's out the window into three feet of snow which saves my life and I know Ruth is up there shutting the window and pulling the curtain so that Shemanski won't see me trying to get my boots off so that I can slip on my pants, then boots again, so cold my dong is the size of a button, with snow everywhere, halfway up my belly, in my pants, filling my boots.

Now I have to sneak away from Ruth's house and into Lenggries looking for hot coffee in a cafe where I can dry out but nothing is open yet and I wander back up to the caserne wondering, Did God put Shemanski on this earth to destroy me entirely?

Now that I'm company clerk I sit at Shemanski's desk and the worst part of the day is typing up the attendance report every morning. Master Sergeant Burdick sits at the other desk drinking coffee and telling me how important this report is, that they're waiting for it over at HQ so that they can add it to the other company reports that go to Stuttgart to Frankfurt to Eisenhower to Washington so that President Truman himself will know the strength of the United States Army in Europe in case of sudden attack by those goddam Russians who wouldn't hesitate if we were short a man, one man, McCourt. They're waiting, McCourt, so get that report done.

The thought of the world waiting for my report makes me so nervous I hit wrong keys and have to start all over. Every time I say, Shit, and pull the report from the typewriter. Sergeant Burdick's eyebrows shoot to his hairline. He drinks his coffee, looks at his watch, loses control of his eyebrows, and I feel so desperate I'm afraid I'll break down and weep. Burdick takes phone calls from HQ to say the colonel is waiting, the general, the Chief of Staff, the President. A messenger is sent to pick up the report. He waits by my desk and that makes it even worse and I wish I could be back in the Biltmore Hotel scouring toilets. When the report is finished without error he takes it away and Sergeant Burdick wipes his forehead with a green handkerchief. He tells me forget the other work, that I'm to stay at this desk all day and practice practice practice till I get these goddam reports down right. They're gonna be talking up at HQ and wondering what kind of asshole he is for taking on a clerk that can't even type a report. All the other clerks knock off that report in ten minutes and he doesn't want Company C to be the laughing stock of the caserne.

So, McCourt, you go nowheres till you type perfect reports. Start typing.

All day and night he drills me, handing me different numbers, telling me, You'll thank me for this.

And I do. In a few days I can type the reports so fast they send a lieutenant from HQ to see if these are made-up numbers done the night before. Sergeant Burdick says, No, no, I'm right on his case, and the lieutenant looks at me and tells him, We got corporal material here, sergeant.

The sergeant says, Yes, sir, and when he smiles his eyebrows are lively.

When Shemanski returns I expect to be re-assigned to Ivan but the captain tells me I'm staying on as clerk in charge of supplies. I'll be responsible for sheets, blankets, pillows and condoms which I'll distribute to dog handler trainees from all over the European Command making sure everything is returned when they're leaving, everything but the condoms, ha ha ha.

How can I tell the captain I don't want to be a clerk down in the basement where I have to requisition everything in language that is backwards, cases, pillow, white, or balls, Pong Ping, counting things and making lists when all I want to do is get back to Ivan and the dog handlers and drink beer and look for girls in Lenggries, Bad Tolz, Munich?

Sir, is there any chance I could be reassigned to the dogs?

No, McCourt. You're a damn fine clerk. Dismissed.

But, sir . . .

Dismissed, soldier.

There are so many dark clouds fluttering in my head I can barely make my way out of his office and when Shemanski laughs and says, He gave you the shaft, eh? Won't let you back to your bow wow? I tell him fuck off and I'm hauled back into the captain's office for a reprimand and told if this ever happens again I'll face a court martial that will make my army record look like Al Capone's arrest record. The captain barks that I'm a private first class now and if I behave myself and keep accurate accounts and control the condoms I could rise to corporal within six months and now get outa here, soldier.

In a week I'm in trouble again and it's because of my mother. When I came to Lenggries I went to the HQ offices to fill out an application for an allotment for my mother. The army would retain half my pay, match it, and send her a check every month.

Now I'm having a beer in Bad Tolz and Davis, the allotment clerk, is in the same room drunk on schnapps and when he calls to me, Hey, McCourt, too bad your mother is up shit creek, the dark clouds in my head are so blinding I throw my beer stein and lunge at him with every wish to strangle him till I'm pulled away by two sergeants and held for the MPs.

I'm locked up for the night in Bad Tolz and taken before a captain in the morning. He wants to know why I'm assaulting corporals who are drinking a beer and minding their own business and when I tell him about the insult to my mother he asks, Who's the allotment clerk?

Corporal Davis, sir.

And you, McCourt, where you from?

New York, sir.

No, no. I mean, where you really from?

Ireland, sir.

Goddam it. I know that. You've got the map on your face. What part?

Limerick, sir.

Oh, yeah? My parents are from Kerry and Sligo. It's a pretty country but it's poor, right?

Yes, sir.

OK, send in Davis.

Davis comes in and the captain turns to the man beside him who is taking notes. Jackson, this is off the record. Now, Davis, you said something about this man's mother in public?

I . . . only . . .

You said something of a confidential nature about the lady's financial problems?

Well . . . sir . . .

Davis, you're a prick and I could send you for a company court martial but I'll just say you had a few beers and your jaw flapped.

Thank you, sir.

And if I ever hear of you making comments like that again I'll ram a cactus up your ass. Dismissed.

When Davis leaves the captain says, The Irish, McCourt. We gotta stick together. Right?

Yes, sir.

In the hallway Davis puts out his hand. Sorry about that, McCourt. I should know better. My mother gets the allotment, too, and she's Irish. I mean, her parents were Irish so that makes me half Irish.

This is the first time in my life anyone ever apologized to me and all I can do is mumble and turn red and shake Davis' hand because I don't know what to say. And I don't know what to say to people who smile and tell me their mothers and fathers and grandparents are Irish. One day they're insulting your mother, the next day they're bragging their own mothers are Irish. Why is it the minute I open my mouth the whole world is telling me they're Irish and we should all have a drink? It's not enough to be American. You always have to be something else, Irish-American, German-American, and you'd wonder how they'd get along if someone hadn't invented the hyphen.

15

When they made me supply clerk the captain didn't tell me that twice a month on Tuesdays I'd have to bundle company bedding and take it by truck to the military laundry outside Munich. I don't mind because it's a day away from the caserne and I can lie on the bundles with two other supply clerks, Rappaport and Weber, and talk about civilian life. Before we leave the caserne we stop at the PX to get our monthly ration of a pound of coffee and a carton of cigarettes to sell to the Germans. Rappaport has to pick up a supply of Kotex to save his bony shoulders from the weight of the rifle when he's on sentry duty. Weber thinks that's funny and tells us he has three sisters but he'd be goddamned if he'd ever step up to a sales clerk and ask for Kotex. Rappaport gives a little smile and says, If you have sisters, Weber, they're still in the rag stage.

No one knows why we're allowed a pound of coffee but the other supply clerks tell me I'm a lucky bastard I don't smoke. They wish they didn't smoke so they could sell the cigarettes to German girls for sex. Weber from Company B says a carton will get you a whole load of poontang and that makes him so excited he burns a hole with his cigarette in a bundle of Company A sheets and Rappaport, the Company A clerk on his first trip like me, tells him watch it or he'll beat the shit out of him. Weber says, Oh, yeah? but the truck stops and Buck the driver says, Everybody out, because we're at a secret little beer place and if we're lucky there might be a few girls in the back room ready to do anything for a few packs from our cartons. The other men are offering me low prices for my cigarettes but Buck tells me, Don't be a goddam fool, Mac, you're a kid, you need to get laid too or you'll get strange in the head.

Buck has grey hair and medals from World War Two. Everyone knows he had a battlefield commission but time and time again he drank and went wild and was busted all the way down to buck private. That's what they say about Buck though I'm learning that no matter what anyone in the army says about anything you have to take it with a grain of salt thrown over your left shoulder. Buck reminds me of Corporal Dunphy back in Fort Dix. They were wild men, they did their bit in the war, they don't know what to do with themselves in peacetime, they can't be sent to Korea with their drinking, and the army is the only home they'll have till they die.

Buck speaks German and seems to know everyone and all kinds of secret little beer places on the road from Lenggries to Munich. There are no girls in the back room anyway and when Weber complains Buck tells him, Aw, fuck off, Weber. Why don't you go out behind that tree and jerk off. Weber says he doesn't have to go behind a tree. It's a free country and he can jerk off anywhere he likes. Buck tells him, All right, Weber, all right, I don't give a shit. Take out your pecker and wave it in the middle of the road for all I care.

Buck tells us get back in the truck and we continue to Munich with no more stops at secret little beer places.

Sergeants shouldn't tell you take the laundry to a place like this without telling you what the place is. They shouldn't tell Rappaport, especially, because he's Jewish, and they shouldn't wait till he looks up from the truck and screams, Oh, Christ, when he sees the name of this place on the gate, Dachau.

What can he do but jump off the truck when Buck slows for the MP at the gate, jump from the truck and run down the Munich road screaming like a madman? Now Buck has to move the truck over and we watch while two MPs chase Rappaport, grab him, push him into the jeep and bring him back. I feel sorry for him the way he's turned white, the way he's shivering like one left out in the cold a long time. He keeps saying, I'm sorry, I'm sorry, I can't, I can't, and the MPs are soft with him. One makes a phone call from the sentry box and when he returns he tells Rappaport, OK, soldier, you don't have to go in. You can stay with a lieutenant near here and wait till your laundry is done. Your buddies can take care of your bundles.

While we unload the trucks I wonder about the Germans who are helping us. Were they in this place in the bad days and what do they know? Soldiers unloading other trucks joke and laugh and hit each other with bundles but the Germans work and don't smile and I know there are dark memories in their heads. If they lived in Dachau or Munich they must have known about this place and I'd like to know what they think about when they come here every day.

Then Buck tells me he can't talk to them because they're not Germans at all. They're refugees, displaced persons, Hungarians, Yugoslavians, Czechs, Romanians. They live in camps all over Germany till someone decides what to do with them.

When the unloading is finished Buck says it's lunch time and he's heading for the mess hall. Weber, too. I can't go to lunch until I walk around and look at this place I've been seeing in newspapers and newsreels since I grew up in Limerick. There are tablets with inscriptions in Hebrew and German and I'm wondering if they're over mass graves.

There are ovens with the doors open and I know what went in there. I saw the pictures in magazines and books and pictures are pictures but these are the ovens and I could touch them if I wanted to. I don't know if I want to touch them but if I went away and never came back to this place with the laundry I'd say to myself, You could have touched the ovens at Dachau and you didn't and what will you say to your children and grandchildren? I could say nothing but what good would that do me when I'm alone and saying to myself, Why didn't you touch the ovens at Dachau?

So I step past the tablets and touch the ovens and wonder if it's proper to say a Catholic prayer in the presence of the Jewish dead. If I were killed by the English would I mind if the likes of Rappaport touched my tombstone and prayed in Hebrew? No, I wouldn't mind after priests telling us that all prayers that are unselfish and not for ourselves reach God's ears.

Still, I can't say the usual three Hail Marys since Jesus is mentioned and He wasn't any way helpful to the Jews in recent times. I don't know if it's proper to say the Our Father touching the door of an oven but it seems harmless enough and it's what I say hoping the Jewish dead will understand my ignorance.

Weber is calling to me from the door of the mess hall, McCourt, McCourt, they're closing down here. You want lunch you get your ass in here.

I take my tray with the bowl of Hungarian goulash and bread to the table by the window where Buck and Weber are sitting but when I look out there are the ovens and I'm not much in the mood for Hungarian goulash anymore and this is the first time in my life I ever pushed food away. If they could see me in Limerick now pushing away the food they'd say I was gone mad entirely but how can you sit there eating Hungarian goulash with open ovens staring at you and thoughts of the people burned there especially the babies. Whenever newspapers show pictures of mothers and babies dying together they show how the baby is laid on the mother's bosom in the coffin and they're together for eternity and there's comfort in that. But they never showed that in the pictures of Dachau or the other camps. The pictures would show babies thrown over to the side like dogs and you could see if they were buried at all it was far from their mothers' bosoms and into eternity alone and I know sitting here that if anyone ever offers me Hungarian goulash in civilian life I'll think of the ovens in Dachau and say, No, thanks.

I ask Buck if there are mass graves under the tablets and he says there's no need for mass graves when you burn everyone and that's what they did at Dachau, the sons-of-bitches.

Weber says, Hey, Buck, I didn't know you were Jewish.

No, asshole. Do you have to be Jewish to be human?

Buck says Rappaport must be hungry and we should bring him a sandwich but Weber says that's the most ridiculous thing he ever heard of. The lunch was goulash and how you gonna make a sandwich outa that? Buck says you can make a sandwich out of anything and if Weber wasn't so stupid he could see that. Weber gives him the finger and says, Your mother, and Buck has to be stopped from attacking him by the duty sergeant who tells us all get out, the place is closed unless we'd like to stick around and do a little mopping.

Buck gets into the cab of the truck and Weber and I take a nap in the back till the laundry is ready and we load up. Rappaport is sitting by the gate reading the *Stars and Stripes*. I want to talk to him about the ovens and the bad things in this place but he's still white and cold-looking.

We're halfway to Lenggries when Buck pulls off the main road and follows a narrow path to some kind of encampment, a place of shacks, lean-tos, old tents where small children are running barefoot in cold spring weather and grown people are sitting on the ground around fires. Buck jumps from the cab and tells us bring our coffee and cigarettes and Rappaport wants to know what for.

To get laid, kid, to get laid. They're not giving it away.

Weber says, Come on, come on, they're only DPs.

The refugees come running, men and women, but all I can look at is the girls. They smile and pull at the coffee cans and cigarette cartons and Buck yells, Hold on, don't let them take your stuff. Weber disappears into a shack with an old woman about thirty-five and I look around for Rappaport. He's still in the truck, looking over the side, pale. Buck signals to one of the girls and tells me, OK, this is your honey, Mac. Give her the cigarettes and keep the coffee and watch your wallet.

The girl has on a ragged dress with pink flowers and there's so little flesh on her it's hard to tell how old she is. She takes me by the hand into a hut and it's easy for her to be naked because there's nothing under the dress. She lies on a pile of rags on the floor and I'm so desperate to be at her I pull my pants down around my legs where they can't go any farther because of the boots. Her body is cold but she's hot inside and I'm so excited I'm finished in a minute. She rolls away and goes to a corner to squat on a bucket and that makes me think of the days in Limerick when we had a bucket in the corner. She gets off the bucket, pulls her dress on, and holds out her hand.

Cigarettes?

I don't know what I'm supposed to give her. Should I give her the whole carton for that one minute of excitement or should I give her a pack of twenty?

She says it again, Cigarettes, and when I look at the bucket in the corner I give her the whole carton.

But she's not satisfied. Coffee?

94

I tell her, No, no. No coffee, but she comes at me, opening my fly and I'm so excited we're down on the rags again and she smiles for the first time over the riches of cigarettes and coffee and when I see her teeth I know why she doesn't smile much.

Buck gets back into the truck cab without a word to Rappaport and I say nothing because I think I'm ashamed of what I did. I try to tell myself I'm not ashamed, that I paid for what I got, even gave the girl my coffee. I don't know why I should be ashamed in the presence of Rappaport. I think it's because he had respect for the refugees and refused to take advantage of them but if that's so why wouldn't he show his respect and sorrow by giving them his cigarettes and coffee?

Weber doesn't care about Rappaport. He goes on about what a great piece of ass that was and how little he paid for it. He gave the woman only five packs and has the rest of his coffee and he can get laid in Lenggries for a week.

Rappaport tells him he's a moron and they trade insults till Rappaport jumps on him and they're all over the laundry with bloody noses till Buck stops the truck and tells them cut it out and all I worry about is the blood that might be on the laundry of Company C.

16

The day after the Dachau laundry detail my neck swells up and the doctor tells me pack a bag, he's sending me back to Munich, that I've got the mumps. He wants to know if I was near children because that's where the mumps come from, children, and when a man gets them it could be the end of his line.

Know what I mean, soldier?

No, sir.

It means you might never have kids yourself.

I'm sent in a jeep with a driver, Corporal John Calhoun, who tells me the mumps is God's punishment for fornicating with German women and I should take this as a sign. He stops the jeep and when he tells me kneel with him by the side of the road to beg God's forgiveness before it's too late I have to obey because of his two stripes. There's froth at the corners of his mouth and I know from growing up in Limerick that's a sure sign of lunacy and if I don't drop to my knees with John Calhoun he might turn violent in the name of God. He raises his arms to the sky and praises God for sending me the gift of the mumps just in time to mend my ways and save my soul and he would like God to keep sending me further gentle reminders of my sinful ways, chickenpox, toothache, measles, severe headaches, and pneumonia if necessary. He knows it was no accident he was chosen to drive me to Munich with my mumps. He knows the Korean

War was started so that he could be drafted and sent to Germany to save my soul and the souls of all the other fornicators. He thanks God for the privilege and promises to watch over the soul of Private McCourt in the mumps ward of the Munich military hospital as long as the Lord desires. He tells the Lord he is happy to be saved, that he's joyous, oh, joyous, indeed, and he sings a song about gathering by the river and pounds the steering wheel and drives so fast I wonder if I'll be dead in a ditch before I'm ever cured of the mumps.

He leads me down the hospital hall, sings his hymns, tells the world I am saved, that the Lord hath sent a sign, yeah verily, the mumps, that I am ready to repent. Praise God. He tells the admissions medic, a sergeant, that I am to be given a Bible and time for prayer and the sergeant tells him get the hell outa heah. Corporal Calhoun blesses him for that, blesses him from the bottom of his heart, promises to pray for the sergeant who is clearly on the side of the devil, tells the sergeant he's lost but if he'll right now drop to his knees and accept the Lord Jesus he'll know the peace that passeth all understanding and he foams so much at the mouth his chin is snow.

The sergeant comes from behind his desk and pushes Calhoun down the hall to the front door with Calhoun telling him, Repent, sergeant, repent. Let us pause, brother, and pray for this Irishman touched by the Lord, touched with the mumps. Oh, let us gather by the river.

He is still pleading and praying when the sergeant propels him into the Munich night.

A German orderly tells me his name is Hans and takes me to a six-bed ward where I'm issued hospital pajamas and two cold bulging ice packs. When he tells me, Zis iss for your neck and zis iss for your bollez, four men in the beds chant, Zis iss for your neck and zis iss for your bollez. He smiles and places one ice pack on my neck, the other in my groin. The men lob ice packs at him for more ice and tell him, Hans, you're so good at catching you could play baseball.

One man in a corner bed whimpers and doesn't throw his ice pack. Hans goes to his bed. Dimino, would you like ice?

No, I don't want ice. What's the use?

Oh, Dimino.

Oh, Dimino, my ass. Goddam krauts. Look what you did to me. Gave me the goddam mumps. I'll never have kids.

Oh, you will haf kids, Dimino.

How would you know? My wife will think I'm a fairy.

Oh, Dimino, you're not a fairy, and Hans turns to the other men, Is Dimino a fairy?

Yeah, yeah, he's a fairy, you're a fairy, Dimino, and he turns to the wall, sobbing.

Hans touches his shoulder. They don't mean it, Dimino.

And the men chant, We mean it, we mean it. You're a fairy, Dimino. We got swollen balls and you got swollen balls but you're a crybaby fairy.

And they chant till Hans pats Dimino's shoulder again, hands him ice packs and tells him, Here, Dimino, keep your bollez cool and you will have many chiltren.

Will I, Hans? Will I?

Oh, you will, Dimino.

Thanks, Hans. You're an OK kraut.

Thanks, Dimino.

Hans, you a fairy?

Yes, Dimino.

That why you like putting ice packs on our balls?

No, Dimino. Iss my job.

I don't mind if you're a fairy, Hans.

Thanks you, Dimino.

You're welcome, Hans.

Another orderly pushes a book cart into the ward and I have a feast of reading. Now I can finish the book I started coming from Ireland on the ship, Dostoyevsky's *Crime and Punishment*. I'd rather read F. Scott Fitzgerald or P. G. Wodehouse but Dostoyevsky is hanging over me with his story of Raskolnikov and the old woman. It makes me feel guilty all over again after the way I stole money from Mrs Finucane in Limerick when she was dead in the chair and I wonder if I should ask for an army chaplain and confess my awful crime.

No. I might be able to confess in the darkness of an ordinary church confession box but I could never do it here in daylight all swollen with the mumps with a screen around the bed and the priest looking at me. I could never tell him how Mrs Finucane was planning to leave her money for priests to say Masses for her soul and how I stole some of that money. I could never tell him about the sins I committed with the girl in the refugee camp. Even while I think of her I get so excited I have to interfere with myself under the blankets and there I am with one sin on top of another. If I ever confessed to a priest now I'd be excommunicated altogether so my only hope is that I'll be hit by a truck or something falling from a great height and that will give me a second to say a perfect Act of Contrition before I die and no priest will be necessary.

Sometimes I think I'd be the best Catholic in the world if they'd only do away with priests and let me talk to God there in the bed.

17

After the hospital two good things happen. I'm promoted to corporal because of my powerful typing when I turn in supply reports and the reward is a two-week furlough to Ireland if I want it. My mother wrote to me weeks ago to say how lucky she was to get one of the new corporation houses up in Janesboro and how lovely it is to have a few pounds for new furniture. She'll have a bathroom with a tub, a sink, a toilet and hot and cold water. She'll have a kitchen with a gas range and a sink and a sitting room with a fireplace where she can sit and warm her shins and read the paper or a nice romance. She'll have a garden in the front for little flowers and plants and a garden in the back for all kinds of vegetables and she won't know herself with all the luxury.

All the way on the train to Frankfurt I'm dreaming of the new house and the comfort it's bringing my mother and my brothers, Michael and Alphie. You'd think that after all the miserable days in Limerick I wouldn't even want to go back to Ireland but when the plane approaches the coast and the shadows of clouds are moving across the fields and it's all green and mysterious I can't stop myself from crying. People look at me and it's a good thing they don't ask me why I'm crying. I wouldn't be able to tell them. I wouldn't be able to describe the feeling that came around my heart about Ireland because there are no words for it and because I never knew I'd feel this way. It's strange to think there are no words for the way I feel unless they're in Shakespeare or Samuel Johnson or Dostoyevsky and I didn't notice them.

My mother is at the railway station to meet me, smiling with her new white teeth, togged out in a bright new frock and shiny black shoes. My brother, Alphie, is with her. He's going on twelve and wearing a grey suit that must have been his confirmation suit last year. You can see he's proud of me, especially my corporal's stripes, so proud he wants to carry my duffel bag. He tries but it's too heavy and I can't let him drag it along the ground because of the cuckoo clock and the Dresden china I brought my mother.

I feel proud myself knowing that people are looking at me in my American army uniform. It isn't every day you see an American corporal getting off the train at the Limerick railway and I can't wait to walk the streets knowing the girls are going to be whispering, Who's that? Isn't he gorgeous? They'll probably think I fought the Chinese hand to hand in Korea, that I'm back for a rest from the serious wound which I'm too brave to show.

When we leave the station and walk to the street I know we're not going the right way. We should be going towards Janesboro and the new house, instead we're walking by the People's Park the way we did when we first came from America and I want to know why we're going to grandma's house in Little Barrington Street. My mother says that, well, the electricity and the gas aren't in the new house yet.

Why not?

Well, I didn't bother?

Why didn't you bother?

Wisha, I don't know.

That puts me in a rage. You'd think she'd be glad to be out of that slum in Little Barrington Street and up there in her new house planting flowers and making tea in her new kitchen that looks out on the garden. You'd think she'd be longing for the new beds with the clean sheets and no fleas and a bathroom. But no. She has to hang on to the slum and I don't know why. She says 'tis hard moving out and leaving her brother, my Uncle Pat, that he's not well in himself and barely hobbling. He still sells papers all around Limerick but, God help him, he's a bit helpless and didn't he let us stay in that house when we were in a bad way. I tell her I don't care, I'm not going back to that house in the lane. I'll stay here in the National Hotel till she gets the electricity and gas up in Janesboro. I hoist my duffel bag to my shoulder and when I walk away she whimpers after me, Oh, Frank, Frank, one night, one last night in my mother's house, sure it wouldn't kill you, one night.

I stop and turn and bark at her, I don't want one night in your mother's house. What the hell is the use of sending you the allotment if you want to live like a pig?

She cries and reaches her arms to me and Alphie's eyes are wide, but I don't care. I sign in at the National Hotel and throw my duffel bag on the bed and wonder what kind of a stupid mother I have who'll stay in a slum a minute more than she has to. I sit on the bed in my American army uniform and my new corporal's stripes and wonder if I should stay here in a fit of rage or walk the streets so that the world can admire me. I look out the window at Tait's clock, the Dominican Church, the Lyric Cinema beyond where small boys are waiting at the entrance to the gods where I used to go for tuppence. The boys are raggedy and rowdy and if I sit at this window long enough I can imagine I'm looking back at my own days in Limerick. It's only ten years since I was twelve and falling in love with Hedy Lamarr up there on the screen with Charles Boyer, the two of them in Algiers and Charles saying, Come wiz me to ze Casbah. I went around saying that for weeks till my mother begged me to stop. She loved Charles Boyer herself and she'd prefer to hear it from him. She loved James Mason, too. All the women in the lane loved James Mason, he was so handsome and dangerous. They all agreed it was the dangerous part they loved. Sure a man without danger is hardly a man at all. Melda Lyons would tell all the women in Kathleen O'Connell's shop how she was mad for James Mason and they'd laugh when she said, Bejesus, if I met him I'd have him naked as an egg in a minute. That would make my mother laugh harder than anyone in Kathleen O'Connell's shop and I wonder if she's over there now telling Melda and the women how her son, Frank, got off the train and wouldn't come home for a night and I wonder if the women will go home and say Frankie McCourt is back in his American uniform and he's too high and mighty now for his poor mother below there in the lane though we should have known for he always had the odd manner like his father.

It wouldn't kill me to walk over to my grandmother's house this one last time. I'm sure my brothers, Michael and Alphie, are bragging to the whole world that I'm coming home and they'll be sad if I don't stroll down the lane in my corporal's stripes.

The minute I go down the steps of the National Hotel the boys at the Lyric Cinema call across Pery Square, Hoi, Yankee soldier, yoo hoo, do you have any choon gum? Do you have a spare shilling in your pocket or a bar of candy in your pocket?

They pronounce candy like Americans and that makes them laugh so hard they fall against each other and the wall.

There's one boy off to the side who stands with his hands in his pockets and I can see he has two red scabby eyes in a face full of pimples and a head shaved to the bone. It's hard for me to admit that's the way I looked ten years ago and when he calls across the square, Hoi, Yankee soldier, turn around so we can all see your fat arse, I want to give him a good fong in his own scrawny arse. You'd think he'd have respect for the uniform that saved the world even if I'm only a supply clerk now with dreams of getting my dog back. You'd think Scabby Eyes would notice my corporal's stripes and have a bit of respect but no, that's the way it is when you grow up in a lane. You have to pretend you don't give a fiddler's fart even when you do.

Still, I'd like to cross the square to Scabby Eyes and shake him and tell him he's the spitting image of me when I was his age but I didn't stand outside the Lyric Cinema tormenting Yanks over their fat arses. I'm trying to convince myself that's the way I was myself, till another part of my mind tells me I wasn't a bit different from Scabby Eyes, that I was just as liable as him to torment Yanks or Englishmen or anyone with a suit or a fountain pen in his top pocket riding around on a new bike, that I was just as liable to throw a rock through the window of a respectable house and run away laughing one minute and raging the next.

All I can do now is walk away keeping myself twisted to the wall so that Scabby Eyes and the boys won't see my arse and have ammunition.

It's all confusion and dark clouds in my head till the other idea comes. Go back to the boys like a GI from the films and give them change from your pocket. It won't kill you.

They watch me coming and they look as if they're about to run though no one wants to be a coward and run first. When I dole out the change all they can say is, Ooh, God, and the different way they look at me makes me feel happy. Scabby Eyes takes his share and says nothing till I'm walking away and he calls after me, Hey, mister, sure you don't have any arse at all at all.

And that makes me feel happier than anything.

The minute I turn off Barrington Street and down the hill to the lane I hear people saying, Oh, God, here's Frankie McCourt in his American uniform. Kathleen O'Connell is at the door of her shop laughing and offering me a piece of Cleeve's toffee. Sure, didn't you always love that, Frankie, even if it destroyed the teeth of Limerick. Her niece is here, too, the one that lost an eye when the knife she was using to open a bag of potatoes slipped and went into her head. She's laughing over the Cleeve's toffee, too, and I'm wondering how you can still laugh with an eye gone.

Kathleen calls down to the little fat woman at the corner of the lane, He's here, Mrs Patterson, a regular film star he is. Mrs Patterson takes my face in her hands and tells me, I'm happy for your poor mother, Frankie, the terrible life she had.

And there's Mrs Murphy who lost her husband at sea in the war, living now in sin with Mr White, nobody in the lanes the slightest bit shocked, and smiling at me, You are a film star, indeed, Frankie, and how's your poor eyes. Sure, they look grand.

The whole lane is out standing at doors and telling me I'm looking grand. Even Mrs Purcell is telling me I'm looking grand and she's blind. But I understand that's what she'd tell me if she could see and when I come near her she holds out her arms and tells me, Come here outa that, Frankie McCourt, and give me a hug for the sake of the days we listened to Shakespeare and Sean O'Casey on the wireless together.

And when she puts her arms around me she says, Arrah, God above, there isn't a pick on you. Aren't they feeding you in the American Army? But what matter, you smell grand. They always smell grand, the Yanks.

It's hard for me to look at Mrs Purcell and the delicate eyelids that barely flutter on the eyes set back in her head and remember the nights when she let me sit in the kitchen listening to plays and stories on the wireless and the way she'd think nothing of giving me a mug of tea and a big cut of bread and jam. It's hard because the people in the lane are at their doors delighted and I'm ashamed of myself for walking away from my mother and sulking on the bed in the National Hotel. How could she explain to the neighbors that she met me at the station and I wouldn't come home? I'd like to walk the few steps to my mother at her door and tell her how sorry I am but I can't say a word for fear the tears might come and she'd say, Oh, your bladder is near your eye.

I know she'd say that to bring on a laugh and keep her own tears back so that we wouldn't all feel shy and ashamed of our tears. All she can do now is say what any mother would in Limerick, You must be famished. Would you like a nice cup of tea?

My Uncle Pat is sitting in the kitchen and when he lifts his face to me it makes me sick to see the redness of his eyes and the yellow ooze. It reminds me of little Scabby Eyes over at the Lyric Cinema. It reminds me of myself.

Uncle Pat is my mother's brother and he's known all over Limerick as Ab Sheehan. Some people call him the Abbot and no one knows why. He says, That's a grand uraform you have there, Frankie. Where's your big gun? He laughs and shows the yellow stubs of teeth in his gums. His hair is black and grey and thick on his head from not being washed and there's dirt in the creases on his face. His clothes, too, shine with the grease of not being washed and I wonder how my mother can live with him and not keep him clean till I remember how stubborn he is about not washing himself and wearing the same clothes day and night till they fall from his body. My mother couldn't find the soap once and when she asked him if he had seen it he said, Don't be blamin' me for the soap. I didn't see the soap. I didn't wash meself in a week. And he said it as if everyone should admire him. I'd like to strip him in the backyard and hose him down with hot water till the dirt left the creases on his face and the pus ran from his eyes.

Mam makes the tea and it's good to see she has decent cups and saucers now not like the old days when we drank from jam jars. The Abbot refuses the new cups. I want me own mug, he says. My mother argues with him that this mug is a disgrace with all the dirt in the cracks where all kinds of diseases might be lurking. He doesn't care. He says, That was me mother's mug that she left to me, and there's no arguing with him when you know he was dropped on his head in his infancy. He gets up to limp out to the backyard lavatory and when he's gone Mam says she did everything to move him out of this house and stay with her for a while. No, he won't go. He's not going to leave his mother's house and the mug she gave him long ago and the little statue of the Infant of Prague and the big picture of the Sacred Heart of Jesus above in the bedroom. No, he's not going to leave all that. What matter. Mam has Michael and Alphie to take care of, Alphie still in school and poor Michael washing dishes down at the Savoy Restaurant, God help him.

We finish our tea and I take a walk with Alphie down O'Connell Street so that everyone will see me and admire me. We meet Michael coming up the street from his job and there's a pain in my heart when I see him, the black hair falling down to his eyes and his body a bag of bones with clothes as greasy as the Abbot's from washing dishes all day. He smiles in his shy way and says, God, you're looking very fit, Frankie. I smile back at him and I don't know what to say because I'm ashamed of the way he looks and if my mother were here I'd yell at her and ask her why Michael has to look like this. Why can't she get him decent clothes or why can't the Savoy Restaurant at least give him an apron to save himself from the grease? Why did he have to leave school at fourteen to wash dishes? If he came from the Ennis Road or the North Circular Road he'd be in school now playing rugby and going to Kilkee on his holidays. I don't know what's the use of coming back to Limerick where children are still running around in bare feet and looking at the world through scabby eyes, where my brother, Michael, has to wash dishes and my mother takes her time moving to a decent house. This is not the way I expected it to be and it makes me so sad I wish I were back in Germany drinking beer in Lenggries.

Some day I'll get them out of here, my mother, Michael, Alphie, over to New York where Malachy is already working and ready to join the air force so that he won't be drafted and sent to Korea. I don't want Alphie to leave school at the age of fourteen like the rest of us. At least he's at the Christian Brothers and not a National school like Leamy's, the one we went to. Some day he'll be able to go to secondary school so that he'll know Latin and other important things. Now at least he has clothes and shoes and food and he needn't be ashamed of himself. You can see how sturdy he is, not like Michael, the bag of bones.

We turn and make our way back up O'Connell Street and I know people are admiring me in my GI uniform till some call out, Jesus, is that you, Frankie McCourt? and the whole world knows I'm not a real American GI, that I'm just someone from the back lanes of Limerick all togged out in the American uniform with the corporal's stripes.

My mother is coming down the street all smiles. The new house will have electricity and gas tomorrow and we can move in. Aunt Aggie sent word she heard I'd arrived and she wants us to come over for tea. She's waiting for us now.

Aunt Aggie is all smiles, too. It's not like the old days when there was nothing in her face but bitterness over not having children of her own and even if there was bitterness she was the one who made sure I had decent clothes for my first job. I think she's impressed with my uniform and my corporal's stripes the way she keeps asking if I'd like more tea, more ham, more cheese. She's not that generous with Michael and Alphie and you can see it's up to my mother to make sure they have enough. They're too shy to ask for more or they're afraid. They know she has a fierce temper from not having children of her own.

Her husband, Uncle Pa Keating, doesn't sit at the table at all. He's over by the coal range with a mug of tea and all he does is smoke cigarettes and cough till he's weak, clutching at himself and laughing, These feckin' fags will kill me in the end.

My mother says, You should give 'em up, Pa, and he says, And if I did, Angela, what would I do with myself? Would I sit here with my tea and stare at the fire?

She says, They'll kill you, Pa.

And if they do, Angela, I won't give a fiddler's fart.

That's the part of Uncle Pa I always loved, the way he doesn't give a fiddler's fart about anything. If I could be like him I'd be free though I wouldn't want his lungs the way they were destroyed by German gas in the Great War, then years working in the Limerick Gas Works and now fags by the fireplace. I'm sad he's sitting there killing himself when he's the only man who ever told the truth. He's the one that told me don't get caught taking tests for the post office when I could save my money and go to America. You could never imagine Uncle Pa telling a lie. It would kill him faster than gas or the fags.

He's still all black from shoveling coke and coal at the Gas Works and there's no flesh on his bones. When he looks up from his place by the fire the whites of his eyes are dazzling around the blue. You can see when he looks over at us he has a special fondness for my brother Michael. I wish he had that fondness for me but he doesn't and it's enough to know he bought me my first pint long ago and told me the truth. I'd like to tell him the way I feel about him. No, I'm afraid someone would laugh.

After the tea at Aunt Aggie's I'm thinking of going back to my room at the National Hotel but I'm afraid my mother will get the hurt look in her eyes again. Now I'll have to doss in my grandmother's bed with Michael and Alphie and I know the fleas will drive me mad. Ever since I left Limerick there hasn't been a flea in my life but now that I'm a GI with a bit of flesh on my bones I'll be eaten alive.

Mam says, No. There's a powder called DDT that kills everything and she has it sprinkled all over the house. I tell her it's what we were sprayed with from small planes flying over our heads in Fort Dix so that we'd be saved from the torment of mosquitoes.

Still, it's crowded in the bed with Michael and Alphie. The Abbot is in his bed across the room grunting and eating from a paper of fish and chips the way he always did. I can't sleep listening to him and thinking of the days when I licked the grease from the newspaper that held his fish and chips. Here I am in the old bed with my uniform hanging over the back of a chair with nothing changed in Limerick but the DDT that keeps the fleas away. It's a comfort to think of the children who can sleep now with the DDT and not have the torment of the fleas.

The next day my mother tries for the last time to get Uncle Pat, her brother, to move up to Janesboro with us. He says, Noah, noah. That's the way he talks from being dropped on his head. He won't go. He'll stay here and when we're all gone he'll move into the big bed, his mother's bed that all of us slept in for years. He always wanted that bed and now he'll have it and he'll have his tea from his mother's mug every morning.

My mother looks at him and the tears are there again. It makes me impatient and I want her to take her things and go. If the Abbot wants to be that stupid and stubborn let him be. She says, You don't know what it is to have a brother like this. You're lucky all your brothers are whole.

Whole? What is she talking about?

Lucky you are to have brothers that are sensible and healthy and never dropped on their heads.

She cries again and asks the Abbot if he'd like a nice cup of tea and he says, Noah.

Wouldn't he like to come up to the new house and have a nice warm bath in the new bathtub?

Noah.

Oh, Pat, oh, Pat, oh, Pat.

She's so helpless with tears she has to sit down and he does nothing but stare at her out of his oozing eyes. He stares at her without a word till he reaches for his mother's mug and says, I'll have me mother's mug and me mother's bed that ye kept me out of all these years.

Alphie goes over to Mam and asks her if we can go to our new house. He's only eleven and he's excited. Michael is already at the Savoy Restaurant washing dishes and when he's finished he can come to the new house where he'll have hot and cold running water and he can take the first bath of his life.

Mam dries her eyes and stands. Are you sure now, Pat, you won't come? You can bring the mug if you like but we can't bring the bed.

Noah.

And that's the end of it. She says, This is the house I grew up in. When I went to America I didn't even look back going up the lane. 'Tis all different now. I'm forty-four years of age and 'tis all different.

She puts on her coat and stands looking at her brother and I'm so tired of her moaning I want to pull her out of the house. I tell Alphie, Come on, and we move out the door so that she has to follow us. Whenever she's hurt her face grows whiter and her nose sharper and that's the way it is now. She won't talk to me, treats me as if I had done something wrong by sending the allotment so that she could have some kind of a decent life. I don't want to talk to her either because it's hard to feel sympathy for someone, even your mother, who wants to stay in a slum with a brother who's simple from being dropped on his head.

She's like that in the bus all the way up to Janesboro. Then, at the door of the new house, she starts foostering in her bag. Oh, God, she says, I must have left the key behind, which shows she didn't want to leave her old house in the first place. That's what Corporal

Dunphy told me once in Fort Dix. His wife had that habit of forgetting keys and when you have that habit it means you don't want to go home. It means you have a dread of your own door. Now I have to knock next door to see if they'll let me go around to the back in case there's a window open for me to climb in.

That puts me in such a bad mood I can barely enjoy the new house. It's different with her. The minute she steps into the hall the paleness goes from her face and the sharpness from her nose. The house is already furnished, at least she did that, and now she says what every mother in Limerick would say, Well, we might as well have a nice cup of tea. She's like Captain Boyle yelling at Juno in *Juno and the Paycock*, Tay, tay, tay, if a man was dyin', you'd be tryin' to make him swally a cup o' tay.

18

All the years I grew up in Limerick I watched people go to dances at Cruise's Hotel or the Stella Ballroom. Now I can go myself and I needn't be a bit shy with the girls with my American uniform and my corporal's stripes. If they ask me was I ever in Korea and was I wounded I'll give them a small smile and act as if I don't want to talk about it. I might limp a little and that might be enough of an excuse for not being able to dance properly which I never could anyway. There might be at least one nice girl who will be sensitive about my wound and take me to a table for a glass of lemonade or stout.

Bud Clancy is up on the stage with his band and recognizes me the minute I walk in. He signals for me to go up to him. How are you, Frankie? Back from the wars, ha ha ha. Would you like us to play a special request?

I tell him "American Patrol" and he talks into the microphone. Ladies and Gentlemen, here's one of our own home from the wars, Frankie McCourt. And I'm in heaven with everyone looking at me. They don't look long because once "American Patrol" starts they're twirling and swinging away on the floor. I stand by the bandstand wondering how they can go on dancing and ignoring an American corporal in their midst. I never thought I'd be ignored like this and now I have to ask a girl to dance to save face. The girls are ranged in seats along the walls, drinking lemonade, chatting, and when I ask them to dance they shake their heads, No, thanks. Only one says yes, and when she gets up I notice she has a limp and that puts me in a quandary wondering if I should postpone my own limp for fear she might think I was mocking her. I can't leave her standing there all night so I lead her out to the dance floor and now I notice everyone looking at me because her limp is so bad she nearly loses her balance every time she steps forward on the right leg that's shorter than the left. It's hard to know what to do when you have to dance with someone with such a serious limp. I know now how foolish it would be for me to put on my false war limp. The whole world would be laughing at us, me going one way, she the other way. What's worse is I don't know what to say to her. I know that if you have the right thing to say you can save any situation but I'm afraid to say anything. Should I say, Sorry for your limp, or, How did you get it? She doesn't give me a chance to say anything. She barks at me, Are you going to stand there gawking all night? and I can't do anything but lead her to the floor with Bud Clancy's band playing "Chattanooga choo choo, won't you hurry me home". I don't know why Bud has to play fast tunes when girls with limps like this are barely able to put one foot before the other. Why couldn't he play "Moonlight Serenade" or "Sentimental Journey" so that I could use the few steps I learned from Emer in New York? Now the girl is asking me if I think this is a funeral and I notice she has the flat accent that shows she's from a poor part of Limerick. Come on, Yank, start swinging, she says, and steps away and twirls on her one good leg as fast as a top. Another couple bumps against us and they tell her, Powerful, Madeline, powerful. You're out on your picky tonight, Madeline. Better than Ginger Rogers herself.

Girls along the wall are laughing. My face is on fire and I wish to God Bud Clancy would play "Three O'Clock in the Morning" so that I could lead Madeline back to her seat and give up dancing forever but, no, Bud starts a slow one, "The Sunny Side of the Street", and Madeline presses herself up against me with her nose in my chest and pushes me around the floor, clumping and limping, till she steps back from me and tells me if this is the way Yanks dance then she'll dance from this day out with the men of Limerick who know how, thank you very much, indeed.

The girls along the wall laugh even harder. Even the men who can't get anyone to dance with them and spend their time drinking pints are laughing and I know I might as well leave because no one will dance with me after the spectacle I made of myself. I have such a desperate feeling and I'm so ashamed of myself that I want them to feel ashamed and the only way to do that is to put on the limp and hope they'll think it's a war wound but when I hobble towards the door the girls shriek and turn so hysterical with laughter I run down the stairs and into the street so ashamed I want to throw myself into the River Shannon.

The next day Mam tells me she heard I went to a dance last night, that I danced with Madeline Burke from Mungret Street and everyone is saying, Wasn't that very good of Frankie McCourt to dance with Madeline the way she is, God help us, an' him in his uniform an' all.

It doesn't matter. I won't go out in my uniform anymore. I'll wear civilian clothes and no one will be looking to see if I have a fat arse. If I go to a dance I'll stand by the bar and drink pints with the men who pretend they don't care when the girls say no.

I have ten days left on my furlough and I wish it was ten minutes so that I could go back to Lenggries and get whatever I want for a pound of coffee and a carton of cigarettes. Mam says I'm acting very dour but I can't explain the strange feelings I have for Limerick after all the bad times of my childhood and now the way I disgraced myself at the dance. I don't care if I was good to Madeline Burke and her limp. That's not what I came back to Limerick for. I'll never try to dance with anyone again without looking to see if they have legs the same length. It should be easy if I watch them going to the lavatory. In the long run it's easier to be with Buck and Rappaport, even Weber, taking the laundry to Dachau.

But I can't tell my mother any of this. It's hard to tell anyone anything especially if it's about coming and going. You have to get used to a big powerful place like New York where you could be dead in your bed for days with a strange odor coming from your room before anyone would notice. Then you're put into the army and you have to get used to men from all over America, all colors and shapes. When you go to Germany you look at people on the streets and in the beer places. You have to get used to them, too. They seem ordinary though you'd like to lean across to the group at the next table and say, Did anyone here kill Jews? Of course we were told in army orientation sessions to keep our mouths shut and treat Germans as allies in the war against godless communism but you'd still like to ask out of pure curiosity or to see the looks on their faces.

The hardest part of all the coming and going is Limerick. I'd like to walk around and be admired for my uniform and corporal's stripes and I suppose I would if I hadn't grown up here but I'm known to too many people because of the time I spent delivering telegrams and working for Eason's and now all I get is, Ah, Jaysus, Frankie McCourt, is that yourself? Aren't you lookin' grand entirely. How're your poor eyes and how's your poor mother? You never looked better, Frankie.

I could be wearing the uniform of a general but all I am to them is Frankie McCourt the scabby-eyed telegram boy with the poor suffering mother.

The best part of being in Limerick is walking around with Alphie and Michael though Michael is usually busy with a girl who's mad about him. All the girls are mad about him with his black hair and blue eyes and shy smile.

Oh, Mikey John, they say, isn't he gorgeous.

If they say it to his face he blushes and that makes them love him even more. My mother says he's a grand dancer, that's what she heard, and no one is better singing "When April showers, they come your way". He was having his dinner one day and the news came on the radio that Al Jolson had died and he got up, crying, and walked away from his dinner. It's a very serious thing when a boy walks away from his dinner and it proved how much Michael loved Al Jolson.

With all his talent I know Michael should be in America and he will because I'll make sure of it.

There are days I walk the streets in civilian clothes by myself. I have a notion that when I visit all the places we lived in I'm in a tunnel through the past where I know I'll be happy to come out at the other end. I stand outside Leamy's School where I got whatever education I have, good or bad. Next door is the St Vincent de Paul Society where my mother went to keep us from starving. I wander the streets from church to church, memories everywhere. There are voices, choirs, hymns, priests preaching or murmuring during confession. I can look at the doors on every street in Limerick and know I delivered telegrams at every one.

I meet schoolmasters from Leamy's National School and they tell me I was a fine boy even if they forget how they whacked me with stick and cane when I couldn't remember the proper answers for the catechism or the dates and names in Ireland's long sad history. Mr Scanlon tells me there's no use in being in America unless I make a fortune for myself and Mr O'Halloran, the headmaster, stops his car to ask me about my life in America and to remind me of what the Greeks said, that there is no royal road to knowledge. He'll be very surprised, he says, if I turn my back on books to join the shopkeepers of the world, to fumble in the greasy till. He smiles with his President Roosevelt smile and drives away.

I meet priests from our own church, St Joseph's, and other churches where I might have gone to confession or delivered telegrams but they pass me. You have to be rich to get a nod from a priest, unless he's a Franciscan.

Still I sit in silent churches to look at altars, pulpits, confessionals. I'd like to know how many Masses I attended, how many sermons frightened the life out of me, how many priests were shocked by my sins before I gave up going to confession altogether. I know I'm doomed the way I am though I'd confess to a kindly priest if I could find one. Sometimes I wish I could be a Protestant or a Jew because they don't know any better. When you belong to the True Faith there are no excuses and you're trapped.

There's a letter from my father's sister, Aunt Emily, to say my grand-mother is hoping I'll be able to travel to the North to see them before I leave for Germany. My father is living with them, working as a farm laborer all around Toome, and he'd like to see me too after all these years.

I don't mind traveling to the North to see my grandmother but I don't know what I'll say to my father. Now that I'm twenty-two I know from walking around Munich and Limerick and looking at children in the streets I could never be the father that walked away from them. He left us when I was ten to work in England and send us money but, as my mother said, he chose the bottle over the babies. Mam says I should go to the North because my grandmother is frail and might not last till the next time I come home. She says there are some things you can do only once and you might as well do them that once.

It's surprising she should talk about my grandmother like this after the cold reception she got when she landed from America with my father and four small children but there are two things she hates in the world, holding grudges and owing money.

If I go to the North in a train I should wear my uniform for the admiration I'm sure to get though I know if I open my gob with my Limerick accent people will turn away or stick their heads in books and newspapers. I could put on an American accent but I already tried that with my mother and she went into hysterics, laughing. She said I sounded like Edward G. Robinson under water.

If anyone talks to me the only thing I can do is nod my head or shake it or put on the look of a secret sadness caused by a severe war wound.

It's all for nothing. The Irish are so used to American soldiers coming and going since the end of the war I might as well be invisible in my corner of the carriage on the train to Dublin and then Belfast. There's no curiosity, no one saying, Are you back from Korea? Aren't those Chinamen terrible? and I don't even want to put on the limp anymore. A limp is like a lie, you have to remember to keep it going.

My grandmother says, Och, don't you look grand in your uniform, and Aunt Emily says, Och, you're a man now.

My father says, Och, you're here. How's your mother?

She's grand.

And your brother Malachy and your brother Michael and your wee brother what's his name?

Alphie.

Och, aye, Alphie. How's your wee brother Alphie?

They're all grand.

He lets out a small Och and sighs, That's grand.

Then he wants to know if I take a drink and my grandmother says, Now, Malachy, enough of that talk.

Och, I only wanted to warn him of the bad company to be found in pubs.

This is my father who left us when I was ten to spend every penny he earned in the pubs of Coventry with German bombs dropping all around him, his family next to starvation in Limerick and here he is putting on the air of one in the grip of sanctifying grace and all I can think of is there must be some truth to the story he was dropped on his head or the other story that he had a disease like meningitis.

That might be an excuse for the drinking, the dropping on the head or the meningitis. German bombs couldn't be an excuse because there were other Limerickmen sending money home from Coventry, bombs or no bombs. There were even men who fell in with English-women and still sent money home though that money would slow down to nothing because Englishwomen are notorious for not wanting their Irishmen to support their families at home when they have three or four snotty-nosed English brats of their own running around demanding bangers and mash. Many an Irishman at the end of the war was so desperate trapped between his Irish and English families there was nothing for him to do but jump on a ship to Canada or Australia never to be heard from again.

That wouldn't be my father. If he had seven children with my mother it was only because she was there in the bed doing her wifely duty. Englishwomen are never that easy. They'd never suffer an Irishman who would leap on them in the bravery of a few pints and that means there are no little McCourt bastards running the streets of Coventry.

I don't know what to say to him with his little smile and his Och aye because I don't know if I'm talking to a man in his right mind or the man dropped on his head or the one with meningitis. How can I talk to him when he gets up, sticks his hands deep into his trouser pockets and marches around the house whistling "Lili Marlene"? Aunt Emily whispers he hasn't had a drink in ages and it's a great struggle for him. I want to tell her it was a greater struggle for my mother to keep us all alive but I know he has the sympathy of his whole family and anyway what use is there going over the past. Then she tells me how he suffered over my mother's disgraceful doings with her cousin, how the story drifted back to the North that they were living as man and wife, that when my father heard about it in Coventry, with the bombs dropping all around him, it drove him so mad he was in the pubs day, night and in between. Men home from Coventry would tell how my father would run into the streets during the air raids lifting his arms to the Luftwaffe and begging them to drop one on his poor tormented head.

My grandmother nods her head, agreeing with Aunt Emily, Och, aye. I want to remind them my father drank long before the bad days in Limerick, that we had to hunt him in pubs all over Brooklyn. I want to tell them that if he'd only sent money we could have stayed in our own house instead of being evicted and having to move in with Mam's cousin.

But my grandmother is frail and I have to control myself. My face feels tight and there are dark clouds in my head and all I can do is stand and tell them my father drank all through the years, drank when babies were born and babies died and drank because he drank.

She says, Och, Francis, and shakes her head as if to disagree with me, as if to defend my father, and that causes such a rage in me I hardly know what to do till I'm pulling my duffel bag down the stairs and out on the road to Toome, Aunt Emily at the hedge calling, Francis, oh, Francis, come back, your grandmother wants to talk to you, but I keep walking though I'm aching to go back, that bad as my father is I'd at least like to know him, that my grandmother was doing only what any mother would do, defending her son who was dropped on his head or had meningitis, and I might go back except that a car stops and a man offers me a lift to the bus station in Toome and once I'm in the car there's no going back.

I'm not in the mood for talk but I have to be polite to the man even when he says the McCourts of Moneyglass are a fine family even if they're Catholics.

Even if they're Catholics.

I'd like to tell the man stop the car and let me out with my duffel bag but if I do I'll be only halfway to Toome and I'd be tempted to walk back to my grandmother's house.

I can't go back. The past won't go away in this family and there would surely be talk again of my mother and her great sin and then we'd have an explosion and I'd be dragging my duffel bag along the Toome road again.

The man lets me out and when I say thanks I wonder to myself if he marches around on the Twelfth of July beating a drum with the other Protestants but he has a kind face and I can't imagine him beating a drum for anything.

All the way on the bus to Belfast and the train from Belfast to Dublin I have the ache to go back to the grandmother I might never see again and to see if I could get past my father's little smiles and the och ayes but once I'm on the train to Limerick there's no going back. My head is cluttered with images of my father, my Aunt Emily, my grandmother, and the sadness of their lives in the farmhouse with seven useless acres. Then there's my mother in Limerick, forty-four years of age with seven children, three dead, and all she wants, as she says, is a little peace, ease and comfort. There's the sadness of Corporal Dunphy's life in Fort Dix and Buck in Lenggries, the two of them who found a home in the army because they wouldn't know what to do with the outside world, and I'm afraid if I don't stop thinking this way the tears will come and I'll disgrace myself in this carriage with five people gawking at me in my uniform saying, Jaysus, who's the Yank weeping in the corner? My mother would say, Your bladder is near your eye, but the people in the carriage might say, Is this a specimen of what's fighting the Chinese hand to hand over there in Korea?

Even if there weren't another soul in the carriage I'd have to control myself because the slightest hint of a tear and the salt in it makes my eyes redder than they are and I don't want to get off the train and walk the streets of Limerick with eyes like two pissholes in the snow.

My mother opens the door and clutches at her chest. Mother o' God, I thought you were an apparition. What are you doing back so soon? Sure, didn't you leave only yesterday morning. Gone one day, back the next?

I can't tell her how I'm home because of the bad things they were saying in the North about her and her terrible sin. I can't tell her how they had my father nearly canonized for his suffering over that same sin. I can't tell her because I don't want to be tormented by the past and I don't want to be trapped between the North and the South, Toome and Limerick.

I have to lie and tell her my father is drinking and that makes her face go white again and her nose pointed. I ask her why she acts so surprised. Isn't this the way he always was?

She says she hoped he might have given up the drink so that we'd have a father we could talk to, even in the North. She'd like Michael and Alphie to see this father they barely knew and she wouldn't want them to see him in his wildness. When he was sober he was the best husband in the world, the best father. He'd always have a song or a story or a comment about the state of the world that made her laugh. Then everything was destroyed with the drink. The demons came, God help us, and children were better off without him. She's better off now by herself with the few pounds coming in and the peace, ease and comfort that's in it and the best thing now would be a nice cup of tea for I must be famished after my travels to the North.

All I can do with the days left in Limerick is walk around again knowing I'll have to make my way in America and I won't return for a long time. I kneel in St Joseph's Church by the box where I made my First Confession. I move to the altar rail to look at the place where the bishop patted my cheek at Confirmation and made me a soldier of the True Church. I wander up to Roden Lane where we lived for years and wonder how families can still live there all sharing the one lavatory. The Downes house is a shell and that's a sign there are other places to go besides the slums. Mr Downes brought his whole family over to England and that's what comes of working and not drinking the wages that should go to wife and children. I could wish I had a father like Mr Downes but I didn't and there's no use complaining.

19

With the months left in Lenggries there is nothing to do most of the day but run the supply room and read books from the base library.

There are no more laundry trips to Dachau. Rappaport told someone about our visit to the refugee camp and when the story reached the captain we were hauled in and reprimanded for unsoldierly conduct and confined to barracks for two weeks. Rappaport says he's sorry. He didn't mean for some asshole to spill the beans but he felt terrible over the women in the camp. He tells me I shouldn't go around with the likes of Weber. Buck is OK but Weber fell out of a tree. Rappaport says I should concentrate on getting an education, that if I were Jewish that's all I'd be thinking about. How would he know about the times I looked at college students in New York and dreamed I'd be like them. He tells me when I'm discharged I'll have the Korean GI Bill and I can go to college but what use is that when I don't even have the high school diploma? Rappaport says I shouldn't think about why I can't do something. I should think about why I *can* do it.

That's the way Rappaport talks and I suppose that's the way it is when you're Jewish.

I tell him I can't go back to New York and go to high school if I have to earn a living.

Nights, says Rappaport.

And how long will it take me to get a high school diploma that way?

A few years.

I can't do that. I can't spend years working by day, going to school by night. I'd be dead in a month.

So what else are you going to do?

I don't know.

So? says Rappaport.

My eyes are red and oozing and Sergeant Burdick sends me on sick call. The army doctor wants to know about my last treatment and when I tell him about the doctor in New York who said I had a disease from New Guinea he says that's it, that's what you got, soldier, go get your head shaved and report back in two weeks. It's not so bad getting your head shaved in the army with the way you have to wear a cap or helmet except that if you go to a *bierstube* the Lenggries girls might call out, Oh, Irishman's got the clap, and if you try to explain it's not the clap they only pat your cheek and tell you come to them any time clap or no clap. In two weeks there's no improvement in my eyes and the doctor says I have to go back to the military hospital in Munich for observation. He doesn't say he's sorry for making a great mistake, for making me get my head shaved, that it probably wasn't the dandruff at all or anything from New Guinea. He says these are desperate times, Russians massing on the border, our troops have to be healthy, and he's not going to take a chance on this eye disease from New Guinea spreading all over the European Command.

They send me in a jeep again but the driver now is a Cuban corporal, Vinnie Gandia, who is asthmatic and plays drums in civilian life. It was hard for him being in the army but the music business was slow and he needed some way to send money to the family in Cuba. They were going to kick him out of the army in basic training because his shoulders were so bony he couldn't carry a rifle or a fifty-millimeter machine gun barrel till he saw a picture of a Kotex on a box and a light went on in his head. Jesus. That was it. Slip the Kotex pads under his shirt as a pad on his shoulders and he was ready for anything the army could throw at him. After remembering Rappaport did the same thing I wonder if Kotex knew how they were helping the fighting men of America. All the way to Munich Vinnie guides the steering wheel with his elbows so that he can tap with his drumsticks on every hard surface. He gasps bits of songs, Mister Whatyoucallit whatcha doin' tonight, and bap bap da do bap do do de do bap to go along with the beat and then he's so excited the asthma hits him and he's gasping so hard he has to stop the jeep and pump his inhaler. He rests his forehead on the steering wheel and when he looks up there are tears on his cheeks from the strain of trying to breathe. He tells me I should be grateful all I have is sore eyes. He wishes he had sore eyes instead of asthma. He could still play the drums without stopping for his goddam inhaler. Sore eyes never stopped a drummer. He wouldn't care if he went blind long as he could play the drums. What's the use of living if you can't play your goddam drums? People don't appreciate not having asthma. They sit around moaning and bitching about life and all the time breathing breathing nice and normal and taking it for granted. Give 'em one day of asthma and they'll spend the rest of their lives thanking God with every breath they take, just one day. He's gonna have to invent some kind of gadget you hang on your head so you can breathe when you play, some kind of helmet maybe, and you're in there breathing like a baby in fresh air and you're rapping away on them drums, shit, man, that would be heaven. Gene Krupa, Buddy Rich, they don't have asthma, lucky bastards. He says if I can still see when I get out of the army he'll take me to joints on Fifty-Second Street, the greatest street in the world. If I can't see he'll still take me. Shit, you don't have to see to hear the sounds, man, and wouldn't that be something, him gasping and me with a white cane or a seeing-eye dog up and down Fifty-Second Street. I could sit with this blind guy, Ray Charles, and we could compare notes. That makes Vinnie laugh and brings on the attack again and when he gets his breath back he says asthma is a bitch because if you think of something funny you laugh and that takes your breath away. That pisses him off, too, the way people go around laughing and taking it for granted and never think what it would be like to play drums with asthma, never think what it's like when you can't laugh. People just don't think about things like that.

The army doctor in Munich says the doctors in New York and Lenggries are full of shit and pours something silvery into my eyes that feels like acid. He tells me stop whining, be a man, you're not the only unit to get this infection, goddamit. I should be thankful I'm not a unit in Korea getting my ass shot off, that half these fat-ass units in Germany should be over there fighting with their *paisans* in Korea. He tells me look up, look down, look right, look left, and that will get the drops into every corner of my eyes. And how the hell, he wants to know, how the hell did they let these two eyes into this man's army? Good thing they sent me to Germany. In Korea I'd need a seeing-eye dog to fight off the goddam Chink units. I'm to stay in the hospital a few days and if I keep my eyes open and my mouth shut I'll be an okay unit.

I don't know why he keeps calling me a unit and I'm beginning to wonder if eye doctors in general are different from other doctors.

The best part of being in the hospital is that even with the bad eyes I can read all day and into the night. The doctor says I'm supposed to rest the eyes. He tells the medic to pour the silvery liquid into the eyes of this unit every day until further notice but the medic, Apollo, tells me the doctor is full of shit and brings a tube of penicillin ointment which he smears on my eyelids. Apollo says he knows a thing or two because he went to medical school himself but had to drop out because of a broken heart.

In a day the infection disappears and now I'm afraid the doctor will send me back to Lenggries and that will be the end of my easy days reading Zane Grey, Mark Twain, Herman Melville. Apollo tells me not to worry. If the doctor comes into my ward I should rub my eyes with salt and they'll look like

Two pissholes in the snow, I say.

Right.

I tell him my mother made me rub salt on my eyes a long time ago to make them look sore so that we'd get money for food from a mean man in Limerick. Apollo says, Yeah, but this is now.

He wants to know about my coffee and cigarette ration which, obviously, I'm not using and he'll be glad to take them off my hands in return for the penicillin ointment and the salt treatment. Otherwise the doctor will come with the silvery stuff and in no time I'll be back in Lenggries counting out sheets and blankets till my discharge in three months. Apollo says Munich is crawling with women and it's easy to get laid but he wants high-class stuff not some whore in a bombed-out building.

The cause of all my misfortunes is a book by Herman Melville called *Pierre, or The Ambiguities* which isn't a bit like *Moby Dick* and so dull it puts me to sleep in the middle of the day and there's the doctor shaking me awake and waving the tube of penicillin left behind by Apollo.

Wake up goddamit. Where did you get this? Apollo, right? That unit, Apollo. That goddam drop-out from a half-ass medical school in Mississippi.

He marches to the door and roars down the hall, Apollo, get your ass in here, and there's Apollo's voice, Yes, sir, yes, sir.

You, goddamit, you. Did you supply this unit with this tube?

In a way, sir, yes, sir.

What the hell are you talking about?

He was suffering, sir, screaming with his eyes.

How the hell do you scream with your eyes?

I mean, sir, the pain. He would scream. I would apply the penicillin.

Who told you, eh? You a goddam doctor?

No, sir. It's just something I saw them doing in Mississippi.

Fuck Mississippi, Apollo.

Yes, sir.

And you, soldier, what are you reading there with those eyes?

Pierre, or The Ambiguities, sir.

Christ. What the hell is it about?

I don't know, sir. I think it's about this Pierre who's caught between a dark-haired woman and a fair-haired woman. He's trying to write a book in a room in New York and he's so cold the women have to heat up hot bricks for his feet.

Christ. You're going back to your outfit, soldier. If you can lie on your ass here reading books about units like that you can be an active unit again. And you, Apollo, you're lucky I don't have your ass before a firing squad.

Yes, sir.

Dismissed.

Next day Vinnie Gandia drives me back to Lenggries and he drives without his drumsticks. He says he can't do it anymore, that he nearly got himself killed after he brought me to Munich the last time. You can't drive, drum and handle your asthma, simple as that. You gotta choose, and the drumsticks had to go. If he got into an accident and had damaged hands and couldn't play he'd stick his head in the oven, simple as that. He can't wait to get back to New York and hang out around Fifty-Second Street, the greatest street in the world. He makes me promise we'll meet in New York and he'll take me to all the great jazz joints, no charge, no cost, because he knows everyone and they know if he didn't have this goddam asthma he'd be right up there with Krupa and Rich, right up there.

There's a law that says I can sign up for another nine months in the army and avoid the six-year army reserve requirement. If I re-up they can't call me back any time the United States decides to defend democracy in distant places. I could stay here in the supply room for the nine months doling out sheets, blankets, condoms, drinking beer in the village, going home with an occasional girl, reading books from the base library. I could journey back to Ireland to tell my grandmother my sorrow over walking out in anger. I could take dancing lessons in Munich so that all the girls in Limerick would be queueing up to get out on the floor with me in my sergeant's stripes which I'd surely get.

But I can't afford another nine months in Germany with the letters coming from Emer telling me how she's counting the days till my return. I never knew she liked me that much and now I like her for liking me because that's the first time in my life I've heard that from a girl. I'm so excited over being liked by Emer I write and tell her I love her and she tells me she loves me, too, and that puts me in heaven and makes me want to pack my duffel bag and jump on a plane to her side.

I write and tell her how I long for her and how I'm here in Lenggries inhaling the perfume from her letters. I dream of the life we'll have in New York, how I'll go to my job every morning, a warm indoor job where I'll sit at a desk and scribble important decisions. Every night we'll have dinner and go to bed early so that we'll have plenty of time for the excitement.

Of course I can't mention the excitement part in the letters because Emer is pure and if her mother ever knew I had such dreams the door would be slammed in my face forever and there I'd be, deprived of the company of the only girl ever to say she liked me.

I can't tell Emer about the way I coveted college girls at the Biltmore Hotel. I can't tell her about the excitement I've had with girls in Lenggries and Munich and the refugee camp. She'd be so shocked she might tell her whole family, especially her big brother Liam, and there would be threats on my life.

Rappaport says that before you get married it's your obligation to tell the bride about all the things you've done with other girls. Buck says, That's bullshit, the best thing in life is to keep your mouth shut especially with someone you're going to marry. It's like the army, never tell, never volunteer.

Weber says, I wouldn't tell nobody nothing, and Rappaport tells him go swing from a tree. Weber says when he gets married he'll do one thing for the girl, he'll make sure he doesn't have the clap because that can be passed on and he wouldn't want any kid of his born with the clap.

Rappaport says, Jesus, the beast has feelings.

The night before I go stateside there's a party in a Bad Tolz restaurant. Officers and non-coms bring their wives and that means ordinary soldiers cannot bring their German girlfriends. Officers' wives would disapprove knowing that certain ordinary soldiers have wives waiting back home and it's not proper to sit with German girls who might be destroying good American families.

The captain makes a speech and says I was one of the finest soldiers he ever had under his command. Sergeant Burdick makes a speech and presents me with a scroll honoring me for my tight control of sheets, blankets, and protective devices.

When he says protective devices there is snickering along the table till the officers give the warning glares that tell the men, Cut it out, our wives are here.

One officer has a wife, Belinda, who is my age. If she didn't have a husband I might have a few beers to give me the courage to talk to her but I don't have to because she leans over and whispers that all the wives think I'm handsome. That makes me blush so hard I have to go out to the lavatory and when I return Belinda is saying something to the other wives that makes them laugh and when they look at me they laugh even harder and I'm sure they're laughing over what Belinda said to me. That makes me blush again and I wonder if there's anyone you can trust in this world.

Somehow Buck seems to know what happened. He whispers, The hell with these women, Mac. They shouldn't mock you like that.

I know he's right but I'm sad that the last memory of Lenggries I'll carry away with me is Belinda and the mocking officers' wives.

20

The day of my discharge from the army at Camp Kilmer I met Tom Clifford at the Breffni Bar on Third Avenue in Manhattan. We had corned beef and cabbage slathered with mustard and beer galore to cool our mouths. Tom had found an Irish bed and breakfast place in the South Bronx, Logan's Boarding House, and once I dropped off my duffel bag there we could come back down and see Emer after work in her apartment at East Fifty-Fourth Street.

Mr Logan seemed to be an old man with a bald head and a meaty red face. He might have been old but he had a young wife, Nora from Kilkenny, and a baby a few months old. He told me he was high up in the Ancient Order of Hibernians and the Knights of Columbus and I should make no mistake about where he stood on religion and morality in general, that none of his twelve boarders could expect a Sunday morning breakfast unless they could show they had attended Mass and, if at all possible, Holy Communion. For those who attended Communion and had at least two witnesses to prove it there would be sausages with the breakfast. Of course every boarder had two other boarders to testify he went to Communion. There was testifying right and left and Mr Logan was so upset over what he had to pay out in sausages he disguised himself in Nora's hat and coat and shuffled up to the middle of the church to discover not only that the boarders hadn't gone to Communion but that Ned Guinan and Kevin Hayes were the only ones to go to Mass at all. The rest were over on Willis Avenue slipping in the back door of a bar for an illegal drink before noon opening time and when they came streeling back for the breakfast, reeking, Mr Logan wanted to smell their breath. They told him feck off, this was a free country, and if they had to get their breaths smelled for the sake of a sausage they'd stay content with the watery eggs and milk, the stale bread and watery tea.

Also, there was to be no swearing or any kind of blaguarding in Mr Logan's house or we'd be asked to desist and depart. He would not allow his wife and child, Luke, to be exposed to any kind of disgraceful behavior from the twelve young Irish boarders. Our beds might be in the basement but he would always know about disgraceful behavior. No, indeed, it takes years to build up a boarding house business and he was not going to let twelve laborers from the Old Country tear it down. Bad enough that Negroes were moving in right and left and destroying a neighborhood, people with no morality, no jobs and no fathers for their children running the streets like savages.

The weekly rate was eighteen dollars for bed and breakfast and if I wanted dinner that would be an extra dollar a day. There were eight beds for twelve boarders and that was because everyone worked different shifts on the docks and various warehouses and what was the use of having extra beds cluttering up the two rooms in the basement, the only time all the beds were filled was Saturday night and then you had to bunk in with someone else. It didn't matter because Saturday night was the night to get drunk up on St Nicholas Avenue and you wouldn't care if you slept with man, woman or sheep.

There was one bathroom for all of us, bring your own soap, and two long narrow towels that used to be white. Each towel had a black line to separate the top from the bottom and that was how you were supposed to use them. There was a handwritten sign on the wall telling you the top was for anything above your navel, the bottom for anything below, signed J. Logan, prop. The towels were changed every two weeks though there were always fights between the boarders who were careful about the rules and the ones who might have had a drink.

Chris Wayne from Lisdoonvarna was the oldest boarder, forty-two, working in construction and saving to bring over his girlfriend, twenty-three, so that they could get married and have children while he still had a tittle of power in himself. The boarders called him Duke because of his last name and because of the silliness in it. He didn't drink or smoke, went to Mass and Communion every Sunday, and avoided the rest of us. He had tufts of grey in his curly black hair and he was gaunt from piety and frugality. He had his own towel, soap, and two sheets he carried around in a bag for fear we might use them. Every night he knelt by his bed and said the entire rosary. He was the only one who had secured a bed of his own since no one, drunk or sober, would climb in with him or use the bed in his absence because of the odor of sanctity around it. He worked from eight to five every work day and ate dinner with the Logans every night. They loved him for that because it brought in an extra seven dollars a week and they loved him even more for the small amounts he put into his scrawny frame. They didn't love him later when he started coughing and spitting and there were specks of blood on his handkerchief. They told him they had a child to think of and he'd better find another place. He told Mr Logan he was a son-of-a-bitch and a pathetic bastard that he felt sorry for. If he thought he was really the father of that child Mr Logan should look around at his boarders and if he wasn't completely blind he'd detect a marked resemblance to the child on the face of one of the boarders. Mr Logan struggled out of his armchair gasping that if he didn't have the bad heart he'd kill Chris Wayne on the spot. He tried to rush at the Duke but his heart wouldn't let him and he had to listen to Nora from Kilkenny screeching at him, begging him to stop or she'd be a widow with an orphan child.

The Duke laughed till he gasped at Nora, Don't worry, that child will always have a father. Sure, isn't he in this room.

He coughed his way out of the room and down the stairs to the basement and no one ever saw him again.

It was hard to live there after that. Mr Logan was suspicious of everyone and you could hear him roaring at Nora from Kilkenny at all hours. He took away one of the towels and saved money by buying old bread at the bakery and serving powdered milk and eggs for breakfast. He wanted to make us all go to confession so that he could watch our faces and know if what the Duke said was true. We refused. There were only four boarders long enough in the house to be suspects and Peter McNamee, the longest one there, told Mr Logan to his face that fooling around with Nora from Kilkenny was the last thing he'd ever think of. She was such a bag of bones from running the house you could hear her rattle and clank coming up the stairs.

Mr Logan gasped in his armchair and told Peter, That hurt me, Peter, that you'd say my wife clanks and you the finest boarder we ever had even if we were fooled a long time by the false piety of the fella that just left, thank God.

I'm sorry to hurt you, Mr Logan, but Nora from Kilkenny is not by any means a morsel. No one here would give her a second look on a dance floor.

Mr Logan looked around the room at us. Is that right, lads? Is that right?

'Tis, Mr Logan.

Are you sure of that, Peter?

I am, Mr Logan.

Thank God for that, Peter.

The boarders earn good money on the docks and in the warehouses. Tom works at Port Warehouses loading and unloading trucks and if he works extra hours he goes on time and a half or double time so that his pay is well over a hundred dollars a week.

Peter McNamee works at Merchants Refrigerating Company unloading and storing the meat from the freezer trucks from Chicago. The Logans like him for the slabs of beef or pork he hauls home every Friday night, drunk or sober, and that meat takes the place of the eighteen dollars. We never see this meat and some boarders swear Mr Logan sells it to a butcher shop on Willis Avenue.

All the boarders drink even though they say they want to save money and go back to Ireland for the peace and quiet that's in it. Only Tom says he'll never go back, that Ireland is a miserable bog of a place, and they take that as a personal insult and offer to settle it if he'll step outside. Tom laughs. He knows what he wants and it's not a life of fighting and drinking and moaning about Ireland and sharing towels in flophouses like this. The only one who agrees with Tom is Ned Guinan and it doesn't matter with him because he has the consumption like the Duke and he's not long for this world. He's saving enough money so that he can go home to Kildare and die in the house he was born in. He has dreams of Kildare where he's leaning on a fence at the Curragh watching the horses training in the morning, trotting through the mist that clouds the track till the sun breaks through and turns the whole world green. When he talks like this his eyes glisten and there's a slight pink flush on his cheeks and he smiles in such a way you'd like to go over and hold him a minute though that's the kind of thing they might frown on in an Irish boarding house. It's remarkable that Mr Logan allows him to stay but Ned is so delicate Mr Logan treats him like a son and forgets the baby who might be threatened by coughs, spits and flecks of blood. It's remarkable the way they keep him on the payroll at the Baker and Williams warehouse where they have him in the office answering the phone because he's so weak he can't lift a feather. When he's not answering the phone he studies French so that he can talk to St Thérèse, the Little Flower, when he goes to heaven. Mr Logan tells him very gently he might be on the wrong track in this matter, that Latin is the language you need in heaven and that leads to a long discussion among the boarders as to what language Our Lord spoke, Peter McNamee declaring for a fact it was Hebrew. Mr Logan says you might be right there, Peter, because he doesn't want to contradict the man who brings the Sunday meat home on a Friday night. Tom Clifford laughs that we should all brush up on our Irish in case we run into St Patrick or St Brigid and everyone glares at him, everyone but Ned Guinan who smiles at everything because it doesn't matter one way or the other when you're dreaming of the horses in Kildare.

Peter McNamee says it's a wonder a single one of us is alive with all the things against us in this world, the weather in Ireland, the TB, the English, the De Valera government, the One Holy Roman Catholic and Apostolic Church, and now the way we have to break our arses to make a few dollars on the docks and the warehouses. Mr Logan begs him to mind his language in the presence of Nora from Kilkenny and Peter says he's sorry, he gets carried away.

Tom tells me of a job unloading trucks at Port Warehouses. Emer says no, I should work in an office where I can use my brains. Tom says warehouse jobs are better than office jobs that pay less and make you wear a suit and tie and have you sitting so much you get an arse on you the size of a cathedral door. I'd like to work in an office but the warehouse pays seventy-five dollars a week and that's more than I ever dreamed of after my thirty-five dollars a week at the Biltmore Hotel. Emer says that's fine as long as I save something and get an education. She talks like that because everyone in her family went to school and she doesn't want me lifting and hauling till I'm a broken old man at the age of thirty-five. She knows from the way Tom and I talk about the boarders that there's drinking and all kinds of blaguarding and she wouldn't like me to be spending my time in bars when I could be making something of myself.

Emer has a clear head because she doesn't drink or smoke and the only meat she eats is an occasional morsel of chicken for her blood. She goes to a business school at Rockefeller Center so that she can earn a living and make something of herself in America. I know her clear head is good for me but I want that warehouse money and I promise her and myself I'll go to school some day.

Mr Campbell Groel who owns Port Warehouses isn't too sure if he wants to hire me, that I might be too scrawny. Then he looks at Tom Clifford who is smaller and scrawnier and the best worker on the platform and if I'm half as strong and fast I have the job.

The platform boss is Eddie Lynch, a fat man from Brooklyn, and when he talks to me or Tom he laughs and puts on a Barry Fitzgerald accent which I don't think is a bit funny though I have to smile because he's the boss and I want the seventy-five dollars every Friday.

At noon we sit on the platform with our lunches from the diner on the corner, long liverwurst and onion sandwiches dripping with mustard and Rheingold beer so cold it gives me a pain in my forehead. The Irish talk about the drinking they did last night and they laugh over their great sufferings in the morning. Italians eat the food they've brought from home and don't know how we can eat that liverwurst shit. The Irish are offended and want to fight except that Eddie Lynch says anyone in a fight on this platform can go looking for a job.

There's one black man, Horace, and he sits away from the rest of us. He smiles once in a while and says nothing because that's the way it is.

When we finish at five someone will say, OK, let's go for a beer, one beer, just one, and we all laugh at the idea of one beer. We drink at bars with longshoremen from the piers who are always fighting over whether their union, the ILA, should join the AFL or the CIO and when they're not fighting about that they're fighting about unfair hiring practices. Hiring bosses and gang foremen go to different bars farther into Manhattan for fear they might have trouble along the waterfront.

There are nights when I stay out so late and I'm so confused with the drink there's no sense going back to the Bronx at all and it's just as easy to sleep on the platform where the bums keep fires going in great drums on the street till Eddie Lynch comes along with his Barry Fitzgerald accent and tells us, Off your awrse and on your feet. Even when I'm hung over I want to tell him arse is pronounced with a flat 'a' but he's from Brooklyn and he's the boss and he'll say awrse forever.

Sometimes there's night work on the piers unloading ships and if there aren't enough longshoremen with ILA cards they'll hire warehousemen like myself with Teamster cards. You have to be careful you're not taking jobs from longshoremen because they think nothing of sinking a baling hook in your skull and pushing you down between ship and dock on the chance you'll be crushed beyond recognition. They make better money on the docks than we do in the warehouses but the work is unsteady and they have to fight for it every day. I carry my own hook from the warehouse but I've never learned to used it for anything but lifting.

After three weeks at the warehouse and all the liverwurst and beer I'm scrawnier than ever. Eddie Lynch says in his Brooklyn brogue, Faith an' begorrah, I could slip you and Clifford through the awrse of a sparrow, two o' youse.

With the nights of drinking and working on the piers my eyes are flaring up again. They're worse when I have to handle sacks of hot Cuban peppers from United Fruit ships. Sometimes the only thing that will give me relief is beer and Eddie Lynch says, Jesus Christ, the kid is so desperate for the beer he's pouring it through his eyes.

The warehouse money is good and I should be content except that there's nothing in my head but confusion and darkness. The Third Avenue El is packed every morning with people in suits and dresses, fresh and clean and happy in themselves. If they're not reading newspapers they're talking and I hear them describing their vacation plans or bragging about how well their children are doing in school or college. I know they'll work every day till they're old and silver-haired and they'll be content with their children and grandchildren and I wonder if I'll ever live like that.

In June the papers are filled with stories about university commencement exercises and pictures of happy graduates and their families. I try to look at the pictures but the train rocks and jolts and I'm thrown against passengers who give me superior looks because of my work clothes. I want to announce that this is only temporary, that one day I'll be going to school and wearing a suit like them.

21

I wish I could be stronger at the warehouse and say no when someone laughs about going for a beer, one beer, just one. I should say no especially when I'm supposed to meet Emer to go to a movie or eat a piece of chicken. Sometimes after hours of drinking I call her and tell her I had to work overtime but she knows better and the more I lie the colder her voice and there's no use calling and lying anymore.

Then, deep into the summer, Tom tells me Emer is going with someone else, she's engaged, she's wearing a big ring from her fiancé, an insurance man from the Bronx.

She won't talk to me on the phone and when I knock on her door she won't let me in. I beg her for a minute so that I can tell her how I'm a changed man, how I'm going to mend my ways and lead a decent life, no more stuffing myself with liverwurst sandwiches, no more guzzling beer till I can hardly stand.

She won't let me in. She's engaged and there's a glint of diamond on her hand that sends me into such a wildness I want to pound the wall, tear out my hair, throw myself on the floor at her feet. I don't want to stumble away from her to Logan's boarding house and the one towel and the warehouses and the docks and the drinking till all hours while the rest of the world, Emer and her insurance man included, lead clean lives with towels galore, all happy on graduation day and smiling with their perfect American teeth brushed after every meal. I want her to take me in so that we can talk about the days before us when I'll have a suit and an office job and we'll have our own apartment and I'll be safe from the world and all temptation.

She won't let me in. She has to go now. She has to see someone and I know it's the insurance man.

Is he inside?

She says no but I know he is and I yell that I want to see him, trot the bugger out and I'll deal with him, I'll lay him out.

Then she shuts the door in my face and I'm so shocked my eyes dry up and all the heat leaves my body. I'm so shocked I wonder if my life is a series of doors closed in my face, so shocked I don't even want to go to the Breffni Bar for a beer. People are passing me on the streets and cars are honking but I feel so cold and alone I could be in a prison cell. I sit on the Third Avenue El to the Bronx and think of Emer and her insurance man, how they're having a cup of tea and laughing at the way I disgraced myself, how clean and whole-some they are, the two of them, not drinking, not smoking, waving away the chicken.

I know that's the way it is around the country, people sitting in their living rooms, smiling, secure, resisting temptation, growing old together because they're able to say, No, thank you, I don't want a beer, not one.

I know Emer is acting like this because of my behavior and I know I'm the one she wants, not this man who's probably sipping tea boring her to distraction with insurance stories. Still, she might like me again and take me back if I give up the warehouse, the docks, the liverwurst, the beer, and get a decent job. There's still a chance for me since Tom told me they won't be getting married till next year and if I improve myself starting tomorrow she'll surely take me back although I don't like thinking of him sitting for months on the couch kissing her and running his paws all over her shoulder blades.

Of course he's an Irish-American Catholic, that's what Tom told me, and of course he'll respect her purity till the wedding night, this insurance man, but I know Irish-American Catholics have filthy minds. They have all the dirty dreams I have myself, especially insurance men. I know Emer's man is thinking of the things they'll be doing on their wedding night though he'll have to confess his dirty thoughts to the priest before he gets married. It's a good thing I'm not getting married myself because I'd have to confess to the things I did with women all over Bavaria and across the border to Austria itself and sometimes even Switzerland.

There's an employment agency advertisement in the paper offering office jobs, steady, secure, well-paid, six-week paid training session, suit and tie required, preference given veterans.

The application form wants to know where I graduated from high school and when and that forces me to lie, Christian Brothers Secondary School, Limerick, Ireland, June 1947.

The agency man tells me the name of the company offering employment, Blue Cross.

Sir, what kind of company is that?

Insurance.

But.

But what?

Oh, it's all right, sir.

It's all right because I realize if I'm hired by this insurance company I might move up in the world and Emer will take me back. All she has to do is choose between two insurance men even if the other one has already given her a diamond ring.

Before I can even talk to her again I have to finish my six-week training course at the Blue Cross. The offices are on Fourth Avenue in a building with an entrance like the door of a cathedral. There are seven men in the training session, all high school graduates, one so badly wounded from the Korean War his mouth has moved around to the side of his head and he dribbles on his shoulder. It takes days to understand what he's trying to say, that he wants to work for Blue Cross so that he can help veterans like himself who were wounded and have no one. Then a few days into the course he discovers he's in the wrong place, that it was the Red Cross he wanted all along and he curses the instructor for not telling him before. We're glad to see him go even after the way he suffered for America but it's hard to be sitting all day with a man whose mouth is on the side of his head.

The instructor is Mr Puglio and the first thing he tells us is that he's studying for his master's degree in business at NYU and, second, all the information we wrote on our application will be carefully checked, so if anyone claims he went to college, and didn't, correct it now or else. The one thing Blue Cross won't tolerate is a lie.

The boarders at Logan's laugh every morning when I put on my suit, shirt, tie. They laugh even harder when they hear what my pay is, forty-seven dollars a week rising to fifty when I finish the training session.

There are only eight boarders left. Ned Guinan went home to Kildare to look at horses and die and two others married waitresses from Schrafft's who are famous for saving up to go home and buy the old family farm. The towel marked Top and Bottom is still there but no one uses it after Peter McNamee caused a sensation by going out and buying a towel of his own. He says he was weary of looking at grown men dripping after their showers walking around and shaking themselves dry like old dogs, men who would squander half their wages on whiskey but couldn't see their way to buying a towel. He says it was the last straw one Saturday when five boarders sat around on their beds drinking duty-free Irish whiskey from Shannon Airport, talking and singing along with an Irish radio program, putting themselves in the mood for a dance in Manhattan that night. After they took showers the towel was useless and instead of walking around to shake themselves dry they began to dance jigs and reels to the music on the radio and they were having a grand time except that Nora from Kilkenny came to replace toilet paper and walked in without knocking and when she saw what she saw she screamed like a banshee and ran up the stairs hysterical to Mr Logan who came down to find the dancers rolling around naked and laughing and not giving a fiddler's fart about Mr Logan and his yelling that they were a disgrace to the Irish nation and Mother Church and he had a good mind to throw the lot of them into the street in their pelts and what kind of mothers did they have at all. He went back upstairs mumbling because he'd never evict five boarders paying eighteen dollars each a week.

When Peter brought his own towel home everyone was astonished and tried to borrow it but he told them bugger off and hid it in various places though hiding it was a problem because a towel, to dry, needs to be hung up and will only grow damp and musty if folded and hidden under the mattress or the bathtub itself. It made Peter bitter that he couldn't hang his towel to dry till Nora from Kilkenny told him she'd take it upstairs and watch over it while it dried, she and Mr Logan were that grateful for the meat he never failed to deliver every Friday night. That was a nice solution till Mr Logan became agitated every time Peter went up for his dry towel and chatted a few minutes with Nora from Kilkenny. Mr Logan would stare at his baby boy, Luke, then at Peter and back again at the baby and his frown would grow so severe his eyebrows met. He could stand it no longer and called up the stairs, Does it take all day, Peter, to get your dry towel? Nora has work to do in this house. Peter would come down the stairs. Ah, sorry, Mr Logan, very sorry, but that doesn't satisfy Mr Logan who is staring at little Luke again and back at Peter. I have something to tell you, Peter. We won't be needing your meat anymore and you'll have to find a way to keep your towel dry yourself. Nora has enough to do without standing guard over your towel while it dries.

That night there is screaming and yelling in the Logan room and next morning Mr Logan pins a note to Peter's towel telling him he'll have to leave, that he's caused too much damage to the Logan family the way he took advantage of their good nature in the matter of drying the towel.

Peter doesn't mind. He's moving out to Long Island to his cousin's house. We'll all miss him, the way he opened up the world of towels to us, and now we all have them, they're hanging everywhere and everyone is honorable about not using other men's towels because they never dry anyway in the dampness of the basement bedroom.

22

It's easier traveling on the train every morning in my suit and tie and the *New York Times* held up so that the world will see I'm not the kind of yob that reads comics in the *Daily News* or the *Mirror*. People will see that this is a man in a suit that can handle big words on his way to an important job in an insurance office.

I might be wearing a suit and reading the *Times* and getting admiring looks but I still can't help committing my daily deadly sin, Envy. I see the college students with the covers on their books, Columbia, Fordham, NYU, CCNY, and I feel empty thinking I'll never be one of them. I'd like to go to one of the bookshops and buy college book covers I could flaunt on the train except I know I'd be found out and laughed at.

Mr Puglio teaches us the different health insurance policies offered by Blue Cross, family, individual, company, widows, orphans, veterans, cripples. When he teaches he becomes excited and tells us it's a wonderful thing to sleep at night knowing people have nothing to worry about if they get sick as long as they have Blue Cross. We sit in a small room where the air is thick with cigarette smoke for lack of a window and it's hard to stay awake on a summer's afternoon with Mr Puglio getting worked up over premiums. Every Friday he gives us a test and it's a misery on Monday when he praises the higher scorers and frowns at the low scorers like me. My scores are low because I don't care about insurance and I wonder if Emer is in her right mind getting engaged to an insurance man when she could be with a man who went from training German shepherds to typing the fastest morning reports in the European Command. I feel like calling her up and telling her now that I'm inside the insurance business it's driving me mad and is she happy she did this to me. I could still be working at Port Warehouses enjoying my liverwurst and beer if she hadn't broken my heart entirely. I'd like to call her but I'm afraid she'll be cold and that will drive me to the Breffni Bar for relief.

Tom is at the Breffni and he says the best thing is to let the wound heal, have a drink, and where did you get that awful suit. It's bad enough to be suffering over the Blue Cross and Emer without having your suit sneered at and when I tell Tom fuck off he laughs and tells me I'll live. He's moving out of the boarding house himself to a small apartment in Woodside, Queens, and if I'd like to share the cost is ten dollars a week, cook our own food.

Once again I feel like calling Emer and telling her about my big job at Blue Cross and the apartment I'm getting in Queens but her face is fading in my memory and there's another place in my mind that tells me I'm glad to be single in New York.

If Emer doesn't want me what's the use of being in the insurance business where I'm suffocated every day in an airless room with Mr Puglio becoming hostile whenever I doze off? It's hard to sit there when he tells us that the first duty of a married man is to train his wife to be a widow and I daydream about Mrs Puglio getting the widow lecture. Does Mr Puglio give her the lecture at the dinner table or sitting up in the bed?

On top of everything my appetite is gone from sitting all day in my suit and if I buy a liverwurst sandwich I throw most of it to the pigeons in Madison Park.

I sit in that park and listen to men in white shirts and ties talking about their jobs, the stock market, the insurance business, and I wonder if they're content knowing this is what they'll be doing till their hair turns grey. They tell each other how they told off the boss, how he didn't have a word to say, his mouth going like this, you know, him stuck to his chair. They'll be bosses themselves some day with people telling them off and how will they like that. There are days I'd give anything to be strolling along the banks of the Shannon or out the Mulcaire River or even climbing the mountains behind Lenggries.

One of the Blue Cross trainees passes me on his way back to the office.

Yo, McCourt, it's two o'clock. You coming?

He says yo because he drove a tank in a cavalry outfit in Korea and that's how they talked when the cavalry had horses. He says yo because that tells the world he wasn't an ordinary infantry soldier.

We walk to the insurance building and I know I can't go through that cathedral entrance. I know I'm not cut out for the world of insurance.

Yo, McCourt, come on, it's late. Puglio will have a shit fit.

I'm not going in.

What?

Not going in.

I walk away down Fourth Avenue.

Yo, McCourt, you crazy, man? You gonna be fired. Shit, man, I gotta go.

I keep going in the bright July sun till I reach Union Square where I sit and wonder what have I done. They say if you quit a job in any big firm or get fired all the other firms are informed and doors are closed to you forever. Blue Cross is a big firm and I might as well give up hope of ever having a big job in any big firm. But it's a good thing I quit now rather than wait to have the lies on my application form discovered. Mr Puglio told us that was such a serious offence you'd not only be fired but Blue Cross would demand repayment of the wages paid for the training session and on top of that your name is sent to all the other big firms with a little red flag waving at the top of the page to warn them. That little red flag, said Mr Puglio, means you're forever barred from the American corporate system and you might as well move to Russia.

Mr Puglio loved talking like that and I'm glad I'm away from him, leaving Union Square to stroll down Broadway with all the other New Yorkers who don't seem to have anything to do. It's easy to see that some have that little red flag on their names, men with beards and jewelry and women with long hair and sandals who would never be allowed inside the door of the American corporate system.

There are New York places I'm seeing today for the first time, City Hall, the Brooklyn Bridge in the distance, a Protestant church, St Paul's, which has the grave of Thomas Addis Emmet, brother of Robert who was hanged for Ireland, and farther down Broadway, Trinity Church, looking the length of Wall Street.

Down where the Staten Island ferries come and go there's a bar, the Bean Pot, where I have the appetite for a whole liverwurst sandwich and a stein of beer because my tie is off and my jacket is over the back of a chair and I feel relieved I escaped with the little red flag on my name. There's something about finishing the liverwurst sandwich that tells me I've lost Emer forever. If she ever hears of my troubles with the American corporate system she might shed a tear of pity for me though she'll be grateful in the long run she settled for the insurance man from the Bronx. She'll be secure knowing she's insured for everything, that she can't take a step that's not covered by insurance.

It's a nickel for the Staten Island ferry and the sight of the Statue of Liberty and Ellis Island reminds me of the morning in October, 1949, I sailed into New York on the *Irish Oak*, past the city and up the river to anchor that night in Poughkeepsie and on the next day to Albany where I took the train back down to New York.

That was nearly four years ago and here I am on the Staten Island ferry with my tie stuffed in the pocket of the jacket hanging from my shoulder. Here I am without a job in the world, my girlfriend gone, and the little red flag waving on my name. I could go back to the Biltmore Hotel and take up where I left off, cleaning the lobby, scouring toilet bowls, laying carpet, but no, a man who was a corporal can never sink that low again.

Looking at Ellis Island and an old wooden ferry rotting between two buildings makes me think of all the people who passed here before me, before my father and mother, all the people escaping the Famine in Ireland, all the people from all over Europe landing here with their hearts in their mouths for fear they might be caught with diseases and sent back and when you think of that a great moaning moves across the water from Ellis Island and you wonder if the people sent back had to return with their babies to places like Czechoslovakia and Hungary. People who were sent back like that were the saddest people in all of history, worse than people like me who might have bad eyes and the little red flag but are still secure with the American passport.

They won't let you stay on the ferry when it docks. You have to go inside, pay your nickel and wait for the next ferry and while I'm there I might as well have a beer at the terminal bar. I keep thinking about my mother and father sailing into this harbor over twenty-five years ago and as I sail back and forth on the ferry, six times, having a beer at each end, I keep thinking of the people with diseases who were sent back and that makes me so sad I leave the ferry altogether to call Tom Clifford at Port Warehouses and ask him to meet me at the Bean Pot so that I'll know how to get home to the small apartment in Queens.

He meets me at the Bean Pot and when I tell him the liverwurst sandwiches here are delicious he says he's finished with liverwurst, he's moving on. Then he laughs and tells me I must have had a few, that I'm having trouble getting my tongue around the word liverwurst and I tell him, no, it's the day I've had with Puglio and the Blue Cross and the airless room and the little red flag and the ones who were sent back, the saddest of all.

He doesn't know what I'm talking about. He tells me my eyes are crossing in my head, put on my jacket, home to Queens and into the bed.

Mr Campbell Groel takes me back at Port Warehouses and I'm glad to be getting decent wages again, seventy-five dollars a week going up to seventy-seven for operating the forklift truck two days a week. Regular platform work means you're on your feet in the truck loading pallets with boxes, crates, sacks of fruits and peppers. Working the forklift is easier. You hoist up the loaded pallets, store them inside and wait for the next load. No one minds if you read the paper while you wait but if you read the *New York Times* they laugh and say, Look at the big intellectual on the forklift.

One of my jobs is to store bags of hot peppers off United Fruit ships in the fumigation room. On a slow day it's a good place to bring in a beer, read the paper, take a nap, and no one seems to mind. Even Mr Campbell Groel on his way out of the office might look in and smile, Take it easy, men. It's a hot day.

Horace, the black man, sits on a bag of peppers and reads a paper from Jamaica or he reads a letter over and over from his son who is in university in Canada. When he reads that letter he slaps his thigh and laughs, Oh, mon, oh, mon. The first time I ever heard him talk his accent sounded so Irish I asked him if he was from County Cork and he couldn't stop laughing. He said, All people from the islands have Irish blood, mon.

Horace and I nearly died together in that fumigation room. The beer and the heat made us so drowsy we fell asleep on the floor till we heard the door slam shut and the gas hissing into the room. We tried to push the door back but it was jammed and the gas was making us sick till Horace climbed up on a mound of pepper sacks, broke a window and called for help. Eddie Lynch was closing up outside and heard us and slid the door back.

You're two lucky bastards, he said, and he wanted to take us up the street for a few beers to clear our lungs and to celebrate. Horace says, No, mon, I can't go to that bar.

What the hell you talking about? says Eddie.

Black man not welcome in that bar.

Fuck that for a story, says Eddie.

No, mon, no trouble. There's another place we have a beer, mon.

I don't know why Horace has to give in like that. He has a son in university in Canada and he can't have a beer himself in a New York bar. He tells me I don't understand, that I'm young and I can't fight the black man's fight.

Eddie says, Yeah, you're right, Horace.

In a few weeks Mr Campbell Groel says the Port of New York is not what it used to be, business is slow, he has to lay off a few men and, of course, I'm the junior man, the first to go.

A few blocks away is Merchants Refrigerating Company and they need a platform man to fill in for men on summer vacation. They tell me, We might be having a heat wave but dress warm.

My job is unloading meat from the freezer trucks that bring sides of beef from Chicago. It's August on the platform but inside where we hang the meat it's freezing. The men laugh and say we're the only workers who travel so fast from the North Pole to the Equator and back.

Peter McNamee is platform boss while the regular man is on vacation and when he sees me he says, What in the name of the crucified Jesus are you doing here? I thought you had a brain in your head.

He tells me I should be going to school, that there's no excuse for me humping sides of beef in and out in and out when I could be using the GI Bill and moving up in the world. He says this is no job for the Irish. They come here and the next thing they're hacking and coughing up blood discovering they had TB all along, the curse of the Irish race but the last generation to be afflicted. It's Peter's job to report if anyone is hacking or coughing all over the sides of beef. Board of Health inspectors would close the place down in a minute and we'd be on the street scratching our arses looking for work.

Peter tells me he's weary of the whole game himself. He couldn't get along with the cousin on Long Island and now he's back in another boarding house in the Bronx and it's the same old game, bring home the side of beef or any kind of meat on a Friday night and he gets the free lodging. His mother torments him with her letters. Why can't he find a nice girl and settle down and give her a grandson or is he waiting for her to sink into the grave? She nags him so much about finding a wife he doesn't want to read her letters anymore.

My second Friday at Merchants Refrigerating Peter wraps the side of beef in newspaper and asks me if I'd like a drink up the street. He rests the side of beef on a bar stool but the meat begins to defrost and there are blood spots and that upsets the bartender. He tells Peter he can't have that kind of thing in the bar and he'd better put it somewhere. Peter says, All right, all right, and when the bartender isn't looking he takes the side of beef into the men's lavatory and leaves it there. He returns to the bar and when he starts talking about the way his mother nags him he shifts from beer to whiskey. The bartender sympathizes with him because they're both from the County Cavan and they tell me I wouldn't understand.

There's a sudden roar from the men's lavatory and a big man stumbles out yelling that there's a huge rat sitting on the toilet seat. The bartender barks at Peter, Damn it to hell, McNamee, is that where you put that goddam meat? Get it outa this bar.

Peter retrieves his meat. Come on, McCourt, that's the end of it. I'm worn out dragging the meat around on Friday nights. I'm going to a dance to get a wife.

We take a taxi to the Jaeger House but they won't let Peter in with the meat. He offers to leave it at the coat check but they won't accept it. He creates a disturbance and when the manager says, Come on, come on, get that meat outa here, Peter swings at him with the side of beef. The manager calls for help and Peter and I are pushed down the stairs by two big men from Kerry. Peter yells that he's only looking for a wife and they should be ashamed of themselves. The Kerrymen laugh and tell him he's an arsehole and if he doesn't behave himself they'll wrap that meat around his head. Peter stands still in the middle of the sidewalk and gives the Kerrymen a peculiar sober look. You're right, he says, and offers them the meat. They won't take it. He offers it to people passing by but they shake their heads and hurry past him.

I don't know what to do with this meat, he says. Half the world is starving but no one wants my meat.

We go to Wright's Restaurant on Eighty-Sixth Street and Peter asks if they'd give us two dinners in exchange for a side of beef. No, they can't do that. Board of Health regulations. He runs to the middle of the street, lays the meat on the center line, runs back and laughs at the way cars swerve to avoid the meat, laughs even more when there's the sound of sirens and a police car and an ambulance scream around the corner and stop with flashing lights and men stand around the meat scratching their heads and then laughing till they drive away with the meat in the back of the police car.

He seems to be sober now and we order eggs and bacon at Wright's. It's Friday, says Peter, but I don't give a shit. That's the last time I'll drag meat through the streets and subways of New York. I'm tired of being Irish anyway. I'd like to wake up in the morning and be nothing or some kind of American Protestant. So will you pay for my eggs because I have to save my money and go to Vermont and be nothing.

And he walks out the door.

23

On a slow day at Merchants Refrigerating we're told we can go home. Instead of taking the train back to Queens I walk up Hudson Street and stop at a bar called the White Horse Tavern. I'm nearly twenty-three but I have to prove I'm eighteen before they'll give me a beer and a knockwurst sandwich. It's quiet in the bar even though I've read in the paper it's a favorite place of poets, especially the wild man, Dylan Thomas. People sitting at tables by the windows look like poets and artists and they're probably wondering why I'm sitting at the bar with trousers caked with beef blood. I wish I could sit there by the windows with a long-haired girl and tell her how I've read Dostoyevsky and how Herman Melville got me thrown out of the hospital in Munich.

There's nothing to do but sit at the bar tormenting myself with questions. What am I doing here with this knockwurst and beer? What am I doing in the world at all? Will I spend the rest of my life hauling sides of beef from truck to freezer and vice versa? Will I end my days in a small apartment in Queens while Emer is happy raising a family in a suburb completely protected by insurance? Will I ride the subways all my life envying people carrying books from universities?

I shouldn't be eating knockwurst at a time like this. I shouldn't be drinking beer when I don't have an answer in my head. I shouldn't be in this bar with poets and artists all sitting there with their serious whispered conversations. I'm weary of knockwurst and liverwurst and the feel of frozen meat on my shoulders every day.

I push the knockwurst away and leave a half stein of beer and walk out the door, across Hudson Street, along Bleecker Street, not knowing where I'm going but knowing I have to keep walking till I know where I'm going, and here I am in Washington Square and there's New York University and I know that's where I have to go with my GI Bill, high school or no high school. A student points to the admissions office and the woman gives me an application. She says I didn't fill it in properly, that they need to know my high school graduation, where and when.

I never went.

You never went to high school?

No, but I have the GI Bill and I've been reading books all my life.

Oh, my, but we require high school graduation or the equivalency.

But I read books. I've read Dostoyevsky and I've read *Pierre, or The Ambiguities*. It's not as good as *Moby Dick* but I read it in a hospital in Munich.

You actually read *Moby Dick*?

I did and *Pierre, or The Ambiguities* got me thrown out of the hospital in Munich.

I can see she doesn't understand. She goes into another office with my application and brings out the Dean of Admissions, a woman with a kind face. The Dean tells me I'm an unusual case and wants to know about my schooling in Ireland. It's her experience that European students are better prepared for college work and she will allow me to enroll at NYU if I can maintain a B average for a year. She wants to know what kind of work I do and when I tell her about the meat she says, My, my, I learn something every day.

Since I'm not a high school graduate and work full time I'm allowed to take only two courses, Introduction to Literature and The History of Education in America. I don't know why I have to be introduced to literature but the woman in the admissions office says it's a requirement even though I've read Dostoyevsky and Melville and that's admirable for someone without a high school education. She says The History of Education in America course will provide me with the broad cultural background I need after my inadequate European education.

I'm in heaven and the first thing to do is buy the required text-books, cover them with the purple and white NYU book jackets so that people in the subway will look at me admiringly.

All I know of university classes is what I saw a long time ago in the movies in Limerick and here I am sitting in one, The History of Education in America, with Professor Maxine Green up there on the platform telling us how the Pilgrims educated their children. All around me are students scribbling away in their notebooks and I wish I knew what to scribble myself. How am I supposed to know what's important out of all the things she's saying up there? Am I supposed to remember everything? Some students raise their hands to ask questions but I could never do that. The whole class would stare at me and wonder who's the one with the accent. I could try an American accent but that never works. When I try it people always smile and say, Do I detect an Irish brogue?

The professor is saying the Pilgrims left England to escape religious persecution and that puzzles me because the Pilgrims were English themselves and the English were always the ones who persecuted everyone else, especially the Irish. I'd like to raise my hand and tell the professor how the Irish suffered for centuries under English rule but I'm sure everyone in this class has a high school diploma and if I open my mouth they'll know I'm not one of them.

Other students are easy about raising their hands and they always say, Well, I think.

Some day I'll raise my hand and say, Well, I think, but I don't know what to think about Pilgrims and their education. Then the professor tells us ideas don't drop fully formed from the skies, that the Pilgrims were, in the long run, children of the Reformation with an accompanying world-view and their attitudes to children were so informed.

There is more notebook scribbling around the room, the women busier than the men. The women scribble as if every word out of Professor Green's mouth were important.

Then I wonder why I have this fat textbook on American education which I carry in the subways so that people can admire me for being a college student. I know there will be examinations, a mid-term and a final, but where will the questions come from? If the professor talks and talks and the textbook is seven hundred pages I'll surely be lost.

There are good-looking girls in the class and I'd like to ask one if she knows what I should know before the mid-term exam in seven weeks. I'd like to go to the university cafeteria or a Greenwich Village coffee shop and chat with the girl about the Pilgrims and their Puritan ways and how they frightened the life out of their children. I could tell the girl how I read Dostoyevsky and Melville and she'd be impressed and fall in love with me and we'd study the history of education in America together. She'd make spaghetti and we'd go to bed for the excitement and then we'd sit up in the bed reading the fat textbook and wondering why people in old New England made themselves so miserable.

Men in the class look at the scribbling women and you know they're not paying the professor a scrap of attention. You know they're deciding which girls they'll talk to afterwards and when this first class ends they move towards the good-looking ones. They smile easily with their fine white teeth and they're used to chatting because that's what they did in high school where boys and girls sit together. A good-looking girl will always have someone waiting for her in the hall outside and the man in the class who started chatting with her will lose his smile.

The lecturer in the Saturday morning class is Mr Herbert. The girls in the class seem to like him and they must know him from other classes because they ask him about his honeymoon. He smiles and jingles the change in his trouser pocket and tells us about his honeymoon and I wonder what this has to do with Introduction to Literature. Then he asks us to write two hundred words on an author we'd like to meet and why. My author is Jonathan Swift and I write that I'd like to meet him because of *Gulliver's Travels*. A man with an imagination like that would be a great one to have a cup of tea or a pint with.

Mr Herbert stands on his platform, looks through the essays, and says, Hmmm, Frank McCourt. Where is Frank McCourt?

I raise my hand and feel my face turning red. Ah, says Mr Herbert, you like Jonathan Swift?

I do.

For his imagination, eh?

Yes.

His smile is gone and his voice doesn't sound friendly and I feel uncomfortable with the way everyone in the class is looking at me. He says, You do know that Swift was a satirist, don't you?

I have no notion of what he's talking about. I have to lie and say, I do.

He says, You do know he was perhaps the greatest satirist in English literature.

I thought he was Irish.

Mr Herbert looks at the class and smiles. Does that mean, Mr McCourt, that if I'm from the Virgin Islands I'm a virgin?

There is laughter around the room and I feel my face on fire. I know they're laughing at me because of the way Mr Herbert toyed with me and put me in my place. Now he tells the class that my essay is a perfect example of a simplistic approach to literature, that while *Gulliver's Travels* may be enjoyed as a children's story it is important in English literature, not Irish, ladies and gentlemen, for its satiric brilliance. He says, When we read great works of literature in college we endeavor to rise above the mundane and the childish, and when he says that he looks at me.

The class ends and the girls gather around Mr Herbert to smile and tell him how they enjoyed his honeymoon story and I feel so ashamed I walk down six flights of stairs so that I don't have to be in the elevator with students who might despise me for enjoying *Gulliver's Travels* for the wrong reasons or even students who might feel sorry for me. I put my books in a bag because I don't care anymore if people in the subway look at me admiringly. I can't hold on to a girl, I can't keep an office job, I make a fool of myself in my first literature class and I wonder why I left Limerick at all. If I'd stayed there and taken the exam I'd be a postman now strolling from street to street, handing out letters, chatting with the women, going home for my tea without a worry in the world. I could have read Jonathan Swift to my heart's content not giving a fiddler's fart whether he was a satirist or a seanachie.

24

Tom is in the apartment singing, making Irish stew, chatting with the wife of the landlord, the Greek downstairs with the dry cleaning shop. The landlord's wife is a thin blonde and I can see she doesn't want me to be there. I walk through Woodside to the library to borrow a book I looked at the last time I was there, Sean O'Casey's *I Knock at the Door*. It's a book about growing up poor in Dublin and I never knew you could write about things like that. It was all right for Charles Dickens to write about poor people in London but his books always end with characters discovering they're the long-lost sons of the Duke of Somerset and everyone lives happily ever after.

There is no happily ever after in Sean O'Casey. His eyes are worse than mine, so bad he can barely go to school. Still he manages to read, teaches himself to write, teaches himself Irish, writes plays for the Abbey Theatre, meets Lady Gregory and the poet Yeats, but has to leave Ireland when everyone turns against him. He would never sit in a class and let someone mock him over Jonathan Swift. He'd fight back and then walk out even if he walked into the wall with his bad eyes. He's the first Irish writer I ever read who writes about rags, dirt, hunger, babies dying. The other writers go on about farms and fairies and the mist that do be on the bog and it's a relief to discover one with bad eyes and a suffering mother.

What I'm discovering now is that one thing leads to another.

When Sean O'Casey writes about Lady Gregory or Yeats I have to look them up in the *Encyclopedia Britannica* and that keeps me busy till the librarian starts turning the light on and off. I don't know how I could have reached the age of nineteen in Limerick ignorant of all that went on in Dublin before my time. I have to go to the *Encyclopedia Britannica* to learn how famous the Irish writers were, Yeats, Lady Gregory, AE, and John Millington Synge who wrote plays where the people talk in a way I never heard in Limerick or anywhere else.

Here I am in a library in Queens discovering Irish literature, wondering why the schoolmaster never told us about these writers till I discover they were all Protestants, even Sean O'Casey whose father came from Limerick. No one in Limerick would want to give Protestants credit for being great Irish writers.

The second week of Introduction to Literature Mr Herbert says that from his personal point of view one of the most desirable ingredients in a work of literature is gusto and that is certainly found in the works of Jonathan Swift and his admirer, our friend Mr McCourt. If there is a certain innocence in Mr McCourt's apprehension of Swift it is leavened with enthusiasm. Mr Herbert tells the class I was the only one of thirty-three people who selected a truly great writer, that it discourages him to think there are people in this class who consider Lloyd Douglas or Henry Morton Robinson great writers. Now he wants to know how and when I first read Swift and I have to tell him how a blind man in Limerick paid me to read Swift to him when I was twelve.

I don't want to talk in class like this because of the shame last week but I have to do what I'm told or I might be kicked out of the university. The other students are looking at me and whispering to each other and I don't know whether they're sneering at me or admiring me. When the class ends I take the stairs again instead of the elevator but I can't get out the door at the bottom because of the sign that says Fire Exit and warns me if I push anything there will be alarms. I climb back to the sixth floor to take the elevator but that door and the doors on the other floors are locked and there's nothing to do but push the door on the ground floor till the alarm goes off and I'm taken to an office to fill out a form and write a statement as to what I was doing in that place causing alarms to go off.

There's no use making a statement about my troubles with the teacher who mocked me the first week and praised me the second week, so I write that even though I dread elevators I'll take them from this day out. I know this is what they want to hear and I learned from the army it's easier to tell people in offices what they want to hear because if you don't there's always someone higher up who wants you to fill out a longer form.

25

Tom says he's tired of New York, he's going to Detroit where he knows people and he can make good money working on assembly lines in car factories. He tells me I should come with him, forget college, I won't get a degree for years and even if I do I won't make much money. If you're fast on the assembly line you're promoted to foreman and supervisor and before you know it you're in an office telling people what to do, sitting there in your suit and tie with your secretary in a chair opposite tossing her hair, crossing her legs and asking if there's anything you'd like, anything.

Of course I'd like to go with Tom. I'd like to have money to drive around Detroit in a new car with a blonde beside me, a Protestant with no sense of sin. I could go back to Limerick in bright American clothes except that they'd want to know what kind of work I was doing in America and I could never tell them I stood all day sticking bits and pieces into Buicks rolling past on the assembly line. I'd prefer to tell them I'm a student at New York University even though some would say, University? How in God's name did you ever get into a university, you that left school at fourteen and never set foot inside secondary school? They might say in Limerick I always had the makings of a swelled head, that I was too big for my boots, that I had a great notion of myself, that God put some of us here to hew wood and draw water and who do I think I am anyway after my years in the lanes of Limerick?

Horace, the black man I nearly died with in the fumigation chamber, tells me if I leave the university I'm a fool. He works to keep his son in college in Canada and that's the only way in America, mon. His wife cleans offices on Broad Street and she's happy because they've got a good boy up there in Canada and they're saving a few dollars for his graduation day in two years. Their son, Timothy, wants to be a child doctor so that he can go back to Jamaica to heal the sick children.

Horace tells me I should thank God I'm white, a young white man with the GI Bill and good health. Maybe a little trouble there with the eyes but still, better in this country to be white with bad eyes than black with good eyes. If his son ever told him he wanted to quit school to stand on an assembly line sticking cigarette lighters into cars he'd go up to Canada and break his head.

There are men in the warehouse who laugh at me and want to know why the hell I sit there with Horace during lunch hour. What is there to talk about with a guy whose grandparents just fell out of a tree? If I sit off at the end of the platform reading a book for my classes they ask if I'm some kind of a fairy and they let their hands go limp at the wrists. I'd like to sink my baling hook into their skulls but Eddie Lynch tells them cut it out, leave the kid alone, that they're ignorant slobs whose grandparents were still in the mud and wouldn't know a tree if it was rammed up their asses.

The men won't answer Eddie but they get back at me when we're unloading trucks by suddenly dropping boxes or crates so that my arms are jerked down and there's pain. If one is operating the forklift he'll try to pin me to the wall and laugh, Whoops, didn't see you there. After lunch they might act friendly and ask how I enjoyed my sandwich and if I say fine they'll say, Shit, man, didn't you taste the pigeon shit Joey spread on your ham?

There are dark clouds in my head and I want to go after Joey with my baling hook but the ham rises in my throat and I'm throwing up off the platform with the men clutching each other and laughing, the only ones not laughing are Joey at the river end of the platform looking at the sky because everyone knows he's not right in the head and Horace at the other end watching and saying nothing.

But after all the ham comes up and the retching stops I know what Horace is thinking. He's thinking that if this were his son,

Timothy, he'd tell him walk away from this and I know that's what I have to do. I walk to Eddie Lynch and pass him my baling hook, making sure to offer him the handle to avoid the insult of the hook itself. He takes it and shakes hands with me. He says, OK, kid, good luck, and we'll send your paycheck. Eddie might be a platform boss with no education who worked his way up but he knows the situation, he knows what I'm thinking. I walk to Horace and shake hands with him. I can't say anything because I have a strange feeling of love for him that makes it hard to talk and I wish he could be my father. He doesn't say anything either because he knows there are times like this when words have no meaning. He pats my shoulder and nods and the last sound I hear at Port Warehouses is Eddie Lynch, Get back to work, you bunch of limp pricks.

On a Saturday morning Tom and I ride the train to the bus station in Manhattan. He's on his way to Detroit and I'm taking my army duffel bag to a boarding house in Washington Heights. Tom gets his ticket, stows his bags in the luggage compartment, steps up on the bus and says, Are you sure? Are you sure you don't want to come to Detroit? You could have a hell of a life.

I could easily get on that bus. Everything I own is in the duffel bag and I could throw it in there with Tom's bags, get a ticket and be on my way to a great adventure with money and blondes and secretaries offering me everything, anything, but I think of Horace telling me what a fool I'd be and I know he's right and I shake my head at Tom before the bus door closes and he makes his way to his seat, smiling and waving.

All the way up to Washington Heights on the A train I'm caught between Tom and Horace, Detroit and New York University. Why couldn't I just get a job in a factory, eight to five, an hour for lunch, two weeks' vacation every year? I could go home in the evening, take a shower, go out with a girl, read a book when I felt like it. I wouldn't have to worry about professors mocking me one week, praising me the next. I wouldn't have to worry about papers and reading assignments from fat textbooks and exams. I'd be free.

But if I traveled on trains and buses in Detroit I might see students with their books and I'd wonder what kind of a fool I was to give up New York University for the sake of making money on the assembly line. I know I'd never be content without a college degree and always wondering what I missed.

Every day I'm learning how ignorant I am especially when I go for a coffee and a grilled cheese sandwich in the cafeteria at NYU. There are always crowds of students who drop their books on the floor and seem to have nothing to do but talk about their courses. They complain about professors and curse them for giving low grades. They brag about how they used the same term paper for more than one course or they laugh over the ways you can fool a professor with papers copied directly from encyclopedias or paraphrased from books. Most of the classes are so big the professors can only skim the papers and if they have assistants they don't know from shit. That's what the students say and going to college seems to be a great game with them.

Everyone talks and no one listens and I can see why. I'd like to be an ordinary student talking and complaining but I wouldn't be able to listen to people talking about something called the grade average. They talk about the average because that's what gets you into good graduate schools and that's what the parents fret over.

When they're not talking about their averages the students argue about the meaning of everything, life, the existence of God, the terrible state of the world, and you never know when someone is going to drop in the one word that gives everyone the deep serious look, existentialism. They might talk about how they want to be doctors and lawyers till one throws up his hands and declares everything is meaningless, that the only person in the world who makes any sense is Albert Camus who says your most important act every day is deciding not to commit suicide.

If ever I'm to sit with a group like this with my books on the floor and turn gloomy over how empty everything is I'll have to look up existentialism and find out who Albert Camus is. That's what I intend to do till the students start talking about the different colleges and I discover I'm in the one everyone looks down on, the School of Education. It's good to be in business school or the Washington Square College of Arts and Sciences but if you're in the School of Ed you're at the bottom of the scale. You're going to be a teacher and who wants to be a teacher. Some of the students' mothers are teachers and they don't get paid shit, man, shit. You break your ass for a bunch of kids who don't appreciate you and what do you get? *Bubkes*, that's what you get.

I know from the way they say it that *bubkes* isn't good and that's another word I have to look up along with existentialism. It gives me a dark feeling sitting there in the cafeteria listening to all the bright talk around me knowing I'll never catch up with the other students. There they are with their high school diplomas and their parents working away to send them to NYU to be doctors and lawyers but do their parents know how much time their sons and daughters spend in the cafeteria going on about existentialism and suicide? Here I am, twenty-three with no high school diploma, bad eyes, bad teeth, bad everything and what am I doing here at all. I feel lucky I didn't try to sit with the clever suicidal students. If they ever found out I wanted to be a teacher I'd be the laughing stock of the group. I should probably sit in some other part of the cafeteria with future teachers from the School of Education though that would show the world I'm with the losers who couldn't get into the good colleges.

The only thing to do is finish my coffee and grilled cheese sandwich and go to the library to look up existentialism and find out what makes Camus so sad, just in case.

26

My new landlady is Mrs Agnes Klein and she shows me a room for twelve dollars a week. It's a real room, not like the end of a hallway Mrs Austin rented me on Sixty-Eighth Street. There's a bed, a desk, a chair, a small couch in the corner by the window where my brother, Michael, can sleep when he comes from Ireland in a few months.

I'm hardly in the door when Mrs Klein is telling me her history. She tells me I'm not to jump to any conclusions. Her name might be Klein but that was her husband who was Jewish. Her own name is Canty and I should know very well you can't get more Irish than that and if I have no place to go at Christmas I can spend it with her and her son, Michael, what's left of him. Her husband, Eddie, was the cause of all her troubles. Just before the war he ran off to Germany with their four-year-old son, Michael, because his mother was dying and he expected to inherit her fortune. Of course they were rounded up, the whole tribe of Kleins, mother and all, and ended up in a camp. No use telling the damn Nazis Michael was an American citizen born in Washington Heights. The husband was never seen again, but Michael survived and, at the end of the war, the poor kid was able to tell the Americans who he was. She tells me what's left of him is in a little room down the hall. She says I should come to her kitchen Christmas Day about two in the afternoon and have a little drink before dinner. There won't be turkey. She'd like to cook European, if I don't mind. She tells me don't say yes unless I mean it, that I don't have to come for Christmas dinner if I have some place to go, some Irish girl making mashed potatoes. Don't worry about her. It wouldn't be her first Christmas with no one but Michael at the end of the hall, what's left of him.

On Christmas Day there are strange smells from the kitchen and there's Mrs Klein pushing things around in a frying pan. Pierogis, she says, Polish. Michael loves them. Have a vodka with a little orange juice. Good for you this time of year with the flu coming on.

We sit in her living room with our drinks, and she talks about her husband. She says we wouldn't be sitting around drinking vodka and cooking up the old pierogis if he were here. For him Christmas was business as usual.

She leans over to adjust a light and her wig falls off and the vodka in me makes me laugh out loud at the sight of her skull with little tufts of brown hair. Go ahead, she says. Some day your mother's wig will fall off and we'll see if you laugh then. And she claps the wig back on her head.

I tell her my mother has a fine head of hair and she says, No wonder. Your mother never had a lunatic husband that walked into the arms of the Nazis, for Christ's sakes. If it wasn't for him Michael what's left of him would be out of that bed there, having a vodka with his poor mouth watering for his pierogis. Oh, my God, the pierogis.

She jumps from her chair and runs to the kitchen. Well, they're a little burned, but that only makes them nice and crisp. My philosophy is, do you want to know my philosophy? is whatever goes against you in the kitchen you can turn it to your advantage. We might as well have another vodka while I cook the sauerkraut and kielbasa.

She pours the drinks and barks at me when I ask her what kielbasa is. She says she can't believe the ignorance in the world. Two years in the US Army and you don't know from kielbasa? No wonder the Communists are taking over. It's Polish, for Christ's sakes, sausage, and you should watch me fry it in case you marry someone who's not Irish, a nice girl who might demand her kielbasa.

We stay in the kitchen with another vodka while the kielbasa sizzles and the sauerkraut stews with a vinegar smell. Mrs Klein puts three plates on a tray and pours a glass of Manischewitz for Michael what's left of him He loves it, she says, loves the Manischewitz with the pierogis and kielbasa.

I follow her through her bedroom into a small dark room where Michael, what's left of him, sits up in the bed, staring ahead. We bring in chairs and use his bed as a table. Mrs Klein turns on the radio and we listen to oompah oompah accordion music. That's his favorite music, she says. Anything European. He gets nostalgic, you know, nostalgic for Europe, for Christ's sakes. Don't you, Michael? Don't you? I'm talking to you. Merry Christmas, Michael, merry goddam Christmas. She tears off her wig and throws it into a corner. No more pretending, Michael. I've had it. Talk to me or next year I cook American. Next year the turkey, Michael, the stuffing, the cranberry sauce, the works, Michael.

He stares straight ahead and the kielbasa grease glistens around his plate. His mother fiddles with the radio till she finds Bing Crosby singing "White Christmas".

Better get used to it, Michael. Next year Bing and the stuffing. To hell with kielbasa.

She pushes her plate aside on the bed and falls asleep with her head by Michael's elbow. I wait awhile, take my dinner to the kitchen, dump it into the garbage, return to my room and fall into my own bed.

Timmy Coin works at Merchants Refrigerating Company and lives at Mary O'Brien's boarding house at 720 West 180 Street around the corner from where I live. He tells me drop in any time for a cup of tea, Mary is that friendly.

It's not a real boarding house, it's a big apartment, and there are four boarders each paying eighteen dollars a week. They get a decent breakfast anytime they like not like Logan's in the Bronx where we had to go to Mass or be in a state of grace. Mary herself would rather sit in her kitchen on a Sunday morning, drinking tea, smoking cigarettes and smiling over the boarders and their stories of how they got these desperate hangovers that make them swear never again. She tells me I can always move in there if one of the boys leaves to go back to Ireland. They're always going back, she says. They think they can get a few dollars together and settle down on the old farm with some girl from the village but what do you do night after night with nothing but the wife opposite you knitting by the light of the fire and you thinking of the lights of New York, the dance halls on the East Side and the lovely cozy bars on Third Avenue.

I'd like to move into Mary O'Brien's to get away from Mrs Agnes Klein who seems to stand forever on the other side of her door waiting for me to turn the key in the lock so that she can shove a vodka and orange juice into my hand. It doesn't matter to her that I have to read or write papers for my classes at NYU. It doesn't matter that I'm worn out from the midnight shift on the piers or warehouse platforms. She wants to tell me the story of her life, how Eddie charmed her ass off better than any Irishman and watch out for the Jewish girls, Frank, they can be very charming, too, and very what-do-you-call-it? very sensual and before you know it you're stepping on the glass.

Stepping on the glass?

That's right, Frank. Do you mind if I call you Frank? They won't marry you without you stepping on the wine glass, smashing it. Then they want you to convert so the kids will be Jewish and inherit everything. But I wouldn't. I was going to but my mother said if I ever turned Jewish she'd throw herself off the George Washington Bridge and between you and me I didn't give a shit if she jumped and bounced off a passing tugboat. She's not the one that stopped me from turning Jewish. I kept the faith for my dad, decent man, little problem with the drink, but what could you expect with a name like Canty that's all over the County Kerry which I expect to see some day if God grants me health. They say the County Kerry is so green and pretty and I never see green. I see nothing but this apartment and the supermarket, nothing but this apartment and Michael what's left of him at the end of the hall. My father said it would break his heart if I became Jewish, not that he had anything against them, poor suffering people, but hadn't we suffered, too, and was I going to turn my back on generations of people getting hanged and burned right and left? He came to the wedding but not my mother. She said what I was doing was putting Christ back up there suffering on the cross, wounds an' all. She said people in Ireland starved to death before they'd take the Protestant soup and what would they say about my behavior? Eddie held me in his arms and told me he had trouble with his family, too, told me when you love someone you can tell the whole world kiss your ass, and look what happened to Eddie, wound up in a goddam oven, God forgive the language.

She sits on my bed, puts her glass on the floor, covers her face with her hands. Jesus, Jesus, she says. I can't sleep thinking what they did to him and what did Michael see? What did Michael see? I saw the pictures in the papers. Jesus. And I know them, the Germans. They live here. They have delicatessens and children and I ask them, Did you kill my Eddie? and they look at me.

She cries, lies back on my bed and falls asleep and I don't know if I should wake her and tell her I'm worn out myself, that I'm paying twelve dollars a week so that she can fall asleep in my bed while I try to sleep on the hard couch in the corner which is waiting for my brother Michael coming here in a few months.

I tell this to Mary O'Brien and her boarders and they get hysterical laughing. Mary says, Ah, God love her. I know poor Agnes and all belongin' to her. There are days she loses her wits entirely and wanders the neighborhood without her wig asking everyone where's the rabbi so that she can convert for the sake of her son, poor Michael in the bed what's left of him.

Every fortnight two nuns come to help Mrs Klein. They wash Michael what's left of him and change his sheets. They clean the apartment and watch over her while she takes a bath. They brush her wig so that it doesn't have that tangled look. She doesn't know it but they weaken her vodka with water and if she gets drunk it's all in her head.

Sister Mary Thomas is curious about me. Do I practice my religion and what school do I go to because she sees books and notebooks? When I tell her NYU she frowns and wonders if I'm not worried about losing my religion in such a place. I can't tell her I stopped going to Mass years ago, she and Sister Beatrice are so good to Mrs Klein and Michael in the bed what's left of him.

Sister Mary Thomas whispers to me something I'm never to tell another soul unless it's a priest, that she took the liberty of baptizing Michael. After all, he's not really Jewish since his mother is Irish Catholic and Sister would hate to think what might happen to Michael if he died without the sacrament. Didn't he suffer enough in Germany, little boy looking at his father being led off or worse? And doesn't he deserve the purification of baptism in case he doesn't wake up some morning in there in the bed?

She wants to know now what is my situation here? Am I encouraging Agnes to drink or is it vice-versa? I tell her I don't have time for anything I'm so busy with school and work and trying to sleep a little. She wants to know if I'd do her a little favor, something to ease her soul. If I have a moment and poor Agnes is sleeping or passed out with the watery vodka would I go down the hall, kneel by Michael's bed and say a few Hail Marys, maybe a decade of the rosary. He might not understand but you never know. With God's help the Hail Marys might sink into his poor troubled brain and help him return to the realm of the living, back to the True Faith which came down to him on his mother's side.

If I do that she'll pray for me. Above all, she'll pray that I leave NYU which everyone knows is a hotbed of Communism where I'm in great danger of losing my immortal soul and what doth it profit a man if he gain the world and lose his immortal soul? God knows there must be a place for me at Fordham or St John's which are not hotbeds of atheistic Communism like NYU. I'd be better off out of NYU before Senator McCarthy goes after it, God bless him and keep him. Isn't that right, Sister Beatrice?

The other nun nods yes because she's always so busy she rarely speaks. While Sister Mary Thomas tries to save my soul from atheistic communism Sister Beatrice is giving Mrs Klein a bath or cleaning Michael what's left of him. Sometimes when Sister Beatrice opens Michael's door the smell that drifts up the hall is enough to make you sick but that doesn't stop her from going in. She still washes him and changes his bedclothes and you can hear her humming hymns. If Mrs Klein has drunk too much and gets cranky over having to take a bath Sister Beatrice holds her, hums her hymns, and strokes the little brown tufts on her skull till Mrs Klein is a child in her arms. That makes Sister Mary Thomas impatient and she tells Mrs Klein, You have no right to waste our time like this. We have other poor souls to visit, Catholics, Mrs Klein, Catholics.

Mrs Klein whimpers, I'm a Catholic. I'm a Catholic.

That's debatable, Mrs Klein.

And if Mrs Klein sobs Sister Beatrice holds her harder, presses her whole open hand on her head and hums away with a little smile towards heaven. Sister Mary Thomas waggles her finger at me and tells me, Beware of marrying outside the True Faith. This is what happens.

27

There's a letter telling me report to my faculty advisor in the English Department, Mr Max Bogart. He says my grades are unsatisfactory, B minus in The History of Education in America and C in Introduction to Literature. I'm supposed to maintain a B average on my year's probation if I want to stay in college. After all, he says, the Dean did you a favor letting you in without a high school diploma and now you let her down.

I have to work.

What do you mean you have to work? Everyone has to work.

I have to work nights, sometimes days, on piers, in warehouses.

He says I have to make a decision, work or college. He'll give me a break this time and put me on probation on top of the probation I already have. Next June he wants to see me with a straight B average or better.

I never thought college would be all numbers and letters and grades and averages and people putting me on probation. I thought this would be a place where kindly learned men and women would teach in a warm way and if I didn't understand they'd pause and explain. I didn't know I'd go from course to course with dozens of students, sometimes over a hundred, with professors lecturing and not even looking at you. Some professors look out the window or up at the ceiling and some stick their noses in notebooks and read from paper that is yellow and crumbling with age. If students ask questions they're waved away. In English novels students at Oxford and Cambridge were always meeting in professors' rooms and sipping sherry while discussing Sophocles. I'd like to discuss Sophocles, too, but I'd have to read him first and there's no time after my nights at Merchants Refrigerating.

And if I'm to discuss Sophocles and get gloomy over existentialism and the Camus suicide problem I'll have to give up Merchants Refrigerating. If I didn't have the night job I might be able to sit in the cafeteria and talk about *Pierre, or The Ambiguities* or *Crime and Punishment* or Shakespeare in general. There are girls in the cafeteria with names like Rachel and Naomi and they're the ones Mrs Klein told me about, Jewish girls who are very sensual. I wish I had the courage to talk to them because they're probably like Protestant girls, all in a state of despair over the emptiness of it all, no sense of sin and ready for all kinds of sensuality.

In the spring of 1954 I'm a full-time student at NYU working only part-time on the docks and the warehouses or when the Manpower agency sends me on a temporary job. The first one is at a hat factory on Seventh Avenue where the owner, Mr Meyer, tells me it's easy work. All I have to do is take these women's hats, neutral colors all of them, dip these feathers into different dye pots, let the feather dry, match the color against the hat, attach feather to hat. Easy, right? Yeah, that's what you'd think, says Mr Meyer, but when I let some of my Puerto Rican help try this job they came up with color combinations that would blind you. These PRs think life is an Easter Parade and it ain't. You gotta have taste when you match a feather with a hat, taste, my friend. Little Jewish ladies in Brooklyn don't want to be wearing the Easter Parade on their heads on Passover, know't I mean?

He tells me I look intelligent enough, college boy, right? Easy job like this shouldn't be a problem. If it is I shouldn't even be in college. He's going away for a few days so I'll be on my own except for the Puerto Rican ladies working on the sewing machines and the cutting tables. Yeah, he says, the PR ladies will take care of you, ha ha.

I want to ask him if there are colors that match and colors that don't but he's gone. I dip feathers into pots and when I attach them to the hats the Puerto Rican women and girls start to giggle and laugh. I finish a batch of hats and they take them to shelves along the walls and bring me another batch. All the time they try not to laugh but they can't help themselves and I can't stop blushing. I try to vary the color schemes by dipping the feathers into different pots for a rainbow effect. I use a feather as a paint brush and on the other feathers I try to make dots, stripes, sunsets, moons waxing and waning, wavy rivers with fish waggling along and birds roosting, and the women laugh so hard they can't operate the sewing machines. I wish I could talk to them and ask them what I'm doing wrong. I wish I could tell them I wasn't put into this world to stick feathers on hats, that I'm a college student who trained dogs in Germany and worked on the piers.

In three days Mr Meyer returns and when he sees the hats he stops inside the door like a man paralyzed. He looks at the women and they shake their heads as if to say there's madness in the world. He says, What did you do? and I don't know what to say back. He says, Jesus. I mean are you Puerto Rican or what?

No, sir.

Irish, right? Yeah, that's it. Maybe you're color blind. I didn't ask you about that. Did I ask you about your color blindness?

No, sir.

If you're not color blind then I don't know how you can explain these combinations. You make the Puerto Ricans look dull, y'know that? Dull. I guess it's the Irish thing, no sense of color, no art, f'Chrissakes. I mean where are the Irish painters? Name one.

I can't.

You heard of Van Gogh, right? Rembrandt? Picasso?

I did.

That's what I mean. You're nice people, the Irish, great singers, John McCormack. Great cops, politicians, priests. Lotta Irish priests but no artists. When didja ever see an Irish painting on the wall? A Murphy, a Reilly, a Rooney? Nah, kid. I think it's because your people know one color, green. Right? So my advice to you is stay away from anything to do with color. Join the cops, run for office, pick up your paycheck and have a nice life, no hard feelings.

They shake their heads in the Manpower office. They thought this would be the perfect job for me, college boy, right? What's so hard about sticking feathers on hats? Mr Meyer called them and said, Don't send me no more Irish college boys. They're color blind. Send me someone stoopid that knows colors and won't mess with my hats.

They say if I could type they'd send me out on all kinds of jobs. I tell them I can type, that I learned in the army and I'm powerful.

They send me to offices all over Manhattan. From nine to five I sit at desks and type lists, invoices, addresses on envelopes, bills of lading. Supervisors tell me what to do and talk to me only when I make mistakes. The other office workers ignore me because I'm only temporary, a temp they say, and I might not even be here tomorrow. They don't even see me. I could die at my desk and they'd talk past me about what they saw on TV last night and how they're getting outa here fast Friday afternoon and heading for the Jersey shore. They send out for coffee and pastries and don't ask me if I have a mouth in my head. Whenever anything unusual happens it's an excuse for a party. There are presents for people being promoted, getting pregnant, people getting engaged or married, and they'll all stand around the other end of the office drinking wine, eating crackers and cheese for the hour before they go home. Women will bring in their new babies and all the other women will rush over to tickle them and say, Isn't she just beautiful? Got your eyes, Miranda, definitely got your eyes. Men will say, Hi, Miranda. Looking good. Nice kid. That's all they can say because men are not supposed to be enthusiastic or excited over babies. I'm not invited to the parties and I feel strange with my typewriter clacking away and everyone having a good time. If a supervisor is giving a small speech and I'm at the typewriter they'll call across the office, Excuse me, you over there, quit the racket a minute, will ya? Can't hear ourselves think here.

I don't know how they can work in these offices day after day, year in, year out. I can't stop looking at the clock and there are times I think I'll just get up and walk away the way I did at the Blue Cross insurance company. The people in their offices don't seem to mind. They go to the water cooler, they go to the toilet, they walk from desk to desk and chat, they call from desk to desk on the telephone, they admire each other's clothes, hair, makeup, and anytime someone loses a few pounds on a diet. If a woman is told she lost weight she smiles for an hour and keeps running her hands over her hips. Office people brag about their children, their wives, their husbands and they dream about the two-week vacation.

I'm sent to an import-export firm on Fourth Avenue. I'm given a pile of papers that have to do with importing Japanese dolls. I'm supposed to copy this paper to that paper. It's nine thirty a.m. by the office clock. I look out the window. The sun is shining. A man and woman are kissing outside a coffee shop across the avenue. It's nine thirty-three a.m. by the office clock. The man and woman separate and walk in opposite directions. They turn. They run towards each other to kiss again. It's nine thirty-six a.m. by the office clock. I take my jacket from the back of the chair and slip it on. The office manager stands at his cubicle door and says, Hey, what's up? I don't answer. People are waiting for the elevator but I head for the stairs and run as fast as I can down seven flights. The kissing people have disappeared and I'm sorry. I wanted to see them once more. I hope they're not going to offices where they'll be typing lists of Japanese dolls or telling everyone they're engaged so that the officer manager will allow them an hour of wine and cheese and crackers.

With my brother Malachy in the air force sending a monthly allotment my mother is comfortable in Limerick. She has the house with gardens front and back where she can grow flowers and onions if she likes. She has enough money for clothes and bingo and excursions to the seaside at Kilkee. Alphie is in school at the Christian Brothers where he'll get a secondary school education and all kinds of opportunities. With the comfort of the new house, beds, sheets, blankets, pillows, he doesn't have to worry about battling fleas all night, there's DDT, and he doesn't have to struggle to light a fire in the grate every morning, there's the gas stove. He can have an egg every day if he likes and not even think about it the way we did. He has decent clothes and shoes and he's warm no matter how bad it is outside.

It's time for me to send for Michael so that he can come to New York and get on in the world. When he arrives he's so thin I want to take him out and fill him with hamburgers and apple pie. He stays with me awhile at Mrs Klein's and works at different jobs but there's the threat of being drafted into the army and he thinks it's better to join the air force because the uniform is a nice shade of blue, more glamorous than the shitty brown of the army uniform and more likely to attract girls. Once Malachy is out of the air force Michael can continue the monthly allotment that will keep my mother going for another three years and I will have only myself to worry about till I finish at NYU.

28

When she saunters into the psychology class the professor himself lets his jaw drop and he grips a piece of chalk so hard it cracks and breaks. He says, Excuse me, miss, and she gives him such a smile all he can do is smile back. Excuse me, miss, he says, but we're seated alphabetically and I'd need to know your name.

Alberta Small, she says, and he points to a row behind me and we don't mind one bit if she takes all day getting to her seat because we're feasting on her blonde hair, blue eyes, luscious lips, a bosom that is an occasion of sin, a figure that makes you throb in the middle of your body. A few rows back she whispers, Excuse me, and there's a shuffle and a flutter where students have to stand to let her get to her seat.

I'd like to be one of the students standing to let her by, to have her brush against me and touch me.

When the class ends I want to make sure I let her pass up the aisle so that I can watch her coming and see her going with that figure you see only in films. She passes and gives me a little smile and I wonder why God is so kind to me that He lets me have a smile from the loveliest girl in all of NYU, so blonde and blue-eyed she must hail from a tribe of Scandinavian beauties. I wish I could say to her, Hi, would you like to go for a cup of coffee and a grilled cheese sandwich and discuss existentialism? but I know that will never happen especially when I see who's meeting her in the hallway, a student the size of a mountain wearing a jacket that says New York University Football.

At the next meeting of the psychology class the professor asks me a question about Jung and the collective unconscious and the moment I open my mouth I know everyone is staring at me as if to say, Who's the one with the Irish brogue? The professor himself says, Oh, do I detect an Irish accent? and I have to admit he does. He tells the class that, of course, the Catholic Church has been traditionally hostile to psychoanalysis. Isn't that right, Mr McCourt? and I feel he's accusing me. Why is he talking about the Catholic Church just because I tried to answer his question on the collective unconscious and am I supposed to defend the Church?

I don't know, Professor.

There's no use telling him that one Redemptorist priest in Limerick ranted from the pulpit on Sunday mornings denouncing Freud and Jung and promising they'd wind up in the deepest hole in hell, the two of them. If I talk in class I know no one is listening to what I'm saying. They're listening only to my accent and there are times when I wish I could reach into my mouth and tear my accent out by the roots. Even when I try to sound American people look puzzled and say, Do I detect an Irish brogue?

At the end of the class I wait for the blonde to pass by but she stops, the blue eyes smile at me, and she says, Hi, and my heart bangs in my chest. She says, My name is Mike.

Mike?

Well, actually, my name is Alberta but they call me Mike.

There is no football player outside and she says she has two hours till her next class and would I like to have a drink at Rocky's?

I have a class in ten minutes but I'm not going to miss this chance to be with this girl everyone is staring at, this girl who picked me out of all the people in the world to say hello to. We have to walk quickly to Rocky's so that we won't run into Bob the football player. He might be upset if he knew she was having a drink with another boy.

I wonder why she calls all males boy. I'm twenty-three.

She says she's kinda engaged to Bob, that they're pinned, and I don't know what she's talking about. She says a girl who's pinned is engaged to be engaged and you can tell if a girl is pinned when she wears her boyfriend's high school graduation ring on a necklace. It makes me wonder why she's not wearing Bob's ring. She says he gave her a gold bracelet with her name on it to wear around her ankle that would show she's taken but she doesn't wear it because it's what Puerto Rican girls do and they're too flashy. The bracelet is what you get just before the engagement ring and she'll wait for that, thank you very much.

She tells me she's from Rhode Island. She was reared there from the age of seven by her father's mother. Her own mother was only sixteen when she was born and her father twenty so you can guess what happened there. Shotgun. When the war came and he was drafted and sent to Seattle it was the end of the marriage. Even though Mike was a Protestant she graduated from a Catholic convent school in Fall River, Massachusetts, and she smiles at the memory of that graduation summer when she had a different date nearly every night. She might be smiling but I feel a great surge of rage and envy and I'd like to kill the boys who ate popcorn with her and probably kissed her in drive-in movies. Now she's living with her father and stepmother up on Riverside Drive and her grandmother is here for a while till she settles in and gets used to the city. She's not a bit shy about telling me she likes my Irish accent and she even liked looking at the back of my head in class the way my hair is black and wavy. This makes me blush and even though it's dark in Rocky's she can see the blush and she thinks it's cute.

I have to get used to the way they say cute in New York. If you say someone is cute in Ireland you're saying he's cunning and sneaky.

I'm in Rocky's and I'm in heaven drinking beer with this girl who could have stepped down from a movie screen, another Virginia Mayo. I know I'm the envy of every man and boy in Rocky's, that it'll be the same on the streets, heads turning and wondering who I am that I'm with the loveliest girl in NYU and Manhattan itself.

After two hours she has to go to her next class. I'm ready to carry her books they way they do in the movies but she says, No, better that I stay here awhile in case we run into Bob who wouldn't be a bit pleased to see her with the likes of me. She laughs and reminds me he's big, thanks for the beer, see you next week in class, and she's gone.

Her glass is still on the table and it's marked with pink lipstick. I put it to my lips for the taste of her and dream that some day I'll kiss the lips themselves. I press her glass against my cheek and think of her kissing the football player and there are dark clouds in my head. Why would she sit with me in Rocky's if she's kinda engaged to him? Is that the way it is in America? If you love a woman you're supposed to be loyal to her at all times. If you don't love her then it's all right to drink beer in Rocky's with someone else. If she goes to Rocky's with me then she doesn't love him and that makes me feel better.

Is it that she feels sorry for me with my Irish accent and my red eyes? Is she able to guess that it's hard for me to talk to girls unless they talk to me first?

All over America there are men who walk up to girls and say, Hi. I could never do that. I'd feel foolish saying Hi in the first place because I didn't grow up with it. I'd have to say Hello or something grown-up. Even when they talk to me I never know what to say. I don't want them to know I never went to high school and I don't want them to know I grew up in an Irish slum. I'm so ashamed of the past that all I can do is lie about it.

The lecturer in English Composition, Mr Calitri, would like us to write an essay on a single object from our childhood, an object that had significance for us, something domestic, if possible.

There isn't an object in my childhood I'd want anyone to know about. I wouldn't want Mr Calitri or anyone in the class to know about the slum lavatory we shared with all those families in Roden Lane. I could make up something but I can't think of anything like the things other students talk about, the family car, Dad's old baseball mitt, the sled they had so much fun with, the old ice box, the kitchen table where they did their homework. All I can think of is the bed I shared with my three brothers and even though I'm ashamed of it I have to write about it. If I make up something that's nice and respectable and don't write about the bed I'll be tormented. Besides, Mr Calitri will be the only one reading it and I'll be safe.

THE BED

When I was growing up in Limerick my mother had to go to the St Vincent de Paul Society to see if she could get a bed for me and my brothers, Malachy, Michael, and Alphie who was barely walking. The man at the St Vincent de Paul said he could give her a docket to go down to the Irishtown to a place that sold secondhand beds. My mother asked him couldn't we get a new bed because you never know what you're getting with an old one. There could be all kinds of diseases.

The man said beggars can't be choosers and my mother shouldn't be so particular.

But she wouldn't give up. She asked if it was possible at least to find out if anyone had died in the bed. Surely that wasn't asking too much. She wouldn't want to be lying in her own bed at night thinking about her four small sons sleeping on a mattress that someone had died on, maybe someone that had a fever or consumption.

The St Vincent de Paul man said, Missus, if you don't want this bed give me back the docket and I'll give it to someone that's not so particular.

Mam said, Ah, no, and she came home to get Alphie's pram so that we could carry the mattress, the spring and the bedstead. The man in the shop in the Irishtown wanted her to take a mattress with hair sticking out and spots and stains all over but my mother said she wouldn't let a cow sleep on a bed like that, didn't the man have another mattress over there in the corner? The man grumbled and said, All right, all right. Bejesus, the charity cases is gettin' very particular these days, and he stayed behind his counter watching us drag the mattress outside.

We had to push the pram up and down the streets of Limerick three times for the mattress and the different parts of the iron bedstead, the head, the end, the supports, and the spring. My mother said she was ashamed of her life and wished she could do this at night. The man said he was sorry for her troubles but he closed at six sharp and wouldn't stay open if the Holy Family came for a bed.

It was hard pushing the pram because it had one bockety wheel that wanted to go its own way and it was harder still with Alphie buried under the mattress screaming for his mother.

My father was there to drag the mattress upstairs and he helped us put the spring and the bedstead together. Of course he wouldn't help us push the pram two miles from the Irishtown because he'd be ashamed of the spectacle. He was from the North of Ireland and they must have a different way of bringing home the bed.

We had old overcoats to put on the bed because the St Vincent de Paul Society wouldn't give us a docket for sheets and blankets. My mother lit the fire and when we sat around it drinking tea she said at least we're all off the floor and isn't God good.

The next week Mr Calitri sits on the edge of his desk on the platform. He pulls our essays from his bag and tells the class, Not a bad set of essays, some a little too sentimental. But there's one I'd like to read you if the author doesn't mind, "The Bed".

He looks towards me and lets his eyebrows go up as if to say, Do you mind? I don't know what to say though I'd like to tell him, No, no, please don't tell the world what I came from, but the heat is in my face already and I can only shrug to him as if I don't care.

He reads "The Bed". I can feel the whole class looking at me and I'm ashamed. I'm glad Mike Small isn't in this class. She'd never look at me again. There are girls in the class and they 're probably thinking they should move away from me. I want to tell them this is a made-up story but Mr Calitri is up there talking about it now, telling the class why he gave it an A, that my style is direct, my subject matter rich. He laughs when he says rich. You know what I mean, he says. He tells me I should continue to explore my rich past, and he smiles again. I don't know what he's talking about. I'm sorry I ever wrote about that bed and I'm afraid everyone will pity me and treat me like a charity case. The next time I have to take a class in English Composition I'll put my family in a comfortable house in the suburbs and I'll make my father a postman with a pension.

At the end of the class students nod to me and smile and I wonder if they're already feeling sorry for me.

Mike Small came from another world, she and her football player. They might be from different parts of America but they were teenagers and it was the same all over. They went on dates on Saturday nights where the boy would have to meet the girl at her house and of course she would never be at the door waiting for him because that would show she was too eager and word would get around and she'd be alone every Saturday night the rest of her life. The boy would have to wait in the living room with a silent dad who always looked disapproving behind his newspaper knowing what he did on dates in the old days himself and wondering what was going to be done to his little daughter. The mother would fuss and want to know what movie they were going to and what time they'd be home because her daughter was a nice girl who needed a good night's sleep to keep that glow in her complexion for church tomorrow morning. At the movies they held hands and if the boy was lucky he might get a kiss and accidentally touch her breast. If that happened she'd give him a sharp look and that meant the body was being reserved for the honeymoon. After the movie they'd have hamburgers and milkshakes at the soda fountain with all the other high school kids, the boys in crewcuts and the girls in skirts and bobbysox. They'd sing along with the jukebox and the girls would squeal over Frankie. If the girl liked the boy she might let him have a long kiss at her door, maybe one dart of a tongue in the mouth, but if he tried to keep the tongue in there she'd back away and tell him goodnight, she had a nice time, thank you, and that was another reminder the body was being reserved for the honeymoon.

Some girls would let you touch and feel and kiss but they wouldn't let you go all the way and they were known as ninety percenters. There was some hope for ninety percenters but the all-the-way girls had such a reputation no one in town would want to marry them and they were the ones who would pack up one day and go to New York where everyone does everything.

That is what I saw in the movies or what I heard in the army from GIs who came from all over the country. If you had a car and a girl said yes she'd go with you to a drive-in movie you knew she was expecting more than popcorn and the doings up there on the screen. There was no sense in just going for a kiss. You could get that in a regular movie house. The drive-in was where you got the tongue into the mouth and the hand on the breast and if she let you get to the nipple, man, she was yours. The nipple was like a key that opened the legs and if you weren't with another couple it was into the back seat and who cared about the goddam movie?

The GIs said there were funny nights when you might be making out but your friend was having trouble in the back seat with his girl who was sitting up and watching the movie or it might be vice versa where your buddy is making out and you're so frustrated you want to explode in your pants. Sometimes your buddy might be finished with his girl and she's ready to take you on and that's pure heaven, man, because not only are you getting laid the one who rejected you is sitting there stonefaced pretending to watch the movie but really listening to you back there and sometimes she can't stand it anymore and climbs on you and you're caught between two broads in the back seat. Goddam.

Men in the army said you'd have no respect later for the girl who let you go all the way and you'd have only a little respect for the ninety percenter. Of course you'd have complete respect for the girl who said no and sat up watching the movie. That's the girl that was pure, not damaged goods, and the girl you'd want to be the mother of your children. If you married a girl who fooled around how would you ever know you were the real father of your kids?

I know that if Mike Small ever went to a drive-in she was the one who sat up and watched the movie. Anything else would be too much of a pain to think about especially when it's hard to think of her even kissing the football player at her own door with her father inside waiting.

The nuns tell me Mrs Klein is losing her wits with the drink and neglecting poor Michael what's left of him. They're moving them to places where they can be cared for, Catholic homes, though it's better not to tell anyone about Michael for fear some Jewish organization would claim him. Sister Mary Thomas is not against Jews but she doesn't want to lose a precious soul like Michael's.

One of Mary O'Brien's boarders is gone back to Ireland to settle on his father's five acres and marry a girl from down the road. I can have his bed for eighteen dollars a week and help myself in the morning to whatever is in the fridge. The other Irish boarders work on the piers and warehouses and they bring home canned fruits or bottles of rum and whiskey from cases that accidentally fell when ships were being unloaded. Mary says isn't it wonderful that when you say there's something you'd like a whole case of it is accidentally dropped the next day on the docks. There are Sunday mornings we don't bother cooking breakfast we're that happy in the kitchen with slices of pine-apple in heavy syrup and glasses of rum to wash it down. Mary reminds us about Mass but we're content enough with our pineapple and rum and soon Timmy Coin is calling for a song even if it's a Sunday morning. He works in Merchants Refrigerating and often brings home a great side of beef on Friday nights. He's the only one who cares about going to Mass though he makes sure he's back in no time for the pineapple and rum which can't last forever.

Frankie and Danny Lennon are twins, Irish-Americans. Frankie lives in another apartment and Danny is a boarder with Mary. Their father, John, lives on the streets, wanders around with a pint of wine in a brown paper bag, and cleans Mary's apartment in exchange for a shower, a sandwich and a few drinks. His sons laugh and sing, "Oh, my papa, to me he was so wonderful".

Frankie and Danny take classes at City College, one of the best colleges in the country and free. Even though they're studying accounting they're always excited over their courses in literature. Frankie talks about seeing a girl on the subway reading James Joyce's *A Portrait of the Artist as a Young Man* and how anxious he was to sit beside her and discuss Joyce. All the way from Thirty-Fourth Street to 181st Street he would leave his seat and move towards her, never having the courage to talk to her, and losing his seat each time to another passenger. At last when the train pulled in to 181st Street he bent to her and said, Great book, isn't it? and she jerked back from him and let out a cry. He wanted to tell her, Sorry, sorry, but the doors were closing and he was out on the platform with people in the train glaring at him.

They love jazz and they're like two mad professors in the living room, putting records on the phonograph, clicking their fingers to the beat, telling me all about the great musicians on this Benny Goodman record, Gene Krupa, Harry James, Lionel Hampton, Benny himself. They tell me this was the greatest jazz concert of all time and the first time a black man was allowed on the Carnegie Hall stage. And listen to him, listen to Lionel Hampton, all velvet and glide, listen to him and Benny coming in, listen, and here comes Harry sending in a few notes to tell you watch out, I'm flying, I'm flying, and Krupa going bap-bap-bap-do-bap-de-bap, hands, feet going, sing sing sing, and the whole damn band wild, man, wild, and the audience, listen to that audience, outa their mind, man, outa their ever-lovin' mind.

They play Count Basie, point their fingers and laugh when the Count hits those single notes, and when they play Duke Ellington they're all over the living room clicking fingers and stopping to tell me, listen, listen to this and I listen because I never listened like this before and now I hear what I never heard before and I have to laugh with the Lennons when the musicians take passages from tunes and turn them upside down and inside out and put them back again as if to say, look, we borrowed your little tune awhile to play our own way but don't worry, here it's back again and you go hum it, honey, you sing that mother, man.

The Irish boarders complain this is just a lot of noise. Paddy Arthur McGovern says, Shure, yeer not Irish at all with that stuff. What about some Irish songs on that machine? What about a few Irish dance tunes?

The Lennons laugh and tell us their father left the bogs a long time ago. Danny says, This is America, men. This is the music. But Paddy Arthur pulls Duke Ellington off the phonograph and puts on Frank Lee's Tara Ceilidhe Band and we sit around the living room, listening, tapping slightly, and not moving our faces. The Lennons laugh, and leave.

29

Sister Mary Thomas somehow found my new address and sent me a note to say it would be very nice if I came over and said goodbye to Mrs Klein and Michael what's left of him and to pick up two books I'd left under my bed. There's an ambulance waiting outside the apartment house and upstairs Sister Mary Thomas is telling Mrs Klein she has to put on her wig and, no, she can't have a rabbi, they don't have rabbis where she's going and she'd be better off on her knees saying a decade of the rosary and praying for forgiveness, and down the hall Sister Beatrice is crooning to Michael what's left of him and telling him a brighter day is dawning, that where he's going there will be birds and flowers and trees and a risen Lord. Sister Mary Thomas calls down the hall, Sister, you're wasting your time. He doesn't understand a word you're saying. But Sister Beatrice answers back, It doesn't matter, Sister. He's a child of the Lord, a Jewish child of the Lord, Sister.

He's not Jewish, Sister.

Does it matter, Sister? Does it matter?

It matters, Sister, and I'd advise you to consult your confessor.

Yes, Sister, I will. And Sister Beatrice goes on with her cheerful words and hymns to Michael what's left of him who may or may not be Jewish.

Sister Mary Thomas says, Oh, I nearly forgot your books. They're under the bed.

She hands me the books and rubs her hands together as if to clean them. Don't you know, she says, that Anatole France is on the Index of the Catholic Church and D. H. Lawrence was a completely depraved Englishman who is now howling in the depths of hell, the Lord save us all? If that's what you're reading at New York University I fear for your soul and I'll light a candle for you.

No, Sister, I'm reading *Penguin Island* for myself and *Women in Love* for one of my classes.

She rolls her eyes to heaven. Oh, the arrogance of youth. I feel sorry for your poor mother.

There are two men in white coats at the door with a stretcher and they go down the hall for Michael what's left of him. Mrs Klein sees them and calls, Rabbi, Rabbi, help me in my hour, and Sister Mary Thomas pushes her back into her chair. They shuffle back down the hall, the men in white with Michael what's left of him on the stretcher and Sister Beatrice stroking the top of his head that looks like a skull. Alannah, alannah, she says in her Irish accent, sure there's nothing left of you. But you'll see the sky now and the clouds in it. She goes down with him in the elevator and I'd like to go myself to get away from Sister Mary Thomas and her remarks on the state of my soul and the terrible things I'm reading but I have to say goodbye to Mrs Klein all dressed up in her wig and hat. She takes my hand, Take care of Michael what's left of him, won't you, Eddie?

Eddie. I feel a fierce pain in my heart because of this and a terrible memory of Rappaport and the laundry at Dachau and I wonder if I'll ever know anything in the world but darkness. Will I ever know what Sister Beatrice promised Michael what's left of him, birds, flowers, trees, and a risen Lord?

What I learned in the army comes in useful at NYU. Never raise your hand, never let them know your name, never volunteer. Students just graduated from high school, eighteen years of age, raise their hands regularly to tell the class and the professor what they think. If professors look directly at me and ask questions I can never finish the answers with the way they always say, Oh, do I detect a brogue? After that I have no peace. Whenever an Irish writer is mentioned, or anything Irish, everyone turns to me as if I'm the authority. Even the professors seem to think I know all about Irish literature and history. If they say anything about Joyce or Yeats they look at me as if I am the expert, as if I should nod and confirm what they say. I nod all the time because I don't know what else to do. If ever I shook my head in doubt or disagreement the professors would dig deeper with their questions and expose my ignorance for all to see, especially the girls.

It's the same with Catholicism. If I answer a question they hear my accent and that means I'm a Catholic and ready to defend Mother Church to the last drop of my blood. Some professors like to taunt me by sneering at the Virgin Birth, the Holy Trinity, the celibacy of St Joseph, the Inquisition, the priest-ridden people of Ireland. When they talk like that I don't know what to say because they have the power to lower my grade and damage my average so that I won't be able to follow the American dream and that might drive me to Albert Camus and the daily decision not to commit suicide. I fear professors with their high degrees and the way they might make me look foolish before the other students, especially the girls.

I'd like to stand up in those classes and announce to the world that I'm too busy to be Irish or Catholic or anything else, that I'm working day and night to make a living, trying to read books for my courses and falling asleep in the library, trying to write term papers with footnotes and bibliographies on a typewriter that betrays me with the letters "a" and "j" so that I have to go back and retype whole pages since it's impossible to avoid "a" and "j", falling asleep on subway trains all the way to the last stop so that I'm embarrassed I have to ask people where I am when I don't even know what borough I'm in.

If I didn't have red eyes and an Irish accent I could be purely American and I wouldn't have to put up with professors tormenting me with Yeats and Joyce and the Irish Literary Renaissance and how clever and witty the Irish are and what a beautiful green country it is though priest-ridden and poor with a population ready to vanish from the face of the earth due to Puritanical sexual repression and what do you have to say to that, Mr McCourt?

I think you're right, Professor.

Oh, he thinks I'm right. And, Mr Katz, what do you say to that?

I guess I agree, Professor. I don't know too many Irish.

Ladies and gentlemen, you must consider what has just been said by Mr McCourt and Mr Katz. Here we have the intersection of the

Celtic and the Hebraic, both ready to accommodate and compromise. Isn't that right, Mr McCourt, Mr Katz?

We nod and I remember what my mother used to say, A nod is as good as a wink to a blind horse. I'd like to say this to the professor but I can't take the risk of offending him with all the power he has to keep me from the American dream and make me look foolish before the class, especially the girls.

Monday and Wednesday mornings in the fall term Professor Middlebrook teaches The Literature of England. She mounts the little platform, sits, places the heavy textbook on the desk, reads from it, comments and looks at the class only to ask an occasional question. She starts with Beowulf and ends with John Milton who, she says, is sublime, somewhat in disfavor in our time but his day will come, his day will come. Students read newspapers, work at crossword puzzles, pass notes to each other, study for other courses. After my all-night shifts at various jobs it's hard to stay awake and when she asks me a question Brian McPhillips jabs me with his elbow, whispers the question and the answer and I stammer it back to her. Sometimes she mutters into the textbook and I know I'm in trouble and that trouble takes the form of a C at the end of the term.

With all my latenesses and absences and falling asleep in class I know I deserve a C and I'd like to tell the professor how guilty I feel and if she failed me completely I wouldn't blame her. I'd like to explain that even if I'm not a model student she should see the way I am with the Literature of England textbook, all excited reading it in the NYU library, on subway trains, even on piers and warehouse platforms during lunch hour. She should know I'm probably the only student in the world who ever got into trouble with men on warehouse platforms over a literature book. The men taunt me, Hey, look at the college boy. Too good to talk to us, eh? and when I tell them about the strangeness of the Anglo-Saxon language they tell me I am full of shit, that isn't English at all and who the fuck do you think you're kiddin', kid? Maybe they never went to college, they said, but they aren't gonna have the wool pulled over their eyes by a half-ass shithead just off the boat from Ireland telling them this is the English language when you could see there wasn't an English word on the whole goddam page.

After that they won't talk to me and the platform boss shifts me inside to run the elevator so that the men won't be pulling tricks on me, dropping loads to jerk the arms out of my sockets or pretending to run me down with forklift trucks.

I'd like to tell the professor how I look at the authors and poets in the textbook and ask myself which of them I'd like to have a pint with in a Greenwich Village pub and the one that stands out is Chaucer. I'd buy him a pint anytime and listen to his stories about the Canterbury pilgrims. I'd like to tell the professor how much I love the sermons of John Donne and how I'd like to buy him a pint except that he was a Protestant priest and not known for sitting in taverns knocking back the pint.

I can't talk about this because it's dangerous to raise your hand in any class to say how much you love anything. The professor will look at you with a pitying little smile and the class will see that and the pitying little smile will travel around the room till you feel so foolish the face turns red and you promise you'll never love anything in college again or if you do keep it to yourself. I can say this to Brian McPhillips sitting next to me but someone in the seat before me turns and says, Aren't we being a little paranoid?

Paranoid. That's another word I have to look up with the way everyone at NYU uses it. From the way this student looks at me with his superior left eyebrow nearly up to his hairline I can only guess he's accusing me of being demented and there's no use trying to answer him till I find out what that word means. I'm sure Brian McPhillips knows what that word means but he's busy talking to Joyce Timpanelli on his left. They're always looking at each other and smiling. That means there's something going on and I can't bother them with the word paranoid. I should carry a dictionary and when anyone throws a strange word at me I could look it up on the spot and shoot back with a smart answer that would collapse the superior eyebrow.

Or I could practise the silence I learned in the army and go my own way which is the best thing of all because people who torment other people with strange words don't like it when you go your own way.

Andy Peters sits next to me in Introduction to Philosophy and tells me about a job in a bank, Manufacturer's Trust Company down on

Broad Street. They're looking for people to work with personal loan applications and I could choose a four to midnight shift or a midnight to eight a.m. He says the best thing about this job is once you finish the work you can leave, that no one works a full eight hours.

There's a typing test and I have no trouble with that because of the way the army dragged me away from my dog and made me a company clerk typist. The bank says, OK, I can work the four to midnight shift so that I can take my classes in the morning and sleep at night. Wednesdays and Fridays I have no classes and I can shape up at the warehouses and piers and make extra money against the day my brother, Michael, is out of the air force and the allotment to my mother ends. I can put the Wednesday-Friday money in a separate account and when the time comes she won't have to be running to the St Vincent de Paul Society for food or shoes.

There are seven women and four men on the shift at the bank and all we have to do is take piles of applications for personal loans and send notices to the applicants that they've been accepted or rejected. Andy Peters tells me during a coffee break that if I ever see an application from a friend that's been rejected I can change it to acceptance. There's a little code the daytime loan officers use and he'll show me how to alter it.

Night after night we see hundreds of applications for loans. People want them for new babies, vacations, cars, furniture, consolidation of debts, hospital expenses, funerals, decorating apartments. Sometimes there are letters attached and if there's a good one we all stop typing and read them back and forth. There are letters that make the women cry and the men want to cry. Babies die and there are expenses and would the bank help. A husband runs away and the applicant doesn't know what to do, where to turn. She never had a job in her life, how could she with raising three kids, and she needs three hundred dollars to tide her over till she finds work and a cheap baby-sitter.

One man promises that if the bank loans him five hundred dollars they can take a pint of his blood every month for the rest of his life and it's a good deal, he says, because he has a rare blood type which he's not ready to divulge at this moment but if the bank helps him out they're getting blood that's as good as gold, the best collateral in the world.

The blood man is rejected and Andy lets it pass but he changes the code for the desperate woman with the three kids who was rejected for having no collateral. Andy says, I don't understand how they can give loans to people who want to spend two weeks lying on the sand at the goddam Jersey shore and then turn down a woman with three kids hanging on by her fingernails. This, my friend, is where the revolution starts.

He changes a few applications every night to prove how stupid a bank can be. He says he knows what happens during the day when asshole loan people go through the applications. Harlem address? Negro? Points off. Puerto Rican? Mucho points off. He tells me there are dozens of Puerto Ricans around New York who think they were accepted for their good credit but it was Andy Peters all the time feeling sorry for them. He says it's a big thing in PR neighborhoods to get out there on the weekend and polish the car. They might never go anywhere but it's the polishing that matters, old guys on the stoop watching the polishing and drinking the old cerveza from bodegas in quart bottles, the radio blasting away with Tito Puente, the old guys checking out the girls shaking their asses along the sidewalks, man, that's living, man, that's living and what more do you want?

Andy talks about Puerto Ricans all the time. He says they're the only people who know how to live in this goddam tight-ass city, that it's a tragedy the Spaniards didn't sail up the Hudson instead of the goddam Dutch and the goddam limeys. We'd have siestas, man, we'd have color. We wouldn't have the Man in the Gray Flannel Suit. If he had his way he'd give a loan to every Puerto Rican applying for a car loan so that all over the city you'd have them polishing their new cars, drinking their beer out of brown paper bags, digging Tito, and flirting with the girls shaking their asses along the sidewalks, girls with those see-through peasant blouses and Jesus medallions nestling in their cleavage, and wouldn't that be a city to live in?

The women in the office laugh at the way Andy talks but they tell him be quiet because they want to finish the work and get outa here. They have kids at home and husbands waiting.

When we finish early we go for a beer and he tells me why he's a thirty-one-year-old student studying philosophy at New York University. He was in the war, not Korea, the big one in Europe, but he has to work nights in this goddam bank because of his dishonorable discharge in the spring of 1945, just before the war ended and isn't that a bitch.

Taking a shit, that's what he was, a nice quiet shit in a French ditch, all wiped and ready to button up when who comes along but a goddam lieutenant and a sergeant and the lieutenant has nothing else to do but march up to Andy and accuse him of an unnatural act with that sheep standing there a few feet away. Andy admits that in a way the lieutenant had a right to jump to the wrong conclusion since just before pulling up his pants Andy had a hard-on which made it difficult to pull up the aforesaid pants and even though he hated anything in the shape of an officer he felt an explanation would help.

Well, Lieutenant, I may have fucked that sheep or I may not have fucked that sheep but what's interesting here is your peculiar concern with me and my relationship with that sheep. There's a war on, Lieutenant. I come out here to take a shit in a French ditch and there's a sheep at eye level and I'm nineteen years old and I haven't been laid since my high school prom and a sheep, especially a French sheep, looks very tempting and if I looked like I was ready to jump on that sheep you're right, Lieutenant, I was, but I didn't. You and the sergeant interrupted a beautiful relationship. I thought the lieutenant would laugh, instead he said I was a goddam liar, that I had sheep written all over me. I wanted sheep all over me. I dreamed of it but it hadn't happened and what he said was so unfair I pushed him, didn't hit him, just pushed, and the next thing, Jesus, they had all kinds of artillery sticking in my face, pistols, carbines, M1 rifles, and before you know it there was a court martial where I had a drunken captain defending me who told me in private that I was a disgusting sheep fucker and he was sorry he couldn't be at the other end prosecuting me because his father was a Basque from Montana where they respected their sheep, and I still don't know if I was sent to the stockade for six months for assaulting an officer or screwing a sheep. What I got out of it was a dishonorable discharge and when that happens you might as well study philosophy at NYU.

30

Because of Mr Calitri I scribble memories of Limerick in notebooks. I make lists of streets, schoolmasters, priests, neighbors, friends, shops.

After "The Bed" essay I'm sure people in Mr Calitri's class are looking at me in a different way. The girls are probably telling each other they'd never go out with someone who spent his life in a bed a man might have died in. Then Mike Small tells me she heard about the essay and how it moved so many people in the class, boys and girls. I didn't want her to know what I came from but now she wants to read the essay and afterwards her eyes fill up and she says, Oh, I never knew. Oh, it must have been awful. It reminds her of Dickens though I don't know how that can be because everything in Dickens always ends well.

Of course I won't say this to Mike Small for fear she might think I'm arguing with her. She might turn on her heel and march back to Bob the football player.

Now Mr Calitri wants us to write a family essay where there's adversity, a dark moment, a setback, and even though I don't want to go into the past there's something that happened to my mother that demands to be written.

THE PLOT

When the war started and food was rationed in Ireland the government offered poor families plots of land in fields outside Limerick. Each family could have a sixteenth of an acre, clear it, and grow whatever vegetables they liked.

My father applied for a plot out the road in Rosbrien and the government lent him a spade and a fork for the work. He took my brother Malachy and me to help him. When my brother Michael saw the spade he cried and wanted to go too but he was only four and he would have been in the way. My father told him, Whisht, that when we came back from Rosbrien we'd bring him berries.

I asked my father if I could carry the spade and I was soon sorry because Rosbrien was miles outside Limerick. Malachy had started out carrying the fork but my father took it away from him because of the way he was swinging it and nearly knocking people's eyes out. Malachy cried till my father said he'd let him carry the spade all the way home. My brother soon forgot the fork when he saw a dog who was willing to chase a stick for miles till he frothed white stuff with the weariness and lay down on the road looking up with the stick between his paws and we had to leave him.

When my father saw the plot he shook his head. Rocks, he said, rocks and stones. And all we did that day was to make a pile by the low wall along the road. My father used the spade to keep digging up rocks and even though I was only nine I noticed two men in the next plots talking and looking at him and laughing in a quiet way. I asked my father why and he gave a small laugh himself and said, The Limerickman gets the dark earth and the man from the North gets the rocky plot.

We worked till the darkness came and we were so weak with hunger we couldn't pick up another rock. We didn't mind one bit if he carried the fork and spade and wished he could carry us, too. He said we were big boys, good workers, our mother would be proud of us, there would be tea and fried bread, and he marched ahead with his long strides till halfway home he stopped suddenly. Your brother Michael, he said. We promised him berries. We'll have to go back out the road to the bushes.

Malachy and I complained so much that we were tired and could hardly walk another step that my father told us go home, he'd get the berries himself. I asked why couldn't he get the berries tomorrow and he said he had promised Michael berries for tonight, not tomorrow, and away he went with the spade and fork on his shoulder.

When Michael saw us he started to cry, Berries, berries. He stopped when we told him, Dad is out the road in Rosbrien getting your berries so will you quit the crying and let us have our fried bread and tea.

We could have eaten a whole loaf between us but my mother said, Leave some for your father. She shook her head. He's such a fool going all the way back there for the berries. Then she looked at Michael the way he was standing at the door looking up the lane for a sign of my father and she shook her head in a smaller way.

Soon Michael spotted my father and he was gone up the lane calling out, Dad, Dad, did you get the berries? We could hear Dad, In a minute, Michael, in a minute.

He stood the spade and fork in a corner and emptied his coat pockets on to the table. Berries he brought, the great black juicy berries you find at the tops and backs of bushes beyond the reach of children, berries he plucked in the dark of Rosbrien. My mouth watered and I asked my mother if I could have a berry and she said, Ask Michael, they're his.

I didn't have to ask him. He handed me the biggest of the berries, the juiciest, and he handed one to Malachy. He offered berries to my mother and father but they said no thanks, they were his berries. He offered Malachy and me another berry each and we took them. I thought if I had berries like that I'd keep them all for myself but Michael was different and maybe he didn't know any better because he was four.

After that we went to the plot every day but Sunday and cleared it of rocks and stones till we reached the earth and helped my father with the planting of potatoes, carrots and cabbage. There were times we left him and roamed the road, hunting for berries and eating so many it gave us the runs.

My father said in no time we'd be digging up our crop but he wouldn't be here to do it. There was no work in Limerick and the English were looking for people to work in their war factories. It was hard for him to think of working for the English after what they did to us but the money was tempting and as long as the Americans had entered the war it was surely a just cause.

He went off to England with hundreds of men and women. Most sent money home but he spent his in the pubs of Coventry and forgot he had a family. My mother had to borrow from her own mother and ask for credit from Kathleen O'Connell's grocery shop. She had to beg for food from the St Vincent de Paul Society or wherever she could get it. She said it would be a great relief to us and we'd be saved when the time came to dig up our spuds, our carrots, our lovely heads of cabbage. Oh, we'd have a right feed then and if God was good He might send us a nice piece of ham and that wasn't asking too much when you lived in Limerick, the ham capital of all Ireland.

The day came and she put the new baby, Alphie, in the pram. She borrowed a coal sack from Mr Hannon next door. We'll fill it, she said. I carried the fork and Malachy the spade so that he wouldn't be knocking people's eyes out with the prongs. My mother said, Don't be swinging those tools or I'll give ye a good clitther on the gob.

A smack in the mouth.

When we arrived at Rosbrien there were other women digging in the plots. If there was a man in the field he was old and not able for the work in England. My mother said hello across the low wall to this woman and that woman and when they didn't answer back she said, They must be all gone deaf with the bending over.

She left Alphie in the pram outside the plot wall and told Michael mind the baby and don't be hunting for berries. Malachy and I jumped over the wall but she had to sit on it, swing her legs over, and get down on the other side. She sat a minute and said, There's nothing in the world like a new potato with salt and butter. I'd give me two eyes for it.

We lifted the spade and fork and went to the plot but for all we got there we might as well have stayed at home. The earth was still fresh from being dug and turned over and white worms crawled in the holes where the potatoes and carrots and heads of cabbage used to be.

My mother said to me, Is this the right plot?

'Tis.

She walked the length of it and back. The other women were busy bending over and picking things out of the ground. I could see she wanted to say something to them but I could see also she knew it was no use. I went to pick up the spade and fork and she barked at me, Leave them. They're no use to us now with everything gone. I wanted to say something but her face was so white I was afraid she'd hit me and I backed away, over the wall.

She came over the wall herself, sitting, swinging her legs, sitting again till Michael said, Mam, can I go hunting berries?

You can, she said. You might as well.

If Mr Calitri likes this story he might make me read it to the class and they'll roll their eyes and say, More misery. The girls might have felt sorry for me over the bed but that's enough, surely. If I go on writing about my miserable childhood they'll say, Stop, stop, life is hard enough, we have our own troubles. So, from now on, I'll write stories about my family moving to the suburbs of Limerick where everyone is well fed and clean from taking a bath at least once a week.

31

Paddy Arthur McGovern warns me that if I keep on listening to that noisy jazz music I'll wind up like the Lennon brothers so American I'll forget I'm Irish altogether and what will I be then. It's no use telling him how the Lennons could be so excited about James Joyce. He'd say, Oh, James Joyce, me arse. I grew up in the County Cavan and no one there ever heard of him and if you don't watch your step you'll be running to Harlem and jitterbuggin' with Negro girls.

He's going to an Irish dance on Saturday night and if I have any sense I'll go with him. He wants to dance only with Irish girls because if you dance with Americans you never know what you're getting.

At the Jaeger House on Lexington Avenue Mickey Carton is up there with his band and Ruthie Morrissey singing "A Mother's Love is a Blessing". A great crystal ball revolves on the ceiling, flecking the ballroom with floating silver spots. Paddy Arthur is no sooner in the door than he's waltzing around with the first girl he asks to dance. He has no trouble getting girls to dance and why should he with his six feet one, his black curly hair, his rich black eyebrows, his blue eyes, the dimple on his chin, the cool way he has of offering his hand that says, Come up, girl, so that the girl would never dream of saying no to this vision of a man and when they move out on the floor, no matter what class of a dance it is, waltz, foxtrot, lindy, two-step, he steers her around with hardly a glance at her and when he leads her back to her seat she's the envy of every giggling girl on the seats along the wall.

He comes to the bar where I'm having a beer for the courage that might be in it. He wants to know why I'm not up dancing. Sure what's the use of coming here if you don't dance with them grand girls along the wall?

He's right. The grand girls sitting along the wall are like the girls in Cruise's Hotel in Limerick except they're wearing dresses the likes of which you'd never see in Ireland, silk and taffeta and materials strange to me, pink, puce, light blue, ornamented here and there with lacy bows, dresses with no shoulders so stiff at the front that when the girl turns to the right the dress stays where it is. Their hair is trapped with pins and combs for fear it might tumble rich to the shoulders. They sit with their hands in their laps holding fancy purses and they smile only when they talk to each other. Some sit dance after dance, ignored by the men, till they're forced to dance with the girls beside them. They clump across the floor and when the dance ends move to the bar for lemonade or orange squash, the drink of girl couples.

I can't tell Paddy I'd rather stay where I am, safe at the bar. I can't tell him that going to any kind of a dance gives me a sick empty feeling, that even if a girl got up to dance with me I wouldn't know what to say to her. I could manage a waltz, oompah oompah, but I could never be like the men on the floor who whisper and make girls laugh so hard they can hardly dance for a whole minute. Buck used to say in Germany that if you can make a girl laugh you're halfway up her leg.

Paddy dances again and comes to the bar with a girl named Maura and tells me she has a friend, Dolores, who's shy because she's Irish-American and would I dance with her since I was born here and we'd make a good match with her ignorance of Irish dancing and my listening to that jazz music all the time.

Maura looks up at Paddy and smiles. He smiles down at her and winks at me. She says, Excuse me. I want to make sure Dolores is OK, and when she's gone Paddy whispers she's the one he's going home with. She's a head waitress in Schrafft's Restaurant with her own apartment, saving money to go back to Ireland and this will be Paddy's lucky night. He says I should be nice to Dolores, you never know, and he winks again. I think I'll be gettin' me hole tonight, he says.

Me hole. Of course that's what I'd like myself but that's not the way I'd say it. I prefer Mikey Molloy's way of saying it in Limerick when he called it the excitement. If you're like Paddy with Irish women jumping into your arms you probably don't remember one from another and they all become one hole until you meet the girl you like and she makes you realize she wasn't put into the world to fall on her back for your pleasure. I could never think about Mike Small like that or even Dolores who's standing there blushing and shy, the way I feel myself. Paddy nudges me and talks out of the side of his mouth. Ask her to dance, for Christ's sake.

All that comes out of me is a mumble and I'm lucky Mickey Carton is playing a waltz with Ruthie singing "There's One Fair County in Ireland", the only dance where I might not make a fool of myself. Dolores smiles at me and blushes and I blush back and there go the two of us blushing around the floor with the little silver spots floating across our faces. If I stumble she steps along with me in such a way that the stumble becomes a dance step and after a while I think I'm Fred Astaire and she's Ginger Rogers and I whirl her around sure the girls along the wall are admiring me and dying for a dance with me.

The waltz stops and even though I'm ready to leave the floor for fear Mickey might start a lindy or a jitterbug Dolores pauses as if to say, Why don't we dance this? And she's so easy on her feet and so light with her touch I look at the other couples, how cool they are, and it's no trouble at all to do it with Dolores, whatever it is, and I push her and pull and twirl her like a top till I'm sure all the girls are eyeing me and envying Dolores till I'm so full of myself I don't notice there's a girl sitting near the door with a crutch sticking out where it shouldn't be and when my foot catches in it I go flying into the laps of the grand girls along the wall who push me off in a rough unfriendly way remarking that some people shouldn't be allowed on the dance floor if they can't hold their drink.

Paddy is at the door with his arm around Maura. He's laughing but she's not. She looks at Dolores as if to sympathize with her but Dolores helps me to my feet, asking me if I'm all right. Maura comes over and whispers to her and turns to me. Will you take care of Dolores?

I will.

She and Paddy leave and Dolores says she'd like to leave, too. She lives in Queens and she says I really don't have to see her all the way home, the E train is safe enough. I can't tell her I'd like to take her home in the hope she might ask me in and there might be some excitement. She surely has her own apartment and she might feel so sorry about the way I tripped over the crutch she wouldn't have the heart to turn me away and we'd be in her bed in no time, warm, naked, mad for each other, missing Mass, breaking the Sixth Commandment over and over and not giving a fiddler's fart.

When the E train rocks or stops quickly we're thrown together and I can smell her perfume and feel her thigh against mine. It's a good sign when she doesn't pull away from me and when she lets me hold her hand I'm in heaven till she starts talking about Nick, her boyfriend in the navy, and I put her hand back in her lap.

I can't understand the women in this world, Mike Small who drinks beer with me in Rocky's and then runs to Bob, now this one who lures me on to the E train all the way to the last stop at 179th Street. Paddy Arthur would never have put up with this. Back at the dance hall he would have made certain there was no Nick in the navy and no one at home to interfere with his all-night plans. If there was any doubt he'd have jumped off the train at the next stop, so why don't I? I was soldier of the week in Fort Dix, I trained dogs, I go to college, I read books, and look at me now sneaking through the streets around NYU to avoid Bob the football player and taking a girl home who's planning to marry someone else. It seems everyone in the world has someone, Dolores her Nick, Mike Small her Bob, and Paddy Arthur is well into his night of excitement with Maura in Manhattan and what kind of a bloody fool am I traveling to the end of the line?

I'm ready to jump off at the next stop and leave Dolores entirely when she takes my hand and tells me how nice I am, that I'm a good dancer, too bad about the crutch, we could have danced all night, that she likes the way I talk, the cute brogue, it's easy to see I was well brought up, it's so nice that I go to college, and she doesn't understand why I'm hanging around with Paddy Arthur who, it was easy to see, had no good on his mind with respect to Maura. She squeezes my hand and tells me I'm so nice to travel all the way home with her and she'll never forget me and I feel her thigh against mine all the way to the last stop and when we stand to leave the train I have to bend to hide the excitement that's throbbing in my trousers. I'm ready to walk her home but she stands by a bus stop and tells me she lives farther out, in Queen's Village, and really, I don't have to go all the way, she'll be all right on the bus. She squeezes my hand again and I wonder if there's any hope that this might be my lucky night and I'll wind up wild in bed like Paddy Arthur.

While we wait for the bus she holds my hand again and tells me all about Nick in the navy, how her father doesn't like him because he's Italian and calls him all kinds of insulting names behind his back, how her mother really likes Nick but would never admit it in case her father might come home in a drunken rage and smash the furniture which wouldn't be the first time. The worst nights are when her brother, Kevin, visits and stands up to her father and you wouldn't believe the swearing and the rolling on the floor. Kevin is a linebacker at Fordham and a good match for her father.

What's a linebacker?

You don't know what a linebacker is?

I don't.

You're the first boy I ever met who didn't know what a linebacker is.

Boy. I'm twenty-four years old and she's calling me a boy and I'm wondering do you have to be forty to be a man in America?

All along I'm hoping that things are so terrible with her father she might have her own place but, no, she lives at home and there go my dreams for a night of excitement. You'd think a girl her age would have her own place so that she could invite in the likes of me who see her to the end of the line. I don't care if she squeezes my hand a thousand times. What's the use of having your hand squeezed on a bus in the middle of the night in Queens if there's no promise of a bit of excitement at the end of the journey?

She lives in a house with a statue of the Virgin Mary and a pink bird on the little front lawn. We stand at the small iron gate and I'm wondering if I should kiss her and get her into such a state we might go behind a tree for the excitement but there's a roar from inside, Goddamit it, Dolores, get your ass in here, hell of a nerve you have coming home at this goddam hour and tell that goddam shithead run for his life, and she says, Oh, and runs inside.

By the time I get back to Mary O'Brien's everyone is up and

having bacon and eggs followed by rum and slices of pineapple in heavy syrup. Mary puffs on her cigarette and gives me the knowing smile.

You look like you had a good time last night.

32

When the day workers at the bank leave their offices Bridey Stokes comes in with her mop and bucket to clean three floors. She pulls a large canvas bag behind her, fills it with trash from the waste paper baskets and drags it to the freight elevator to empty it somewhere in the basement. Andy Peters tells her she should have extra canvas bags so that she won't have to travel up and down so much and she says the bank won't supply even one more canvas bag they're that cheap. She could buy them herself but she's working nights to keep her son, Patrick, at Fordham University and not to be supplying the Manufacturer's Trust Company with canvas bags. Every night on each floor she fills the bag twice and that means six trips to the basement. Andy tries to explain to her that if she had six canvas bags she could fill the elevator once and that would save so much time and energy she could finish earlier and go home to Patrick and her husband.

Husband? He drank himself to death ten years ago.

I'm sorry to hear that, says Andy.

I'm not a bit sorry. He was too handy with his fists and I bear the marks to this day. Patrick, too. He'd think nothing of knocking little Patrick around the house till the little fella couldn't even cry anymore and it was so bad one night I took him from the house and begged the man in the subway booth to let us in and I asked a cop where was Catholic Charities and they took care of us and got me this job and I'm grateful even if there's only one canvas bag.

Andy tells her she doesn't have to be a slave.

I'm not a slave. I'm up in the world since I got away from that lunatic. God forgive me but I didn't even go to his funeral.

She lets out a sigh and leans on the handle of the mop which comes up to her chin she's that small. She has large brown eyes and no lips and when she tries to smile there's nothing to smile with. She's so thin that when Andy and I go out to the coffee shop we bring her a cheeseburger with french fries and a milkshake to see if we could put some fat on her bones till we realize she's not touching the food but taking it home to Patrick who's studying accounting at Fordham.

Then one night we find her crying and stuffing the freight elevator with six bulging canvas bags. There's room for us with the bags and we ride down with her wondering if the bank suddenly turned generous and lavished canvas bags on her.

No. 'Tis my Patrick. One more year and he'd be graduated from Fordham but he left me a note to say he's in love with a girl from Pittsburgh and they're gone off to start a new life in California and I said to myself if that's the way I'm going to be treated I'm not going to kill myself with the one canvas bag anymore and I went up and down the streets of Manhattan till I found a place on Canal Street that sells them, a Chinese place. You'd think in a city like this you wouldn't have trouble finding canvas bags and I don't know what I'd do without the Chinese.

She cries harder and pulls the sleeve of her sweater across her eyes. Andy says, All right, Mrs Stokes.

Bridey, she says. I'm Bridey now.

All right, Bridey. We'll go across the street and you can eat something for your strength.

Ah, no. I have no appetite.

Take off the apron, Bridey. We're going across the street.

She tells us in the coffee shop she doesn't even want to be Bridey anymore. She's Brigid. Bridey is a name for skivvies and Brigid has the bit of dignity. No, she could never manage a cheeseburger but she eats it and all the french fries slathered with ketchup and tells us her heart is broken while she sucks her milkshake through a straw. Andy wants her to explain why she suddenly decided to get the canvas bags. She doesn't know. There was something about Patrick leaving like that and the memories of the way her husband beat her that opened a little door in her head and that's all she can say about it. The days of the one bag are over. Andy says there's no rhyme nor reason to it. She agrees but she doesn't care anymore. She got off the *Queen Mary* over twenty years ago, a healthy girl excited over America, and look at her now, a scarecrow. Well, her scarecrow days are over, too, and she'd love a piece of apple pie if they have it. Andy says he studies rhetoric, logic, philosophy but this is beyond him and she says they're very slow with the apple pie.

There are books to be read, term papers written, but I'm so obsessed with Mike Small I sit at the library window and watch her movements along Washington Square between the main university building and the Newman Club where she goes between classes even though she's not a Catholic. When she's with Bob the football player my heart sinks and that song runs through my head, "I Wonder Who's Kissing Her Now?" though I know very well who's kissing her now, Mr Football Player himself, two hundred pounds of him bending to plant his lips on her and even though I know I'd like him if there were no Mike Small in the world, he's that decent and good-humored, I still want to find the back of a comic book where Charles Atlas promises to help me build muscles that will let me kick sand in Bob's face the first time I meet him at a beach.

When summer comes he puts on his ROTC uniform and travels to North Carolina for training and Mike Small and I are free to meet and roam Greenwich Village, eating at Monte's on MacDougal Street, drinking beer at the White Horse or the San Remo. We ride the Staten Island Ferry and it's lovely to stand on deck, hand in hand, to watch the Manhattan skyline recede and loom even though I can't stop thinking again of the ones who were sent back with the bad eyes and the bad lungs and wondering what it was like for them in towns and villages all over Europe once they had a glimpse of New York, the tall towers over the water and the way the lights twinkle at dusk with tugboats hooting and ships blaring in the Narrows. Did they see and hear all this through the windows at Ellis Island? Did the memory bring pain and did they ever again try to slip into this country through a place where there weren't men in uniform rolling back their eyelids and tapping at their chests?

When Mike Small says, What are you thinking about? I don't know what to say for fear she might think I'm peculiar the way I wonder about the ones who were sent back. If my mother or father had been sent back I wouldn't be on this deck with the lights of Manhattan a sparkling dream before me.

Besides, it's only Americans who ask questions like that, What are you thinking about? or What do you do? In all my years in Ireland no one ever asked me such questions and if I weren't madly in love with Mike Small I'd tell her mind her own business about what I'm thinking or what I do for a living.

I don't want to tell Mike Small too much about my life because of the shame and I don't think she'd understand especially when she grew up in a small American town where everyone had everything. But when she starts talking about her days in Rhode Island with her grandmother there are clouds. She talks about swimming in the summer, ice skating in the winter, hay rides, trips to Boston, dates, proms, editing her high school yearbook, and her life sounds like a Hollywood movie till she goes back to the time her father and mother separated and left her with his mother in Tiverton. She talks about how much she missed her mother and how she cried herself to sleep for months and now she cries again. This makes me wonder if ever I had been sent to live in comfort with a relation would I have missed my family? It's hard to think I would have missed the same tea and bread every day, the collapsed bed swarming with fleas, a lavatory shared by all the families in the lane. No, I wouldn't have missed that but I would have missed the way it was with my mother and brothers, the talk around the table and the nights around the fire when we saw worlds in the flames, little caves and volcanoes and all kinds of shapes and images. I would have missed that even if I lived with a rich grandmother and I felt sorry for Mike Small who had no brothers and sisters and no fire to sit at.

She tells me how excited she was the day she graduated from elementary school, how her father was to travel all the way up from New York for the party but called at the last minute to say he had to go to a picnic for tugboat men and the memory of that brings the tears again. That day on the phone her grandmother blasted her father, told him he was a no-good skirt-chasing bastard and not to set foot in Tiverton again. At least her grandmother was there. She was there for everything, always. She wasn't much for the kissing and hugging and tucking in but she kept the house clean, the clothes laundered, the lunch box well stuffed every day for school.

Mike wipes her tears and says you can't have everything and even if I say nothing I wonder why you can't have everything or at least give everything. Why can't you clean the house, launder the clothes, stuff the lunch box and still kiss, hug, and tuck in? I can't say this to Mike because she admires her grandmother for being tough and I'd prefer to hear that grandma might have hugged, kissed, and tucked in.

With Bob away at ROTC camp Mike invites me to visit her family. She lives on Riverside Drive near Columbia University with her father, Allen, and her new stepmother, Stella. Her father is a tugboat captain for the Dalzell Towing Company in New York harbor. Her stepmother is pregnant. Her grandmother, Zoe, is here from Rhode Island for a while till Mike settles in and gets used to New York.

Mike tells me her father likes to be called Captain and when I say, Hello, Captain, he growls till the phlegm rattles in his throat and squeezes my hand till the knuckles crack so that I'll know how manly he is. Stella says, Hi, honey, and kisses my cheek. She tells me she's Irish, too, and it's nice to see Alberta going out with Irish boys. Even she says boys and she's Irish. Grandmother lies on the living room couch with her hands joined under her head and when Mike introduces me Zoe's hairline twitches forward and she says, Howya doin'?

It slips out of my mouth, Nice easy life you have there on the couch.

She glares at me and I know I've said the wrong thing and it's awkward when Mike and Stella go to another room to look at a dress and I'm left standing in the middle of the living room with the Captain smoking a cigarette and reading the *Daily News*. No one speaks to me and I'm wondering how Mike Small can go off and leave me standing here with the father and the grandmother ignoring me. I never know what to say to people at times like this. Should I say, How's the tugboat business? or should I tell the grandmother she did a wonderful job raising Mike.

My mother in Limerick would never leave anyone standing in the middle of the room like this. She'd say, Sit down there and we'll have a nice cup of tea, because in the lanes of Limerick it's a bad thing to ignore anyone and even worse to forget the cup of tea.

It's strange that a man with a good job like the Captain and his mother on the couch wouldn't bother to ask me if I had a mouth in my head or if I'd like to sit down. I don't know how Mike can leave me standing like this though I know if this ever happened to her she'd simply sit down and make everyone feel cheerful the way my brother Malachy does.

What would happen if I sat down? Would they say, Oh, you're feeling pretty relaxed sitting down without being asked? Or would they say nothing and wait till I leave to talk behind my back?

They'll talk behind my back anyway and tell each other Bob is a much nicer boy and looks handsome in his ROTC uniform though they might have said as much if they'd seen me in my summer khakis with my corporal's stripes. I doubt it. They probably prefer him with his high school diploma and his clear healthy eyes and his bright future and his cheerful nature all done up in his officer's uniform.

And I know from the history books the Irish were never liked up there in New England, that there were signs everywhere saying, No Irish Need Apply.

Well, I don't want to beg anyone for anything and I'm ready to turn on my heel and walk out when Mike bounces down the hall all blonde and smiling and ready for a walk and dinner in the Village. I'd like to tell her I don't want to have anything to do with people who leave you standing in the middle of the floor and hang out signs rejecting the Irish but she's so bright and blue-eyed and cheerful, so clean and American, I think if she told me stand there forever I'd be like a dog and wag my tail and do it.

Then on the way down in the elevator she tells me I said the wrong thing to grandma, that grandma is sixty-five and works very hard cooking and keeping the house clean and doesn't like people's smartass remarks about taking a few minutes on the couch.

What I want to say is this, Oh, fuck your grandma and her cooking and cleaning. She has plenty of food and drink and clothes and furniture and hot and cold running water and no shortage of money and what the bloody hell is she complaining about? There are women all over the world raising large families and not whining and there's your grandmother lying on her arse complaining she has to take care of an apartment and a few people. Fuck your grandma again.

That is what I want to say except that I have to swallow my words in case Mike Small might be offended and never see me again and it's very hard going through life not saying what comes to your tongue. It's hard being with a beautiful girl like her because she'd never have any trouble getting someone else and I'd probably have to find a girl not as good-looking who didn't mind my bad eyes and my lack of a high school diploma though a girl not as good-looking might offer me a chair and a cup of tea and I wouldn't have to swallow my words all the time. Andy Peters is always telling me life is easier with plain-looking girls, especially ones with small tits or no tits, because they're always grateful for the least bit of attention and one might even love me for myself, as they say in the movies. I can't even think of Mike Small having tits the way she's reserving the whole body for the wedding night and the honeymoon and it gives me a pain to picture Bob the football player having the excitement with her on the wedding night.

The platform boss from the Baker and Williams Warehouse sees me on the subway train and tells me I can get work during the summer with men going on vacation. He lets me work eight to noon and when I'm finished on the second day I walk over to Port Warehouses to see if I can have a sandwich with Horace. I often think he's the father I'd like to have even if he's black and I'm white. If ever I said that to anyone at the warehouse I'd be laughed off the platform. He must know himself the way they talk about black people and he surely hears the word nigger floating through the air. When I worked on the platform with him I wondered how he could keep his fists to himself. Instead he'd put his head down and have a little smile and I thought he might be a bit deaf or simple in his mind but I knew he wasn't deaf and the way he talked about his son getting an education in Canada showed that if he'd had a chance he would have been in a university himself.

He's coming out of a diner on Laight Street and when he sees me he smiles, Oh, mon. I must have known you were coming. I got a hero sandwich a mile long and beer. We eat on the pier, okay?

I'm ready to walk back down Laight Street to the pier but he steers me away. He doesn't want the men at the warehouse to see us. They'd ride him all day. They'd laugh and ask Horace when he knew my mother. That makes me want to defy them and walk Laight Street even more. No, mon, he says. Save your emotions for bigger things.

This is a big thing, Horace.

It's nothing, mon. It's ignorance.

We should fight back.

No, son.

God, he's calling me son.

No, son. I don't have time for fighting back. I won't step on their ground. I pick my own fights. I have a son in college. I have a wife who is ailing and still cleaning offices at night on Broad Street. Eat your sandwich, mon.

It's ham and cheese slathered with mustard and we wash it down with a quart of Rheingold passing the bottle back and forth, and I have a sudden thought and a feeling that I'll never forget this hour on the pier with Horace with seagulls circling for what might come and ships strung along the Hudson waiting for tugboats to dock them or push them out to the Narrows, traffic rushing behind us and over our heads on the West Side Highway, a radio in a pier office with Vaughn Monroe singing "Buttons and Bows", Horace offering me another chunk of sandwich telling me I could use a few pounds on my bones and his surprised look when I nearly drop the sandwich, nearly drop it because of the weakness in my heart and the way tears are dropping on the sandwich and I don't know why, can't explain it to Horace or myself with the power of this sadness that tells me this won't come again, this sandwich, this beer on the pier with Horace that makes me feel so happy all I can do is weep with the sadness in it and I feel so foolish I'd like to rest my head on his shoulder and he knows that because he moves closer, puts his arm around me as if I were his own son, the two of us black or white or nothing, and it doesn't matter because there's nothing to do but put down the sandwich where a seagull swoops in and gobbles it and we laugh, Horace and I, and he puts in my hand the whitest handkerchief I've ever seen and when I offer it back he shakes his head, keep it, and I tell myself I'll keep that handkerchief till my last breath.

I tell him what my mother used to say when we cried, Oh, your bladder must be near your eye, and he laughs. He doesn't seem to mind if we go back up Laight Street, and the men on the platform say nothing about him and my mother because it's hard to hurt people already laughing and beyond you.

33

Sometimes she's invited to cocktail parties. She takes me along and I'm confused with the way people stand nose to nose chatting and eating little things on bits of stale bread and crackers, no one singing or telling a story the way they did in Limerick, till they start looking at their watches and saying, Are you hungry? Wanna go eat something? and out they drift and that's what they call a party.

That's the uptown New York and I don't like it one bit especially when a man in a suit talks to Mike, tells her he's a lawyer, nods towards me, asks her why in heaven's name she's going out with someone like me and invites her to go to dinner as if she should walk away and leave me with the empty glass, everything stale, and nobody singing. Of course she says, No, thanks, though you can see she's flattered and I often wonder if she'd like to go with Mr Lawyer in the Suit rather than stay with me, a man from a slum who never went to high school and gawks at the world with two eyes like pissholes in the snow. Surely she'd like to marry someone with clear blue eyes and spotless white teeth who would take her to cocktail parties and move to Westchester where they'd join the country club, play golf and drink martinis, and frolic in the night in the grip of the gin.

I know already what I prefer myself, the downtown New York where men with beards and women with long hair and beads are reading poetry in coffee houses and bars. Their names are in the papers and magazines, Kerouac, Ginsberg, Brigid Murnaghan. When they're not living in lofts and tenements they roam the country. They drink wine from great jugs, they smoke marijuana, they lie on floors and dig the jazz. Dig. That's the way they talk and they click their fingers, cool, man, cool. They're like my Uncle Pa in Limerick, they don't give a fiddler's fart about anything. If they had to go to a cocktail party or wear a tie they'd die.

A tie was the cause of our first disagreement and the first time I saw Mike Small's temper. We were to go to a cocktail party and when I met her outside her apartment building on Riverside Drive she said, Where's your tie?

It's at home.

But this is a cocktail party.

I don't like wearing ties. They don't wear them down in the Village.

I don't care what they wear in the Village. This is a cocktail party and all the men will be wearing ties. You're in America now. Let's go up to a men's store on Broadway and get you a tie.

Why should I buy a tie when I have one at home?

Because I'm not going to that party with you in that condition.

She walked away from me, up 116th Street to Broadway, stuck her hand out, jumped into a taxi without giving me a second look to see if I was coming.

I took the Seventh Avenue train to Washington Heights in a blind agony, cursing myself for my stubbornness and worrying she might give me up completely for a Mr Lawyer in a Suit, that she might spend the rest of the summer going to cocktail parties with him till Bob the football player returned from ROTC. She might even give up Bob for the lawyer, finish college and move to Westchester or Long Island where all the men wear ties, where some have ties for every day of the week and social functions on top of it. She might be happy going to the country club all dressed up and remembering what her father said, A lady is not properly dressed till she has white gloves up to her elbows.

Paddy Arthur was coming down the stairs, all dressed up, no tie, on his way to an Irish dance and why didn't I go with him, I might meet Dolores again, ha ha.

I turned and went back downstairs telling him I didn't care if I never saw Dolores again in this life or the next after what she did luring me on to the E train and all the way to Queens Village letting me think there might be a bit of excitement at the end of the night. Before getting on the downtown train Paddy and I stopped for a beer at a Broadway bar and Paddy said, Jesus, what's up with you? Is it some kind of a bee you have up your arse?

When I told him about Mike Small and the tie he wasn't a bit sympathetic. He said that's what I get for running around with them fookin' Protestants and what would my poor mother say back in Limerick.

I don't care what my mother would say. I'm mad about Mike Small.

He asked for a whiskey and told me I should have one, too, loosen me up, calm me down, clear my head, and once I had two whiskeys in my system I told him how I'd like to lie on a Greenwich Village floor smoking marijuana, sharing a jug of wine with a long-haired girl, Charlie Parker on the phonograph floating us to heaven and easing us down again on a long low sweet wail.

Paddy gave me the fierce look. Arrah, for Jasus' sake, is it coddin' me you are? Do you know the trouble with you? Protestants and Negroes. Next thing it'll be Jews and then you're doomed altogether.

There was an old man smoking a pipe on the stool beside Paddy and he said, That's right, son, that's right. Tell your friend there that you have to stick with your own. All me life I stuck with me own, dug holes for the phone company, all Irish, never a bit of trouble because, by Jesus, I stuck with me own and I seen young fellas comin' over marryin' all kinds an' losin' their faith an' the next thing they're goin' to baseball games an' that's the end of them.

The old man said he knew a man from his own town who worked twenty-five years in a pub in Czechoslovakia and came home to settle down without a word of Czechoslovakian in his head and all because he stuck to his own kind, the few Irishmen he could find there, all sticking together, thank God an' His Blessed Mother. The old man said he'd like to buy us a drink to honor the men and women of Ireland who stick with their own so that when a child is born they know who the father is and that, by Christ, God forgive the language, is the most important thing of all, knowing who the father is.

We raised the glasses and toasted all who stick with their own and know who the father is. Paddy leaned towards the old man and they talked about home, which is Ireland, though the old man hadn't seen it for forty years and hoped to be buried in the lovely town of Gort beside his poor old Irish mother and his father who did his bit in the long struggle against the perfidious Saxon tyrant, and he raised his glass to sing,

> God save Ireland, sez the heroes,
> God save Ireland, sez 'em all,
> Whether on the scaffold high
> Or the battlefield we die,
> Oh, what matter when for Erin's sake we fall.

They sank deeper and deeper into their whiskey and I stared into the bar mirror wondering who's kissing Mike Small now, wishing I could be parading the streets with her so that heads would turn and I'd be the envy of one and all. Paddy and the old man talked to me only to remind me that thousands of men and women died for Ireland who'd hardly be happy with my behavior the way I run around with Episcopalians betraying the cause. Paddy gave me his back again and I was left to gawk at what I could see of myself in the mirror and wonder at the world I found myself in. From time to time the old man leaned around Paddy to tell me, Stick to your own, stick to your own. I'm in New York, land of the free and home of the brave but I'm supposed to behave as if I were still in Limerick, Irish at all times. I'm expected to go out only with Irish girls who frighten me with the way they're always in a state of grace saying no to everything and everyone unless it's a Paddy Muck who wants to settle on a farm of land in Roscommon and bring up seven children, three cows, five sheep and a pig. I don't know why I returned to America if I have to listen to the sad stories of Ireland's sufferings and dance with country girls, Mullingar heifers, beef to the heels.

There's nothing in my head but Mike Small, blonde, blue-eyed, delicious, sailing through life in her easy Episcopalian way, the all-American girl, with sweet memories of Tiverton in her head, the small town in Rhode Island, the house where her grandmother reared her, the bedroom with little curtains moving gently at the windows that looked out on the Narragansett River, the bed dressed with sheets, blankets, pillows galore, blonde head on pillow filled with dreams of outings, hayrides, trips to Boston, boys boys boys, and grandma in the morning setting out the nourishing all-American breakfast so that her little girl can move through the day charming the arse off every boy, girl, teacher and anyone she meets including me and mostly me as I sit stricken on the bar stool.

There was a darkness in my head from the whiskey and I was ready to tell Paddy and the old man, I'm weary of Ireland's sufferings and I can't live in two countries at the same time. Instead I left them, the two of them colloguin' on their bar stools, and walked from 179th Street down Broadway to 116th Street hoping that if I waited long enough I'd have one glimpse of Mike Small being brought home by Mr Lawyer in a Suit, a glimpse I want and don't want, till a cop in a patrol car calls to me and tells me, Move on, buddy, all the Barnard girls are gone to bed.

Move on, says the cop, and I did because there was no use trying to tell him I know who's kissing her now, that she's surely at a movie with the lawyer's arm around her, the tips of his fingers dangling at the border of her breast which is reserved for the honeymoon, that there might be a kiss or a squeeze between popcorn munches, and I'm here on Broadway looking at the gates of Columbia University across the street and I don't know which way to turn, wishing I could find a girl from California or Oklahoma, all blonde and blue-eyed like Mike Small, all cheerful with teeth that never knew an ache or cavity, all cheerful because her life is laid out so that she'll graduate from college and marry a nice boy, boy she calls him, and settle down in peace, ease and comfort, as my mother used to say.

The cop came at me again and told me keep moving, pal, and I tried to cross 116th Street with a bit of dignity so that he wouldn't be able to point the finger and tell his partner, There goes another whiskey-head Mick from the Old Country. They didn't know and wouldn't care that all this was happening because Mike Small wanted me to wear a tie and I refused.

The West End Bar was packed with Columbia students and I thought if I had a beer I might merge in and be mistaken for one of them, higher on the scale than NYU students. A blonde might take a fancy to me and get my mind off Mike Small though I didn't think I could shrug her off even if Brigitte Bardot herself slipped between my sheets.

I might as well be in the NYU cafeteria the way these Columbia students argued at the top of their voices about the emptiness of life, how absurd everything is and how all that matters is grace under pressure, man. When that bull's horn comes at you and grazes your hip you know that's the moment of truth, man. Read your Hemingway, man, read your J. Paul Sartre, man. They know the score.

If I didn't have to work in banks, docks, warehouses, I'd have time to be a proper college student and moan over the emptiness. I wish my father and mother had lived respectable lives and sent me to college so that I could spend my time in bars and cafeterias telling everyone how I admired Camus for his daily invitation to suicide and Hemingway for risking the bull's horn in the side. I know if I had money and time I'd be superior to every student in New York in the despair department though I could never mention any of this to my mother because she'd say, Arrah, for God's sake, don't you have your health and shoes and a fine head o' hair and what more do you want?

I drank my beer and wondered what kind of a country is this where cops keep telling you move on, where people put pigeonshit in your ham sandwich, where a girl who's engaged to be engaged to a football player walks away from me because I'm not wearing a tie, where a nun will baptize Michael what's left of him though he suffered in a concentration camp and deserves to be left in his Jewish condition bothering no one, where college students eat and drink to their hearts' content and moan about existentialism and the emptiness of everything, and cops tell you once again, Move on.

I walked back up Broadway past Columbia into Washington Heights and over to the George Washington Bridge where I could look up and down the Hudson River. My head was filled with dark clouds and noises and a coming and going of Limerick and Dachau and Ed Klein where Michael what's left of him, a piece of offal, was saved by GIs, and my mother moved in and out of my head with Emer from Mayo and Mike Small from Rhode Island, and Paddy Arthur laughed and said you'll never dance with Irish girls with them two eyes like pissholes in the snow, and I looked up and down the river and felt sorry for myself till the sky brightened beyond and the sun coming up traveled from tower to tower turning Manhattan into pillars of gold.

34

A few days later she calls me in tears. She's out on the street and would I come and get her at 116th and Broadway. There was trouble with her father, she has no money and doesn't know what to do. She's waiting on the corner and on the train she tells me how she got dressed with every intention of calling me and meeting me even though I had strong feelings about ties but her father said no, she wasn't going out and she said yes, she was going out and he punched her on the mouth which, as I can see, is swelling. She ran from her father's house and there's no going back. Mary O'Brien says she's in luck. One of the boarders is gone back to Ireland to marry the girl down the road and his room is available.

In a way I'm glad her father punched her because she came to me instead of Bob and that surely means she prefers me. Of course Bob is unhappy and in a few days there he is at the door calling me a sneaky little bogtrotter and telling me he's going to break my head but I move my head to one side and his fist crashes into the wall and he has to go to the hospital for a cast. On the way out he threatens he'll see me again and I'd better make my peace with my Maker though when I run into him a few days later at NYU he offers his good hand in friendship and I never see him again. He may be calling Mike Small behind my back but it's too late and she shouldn't even be talking to him since she already allowed me into her room and into her bed forgetting how she was reserving the body for the wedding night and the honeymoon. The night of our first excitement she tells me I've taken her virginity and if I should feel guilty or sad I can't especially when I know I'm the first, the one that stays forever in any girl's memory, as they used to say in the army.

We can't stay at Mary O'Brien's because we can't resist the temptation to be in the same bed and there are knowing looks. Paddy Arthur stops talking to me altogether and I'm not sure if he's being pious or patriotic, angry that I'm with someone neither Catholic nor Irish.

The Captain sends word he's ready to give Mike a certain amount of money every month and that means she can rent a small apartment in Brooklyn. I'd like to live with her but the Captain and the grandmother would think that disgraceful, so I rent my own cold water flat at 46 Downing Street in Greenwich Village. They call it a cold water flat and I don't know why. It has hot water but no heat except for a large kerosene heater which turns so red I'm afraid it might blow up. The only thing I can do to keep warm is to buy an electric blanket at Macy's and plug it into a long cord that lets me wander around. There's a bath tub in the kitchen, and a lavatory in the hallway I must share with an old Italian couple across the hall. The old Italian man knocks on my door to tell me I'm to put my own toilet paper on the holder in the lavatory and I'm to keep my hands off his. He and his wife mark their toilet paper and they'll know if I try to use it so watch out. His English is poor and when he starts to tell me of the troubles he had with the previous tenants in my flat he becomes so frustrated he shakes his fist in my face and warns me I could be in big trouble if I touch his toilet paper, big trouble, yet gives me a roll to start me off, to make sure I don't touch his. He says his wife is a nice woman and giving me the roll is her idea, that she's a sick woman who wants a quiet life and no trouble. Capice?

Mike finds a small apartment on Henry Street in Brooklyn Heights. She has her own bathroom and no one torments her over toilet paper. She says my apartment is a disgrace and she doesn't know how I can live like that, no heat, no place to cook, Italians yelling over toilet paper. She feels sorry for me and lets me stay over. She makes delicious dinners even though she didn't even know how to make coffee when her father punched her out of the house.

When classes end she goes back to Rhode Island to have her dentist examine the abscess caused by her father's fist. I'm taking summer session courses at NYU, reading, studying, writing term papers. I'm working at the bank, the midnight to eight shift, and operating the forklift at the Baker and Williams warehouse two days a week, dreaming of Mike Small nice and cozy with her grandmother in Rhode Island.

She calls to tell me her grandmother isn't that angry with me anymore over what I said about her easy life. Grandma even said something nice about me.

What was that?

She said you have a nice head of black curly hair and she feels so sorry about the thing with my father she doesn't mind if you come here for a day or two.

After what happened to me in the bank I could go to Rhode Island for a week. A man sat next to me in a coffee shop on Broad Street near where I worked, told me he had heard me talk the night before and figured I was Irish, right?

I am.

Yeah, well, I'm Irish, too, Irish as Paddy's pig, father from Carlow, mom from Sligo. I hope you don't mind but I got your name from someone and found you're a member of the Teamsters and the ILA.

My ILA card expired.

That's okay. I'm an organizer and we're trying to break into these fucking banks, excuse the language. Are you on for that?

Oh, sure.

I mean you're the only one we could get on your shift with any kind of union history and what we'd like you to do is just drop little hints. You know and they know the banks pay shit wages. So, just a little hint here and there, not too many, not too soon, and I'll see you in a few weeks. Here, I'll take care of the bill.

Next night is Thursday, pay night, and when we receive our checks the supervisor says, You've got the rest of the night off, McCourt.

He makes sure everyone on the shift hears him. You're off tonight, McCourt, and all the other nights and you can tell that to your union friends. This is a bank and we don't need any goddam unions.

They say nothing, the typists, the clerks. They nod. Andy Peters would say something but he's still on the four to twelve shift.

I take my check and as I wait for the elevator an executive comes out of his office. McCourt, right?

I nod.

So, you're finishing college, right?

I am.

Ever think of joining us here? You could come aboard and we'd have you up to a nice five-figure salary in three years. I mean you're one of our own, right? Irish?

I am.

Me, too. Father from Wicklow, mom from Dublin, and when you work at a bank like this doors open, you know, AOH, Knights of Columbus, all that there. We take care of our own. If we don't, who will?

I was just fired.

Fired? What the hell you talking about? Fired for what?

For letting a union organizer talk to me in a coffee shop.

You did that? Let a union organizer talk to you?

I did.

That was a stupid damn thing to do. Look, pal, we're outa the coal mines, we're outa the kitchens and the ditches. We don't need unions. Will the Irish ever get sense? Asking you a question. Talkin' a yeh.

I say nothing here and on the elevator going down. I say nothing because I've been fired from this bank and there's nothing to say anyway. I don't want to talk about the Irish getting sense and I don't know why everyone I meet has to tell me where his father and mother came from in Ireland.

The man wants to argue with me but I won't give him the satisfaction. It's better to walk away and leave him to the height he grew, as my mother used to say. He calls after me to tell me I'm an asshole, that I'll wind up digging ditches, delivering beer barrels, pouring whiskey for boozy micks in a Blarney Stone bar. He says, Jesus, is there anything wrong with looking after your own kind? and the strange thing is there's something in his voice that's sad as if I were a son that disappointed him.

Mike Small meets my train in Providence, Rhode Island, and takes me by bus to Tiverton. On the way we stop at a liquor store for a bottle of Pilgrim's rum, grandma's favorite. Zoe, the grandmother, says hi but doesn't offer hand or cheek. It's dinner time and there's corned beef and cabbage and boiled potatoes because that's what the Irish like to eat, according to Zoe. She says I must be tired from the trip and surely I'd like a drink. Mike looks at me and smiles and we know it's Zoe who wants a drink, rum and Coke.

How about you, grandma? Would you like a drink?

Well, I dunno, but all right. Are you making the drinks, Alberta? Yes.

Well, go easy with the Coke. It kills my stomach.

We sit in a living room dark from layers of blinds, curtains, drapes. There are no books, magazines, newspapers and the only pictures are of the Captain in his army lieutenant's uniform and one of Mike, a blonde angel of a child.

We sip our drinks and there's a silence because Mike is in the hallway answering the phone and Zoe and I have nothing to say to each other. I wish I could say, This is a nice house, but I can't because I don't like the darkness of this room when the sun is beaming outside. Then Zoe calls out, Alberta, you gonna stay on that goddam phone all night? You have a guest. She says to me, That's Charlie Moran she's talking to. They was great friends all through school but goddam he likes to talk.

Charlie Moran, is it? Mike leaves me here in this gloomy room with grandma while she chatters away with her old boyfriend. All these weeks in Rhode Island she's been having a grand time of it with Charlie while I'm slaving away in banks and warehouses.

Zoe says, Make yourself another drink, Frank. That means she wants one, too, and when she tells me go easy on the Coke, it kills her stomach, I double her rum dosage hoping it will knock her out so that I can have my way with her granddaughter.

But no, the drink makes her livelier and after a few swallows she says, Let's eat, goddamit. Irishmen like to eat, and while we're eating, she says, Do you like that, Frank?

I do.

Well, then, eat it. You know what I always say. A meal ain't a meal without a potato and I'm not even Irish. No, goddamit, not a drop of Irish though there's a bit of Scotch. MacDonald was my mother's name. That's Scotch, isn't it?

'Tis.

Not Irish?

No.

After dinner we watch television and she falls asleep in her armchair after telling me that Louis Armstrong there on the screen is ugly as sin and can't sing worth a damn. Mike shakes her and tells her go to bed.

Don't tell me go to bed, goddamit. You might be a college student but I'm still your grandmother, isn't that right, Bob?

I'm not Bob.

You're not? Well, who are you?

I'm Frank.

Oh, the Irishman. Well, Bob's a nice fellow. He's gonna be an officer. What are you gonna be?

A teacher.

A teacher? Oh, well, you won't be drivin' no Cadillac, and she pulls herself up the stairs to bed.

Now, surely, with Zoe snoring away in her room Mike will visit my bed but, no, she's too nervous. What if Zoe woke suddenly and discovered us? I'd be out on the road hailing the bus to Providence. It's a torment when Mike comes to kiss goodnight and even in the dark I know she's in her pink baby doll pajamas. She won't stay, oh, no, grandma might hear and I tell her I wouldn't care if God Himself were in the next room. No, no, she says, and leaves, and I wonder what kind of world is this where people will walk away from a chance of a wild fling in the bed.

At dawn Zoe runs the vacuum cleaner upstairs and downstairs and complains, This goddam house looks like Hogan's Alley. The house is spotless because she has nothing else to do but clean it and she barks about Hogan's Alley to put me in my place because she knows I know it was a dangerous Irish slum in New York. She complains the vacuum cleaner doesn't pick up the way it used to though it's easy to see there's nothing to pick up. She complains that Alberta sleeps too late and is she supposed to make three separate breakfasts, her own, mine, Alberta's?

Her neighbor, Abbie, drops in and they drink coffee and complain about kids, dirt, television, that goddam ugly Louis Armstrong who can't sing, dirt, the price of food and clothes, kids, the goddam Portuguese taking over everything in Fall River and surrounding towns, bad enough when the Irish ran everything, at least they could speak English long as they were sober. They complain about hairdressers who charge a fortune and can't tell a decent hairdo from a donkey's ass.

Oh, Zoe, says Abbie, your language.

Well, I mean it, goddamit.

If my mother were here she'd be puzzled. She'd wonder why these women complain. Lord above, she'd say, they have everything. They're warm and clean and well fed and they complain about everything. My mother and the women in the slums of Limerick had nothing and rarely complained. They said it was the will of God.

Zoe has everything but complains with the music of the vacuum cleaner and that may be her way of prayer, goddamit.

In Tiverton Mike is Alberta. Zoe complains she doesn't know why a girl would want to use a goddam name like Mike when she has her own name, Agnes Alberta.

We walk around Tiverton and I imagine again what it would be like to be a teacher here, married to Alberta. We'd have a sparkling kitchen where every morning I'd have my coffee and an egg and read the *Providence Journal*. We'd have a big bathroom with plenty of hot water and thick towels with powerful naps and I might loll there in the tub and gaze on the Narragansett River through little curtains billowing gently in the morning sun. We'd have a car for trips to Horseneck Beach and Block Island, and we'd visit Alberta's mother's relations in Nantucket. As the years passed my hair would recede, my belly protrude. Friday nights we'd attend local high school basketball games and I'd meet someone who might sponsor me for the country club. If they admitted me I'd have to take up golf and that would surely be the end of me, the first step towards the grave. A visit to Tiverton is enough to drive me back to New York.

35

In the summer of 1957 I complete my degree courses at NYU and in the autumn pass the Board of Education exams for teaching high school English.

An afternoon newspaper, *The World-Telegram and Sun*, has a School Page where teachers can find jobs. Most of the vacancies are for vocational high schools and friends have already warned me, Don't go near those vocational high schools. The kids are killers. They'll chew you up and spit you out. Look at that movie, *The Blackboard Jungle*, where a teacher says vocational schools are the garbage cans of the school system and the teachers are there to sit on the lids. See that movie and you'll run in the other direction.

There is a vacancy for an English teacher at Samuel Gompers Vocational High School in the Bronx but the chairman of the Academic Department tells me I look too young and the kids would give me a hard time. He says his father was from Donegal, his mother from Kilkenny, and he'd like to help me. We should take care of our own but his hands are tied and the way he shrugs and extends his open palms contradicts what he said entirely. Still, he heaves himself from his chair and walks me to the front door with his arm across my shoulders, tells me I should try Samuel Gompers again, maybe in a year or two I'd fill out and lose that innocent look, and he'd keep me in mind though I needn't bother to come back if I grew a beard. He can't stand beards and he wants no goddam beatniks in his department. Meanwhile, he says, I might try the Catholic high schools where the pay wasn't that good but I'd be with my own kind of people and a nice Irish kid should stick with his own.

The Academic Chairman at Grady Vocational High School in Brooklyn says, Yeah, he'd like to help me out but, you know, with that brogue you'd have trouble with the kids, they might think you talk funny and teaching is hard enough when you speak properly and doubly hard with a brogue. He wants to know how I passed the speech part of the teachers' license examination and when I tell him I was issued a substitute license on condition I take remedial speech he says, Yeah, maybe you could come back when you don't sound like Paddy-off-the-boat, ha ha ha. He tells me in the meantime I should stick with my own people, he's Irish himself, well, three-quarters Irish and you never know with other people.

When I meet Andy Peters for a beer I tell him I can't get a teaching job till I fill out and look older and talk like an American and he says, Shit. Forget the teaching. Go into business. Specialize in something. Hubcaps. Corner the market. Get a job in a garage and learn all you can about hubcaps. People come into the garage and hubcaps are mentioned and everyone turns to you. A hubcap crisis, you know? where a hubcap falls off, flies through the air and decapitates a model housewife and all the TV stations call you for your expert opinion. Then you go out on your own. McCourt's Hubcap Emporium. Foreign and Domestic Hubcaps New and Old. Antique Hubcaps for the Discerning Collector.

Is he serious?

Maybe not about hubcaps. He says, Look at what they do in the academic world. You corner a half-acre of human knowledge, Chaucer's phallic imagery in *The Wife of Bath*, or Swift's devotion to shit, and you build a fence around it. Decorate the fence with footnotes and bibliographies. Post a sign, Keep off, Trespassers Will Lose Their Tenure. I'm engaged, myself, in a noble search for a Mongolian philosopher. I thought of cornering the market on an Irish philosopher but all I could find was Berkeley and they've got their claws into him already. One Irish philosopher, for Christ's sakes. One. Don't you people ever ponder? So I'm stuck with the Mongolians or the Chinese and I'll probably have to learn Mongolian or Chinese or whatever the hell they speak there and when I find him he'll be my very own.

When was the last time you heard a Mongolian philosopher mentioned at those East Side cocktail parties you like so much? I'll get my PhD, write a few articles on my Mongolian in obscure scholarly journals. I'll deliver learned lectures to drunken Orientalists at MLA conventions and wait for the job offers to pour in from the Ivy League and its cousins. I'll get a tweed jacket, a pipe, and a pompous manner, and faculty wives will be throwing themselves at me, begging me to recite, in English, erotic Mongolian verses smuggled into the country up the ass of a yak or a panda at the Bronx Zoo. And I'll tell you another thing, piece of advice in case you go to graduate school. When you take a course always find out what the professor wrote his doctoral dissertation on and give it back to him. If the guy specializes in Tennyson's water images then pour it all over him. If the guy specializes in George Berkeley give him the sound of one hand clapping while a tree falls in the forest. How do you think I got through these fucking philosophy courses at NYU? If the guy's a Catholic I give him Aquinas. Jewish? I give him Maimonides. Agnostic? You never know what to tell an agnostic. You never know where you stand with them though you can always try old Nietzsche. You can bend that old fucker any way you like.

Andy tells me Bird was the greatest American who ever lived, right up there with Abraham Lincoln and Max Kiss, the guy who invented Ex-Lax. Bird should be given the Nobel Prize and a seat in the House of Lords.

Who's Bird?

For Christ's sakes, McCourt. I worry about you. You tell me you love jazz and you don't know Bird. Charlie Parker, man. Mozart. You listenin' to me? You dig? Mozart, for Christ's sakes. That's Charlie Parker.

What does Charlie Parker have to do with teaching jobs or hubcaps or Maimonides or anything else?

You see, McCourt, that's your problem, always looking for relevance, a sucker for logic. That's why the Irish don't have philosophers. Lotta goddam barroom theologians and shithouse lawyers. Loosen up, man. Thursday night I finish early and we'll take a trip to Fifty-Second Street for a little music. Okay?

We go from club to club till we come to one place where a black woman in a white dress croaks into a microphone and holds on to it as if she were on a swaying ship. Andy whispers, That's Billie and it's a disgrace they're letting her make an ass of herself up there.

He marches to the stage and tries to take her hand to help her down but she curses him and swings at him till she stumbles and falls off the stage. Another man leaves his barstool and leads her out the door and I know from the clear sounds between her croaks that was Billie Holiday, the voice I heard on the Armed Forces Network when I was a boy in Limerick, a pure voice telling me, "I Can't Give You Anything But Love, Baby."

Andy says, That's what happens.

What do you mean, that's what happens?

I mean that's what happens, that's all. Jesus, do I have to write a book?

How is it you know Billie Holiday?

I have loved Billie Holiday since I was a child. I come to Fifty-Second Street to catch glimpses of her. I would hold her coat. I would scour her toilet bowl. I would run her bath water. I would kiss the ground she walks on. I told her I got a dishonorable discharge for not fucking a French sheep and she thought it should be made into a song. I don't know what God intends to do with me in the next life but I'm not going unless I can sit between Billie and Bird for eternity.

In the middle of March, 1958, there's another notice in the paper, Vacancy for English teacher at McKee Vocational and Technical High School, Staten Island. The assistant principal, Miss Seested, examines my license and takes me to see the principal, Moses Sorola, who doesn't move from his chair behind the desk where he squints at me through a cloud of smoke drifting from his nose and from the cigarette in his hand. He says this is an emergency situation. The teacher I'd be replacing, Miss Mudd, has made an abrupt decision to retire in the middle of the term. He says teachers like that are inconsiderate and make life hard for a principal. He doesn't have a full English program for me, that I'd have to teach three classes in Social Studies every day, two in English.

But I don't know anything about Social Studies.

He puffs and squints and says, Don't worry about it, and takes me to the office of the Academic Chairman, Acting, who says I'd be teaching three classes of Economic Citizenship and here's the text-book, *Your World and You.* Mr Sorola smiles through the smoke and says, *Your World and You*. That should cover just about everything.

I tell him I know nothing about economics or citizenship and he says, Just stay a few pages ahead of the kids. Everything you tell them will be news. Tell them this is 1958, tell them their names, tell them they live on Staten Island, and they'll be surprised and grateful for the information. By the end of the year even your name will be news to them. Forget your college literature courses. This is not high IQ plateau.

He takes me to see Miss Mudd, the teacher I'm replacing. When he opens the classroom door boys and girls are leaning out the windows calling to others across the schoolyard. Miss Mudd sits at her desk, reading travel brochures, ignoring the paper airplane that zooms over her head.

Miss Mudd has retired.

Mr Sorola leaves the room and she says, That's right, young man. I can't wait to get outa here. What's this? Wednesday? Friday's my last day and you're welcome to this looney bin. Thirty-two years I've been at this and who cares? The kids? Parents? Who, young man, gives a shit, forgive my French? We teach their brats and they pay us like dishwashers. What was the year? Nineteen and twenty-six. Calvin Coolidge was in. I came in. I worked right through him and the Depression man, Hoover, and Roosevelt and Truman and Eisenhower. Look out that window. You got a good view of New York Harbor from here and Monday morning if these kids aren't driving you crazy you'll see a big ship sailing by and that'll be me on the deck waving, son, waving and smiling, because there's two things I never want to see again in my life, with God's help, Staten Island and kids. Monsters, monsters. Look at 'em. You'd be better off working with chimpanzees in the Bronx Zoo. What's this? Nineteen and fifty-eight. How did I ever last? You'd need to be Joe Louis. So, good luck, son. You're gonna need it.

36

Before I leave Mr Sorola says I should return next day to observe Miss Mudd with her five classes. I'd learn something about procedure. He says half of teaching is procedure and I don't know what he's talking about. I don't know what to make of the smile through the cigarette smoke and I wonder if he's joking. He pushes my typed program across the desk, three classes of EC, Economic Citizenship, two classes of E4, sophomore English in the fourth term. The top of the program card says, Official Class, PRA, and at the bottom, Building Assignment, School Cafeteria, fifth period. I don't ask Mr Sorola what these mean for fear he might think I'm ignorant and change his mind about hiring me.

As I make my way down the hill to the ferry a boy's voice calls, Mr McCourt, Mr McCourt, are you Mr McCourt?

I am.

Mr Sorola would like to see you again.

I follow the student up the hill and I know why Mr Sorola wants to see me again. He has changed his mind. He's found someone with experience, someone with a grasp of procedure, someone who knows what an official class is. If I don't get this job I'll have to start my search again.

Mr Sorola waits at the front door of the school. He lets his cigarette dangle from his mouth and puts his hand on my shoulder. He says, I have good news for you. The job is opening sooner than we expected. Miss Mudd must have been impressed by you because she decided to leave today. In fact she's gone, out the back door, and it's barely noon. So we're wondering if you can take over tomorrow and then you won't have to wait till Monday.

But I . . .

Yeah, I know. You're not ready. That's okay. We'll give you some stuff to keep the kids busy till you get the hang of it and I'll look in from time to time to keep them in line.

He tells me this is my golden opportunity to jump right in and start my teaching career, I'm young, I'll like the kids, they'll like me, McKee High School has a hell of a faculty all ready to help and support.

Of course I say yes, I'll be in tomorrow. It isn't the teaching job of my dreams but it will have to do since I can't get anything else. I sit on the Staten Island ferry thinking of teacher recruiters from suburban high schools at NYU, how they told me I seemed intelligent and enthusiastic but really my accent would be a problem. Oh, they had to admit it was charming, reminded them of that nice Barry Fitzgerald in *Going My Way* but but but. They said they had high standards of speech in their schools and it wouldn't be possible to make an exception in my case since the brogue was infectious and what would parents say if their kids came home sounding like Barry Fitzgerald or Maureen O'Hara?

I wanted to work in one of their suburban schools, Long Island, Westchester, where the boys and girls were bright, cheerful, smiling, attentive, their pens poised as I discoursed on *Beowulf*, *The Canterbury Tales*, the Cavalier Poets, the Metaphysicals. I'd be admired and once the boys and girls had passed my classes their parents would surely invite me to dinner at the finest houses. Young mothers would come to see me about their children and who could tell what might happen when husbands were absent, the men in grey flannel suits, and I trolled the suburbs for lonely wives.

I'll have to forget the suburbs. I have here on my lap the book that will help me through my first day of teaching, *Your World and You*, and I flip the pages through a short history of the United States from an economic point of view, chapters on American government, the banking system, how to read the stock market pages, how to open a savings account, how to keep household accounts, how to get loans and mortgages.

At the end of each chapter there are questions of fact and questions for discussion. What caused the stock market crash of 1929? How can this be avoided in future? If you wanted to save money and gain interest would you a) keep it in a glass jar b) invest in the Japanese stock market c) keep it under your mattress d) put it in a savings bank account.

There are suggested activities, with insertions penciled in by a former student. Call a family meeting and discuss your family finances with Dad and Mom. Show them from your study of this book how they might improve their bookkeeping. (Insertion, Don't be surprised if they beat you up.) Take a tour of the New York Stock Exchange with your class. (They'll be glad to get out of school for a day.) Think of a product your community might need and start a small company to supply it. (Try Spanish fly.) Write to the Federal Reserve Board and tell them what you think of them. (Tell them leave a little for the rest of us.) Interview a number of people who remember the crash of 1929 and write a one-thousand-word report. (Ask them why they didn't commit suicide.) Write a story in which you explain the gold standard to a ten-year-old child. (It'll help him sleep.) Write a report on what it cost to build the Brooklyn Bridge and what it might cost now. Be specific. (Or else.)

The ferry sails by Ellis Island and the Statue of Liberty and I'm so worried about Economic Citizenship I don't even think of the millions who landed here and the ones who were sent back with the bad eyes and the weak chests. I don't know how I'll be able to stand before these American teenagers and talk to them about the branches of government and preach the virtues of saving when I owe money everywhere myself. And with the ferry sliding into its slip and the day that's facing me tomorrow why shouldn't I treat myself to a few beers at the Bean Pot bar and after those few beers why shouldn't I take a train to the White Horse Tavern in Greenwich Village to chat with Paddy and Tom Clancy and listen to them sing in the back room? When I call Mike to tell her the good news about the new job she wants to know where I am and gives me a lecture on the stupidity of staying out drinking beer the night before the most important day of my life and I'd better get my ass home if I know what's good for me.

Sometimes she talks like her grandmother who always tells you what to do with your ass. Get your ass in here. Get your ass out of that bed.

Mike is right but she graduated from high school and she'll know what to say to her classes when she starts teaching and even though I have a college degree I don't know what I'm going to say to Miss Mudd's classes. Should I be Robert Donat in *Goodbye, Mr Chips* or Glenn Ford in *The Blackboard Jungle*? Should I swagger into the classroom like James Cagney or march in like an Irish schoolmaster with a stick, a strap and a roar? If a student sends a paper airplane zooming at me should I shove my face into his and tell him try that one more time, kid, and you're in trouble? What am I to do with the ones looking out the window calling to their friends across the yard? If they're like some of the students in *The Blackboard Jungle* they'll be tough and they'll ignore me and the rest of the class will despise me.

Paddy Clancy leaves his singing in the back room of the White Horse and tells me he wouldn't be in my shoes for anything. Everyone knows what the high schools in this country are like, that's right, blackboard jungles. With my college degree why didn't I become a lawyer or a businessman or something where I could make some money? He knows a few teachers around the Village and they're getting out of it the first opportunity.

He's right, too. Everybody is right and I'm too muddled with all the beer in my body to worry anymore. I go to my apartment and fall into bed with all my clothes on and even though I'm worn out with the long day and the beer I can't sleep. I keep getting up to read chapters of *Your World and You*, testing myself with questions of fact, imagining what I'm going to say about the stock market, the differences between stocks and bonds, the three branches of government, the recession of this year, the depression of that year, and I might as well get up, go out, and fill myself with coffee to keep me going the rest of the day.

At dawn I sit in a coffee shop on Hudson Street with longshoremen, truck drivers, warehousemen, checkers. Why shouldn't I live like them? They work their eight hours a day, read the *Daily News*, follow baseball, have a few beers, go home to their wives, raise their kids. They're paid better than teachers and they don't have to worry about *Your World and You* and sex-crazed teenagers who don't want to be in your class. In twenty years workingmen can retire and sit in the Florida sun, waiting for lunch and dinner. I could call McKee Vocational and

Technical High School and tell them, Forget it, I want an easier life. I could tell Mr Sorola they're looking for a checker at the Baker and Williams Warehouse, a job I could easily get with my college degree, and all I'd have to do the rest of my life is stand on the platform with manifests on a clipboard checking what comes and what goes.

Then I think of what Mike Small would say if I told her, No, I didn't go to McKee High School today. I took a job as checker with Baker and Williams. She'd have a tantrum. She'd say, All that work in college to be a goddam checker down at the docks? She might throw me out of the house and return to the arms of Bob the football player and I'd be alone in the world, forced to go to Irish dances and take home girls reserving their bodies for the wedding night.

I'm ashamed of myself that I'm going to my first day of teaching in this condition, hung over from the White Horse Tavern, jumping out of my skin from seven cups of coffee this morning, my eyes like two pissholes in the snow, two days of black hair sprouting on my face, my tongue furry from lack of a toothbrush, my heart banging in my chest from fatigue and fear of dozens of American adolescents. I'm sorry I ever left Limerick. I could be back there with a pensionable job in the post office, postman respected by one and all, married to a nice girl named Maura, raising two children, confessing my sins every Saturday, in a state of grace every Sunday, a pillar of the community, a credit to my mother, dying in the bosom of Mother Church, mourned by a large circle of friends and relations.

There's a longshoreman at a table in the diner telling his friend how his son is graduating from St John's University in June, how he worked his ass off all these years to send the kid to college and he's the luckiest man in the world because his son appreciates what he's doing for him. Graduation Day he'll give himself a pat on the back for surviving a war and sending a son to college, a son who wants to be a teacher. His mother is so proud of him because she always wanted to be a teacher herself but never had the chance and this is the next best thing. Graduation Day they'll be the proudest parents in the world and that's what it's all about, right?

If this longshoreman and Horace down at Port Warehouses knew what I was thinking they'd have no patience with me. They'd tell me how lucky I am to have a college degree and a chance to teach.

★   ★   ★

The school secretary tells me see Miss Seested who tells me see Mr Sorola who tells me see the chairman of the Academic Department who says I have to check in with the school secretary to get my time card and why were they sending me to him in the first place?

The school secretary says, Oh, back already? and shows me how to dip my time card into the time clock, how to place it in my slot on the In Side and how to move it to the Out side. She says that if I have to leave the building for any reason whatsoever, even during my lunch period, I'm to sign out and back in with her because you never know when you might be needed, never know when there might be an emergency and you can't have teachers wandering in and out, back and forth at will. She tells me see Miss Seested who looks surprised. Oh, you're back, she says, and gives me a red Delaney book, the attendance book for my classes. She says, Of course you know how to use this, and I pretend I do for fear of being thought stupid. She sends me back to the school secretary for my home room attendance book and I have to lie to the secretary too and tell her I know how to use it. She says if I have any problems ask the kids. They know more than the teachers.

I'm trembling from the hangover and the coffee and the fear of what lies ahead of me, five classes, a home room, a Building Assignment, and I wish I were on the ferry to Manhattan where I could sit at a desk in a bank and make decisions about loans.

Students jostle me in the hallway. They push and scuffle and laugh. Don't they know I'm a teacher? Can't they see under my arm two attendance books and *Your World and You*? The schoolmasters in Limerick would never tolerate this carryon. They'd march up and down the halls with sticks and if you didn't walk properly you'd get that stick across the backs of your legs so you would.

And what am I supposed to do with this class, the first in my whole teaching career, students of Economic Citizenship, pelting each other with chalk, erasers, bologna sandwiches? When I walk in and place my books on the teacher's desk they'll surely stop throwing things. But they don't. They ignore me and I don't know what to do till the words come out of my mouth, the first words I ever utter as a teacher, Stop throwing sandwiches. They look at me as if to say, Who's this guy?

The bell signals the start of the class and the students slide into

233

their seats. They whisper to each other, they look at me, laugh, whisper again and I'm sorry I ever set foot on Staten Island. They turn to look at the blackboard along the side of the room where someone has printed in a large scrawl, Miss Mudd Is Gone. The Old Bag Reetired, and when they see me looking at it they whisper and laugh again. I open my copy of *Your World and You* as if to start a lesson till a girl raises her hand.

Yes?

Teacher, ain'tcha gonna take the attendance?

Oh, yes, I am.

That's my job, teacher.

When she sways up the aisle to my desk the boys make woo woo sounds and, Whaddya doin' the rest of my life, Daniela? She comes behind my desk, faces the class, and when she leans over to open the Delaney book it's easy to see her blouse is too small and that starts the woo woo all over again.

She smiles because she knows what the psychology books told us at NYU, that a fifteen-year-old girl is years ahead of a boy that age and if they want to shower her with woo woos it means nothing. She whispers to me she's already going out with a senior, a football player up at Curtis High School, where all the kids are smart, not a bunch of automechanic grease monkeys like the ones in this class. The boys know this, too, and that's why they pretend to clutch their hearts and faint when she calls out their names from the Delaney cards. She takes her time with the attendance book and I'm a fool standing off to the side, waiting. I know she's teasing the boys and I wonder if she's toying with me, too, showing her control of the class with a well-filled blouse and keeping me from whatever I might want to do with Economic Citizenship. When she calls the name of someone who was absent yesterday she demands a parent's note and if the absentee doesn't have it she reprimands him and writes N on the card. She reminds the class that five Ns could get you an F on your report card and turns to me, Isn't that right, teacher?

I don't know what to say. I nod. I blush.

Another girl calls out, Hey, teach, you cute, and I blush harder than ever. The boys roar and slap the desks with their open palms and the girls smile at each other. They say, You crazy, Yvonne, to the one who called me cute, and she tells them, But he is, he's really cute, and I wonder if the redness will ever leave my face, if I'll ever

234

be able to stand here and talk about Economic Citizenship, if I'll be forever at the mercy of Daniela and Yvonne.

Daniela says she's finished with the attendance and now she needs the pass to go to the bathroom. She takes a piece of wood from a drawer and wiggles her way out the door to another woo woo chorus and one boy calling to another, Joey, stand up, Joey, let's see how much you love her, let's see you stand, Joey, and Joey blushes so hard there's a wave of laughter and giggling across the room.

We're halfway through the period and I haven't said a word about Economic Citizenship. I try to be a teacher, a schoolmaster. I pick up *Your World and You* and tell them, OK, open your book to chapter, ah, what chapter were you up to?

We weren't up to no chapter.

You mean you weren't up to any chapter? Any chapter.

No, I mean we weren't up to no chapter. Miss Mudd didn't teach us nothing.

Miss Mudd didn't teach you anything. Anything.

Hey, teacher, why you repeating everything I'm sayin'? Nothing, anything. Miss Mudd never bothered us like that. Miss Mudd was nice.

They nod and murmur, Yeah, Miss Mudd was nice, and I feel I have to compete with her even if they drove her into retirement.

A hand is up.

Yes?

Teacher, you Scotch or somethin'?

No. Irish.

Oh, yeah? Irish like to drink, eh? All that whiskey, eh? You gonna be here Paddy's Day?

I'll be here on St Patrick's Day.

You not gonna be drunk an' throwin' up at the parade like all the Irish?

I said I'll be here. All right, open your books.

A hand.

What books, teacher?

This book, *Your World and You.*

We ain't got that book, teacher.

We don't have that book.

There you go again repeatin' everything we say.

We have to speak proper English.

Teacher, this ain't no English class. This is Ecanawmic Cizzenship. We supposed to be learnin' about money an' all an' you ain't teachin' us about money.

Daniela returns just as another hand is raised. Teacher, what's your name? Daniela returns the pass to the desk and tells the class. His name is McCoy. I just found out in the bathroom an' he ain't married.

I print my name on the blackboard, Mr McCourt.

A girl in the back of the room calls out, Mister, you got a girl-friend?

They laugh again. I blush again. They nudge each other. The girls say, Isn't he cute? and I take refuge in *Your World and You*.

Open your books. Chapter One. We'll start at the beginning. "A Brief History of the United States of America."

Mr McCoy.

McCourt. McCourt.

OK, yeah, we know all that about Columbus an' everything. We get that in history class with Mr Bogard. He'll be mad if you teach history an' he's gettin' paid to teach it an' that's not your job.

I have to teach what's in the book.

Miss Mudd didn't teach what's in the book. She didn't give a shit, excuse me, Mr McCoy.

McCourt.

Yeah.

And when the bell rings and they rush from the room Daniela comes to my desk and tells me not to worry, don't lissena to these kids, they're all so stoopid, she's taking the commercial course to be a legal secretary, and who knows she might be a lawyer herself some day, she'll take care of the attendance and everything. She tells me, Don't take no shit from nobody, Mr McCoy, excuse the language.

There are thirty-five girls in the next class, all dressed in white with buttons down the front from neck to hem. Most have the same hairstyle, the beehive. They ignore me. They set up little boxes on their desks and peer into mirrors. They pluck their eyebrows, they dab at their cheeks with powder puffs, they apply lipstick and pull their lips back between their teeth, they file their nails and blow at the nail dust. I open the Delaney book to call their names and they look surprised. Oh, you the substitute? Where's Miss Mudd?

She has retired.

Oh, you gonna be our regular teacher?

Yes.

I ask them what shop they're in, what they're studying.

Cosmetology.

What's that?

Beauty Culture. And what's your name, teacher?

I point to my name on the board. Mr McCourt.

Oh, yeah. Yvonne said you was cute.

I let this pass. If I attempt to correct every grammatical error in these classes I'll never get to Economic Citizenship and, worse, if I'm asked to explain the rules of grammar I'm bound to show my ignorance. I will put up with no distractions. I will begin with Chapter One from *Your World and You*, "A Brief History of the United States". I flip the pages from Columbus to the Pilgrims to the War of Independence, the War of 1812, the Civil War, and there's a hand and a voice in the back of the room.

Yes?

Mr McCourt, why you telling us this stuff?

I'm telling you this because you can't understand Economic Citizenship unless you have a grasp of the history of your country.

Mr McCourt, this is an English class. I mean you're the teacher an' you don't even know what class you're teaching.

They pluck their eyebrows, they file their nails, they shake their beehives, they pity me. They tell me my hair is a mess and it's easy to see I never had a manicure in my life.

Why don'tcha come up to Beauty Culture Shop an' we'll do you?

They smile and nudge each other and my face is on fire again and they say that's cute, too. Aw, gee, lookit him. He's shy.

I have to take control. I have to be the teacher. After all, I was once a corporal in the United States Army. I told men what to do and if they didn't do it I'd have their ass because they were in direct defiance of military regulations and subject to court martial. I will simply tell these girls what to do.

Put everything away and open your books.

What books?

Whatever books you have for English.

All we got is this *Giants in the Earth* and that's the most boring book in the world. And the whole class chants, Uh, huh, boring, boring, boring.

They tell me it's about some family from Europe out there on

237

the prairie and everyone is depressed and talking about suicide and no one in the class can finish this book because it makes you want to commit suicide yourself. Why can't they read a nice romance where you don't have all these Europe people all gloomy on the prairie? Or why couldn't they watch movies? They could watch James Dean, oh, gawd, James Dean, can't believe he's dead, they could watch him and talk about him. Oh, they could watch James Dean forever.

When the Beauty Culture girls leave there is homeroom, an eight-minute period when I have to take care of the clerical work for thirty-three students from printing shop. They swarm in, all boys, and they're helpful. They tell me what has to be done and not to worry. I am to take attendance, send a list of absentees to Miss Seested, collect absentee excuse notes supposedly written by parents and doctors, distribute transportation passes for bus, train, ferry. One boy brings the contents of Miss Mudd's mail box in the office. There are notes and letters from various officials in and out of the school, notes summoning wayward students for counseling, requests and demands for lists and forms and second and third reminders for everything. Miss Mudd seems to have ignored everything in her mail box for weeks and my head feels heavy with the thought of the work she's left me.

The boys tells me I don't have to take attendance every day but once I start I can't stop. Most are Italian and taking the attendance is light opera: Adinolfi, Buscaglia, Cacciamani, DiFazio, Esposito, Gagliardo, Miceli.

I'm supposed to lead the class in reciting the Pledge of Allegiance and singing "The Star Spangled Banner". I barely know them but that doesn't matter. The boys stand, place their hands on their hearts and recite their own version of the Pledge, I pledge allegiance to the flag of Staten Island, and to one night stands, one girl under me, invisible to all, with love and kisses for me only me.

When they sing "The Star Spangled Banner" some hum along with "You ain't nothin' but a hounddog".

There's a note from the Academic chairman requesting I go to his office next period, the third, my prep period when I'm supposed to plan my lessons. He tells me I should have a lesson plan for every class and there is a standard form for lesson plans, I should insist all students keep notebooks that are clean and neat, I should make sure their textbooks are covered, points off if they don't, I should check to see that windows are open six inches from the top, I should send a student around the room at the end of every period to collect litter, I should stand at the door to greet classes entering and again leaving, I should print clearly on the blackboard the title and aim of every lesson, I should never ask a question requiring a yes or no answer, I shouldn't allow unnecessary noise in the room, I should require all students to stay in their seats unless they raise their hands for the bathroom pass, I should insist on boys removing their hats, I should make it clear that no student is allowed to speak without first raising his hand. I should make sure all students stay till the end of the period, that they're not to be allowed out of the room at the warning bell which, for my information, rings five minutes before the end of the period. If my students are caught in the hallways before the end of the period I'll have to answer to the principal himself. Any questions?

The chairman says there will be mid-term exams in two weeks and my teaching should focus on the areas that will be covered in the exams. Students in English should have mastered spelling and vocabulary lists, one hundred of each which they are supposed to have in their notebooks and if they don't, points off, and be prepared to write essays on two novels. Economic Citizenship students should be more than halfway through *Your World and You*.

The bell rings for the fifth period, my Building Assignment, the school cafeteria. The chairman tells me that's an easy assignment. I'll be up there with Jake Homer, the teacher the kids fear most.

I climb the stairs to the cafeteria, my head throbbing, my mouth dry and I wish I could sail away with Miss Mudd. Instead I'm pushed and jostled by students on the staircase and stopped by a teacher who demands to see my pass. He's short and broad and his bald head sits, neckless, on his shoulders. He glares at me through thick glasses and his chin is a challenging jut. I tell him I'm a teacher and he won't believe me. He wants to see my program card. Oh, he says, I'm sorry. You're McCourt. I'm Jake Homer. We'll be in the cafeteria together. I follow him upstairs and along the hallway to the students' cafeteria. There are two lines waiting to be served in the kitchen, a boys and a girls. Jake tells me that's one of the big problems, keeping the boys and girls separated. He says they're animals at this age, especially the boys, and it's not their fault. It's nature. If he had his way he'd have the girls in a separate cafeteria altogether. The boys are always strutting and showing off and if two like the same girl there's bound to be a fight. He tells me if there is a fight don't interfere right away. Let the little bastards go at it and get it out of their systems. It's worse in the warm weather, May, June, when the girls take off their sweaters and the boys go tit crazy. The girls know what they're doing and the boys are like lap dogs, panting. Our job is to keep them separated and if a boy wants to visit the girls' section he has to come over here for permission. Otherwise you'll have two hundred kids going at it in broad daylight. We also have to patrol the cafeteria and make sure the kids take their trays and garbage back to the kitchen, make sure they clean the area around their tables.

Jake asks if I'd ever been in the army and when I tell him yes he says, Bet you didn't know you'd be pulling this kind of shit detail when you decided to become a teacher. Bet you didn't know you'd be a cafeteria guard, a garbage supervisor, a psychologist, a babysitter, eh? Tells you what they think of teachers in this country that you have to spend hours of your life looking at these kids eating like pigs and telling them clean up afterwards. Doctors and lawyers don't run around telling people clean up. You won't find teachers in Europe stuck with this kind of crap. Over there a high school teacher is treated like a professor.

A boy carrying his tray to the kitchen doesn't notice that an ice cream wrapper has fallen from his tray. On the way back to his table Jake calls him over.

Kid, pick up that ice cream wrapper.

The boy is defiant. I didn't drop that.

Kid, I didn't ask you that. I said pick it up.

I don't have to pick it up. I know my rights.

Come here, kid. I'll tell you your rights.

It is suddenly quiet in the cafeteria. With everyone looking on Jake grabs the skin over the boy's left shoulder blade and twists it clockwise. Kid, he says, you have five rights. Number one, you shut up. Number two, you do what you're told, and the other three don't count.

As Jake twists the skin the boy tries not to grimace, tries to look good, till Jake twists so hard the boy's knees buckle and he cries, All right, all right, Mr Homer, all right. I'll pick up the paper.

Jake releases him. Okay, kid. I can see you're a reasonable kid.

The boy slouches back to his seat. He's ashamed and I know he needn't be. When a master in Leamy's National School in Limerick tormented a boy like that we were always against the master and I can feel that's how it is here the way students, boys and girls, glare at Jake and me. It makes me wonder if I'll ever be as hard as an Irish schoolmaster or as tough as Jake Homer. The psychology teachers at NYU never told us what we should do in such cases and that's because university professors never have to supervise students in high school cafeterias. And what will happen if Jake is ever absent and I'm the only teacher here trying to keep two hundred students under control? Surely if I tell a girl pick up a piece of paper and she refuses I can't twist the skin of her shoulder blade till her knees tremble. No, I'll have to wait till I'm old and tough like Jake, though even he surely wouldn't twist the skin of a girl's shoulder blade. He's more polite with the girls, calls them dear, and would they mind helping keep this place clean. They say, Yes, Mr Homer, and he waddles away smiling.

He stands by me near the kitchen and tells me, You gotta come down on the little bastards like a ton of bricks. Then he says to a boy standing before us, Yes, son?

Mr Homer, I gotta give you back the dollar I owe you.

What was that, son?

Day I didn't have lunch money last month. You gave me a lend of a buck.

Forget it, son. Get yourself an ice cream.

But, Mr Homer.

Go on, son. Get yourself a treat.

Thanks, Mr Homer.

Okay, kid.

He tells me, That's a nice kid. You wouldn't believe what a hard time he has, still comes to school. His father tortured, nearly killed by a Mussolini gang in Italy. Jesus, you wouldn't believe the hard times they have, these kids' families, and this is the richest country in the world. Count your blessings, McCourt. Mind if I call you Frank?

Not at all, Mr Homer.

Call me Jake.

Okay, Jake.

It's my lunch hour and he directs me to the teachers' cafeteria on the top floor. Mr Sorola sees me and introduces me to teachers at different tables, Mr Rowantree, Printing, Mr Kriegsman, Health Ed., Mr Gordon, Machine Shop, Miss Gilfinane, Art, Mr Garber, Speech, Mr Bogard, Social Studies, Mr Maratea, Social Studies.

I take my tray with sandwich and coffee and sit at an empty table but Mr Bogard comes over, tells me his name is Bob, and invites me to sit with him and the other teachers. I'd like to stay by myself because I don't know what to say to anyone and as soon as I open my mouth they'll say, Oh, you're Irish, and I'll have to explain how that happened. It's not as bad as being black. You can always change your accent but you can never change the color of your skin and it must be a nuisance when you're black and people think they have to talk about black matters just because you're there with that skin. You can change your accent and people will stop telling you where their parents came from in Ireland but there's no escape when you're black.

But I can't say no to Mr Bogard after he went to all the trouble of coming to my table and, when I'm settled with my coffee and sandwich, the teachers introduce themselves again with first names. Jack Kriegsman says, Your first day, eh? You sure you want to do this?

Some teachers laugh and shake their heads as if to say they're sorry they ever got into this. Bob Bogard doesn't laugh. He leans across the table and says, If there's any profession more important than teaching I'd like to know what it is. No one seems to know what to say after that till Stanley Garber asks me what subject I teach.

English. Well, not exactly. They have me teaching three classes of Economic Citizenship, and Miss Gilfinane says, Oh, you're Irish. It's so nice to hear the brogue here.

She tells me her ancestry and wants to know where I came from, when I came, will I ever go back, and why are the Catholics and Protestants always fighting in the Old Country. Jack Kriegsman says they're worse than the Jews and the Arabs and Stanley Garber disagrees. Stanley says at least the Irish on both sides have one thing in common, Christianity, and the Jews and the Arabs are as different as day and night. Jack says, Bullshit, and Stanley comes back with a sarcastic, That's an intelligent comment.

When the bell rings Bob Bogard and Stanley Garber walk me downstairs and Bob tells me he knows the situation in Miss Mudd's classes, that the kids are wild after weeks where there was no teaching, and if I need help to let him know. I tell him I do need help. I'd like to know what the hell I'm supposed to do with Economic Citizenship classes facing mid-term exams in two weeks who haven't even looked at the book. How am I supposed to give grades on report cards based on nothing?

Stanley says, Don't worry. A lot of the report card grades in this school are based on nothing anyway. There are kids here reading on a third grade level and it's not your fault. They should be in elementary school but they can't be kept there because they're six feet tall, too big for the furniture and trouble for the teachers. You'll see.

He and Bob Bogard look at my program and shake their heads. Three classes at the end of the day That's the worst possible program you can get, an impossible one for a new teacher. The kids have had their lunch and they're all charged up with protein and sugar and they want to be outside horsing around. Sex. That's all it is, says Stanley. Sex, sex, sex. But that's what happens when you arrive in the middle of the term and take over for the Miss Mudds of the world.

Good luck, says Stanley.

Let me know if I can help, says Bob.

I grapple with the protein and the sugar and the sex sex sex in periods six, seven, and eight but I'm silenced by a hail of questions and objections. Where's Miss Mudd? She dead? She eloped? Ha ha ha. You our new teacher? You gonna be with us forever and ever? You gotta girlfriend, teacher? No, we don't have no *World and You*. Dumb book. Why can't we talk about movies? I had a teacher in fifth grade talked about movies all the time and they fired her. She was a great teacher. Teacher, don't forget to take the attendance. Miss Mudd always took the attendance.

Miss Mudd didn't have to take the attendance because in every class there is a monitor to do it. The monitor is usually a shy girl with a neat notebook and good handwriting. For taking the attendance she gets service credits and that impresses employers when she goes looking for a job in Manhattan.

The sophomore English students break into cheers at the news that Miss Mudd is gone forever. She was mean. She tried to make them read that boring book, *Giants in the Earth*, and she said when they were finished with that they'd have to read *Silas Marner* and Louis by the window who reads lots of books told everyone it's a book about a dirty old man in England and a little girl and that's the kind of book we shouldn't be reading in America.

Miss Mudd said they'd have to read *Silas Marner* because there was a mid-term exam coming up and they'd have to write an essay comparing it with *Giants in the Earth* and the students in eighth-period sophomore English would like to know where does she get off thinking you can compare a book about gloomy people on the prairie with a book about a dirty old man in England?

They cheer again. They tell me, We don't want to read no dumb books.

You mean you don't want to read any dumb books.

What?

Oh, nothing. The warning bell rings and they gather up their coats and bags to pile out the door. I have to shout, Sit down. That's the warning bell.

They look surprised. What's up, teacher?

You're not supposed to leave at the warning bell.

Miss Mudd let us leave.

I'm not Miss Mudd.

Miss Mudd was nice. She let us leave. Why you so mean?

They're out the door and I can't stop them. Mr Sorola is in the hallway to tell me my students are not supposed to leave at the warning bell.

I know, Mr Sorola. I couldn't stop them.

Well, Mr McCourt, a little more discipline tomorrow, eh?

Yes, Mr Sorola.

Is this man serious or is he pulling my leg?

37

Old Italian men patrol the Staten Island Ferry for shoeshine customers. I've had a hard night and a harder day and is there any reason why I shouldn't spend a dollar plus a quarter tip on a shoeshine even if this old Italian shakes his head and tells me in his broken English I should buy a new pair of shoes from his brother who sells them on Delancey Street and would give me a good price if I mention Alfonso on the ferry.

When he finishes he shakes his head and says he'll charge me only fifty cents because these are the worst shoes he's seen in years, a bum's shoes, shoes you wouldn't put on a dead man, and I should go to Delancey Street and don't forget to tell his brother who sent me. I tell him how I don't have the money for a new pair, I just started a new job, and he says, Alla right, alla right, gimme a dolla. He says, You teacha, right? and I say, How do you know? Teachas always have the lousy shoes.

I give him the dollar and the tip and he walks away shaking his head and calling Shine, shine.

It's a bright March day and pleasant to sit on the deck outside to watch tourists excited with their cameras over the Statue of Liberty, the long finger of the Hudson River ahead and the Manhattan skyline drifting toward us. The water is alive with little choppy white waves and there's a warm spring touch in the breeze blowing up the Narrows.

Oh, it's good and I'd like to stand up there on the bridge steering this old ferry back and forth back and forth through the tugs and scows and freighters and liners that heave the harbor into swells that plash against the ferry car deck.

That would be a pleasant life, easier than facing dozens of high school kids every day with their secret little nudges, winks and laughs, their complaints and objections, or the way they have of ignoring me as if I were a piece of furniture. A memory floats into my head from a morning at NYU, a face saying, Aren't we being a little paranoid?

Paranoid. I looked it up. If I'm standing before a class and one kid whispers something to another and they laugh will I think they're laughing at me? Will they sit in the cafeteria imitating my accent and joking about my red eyes? I know they will because we did the same thing in Leamy's National School and if I'm going to worry about it I might as well spend my life in the loan department of the Manufacturer's Trust Company.

Is this what I'll do the rest of my life, take the subway then the ferry to Staten Island, climb the hill to McKee Vocational and Technical High School, punch in at the time clock, extract a bulge of paper from my mail box, tell my students class after class day after day, Sit down, please, open your notebooks, take out your pens, you don't have paper? here's paper, you don't have a pen? borrow one, copy the notes on the board, you can't see from there? Joey would you change seats with Brian? come on, Joey, don't be such a, no, Joey, I didn't call you a jerk, I just asked you to change seats with Brian who needs glasses, you don't need glasses, Brian? well, why do you have to move, never mind, Joey, just move, will you? Freddie, put that sandwich away, this isn't the lunchroom, I don't care if you're hungry, no, you can't go to the bathroom to eat your sandwich, you're not supposed to be eating sandwiches in the toilet, what is it, Maria? you're sick, you have to see the nurse? OK, here's a pass, Diane, would you take Maria to the nurse's office and let me know what the nurse says, no, I know they won't tell you what's wrong with her, I just want to know if she'll be coming back to class, what is it, Albert, you're sick, too? no, you're not, Albert, you just sit there and do your work, you gotta see the nurse, Albert? you're really sick? you have diarrhea? well, here, here's the pass to the boys' room and don't stay there all period, the rest of you finish copying the notes on the board, there will be a test, you know that, don't you? there will be a test, what's that, Sebastian, your pen ran out of ink? well, why didn't you say something? yes, you're saying it now but you could have said it ten minutes ago, oh, you didn't want to interrupt all these sick people? that's nice of you, Sebastian, does anyone have a pen to loan Sebastian? oh, come on, what's that, Joey? Sebastian is a what? a what? you shouldn't say things like that, Joey, Sebastian sit down, no fighting in the classroom, what's that, Ann? you gotta go? go where, Ann? oh, you got your period? you're right, Joey, she doesn't have to tell the whole world, yes, Daniela? you want to take Ann to the bathroom? why? oh, she don't ah doesn't speak good English, so what does that have to do with her having her? what's that, Joey? you don't think girls should talk like that, easy, Daniela, easy, you don't have to be insulting, what's that, Joey? you're religious and people shouldn't talk like that, okay, easy, Daniela, I know you're defending Ann who needs to go to the toilet, the bathroom, so go, take her there, and the rest of you copy the notes on the board, oh, you can't see, either? you want to move up? ok, move up, here's an empty seat but where's your notebook? you left it on the bus, all right, you need paper, here's paper, you need a pen? here's a pen? you need to go to the bathroom? well, go go go to the bathroom, eat a sandwich, hang out with your friends, Jesus.

Mr McCoy.

McCourt.

You shun't swear like dat. You shun't say God's name like dat.

They say, Oh, Mr McCourt, you should take off tomorrow, Paddy's Day. Gee, you're Irish. You should go to the parade.

If I took off and stayed in bed all day they'd be just as pleased. Substitutes for absent teachers rarely bother with attendance and students simply cut class. Aw, come on, Mr McCourt, you need a holiday with your Irish friends. I mean you wouldn't come to school if you was in Ireland, would you?

They groan when I appear on the day. Aw, shit, man, excuse the language, what kinda Irishman are you? Hey, teacher, maybe you'll go out tonight with all the Irish an' maybe you won't be in tomorrow?

I'll be here tomorrow.

They bring me green things, a potato sprayed, a green bagel, a bottle of Heineken because it's green, a head of cabbage with holes for eyes, nose, mouth, wearing a little green leprechaun cap made in the art room. The cabbage is Kevin and has a girl friend, an eggplant named Maureen. There is a greeting card two feet by two wishing me Happy St Paddy's Day with a collage of green paper things, shamrocks, shillelaghs, whiskey bottles, a drawing of a green corned beef, St Patrick holding a glass of green beer instead of a crozier and saying, Faith an' Begorrah, it's a great day for the Irish, a drawing of me with a balloon saying, Kiss Me I'm Irish. The card is signed by dozens of students from my five classes and decorated with happy faces shaped like shamrocks.

The classes are noisy. Hey, Mr McCourt, how come you ain't wearin' green? Because he don't have to, stoopid, he's Irish. Mr McCourt, whyn't you goin' to the parade? Because he just started this job. Chrissakes, he's here only a week.

Mr Sorola opens the door. Is everything all right, Mr McCourt? Oh, yes.

He comes to my desk, looks at the card, smiles. They must like you, eh? And you've been here how long? A week?

Almost.

Well, this is very nice but see if you can get them back to work. He goes towards the door and he's followed by, Happy Paddy's Day, Mr Sorola, but he leaves without turning around. When someone at the back of the room says, Mr Sorola is a miserable guinea, there is a scuffle that ends only when I threaten them with a test on *Your World and You*. Then someone says, Sorola ain't no Italian. He's Finnish.

Finnish? What's Finnish?

Finland, stoopid, where it's dark all the time.

He don't look Finnish.

So, shithead, what does Finnish look like?

I dunno but he don't look it. He could be Sicilian.

He's not Sicilian. He's Finnish and I'm layin' a dollar bet. Anyone wanna bet?

No one wants to challenge the bet and I tell them, All right, open your notebooks.

They're indignant. Open our notebooks? Paddy's Day an' you're telling' us open our notebooks after we got you the card an' everything.

I know. Thank you for the card but this is a regular schoolday, there will be tests and we have to cover *Your World and You*.

There is a groaning around the room and the green is gone out of the day. Oh, Mr McCourt, if you only knew how we hate that book.

Oh, Mr McCourt, can't you tell us about Ireland or something?

Mr McCourt, tell us about your girlfriend. You must have a nice girlfriend. You're real cute. My mother is divorced. She'd like to meet you.

Mr McCourt, I got a sister your age. She got a big job in a bank. She likes all that old music, Bing Crosby an' all.

Mr McCourt, I seen this Irish movie, *The Quiet Man*, on TV an' John Wayne was beatin' up his wife, what's her name, and is that what they do in Ireland, beat up their wives?

They would do anything to avoid *Your World and You*. Mr McCourt, did you keep pigs in your kitchen?

We didn't have a kitchen.

Yeah, but if you didn't have a kitchen how could you cook?

We had a fireplace where we boiled water for tea and we ate bread.

They couldn't believe we had no electricity and wanted to know how we kept food refrigerated. The one who asked about pigs in the kitchen said everyone has a refrigerator till another boy told him he was wrong, that his mother grew up in Sicily and didn't have a refrigerator and if the pigs-in-the-kitchen boy didn't believe him they'd meet in a dark alley after school and only one of them would come out. Some girls in the class told them cool it and one said she felt so sorry for me growing up like that if she could go back in time she'd take me home and let me take a nice bath as long as I liked and then I could eat everything in the refrigerator, everything. The girls nodded and the boys were quiet and I was glad the bell rang so that I could escape to the teachers' toilet with my strange emotions.

I am learning the art of the high school students' delaying tactics, how they seize on any occasion to avoid the work of the day. They flatter and cajole and hold their hands over their hearts declaring they are desperate to hear all about Ireland and the Irish, they would have asked days ago but they delayed till St Patrick's Day knowing I'd want to celebrate my heritage and religion and everything and would I tell them about Irish music and is it true Ireland is green all the time and the girls have those cute little upturned noses and the men drink drink drink, is it true, Mr McCourt?

There are muttered threats and promises around the room. I ain't stayin' in school today. I'm goin' to the parade in the city. All the Catlic schools have the day off. I'm Catlic. Why shun't I have the day off? Fuck this. End of this period you'll see my ass on the ferry. You comin,' Joey?

Nah. My mother would kill me. I'm not Irish.

So what? I'm not Irish neither.

Irish only want Irish in that parade.

Bullshit. They got Negroes in the parade an' if they got Negroes why should I be sittin' here an' I'm Italian Catlic?

They won't like it.

I don't care. Irish wouldn't even be here 'cept Columbus discovered this country an' he was Italian.

My uncle said he was Jewish.

Oh, kiss my ass, Joey.

There's a ripple of excitement in the room and calls for, Fight, fight, hit him, Joey, hit him, because a fight is another way of passing the time and keeping the teacher from the lesson.

It is time for teacher intervention, All right, all right, open your notebooks, and there are cries of pain, Notebooks, notebooks, Mr McCourt, why you doin' this to us? An' we don't want no *Your World an' You* on Paddy's Day. My mother's mother was Irish an' we should have respect. Why can't you tell us about school in Ireland, why?

All right.

I'm a new teacher and I've lost the first battle and it's all the fault of St Patrick. I tell this class and all my classes the rest of the day about school in Ireland, about the masters with their sticks, straps, canes, how we had to memorize everything and recite, how the masters would kill us if we ever tried to fight in their classrooms, how we were not allowed to ask questions nor have discussions, how we left school at fourteen and became messenger boys or unemployed.

I tell them about Ireland because I have no choice. My students have seized the day and there's nothing I can do about it. I could threaten them with *Your World and You* and *Silas Marner* and satisfy myself that I was in control, that I was teaching, but I know there would be a flurry of requests for passes for the toilets, the nurse, the guidance counselor, and, Can I have the pass to call my aunt who's dying of cancer in Manhattan? If I insisted on hewing to the curriculum today I'd be talking to myself and my instincts tell me one group of experienced students in an American classroom can break one inexperienced teacher.

How about high school, Mr McCourt?

I didn't go.

Sebastian says, Yeah, it shows. And I promise myself, I'll get you later, you little bastard.

They tell him, Shut up, Sebastian.

Mr McCourt, didn't they have no high school in Ireland?

They had dozens of high schools but kids from my school weren't encouraged to go.

Man, I'd like to live in a country where you didn't have to go to high school.

In the teachers' cafeteria there are two schools of thought. The old timers tell me, You're young, you're new but don't let these damn kids ride all over you. Let 'em know who's boss in the classroom and remember, you are the boss. Control is the big thing in teaching. No control and you can't teach. You have the power to pass and fail and they know goddam well if they fail there's no place for them in this society. They'll be sweeping the streets and washing the dishes and it'll be their own fault, the little bastards. Just don't take shit. You're the boss, the man with the red pen.

Most of the old-timers survived the Second World War. They won't talk about it except to hint at bad times at Monte Cassino, the Battle of the Bulge, Japanese prisoner of war camps, riding a tank into a German town and searching for your mother's family. You see all this and you're not gonna take shit from these kids. You fought so they could sit on their asses in school every day and get the school lunch they whine about all the time and that's more than your own father and mother ever had.

Younger teachers are not so sure. They've taken courses in Educational Psychology and The Philosophy of Education, they've read John Dewey, and they tell me these children are human beings and we have to meet their felt needs.

I don't know what a felt need is and I don't ask for fear of exposing my ignorance. The younger teachers shake their heads over the older ones. They tell me the war is over, these children are not the enemy. They are our children, for God's sakes.

An older teacher says, Felt needs, my ass. Jump from a plane into a field full of krauts and you'll know what a felt need is. And John Dewey can kiss my ass, too. Just like the rest of these goddam college professors bullshittin' about teaching in high schools and they wouldn't know a high school kid if he walked up and pissed on their leg.

Stanley Garber says, That's right. Every day we put on our armor and go into battle. Everyone laughs because Stanley has the easiest job in the school, speech teacher, no paper work, no books, and what the hell would he know about going into battle? He sits behind his desk and asks his small classes what they'd like to talk about today and all he has to do is correct their pronunciation. He tells me it's really too late to help them by the time they get to high school. This is not *My Fair Lady* and he's not Professor Henry Higgins. On days when he's not in the mood or they don't want to talk he tells them get lost and he comes to the cafeteria to discuss the terrible state of American education.

Mr Sorola smiles at Stanley through his cigarette smoke. So, Mr Garber, he says, how does it feel to be retired?

Stanley smiles back. You should know, Mr Sorola. You've been retired for years.

We'd all like to laugh but you never know with principals.

When I tell my students bring their books to class they claim, Miss Mudd never gave us no books. Economic Citizenship classes say, We don't know nothin' about *Your World and You,* and English classes say they never saw *Giants in the Earth* or *Silas Marner.* The chairman of the Academic Department says, Of course they got books and when they got them they had to fill out book receipts. Look in Miss Mudd's desk, excuse me, your desk, and you'll find them.

There are no book receipts in the desk. There are travel brochures, crossword puzzle books, an assortment of forms, directives, letters Miss Mudd wrote and never sent, a few letters to her from former students, a life of Bach in German, a life of Balzac in French, and there are innocent looks around the room when I say, Didn't Miss Mudd hand out books and didn't you fill in book receipts? They look at one another and shake their heads. Did you get a book? I don't remember getting a book? Miss Mudd, she never did nothin'.

I know they're lying because in each class there are two or three with books and I know they got the books in the normal way. Teacher distributes them. Teacher gets books receipts. I don't want to embarrass the students who have the books by asking them how they came by them. I can't ask them to make liars of their classmates.

The chairman stops me in the hallway. Well, how about those books? and when I tell him how I can't embarrass the students who have the books he says, Bullshit, and storms into my class next period. All right, the ones who have books, raise your hands.

There is one hand.

All right, where did you get that book?

Ah, I got it, ah, from Miss Mudd.

And you signed a receipt?

Ah, yeah.

What's your name?

Julio.

And when you got that book didn't the rest of the class get books, too?

I feel my heart beating hard and I'm angry that even if I'm a new teacher this is my class and no one should barge in here and embarrass one of my students and, Christ, I have to say something. I have to come between this boy and this chairman. I tell the chairman, I already asked Julio about that. He was absent and got the book from Miss Mudd at the end of the day.

Oh, yeah. Is that right, Julio?

Yeah.

And the rest of you. When did you get your books?

There is silence. They know I lied and Julio knows I lied and the chairman surely suspects me of lying but he doesn't know what to do. He says, We'll get to the bottom of this, and leaves.

The word goes from class to class and next day there is a book on every desk, *Your World and You* and *Silas Marner*, and when the chairman returns with Mr Sorola he doesn't know what to say. Mr Sorola gives his little smile. So, Mr McCourt, we're back in business, eh?

There may be books on every desk this one day when students and teacher present a united front to the outsiders, the chairman, the principal, but once they leave the honeymoon ends and there is a chorus of complaints about these books, how boring they are, how heavy, and why do they have to bring them to school every day? The

English students say, Oh, *Silas Marner*'s a small book, but if they have to carry *Giants in the Earth* you need a big breakfast, it's such a big book and it's so boring. Will they have to carry it every day? Why can't they leave it in the classroom closet?

If you leave it in the closet how are you going to read it?

Why can't we read it in class? All the other teachers tell their classes, Okay, Henry, you read page nineteen, okay, Nancy, you read page twenty, an' that's how they finish the book and when they're reading we can put our heads down an' take a nap ha ha ha, just kidding, Mr McCourt.

38

In Manhattan my brother, Malachy, is running a bar called Malachy's with two partners. He acts with the Irish Players, appears on radio and television and gets his name into the newspapers. That brings me fame at McKee Vocational and Technical High School. Now my students know my name and I'm not Mr McCoy anymore.

Hey, Mr McCourt, I seen your brother on TV. He's a crazy guy.

Mr McCourt, my mother seen your brother on TV.

Mr McCourt, how come you're not on TV? How come you're just a teacher?

Mr McCourt, you got an Irish accent. Why can't you be funny like your brother?

Mr McCourt, you could be on TV. You could be in a love story with Miss Mudd, holding her hands on a ship and kissing her old wrinkly face.

Teachers who venture into the City, Manhattan, tell me they see Malachy in plays.

Oh, he's funny, your brother. We said hello to him after the play and told him we teach with you and he was very nice but, boy, does he like to drink.

★   ★   ★

My brother, Michael, is out of the air force and working behind the bar with Malachy. If people want to buy my brothers a drink who are they to say no. It's cheers, bottoms, up, *slainte* and *skoal*. When the bar closes they don't have to go home. There are after-hours joints where they can drink and trade stories with police inspectors and gracious madams from the finest brothels on the Upper East Side. They can breakfast at Rubin's on Central Park South where there are always celebrities to keep your neck swiveling.

Malachy was famous for his, Come in, girls, and to hell with the old farts up and down Third Avenue. The old bar owners looked with suspicion on a woman alone. She was up to no good and there was no place at the bar for her. Put her over there in a dark corner and give her no more than two drinks and if there's a hint of a man going near her out she goes on the sidewalk and that's that.

When Malachy's Bar opened the word spread that girls from the Barbizon Women's Residence were actually sitting up on his barstools and soon the men flocked in from P. J. Clarke's, Toots Shor's, El Morocco, to be trailed by a snoop of gossip columnists eager to report celebrity sightings and Malachy's latest wild doings. There were playboys and their ladies, pioneers of the jet set. There were heirs to fortunes so old and deep their tendrils curled in the dark depths of South African diamond mines. Malachy and Michael were invited to parties in Manhattan apartments so vast that guests emerged days later from forgotten rooms. There were skinny-dipping parties in the Hamptons and parties in Connecticut where rich men rode the rich women who rode the thoroughbred horses.

President Eisenhower takes time out from his golf to sign an occasional bill and to warn us of the industrial-military complex and Richard Nixon watches and waits while Malachy and Michael pour the drinks and keep everyone laughing and demanding more, more drinks, Malachy, more stories, Michael, you two are a riot.

Meanwhile my mother Angela McCourt, drinks tea in her comfortable kitchen in Limerick, hears stories from visitors about the great times in New York, sees newspaper clippings about Malachy on *The Jack Paar Show*, and she has nothing else to do but drink that tea, keep the house and herself nice and warm, look after Alphie now that he's out of school and ready for a job whatever that may be, and wouldn't it be lovely if she and Alphie could take a little trip to New

York because she hasn't been there in ages and her sons, Frank, Michael, Malachy are there and doing so well.

My cold water flat on Downing Street is uncomfortable and there's nothing I can do about it because of my small teacher's salary and the few dollars I send my mother till my brother Alphie gets a job. When I moved in I bought kerosene for my cast-iron stove from the little Italian hunchback on Bleecker Street. He said, You ony need a leetle in the stove, but I must have put in too much because the stove turned into a great red living thing in my kitchen and since I didn't know how to turn it down or off I fled the flat and went to the White Horse Tavern where I sat all afternoon in a terrible state of nerves waiting for the boom of the explosion and the wailing and honking of fire engines. I would have to decide then if I should go back to the smoking remains of 46 Downing Street with charred bodies being brought out and face fire inspectors and police or if I should call Alberta in Brooklyn, tell her my building was in ashes, my belongings all gone, and could she see her way to putting me up for a few days till I could find another cold water flat.

There was no explosion, no fire, and I felt so relieved I thought I deserved a bath, time in the tub, a little peace, ease and comfort, as my mother would say.

It's all right to loll in a tub in a cold water flat but there's a problem with the head. The flat is so cold that if you stay in the tub long enough your head begins to freeze and you don't know what to do with it. If you slip under the water, head and all, you suffer when you emerge and the hot water on your head freezes and then you're shivering and sneezing from the chin up.

And you can't read in comfort in a tub in a cold water flat. The body submerged in the hot water might grow pink and wrinkled from the heat but the hands holding the book turn purple from the cold. If it's a small book you can alternate the hands, holding the book with one hand while the other is in warm water. This could be a solution to the reading problem except that the hand that was in the water is now wet and threatening to make the book soggy and you can't reach for the towel every few minutes because you want that towel to be warm and dry at the end of your time in the tub.

I thought I could solve the head problem by wearing a knitted skier's cap and the hand problem with a pair of cheap gloves but then I worried that if I ever died of a heart attack the ambulance people would wonder what I was doing wearing cap and gloves in the tub and of course they'd slip this discovery to the *Daily News* and I'd be the laughing stock of McKee Vocational and Technical High School and the patrons of various bars.

I bought the cap and gloves anyway and on the day of no explosion I filled the tub with hot water. I decided to be good to myself, forget the reading and slide under the water as often as I liked to keep the head from freezing. I turned on the radio to music suitable for a man who had survived a nerve-racking afternoon with a dangerous stove, plugged in my electric blanket and draped it across a chair beside the tub so that I could step out, dry myself quickly with the pink towel Alberta had given me, wrap myself in the electric blanket, put on my cap and gloves and lay on the bed cozy and warm. I watched the snow beat against my window, thanked God the stove had cooled by itself and read myself to sleep with *Anna Karenina*.

The tenant under me is Bradford Rush who moved into the flat when I told him about it on the midnight shift at the Manufacturer's Trust Company. If anyone at the bank called him Brad he snapped at them, Bradford, Bradford, my name is Bradford, so mean that no one ever wanted to talk to him and when we went out for breakfast or lunch or whatever we called it at three a.m. he was never invited to join us. Then one of the women who was leaving to get married invited him to have a drink with us and he told us, after three drinks, he was from Colorado, a graduate of Yale and living in New York to get over the suicide of his mother who screamed for six months with bone cancer. The woman leaving to get married burst into tears over this story and we wondered why the hell Bradford had to hang such a cloud over our small party. That's what I asked him on the train to Downing Street that night but all I got was a little smile and I wondered if he was right in the head. I wondered why he did clerical work in a bank when he had an Ivy League degree and could have been on Wall Street with his own kind.

Later I wondered why he didn't just say no to me in my time of crisis, the bitter February day my electricity was turned off for nonpayment. I came home to give myself the peace, ease and comfort of a hot bath in the kitchen tub. I draped the electric blanket over the chair, I turned on the radio. There was no sound. There was no warmth in the blanket, no light from the lamp.

The water was steaming into the tub and I was naked. Now I had to put on cap, gloves and socks, wrap myself in an electric blanket with no heat and curse the company that turned off my electricity. It was still daylight but I knew I couldn't stay in that condition.

Bradford. Surely he wouldn't mind doing me a little favor.

I knocked on his door and he opened it with his usual grimness. Yes?

Bradford, I have a bit of a crisis upstairs.

Why are you wrapped up in that electric blanket?

That's what I came to talk to you about. They cut off my electricity and I have no heat but this blanket and I wondered if I dropped a long extension cord out my window you might take it and plug it in and I'd have electricity till I can pay my bill which I promise you will be very soon.

I could tell he didn't want to do it but he gave a little nod and pulled in my extension cord when I dropped it. I knocked on the floor three times hoping he'd understand that I was saying thank you but there was no response and whenever I saw him on the stairs he barely acknowledged me and I knew he was brooding on the extension cord. The Electrical Shop teacher at McKee told me an arrangement like this would cost a few measly pennies a day and couldn't understand why anyone would resent it. He said I could offer the cheap bastard a few dollars for the great inconvenience of having a cord plugged into an outlet but people like that were so miserable anyway it wasn't the money. It was the way they had of not being able to say no so that that no turned into acid in their guts and destroyed their lives.

I thought the Electrical Shop teacher was exaggerating till I noticed Bradford was becoming more and more hostile. He used to smile a little or nod or grunt something. Now he passes me without a word and I'm worried because I still don't have the money for the bills and I don't know how long our arrangement will last. It makes me so nervous I always turn on the radio to make sure I can take a bath and have the blanket warming up.

My cord stayed in his outlet for two months and then on a bitter night at the end of April there was an act of treachery. I turned on the radio, laid my electric blanket on a chair to warm up, put towel, cap and gloves on the blanket so that they'd be warm too, filled the tub, soaped myself and lay back listening to the *Symphonie fantastique* of Hector Berlioz and in the middle of the second movement when I'm ready to float out of the tub with the excitement everything stops, the radio is off, the light is out and I know the blanket will grow cold on the back of the chair.

And I knew what he did, this Bradford, pulled the cord on a man in a tub of hot water in a cold water flat. I knew I could never have done that to him or anyone else. I might do it to someone with central heating but never to a fellow cold water flat tenant, never.

I leaned over the side of the tub and knocked on the floor hoping he might have made a mistake, that he'd have the decency to plug me back in, but no, not a sound from him and no radio, no light. The water was still warm so I could lie there awhile thinking about the villainy of the human race, how a man with a degree from Yale could deliberately take hold of an electric cord and yank it from the outlet leaving me to freeze to death upstairs. One act of treachery like that is enough to make you give up hope and think of revenge.

No, it wasn't revenge I wanted. It was electricity and I'd have to find another way to bring Bradford to his senses. There was a spoon and there was a long piece of string and if I tied string to spoon I could open the window and dangle spoon so that it tapped against Bradford's window and he might understand that I was up there at the other end of the string, tapping, tapping for the gift of electricity. He might be annoyed and ignore my spoon but I remembered how he once told me that a dripping faucet was enough to keep him awake all night and if necessary I'd tap on his window with my spoon till he could stand it no longer. He could have climbed the stairs and banged on my door and told me to stop but I knew he could never be that direct and I knew I had him cornered. I felt sorry for him and the way his mother screamed for six months with bone cancer and I'd try to make all this up to him some day but this was a crisis and I needed my radio, my light, my electric blanket or I'd have to call Alberta for a night's lodgings and if she asked me why I could never tell her about Bradford plugging me in all these weeks. She'd get into a state of righteous indignation, the New England kind, and tell me I should be paying my bills and not tapping on people's windows with spoons on bitter nights, especially the windows of people whose mothers had died screaming of bone cancer. Then I'd tell her there was no connection between my spoon and Bradford's dead mother and that would lead to more disagreement and a fight and I'd have to storm out, back to my flat in the cold and the dark.

It was a Friday night, his night off from the bank, and I knew he couldn't escape by going to work. I imagined him downstairs with the cord in his hand trying to decide what to do with the spoon at his window. He could have gone out but where would he go? Who would want to have a beer with him in a bar and listen to how his mother died screaming? On top of that he'd probably tell the world someone upstairs was tormenting him with a spoon and anyone in a bar with a beer would move away from him.

I tapped on and off for a few hours and and suddenly there was light and music from the radio. *Symphonie fantastique* was long over and that irritated me but I turned the dial up on the electric blanket, put on cap and gloves and got back into bed with *Anna Karenina* which I couldn't read because of the darkness in my head over Bradford and his poor mother in Colorado. If my mother were dying of bone cancer in Limerick and someone upstairs tormented me with a spoon at my window I'd go up and kill him. I felt so guilty now I thought of knocking on Bradford's door and telling him, I'm sorry over the spoon and your poor mother and you can pull the plug, but I was so warm and cozy in the bed I fell asleep.

The following week I met him loading his things into a van. I asked if I could help and all he said was, Prick. He moved out but he left me plugged in and I had weeks of electricity till I blew the cord with an electric heater and had to go to Beneficial Finance Company for a loan to pay my electricity bills so that I wouldn't freeze to death.

39

The old-timers in the teachers' cafeteria say the classroom is a battleground, that teachers are warriors bringing the light to these damn kids who don't want to learn, who just want to sit on their asses and talk about movies and cars and sex and what they're gonna do Saturday night. That's the way it is in this country. We've got free education and no one wants it. Not like Europe where there's respect for teachers. Parents of kids in this school don't care because they never went to high school themselves. They were too busy struggling with the Depression and fighting wars, World War Two and Korea. Then you have all these bureaucrats who never liked teaching in the first place, all these goddam principals and assistant principals and chairmen who got out of the classroom as fast as their little legs could carry them and now spend their lives harassing the classroom teacher.

Bob Bogard is at the time clock. Ah, Mr McCourt, would you like to go for some soup?

Soup?

He has a little smile and I know he means something else. Yes, Mr McCourt. Soup.

We walk down the street and turn into the Meurot Bar.

Soup, Mr McCourt. Would you like a beer?

We settle on our bar stools and drink beer after beer. It's Friday and other teachers drift in and the talk is kids, kids, kids and the school, and I learn that in every school there are two worlds, the world of the classroom teacher and the world of the administrator and supervisor, that these worlds are forever at sword's point, that when anything goes wrong the teacher is the scapegoat.

Bob Bogard tells me don't worry about *Your World and You* and the mid-term test. Go through the motions. Distribute the test, watch the kids scribble what they don't know, retrieve the tests, give the kids passing grades, it isn't their fault Miss Mudd neglected them, the parents will be satisfied, and the chairman and principal will stay off my back.

I should be leaving the Meurot and taking the ferry to Manhattan where I'm having dinner with Alberta but the beers keep coming and it's hard to say no to such generosity and when I leave my barstool to call Alberta she screams at me that I'm a common Irish drunk and that's the last time she'll ever wait for me because she's finished with me forever and there are plenty of men who'd like to go out with her, goodbye.

All the beer in the world won't relieve my misery. I struggle with five classes a day, I live in a flat Alberta calls a hovel, and now I'm in danger of losing her because of my hours at the Meurot. I tell Bob I have to go, it's nearly midnight, we've been on the barstools for nine hours and I have dark clouds fluttering in my head. He says, One more and then we'll eat. You can't go on that ferry without eating. He says it's important to eat the kind of food that will ward off any unpleasant feeling in the morning, and the food he orders at the St George Diner is fish with eggs sunny-side up, hash brown potatoes, toast and coffee. He says the combination of fish and eggs after a day and night of beer is miraculous.

I'm on the ferry again where the old Italian patroling for shoeshine customers tells me my shoes look worse than ever and there's no use telling him I can't afford his offer of a shine, half price, if I'll buy shoes from his brother up on Delancey Street.

No, I don't have money for shoes. I don't have money for a shine.

Ah, *professore, professore*, I give you free shine. Make you feel good, the shine. You go see my brother for the shoes.

He sits on his box, pulls my foot to his lap and looks up at me.

I smella beer, *professore*. Teacher come home late, eh? Terrible shoes, terrible shoes, but I shine. He dabs on the polish, draws the brush around the shoe, snaps the polishing cloth across the toe, taps my knee to say it's done, replaces his things in the box and stands. He waits for the question and I don't ask because he knows it, What about my other shoe?

He shrugs. You go see my brother and I do your other shoe.

If I buy new shoes from your brother I won't need a shine for this.

He shrugs again. You are the *professore*. You smart, eh, with the brains? You teach and think about the shine and the no shine.

And he waddles away humming and calling shine shine to sleeping passengers.

I'm a teacher with a college degree and this old Italian, with little English, toys with me and sends me ashore with one shoe shined, the other streaked with marks of rain, snow, mud. If I grabbed him and demanded a shine for the dirty shoe he might yell and bring crew members to his aid and how would I explain the offer of a free shine, the shining of one shoe and then the trick? I'm sober enough by now to know you can't force an old Italian to shine your dirty shoe, that I was foolish to let him at my foot in the first place. If I protested to the crew members he might tell them he smelled beer and they'd laugh and walk away.

He waddles up and down the aisles. He keeps saying shine to the other passengers and I have a great urge to grab him and his box and heave him over the side. Instead, when I'm leaving the ferry, I tell him, I'll never buy shoes from your brother on Delancey Street.

He shrugs. I don't have a no brother on Delancey. Shine, shine.

When I told the shoeshine man I had no money I wasn't lying. I don't have fifteen cents for the subway fare. Whatever I had went for beer and when we went to the St George Diner I asked Bob Bogard to pay for my fish and eggs and I'll pay him back next week and it won't do me any harm to walk home, up Broadway, past Trinity Church and St Paul's Church where Robert Emmet's brother, Thomas, is buried, past City Hall, up to Houston Street and over to my cold water flat on Downing Street.

It is two o'clock in the morning, few people, an occasional car. Broad Street, where I worked at the Manufacturer's Trust Company, is over to my right and I wonder what became of Andy Peters and

Brigid formerly Bridey. I walk and look back over the eight and a half years since I arrived in New York, days at the Biltmore Hotel, the army, NYU, jobs in warehouses, on the docks, in banks. I think of Emer and Tom Clifford and wonder what became of Rappaport and the men I knew in the army. I never dreamed I'd be able to get a college degree and become a teacher and now I'm wondering if I can survive a vocational high school. The office buildings I pass are dark now but I know that during the day people sit at desks, study the stock market and make millions. They wear suits and ties, they carry briefcases, they go to lunch and talk about money money money. They live in Connecticut with their long-legged Episcopalian wives, who probably lolled in the lounge of the Biltmore Hotel when I cleaned up for them, and they drink martinis before dinner. They play golf at the country club and they have affairs and no one cares.

I could do that. I could spend time with Stanley Garber to get rid of my accent though he told me already I'd be an ass to lose it. He said the Irish accent is charming, opens doors, reminds people of Barry Fitzgerald. I told him I didn't want to remind people of Barry Fitzgerald and he said, Would you prefer to have a Jewish accent and remind people of Molly Goldberg? I asked him who Molly Goldberg was and he said if you don't know who Molly Goldberg is there's no use talking to you.

Why can't I have a bright carefree life like my brothers Malachy and Michael, uptown in the bar serving drinks to beautiful women and bantering with Ivy League graduates? I'd make more money than this forty-five-hundred dollars a year for regular substitute teachers. There would be large tips, all the food I could eat, and nights in the beds of Episcopalian heiresses frolicking and dazzling them with bits of poetry and scraps of wit. I'd sleep late, have lunch at a romantic restaurant, walk the streets of Manhattan, there would be no forms to fill out, no papers to correct, the books I'd read would be for my own pleasure and I'd never have to worry about sullen high school teenagers.

And what would I say if I ever met Horace again? Would I be able to tell him I went to college and became a teacher for a few weeks and it was so hard I became a bartender so that I could meet a better class of people on the Upper East Side? I know he'd shake his head and probably thank God I wasn't his son.

I think of the longshoreman in the coffee shop working for years so that his son can go to St John's University to become a teacher. What would I say to him?

If I told Alberta I was planning to leave teaching for the exciting world of the bars she'd surely run off and marry a lawyer or a football player.

So I won't give up teaching, not because of Horace or the long-shoreman or Alberta, but because of what I might say to myself at the end of a night of serving drinks and amusing the customers. I'd accuse myself of taking the easy way and all because I was defeated by boys and girls resisting *Your World and You* and *Giants in the Earth*.

They don't want to read and they don't want to write. They say, Aw, Mr McCourt, all these English teachers want us to write about dumb things like our summer vacation or the story of our life. Boring. Every year since our first grade we write the story of our life and teachers just give us a check mark and they say, Very Nice.

In the English classes they're cowed by the mid-term test with its multiple choice questions on spelling, vocabulary, grammar and reading comprehension. When I hand out the tests in Economic Citizenship there is muttering. There are hard words against Miss Mudd and how her ship should hit a rock and she should become fish food. I tell them, Do your best, and I'll be reasonable with report card grades, but there is a coldness and resentment in the room as if I had betrayed them by forcing this test on them.

Miss Mudd saves me. While my classes are taking the mid-term test I explore the closets at the back of the room and find them stuffed with old grammar books, newspapers, Regents exams and hundreds of pages of uncorrected student compositions going back to 1942. I'm about to dump everything into the trash till I start reading the old compositions. The boys back then yearned to fight, to avenge the deaths of brothers, friends, neighbors. One wrote, I'm gonna kill five Japs for every one they killed from my neighborhood. Another wrote, I don't want to go in the army if they tell me kill Italians because I'm Italian. I could be killing my own cousins and I won't fight unless they let me kill Germans or Japs. I'd prefer to kill Germans because I don't want to go to the Pacific where there's all kinds of jungles with bugs and snakes and crap like that.

The girls would wait. When Joey comes home me and him gonna

get married and move to Jersey and get away from his crazy mother.

I pile the crumbling papers on my desk and begin reading to my classes. They sit up. There are familiar names. Hey, that was my father. He was wounded in Africa. Hey, that was my Uncle Sal that was killed in Guam.

While I read the essays aloud there are tears. Boys run from the room to the toilets and return red-eyed. Girls weep openly and console one another.

Dozens of Staten Island and Brooklyn families are named in these papers so brittle we worry they'll fall apart. We want to save them and the only way is to copy them by hand, the hundreds still stacked in the closets.

No one objects. We are saving the immediate past of immediate families. Everyone has a pen and all through the rest of the term, April till the end of June, they decipher and write. Tears continue and there are outbursts. This is my father when he was fifteen. This is my aunt and she died when she was having a baby.

They are suddenly interested in compositions with the title, My Life, and I want to say, See what you can learn about your fathers and uncles and aunts? Don't you want to write about your lives for the next generation?

But I let it pass. I don't want to interfere with a room so quiet Mr Sorola has to investigate. He walks around the room, looks at what the class is doing and says nothing. I think he's grateful for the silence.

In June I give everyone a passing grade, thankful I've survived my first months of teaching in a vocational high school, though I wonder what I would have done without the crumbling compositions.

I might have had to teach.

40

Since I long ago lost the key the door of my flat is always open and it doesn't matter because there's nothing to steal. Strangers begin to appear, Walter Anderson, an aging public relations man, Gordon Patterson, aspiring actor, Bill Galetly, man in search of the truth. They are homeless bar patrons sent by Malachy in the largeness of his heart.

Walter begins to steal from me. Goodbye, Walter.

Gordon smokes in bed and causes a fire but worse than that his girlfriend complains to me at Malachy's bar about Gordon's discomfort and my hostility. He, too, goes.

School is over and I have to work again, day by day, on piers and warehouse platforms. Every morning I shape up to replace men on vacation, men out sick, or when there's a sudden rush of business and they need more help. When there's no work I roam the docks and the streets of Greenwich Village. I can make my way to Fourth Avenue to browse in one bookshop after another and dream of the day I'll come here and buy all the books I like. All I can afford now is cheap paperbacks and I'm content on my way home with my package of F. Scott Fitzgerald's *This Side of Paradise*, D. H. Lawrence's *Sons and Lovers*, Ernest Hemingway's *The Sun Also Rises*, Herman Hesse's *Siddhartha*, a weekend of reading. I'll heat up a can of beans on my electric ring and boil water for tea and read in the light that comes from the flat below. I'll start with Hemingway because I saw the film with Errol Flynn and Tyrone Power, everyone having a fine time of it in Paris and Pamplona, everyone drinking, going to bullfights, falling in love even if there was a sadness between Jake Barnes and Brett Ashley over his condition. It's the way I'd like to live, roaming the world without a care, though I wouldn't want to be Jake.

I take my books home and there is Bill Galetly. After Walter and Gordon I want no more interlopers but Bill is harder to dislodge and after a while I don't mind if he stays. He has already installed himself by the time Malachy calls to say his friend, Bill, who has renounced the world, left his job as an executive in an advertising agency, divorced his wife, sold his clothes books records, needs shelter for a short time and surely I won't mind.

Bill stands naked on a bathroom scale before a long mirror propped against the wall. On the floor are two flickering candles. He looks from the mirror to the scale and back again and again. He shakes his head and turns to me. Too much, he says. This too, too solid flesh. He points to his body, a collection of bones topped with a head of lank black hair and a bushy black beard flecked with grey. His eyes are blue wide staring. You're Frank, eh? Hi. He steps from the scale, stands with his back to the mirror, twists to look at himself over his shoulder and tells himself, Thou art fat and pursy, Bill.

He asks me if I've ever read *Hamlet* and tells me he's read it thirty times.

And I've read *Finnegans Wake*, that's if anyone can read *Finnegans Wake*. I've spent seven years with the damn book and that's why I'm here. Yeah, you're wondering. Read *Hamlet* thirty times and you start talking to yourself. Read *Finnegans Wake* for seven years and you want to put your head under water. The thing to do with *Finnegans Wake* is to chant it. It might take you seven years but it's something you'll be able to tell your grandchildren. They'll look up to you. What's that you have there, beans?

Would you like some? I'm heating them on the ring there.

No, thanks. No beans for me. You have your beans and I'll give you the message while you're eating. I'm trying to reduce the body to bare necessity. The world is too much with me. Know what I mean? Too much flesh.

I don't see it.

There you are. Through prayer, fasting and meditation I will drop below one hundred pounds, the despicable three digits. I want to be ninety-nine or nothing. Want. Did I say want? I shouldn't say want. I shouldn't say shouldn't. You're confused? Oh, have your beans. I'm trying to eliminate my ego but that action is ego itself. All action is ego. Are you following me? I'm not here with my mirror and scale for the good of my health.

From the next room he brings two books and tells me all my questions will be answered in Plato and the Gospel According to St John. Excuse me, he says, I gotta take a leak.

He takes the key and goes naked to the hall toilet. He returns to stand on the scale to see how much he lost with the leak. Quarter pound, he says, and lets out a sigh of relief. He squats on the floor, faces the mirror again flanked by the candles, with Plato on his left, St John on his right. He studies himself in the mirror and talks to me. Go ahead. Eat your beans. Books. That's what you have there, eh?

I eat my beans and when I tell him the book titles he shakes his head. Oh, no, oh, no. Hesse, maybe. Forget the rest. All Western ego. All Western crap. I wouldn't wipe my ass with Hemingway. But I shouldn't say that. Arrogant. Ego stuff. I take it back. No, wait. I said it. I'll leave it out there. It's gone. I read *Hamlet*. I read *Finnegans Wake* and here I am sitting on a floor in Greenwich Village with Plato, John and a man eating beans. What do you make of those ingredients?

I don't know.

I despair sometimes and you know why?

Why?

I despair I might push too far with Plato and John and find them wanting. I might come to a nowhere. You know?

No.

You ever read Plato?

I did.

St John?

They read the gospels all the time at Mass.

Not the same. You have to sit down and read St John, hold him in your hands. No other way. John is an encyclopedia. He changed my life. Promise me you'll read John and not that goddam stuff you brought home in the bag. Sorry, there's that ego popping up again.

He cackles into the mirror, pats himself where his belly should be, and rocks from book to book reading verses from John and paragraphs from Plato, squeaks with pleasure, Eek, eek, oh the Greek and the Jew, the Greek and the Jew.

He talks to me again. I take it back, he says. There's no nowhere with these guys. No nowhere. The form, the cave, the shadow, the cross. Jesus, I need a banana. He takes half a banana from behind the mirror and after mumbling something over it eats it. He crosses his legs under him, rests the backs of his hands on his knees, lotus position. When I cross behind him to drop my bean can into the garbage I can see he's staring at the tip of his nose. When I tell him goodnight he doesn't respond and I know I'm not in his world anymore, that I might as well go to bed and read. I'll read Hesse to keep the mood.

41

Alberta talks about marriage. She'd like to settle down, have a husband, go to antique shops on weekends, make dinner, get a decent apartment some day, be a mother.

But I'm not ready yet. I see Malachy and Michael having their grand times uptown. I see the Clancy Brothers singing in the back room of the White Horse Tavern, acting in plays at the Cherry Lane Theatre, recording their songs, being discovered and moving on to glamorous clubs where beautiful women invite them to parties. I see the Beats in cafes all over the Village reading their work with jazz musicians in the background. They're all free and I'm not.

They drink. They smoke pot. The women are easy.

Alberta follows her grandmother's Rhode Island routines. Every Saturday you make coffee, smoke a cigarette, put your hair up in pink curlers, go to the supermarket, get a big order, stock the refrigerator, take soiled things to the laundromat and wait till they're cleaned and ready to be folded, go to the dry cleaner with garments which look clean to me and when I object she simply says, What would you know about dry cleaning? clean the house whether it needs it or not, have a drink, make a big dinner, go to a movie.

Sunday morning you sleep late, have a big lunch, read the paper, look at antiques on Atlantic Avenue, come home, prepare lessons for the week, correct papers, make a big dinner, have a drink, correct more papers, have tea, smoke a cigarette, go to bed.

She works harder at teaching than I do, prepares her lessons carefully, corrects papers conscientiously. Her students are more academic than mine and she can encourage them to talk about literature. If I mention books, poetry, plays my students groan and whine for the lavatory pass.

The supermarket depresses me because I don't want a big dinner every night. It exhausts me. I want to roam the city, drink coffee in cafés and beer in bars. I don't want to face the Zoe routine every weekend the rest of my life.

Alberta tells me things have to be taken care of, that I have to grow up and settle down or I'll be like my father, a mad wanderer drinking myself to death.

This leads to an argument where I tell her I know my father drank too much and abandoned us but he's my father, not hers, and she'll never understand how it was when he didn't drink, mornings I had with him by the fire, listening to his talk about Ireland's noble past and Ireland's great sufferings. She never had mornings like that with her father who left her with Zoe when she was seven and I wonder how she could ever get over that. How could she ever forgive her mother and father for dumping her on the grandmother?

The argument is so bad I walk out and live in my Village flat, ready for the wild bohemian life. Then I hear she has found someone else and suddenly I want her, I'm desperate, I'm mad for her. I can think only of her virtues, her beauty and energy and the sweetness of her weekend routines. If she takes me back I'll be the perfect husband. I'll take coupons to the supermarket, wash the dishes, vacuum the whole apartment every day of the week, chop vegetables for the big dinners every night. I'll wear a tie, polish my shoes, turn Protestant. Anything.

I don't care anymore about the wild life of Malachy and Michael uptown, the scruffy Beats in the Village with their useless lives. I want Alberta, crisp and bright and womanly, all warm and secure. We'll be married, oh we will, and we'll grow old together.

She agrees to meet me in Louis' Bar near Sheridan Square and when she walks in the door she's more beautiful than ever. The bartenders stop pouring to look at her. Necks are craned. She's wearing the rich blue coat with a light grey fur collar her father bought her as a peace offering after he punched her in the mouth years ago. There's a silken lavender scarf over the collar and I know I'll never look at that color again without thinking of this moment, that scarf. I know she's going to sit on the stool beside me and tell me it was all a mistake, that we were made for each other and I should come with her now to her apartment, she'll make dinner and we'll live happily ever after.

Yes, she'll have a martini and no she won't go with me to my apartment and no I won't go with her to her apartment because it's over. She's had enough of me and my brothers, the uptown scene and the Village scene, and she wants to get on with her life. It's hard enough teaching every day without the strain of putting up with me and my whining about how I want to do this that and the other thing, how I want to be everything but responsible. Too much complaining, she says. Time to grow up. She tells me I'm twenty-eight years old but I act like a kid and if I want to waste my life in bars like my brothers it's my business but she'll have no part of it.

The more she talks the angrier she grows. She won't let me hold her hand or even kiss her on the cheek and, no, she won't have another martini.

How can she talk to me like this with my heart breaking there on the barstool? She doesn't care that I was the first man in her life, the first ever in the bed, the one a woman never forgets. All that doesn't matter because she's found someone who is mature, who loves her, who will do anything for her.

I'll do anything for you.

She says it's too late. You had your chance.

My heart is banging away, and there's a great pain in my chest and all the dark clouds in the world are gathered in my head. I want to cry into my beer there in Louis' Bar but there would be talk, oh, yeah, another lovers' quarrel and we'd be asked to leave or at least I would. I'm sure they'd like Alberta to stay to adorn the place. I don't want to be out on the street with all those happy couples strolling to dinners and movies and a little snack later before they climb into the bed all naked and, Jesus, is this her plan for tonight when I'm alone in my cold water flat and no one in the world to talk to but Bill Galetly?

I appeal to her. I invoke my miserable childhood, brutal school-masters, the tyranny of the Church, my father who chose the bottle over the babies, my defeated mother moaning by the fire, my eyes blazing red, my teeth crumbling in my head, the squalor of my flat, Bill Galetly tormenting me with people in Platonic caves and the Gospel According to St John, my hard days at McKee Vocational and Technical High School, older teachers telling me whip the little bastards into shape, the younger ones declaring our students are real people and it's up to us to motivate them.

I plead with her to have another martini. It might soften her so much she'll come to my apartment where I'll tell Bill, Take a walk, Bill, we need privacy. We want to sit in the candlelight and plan a future of Saturday shopping, vacuuming, cleaning, Sunday antique hunting, lesson planning and hours romping in the bed.

No, no, she won't have another martini. She's meeting her new man and she has to go.

Oh, God, no. It's a knife in my heart.

Stop the whining. I've heard enough about you and your miserable childhood. You're not the only one. I was dumped on my grandmother when I was seven. Do I complain? I just get on with it.

But you had hot and cold running water, thick towels, soap, sheets on the bed, two clear blue eyes and fine teeth and your grandmother packed your little lunch box to capacity every day.

She climbs from the bar stool, lets me help her with her coat, drapes the lavender scarf around her neck. She has to go.

Oh, Christ. I could easily whimper like a kicked dog. My belly is cold and there's nothing in the world but dark clouds with Alberta in the middle all blonde, blue-eyed, lavender-scarved, ready to leave me forever for her new man and it's worse than having doors shut in my face, worse than dying itself.

Then she kisses my cheek. Goodnight, she says. She doesn't say goodbye. Does that mean she's leaving a door open? Surely if she's finished with me forever she should be saying goodbye.

It doesn't matter. She's gone. Out the door. Up the steps with every man in the bar looking at her. It's the end of the world. I might as well be dead. I might as well jump into the Hudson River and let it carry my corpse past Ellis Island and the Statue of Liberty across the Atlantic and up the River Shannon where at least I'd be among my own people and not rejected by Rhode Island Protestants.

The bartender is about fifty and I'd like to ask him if he's ever suffered the way I'm suffering now and what did he do about it?

Is there a cure? He might even be able to tell me what it means when a woman who's leaving you forever says goodnight instead of goodbye.

But this man has a great bald head and massive black eyebrows and I have a feeling he has his own troubles and there's nothing for it but to get off the barstool and leave. I could go uptown and join Malachy and Michael in their exciting lives but I walk home to Downing Street instead hoping happy passing couples won't hear the escaping whimpers of a man whose life is over.

Bill Galetly is there with his candles, his Plato, his Gospel According to St John and I wish I could have my own place to myself for a night of whimpering into my pillow but he's sitting on the floor staring at himself in the mirror and pinching whatever flesh he can find on his belly. He looks up and tells me I look heavy-laden.

What do you mean?

The burden of the ego. You're sagging. Remember, the Kingdom of God is within you.

I don't want God or His Kingdom. I want Alberta. She gave me up. I'm going to bed.

Bad time to go to bed. To lie down is to lie down.

It irritates me to have to listen to the obvious and I tell him, Of course it is. What are you talking about?

To lie down is to succumb to gravity at a time when you could spiral to the perfect form.

I don't care. I'm lying down.

Okay. Okay.

I'm in the bed a few minutes when he sits on the edge and tells me of the madness and emptiness of the advertising business. Plenty of money and everyone wretched with stomach ulcers. All ego. No purity. He tells me I'm a teacher and I could save many lives if I studied Plato and St John but first I have to save my own life.

I'm not in the mood.

Not in the mood to save your own life?

No, I don't care.

Yeah, yeah, that's what happens when you're rejected. You take it personally.

Of course I take it personally. How else would I take it?

Look at her side of the story. She's not rejecting you, she's accepting herself.

He's going around in circles and the Alberta pain is so great I have to get away. I tell him I'm going out.

Oh, you don't have to go out. Sit on the floor with the candle behind. Look at the wall. Shadows. Are you hungry?

No.

Wait, and he brings a banana from the kitchen. Have this. The banana is good for you.

I don't want a banana.

It makes you peaceful. All that potassium.

I don't want a banana.

You only think you don't want a banana. Listen to your body.

He follows me into the hallway preaching bananas. He's naked but he follows me down the stairs, three flights, along the hallway that leads to the front door. He keeps talking about bananas, the ego and Socrates happy under a tree in Athens and when we reach the front door he stands on the top step waving the banana while children playing hopscotch on the sidewalk whoop and scream and point and women with bosoms and elbows resting on windowsill pillows scream at him in Italian.

Malachy isn't at his bar. He's at home and happy with his wife, Linda, planning the life of the baby to come. Michael is off for the night. There are women at the bar and the tables but they're with men. The bartender says, Oh, you're Malachy's brother, and won't let me pay for my drinks. He introduces me to couples at the bar, This is Malachy's brother.

Really? We didn't know he had another brother. Oh, yeah, we know your brother Michael. And your name is?

Frank.

And what do you do?

I'm a teacher.

Really? You're not in the bar business?

They laugh. And when do you think you'll go into the bar business?

When my brothers become teachers.

That's what I say but what flows through my head is different. I want to tell them they're condescending twits, that I knew their likes in the lobby of the Biltmore Hotel, that they probably flicked their cigarette ash on the floor for me to clean up and looked through me the way you look through people who clean up. I'd like to tell them to kiss my arse and if I had a few more drinks I would but I know that inside I'm still plucking at my forelock and shuffling my feet in the presence of superior people, that they'd laugh at anything I said to them because they know what I am inside and if they don't know they don't care. If I fell dead off the barstool they'd move to a table to avoid the unpleasantness and tell the world later how they ran into a drunken Irish schoolteacher.

None of this matters anyway. Alberta is surely in a romantic little Italian restaurant with her new man, the two of them smiling at each other across the glow of the light from the candle stuck in a Chianti bottle. He's telling her what's good on the menu and after they order their dinner they talk about what they'll do tomorrow, maybe tonight, and if I think about that my bladder will move near my eye.

Malachy's Bar is at Sixty-Third Street and Third Avenue, five blocks from my first furnished room at Sixty-Eighth Street. Instead of going home straightway I can sit on Mrs Austin's steps and look back over the contents of my ten years in New York, the trouble I had trying to see *Hamlet* at the Sixty-Eighth Street Playhouse with my lemon meringue pie and my bottle of ginger ale.

Mrs Austin's house is gone. There's a large new building, the New York Foundling Hospital, and it brings me to tears the way they're tearing down my early days in the city. At least the cinema is here and it must be the night of beer because I have to press my whole body against the cinema wall with arms stretched out till a head calls from a police car, Hey, buddy, what's going on?

What if I told him about *Hamlet* and the pie and Mrs Austin and the night of glug and how her house is gone and my furnished room with it and how the woman in my life is with another man and is it against the law, Officer, to kiss a cinema of sad and happy memories when it's the only comfort you have left, is it, Officer?

Of course I'm not going to say this to a New York cop or anyone else. I just tell him, It's all right, Officer, and he tells me move on, the favorite words of the police department.

I move on and all along Third Avenue music pours through the doors of Irish pubs with the smells of beer and whiskey and snatches of talk and laughter.

Good man yourself, Sean.

Arrah, Jasus, we might as well be drunk as the way we are.

God above, I can't wait to get back to Cavan for the decent pint that's in it.

Do you think you'll ever go back, Kevin?

I will when they build a bridge.

They laugh and Mickey Carton on the jukebox pumps his accordion with Ruthie Morrissey's voice sailing over all the noise of the night, It's my old Irish home, far across the foam, and I'm tempted to turn in, sit up on a stool and tell the bartender, Give us an oul' drop of the craythur there, Brian, or make it two because bird never flew on one wing, good lad yourself. And wouldn't that be better than sitting on Mrs Austin's steps or kissing the walls of the Sixty-Eighth Street Playhouse and wouldn't I be among my own, wouldn't I?

My own. The Irish.

I could drink Irish, eat Irish, dance Irish, read Irish. My mother often warned us, Marry your own, and now old-timers tell me, Stick with your own. If I listened to them I wouldn't be rejected by a Rhode Island Episcopalian who once said, What would you do with yourself if you weren't Irish? And when she said that I would have walked out except that we were halfway through the dinner she'd cooked, stuffed chicken with a bowl of pink new potatoes tossed in salt butter and parsley and a bottle of Bordeaux that gave me such shivers of pleasure I could have tolerated any number of barbs at myself and the Irish in general.

I'd like to be Irish when it's time for a song or a poem. I'd like to be American when I teach. I'd like to be Irish-American or American-Irish though I know I can't be two things even if Scott Fitzgerald said the sign of intelligence is the ability to carry opposed thoughts at the same time.

I don't know what I'd like to be and what does it matter with Alberta over in Brooklyn with her new man?

Then in a shop window I catch a glimpse of my sad face and I laugh when I remember what my mother would have called it, the gloomy puss.

At Fifty-Seventh Street I walk west towards Fifth Avenue for a taste of America and the richness that's in it, the world of the people who sit in the Palm Court of the Biltmore Hotel, people who don't have to go through life carrying ethnic hyphens. You could wake them in the middle of the night, ask them what they are and they'd say, Tired.

I turn the gloomy puss south on Fifth Avenue and there's the dream I had all those years in Ireland, the avenue nearly deserted at this hour of the morning except for double-decker buses, one going north, the other south, jewelry shops, bookshops, women's shops with mannequins all dressed up for Easter, rabbits and eggs everywhere in windows and not a sign of the risen Jesus, and far down the avenue the Empire State Building, and I have my health, don't I? a little weak in the eye and teeth department, a college degree and a teaching job and isn't this the country where all things are possible, where you can do anything you like as long as you stop complaining and get off your ass because life, pal, is not a free lunch.

If only Alberta came to her senses and back to me.

Fifth Avenue tells me how ignorant I am. There are the window mannequins in their Easter garb and if one of them came to life and asked me what kind of fabric she was wearing I wouldn't have a notion. If they wore canvas I'd spot it straightway because of the coal bags I delivered in Limerick and used for cover when they were empty and the weather was desperate. I might be able to recognize tweed because of the coats people wore winter and summer though I'd have to admit to the mannequin I don't know the difference between silk and cotton. I could never point to a dress and say that's satin or wool and I'd be lost entirely if challenged to identify damask or crinoline. I know novelists like to hint at the wealth of their characters by dwelling on damask drapes though I don't know if anyone wears such material unless the characters fall on hard times and take the scissors to the damask. I know you can hardly pick up a novel set in the South where there isn't a white plantation family lolling on the verandah sipping bourbon or lemonade listening to the darkies singing "Swing Low, Sweet Chariot", the verandah women fanning themselves against the crinoline heat.

Down in Greenwich Village I buy shirts and socks in shops called haberdasheries and I don't know what material they're made of even though there are people telling me you have to be careful what you put on your body nowadays, you might have allergies and break out in a rash. I never worried about such things in Limerick but here danger lurks even in the buying of socks and shirts.

Things in shop windows have names I don't know and I don't know how I traveled this far in life in such a state of ignorance. There are florist shops along the avenue and all I can name beyond these windows is geraniums. Respectable people in Limerick were mad for the geraniums and when I delivered telegrams there were often notes on the front door, Please slide the window up and leave messages under the geranium pot. It's strange to stand at a florist's shop on Fifth Avenue remembering how delivering telegrams helped me become an expert on geraniums and now I don't even like them. They never excited me like other flowers in people's gardens with all that color and fragrance and the sadness of their dying in the autumn. Geraniums have no fragrance, they live forever and the taste makes you sick though I'm sure there are people over there on Park Avenue who would take me aside and spend an hour persuading me of the glories of the geranium and I suppose I'd have to agree with them because everywhere I go people know more about everything than I do and it's not likely you'd be rich and living on Park Avenue unless you had a profound knowledge of geraniums and growing things in general.

All along the avenue there are shops with gourmet foods and if I ever enter such a place I'll have to bring someone who grew up respectable and knows the difference between pâté de foie gras and mashed potatoes. All these shops are obsessed with French and I don't know what they're thinking of. Why can't they say spuds instead of pommes or is it that you pay more for something printed in French?

There's no sense at all looking in the windows of antique furniture shops. They'll never let you know the price of something till you ask and they'll never plant a sign on a chair to tell you what it is or where it came from. Most of the chairs you wouldn't want to sit in anyway. They're so upright and stiff they'd give you such a pain in your back you'd wind up in the hospital. Then there are little tables with curved legs so delicate they'd collapse under the weight of a pint and destroy a priceless carpet from Persia or wherever people sweat for the pleasure of rich Americans. There are delicate mirrors, too, and you wonder what it's like in the morning to see your face in a frame agog with little Cupids and maidens frolicking and where would you look in such confusion? Would I look at the stuff oozing from my eyes or would I be enchanted with a maiden succumbing to a Cupid arrow?

With the dawn glimmering far down in Greenwich Village Fifth Avenue is nearly deserted except for people making their way to St Patrick's Cathedral to save their souls, mostly old women who seem to have greater fear than the old men mumbling along beside them or it may be that old women live longer and there are more of them. When the priest dispenses Communion the pews empty and I envy the people coming back down the aisles with the wafers in their mouths and the holy look that tells you they're in a state of grace. They can go home now and have the big breakfast and if they fall dead while eating sausages and eggs they go straight to heaven. I'd like to make my peace with God but my sins are so terrible any priest would drive me from the confessional and I know once again my only hope for salvation is that I'll have an accident where I'll linger for a few minutes so that I can make an Act of Perfect Contrition that will open the gates of heaven.

Still, it's comforting to sit in the cathedral in the hush of a dawn Mass especially when I can look around and put names on what I see, pews, the Stations of the Cross, the pulpit, the tabernacle with the monstrance holding the Eucharist inside, the chalice, the ciborium, the cruets for wine and water at the altar's right side, the paten. I know nothing about jewelry and the flowers in the shop but I can recite the priestly vestments, the amice, the alb, the girdle, the maniple, the stole, the chasuble, and I know the priest up there wearing the purple chasuble of Lent will change to white on Easter Sunday when Christ is risen and Americans give their children chocolate rabbits and yellow eggs.

After all the Sunday mornings in Limerick I can skip as easily as an altar boy from the Introit of the Mass to the Ite, missa est, Go, you are dismissed, the signal for the thirsty men of Ireland to rise from their knees and flock to the pubs for the Sunday pint, cure for the woes of the night before.

I can name the parts of the Mass and the priestly vestments and the parts of a rifle like Henry Reed in his poem but what use is all this if I rise in the world and sit in a stiff chair at a table where they're serving fancy food and I can't tell the difference between mutton and duck?

It's full daylight on Fifth Avenue and there's no one but myself sitting on the steps between the two great lions of the Forty-Second Street Public Library where Tim Costello told me to go nearly ten years ago to read *The Lives of the Poets*. There are little birds of different sizes and colors flitting from tree to tree telling me spring will soon be here and I don't know their names either. I can tell the difference between a pigeon and a sparrow and there it ends except for the seagull.

If my students at McKee High School could look into my head they'd wonder how I ever became a teacher at all. They know already I never went to high school and they'd say, That's it. Here's a teacher who stands up there giving us vocabulary lessons and he doesn't even know the names of the birds in the trees.

The library will be open in a few hours and I could sit in the Main Reading Room with big picture books that tell me the names of things but it's still early morning and it's a long way to Downing Street, Bill Galetly cross-legged and squinting at himself in the mirror, Plato and the Gospel According to St John.

He's flat on his back on the floor, naked and snoring, a candle guttering by his head, banana peels everywhere. It's cold in the flat but when I place a blanket over him he sits up and pushes it away. Sorry about the bananas, Frank, but I had a little celebration this morning. Big breakthrough. Here it is.

He points to a passage in St John. Read it, he says. Go ahead, read it.

And I read, It is the spirit that quickeneth, the flesh profiteth nothing, the words that I speak unto you, they are the spirit, and they are the life.

Bill stares at me. So?

What?

You get it? You dig?

I don't know. I'd have to read it a few times and it's nearly nine o'clock in the morning. I've been up all night.

I fasted for three days to get inside that. You have to get inside things. Like sex. But I'm not finished. I'm looking for the parallel world in Plato. Guess I'll have to go to Mexico.

Why Mexico?

Great shit there.

Shit?

You know. Variety of chemicals to help the seeker.

Oh, yes. I'm going to bed for a while.

Wish I could offer you a banana but I had the celebration.

I sleep a few hours this Sunday morning and when I awake he's gone leaving behind nothing but banana skins.

42

Alberta is back. She calls me and asks me to meet her over at Rocky's for the sake of old times. She's wearing a light spring coat with the lavender scarf she wore when she said good-night instead of good-bye and this meeting must have been what she had in mind all the time.

All the men in Rocky's stare at her and their women glare at them to stop looking at someone else and look back at them.

She slips off her coat and sits with the lavender scarf on her shoulders and my heart is beating so hard I can hardly talk. She'll have a martini straight up with a twist and I'll have a beer. She tells me it was all a mistake going off with someone else but he was mature and ready to settle down and I acted all the time like a single man with the hovel in the Village. She realized in no time it was me she loved and even though we have our differences we can work them out especially if we settle down and get married.

When she mentions marriage there's a different sharp pain in my chest from the fear I'll never have that free life I see everywhere in New York, the kind of life they had in Paris where everyone sat in cafés drinking wine, writing novels, sleeping with other men's wives and beautiful rich American women eager for the passion.

If I say anything like this to Alberta she'll say, Oh, grow up. You're twenty-eight going on twenty-nine not a goddam beatnik.

Of course neither one of us is going to talk like this in the middle of our reconciliation especially since I have a nagging feeling she's right and I might be just a drifter like my father. Even though I've been a teacher for a year I still envy people who can sit in coffee shops and pubs and go to parties where there are artists and models and a jazz combo in the corner blowing cool and lowdown.

No use telling her anything of my freedom dreams. She'd say, You're a teacher. You never dreamed when you got off the boat you'd come this far. Get on with it.

Once in Rhode Island we argued over something and Zoe the grandmother said, You're nice people, but not together.

She won't come to my cold water flat, the hovel, and she won't let me come to hers with her father there for a short time because of a rift with his wife, Stella. She puts her hand on mine and we look at each other so hard she has tears and I'm ashamed of the redness she must be seeing and the oozing.

On the way to the subway she tells me that when the school term ends in a few weeks she's going to Rhode Island to be with her grandmother for a while and sort out her life. She knows there's a question in the air, Will I be invited? and the answer is no, I'm not in favor with the grandmother at this moment. She kisses me goodnight, tells me she'll talk to me on the phone soon, and after she disappears into the subway I walk across Washington Square Park torn between my yearning for her and my dreams of the free life. If I don't fit in with the way she wants to live, clean, organized, respectable, I'll lose her and I'll never find anyone like her. I never had women throwing themselves at me in Ireland, Germany or the USA. I could never tell the world about the weekends in Munich where I consorted with the lowest whores in Germany or the time when I was fourteen and a half frolicking with a dying girl on a green sofa in Limerick. All I have is dark secrets and shame and it's a wonder Alberta has anything to do with me at all. If I had any belief left in anything I could go to confession but where is the priest who could hear my sins without throwing his hands up in disgust and sending me to the bishop or some part of the Vatican reserved for the doomed?

The man at the Beneficial Finance Company says, Do I detect a brogue? He tells me where his mother and father came from in Ireland

and how he plans to visit himself though that'd be hard with six kids, ha ha. His mother comes from a family of nineteen. Can you believe that? he says. Nineteen kids. Of course seven died but what the hell. That's how it was in the old days in the Old Country. They had kids like rabbits.

So, back to the application. You want to borrow three hundred and fifty dollars to visit the Old Country, eh? You haven't seen your mother in what, six years? The man congratulates me on wanting to see my mother. Too many people nowadays forget their mothers. But not the Irish. No, not us. We never forget our mothers. The Irishman that forgets his mother is no Irishman and should be drummed out, goddamit, excuse the language, Mr McCourt. I see you're a teacher and I admire you for that. It must be rough, big classes, low pay. Yeah, all I have to do is look at your application to see the low pay. Don't know how you can live on it and that, I'm sorry to tell you, is the problem. That's what causes the hitch in this application, the low pay and absence of any collateral if you know what I mean. They're gonna shake their heads at the head office over this application but I'm gonna push it because you got two things in your favor, you're an Irishman that wants to see his mother in the Old Country and you're a teacher killing himself in a vocational high school and, as I say, I'm going to bat for you.

I tell him I'll be shaping up at the warehouses in July to replace men going on vacation but that means nothing to the Beneficial Finance Company unless there's proof of steady employment. The man advises me to say nothing about sending money to my mother. They'd shake their heads at the main office if there was anything that might threaten my monthly payments on the loan.

The man wishes me good luck. He says, it's such a pleasure to do business with one of my own.

The platform boss at Baker and Williams looks surprised. Jesus, you back again. I thought you became a teacher or some goddam thing.

I did.

So what the hell you doin' here?

I need the money. The teacher's pay is not princely.

You shoulda stood in the warehouses or drove a truck or somethin'

287

an' you'd be makin' money an' not strugglin' with them goddam kids that don't care.

Then he asks, Didn't you used to hang around with that guy, Paddy McGovern?

Paddy Arthur?

Yeah. Paddy Arthur. So many Paddy McGoverns they have to get another name. You know what happened to him?

I don't.

Dumb bastard is on the A train platform at 125th Street. Harlem, you know. What the hell was he doin' in Harlem? Lookin' for a little of that black stuff. So he gets bored standing on the platform like everybody else and decides to wait for the train down on the tracks. On the goddam tracks, avoiding the third rail. You could get killed with the third rail. Lights a cigarette and stands there with that stupid smile on his face till the A train comes in and ends his troubles. That's what I heard. What was it with that dumb bastard?

He must have been drinking.

Course he was drinking. Goddam Irish are always drinking but I never heard of no Irishman waiting for the train on the tracks before. But your friend there, Paddy, always said he was going back. He'd save enough money and live in the Old Country. What happened? Know what I think? You wanna know what I think?

What do you think?

Some people should stay where they are. This country could drive you crazy. It drives people crazy that was born here. How come you're not crazy? Or maybe you are, eh?

I don't know.

Lissena me, kid. I'm Italian an' Greek an' we have our problems but my advice to a young Irishman is this, Stay away from the booze an' you won't have to wait for the train on the tracks. You got me?

I do.

At lunch I see a figure from the past washing dishes in the diner kitchen, Andy Peters. He sees me and tells me hold on, try the meatloaf and the mashed potatoes and he'll be out in a minute. He sits beside me on a counter stool and asks how I like the gravy.

Fine.

Yeah, well I made it. It's my practice gravy. I'm really the dishwasher

288

here but the cook is a drunk and he lets me do gravy and salads though there isn't much call for salads around here. Guys from docks and warehouses think salads are for cows. I came here to wash dishes so I can think, finished with that fucking NYU. I need to clear my head. What I'd really like to do is get a job vacuuming. I've gone from hotel to hotel offering to vacuum but there's always the form, always the shitass investigation into my past which reveals my dishonorable discharge for not having congress with a sheep and that puts the kibosh on vacuuming. You take a shit in a French ditch and your life is ruined till you hit on the brilliant solution of re-entering American life on the lowest level, dishwashing, and watch my speed, man. I'll be the dishwasher supremo. They'll blink in amazement and before you know it I'll be salad man. How? Learning, watching in an uptown kitchen, promoted to salad man, assistant assistant chef and before you know it I'll be on sauces. Sauces, for Christ's sakes, because the sauce is the great bullshit ingredient in French cooking and Americans are suckers for it. So watch my style, Frankie boy, watch for my name in the papers, André Pierre, pronounced in the proper French way with your eyebrows up to your hairline, sauce man supreme, wizard with pot pan and wire whisk, yacking away on all the talk shows on TV with no one giving a damn if I diddled every sheep in France and adjoining monarchies. People in fancy restaurants will ooh and ah, compliments to the chef, me, and I'll be invited to visit their tables so they can patronize me in my white hat and apron and of course I'll let the word slip out I was this close to a PhD at NYU and the Park Avenue wives will have me up for sauce consultations and the meaning of it all while the husbands are in Saudi Arabia buying oil and I'm with their wives drilling for gold.

He takes a moment to ask me what I'm doing with my life.

Teaching.

I was afraid of that. I thought you wanted to be a writer.

I do.

So?

I have to earn a living.

You're falling into the trap. I beg you, don't fall into the trap. I nearly fell into it myself.

I have to earn a living.

You'll never write while you're teaching. Teaching is a bitch. Remember Voltaire? Cultivate your garden.

I remember.

And Carlyle? Make money and forget the universe.

I'm earning a living.

You're dying.

A week later he is gone from the diner and no one knows where.

With the money from the Beneficial Finance Company and the wages from the warehouses I'm able to spend a few weeks in Limerick and it's the same old feeling when the plane descends and follows the Shannon Estuary to the airport. The river gleams silver and the fields rolling away are somber shades of green except where the sun shines and emeralds the land. It's a good time to be sitting near a window in case there are tears.

She's at the airport with Alphie and a hired car and the morning is fresh and dewy on the road to Limerick. She tells me about Malachy's visit with his wife, Linda, and what a wild party they had with Malachy going out to a field and riding home on a horse which he wanted to bring into the house till everyone persuaded him a house was no place for a horse. There was plenty of drink that night and more than drink, poteen, which someone got from a man out in the country and 'twas the luck o' God the guards never came near the house for the possession of poteen is a serious offense that could land you in the Limerick Jail. Malachy said she and Alphie might be able to come to New York for a visit at Christmas and wouldn't that be grand, we'd all be together.

They meet me on the streets and tell me I look grand, that I look more like a Yank all the time. Alice Egan argues, Frankie McCourt hasn't changed one hour, not one hour. Isn't that right, Frankie?

I don't know, Alice.

You don't have the slightest bit of an American accent.

Whatever friends I had in Limerick are gone, dead or emigrated, and I don't know what to do with myself. I could read all day in my mother's house but why did I come all the way from New York to sit on my arse and read? I could sit in pubs all night and drink but I could have done that in New York, too.

I walk from one end of the city to the other and out into the country where my father walked endlessly. People are polite but they're working and they have families and I'm a visitor, a returned Yank.

Is that yourself, Frankie McCourt?

'Tis.

When did you come?

Last week.

And when are you going back?

Next week.

That's grand. I'm sure your poor mother is glad to have you at home and I hope the weather keeps fine for you.

They say, I suppose you notice all kinds of changes in Limerick?

Oh, yes. More cars, fewer snotty noses and scabby knees. No barefoot children. No women in shawls.

Jesus, Frankie McCourt, them's peculiar things to be noticing.

They'll watch to see if I put on airs and they'll cut me down but I have none to put on. When I tell them I'm a teacher they seem disappointed.

Only a teacher. Lord above, Frankie McCourt, we thought you'd be a millionaire by now. Sure wasn't your brother Malachy here with his glamorous model of a wife and isn't he an actor and everything.

The plane lifts into a western sun which touches the Shannon with gold and even though I'm happy to be returning to New York I hardly know where I belong anymore.

43

Malachy's bar is so successful he provides passage for my mother and my brother, Alphie, on the SS *Sylvania* which arrives in New York on December 21st, 1959.

When they emerge from the customs shed there's a piece of broken leather flapping from Mam's right shoe so that you can see the small toe of a foot that was always swollen. Does it ever end? Is this the family of the broken shoe? We embrace and Alphie smiles with broken blackened teeth.

The family of broken shoes and teeth destroyed. Will this be our coat of arms?

Mam looks past me to the street beyond. Where's Malachy?

I don't know. He should be here in a minute.

She tells me I look fine, that it didn't do me any harm to put on a bit of weight though I should do something about my eyes they're that red. That irritates me because I know that if I even think of my eyes or anyone mentions them I can feel them flush red and of course she notices.

See, she says. You're a bit old to be having bad eyes.

I want to snap at her that I'm twenty-nine and I don't know the proper age for not having bad eyes and is this what she wants to talk about the minute she arrives in New York? but Malachy arrives in a taxi with his wife, Linda. More smiles and embraces. Malachy keeps the taxi while we retrieve the suitcases.

Alphie says, Will we put these in the boot?

Linda smiles. Oh, no, we put them in the trunk.

Trunk? We didn't bring a trunk.

No, no, she says, we put your bags in the trunk of the taxi.

Isn't there a boot in the taxi?

No, that's the trunk.

Alphie scratches his head and smiles again, a young man understanding lesson number one in American English.

In the taxi Mam says, Lord above, look at all those motor cars. The roads are packed. I tell her it's not so bad now. An hour earlier it was the height of the rush hour and traffic was even worse. She says she doesn't see how it could ever be worse. I tell her it's always worse earlier and she says, I don't see how it could be worse than this the way the motor cars are crawling along this minute.

I am trying to be patient and I speak slowly. I am telling you, Mam, this is how the traffic is in New York. I live here.

Malachy says, Oh, it doesn't matter. It's a lovely morning, and she says, I lived here, too, in case you've forgotten.

You did, I tell her. Twenty-five years ago and you lived in Brooklyn, not Manhattan.

Well, it's still New York.

She won't give up and I won't though I'm looking at the pettiness of the two of us and wondering why I'm arguing instead of celebrating the arrival of my mother and my youngest brother in the city all of us dreamed of all our lives. Why does she pick on my eyes and why do I have to contradict her over the traffic?

Linda tries to ease the moment. Well, as Malachy says, it is a beautiful day.

Mam gives a little begrudging nod. 'Tis.

And how was the weather when you left Ireland, Mam?

A begrudging word, Raining.

Oh, it's always raining in Ireland, isn't it, Mam?

No, it's not, and she folds her arms and stares straight ahead at the traffic that was much busier an hour earlier.

At the apartment Linda makes breakfast while Mam dandles the new baby, Siobhan, and croons to her the way she crooned to seven of us. Linda says, Mam, would you like tea or coffee?

Tea, please.

When the breakfast is ready Mam puts the baby down, comes to the table and wants to know what is that thing floating around in her cup. Linda tells her it's a tea bag and Mam puts her nose in the air. Oh, I wouldnt drink that. Sure, that's not proper tea at all.

Malachy's face tightens and he tells her through his teeth, That's the tea we have. That's the way we make it. We don't have a pound of Lyons' tea and a teapot for you.

Well, then, I won't have anything. I'll just eat my egg. I don't know what kind of country this is where you can't get a decent cup of tea.

Malachy is ready to say something but the baby cries and he goes to lift her from her crib while Linda flutters around Mam, smiling, trying to please. We could get a teapot, Mam, and we could get loose tea, couldn't we, Malachy?

But he's parading the living room with the baby whimpering on his shoulder and you can see that in the matter of tea bags he won't yield, not this morning anyway. Like anyone who has ever had a decent cup of tea in Ireland he despises tea bags but he has an American wife who knows nothing but tea bags, he has a baby and things on his mind and little patience with this mother with her nose in the air over tea bags her first day in the United States of America and he doesn't know why, after all his expense and trouble, he has to tolerate her picky ways for the next three weeks in this small apartment.

Mam pushes away from the table. Lavatory? she asks Linda. Where's the lavatory?

What?

Lavatory. WC.

Linda looks at Malachy. The toilet, he says. The bathroom.

Oh, says Linda. In there.

While Mam is in the bathroom Alphie tells Linda the teabag wasn't that bad after all. If you didn't see it floating in the cup you'd think it was all right, and Linda smiles again. She tells him that's why the Chinese don't serve great chunks of meat. They don't like looking at the animal they're eating. If they cook chicken they chop it into little pieces and mix it with other things so you barely know it's chicken. That's why you never see a chicken leg or breast in a Chinese restaurant.

Is that right? Alphie says.

The baby is still whimpering on Malachy's shoulder but all is sweet at the table with Alphie and Linda discussing teabags and the delicacy of Chinese cooking. Then Mam comes from the bathroom and tells Malachy, That child is full of wind, so she is. I'll take her.

Malachy hands over Siobhan and sits at the table with his tea. Mam walks the floor with the piece of leather flapping from her broken shoe and I know I'll have to take her down Third Avenue to a shoe shop. She pats the baby and there's a powerful burp that makes us all laugh. She puts the baby back in the crib and leans over her. There, there, leanv, there, there, and the baby gurgles. She returns to the table, rests her hands in her lap and tells us, I'd give me two eyes for a decent cup of tea, and Linda tells her she'll go out today and get a teapot and loose tea, right, Malachy?

He says, Right, because he knows in his heart there's nothing like tea made in a pot which you rinse with water boiling madly, where there's a heaping spoon for each cup, where you pour in the madly boiling water, keeping the pot warm with a tea cozy while the tea brews for six minutes exactly.

Malachy knows that's how Mam will make tea and he softens his stand on teabags. He knows also that in the matter of baby burping she has finer instincts and superior ways and it's a fair exchange, a decent cup of tea for her and comfort for the baby Siobhan.

For the first time in ten years we're all together, Mam and her four sons. Malachy has his wife, Linda, and his baby, Siobhan, the first of a new generation. Michael has a girlfriend, Jan, and Alphie will soon find one, too. I'm reconciled with Alberta and living with her in Brooklyn.

Malachy is the life of the party in New York and no party can start without him. If he doesn't appear there's restlessness and whimpering, Where's Malachy? Where's your brother? and when he roars in they're happy. He sings and drinks and passes his glass for more drink and sings again till he rushes off to the next party.

Mam loves the life, the excitement of it. She loves having a highball at Malachy's Bar and being introduced as Malachy's mother. Her eyes twinkle and her cheeks glow and she dazzles the world with a flash of false teeth. She follows Malachy to the parties, the oul' hooleys, she calls them, basks in the mother spotlight and tries to join in

Malachy's songs till she runs out of breath with the first signs of emphysema. After all the years sitting by the fire in Limerick wondering where the next loaf of bread was coming from she's having a lovely time and isn't this a grand country altogether? Ah, maybe she'll stay a little longer. Sure, what's the use of going back to Limerick in the middle of the winter with nothing to do but sit there by the fire warming her poor shins? She'll go back when the weather warms up, Easter maybe, and Alphie can get a job here to keep them going.

Malachy has to tell her if she wants to stay in New York even for a short time she can't stay with him in his small apartment with Linda and the baby, four months old.

She calls me at Alberta's and tells me, I'm hurted, so I am. Four sons in New York and no place for me to lay my head.

But we all have small apartments, Mam. No room.

Well, one would wonder what ye're all doing with the money ye're making. Ye should have told me this before ye dragged me from my own comfortable fireplace.

No one dragged you. Didn't you say over and over you wanted to come for Christmas and didn't Malachy pay your fare?

I came because I wanted to see my first grandchild and, don't worry, I'll pay Malachy back if I have to get down on my two knees and scrub floors. If I knew the way I was going to be treated here I would have stayed in Limerick and had a nice goose for myself and a roof over my head.

Alberta whispers I should invite Mam and Alphie for dinner on Saturday night. There's a silence at the other end and then a sniffle.

Well, I don't know what I'll be doing on Saturday night. Malachy said there might be a party.

All right. We invited you to dinner but if you want to go to another party with Malachy, go.

You don't have to sound so huffy. It's an awful long distance to Brooklyn. I know because I used to live there.

It's less than half an hour.

She whispers something to Alphie and he takes the phone. Francis? We'll come.

When I open the door she brings her own chill along with the January chill. She acknowledges Alberta's existence with a nod and asks if I have a match for her cigarette. Alberta offers her a cigarette but she says, no, she has her own and these American cigarettes barely have any taste anyway. Alberta offers her a drink and she'll have a highball. Alphie says he'll have a beer and Mam says, Oh, you're starting, are you?

I tell her it's only a beer.

Well, that's how it starts. One beer and the next thing ye're roaring and singing and waking the child.

There's no child here.

There is in Malachy's house and the roaring and singing, too.

Alberta calls us into dinner, tuna casserole with green salad. Mam takes her time coming to the table. She has to finish her cigarette and what's the hurry anyway.

Alberta says it's nice to eat casserole when it's good and hot.

Mam says she hates hot food that burns the roof of your mouth.

I tell her, For Christ's sake, finish your cigarette and come to the table.

She comes with her offended look. She pulls her chair in and pushes the salad away. She doesn't like the lettuce in this country. I try to control myself. I ask her what the hell is the difference between the lettuce in this country and the lettuce in Ireland. She says there's a big difference, that the lettuce in this country is tasteless.

Alberta says, Oh, never mind. Not everyone likes lettuce anyway.

Mam stares at her casserole and forks noodles and tuna aside while she hunts for peas. She says she loves peas though these are not as good as the ones in Limerick. Alberta asks if she'd like more peas.

No, thank you.

After which she probes the noodles for bits of tuna.

I ask her, Don't you like the noodles?

What?

The noodles. Don't you like them?

I don't know what they are but I'm not fond of 'em.

I want to lean into her face and tell her she's acting like a savage, that Alberta went to great lengths thinking of something that might please her and all she can do now is to sit with her nose in the air as if someone had done something to her and if she doesn't like it she can put on her damn coat and go back to Manhattan to the party she's missing and I'll never bother her again with an invitation to dinner.

I want to say all this but Alberta makes peace. Oh, that's all right. Maybe Mam is tired with the excitement of coming to New York and if we have a nice cup of tea and a piece of cake we'll all relax.

Mam says, No, thank you to the cake, she couldn't eat another morsel but she would like a cup of tea till, again, she sees the tea bag in her cup and tells us this isn't a proper cup of tea at all.

I tell her that's what we have and that's what she's getting though what I don't tell her is that I'd like to throw the tea bag between her eyes.

She said no to the cake but here she is pushing it into her mouth and swallowing with hardly a chew and then picking up and eating the crumbs from around her plate, the woman who didn't want the cake.

She glances at the tea cup. Well, if that's the only tea ye have I suppose I'll have to drink it. She lifts the tea bag on her spoon and squeezes it till the water turns brown and wants to know why there's a lemon on her saucer.

Alberta says some people like lemon with their tea.

Mam says she never heard the likes of that, it's disgusting.

Alberta removes the lemon and Mam says she'd like milk and sugar, if you don't mind. She asks for a match for her cigarette and smokes while she drinks only half the tea to show she doesn't care for it.

Alberta asks if she and Alphie would like to see a movie in the neighborhood but Mam says, no, they have to be getting back to Manhattan and it's too late.

Alberta says it isn't that late and Mam says it's late enough.

I walk with my mother and Alphie up Henry Street and over to the subway at Borough Hall. It's a bright January night and all along the street there are still Christmas lights glowing and flickering in the windows. Alphie talks about the elegance of the houses and says thanks for the dinner. Mam says she doesn't know why people can't put the dinner in a bowl and give it to you without a plate under it. She thinks that kind of thing is putting on airs.

When the train comes in I shake hands with Alphie. I bend over to kiss my mother and hand her a twenty-dollar bill but she pulls her face away and sits in the train with her back to me and I walk away with the money back in my pocket.

44

For eight years I traveled on the Staten Island Ferry. I would take the RR train from Brooklyn to Whitehall Street in Manhattan, walk to the terminal, slip a nickel into a turnstile slot, buy coffee and a doughnut, plain no sugar, and wait on a bench with a newspaper filled with yesterday's disasters.

Mr Jones taught music at McKee High School though when you saw him on the ferry you might have thought he was a university professor or head of a law firm. You might have thought that even though he was a Negro who would become a black and, in later years, an African-American. Every day he wore a different three-piece suit and a hat to match. He wore shirts with collars or held in place with gold stick pins. His watch and rings were gold, too, and delicate. The old Italian shoeshine men loved him for the daily trade and generous tips and they left his shoes dazzling. Every morning he read the *Times* and held it with fingers protruding from little leather gloves that covered the area below the wrist to beyond the knuckles. He smiled when he told me of concerts and operas he'd attended the night before or of summer trips to Europe especially to Milan and Salzburg. He put his hand on my arm and told me I must not die before I sit in La Scala. Another teacher joked one morning that the kids at McKee must be impressed with his clothes, all that elegance, you know, and Mr Jones said, I dress for what I am. The teacher shook his head and Mr Jones went back to his *Times*. On the ferry back that day the other teacher told me Mr Jones didn't see himself as a Negro at all, that he'd call to the black kids to stop bopping down the hall. The black kids didn't know what to make of Mr Jones with all that elegance. They knew that whatever music they liked Mr Jones would be up there talking about Mozart, playing his music on the phonograph or illustrating passages on the piano, and when it was time for the Christmas assembly he'd have his boys and girls up on the stage caroling like angels.

Every morning on the ferry I passed the Statue of Liberty and Ellis Island and thought of my mother and father coming to this country. When they sailed in were they excited as I was that first sunny October morning? Teachers going to McKee and other schools on Staten Island sat on the ferry and looked towards the Statue and the island. They must have thought of their parents and grandparents coming into this place and they might have thought of all the hundreds who were sent back. It must have saddened them the way it saddened me to see Ellis Island neglected and crumbling and that ferry docked by the side low in the water, the ferry that took the immigrants from Ellis Island to the island of Manhattan and if they looked hard enough they saw ghosts hungry for the landing.

Mam had moved with Alphie to an apartment on the West Side. Then Alphie left to be his own man in the Bronx and Mam moved to Flatbush Avenue near Grand Army Plaza in Brooklyn. Her building was shabby but she felt comfortable having a place of her own where she'd be under obligation to nobody. She could walk to any number of bingo games and she was content, thank you.

In my early years at McKee High School I enrolled at Brooklyn College for classes leading to a master's degree in English. I started with summer courses and continued with afternoon and evening classes into the academic year. I would take the ferry from Staten Island to Manhattan and walk to a subway train at Bowling Green that took me to the end of the Flatbush line near Brooklyn College. On ferry and train I could read for my classes or correct the work of my students at McKee.

I told my students I wanted neat, clean, legible work but they handed in whatever they had scribbled quickly on buses and trains, in shop classes when the teacher wasn't looking, or in the cafeteria. The papers were dotted with the stains of coffee, Coke, ice cream, ketchup, sneezes, and a lusciousness where girls had blotted their lips. A set of such papers would so irritate me I'd fling them over the side of the ferry and watch with satisfaction while they sank below the water to create a Sargasso of illiteracy.

When they asked for their papers I told them they were so bad that if I had returned them each paper would have been given a zero and would they prefer that to nothing at all?

They weren't sure and when I thought of it I wasn't sure myself. Zero or nothing at all? We discussed it for a whole period and decided that nothing at all was better than zero on your report card because you can't divide nothing at all by anything and you can divide zero if you use algebra or something like that because a zero is something and nothing at all is nothing at all and nobody could argue with that. Also, if your parents see a zero on your report card they're upset, the ones who care, but if they see nothing they don't know what to think and it's better to have a father and mother who don't know what to think than a father and mother looking at a zero and giving you a punch upside your head.

After my classes at Brooklyn College I would sometimes leave the train at Bergen Street to visit my mother. If she knew I was coming she'd make soda bread so warm and delicious it melted in the mouth as fast as the butter she slathered on it. She made tea in a teapot and couldn't help sniffing at the idea of tea bags. I told her tea bags were just a convenience for people with busy lives and she said no one is so busy they can't take time to make a decent cup of tea and if you are that busy you don't deserve a decent cup of tea for what is it all about anyway? Are we put into this world to be busy or to chat over a nice cup of tea?

My brother Michael married Donna from California in Malachy's apartment on West Ninety-Third Street. Mam bought a new dress for the occasion but you could see she didn't approve of the proceedings. There was her lovely son Michael getting married and no sign of a priest, nothing but a Protestant minister in the living room who could pass for a grocer or an off-duty policeman in his collar and tie. Malachy had rented two dozen folded chairs and when we took our places I noticed Mam's absence. She was in the kitchen smoking a cigarette. I told her the wedding was about to begin and she told me she had to finish her cigarette. Mam, for Christ's sake, your son is getting married. She said that was his problem, she had to finish her fag and when I told her she was keeping everyone waiting her face tightened, the nose went up in the air; she stubbed out her butt in the ashtray and took her time going to the living room. On the way in she whispered she had to go to the bathroom and I hissed at her that she'd bloody well have to wait. She sat in her chair and stared over the head of the Protestant minister. No matter what was said, no matter what softness or sweetness surged here, she wouldn't be part of it, wouldn't yield, and when bride and groom were kissed and hugged Mam sat with her purse in her lap staring straight ahead so that the world would know she was seeing nothing, especially the sight of her lovely son Michael falling into the clutches of Protestants and their ministers.

When I visited Mam on Flatbush Avenue and we had the tea she said wasn't it a peculiar thing she was back in this part of the world after all these years, a place where she had five children, though three would die, the little girl here in Brooklyn, and twin boys in Ireland. It might have been too much for her to think about that little girl, dead at twenty-one days, a short distance from here. She knew that if you walked down Flatbush Avenue to where it crossed Atlantic Avenue you'd still see the bars my father went wild in, spending his wages, forgetting his children. No, she wouldn't talk about that, either. When I asked her about her days in Brooklyn she doled out scraps and then went silent. What was the use? The past is the past and it's dangerous to go back.

She must have had nightmares alone in that apartment.

45

Stanley spends more time in the teachers' cafeteria than anyone. When he sees me he sits with me, drinks coffee, smokes cigarettes and delivers monologues on everything.

Like most teachers he has five classes but his speech therapy students are often absent because of the shame of stammering and trying to make themselves understood with cleft palates. Stanley gives them inspirational speeches and even though he tells them they're as good as anyone else they don't believe him. Some are in my regular English classes and they write compositions saying it's all right for Mr Garber to talk, he's a nice guy and all, but he doesn't know what it's like to walk up to a girl and ask her to dance when you can't get the first word out of your mouth. Oh, yeah, it's all right for Mr Garber to help their stammer with singing in his class but what good is that when you go to the dance?

In the summer of 1961 Alberta wanted to be married at Grace Episcopal Church in Brooklyn Heights. I refused. I told her I'd rather be married in City Hall than in some pale imitation of the One, Holy, Roman, Catholic and Apostolic Church. Episcopalians irritated me. Why couldn't they stop the damned nonsense? They're up there with their statues and crosses and holy water and even confession, so why don't they call Rome and tell them they want to return?

Alberta said, All right, all right, and we went to the Municipal Building in Manhattan. It wasn't required but we had Brian McPhillips as best man and his wife, Joyce, as bridesmaid. Our ceremony was delayed because of a quarrel between the couple ahead of us. She said to him, You goin' be married to me with that green umbrella on you arm? He said that was his umbrella and he wasn't going to leave it out in this office to be stolen. She nodded towards us and told him, These people ain't gonna steal you goddam green umbrella, excuse the language on my wedding day. He said he wasn't accusin' nobody of nothin' but goddam he paid a lot for that umbrella on Chambers Street from a guy that steals them and he wasn't givin' it up for nobody. She told him, Well, then, marry you damn umbrella, and she picked up her bag and walked out. He told her if she walked out now that was the end and she turned to the four of us and the woman behind the desk and the official coming out of the small wedding chapel and said, The end? What you talkin' about, man? We be livin' together three years an' you tell me this is the end? You don't tell me this is the end. I tell you and I'm tellin' you that umbrella ain't goin' to my weddin' an' if you insist there's a certain party in South Carolina, a certain ex-wife, that would like to know where you at an' I be glad to tell her if you know what I mean, certain party lookin' for alimony an' child support. So take you choice, Byron, me in that little room with the man an' no umbrella or you back in South Carolina with you umbrella standin' before a judge tellin' you, Pay up, Byron, support you wife an' child.

The official at the door of the wedding chapel asked if they were ready. Byron asked me if I was the one getting married today and would I mind holding his umbrella because he could see that I was like him, going nowhere but into that little room. End of the road, man, end of the road. I wished him good luck but he shook his head and said, Damn, why we all whupped like this?

In a few minutes they were back to sign papers, the bride smiling, Byron grim. We all wished them good luck again and followed the official into the room. He smiled and said, Are we all atthembled?

Brian looked at me, raised his eyebrows.

The official said, Do you promith to love, honor, cherith? and I struggled to keep myself from laughing. How could I survive this wedding conducted by a man with such a powerful lisp? I'd have to think of some way of controlling myself. That's it. The umbrella on my arm. Oh, God, I'll fall apart. I'm caught between the lisp and the umbrella and I can't laugh. Alberta would kill me for laughing at our own wedding. You're allowed to weep with joy but you must never laugh and here I am made helpless by this man with the lisp, promi-thing thith and that, first man ever in New York to be married with a green umbrella on his arm, solemn thought that kept me from laughing, and the ceremony was over, the ring on Alberta's finger, groom and bride kissing and being congratulated by Brian and Joyce till the door opened and there was Byron. Man, you got my umbrella? You did that for me? Kep' it right here? Wanna have a drink? Celebrate?

Alberta signaled no to me with a little shake of her head.

I told Byron I was sorry. We were meeting friends who were giving us a party.

You lucky, man, you have friends. Me an' Selma goin' out to have a sangwidge an' go to a movie. I don't mind. Movie keeps her quiet, ha ha ha. Thanks for watchin' my umbrella.

Byron and Selma left and I fell against the wall, laughing. Alberta tried to keep a bit of dignity in the occasion but she gave way when she saw Brian and Joyce laughing, too. I tried to tell them how the thought of the green umbrella saved me from laughing over the lisp but the more I tried to talk the more helpless I became till we were clutching each other going down in the elevator and wiping our eyes outside in the August sun.

It was a short walk to Diamond Dan O'Rourke's Saloon for drinks and sandwiches with friends, Frank Schwake and his wife, Jean, and Jim Collins and his new wife, Sheila Malone. After that there was to be a party out in Queens given by Brian and Joyce who would drive Alberta and me in their Volkswagen.

Schwake bought me a drink. So did Collins and Brian. The bartender bought us a round and I bought him a drink and left him a big tip. He laughed and said I should get married every day. I bought drinks for Schwake and Collins and Brian and they all wanted to buy me one again. Joyce whispered to Brian and I knew she was worried about the drinking. Alberta told me to slow down. She understood it was my wedding day but it was early and I should have respect for her and the guests at the reception later. I told her we were married barely five minutes and she was already telling me what to do. Of course I had respect for her and the guests. That's all I ever had was respect and I was weary of having respect. I told her back off and there was such a state of tension Collins and Brian intervened. Brian said it was his job, that's what best men are for. Collins said he knew me longer than Brian but Brian said, No, you don't. I went to college with him. Collins said he didn't know that. McCourt, how come you never told me you went to college with McPhillips? I told him I never saw a need to tell the world who I went to college with and for some reason that made us all laugh. The bartender said it was nice to see people happy on their wedding day and we laughed even harder thinking of lisps and green umbrellas and Alberta telling me have respect for her and the guests. Of course I had respect for her on our wedding day till I went to the toilet and started thinking of how she rejected me for another man and I was ready to go out and confront her till I slipped on the slimy floor of the toilet in Diamond Dan O'Rourke's and banged my head so hard against the big urinal I had a headache that made me forget the rejection. Alberta wanted to know why the back of my jacket was damp and when I told her there was a leak in the men's room she didn't believe me. You fell, didn't you? No, I didn't fall. There was a leak. She wouldn't believe me, told me I was drinking too much and that so irritated me I was ready to walk out and live with a ballerina in a loft in Greenwich Village till Brian said, Oh, come on, don't be an ass, it's Alberta's wedding day, too.

Before going out to Queens we had to pick up a wedding cake at Schrafft's on West Fifty-Seventh Street. Joyce said she'd drive because Brian and I had been too enthusiastic with the celebrations at Diamond Dan's while she and Alberta were saving themselves for the party that night. She stopped opposite Schrafft's and said no when Brian offered to get the cake but he insisted and dodged the traffic. Joyce shook her head and said he was going to get killed. Alberta told me go help him but Joyce shook her head again and said that would only make things worse. Brian came out of Schrafft's holding a big cake box against his chest and once more dodged cars till a taxi sideswiped him slightly at the street's dividing line and the box fell to the ground. Joyce put her forehead against the steering wheel. Oh, God, she said, and I said I was going to help my best man, Brian. No, no, Alberta said, I'll go. I told her this was man's work, that I wouldn't risk her life with these mad taxis on Fifty-Seventh Street and I went to help Brian who was on his hands protecting the wrecked cake from the traffic zooming by him right and left. I knelt with him, tore a cardboard flap from the box, and we shoveled the cake back in with bits hanging here and there. The little bride and groom figures looked sad but we wiped them off and stuck them back on the cake, not the top, because we didn't know where the top was anymore, but somewhere in the cake where we could push them in for the security. Joyce and Alberta called to us from the car that we'd better get off the street before the police came or we were killed and they were tired of waiting anyway, hurry up. When we got into the car Joyce told Brian pass the cake back to Alberta for safekeeping but he turned stubborn and said no, after all his troubles he'd hold on to it till we were at the apartment, and he did even if he had bits of cream and little green and yellow decorations all over his lap and his suit in general.

The wives treated us coolly the rest of the way in the car, talking only to each other and making comments on the Irish and how you can't trust them with a simple task like crossing a street with a wedding cake, how these Irish couldn't have one or two drinks and be content till the reception, oh, no, they had to talk and treat each other to rounds till they're in such a condition you couldn't send them to the grocery for a quart of milk.

Look at him, Joyce said, and when I saw Brian dozing away with his chin on his chest I nodded off while the wives went on with their lamentation about the Irish in general and this day in particular, Alberta saying, Everyone warned me that the Irish are great to go out with but never marry them. I would have defended my race and told her how her Yankee ancestors had nothing to be proud of the way they treated the Irish with those signs everywhere that said, No Irish Need Apply, except that I was weary from the strain of being married by a man with a lisp while I carried Byron's green umbrella and my heavy responsibility as groom and host at Diamond Dan O'Rourke's. If I hadn't slumped with the weariness I would have reminded her how her ancestors hanged women right and left for being witches, how they were a dirty-minded lot, rolling their eyes in shock and horror at the mention of sex, but having a grand time between their thighs listening in court to hysterical Puritan maidens claiming the devil appeared in various forms and frolicked with them in the woods and how they became so devoted to him all decency went out the window.

I would have told Alberta how the Irish never carried on like that. In the whole history of Ireland only one witch was hanged and she was probably English and deserved it. And, just to clinch it, I would have told her the first witch to be hanged in New England was Irish and they did it to her because she said her prayers in Latin and wouldn't stop.

Instead of saying all this I fell asleep till Alberta shook me and told me we were there. Joyce insisted on taking the cake from Brian. She didn't want him to fall forward on the stairs and crush the cake entirely and she still had hopes of reconstructing it so that we'd have some resemblance of a cake and people could sing, The bride cuts the cake.

People arrived and there was eating, drinking, dancing and misunderstandings between all the couples, married and unmarried. Frank Schwake wouldn't talk to his wife, Jean. Jim Collins quarrelled in a corner with his wife, Sheila. There was still a coolness between Alberta and me and between Brian and Joyce. Other couples were affected and there were islands of tension all over the apartment. The night would have been ruined except for the way we all united against an outside danger.

One of Alberta's friends, a German named Dietrich, drove off in his Volkswagen to replenish the beer supply and when he returned there was trouble with the owner of a Buick he had backed into. Someone told me about the trouble outside and since I was the bridegroom it was my duty to make peace. The Buick man was a giant and poking his fist into the face of Alberta's friend. When I stepped between them he let loose with his big punch. His arm swung around the back of my head, into Dietrich's eye and we all fell to the ground. We wrestled a bit, one with another, no one a bit particular, till Schwake, Collins and McPhillips separated us with the Buick man threatening to tear Dietrich's head from his shoulders. When we dragged the German inside I discovered my trouser knee was ripped, the kneecap bleeding. The knuckles of my right hand bled, too, from being scraped along the ground.

Upstairs Alberta started to cry, telling me I was ruining the whole night. My blood boiled a bit and I told her I was only trying to be a peacemaker and it wasn't my fault if I was knocked down by that baboon next door. Besides, I was helping her German friend and she should be grateful.

The argument would have continued if Joyce hadn't stepped in to call everyone to the table for the cutting of the cake. When she slipped off the covering cloth Brian laughed and kissed her for being such a genius of an artist you'd never know this cake was scooped off the street a short time ago. The little bride and groom were secure though his head wobbled and fell and I told Joyce, Uneasy lies the groom that wears a head. Everyone sang, The bride cuts the cake, the groom cuts the cake, and Alberta looked mollified even though we couldn't cut proper slices and the cake had to be dished out in chunks.

Joyce said she was making coffee and Alberta said that would be nice but Brian said we should have one more drink to toast the newlyweds and I agreed and Alberta got so angry she ripped the wedding ring from her finger and threw it out the window though she remembered suddenly that was her grandmother's wedding ring from early in the century and now it was out the window, God knows where in Queens and what was she going to do, it was all my fault, and her great mistake for marrying me. Brian said we'd have to find that ring. We didn't have a flashlight but we were able to light up the night with matches and cigarette lighters as we crawled across the lawn below Brian's window till Dietrich shouted he had the ring and everyone forgave him for stirring up trouble with the big Buick man. Alberta refused to replace the ring on her finger. She'd keep it in her purse till she was sure of this marriage. She and I took a taxi with Jim Collins and Sheila. They would drop us at our apartment in Brooklyn and continue in to Manhattan. Sheila wasn't talking to Jim and Alberta wasn't talking to me but as we swung into State Street I grabbed her and told her, I'm going to consummate this marriage tonight.

She said, Oh, consummate my ass, and I said, That'll do.

The taxi stopped and I climbed from the back seat I had shared with Sheila and Alberta. Jim got out of the seat by the driver and came to where I stood on the sidewalk. He intended to say goodnight and get back in with Sheila but Alberta pulled the door shut and the taxi drove away.

Christ Almighty, said Collins, this is your goddam wedding night, McCourt. Where is your bride? Where is mine?

We climbed the stairs to my apartment, found a six-pack of Schlitz in the refrigerator, sat on the couch, the two of us, and watched television Indians drop from the bullets of John Wayne.

46

In the summer of 1963 Mam called to say she had a letter from my father. He claimed he was a new man, that he hadn't had a drink in three years and worked now as a chef in a monastery.

I told her if my father was a monastery chef the monks must have been on a permanent fast.

She didn't laugh and that said she was troubled. She read from the letter where he said he was coming with a three-week return ticket on the *Queen Mary* and how he looked forward to the day when we could all be together again, he and she sharing a bed and a grave for he knew and she knew that whatever God hath joined let no man put asunder.

She sounded uncertain. What should she do? Malachy had already told her, Why not? She wanted to know what I thought. I put it back to her. What do you think? After all, this was the man who put her through hell in New York and Limerick and now he wants to sail to her side, a safe harbor in Brooklyn.

I don't know what to do, she said.

She didn't know what to do because she was lonely in that dingy place on Flatbush Avenue and she was now illustrating that Irish saying, Contention is better than loneliness. She could take back this man or, at fifty-five, face the years alone. I told her I'd meet her for coffee at Junior's Restaurant.

She was there before me, puffing and gasping on a strong American cigarette. No, she wouldn't have tea. The Americans can send a man into space but they can't make a decent cup of tea, so she'd have coffee and some of that nice cheesecake. She drew on the cigarette, sipped the coffee and told me she didn't know under God what to do. She said the whole family was falling apart with Malachy separated from his wife, Linda, and the two small children, Michael off to California with his wife, Donna, and their child, Alphie disappeared into the Bronx. She said she could have a nice life for herself in Brooklyn with the bingo and the odd meeting of the Limerick Ladies' Association in Manhattan and why should she let the man from Belfast upset that life.

I drank my coffee and ate my strudel knowing she'd never admit she was lonely though she might have been thinking, Ah, sure if it wasn't for the drink he wouldn't be bad to live with at all, at all.

I told her what I was thinking. Well, she said, he'd be company for me if he's not drinking, if he's a new man. We could take walks in Prospect Park and he could meet me after the bingo.

All right. Tell him to come for the three weeks and we'll see if he's a new man.

On the way back to her apartment she stopped often to press her hand against her chest. 'Tis my heart, she said, going a mile a minute so 'tis.

It must be the cigarettes.

Oh, I don't know.

Then it must be nervousness over that letter.

Oh, I don't know. I just don't know.

At her door I kissed her cold cheek and watched her gasping her way upstairs. My father had put years on her.

When Mam and Malachy went to meet the new man at the pier he arrived so drunk he had to be helped off the ship. The purser told them he had gone wild with the drink and had to be kept in restraint.

I was away that day and when I returned I took the subway to see him at Mam's apartment but he had gone with Malachy to a meeting of Alcoholics Anonymous. We drank tea and waited. She said again she didn't know under God what to do. He was the same lunatic with the drink and all that talk about being a new man was a lie and she was glad he had a three-week return ticket. Still, there was a darkness in her eyes that told me she must have had hopes of a normal family, her man by her side with sons and grandchildren coming to her from all over New York.

They returned from the meeting, Malachy big, red-bearded and sober because of his troubles, my father older and smaller. Malachy had tea. My father said, Och, no, and lay on the couch with his hands joined under his head. Malachy left his tea to stand over him and lecture him. You have to admit you're an alcoholic. That's the first step.

Dad shook his head.

Why are you shaking your head? You are an alcoholic and you have to admit it.

Och, no. I'm not an alcoholic like those poor people at the meeting. I don't drink kerosene.

Malachy threw up his hands and returned to his tea at the table. We didn't know what to say to each other in the presence of this man on the couch, husband, father. I had my memories of him, mornings by the fire in Limerick, his stories and songs, his cleanliness, neatness and sense of order, the way he helped us with our schoolwork, his insistence on obedience and attention to our religious duties, all destroyed by his payday madness when he threw his money around the pubs buying pints for every hanger-on while my mother despaired by the fire knowing the next day she'd have to stick her hand out for charity.

I knew in the days that followed that if blood called to blood I'd drift to my father's side of the family. My mother's people had often said in Limerick I had the odd manner of my father and a strong streak of the North in my character. They may have been right because whenever I went to Belfast I felt at home.

The night before he left he asked if we'd like to go for a walk. Mam and Malachy said no, they were tired. They had spent more time with him than I and must have been weary of his shenanigans. I said yes because this was my father and I was a nine-year-old thirty-three-year-old.

He put on his cap and we walked down Flatbush Avenue. Och, he said, it's a very warm kind of a night.

'Tis.

Very warm, he said. You'd be in danger of drying up on a night like this.

Ahead of us was the Long Island Railroad Station ringed with bars for the thirsty commuters. I asked if he remembered the bars.

Och, he said, why should I remember such places?

Because you drank in them and we searched for you.

Och, well, I might have worked in one or two when times were hard for the bread and meat they gave me to take home to you childer.

He remarked again on the heat of the night and surely it wouldn't do us any harm to cool ourselves in one of these places.

I thought you didn't drink.

That's right. Gave it up.

Well, what about the ship? You had to be carried off.

Och, that was the sea sickness. We'll have something here for the coolness.

While we drank our beer he told me my mother was a fine woman and I should be good to her, that Malachy was a fine big lad though you'd hardly know him with that red beard and where did it come from, that he was sorry to hear I had married a Protestant though it wasn't too late for her to convert nice girl that she was and he was happy to hear I was a teacher like all his sisters in the North and would there be any harm in having another beer?

No, there wouldn't be any harm and there wasn't any harm in the beers we had up and down Flatbush Avenue and when we arrived back at my mother's apartment I left him at the door because I didn't want to see the looks on the faces of Mam and Malachy that would accuse me of leading my father astray or vice versa. He wanted to continue the drinking up towards Grand Army Plaza but my guilt told me to say no. He was supposed to leave next day on the *Queen Mary* though he hoped my mother would say, Ah, stay. Sure we'll find some way of getting along.

I said that would be lovely and he said we'd all be together again and things would be better because he was a new man. We shook hands and I left.

Next morning Mam called and said, He went pure mad, so he did.

What did he do?

You brought him home drunk as a lord.

He wasn't drunk. He had a few beers.

He had more than that and I was here by myself with Malachy gone into Manhattan. A bottle of whiskey he had, your father, that he brought from the ship and I had to call the cops and he's gone now, bag and baggage, and sailed away today on the *Queen Mary* because I called Cunard and they told me, oh, yes, they had him on board and they'd be watching closely for any signs of the lunacy he came with.

What did he do?

She wouldn't tell me and she didn't have to because it was easy to guess. He probably tried to get into bed with her and that was not part of her dream. She hinted and suggested that if I hadn't spent hours with him in saloons he would have behaved himself and wouldn't be on the *Queen Mary* now heading out into the Atlantic. I told her his drinking wasn't my fault but she was sharp with me. Last night was the last straw, she said, and you were part of it.

47

For teachers Fridays are bright. You leave the school with a bag filled with papers to read and correct, books to read. This weekend you will surely catch up with all those uncorrected, unmarked papers. You don't want to let them pile up in the closets like Miss Mudd so that decades hence a young teacher will pounce on them to keep his classes busy. You will take the papers home, pour a glass of wine, stack Duke Ellington, Sonny Rollins and Hector Berlioz on the phonograph and try to read a hundred and fifty student compositions. You know that some don't care what you do with their work as long as you give them a decent grade so that they can pass and get on with real life in their shops. Others fancy themselves as writers and want their papers back corrected and graded high. The class Romeos would like you to comment on their papers and read them aloud so that they can bask in the admiring glances of the girls. The ones who don't care are sometimes interested in the same girls and verbal threats are passed from desk to desk because the ones who don't care are weak in written expression. If a boy is a good writer you have to be careful about praising him too much because of the danger of accidents on the stairs. The ones who don't care hate goody-goodies.

You intend to go straight home with your bag but you then discover Friday afternoon is the time for beer and teacher enlightenment. An occasional teacher might say he has to go home to his wife till he finds Bob Bogard standing by the time clock to remind us of first things first, that the Meurot Bar is a few steps away, next door in fact, and what harm would there be in one beer, one? Bob is not married and may not understand the dangers for a man who might go beyond the one beer, a man who might have to face the wrath of a wife who has cooked a fine Friday fish and now sits in the kitchen watching the grease congeal.

We stand at the Meurot Bar and order our beers. There is teacher small talk. When there's a mention of good-looking women on our staff or even nubile students we roll our eyes. What we wouldn't do if we were high school kids nowadays. We talk tough at the mention of troublesome boys. One more word out of that goddam kid and he's gonna beg for a transfer. We unite in our hostility to authority, all the people who emerge from their offices to supervise and observe us and tell us what to do and how to do it, people who spent as little time as possible in the classroom themselves and don't know their ass from their elbow about teaching.

A young teacher might drop in, just graduated from college, newly licensed. The drone of university professors and the chatter from college cafeterias is still in his ears and if he wants to discuss Camus and Sartre and how existence precedes essence or vice versa he'll be talking to himself in the mirror of the Meurot Bar.

None of us had followed the Great American Path, elementary school, high school, college, and into teaching at twenty-two. Bob Bogard fought in the war in Germany and was probably wounded. He won't tell you. Claude Campbell served in the navy, graduated from college in Tennessee, published a novel when he was twenty-seven, teaches English, has six children with his second wife, took a master's degree at Brooklyn College with a thesis, *Ideational Trends in the American Novel*, fixes everything in his house, wiring, plumbing, carpentry. I look at him and think of Goldsmith's lines on the village schoolmaster, "And all around the wonder grew/That one small head could carry all he knew." And Claude hasn't even reached the age of Christ at his crucifixion, thirty-three.

When Stanley Garber drops in for a Coke he tells us he often feels he made a mistake by not going into college teaching where you amble through life thinking you shit cream puffs and suffering if you have to teach more than three hours a week. He says he could have written a bullshit PhD dissertation on the bilabial fricative in the middle period of Thomas Chatterton who died when he was seventeen because that's the kind of crap that goes on in colleges while the rest of us hold the front lines with kids who won't get their heads out from between their thighs and supervisors content to keep their heads up their asses.

There will be trouble tonight in Brooklyn. I'm supposed to have dinner with Alberta at an Arabic restaurant, the Near East, bring your own wine, but it's six going on seven and if I call now she'll complain she's been waiting for hours, that I'm just an Irish drunk like my father and she doesn't care if I stay on Staten Island the rest of my life, goodbye.

So I won't call. Better not to. No use having two rows, one on the phone now, another when I get home. It's easier to sit at the bar where's there's a glow and important matters are discussed.

We agree that teachers are sniped at from three fronts, parents, kids, supervisors, and you either have to be diplomatic or tell them all kiss your ass. Teachers are the only professionals who have to respond to bells every forty-five minutes and come out fighting. All right, class, sit down. Yes, you, sit down. Open your notebooks, that's right, your notebooks, am I speaking a foreign language, kid? Don't call you kid? Okay, I won't call you kid. Just sit down. Report card grades are just around the corner and I can put you on the welfare rolls. All right, bring in your father, bring in your mother, bring in your whole damn tribe. You don't have a pen, Pete? Okay, here's a pen. Goodbye, pen. No, Phyllis, you can't have the pass. I don't care if you're having a hundred periods, Phyllis, because what you really want to do is meet Eddie and disappear into the basement where your future could be determined by one smooth panty drop and one swift upward stroke from Eddie's impatient member, the start of a little nine-month adventure that will end with you squawking Eddie better marry you, the shotgun aimed at his lower frontal region and his dreams dead. So I'm saving you, Phyllis, you and Eddie and no, you don't have to thank me.

This is talk along the bar that will never be heard in the classroom unless a teacher loses his wits entirely. You know you can never deny the lavatory pass to a menstrual Phyllis for fear of being dragged before the highest court in the land where the black robes, all men, will excoriate you for insulting Phyllis and the future mothers of America.

There is talk along the bar about certain efficient teachers and we agree we don't like them and the way their classes are so organized they hum from bell to bell. In these classes there are monitors for every activity, every part of the lesson. There is the monitor who goes immediately to the board to write the number and title of the day's lesson, Lesson #32, Strategies in Dealing with the Dangling Participle. Efficient teachers are known for their strategies, the darling new word at the Board of Education.

The efficient teacher has rules for taking notes and the organization of the notebook and there are notebook monitors who roam the classroom to check for proper form, top of page filled with student's name, homeroom class, title of course and date with the month written out, not numbers, it must be written out so that the student will have practice in writing out because there are too many people in this world that we live in, business people and others, who are too lazy to write out the months. There are to be prescribed margins and no scribbling. If the notebook doesn't adhere to the rules the monitor will enter demerits on the student's card and when report card time rolls around there will be suffering and no mercy.

Homework monitors collect and return assignments, attendance monitors preside over the little cards in the attendance book and collect excuses for absences and latenesses. Failure to submit written excuses leads to further suffering and no mercy.

Some students are known for their skill in writing excuse notes from parents and doctors and they'll do it in return for favors in the cafeteria or the far reaches of the basement.

Monitors who take blackboard erasers to the basement to knock out the chalk must first promise they're not taking this important job to sneak a smoke or make out with the boy or girl of their choice. The principal is already complaining there is too much activity in the basement and he'd like to know what's going on there.

There are monitors to distribute books and collect receipts, monitors to handle the lavatory pass and the sign-in sign-out sheet, monitors to put everything in the room in alphabetical order, monitors to carry the trash can along the aisles in the war against litter, monitors who decorate the room to make it so bright and cheerful the principal brings in visitors from Japan and Liechtenstein.

The efficient teacher is monitor of monitors though he may lighten his monitor load by appointing monitors who monitor the other monitors or he may have dispute monitors who settle arguments between monitors accusing other monitors of interfering with their jobs. The dispute monitor has the most dangerous job of all because of what might happen on the stairs or the street.

A student caught trying to bribe a monitor is immediately reported to the principal who will enter a remark on his permanent record that will blacken his reputation. This is a warning to others that such a blot could be an impediment to a career in sheet metal, plumbing, automechanics, anything.

Stanley Garber snorts that with all this efficient activity there is little time for instruction but what the hell, the students are in their seats, completely monitored and behaving themselves, and that pleases the teacher, the chairman, the principal and his assistants, the superintendent, the Board of Education, the Mayor, the Governor, the President, and God Himself.

So says Stanley.

If a university professor discusses *Vanity Fair* or anything else his classes listen with notebooks open and pens poised. If they dislike the novel they won't dare complain for fear of lowered grades.

When I distributed *Vanity Fair* to my junior class at McKee Vocational and Technical High School there was moaning in the room. Why do we have to read this dumb book? I told them it was about two young women, Becky and Amelia, and their adventures with men, but my students said it was written in that old English and who can read that? Four girls read it and said it was beautiful and should be made into a movie. The boys pretended to yawn and told me English teachers were all the same. They just wanted to make you read that old stuff and how was that gonna help you if you was fixin' a car or a busted air conditioner, ah?

I could threaten them with failure. If they refused to read this book they'd fail the course and they wouldn't graduate and everyone knew girls didn't want to go out with anyone who wasn't a high school graduate.

For three weeks we toiled through *Vanity Fair*. Every day I tried to motivate and encourage them, to draw them into a discussion of what it's like to make your way through the world when you're a young nineteenth-century woman, but they didn't care. One wrote on the board, Becky Sharp Drop Dead.

Then, as decreed by the school syllabus, it was on to *The Scarlet Letter*. This would be easier. I'd talk about the New England witch hunts, the accusations, the hysteria, the hangings. I'd talk about Germany in the 1930s and how a whole nation was brainwashed.

Not my students. They'd never be brainwashed. No, sir, they'd never be able to get away with that here. They'd never fool us like that.

I chanted to them, Winston tastes good like . . . and they finished the sentence.

I sang, My beer is Rheingold the dry beer . . . and they finished the jingle.

I chanted again, You wonder where the yellow went when . . . and they finished the line.

I asked if they knew any more and there was an eruption of jingles from radio and television, proof of the power of advertising. When I told them they were brainwashed they were indignant, Oh, no, they weren't brainwashed. They could think for themselves and nobody could tell them what to do. They denied they'd been told what cigarette to smoke, what beer to drink, what toothpaste to use though they'd admit that when you're in a supermarket you'll buy the brand in your head. No, you'd never buy a cigarette called Turnip.

Yeah, they heard about Senator McCarthy and all that but they were too young and their fathers and mothers said he was a great man for getting rid of the Communists.

From day to day I struggled to make connections between Hitler and McCarthy and the New England witch hunts, trying to soften them up for *The Scarlet Letter*. From parents there were indignant calls. What is this guy telling our kids about Senator McCarthy? Tell him back off. Senator McCarthy was a good man, fought for his country. Tailgunner Joe. Got rid of the Communists.

Mr Sorola said he didn't want to interfere but would I please tell him was I teaching English or was I teaching history. I told him about my troubles trying to get the kids to read anything. He said I shouldn't listen to them. Just tell them, You're going to read *The Scarlet Letter* whether you like it or not because this is high school and that's what we do here and that's that and if you don't like it, kid, you fail.

They complained when I distributed the book. Here we go again with the old stuff. We thought you was a nice guy, Mr McCourt. We thought you was different.

I told them this book was about a young woman in Boston who got into trouble over having a baby with a man who wasn't her husband though I couldn't tell them who the man was in case it might ruin the story. They said they didn't care who the father was. One boy said you never know who your father is anyway because he had a friend who discovered his father wasn't his father at all, that his real father was killed in Korea, but the pretend father was the one he grew up with, a good guy, so who gives a shit about this woman in Boston.

Most of the class agreed though they wouldn't want to wake up in the morning to find their fathers weren't their real fathers. Some wished they had other fathers, their own fathers were so mean they made them come to school and read dumb books.

But that's not the story of *The Scarlet Letter*, I said.

Aw, Mr McCourt, do we have to talk about that old stuff? This guy Hawthorne don't even know how to write so's we can understand and you're always saying write simple, write simple. Why can't we read the *Daily News*? They have good writers. They write simple.

Then I remembered I was broke and that's what led to *Catcher in the Rye* and *Five Great Plays of Shakespeare* and a change in my teaching career. I had forty-eight cents to get me home on the ferry and the subway, no money for lunch, not even for a cup of coffee on the ferry and I blurted to the class that if they wanted to read a good book that didn't have big words and long sentences and was all about a boy their age who was mad at the world I'd get it for them but they'd have to buy it, a dollar twenty-five each which they could pay in instalments starting now, so if you have a nickel or a dime or more you can pass it up and I'll write your name and amount on a sheet of paper and order the books today from the Coleman Book Company in Yonkers, and they'd never know, my students, I'd have a pocketful of change for lunch and maybe a beer at the Meurot next door, though I didn't tell them that, they'd be shocked.

Small change was passed up and when I called the book company I saved a dime by using the assistant principal's phone because it's illegal to have students buy books when bookrooms are spilling over with copies of *Silas Marner* and *Giants in the Earth*.

Catcher in the Rye arrived in two days and I passed them out, paid for or not. Some students never offered a penny, others less than their share, but the money collected kept me going till pay day when I'd satisfy the book company.

When I handed out the books someone discovered the word crap on the first page and that brought silence to the room. That's a word you'd never find in any book in the English bookroom. Girls covered their mouths and giggled and boys tittered over shocking pages. When the bell rang there was no stampede to the door. I had to ask them to leave, another class was coming in.

The class coming in were curious about the class going out and why was everyone looking at this book and if it was that good why couldn't they read it. I reminded them they were seniors and the class going out were juniors. Yeah, but why couldn't they read that small book instead of *Great Expectations*? I told them they could but they'd have to buy it and they said they'd pay anything not to read *Great Expectations*, anything.

Next day Mr Sorola came into the room with his assistant, Miss Seested. They went from desk to desk snatching copies of *Catcher in the Rye* and dropping them into two shopping bags. If the books weren't on the desks they demanded the students take them from their bags. They counted the books in the shopping bags and compared them with the class attendance and threatened the four students who hadn't turned in their books with big trouble. Raise your hands, the four people who still have the book. No hands were raised and on the way out Mr Sorola told me I was to see him in his office right after this class, not a minute later.

Mr McCourt, you in trouble?

Mr McCourt, that's the only book I ever read and now that man took it.

They complained about the loss of their books and told me if anything happened to me they'd go on strike and that would teach the school a lesson. They nudged and winked over the strike and they knew I knew it would simply be another excuse for avoiding school and not any great concern for me.

Mr Sorola sat behind his desk reading *Catcher in the Rye*, puffing on his cigarette and letting me wait while he turned the page, shook his head and put the book down.

Mr McCourt, this book is not on the syllabus.

I know, Mr Sorola.

You know I've had calls from seventeen parents and you know why?

They didn't like the book?

That's right, Mr McCourt. There's a scene in this book where the kid is in a hotel room with a prostitute.

Yes, but nothing happens.

That's not what the parents think. You telling me that kid was in that room to sing? The parents don't want their kids reading this kind of trash.

He warned me to be careful, that I was endangering my satisfactory rating on the yearly performance report and we wouldn't want that, would we? He would have to place a note in my file as a record of our meeting. If there were no further incidents in the near future the note would be removed.

Mr McCourt, what are we gonna read next?

The Scarlet Letter. We have tons of them in the bookroom.

Their faces fell. Aw, Gawd, no. All the kids in the other classes told us it's that old stuff again.

All right, I said, jokingly. We'll read Shakespeare.

Their faces fell even farther and the room was filled with moans and hisses. Mr McCourt, my sister went to college for a year and dropped out because she couldn't read Shakespeare and she can speak Italian and everything.

I said it again, Shakespeare. There was fear in the room and I felt myself drawn to the edge of a cliff with something in my head demanding, How can you move from Salinger to Shakespeare?

I told the class, It's Shakespeare or *The Scarlet Letter*, kings and lovers or a woman having a baby in Boston. If we read Shakespeare we'll act out the plays. If we read *The Scarlet Letter* we'll sit here and discuss the deeper meaning and I'll give you the big exam they keep in the department office.

Oh, no, not the deeper meaning. English teachers always be going on about the deeper meaning.

All right. It's Shakespeare, no deeper meaning and no exams except what you decide. So, write your name on this paper and the amount you're paying and we'll get the book.

They passed up their nickels and dimes. They groaned when they thumbed the book, *Five Great Plays of Shakespeare*. Man, I can't read this old English.

I wished I could have dominated my classes like other teachers, imposed on them classic English and American literature. I failed. I caved in and took the easy way with *Catcher in the Rye* and when that was taken dodged and danced my way to Shakespeare. We'd read the plays and enjoy ourselves and why not? Wasn't he the best?

Still my students complained till someone called out, Shit, man, excuse the language, Mr McCourt, but here's this guy saying Friends, Romans, countrymen, lend me your ears.

Where? Where? The class wanted to know the page number and all around the room boys declaimed Mark Antony's speech, flung out their arms and laughed.

Another discovered Hamlet's To be or not to be soliloquy and soon the room was filled with ranting Hamlets.

The girls raised their hands. Mr McCourt, the boys have all these great speeches and there's nothing for us.

Oh, girls, girls, there's Juliet, Lady Macbeth, Ophelia, Gertrude.

We spent two days plucking morsels from the five plays, *Romeo and Juliet, Julius Caesar, Macbeth, Hamlet, Henry IV*, Part One.

My students led and I followed because there was nothing else to do. Remarks had been passed in the hallways, in the students' cafeteria.

Hey, wass dat?

It's a book, man.

Oh, yeah? What book?

Shakespeare. We're reading Shakespeare.

Shakespeare? Shit, man, you not reading Shakespeare.

When the girls wanted to act out *Romeo and Juliet* the boys yawned and obliged. This would be sissy romantic stuff till the fight scene where Mercutio dies in style, telling the world about his wound.

> *Tis not so deep as a well, nor so wide as a church door,*
> *But 'tis enough, 'twill serve.*

★ ★ ★

To be or not to be was the passage everyone memorized but when they recited it they had to be reminded this was a meditation on suicide and not an incitement to arms.

Oh, yeah?

Yeah.

The girls wanted to know why everyone picked on Ophelia especially Laertes, Polonius, Hamlet. Why didn't she fight back? They had sisters like that who were married to bastard sons o' bitches, excuse the language, and you wouldn't believe what they put up with.

A hand went up. Why didn't Ophelia run away to America?

Another hand. Because there was no America in the old days. It had to be discovered.

Whadda you talkin' about? There was always an America. Where do you think the Indians lived?

I told them they'd have to look it up and the opposing hands agreed to go to the library and report next day.

One hand, There was an America in Shakespeare's time and she coulda went.

The other hand. There was an America in Shakespeare's time but no America in Ophelia's time and she cuddena went. If she went in Shakespeare's time there was nothing but Indians and Ophelia woulda been uncomfortable in a tepee which is what they called their houses.

We moved on to *Henry IV*, Part One, and all the boys wanted to be Hal, Hotspur, Falstaff. The girls complained again there was nothing for them except for Juliet, Ophelia, Lady Macbeth and Queen Gertrude and look what happened to them. Didn't Shakespeare like women? Did he have to kill everyone who wore a skirt?

The boys said that's the way it is and the girls snapped back they were sorry we didn't read *The Scarlet Letter* because one of them had read it and told the rest how Hester Prynne had her beautiful baby, Pearl, and the father was a jerk who died miserable and Hester got her revenge on the whole town of Boston and wasn't that much better than poor Ophelia floating down a stream, out of her mind, talking to herself and throwin' flowers around, wasn't it?

Mr Sorola came to observe me with the new head of the Academic Department, Mrs Popp. They smiled and didn't complain about this Shakespeare book not being on the syllabus though the next term Mrs Popp took this class away from me. I lodged a grievance and had a hearing before the superintendent. I said that was my class, I had started them reading Shakespeare and I wanted to continue in the next term. The superintendent ruled against me on the grounds that my attendance record was spotty and erratic.

My Shakespeare students were probably lucky in having the head of the department as their teacher. She was surely more organized than I and more likely to discover deeper meanings.

48

Paddy Clancy lived around the corner from me in Brooklyn Heights. He called to see if I'd like to go to the opening of a new bar in the Village, the Lion's Head.

Of course I'd like to go and I stayed till the bar closed at four a.m. and missed work the next day. The bartender, Al Koblin, thought for a while I was one of the singing Clancy Brothers and charged me nothing for the drinks till he discovered I was only Frank McCourt, a teacher. Now even though I had to pay for my drinks I didn't mind because the Lion's Head became my home away from home, a place where I could feel comfortable the way I never did in uptown bars.

Reporters from the first office of the *Village Voice* drifted in from next door and they attracted journalists from everywhere. The wall opposite the bar was soon adorned with the framed book jackets of writers who were regular customers.

That was the wall I coveted, the wall that haunted me and had me dreaming that some day I'd look up at a framed book jacket of my own. Up and down the bar writers, poets, journalists, playwrights talked about their work, their lives, their assignments, their travels. Men and women would have a drink while waiting for cars to planes that would take them to Vietnam, Belfast, Nicaragua. New books came out, Pete Hamill, Joe Flaherty, Joel Oppenheimer, Dennis Smith, and went up on the wall, while I hung on the periphery of the accomplished, the ones who knew the magic of print. At the Lion's Head you had to prove yourself in ink or be quiet. There was no place here for teachers and I went on looking at the wall, envious.

Mam moved into a small apartment across the street from Malachy on the Upper West Side of Manhattan. Now she could see Malachy, his new wife, Diana, their sons, Conor and Cormac, my brother, Alphie, his wife, Lynn, and their daughter, Allison.

She could have visited all of us as often as she liked and when I asked her why she didn't she barked at me, I don't want to be beholden to anyone. It irritated me always when I called and asked her what she was doing and she said, Nothing. If I suggested that she get out of the house and visit a community center or a senior citizens' center she'd say, Arrah, for the love o' Jesus, will you leave me alone. Whenever Alberta invited her to dinner she always made a point of being late, complaining of the long journey from her Manhattan apartment to our house in Brooklyn. I wanted to tell her she didn't have to come at all if it was such a bother to her and the last thing she needed anyway was a dinner she was getting that fat, but I curbed my tongue so that there wouldn't be tension at the table. Unlike the first time she came to dinner and pushed the noodles aside she now devoured everything before her though if you offered her a second helping she'd look prim and say no thanks as if she had the appetite of a butterfly and then pick at the crumbs on the table. If I told her she didn't have to pick at crumbs, there was more food in the kitchen, she'd tell me leave her alone, that I was getting to be a right bloody torment. If I told her she'd be better off if she'd stayed in Ireland she'd bristle, What do you mean I'd be better off?

Well, you wouldn't be lying in bed half the day with the radio stuck to your ear listening to every half-witted show they have.

I listen to Malachy on the radio and what's wrong with that?

You listen to everything. You do nothing.

Her face would grow pale, her nose pointed, she'd pick at crumbs no longer there and there might be a hint of watery eyes. Then I'd be pricked with guilt and invite her to stay for the night so that she wouldn't have to take that long subway ride to Manhattan.

No, thank you, I'd rather be in my own bed, if you don't mind.

Oh, I suppose you're afraid of the sheets, all those diseases from foreigners in the Laundromat?

And she'd say, I think now 'tis the drink talking. Where's my coat?

Alberta would try to soften the moment with another invitation to stay, that we had new sheets and Mam needn't be nervous.

'Tisn't the sheets at all. I just want to go home, and when she saw me put on my coat she'd say, I don't need anyone to walk me to the subway. I can find my own way.

You're not going to walk these streets by yourself.

I walk the streets by myself all the time.

It was a long silent walk up Court Street to the subway at Borough Hall. I wanted to say something to her. I wanted to get past my irritation and my anger and ask her that simple question, How are you, Mam?

I couldn't.

When we reached the station she said I didn't have to pay a fare to get through the turnstiles. She'd be all right on the platform. There were people there and she'd be safe. She was used to it.

I went in with her thinking we might say something to each other but when the train arrived I let her go without even an attempt at a kiss and watched her stumble towards a seat as the train pulled from the station.

Down near Court Street and Atlantic Avenue I remembered something she had told me months ago while we sat waiting for Thanksgiving dinner. Isn't it remarkable, she said, the way things turn out in people's lives?

What do you mean?

Well, I was sitting in my apartment and I was feeling lonesome so I went up and sat on one of those benches they have in the grassy island in the middle of Broadway and this woman came along, a shopping bag woman, one of the homeless ones, all tattered and greasy, rootin' around in the garbage can till she found a newspaper and sat beside me reading it till she asked me if she could borrow my glasses because she could only read the headlines with the sight she had and when she talked I noticed she had an Irish accent so I asked her where she came from and she told me Donegal a long time ago and wasn't it lovely to be sitting on a bench in the middle of Broadway with people noticing things and asking where you came from. She asked if I could spare a few pennies for soup and I said instead she could come with me to the Associated supermarket and we'd get some groceries and have a proper meal. Oh, she couldn't do that, she said, but I told her that's what I was going to do anyway. She wouldn't come inside the store. She said they wouldn't want the likes of her. I got bread and butter and rashers and eggs and when we got home I told her she could go in and have a nice shower and she was delighted with herself though there wasn't much I could do about her clothes or the bags she carried. We had our dinner and watched television till she started falling asleep on me and I told her lie down there on the bed but she wouldn't. God knows the bed is big enough for four but she laid down on the floor with a shopping bag under her head and when I woke up in the morning she was gone and I missed her.

I know it wasn't the dinner wine that had me against the wall in a fit of remorse. It was the thought of my mother being so lonesome she had to sit on a street bench, so lonesome she missed the company of a homeless shopping bag woman. Even in the bad days in Limerick she always had an open hand and an open door and why couldn't I be like that to her?

49

Teaching nine hours a week at New York Community College in Brooklyn was easier than twenty-five hours a week at McKee Vocational and Technical High School. Classes were smaller, students older, and there were none of the problems a high school teacher has to deal with, the lavatory pass, the moaning over assignments, the mass of paperwork created by bureaucrats who have nothing to do but create new forms. I could supplement my reduced salary by teaching at Washington Irving Evening High School or substituting at Seward Park High School and Stuyvesant High School.

The chairman of the English Department at the Community College asked me if I'd like to teach a class of paraprofessionals. I said yes though I had no notion of what a paraprofessional was.

That first class I found out. Here were thirty-six women, African-American with a sprinkling of Hispanics, ranging in age from early twenties to late fifties, teacher aides in elementary schools and in college now with government help. They'd get two-year associate degrees and, perhaps, continue their education so that some day they might become fully qualified teachers.

That night there was little time for teaching. After I had asked the women to write a short autobiographical essay for the next class they gathered up their books and filed out, apprehensive, still unsure of themselves, of each other, of me. I had the whitest skin in the room.

When we met again the mood was the same except for one woman who sat with her head on the desk, sobbing. I asked what was the matter. She raised her head, tears on her cheeks.

I lost my books.

Oh, well, I said, you'll get another set of books. Just go to the English Department and tell them what happened.

You mean I won't get throwed out of college?

No, you won't be throwed, thrown out of college.

I felt like patting her head but I didn't know how to pat the head of a middle-aged woman who has lost her books. She smiled, we all smiled. Now we could begin. I asked for their compositions and told them I'd read some aloud though I wouldn't use their real names.

The essays were stiff, self-conscious. As I read I wrote some of the more common misspelled words on the chalkboard, suggested changes in structure, pointed out grammatical errors. It was all dry and tedious till I suggested the ladies write simply and clearly. For their next assignment they could write on anything they liked. They look surprised. Anything? But we don't have anything to write about. We don't have no adventures.

They had nothing to write about, nothing but the tensions of their lives, summer riots erupting around them, assassinations, husbands who so often disappeared, children destroyed by drugs, their own daily grind of housework, jobs, school, raising children.

They loved the strange ways of words. During a discussion on juvenile delinquency Mrs Williams sang out, No kid o' mine gonna be no yoot.

Yoot?

Yeah, you know. Yoot. She held up a newspaper where the headline howled, Youth Slays Mom.

Oh, I said, and Mrs Williams went on, These yoots, y'know, runnin' around slayin' people. Killin' 'em, too. Any kid o' mine come home actin' like a yoot an' out he go on his you-know-what.

The youngest woman in the class, Nicole, turned the tables on me. She sat in the back in a corner and never spoke till I asked the class if they'd like to write about their mothers. Then she raised her hand. How about your mother, Mr McCourt?

Questions came like bullets. Is she alive? How many children did she have? Where's your father? Did she have all those children with one man? Where is she living? Who's she living with? She's living alone? Your mother's living alone and she has four sons? How come?

They frowned. They disapproved. Poor lady with four sons shouldn't be living alone. People should take care of their mothers but what do men know? You can never tell a man what it's like to be a mother and if it wasn't for the mothers America would fall apart.

In April Martin Luther King was killed and classes were suspended for a week. When we met again I wanted to beg forgiveness for my race. Instead I asked for the essays I had already assigned. Mrs Williams was indignant. Look, Mr McCourt, when they tryin' to burn your house down you ain't sittin' around writin' no cawm-po-zishuns.

In June Bobby Kennedy was killed. My thirty-six ladies wondered what was happening to the world but they agreed you have to carry on, that education was the only road to sanity. When they talked about their children their faces brightened and I became irrelevant to their talk. I sat on my desk while they told each other that now they were in college themselves they stood over their kids to make sure the homework was done.

On the last night of classes in June there was a final examination. I watched those dark heads bent over papers, the mothers of two hundred and twelve children, and I knew that, no matter what they wrote or didn't write on those papers, no one would fail.

They finished. The last paper had been handed in but no one was leaving. I asked if they had another class here. Mrs Williams stood and coughed. Ah, Mr McCourt, I must say, I mean we must say, it was a wonderful thing to come to college and learn so much about English and everything and we got you this little something hopin' you'll like it an' all.

She sat down, sobbing, and I thought, This class begins and ends in tears.

The gift was passed up, a bottle of shaving lotion in a fancy red and black box. When I sniffed it I was nearly knocked over but I sniffed again with gusto and told the ladies I'd keep the bottle forever in memory of them, this class, their yoots.

Instead of going home after that class I took the subway to West Ninety-Sixth Street in Manhattan and called my mother from a street telephone.

Would you like to have a snack?

333

I don't know. Where are you?

I'm a few blocks away.

Why?

I just happened to be in the neighborhood.

Visiting Malachy?

No. Visiting you.

Me? Why should you be visiting me?

For Christ's sake, you're my mother and all I wanted to do was invite you out for a snack. What would you like to eat?

She sounded doubtful. Well, I love them jumbo shrimps they have in the Chinese restaurants.

All right. We'll have jumbo shrimps.

But I don't know if I'm able for them this minute. I think I'd prefer to go to the Greeks for a salad.

All right. I'll see you there.

She came into the restaurant gasping for breath and when I kissed her cheek I could taste the salt of her sweat. She said she'd have to sit a minute before she could even think of food, that if she hadn't given up the cigarettes she'd be dead now.

She ordered the feta salad and when I asked her if she liked it she said she loved it, she could live on it.

Do you like that cheese?

What cheese?

The goat cheese.

What goat cheese?

The white stuff. The feta. That's goat cheese.

'Tis not.

'Tis.

Well, if I knew that was goat cheese I'd never touch it because I was attacked by a goat once out the country in Limerick and I'd never eat a thing that attacked me.

It's a good thing you were never attacked by a jumbo shrimp.

50

In 1971 my daughter Maggie was born at Unity Hospital in the
Bedford-Stuyvesant area of Brooklyn. There would be no problem
taking home the right infant since she seemed to be the only white
one in the nursery.

Alberta wanted a natural Lamaze childbirth but the doctors and
nurses at Unity Hospital had no patience with middle-class women and
their peculiarities. They had no time for this woman and her breathing
exercises and jabbed her with an anaesthetic to hasten the birth. Instead,
that slowed the rhythm so much the impatient doctor clamped forceps
on Maggie's head and yanked her from her mother's womb and I
wanted to punch him for the flatness he left on her temples.

The nurse took the child to a corner to clean and wash her and
when she finished beckoned that I might now see my daughter with
her red astonished face and her black feet.

The soles of her feet were black.

God, what kind of a birthmark have you inflicted on my child?
I couldn't say anything to the nurse because she was black and might
be offended that I didn't find my daughter's black feet attractive. I
had a vision of my child as a young woman lolling on a beach, lovely
in a bathing suit, but forced to wear socks to conceal her disfigurement.

The nurse asked if the baby was to be breast-fed. No. Alberta had
said she wouldn't have the time when she went back to work and

the doctor did something to dry up her milk. They wanted to know the child's name and even though Alberta had toyed with Michaela she was still under anaesthetic and powerless and I told the nurse, Margaret Ann, for my two grandmothers and my sister who had died at twenty-one days in this very borough of Brooklyn.

Alberta was wheeled back to her room and I called Malachy to tell him the good news, that a child had been born but that she was afflicted with black feet. He laughed in my ear and told me I was an ass, that the nurse probably took footprints instead of fingerprints. He said he'd meet me at the Lion's Head where everyone bought me a drink and I got stocious drunk, so drunk Malachy had to hoist me home in a taxi which made me so sick I threw up the length of Broadway with the driver yelling that would cost me twenty-five dollars for the cleaning of the cab, an unreasonable demand that deprived him of a tip and had him threatening to call the cops and, What are you going to tell them? said Malachy, are you going to tell them that you're a zigzag driver going from one side of Broadway to the other and making everyone sick, is that what you're going to tell them? and the driver was so angry he wanted to step out and confront Malachy but changed his mind when my brother, holding me up, stood large and red-bearded on the sidewalk and asked the driver politely if he had any more comments before he went to meet his Maker. The driver uttered obscenities about us and the Irish in general and drove through a red light, his left arm at the window, middle finger rigid in the air.

Malachy brought me aspirins and vitamins and told me I'd be as right as rain in the morning and I wondered what that meant, right as rain, though that question was pushed from my head by the image of Maggie and the forcep flatness of her temples and I was ready to jump from the bed to hunt down that damn doctor who wouldn't let my daughter be born in her own good time but my legs wouldn't oblige me and I fell asleep.

Malachy was right. There was no hangover, only delight that a little child in Brooklyn had my name and I'd have a lifetime watching her grow and when I called Alberta I could hardly talk with the tears in my throat and she laughed and quoted my mother, Your bladder is near your eye.

★   ★   ★

That same year Alberta and I bought the brownstone house where we'd been tenants on the parlor floor. We were able to buy it only because our friends, Bobby and Mary Ann Baron, lent us money and because Virgil Frank had died and left us eight thousand dollars.

When we lived at 30 Clinton Street on Brooklyn Heights Virgil was two floors below us. He was over seventy, had a full head of combed-back white hair, a strong nose, his own teeth and hardly a scrap of flesh on his bones. I visited him regularly because an hour with him was better than movies, television and most books.

His apartment was one narrow room with a kitchenette and a bathroom. His bed was a cot against the wall and beyond that a desk and a window with an air conditioner. Opposite the bed was a bookcase filled with volumes on flowers, trees and birds which, he said, he'd get around to some day as soon as he bought a pair of binoculars. You have to be careful about buying binoculars because you go into a store and how are you gonna test them? Salesmen in the store say, Oh, they're okay, they're strong, and how can you tell? They won't let you take them outside to look up and down Fulton Street in case you make a run for it with the binoculars and that's dumb. How the hell you gonna make a run for it when you're seventy? In the meantime he'd like to be able to see birds out his window but all you can see from his apartment is pigeons fornicating on top of his air conditioner and that pisses him off.

He watches them, oh, yeah, he watches them, bangs on the window with a fly swatter, tells them, Get outa here, goddam pigeons. Go fornicate on someone else's air conditioner. He tells me they're just rats with wings, all they do is eat and fornicate and when they're finished with fornicating they drop a load on the air conditioner, one load after another, like that crap the boids, I mean the birds, damn, I'm talkin' Brooklyn again and that ain't good when you're selling water coolers, like that bird crap in South America where the mountains are covered with it, what is it? guano, yeah, which is good for growing things but not for air conditioners.

Besides the books on outdoor life he had a three-volume set of the *Summa Theologica of St Thomas Aquinas* and when I opened a volume he said, I didn't know you liked that stuff. Wouldn't you prefer the birds? I told him you can always get bird books but his *Summa* was rare and he said I could have it except I'd have to wait till he died. But don't worry, Frank, I'll put it in my will.

337

He also promised to leave me his collection of ties which dazzled me whenever he opened his closet door, the loudest, most colorful ties I had ever seen.

You like 'em, eh? Some of these ties go all the way back to the twenties and on down to the thirties and forties. Men knew how to dress then. They didn't go around tippy-toe like the Man in the Gray Flannel Suit afraid of a little color. I always said never stint on the tie and the hat because you have to look good when you're selling water coolers which I did for forty-five years. I'd go into an office and I'd say, What? What? You telling me you still drinking tap water from these old cups and glasses. Don't you know the danger to your health?

And Virgil would stand between bed and bookcase rocking like a preacher and delivering his sales spiel on water coolers.

Yes, sir, I sell water coolers and I wanna tell you there's five things you can do with water. You can clean it, you can pollute it, you can heat it, you can cool it and, ha ha, you can sell it. You know and I don't have to tell you, Mr Office Manager, you can drink it and you can swim in it though there isn't much call for swimming water in the average American office. I wanna tell you my company has made a study of offices that drink our water and offices that don't drink our water and, you're right, you're right, Mr Office Manager, the people who drink our water are healthier and more productive. Our water drives away the flu and improves digestion. We're not saying, no we're not saying, Mr Office Manager, that our water is solely responsible for the great productivity and the prosperity of America but we are saying that our studies show offices without our water are barely hanging on, desperate and wondering why. A copy of our study is available when you sign our yearly contract. At no extra charge we'll survey your staff and give you an estimate of water consumption. I am happy to observe you don't have air conditioning because that means you'll need extra drinking water for your fine staff. And we know, Mr Office Manager, that our water coolers bring people together. Problems are settled over a paper cup of water. Eyes meet. Romances flourish. Everybody happy, everybody eager to come to work every day. Increased productivity. We get no complaints. Sign right here. A copy for you, a copy for me and we're in business.

A knock on the door interrupted him.

Who is it?

A faint old voice. Virgil, it's Harry.

Can't talk to you now, Harry. I got the doctor here and I'm naked getting examined.

All right, Virgil. I'll come back later.

Tomorrow, Harry, tomorrow.

Okay, Virgil.

He told me that was Harry Ball, eighty-five years old, so old you can't hear his voice over a clothesline, who drives Virgil crazy with his parking problems. He's got this big car, a Hudson that they don't make no more, is that right, no more or anymore? You're an English teacher. I dunno. Never went beyond the seventh grade. Ran away from the Sisters of St Joseph Orphanage even if I'm leaving them money in my will. Anyway, Harry's got this car and he goes nowhere with it. Says some day he's gonna drive it to Florida to see his sister but he's going nowhere because that car is so old it wouldn't make it across the Brooklyn Bridge and that goddam Hudson is his life. He moves it from one side of the street to the other, back and forth, back and forth. Sometimes he brings the little aluminum beach chair and sits near his car looking for a parking spot to open for next day. Or he walks around the neighborhood looking for a spot and if he finds one he gets excited and gives himself a heart attack rushing to his car to drive it to the new spot which is now gone and so is the one he was in and there he is driving around with no spot, cursing the government. I was with him once and he nearly ran down a rabbi and two old women and I said, Christ, Harry, lemme out, and he wouldn't, but I jumped out at the first red light and he yelled after me I was the type that flashed lights so the Japs could find Pearl Harbor till I told him he was a dumb bastard that didn't know Pearl Harbor was bombed in broad daylight and he sat there contradicting me with the light turning green and people honking and yelling who gives a shit about Pearl Harbor, buddy, move your goddam Hudson. He could park that car in a garage for eighty-five bucks a month but that's more than he pays for rent and that'll be the day Harry Ball ever wastes a penny. I'm frugal myself, I admit that, but he could make Scrooge look like a spendthrift. Is that the right word, spendthrift? I ran away from the orphanage in seventh grade.

He asked me to go with him to a hardware store on Court Street so that he could get an egg timer for the telephone just installed.

An egg timer?

Yeah, this is a kind of hourglass with sand that runs for three minutes and that's the way I like my egg and when I use the telephone I'll know when the three minutes is up because that's how they charge you at the phone company, the bastards. I'll have the egg timer on my desk and I'll hang up at the last grain of sand.

On Court Street I asked him if he'd like a beer and a sandwich at the Blarney Rose. He never went to bars and was shocked at the prices of beer and whiskey. Ninety cents for a little shot of whiskey. Never.

I went with him to a liquor store where he ordered cases of Irish whiskey and told the salesman his friend Frank liked it, and cases of wine, vodka and bourbon because he liked it himself. He told the man he wouldn't pay the lousy taxes on his purchase. I'm giving you a big order here and you want me to support the goddam government on top of it. No, sir. Pay it yourself.

The man agreed and said he'd deliver the twenty-five cases.

Virgil called me next day. Even though his voice was weak he told me, I got the eggtimer goin' here, so I have to talk fast. Can you come down? I need a little help. The door is open.

He was sitting in his armchair in his bathrobe. I didn't get a wink of sleep last night. Couldn't get into the bed.

He couldn't get into the bed because the liquor store man had piled up the twenty-five cases around his bed so high that Virgil couldn't climb over. He said he had to try some of the Irish whiskey and the wine and that didn't help much when it was time to climb. He said he needed soup, something in his stomach to keep him from being sick. When I opened a can of soup and poured it into a pot with an equal amount of water he asked if I'd read the instructions on the can.

No.

Well, how do you know what to do?

It's common sense, Virgil.

Common sense, my ass.

He was hangover cranky. Listen to me, Frank McCourt. You know why you'll never be a success?

Why?

You never follow the instructions on the package. That's why I have money in the bank and you don't have a pot to piss in. I always followed the instructions on the package.

340

Another knock on the door. What? What? said Virgil.

Voigel, it's me. Pete.

Pete who? Pete who? I can't see through the door.

Pete Buglioso. I got something for you, Voigel.

Don't talk Brooklyn to me, Pete. My name is Virgil, not Voigel. He was a poet, Pete. You should know, you're Italian.

I don't know nothin' about that, Voigel. I got somethin' for you, Voigel.

I don't want nothin', Pete. Call back next year.

But, Voigel, you'll like what I have. Cost you a coupla bucks. What is it?

Can't tell you through the door, Voigel.

Virgil heaved himself from the armchair and stumbled to the egg timer on his desk. All right, Pete, all right. You can come in for three minutes. I'm setting my egg timer.

He tells me open the door and tells Pete the egg timer is working and even though grains of sand have already dropped Pete still has three minutes, so start talking, Pete, start talking and make it snappy.

All right, Voigel, all right, but how the hell can I talk when you're talking. You talk more than anyone.

You're wasting your time, Pete. You're hanging yourself. Look at the egg timer. Look at that sand. Sands of time, Pete, sands of time.

Whadda you doin' with all them boxes, Voigel. Rob a truck or somethin'?

The egg timer, Pete, the egg timer.

All right, Voigel, what I got here is, will you stop lookin' at the goddam egg timer, Voigel, an' lissena me. What I got here is prescription pads from a doctor's office on Clinton Street.

Prescription pads. You been robbing them doctors again, Pete.

I didn't rob 'em. I know a receptionist. She likes me.

She must be deaf dumb and blind. I don't need no prescription pads.

Come on, Voigel. You never know. You might have a disease or a bad hangover and you'll need something.

Bullshit, Pete. Your time is up. I'm busy.

But, Voigel.

Out, Pete, out. I have no control over that egg timer once it gets goin' and I don't want no prescription pads.

He pushed Pete out the door and yelled after him, You could get me in jail and you're gonna wind up in jail yourself selling stolen prescription pads.

He slumped back into his armchair and said he'd try the soup even though I hadn't followed the instructions on the can. He needed it to settle his stomach but if he didn't like it he'd have a little wine and that would do the job. He tasted the soup and said, yeah, it was okay and he'd have it and the wine, too. When I popped the wine cork he barked that I was not to pour the wine now, I was to let it breathe, didn't I know that and if I didn't how could I teach school. He sipped his wine and remembered he had to call the air conditioning company about his problems with pigeons. I told him stay in his chair and handed him the telephone and the number of the company but he wanted the egg timer, too, so that he could tell them they had three minutes to give him the information he needed.

Hello, you listenin' to me? I got the egg timer goin' and you got three minutes to tell me how I can stop these goddam pigeons, excuse the language, miss, how I can stop these pigeons from making love on the outside part of my air conditioner. They're driving me crazy with the coo coo coo all day and they shit all over the window. You can't tell me that now? You have to look it up? Whaddaya have to look up? Pigeons fornicating on my air conditioner and you have to look it up. Sorry, egg timer ran out and that's the three minutes. Good-bye.

He handed me back the telephone. And I'll tell you something else, he said. It's that goddam Harry Ball that's responsible for all them pigeons shitting on my air conditioner. He sits in his goddam aluminum beach chair when he's looking for a parking spot and feeds them pigeons over at Borough Hall. I told him once cut it out, that they were just rats with wings, and he got so mad he wouldn't talk to me for weeks and that suited me fine. These old guys feed pigeons because they don't have wives no more, anymore? I dunno. I ran away from the orphanage but I don't feed pigeons.

He knocked on our door one night and when I opened it he was in his ragged bathrobe, holding a sheaf of papers, and drunk. It was his will and he wanted to read me part of it. No, he wouldn't have coffee. It killed him, but he'd have a beer.

So, you helped me out and Alberta had me up for dinner and no one ever has old guys up for dinner so I'm leaving you four thousand dollars and Alberta four thousand and I'm leaving you my Thomas

Aquinas and my ties. Here's what it says in the will, To Frank McCourt I leave my collection of ties which he has admired and which are anything but somber.

When we moved to Warren Street we lost touch with Virgil for a while though I wanted him to be godfather at Maggie's christening. Instead there was a call from a lawyer telling me of Virgil Frank's death and the terms of his will as it pertained to us. However, said the lawyer, he changed his mind about the *Summa Theologica* and the ties, so all you get is the money. Do you accept this?

Sure, yes, but why did he change it?

He heard you went to Ireland for a visit and that upset him because you contributed to the gold flow.

What do you mean?

According to Mr Frank's will President Johnson said a few years ago that Americans traveling abroad were draining the country of gold and weakening the economy and that's why you're not getting the ties that are anything but somber and the three volumes of Aquinas. Okay?

Oh, sure.

Now that we had a portion of a down payment we searched the neighborhood for a house. Our landlady, Hortensia Odones, heard we'd been looking and one day she climbed the outside fire escape at the back of the house and startled me when I saw her head at the kitchen window with the great curly wig.

Frankie, Frankie, open the window. It's cold out here. Lemme in.

I reached out to help her in but she yelled, Watch my hair, watch my hair, and I had to do the heavy work of hauling her in the kitchen window while she hung on to her wig.

Whoo, she said, whoo. Frankie, you got any rum?

No, Hortensia, only wine or Irish whiskey.

Gimme a whiskey, Frankie. My ass is frozen.

Here, Hortensia. Tell me, why don't you come up the stairs?

Because it's dark down there, that's why, and I can't afford to keep lights goin' night an' day an' I can see the fire escape day an' night.

Oh.

And what's this I hear? You an' Alberta lookin' for a house? Why don't you buy this one?

How much?

Fifty thousand.

Fifty thousand?

That's right. Is that too much?

Oh, no. That's fine.

The day we signed the agreement we drank rum with her while she told us how sad she was to leave this house after all the years she was there, not with her husband, Odones, but her boyfriend, Louis Weber, who was famous for running the numbers game in the neighborhood and even though he was Puerto Rican he was afraid of nobody, not even the Cosa Nostra who tried to take over till Louis walked into the Don's house down in Carroll Gardens and said, What is this shit? excuse the language, and the Don admired Louis for his balls and told his goombahs back off, don't bother Louis, and you know, Frankie, no one messes with the Italians in Carroll Gardens. You don't see no coloreds or PRs down there, no sir, and if you do they're passing through.

The Mafia might have backed away from Louis but Hortensia said you couldn't trust them and anytime she and Louis went for a drive they rode with two guns between them, his and hers, and he told her if anyone came with trouble and put him out of commission she was to take the steering wheel and yank it towards the sidewalk so that they'd hit a pedestrian instead of traffic and the insurance company would take care of things and if they didn't and gave Hortensia any trouble he'd leave her with a set of phone numbers of a few guys, PRs, the goddam Mafia wasn't the only game in town, and these guys would take care of the insurance companies, the greedy bastards, excuse the language, Alberta, is there any rum left, Frankie?

Poor Louis, she said, the Kefauver Commission was bothering him but he died in his bed and I never go for a ride no more but he left me a gun downstairs, you wanna see my gun, Frankie, no? well, I have it and anyone comes into my apartment without an invitation gets it, Frankie, right between the eyes, bang, boom, he's gone.

Neighbors smiled and nodded and told us we had bought a gold mine, that everyone knew Louis had buried money in the basement of our new house where Hortensia still lived, or over our heads in the false ceiling of the living room. All we had to do was pull down that ceiling and we'd be up to our armpits in hundred-dollar bills.

When Hortensia moved out we dug up the basement to install a new waste line. No buried money. We pulled down false ceilings, exposed bricks and beams. We tapped on walls and someone suggested we consult a psychic.

We found an old doll with tufts of hair, no eyes, no arms, one leg. We kept it for our two-year-old, Maggie, who called it The Beast and loved it over all her other dolls.

Hortensia moved to a small street-level apartment on Court Street and stayed there till she died or moved back to Puerto Rico. I often wished I had spent more time with her and a bottle of rum or that I had introduced her to Virgil Frank so that we could have rum and Irish whiskey and talk about Louis Weber and the gold flow and ways of reducing your telephone bills with an egg timer.

51

It's 1969 and I'm substitute teaching for Joe Curran who is out for a few weeks with the drink. His students ask if I know Greek and seem disappointed that I don't. After all, Mr Curran would sit at his desk and read or recite from memory long passages from *The Odyssey*, yeah, in Greek, and he'd remind his students daily he was a graduate of Boston Latin School and Boston College and tell them anyone who didn't know his Greek or Latin couldn't consider himself educated, could never lay claim to being a gentleman. Yes, yes, this might be Stuyvesant High School, says Mr Curran, and you might be the brightest kids from here to the foothills of the Rockies, your heads stuffed with science and mathematics, but all you need in this life is your Homer, your Sophocles, your Plato, your Aristotle, your Aristophanes for the lighter moments, your Virgil for the dark places, your Horace to escape the mundane, and your Juvenal when you're completely pissed off with the world. The grandeur, boys, the grandeur that was Greece and the glory that was Rome.

It wasn't the Greeks or the Romans his students loved, it was the forty minutes when Joe droned or declaimed and they could daydream, catch up on homework for other classes, doodle, nibble at sandwiches from home, carve their initials on desks that might have been occupied by James Cagney, Thelonious Monk or certain Nobel Laureates. Or they could dream of the nine girls who had just been admitted for the first time in the school's history. The nine Vestal Virgins, Joe Curran called them, and there were complaints from parents that the suggestiveness of his language was inappropriate.

Oh, inappropriate my ass, said Joe. Why can't they speak simple English? Why can't they use a simple word like wrong?

His students said, Yeah, wasn't it something to see the girls in the hallway, nine girls, nearly three thousand boys and what about the boys in the school, fifty percent for Chrissakes, who didn't want the girls, what about that? They had to be dead from the waist down, didn't they?

Then you'd wonder about Mr Curran himself up there shifting into English to talk about *The Iliad* and the friendship of Achilles and Patroclus, he couldn't stop talking about those two old Greeks, and how Achilles was so furious with Hector for killing Patroclus he killed Hector and dragged his body behind his chariot to show the power of his love for his dead friend, the love that dare not speak its name.

But, boys oh boys, is there a sweeter moment in all of literature than that moment when Hector removed his helmet to calm the fears of his child? Oh, if only all our fathers removed their helmets. And when Joe blubbered into his grey handkerchief and used words like piss you knew he'd left the school at lunch hour for a little tot around the corner at the Gashouse Bar. There were days he returned so excited from thoughts that had come to him on the barstool he wanted to thank God for leading him to teaching so that he could forget the Greeks for a while to sing the praises of the great Alexander Pope and his "Ode on Solitude".

> *Happy the man whose wish and care*
> *A few paternal acres bound*
> *Content to breathe his native air,*
> *In his own ground.*

And remember, boys and girls, is there a girl here? raise your hand if you're a girl, no girls? remember, boys, that Pope was indebted to Horace, and Horace was indebted to Homer and Homer was indebted to God knows who. Will you promise on your mothers' heads to remember that? If you remember Pope's debt to Horace you'll know no one springs full-blown from his father's head. Will you remember?

We will, Mr Curran.

What am I to tell Joe's students who complain that they have to read *The Odyssey* and all this old stuff? Who cares what happened in ancient Greece or Troy with men dying right and left over that stupid Helen? Who cares? Boys in the class say you wouldn't catch them fighting to the death over some girl that didn't want them. Yeah, they could understand *Romeo and Juliet* because a lotta families are dumb about you going out with someone from another religion and they could understand *West Side Story* and the gangs but they could never believe grown men would leave home the way Odysseus left Penelope and Telemachus and go off to fight over this stupid chick who didn't know enough to come inside. They have to admit Odysseus was cool the way he tried to dodge the draft, acting crazy an' all and they like the way Achilles fooled him because Achilles is nowhere near as smart as Odysseus but like they can't believe he'd stay away twenty years fighting and fooling around and expect Penelope to like sit there spinning and weaving and telling the suitors get lost. Girls in the class say they can believe it, they really can, that women can be true forever because that's the way women are, and one girl tells the class what she read in a Byron poem, that man's love is of his life a thing apart, 'tis woman's whole existence. Boys hoot at this but girls applaud and tell them what all the psychology books say, that boys their age are three years behind in mental development though there are some in this class who must be at least six years behind and they should there-fore shut up. The boys try to be sarcastic, raising their eyebrows and telling each other, Oh, law de daw, smell me, I'm developed, but the girls look at each other, shrug, toss their hair and ask me in a lofty tone if we could please get back to the lesson.

Lesson? What are they talking about? What lesson? All I can remember is the usual high school whine about why we have to read this and why we have to read that and my irritation, my unspoken response, is that you have to read it, goddamit, because it's part of the curriculum and because I'm telling you read it, I'm the teacher, and if you don't cut the whining and complaining you'll get an English grade on your report card that will make zero look like a gift from the gods because I'm standing here listening to you and looking at you, the privileged, the chosen, the pampered, with nothing to do but go to school, hang out, do a little studying, go to college, get into a moneymaking racket, grow into your fat forties, still whining, still complaining, when there are millions around the world who'd offer fingers and toes to be in your seats, nicely clothed, well-fed, with the world by the balls.

That's what I'd like to say and never will because I might be accused of using inappropriate language and that would give me a Joe Curran fit. No. I can't talk like that because I have to find my way in this place, a far cry from McKee Vocational and Technical High School.

In the spring of 1972 the English Department chairman, Roger Goodman, offers me a permanent position at Stuyvesant High School. I'll have my own five classes and a building assignment where, once more, I'll keep order in the students' cafeteria and make sure no one drops ice cream wrappers or bits of hot dog on the floor though boys and girls are allowed to sit together here and romance kills appetites.

I'll have a small homeroom, the first nine girls, seniors and ready to graduate. The girls are kind. They bring me coffee, bagels, newspapers. They're critical. They say I should do something about my hair, let the sideburns grow, this is 1972 and I should get with it, be cool, and do something about my clothes. They say I dress like an old man, and even though I have a few grey hairs I don't have to look so old. They tell me I look uptight and one of them kneads my neck and shoulders. Relax, she says, relax, we're harmless, and they laugh the way women laugh when they share a secret and you think it's about you.

I'll have five classes a day five days a week where I have to memorize the names of one hundred and seventy-five students along with the names of a full homeroom class next year, another thirty-five, and I'll have to be particularly careful with the Chinese and Korean students with their sarcastic, That's okay if you don't know our names, Mr McCourt, we all look the same. Or they might laugh, Yeah, and all you white people look the same.

I know all this from my days as a substitute teacher but now I watch my students, my very own, stream into my room this first day of February 1972, Feast of St Brigid, and I'm praying to you, Brigid, because these are kids I'll be seeing five days a week for five months and I don't know if I'm up to it. The times they are a-changin' and you can see these Stuyvesant kids are worlds and years away from the ones I first met at McKee. We've had wars and assassinations since then, the two Kennedys, Martin Luther King, Medgar Evers. Boys at McKee wore short hair or pompadours greased back to a duck's ass. Girls had blouses and skirts and their hair was permed to the stiffness of a helmet. Stuyvesant boys wear hair so long people on the streets sneer, You can hardly tell them from the girls, ha ha. They wear tie-dye shirts, jeans and sandals so that no one will ever guess they come from comfortable families all over New York. Stuyvesant girls let hair and breasts hang loose and drive the boys mad with desire and cut their jeans at the knees for that cool poverty effect because like you know they've had it with all that middle-class crap.

Oh, yeah, they're cooler than the McKee kids because they've got it made. In eight months they'll be at colleges and universities all over the country, Yale, Stanford, MIT, Williams, Harvard, lords and ladies of the earth, and here in my classroom they sit where they like, chatting, ignoring me, giving me their backs, one more teacher obstructing their way to graduation and the real world. Some stare as if to say, Who is this guy? They slump and slouch and gaze out the window or over my head. Now I have to get their attention and that's what I say, Excuse me, may I have your attention? A few stop talking and look at me. Others look offended at the interruption and turn away again.

My three senior classes groan with the burden of the textbook they have to carry every day, an anthology of English literature. The juniors complain over the weight of their anthology of American literature. The books are sumptuous, richly illustrated, designed to challenge, motivate, illuminate, entertain, and they're expensive. I tell my students that carrying textbooks strengthens their upper bodies and hope the contents seep up to their minds.

They glare at me. Who is this guy?

There are teaching guides so detailed and comprehensive I need never think for myself. They are packed with enough quizzes, tests, examinations to keep my students in a constant state of nervous tension. There are hundreds of multiple choice questions, true or false questions, fill in the blank spaces, match column A with column B, peremptory questions ordering the student to explain why Hamlet was mean to his mother, what Keats meant by negative capability, what Melville was getting at in his chapter on the whiteness of the whale.

I'm ready, boys and girls, to march through the chapters from

Hawthorne to Hemingway, from *Beowulf* to Virginia Woolf. Tonight you are to read the pages assigned. Tomorrow we'll discuss. There may be a quiz. Then again there may not be a quiz. Just don't gamble on it. Only the teacher knows for sure. On Tuesday there will be a test. Three Tuesdays from now there will be an exam, a big exam, and yes, it will count. Your whole report card grade hinges on this exam. You also have tests on physics and calculus? Sorry for your troubles. This is English, the queen of the curriculum.

And you don't know it, boys and girls, but I am armed with my teaching guides on American and English literature. I have them safe here in my bag, all the questions that will have you scratching your little heads, gnawing your pencils, dreading report card day, and, I suppose, hating me because I'm the one who can thwart your high Ivy League ambitions. I'm the one who skulked around the lobby of the Biltmore Hotel cleaning up for your fathers and mothers.

This is Stuyvesant and isn't this the best high school in the city, some say the best in the country? You asked for it. You could have gone to your neighborhood high schools where you'd be kings and queens, numero uno, top of your class. Here you're just one of the crowd, scrambling for grades to bolster the precious average that will slip you into the Ivy League. It's your great god, isn't it, the average? Down in the Stuyvesant basement they should construct a sanctum with an altar. They should mount on that altar a great red blinking neon 9, blink blink blink, the sacred initial digit you're desperate for on every grade, and you should pray and worship there. Oh, God, send me As and nineties.

Mr McCourt, how come you only gave me a ninety-three on my report card?

I was kind.

But I did all the work, handed in the papers you assigned.

You were late with two papers. Two points off for each one.

But, Mr McCourt, why two points?

That's it. That's your grade.

Aw, Mr McCourt, how come you're so mean?

It's all I have left.

I followed the teacher guides. I launched the prefabricated questions at my classes. I hit them with surprise quizzes and tests and destroyed them with the ponderous detailed examinations concocted by college professors who assemble high school textbooks.

My students resisted and cheated and disliked me and I disliked them for disliking me. I learned their cheating games. Oh, the casual glance at the papers of students around you. Oh, the discreet little morse code cough for your girlfriend and her sweet smile when she catches the multiple choice answer. If she's behind you splay your fingers on the back of your head, three splays of five fingers would be question fifteen, a forefinger scratching the right temple is answer A and other fingers represent other answers. The room is alive with coughs and body movements and when I catch the cheaters I hiss in their ears they'd better cut it out or their papers will be shredded into the waste basket, their lives ruined. I am lord of the classroom, a man who would never cheat, oh, no, not if they flashed the answers in green letters on the bright side of the full moon.

Every day I taught with my guts in a knot, lurking behind my desk at the front of the room playing the teacher game with the chalk, the eraser, the red pen, the teacher guides, the power of the quiz, the test, the exam, I'll call your father, I'll call your mother, I'll report you to the Governor, I'll damage your average so badly, kid, you'll be lucky to get into a community college in Mississippi, weapons of menace and control.

A senior, Jonathan, bangs his forehead on his desk and wails, Why? Why? Why do we have to suffer with this shit? We've been in school since kindergarten, thirteen years, and why do we have to know what color shoes Mrs Dalloway was wearing at her goddam party and what are we supposed to make of Shakespeare troubling deaf heaven with his bootless cries and what the hell is a bootless cry anyway and when did heaven turn deaf?

Around the room rumbles of rebellion and I'm paralyzed. They're saying Yeah, yeah to Jonathan who halts his head banging to ask, Mr McCourt, did you have this stuff in high school? and there's another chorus of yeah yeah and I don't know what to say. Should I tell them the truth, that I never set foot in a high school till I began teaching in one or should I feed them a lie about a rigorous secondary school education with the Christian Brothers in Limerick?

I'm saved, or doomed, by another student who calls out, Mr McCourt, my cousin went to McKee on Staten Island and she said you told them you never went to high school and they said you were an okay teacher anyway because you told stories and talked and never bothered them with all these tests.

Smiles around the room. Teacher unmasked. Teacher never even went to high school and look what he's doing to us, driving us crazy with tests and quizzes. I'm branded forever with the label, teacher who never went to high school.

So, Mr McCourt, I thought you had to get a license to teach in the city.

You do.

Don't you have to get a college degree?

You do.

Don't you have to graduate high school?

You mean graduate from high school, from high school, from from from.

Yeah, yeah. Okay. Don't you have to graduate from high school to get into college?

I suppose you do.

Tyro lawyer grills teacher, carries the day, and word spreads to my other classes. Wow, Mr McCourt, you never went to high school and you're teaching at Stuyvesant? Cool, man.

And into the trash basket I drop my teaching guides, my quizzes, tests, examinations, my teacher-knows-all mask.

I'm naked and starting over and I hardly know where to begin.

In the 1960s and early 70s students wore buttons and headbands demanding equal rights for women, blacks, Native Americans and all oppressed minorities, an end to the war in Vietnam, the salvation of the rain forests and the planet in general. Blacks and curly-haired whites sprouted Afros, and the dashiki and the tie-dye shirt became the garb of the day. College students boycotted class, taught in, rioted everywhere, dodged the draft, fled to Canada or Scandinavia. High school students came to school fresh from images of war on television news, men blown to bits in rice paddies, helicopters hovering, tentative soldiers of the Viet Cong blasted out of their tunnels, their hands behind their heads, lucky for the moment they weren't blasted back in again, images of anger back home, marches, demonstrations, hell no we won't go, sit-ins, teach-ins, students falling before the guns of the National Guard, blacks recoiling from Bull Connor's dogs, burn baby burn, black is beautiful, trust no one over thirty, I have a dream and, at the end of it all, your President is not a crook.

On streets and in subways I'd meet former students from McKee High School who would tell me of the boys who went to Vietnam, heroes when they left and now home in body bags. Bob Bogard called to tell me about the funeral of a boy who had been in both our classes but I didn't go because I knew that on Staten Island there would be pride in this blood sacrifice. The boys from Staten Island would fill more body bags than Stuyvesant could ever imagine. Mechanics and plumbers had to fight while college students shook indignant fists, fornicated in the fields of Woodstock and sat in.

In my classroom I wore no buttons, took no sides. There was enough ranting all around us and, for me, picking my way through five classes was minefield enough.

Mr McCourt, why can't our classes be relevant?

Relevant to what?

Well, you know, look at the state of the world. Look at what's happening.

There's always something happening in the world and we could sit in this classroom for four years clucking over headlines and going out of our minds.

Mr McCourt, don't you care about the babies burned with napalm in Vietnam?

I do, and I care about the babies in Korea and China, in Auschwitz and Armenia, and the babies impaled on the swords of Cromwell's soldiers in Ireland. I told them what I'd learned from my part-time teaching at New York Technical College in Brooklyn, from my class of twenty-three women, most from the Islands, and from my five men. There was a fifty-five-year-old working for a college degree so that he could return to Puerto Rico and spend the rest of his life helping children. There was a young Greek studying English so that he could work towards a PhD in the literature of Renaissance England. There were three young African-American men in the class and when one, Ray, complained he'd been bothered by the police on a subway platform because he was black the women from the Islands had no patience with him. They told him if he stayed home and studied he wouldn't be getting into trouble and no kid of theirs would come home with a story like that. They'd break his head. Ray was quiet. You don't talk back to women from the Islands.

Denise, now in her late twenties, was often late to class and I threatened her with failure till she wrote an autobiographical essay which I asked her to read to the class.

Oh, no, she couldn't do that. She'd be ashamed to let people know she had two children whose father had left her to return to Montserrat and never sends her a penny. No, she wouldn't mind if I read the essay to the class if I didn't tell who wrote it.

She had described a day in her life. She'd wake early to do her Jane Fonda video exercises while thanking Jesus for the gift of another day. She'd take a shower, get her children up, her eight-year-old, her six-year-old, and take them to school and after that she'd rush to her college classes. In the afternoon she'd go straight to her job at a bank in downtown Brooklyn and from there to her mother's house. Her mother had already picked up the children from school and without her Denise didn't know what she'd do especially when her mother had that terrible disease that makes your fingers curl up in knots and Denise didn't know how to spell. After taking the children home, putting them to bed and getting their clothes ready for the next morning Denise would pray by the side of her bed, look up at the cross, thank Jesus once more for another wonderful day and try to fall asleep with his suffering image in her dreams.

The women from the Islands thought that was a wonderful story and looked at each other wondering who wrote it and when Ray said he didn't believe in Jesus they told him shut up, what did he know hanging around subway platforms? They worked, took care of their families, went to school and this was a wonderful country where you could do what you liked even if you were black like the night and if he didn't like it he could go back to Africa if he could ever find it without getting hassled by the police.

I told the women they were heroes. I told the Puerto Rican man he was a hero and I told Ray if he ever grew up he could be a hero, too. They looked at me, puzzled. They didn't believe me and you could guess what was running through their minds, that they were doing only what they were supposed to do, getting an education, and why was this teacher calling them heroes?

My Stuyvesant students were not satisfied. Why was I telling them stories of women from the Islands and Puerto Ricans and Greeks when the world was going to hell?

Because the women from the Islands believe in education. You can demonstrate and shake your fists, burn your draft cards and block the traffic with your bodies, but what do you know in the end? For the ladies from the Islands there is one relevance, education. That is all they know. That is all I know. That is all I need to know.

Still there was a confusion and a darkness in my head and I had to understand what I was doing in this classroom or get out. If I had to stand before those five classes I couldn't let days dribble by in the routine of high school grammar, spelling, vocabulary, digging for the deeper meaning in poetry, bits of literature doled out for the multiple choice tests that would follow so that universities can be supplied with the best and the brightest. I had to begin enjoying the act of teaching and the only way I could do that was to start over, teach what I loved and to hell with the curriculum.

The year Maggie was born I told Alberta something my mother used to say, that a child gains her vision at six weeks and if that was true we should take her to Ireland so that her first image would be of moody Irish skies, a passing shower with the sun shining through.

Paddy and Mary Clancy invited us to stay on their farm in Carrick-on-Suir but newspapers were saying Belfast was in flames, a nightmare city, and I was anxious to see my father. I traveled north with Paddy Clancy and Kevin Sullivan and the night we arrived we walked the streets of Catholic Belfast. The women were out banging on the pavements with the lids of garbage cans, warning their men of approaching army patrols. They were suspicious of us till they recognized Paddy of the famous Clancy Brothers and we passed on without trouble.

Next day Paddy and Kevin stayed in the hotel while I went to my Uncle Gerard's house so that he could take me to my father in Andersonstown. When my father opened his door he nodded at Uncle Gerard and looked through me. Uncle said, This is your son.

My father said, Is it little Malachy?

No. I'm your son Frank.

Uncle Gerard said, It's a sad thing when your own father doesn't know you.

My own father said, Come in. Sit down. Will you have a cup of tea?

He offered the tea but showed no signs of making it in his little kitchen till a woman came from next door and did it. Uncle Gerard whispered, See that. He never lifts a finger. He doesn't have to with the way the ladies of Andersonstown wait on him hand and foot. They tempt him daily with soup and dainty things.

My father smoked his pipe but never touched his mug of tea. He was busy asking about my mother and three brothers. Och, your brother, Alphie, came to see me. Quiet lad your brother Alphie. Och, aye. Quiet lad. And you're all well in America? Attending to your religious duties? Och, you have to be good to your mother and attend to your religious duties.

I wanted to laugh. Jesus, is this man preaching? I wanted to say, Dad, have you no memory?

No, what's the use. I'd be better off leaving my father to his demons though you could see from the peaceful way he had with his pipe and his mug of tea that the demons wouldn't cross his threshold. Uncle Gerard said we ought to leave before darkness fell on Belfast and I wondered how I should say goodbye to my father. Shake his hand? Embrace him?

I shook his hand because that's all we ever did except for one time when I was in hospital with typhoid and he kissed my forehead. Now he drops my hand, reminds me once more to be a good boy, to obey my mother and remember the power of the daily rosary.

When we returned to his house I told my uncle I'd like to walk through the Protestant area, the Shankill Road. He shook his head. Quiet man. I said, Why not?

Because they'll know.

What will they know?

They'll know you're a Catholic.

How will they know?

Och, they'll know.

His wife agreed. She said, They have ways.

Do you mean to say you could spot a Protestant if he walked down this street?

We could.

How?

And my uncle smiled. Och, years of practice.

While we had another cup of tea there was shooting down Leeson Street. A woman screamed and when I went to the window Uncle

Gerard said, Och, get your head away from the window. One little movement and the soldiers are so nervous they'll spray it.

The woman screamed again and I had to open the door. She had a child in her arms and another one clinging to her skirt and she was being forced back by a soldier pushing his slanted rifle. She begged him to let her cross Leeson Street to her other children. I thought I'd help by carrying the child clinging to her but when I went to pick her up the woman dashed around the soldier and across the street. The soldier swung on me and put his rifle barrel against my forehead. Get inside, Paddy, or I'll blow your fawking head off.

My uncle and his wife, Lottie, told me that was a foolish thing I did and it helped no one. They said that whether you were Catholic or Protestant there was a way of handling things in Belfast that outsiders would never understand.

Still, on my way back to the hotel in a Catholic taxi, I dreamed I could easily roam Belfast with an avenging flamethrower. I'd aim it at that bastard in his red beret and reduce him to cinders. I'd pay back the Brits for the eight hundred years of tyranny. Oh, by Jesus, I'd do my bit with a fifty-caliber machine gun. I would, indeed, and I was ready to sing "Roddy McCorley goes to die on the bridge of Toome today", till I remembered that that was my father's song and decided instead I'd have a nice quiet pint with Paddy and Kevin in the bar of our Belfast hotel and before I went to sleep that night I'd call Alberta so that she could hold the phone to Maggie and I'd carry my daughter's gurgle into my dreams.

Mam flew over and stayed with us awhile at our rented flat in Dublin. Alberta went shopping on Grafton Street and Mam strolled with me to St Stephen's Green with Maggie in her pram. We sat by the water and threw crumbs to ducks and sparrows. Mam said it was lovely to be in this place in Dublin in the latter end of August the way you could feel autumn coming in with the odd leaf drifting before you and the light changing on the lake. We looked at children wrestling in the grass and Mam said it would be lovely to stay here a few years and see Maggie grow up with an Irish accent, not that she had anything against the American accent, but wasn't it a pure pleasure to listen to these children and she could see Maggie growing and playing on this very grass.

When I said it would be lovely a shiver went through me and she said someone was walking on my grave. We watched the children play and looked at the light on the water and she said, You don't want to go back, do you?

Back where?

New York.

How do you know that?

I don't have to lift the lid to know what's in the pot.

The porter at the Shelbourne Hotel said it would be no bother at all to keep an eye on Maggie's pram against the railings outside while we sat in the lounge, a sherry for Mam, a pint for me, a bottle of milk for Maggie on Mam's lap. Two women at the next table said Maggie was a dote, a right dote she was, oh gorgeous, and wasn't she the spittin' image of Mam herself. Ah, no, said Mam, I'm only the grandmother.

The women were drinking sherry like my mother but the three men were lowering pints and you could see from their tweed caps, red faces and great red hands they were farmers. One, with a dark green cap, called to my mother, The little child might be a lovely child, missus, but you're not so bad yourself.

Mam laughed and called back to him, Ah, sure, you're not so bad either.

Begod, missus, if you were a little older I'd run away with you.

Well, said Mam, if you were a little younger I'd go.

People all around the lounge were laughing and Mam threw her head back and laughed herself and you could see from the shine in her eyes she was having the time of her life. She laughed till Maggie whimpered and Mam said the child had to be changed and we'd have to go. The man with the dark green cap put on a begging act. Yerra, don't go, missus. Your future is with me. I'm a rich widow man with a farm o' land.

Money isn't everything, said Mam.

But I have a tractor, missus. We could ride together and how would that suit you?

It stirs me, said Mam, but I'm still a married woman and when I put on the widow's weeds you'll be the first to know.

Fair enough, missus. I live in the third house on the left as you enter the south west coast of Ireland, a grand place called Kerry.

I heard of it, said Mam. 'Tis known for sheep.

And powerful rams, missus, powerful.

You're never short of an answer, are you?

Come to Kerry with me, missus, and we'll walk the hills wordless.

Alberta was already at the flat making lamb stew and when Kevin Sullivan dropped in with Ben Kiely, the writer, there was enough for everyone and we drank wine and sang because there isn't a song in the world Ben doesn't know. Mam told the story of our time in the Shelbourne Hotel. Lord above, she said, that man had a way with him and if it wasn't for Maggie needing to be changed and wiped I'd be on my way to Kerry.

In the 1970s Mam was in her sixties. The emphysema that came from years of smoking left her so breathless she dreaded leaving her apartment anymore and the more she stayed at home the heavier she grew. For a while she came to Brooklyn to take care of Maggie on weekends but that stopped when she could no longer climb the subway stairs. I accused her of not wanting to see her granddaughter.

I do want to see her but 'tis hard for me to get around anymore.

Why don't you lose weight?

'Tis hard for an elderly woman to lose weight and anyway why should I?

Don't you want to have some kind of life where you're not sitting in your apartment all day looking out the window?

I had my life, didn't I, and what use was it? I just want to be left alone.

There were attacks which left her gasping and when she visited Michael in San Francisco he had to rush her to the hospital. We told her she was ruining our lives the way she always got sick on holidays, Christmas, New Year's Eve, Easter. She shrugged and laughed and said, Pity about ye now.

No matter how her health was, no matter how breathless, she climbed the hill to the Broadway bingo hall till she fell one night and broke her hip. After the operation she was sent to an upstate convalescent home and then stayed with me at a summer bungalow in Breezy Point at the tip of the Rockaway Peninsula. Every morning she slept late and when she woke sat slumped on the side of her bed, staring out the window at a wall. After a while she'd drag herself into the kitchen for breakfast and when I barked at her for eating too much bread and butter, that she'd be the size of a house, she barked back at me, For the love o' Jesus, leave me alone. The bread and butter is the only comfort I have.

52

When Henry Wozniak taught Creative Writing and English and American Literature he wore a shirt, a tie and a sports jacket every day. He was faculty advisor to the Stuyvesant High School literary magazine, *Caliper*, and to the students' General Organization and he was active in the union, the United Federation of Teachers.

He changed. On the first day of school in September, 1973, he roared up Fifteenth Street on a Harley Davidson motor bike and parked it outside the school. Students said, Hi, Mr Wozniak, though they hardly recognized him with his shaved head, his earring, his black leather jacket, black collarless shirt, worn jeans so tight they didn't need the wide belt with the large buckle, the bunch of keys that dangled from that belt, his black leather boots with the elevated heels.

He said Hi back to the students but he didn't linger and smile the way he used to when he didn't mind if students called him The Woz. Now he was reserved with them and with teachers at the time clock. He told the English Department chairman, Roger Goodman, he wanted regular English classes, that he would even take freshmen and sophomores and drill them in grammar, spelling, vocabulary. He told the principal he was withdrawing from all non-teaching activities.

★　★　★

Because of Henry I became the Creative Writing teacher. You can do it, said Roger Goodman, and he bought me a beer and a hamburger at the Gashouse Bar around the corner to fortify me. You can handle it, he said. After all, hadn't I written pieces for the *Village Voice* and other papers and wasn't I planning to write more?

All right, Roger, but what the hell is Creative Writing and how do you teach it?

Ask Henry, said Roger, he did it before you.

I found Henry in the library and asked him how you teach creative writing.

Disneyland, he said.

What?

Take a trip to Disneyland. Every teacher should do it.

Why?

It's an enlarging experience. In the meantime, remember one little nursery rhyme and take it as your mantra.

> *Little BoPeep has lost her sheep*
> *And cannot know where to find them.*
> *Leave them alone. and they'll come home*
> *Wagging their tails behind them.*

That was all I got from Henry and, except for an occasional hallway Hi, we never talked again.

I write my name on the board and think of Mr Sorola's remark that fifty percent of teaching is procedure and if so how should I proceed? This class is an elective and that means they're here because they asked for it and if I ask them to write something there should be no whining.

I have to give myself breathing room. I write on the board, Funeral Pyres, two hundred words, do now.

What? Funeral pyres? What kinda topic is that to write about? What's a funeral pyre anyway?

You know what a funeral is, don't you? You know what a pyre is. You've seen pictures of women in India climbing on their husbands' funeral pyres, haven't you? It's called suttee, a new word for your vocabulary.

A girl calls out, That's disgusting, that's really disgusting.

What?

Women killing themselves just because their husbands are dead. That really sucks.

It's what they believe. Maybe it shows their love.

How could it show their love when the man is dead? Don't these women have any self-respect?

Of course they do and they show it by committing suttee.

Mr Wozniak would never tell us to write stuff like this.

Mr Wozniak isn't here, so write your two hundred words.

They write and hand in their scribbled line and I know I've started off on the wrong foot though I know also that if I ever want a lively class discussion there's always suttee.

On Saturday mornings my daughter Maggie watches television cartoons with her friend Claire Ficarra from down the street. They giggle, scream, clutch each other, jump up and down while I sneer in the kitchen and read the paper. Between their chatter and the television noise I catch snatches of a Saturday morning all-American mythology, names repeated weekly, Road Runner, Woody Woodpecker, Donald Duck, the Partridge Family, Bugs Bunny, the Brady Bunch, Heckel and Jeckel. The idea of mythology loosens my sneer and I take my coffee to join the girls before the television set.

Oh, Dad, are you going to watch with us?

I am.

Wow, Maggie, says Claire, your Dad is cool.

I'm sitting with them because they helped me yoke violently two disparate characters, Bugs Bunny and Odysseus.

Maggie had said, Bugs Bunny, he's so mean to Elmer Fudd, and Claire had said, Yeah, Bugs is nice and funny and clever but why is he so mean to Elmer?

When I returned to my classes on Monday morning I announced my great discovery, the similarities between Bugs Bunny and Odysseus, that they were devious, romantic, wily, charming, that Odysseus was the first draft dodger while Bugs showed no evidence of ever having served his country or of ever having done anything for anyone except to cause mischief, that the major difference between them was that Bugs simply drifted from one mischief to another while Odysseus had a mission, to get home to Penelope and Telemachus.

What prompted me then to ask the simple question that caused the class to explode, When you were a child what did you watch on Saturday mornings?

An eruption of Mickey Mouse, Flotsam and Jetsam, Tom and Jerry, Mighty Mouse, Crusader Rabbit, dogs, cats, mice, monkeys, birds, ants, giants.

Stop. Stop.

I threw out pieces of chalk. Here, you and you and you, go to the board. Write the names of these cartoons and shows. Put them in categories. This is what scholars will be poring over a thousand years hence. This is your mythology. Bugs Bunny. Donald Duck.

The lists covered all the boards and there still wasn't enough room. They could have covered floor and ceiling and continued into the hallway, thirty-five students in each class dredging up the detritus of countless Saturday morning shows. I called above the din, Did these shows have theme songs and music?

Another eruption. Songs, hummings, mood music, reminiscences of favorite scenes and episodes. They could have sung and chanted and acted well past the bell and into the night. From the board they copied lists into their notebooks and they didn't ask why, they didn't complain. They told each other and me they couldn't believe they'd watched so much television in their lives. Hours and hours. Wow. I asked them, How many hours? and they said days, months, maybe years. Wow again. If you were sixteen you probably spent three years of your life before a TV set.

53

Before Maggie was born I dreamed of being a Kodak daddy. I'd wield a camera and assemble an album of milestone pictures, Maggie moments after her birth, Maggie on her first day of kindergarten, Maggie graduating from kindergarten, from elementary school, high school and, above all, college.

The college wouldn't be some sprawling urban affair, NYU, Fordham, Columbia. No, my lovely daughter would spend four years in one of those sweet New England colleges so exquisite they find the Ivy League vulgar. She'd be blond and tanned, strolling the greensward with an Episcopalian lacrosse star, scion of a Boston Brahmin family. His name would be Doug. He'd have bright blue eyes, powerful shoulders, a frank direct look. He'd call me sir and crush my hand in his manly honest way. He and Maggie would be married in the honest stone Episcopalian church on campus, showered with confetti under an arch of lacrosse sticks, the sport of a better class of people.

And I'd be there, proud Kodak dad, awaiting my first grandchild, half Irish Catholic, half Boston Brahmin Episcopalian. There would be a christening and a garden party, and I'd be snapping away with my Kodak, white tents, women in hats, everyone pastelled, Maggie with child, comfort, class, security.

That's what I dreamed when I held her bottle, changed her diapers, bathed her in the kitchen sink, taped her infant gurglings. The first three years I secured her in a little basket and rode my bicycle around Brooklyn Heights. When she toddled I took her to the playground and while she discovered sand and other children I eavesdropped on mothers around me. They talked about kids, husbands, how they couldn't wait to get back to their own careers in the real world. They'd lower their voices and whisper about affairs and I'd wonder if I should make a move. No. They were already suspicious of me. Who was this guy sitting around with mothers on a summer morning when real men were at work?

They didn't know I was born lower-class, using daughter and wife to ease myself into their world. They worried about something that comes before kindergarten, pre-school, and I was learning that kids have to be kept busy. A few wild minutes in the sandbox is okay but play should really be structured and supervised. You just can't have enough structure. If a child is aggressive you have to worry. Quiet? Same worry. It's all anti-social behavior. Kids must learn to adjust, or else.

I wanted to send Maggie to a public elementary school or even the Catholic school down the street but Alberta insisted on an ivy-covered pile that had once been a school for Episcopalian girls and I didn't have the stomach for a fight. It would surely be more respectable and we'd meet a better class of people.

Oh, we did. There were stockbrokers, investment bankers, engineers, heirs to old fortunes, professors, obstetricians. There would be parties where they'd say, And what do you do? and when I said I was a teacher they'd turn away. It didn't matter that we had a mortgage on a Cobble Hill brownstone, that we kept in step with other gentrifying couples, exposing our bricks, our beams, ourselves.

It was too much for me. I didn't know how to be a husband, a father, a house owner with two tenants, a certified member of the middle class. I didn't know how to proceed, how to dress, how to chatter of the stockmarket at parties, how to play squash or golf, how to give a testosteronic handshake and look my man in the eye with a Pleasure to meet you, sir.

Alberta would say she wanted nice things and I never knew what that meant. Or I didn't care. She'd want to go antiquing along Atlantic Avenue and I'd want to chat with Sam Colton in his Montague Street bookshop or have a beer at the Blarney Rose with Yonk Kling. Alberta would talk about Queen Anne tables, Regency sideboards, Victorian ewers and I didn't give a fiddler's fart. Her friends talked about good taste and rounded on me when I said good taste was what pops up when the imagination dies. The air was thick with good taste and I felt suffocated.

The marriage had become a sustained squabble and there was Maggie, trapped in the middle of it. After school every day she had to follow the routine passed down by a Yankee grandmother in Rhode Island. Change your clothes, drink milk, eat cookies, do your homework because you're not getting out of the house till you do. That's what you're supposed to do. That's what your mother did. Then you can play with Claire till it's dinnertime where you have to sit with parents who are civil only because of you.

Mornings redeemed the nights. When Maggie grew from toddler to walker to talker she'd come to the kitchen in her dream state, talking dream talk of a flight over the neighborhood with Claire and a landing in the street outside. In April she'd look at the magnolia tree that bloomed beyond the kitchen window and want to know why we couldn't have that color forever. Why did the green leaves drive away the lovely pink? I told her all the colors must have their day in the world and that seemed to satisfy her.

Mornings with Maggie were as golden or pink or green as the mornings I had with my father in Limerick. Till he went away I had him to myself. Till everything fell apart I had Maggie.

Weekdays I'd walk her to school and then take the train to my classes at Stuyvesant High School. My teenage students wrestled with hormones or struggled with family problems, divorces, custody battles, money, drugs, the death of faith. I felt sorry for them and their parents. I had the perfect little girl and I'd never have their problems.

I did and Maggie did. The marriage crumbled. Slum-reared Irish Catholics have nothing in common with nice girls from New England who had little curtains at their bedroom windows, who wore white gloves right up to their elbows and went to proms with nice boys, who studied etiquette with French nuns and were told, Girls, your virtue is like a dropped vase. You may repair the break but the crack will always be there. Slum-reared Irish Catholics might have recalled what their fathers said, After a full belly all is poetry.

The old Irish had told me, and my mother had warned me, Stick with your own. Marry your own. The devil you know is better than the devil you don't know.

When Maggie was five I walked out and stayed with a friend. It didn't last. I wanted my mornings with my daughter. I wanted to sit on the floor before the fire, tell her stories, listen to *Sergeant Pepper's Lonely Hearts Club Band*. Surely, after all these years, I could work on this marriage, wear a tie, escort Maggie to birthday parties around Brooklyn Heights, charm wives, play squash, pretend an interest in antiques.

I walked Maggie to school. I carried her bookbag, she toted her Barbie lunch box. Around her eighth year she announced, Look, Dad, I want to go to school with my friends. Of course, she was pulling away, going independent, saving herself. She must have known her family was disintegrating, that her father would soon leave forever as his father had long ago and I left for good a week before her eighth birthday.

54

When I look at the framed book jackets on the wall at the Lion's Head I suffer with envy. Will I ever be up there? The writers travel the land, signing books, appearing on television talk shows. There are parties and women and romance everywhere. People listen. No one listens to teachers. They are pitied for their sad salaries.

But there are powerful days in room 205 at Stuyvesant High School, when discussion of a poem opens the door to a blazing white light and everyone understands the poem and understands the understanding and when the light fades we smile at each other like travelers returned.

My students don't know it but that classroom is my refuge, sometimes my strength, the setting for my delayed childhood. We dip into the *Annotated Mother Goose* and the *Annotated Alice in Wonderland*, and when my students bring in the books of their early years there is delight in the room. You read that book, too? Wow.

A wow in any classroom means something is happening.

There is no talk of quizzes or tests and if grades have to be assigned for the bureaucrats well then students are capable of evaluating themselves. We know what's going on in *Little Red Riding Hood*, that if you don't follow the path the way your mother tells you you're gonna meet that big bad wolf and there will be trouble, man, trouble, and like how come everyone complains about violence on television and no one says a word about the viciousness of the father and step-mother in *Hansel and Gretel*, how come?

From the back of the room a boy's angry cry, Fathers are such assholes.

And for a whole class period there's a heated discussion of "Humpty Dumpty."

> *Humpty Dumpty sat on the wall.*
> *Humpty Dumpty had a great fall;*
> *All the king's horses,*
> *And all the king's men*
> *Couldn't put Humpty together again.*

So, I ask, what's going on in this nursery rhyme? The hands are up. Well, like, this egg falls off the wall and if you study biology or physics you know you can never put an egg back together again. I mean, like, it's common sense.

Who says it's an egg? I ask.

Of course it's an egg. Everyone knows that.

Where does it say it's an egg?

They're thinking. They're searching the text for egg, any mention, any hint of egg. They won't give in.

There are more hands, impassioned assertions of egg. All their lives they knew this rhyme and there was never a doubt that Humpty Dumpty was an egg. They're comfortable with the idea of egg and why do teachers have to come along and destroy everything with all this analysis.

I'm not destroying. I just want to know where you got the idea that Humpty is an egg.

Because, Mr McCourt, it's in all the pictures and whoever drew the first picture musta known the guy who wrote the poem or he'd never have made it an egg.

All right. If you're content with the idea of egg we'll let it be but I know the future lawyers in this class will never accept egg where there is no evidence of egg.

As long as there's no threat of grades they're comfortable with the matter of childhood and when I suggest they write their own children's books they don't complain, they don't resist.

Oh, yeah, yeah, what a great idea.

They are to write, illustrate and bind their books, original work, and when they're finished I take them to an elementary school down the street on First Avenue to be read and evaluated by real critics, the ones who would read such books, third and fourth graders.

Oh, yeah, yeah, the little ones, that'd be cute.

On a bitter January day the little ones are brought to Stuyvesant by their teacher. Aw, gee, look at 'em. So c-u-t-e. Look at their little coats and earmuffs and mittens and their little colored boots and their little frozen faces. Aw, cute.

The books are laid out on a long table, books of all sizes, shapes, and the room blazes with color. My students sit and stand, giving up their seats to their little critics who sit on desks, their feet dangling far above the floor. One by one they come to the table to select the books they read and to comment. I've already warned my students these small children are poor liars, all they know for the moment is the truth. They read from sheets their teacher helped them prepare.

The book I read is *Petey and the Space Spider*. This book is okay except for the beginning, the middle and the end.

The author, a tall Stuyvesant junior, smiles weakly and looks at the ceiling. His girlfriend hugs him.

Another critic. The book I read was called *Over There* and I didn't like it because people shouldn't write about war and people shooting each other in the face and going to the bathroom in their pants because they're scared. People shouldn't write about things like that when they can write about nice things like flowers and pancakes.

For the little critic there is wild applause from her classmates, from the Stuyvesant authors a stony silence. The author of *Over There* glares over the head of his critic.

Their teacher had asked her pupils to answer the question, Would you buy this book for yourself or anyone else?

No, I wouldn't buy this book for me or anyone. I already have this book. It was written by Dr Seuss.

The critic's classmates laugh and their teacher tells them shush but they can't stop and the plagiarist, sitting on the window sill, turns red and doesn't know what to do with his eyes. He's a bad boy, did the wrong thing, gave the little ones ammunition for their jeers, but I want to comfort him because I know why he did that bad thing, that he could hardly be in the mood for creating a children's book when his parents separated during the Christmas break, that he's caught in

372

the bitterness of a custody battle, doesn't know what to do when mother and father pull him in opposite directions, that he feels like running to his grandfather in Israel, that with all this he can meet his English assignment only by stapling together a few pages on which he has copied a Dr Seuss story and illustrating it with stick figures, that this is surely the lowest point in his life and how do you handle the humiliation when you're caught in the act by this smartass third-grader who stands there laughing in the spotlight. He looks at me across the room and I shake my head, hoping he understands that I understand. I feel I should go to him, put my arm around his shoulder, comfort him, but I hold back because I don't want third-graders or high school juniors to think I condone plagiarism. For the moment I have to hold the high moral ground and let him suffer.

The little ones get into their winter clothes and leave and my classroom is quiet. A Stuyvesant author who suffered negative criticism says he hopes those damn kids get lost in the snow. Another tall junior, Alex Newman, says he feels okay because his book was praised but what those kids did to a few of the authors was disgraceful. He says some of those kids are assassins and there is agreement around the room.

But they're softened up for the American Literature of the junior year, ready for the rant of *Sinners in the Hands of an Angry God*. We chant Vachel Lindsay and Robert Service and T. S. Eliot who can be recruited for either side of the Atlantic. We tell jokes because every joke is a short story with a fuse and an explosion. We journey back into childhood for games and street rhymes, Miss Lucy and Ring-around-a-rosy, and visiting educators wonder what's going on in this classroom.

And tell me, Mr McCourt, how does that prepare our children for college and the demands of society?

55

On the table by the bed in my mother's apartment there were bottles of pills, tablets, capsules, liquid medicines, take this for that and that for this three times a day when it's not four but not when you're driving or operating heavy machinery, take before during and after meals avoiding alcohol and other stimulants and be sure you don't mix your medications, which Mam did, confusing the emphysema pills with the pills for the pain of her new hip and the pills that put her to sleep or woke her up and the cortisone that bloated her and caused hair to grow on her chin so that she was terrrified to leave the house without her little blue plastic razor in case she might be away a while and in danger of sprouting all kinds of hair and she'd be ashamed of her life, so she would, ashamed of her life.

The city provided a woman to care for her, bathe her, cook, take her for walks if she was able for it. When she wasn't able for it she watched television and the woman watched with her though she reported later that Mam spent much of her time staring at a spot on the wall or looking out the window delighting in the times her grandson, Conor, called up to her and they chatted while he hung from the iron bars that secured her windows.

The woman from the city lined up the pill bottles and warned Mam to take them in a certain order during the night but Mam would forget and become so confused no one knew what she might have done to herself and the ambulance would have to take her to Lenox Hill Hospital where she was now well known.

The last time she was in the hospital I called her from my school to ask how she was.

Ah, I dunno.

What do you mean you dunno?

I'm fed up, They're sticking things in me and pulling things out of me.

Then she whispered, If you're coming to see me, would you do me a favor?

I would. What is it?

You're not to tell anyone about this.

I won't. What is it?

Will you bring me a blue plastic razor?

A plastic razor? For what?

Never mind. Couldn't you just bring it and stop asking questions? Her voice broke and there was sobbing.

All right, I'll bring it. Are you there?

She could barely talk with the sobbing. And when you come up give the razor to the nurse and don't come in till she tells you.

I waited while the nurse took in the razor and screened Mam from the world. On her way out, the nurse whispered, She's shaving. It's the cortisone. She's embarrassed.

All right, said Mam, you can come in now and don't be asking me any questions even if you didn't do what I asked you.

What do you mean?

I asked you for a blue plastic razor and you brought me a white one.

What's the difference?

There's a big difference but you wouldn't know. I won't say another word about it.

You look fine.

I'm not fine. I'm fed up, I told you. I just want to die.

Oh, stop. You'll be out by Christmas. You'll be dancing.

I will not be dancing. Look, there's women running around this country getting abortions right and left and I can't even die.

What in God's name is the connection between you and women getting abortions?

Her eyes filled. Here I am in the bed, dying or not dying, and you're tormenting me with theology.

My brother, Michael, came into the room, all the way from San Francisco. He prowled the area around her bed. He kissed her and massaged her shoulders and feet. That'll relax you, he said.

I'm relaxed, she said. If I was any more relaxed I'd be dead and wouldn't that be a relief.

Michael looked at her and at me and around the room and his eyes were watery. Mam told him he should be back in San Francisco with his wife and children.

I'll be going back tomorrow.

Well, it was hardly worth your while, all this traveling, was it?

I had to see you.

She drifted off and we went to a bar on Lexington Avenue for a few drinks with Alphie and Malachy's son, young Malachy. We didn't talk about Mam. We listened to young Malachy who was twenty and didn't know what to do with his life. I told him since his mother was Jewish he could go to Israel and join the army. He said he wasn't Jewish but I insisted he was, that he had the right of return. I told him if he went to the Israeli Consulate and announced he wanted to join the Israeli army it would be a publicity coup for them. Imagine, young Malachy McCourt, a name like that, joining the Israeli army. He'd be on the front page of every paper in New York.

He said no, he didn't want his ass shot off by those crazy Arabs. Michael said he wouldn't be up there on the front lines, he'd be back where he could be used for propaganda purposes and all those exotic Israeli girls would be throwing themselves at him.

He said no again and I told him it was a waste of time buying him drinks when he wouldn't do a simple thing like joining the Israeli army and carving out a career for himself. I told him if I had a Jewish mother I'd be in Jerusalem in a minute.

That night I returned to Mam's room. A man stood at the end of her bed. He was bald, he had a grey beard and a grey three-piece suit. He jingled the change in his trouser pocket and told my mother, You know, Mrs McCourt, you have every right to be angry when you're ill and you do have a right to express it.

He turned to me. I'm her psychiatrist.

I'm not angry, said Mam. I just want to die and ye won't let me.

She turned to me. Will you tell him go away?

Go away, doctor.

Excuse me, I'm her doctor.

Go away.

He left and Mam complained they were tormenting her with priests and psychiatrists and even if she was a sinner she'd done penance a hundred times over, that she was born doing penance. I'm dying for something in my mouth, she said, something tarty like lemonade.

I brought her an artificial lemon filled with concentrated juice and poured it into a glass with a little water. She tasted it. I asked you for lemonade and all you gave me was water.

No, that's lemonade.

She's tearful again. One little thing I ask you, one little thing and you can't do it for me. Would it be too much to ask you to shift my feet, would it? They're in the one place all day.

I want to ask her why she doesn't move her feet herself but that will only lead to tears so I move them.

How's that?

How's what?

Your feet.

What about my feet?

I moved them.

You did? Well, I didn't feel it. You won't give me lemonade. You won't shift my feet. You won't bring me a proper blue plastic razor. Oh, God, what use is it having four sons if you can't get your feet shifted?

All right. Look. I'm moving your feet.

Look? How can I look? 'Tis hard for me to lift my head from the pillow to be looking at my feet. Are you done tormenting me?

Is there anything else?

It's a furnace in here. Would you open the window?

But it's freezing outside.

There are tears. Can't get me lemonade, can't . . .

All right, all right. I open the window to a blast of cold air from Seventy-Seventh Street that freezes the sweat on her face. Her eyes are closed and when I kiss her there is no taste of salt.

Should I stay a while or even all night? The nurses don't seem to mind. I could push this chair back, rest my head against the wall and doze. No. I might as well go home. Maggie will be singing tomorrow with the choir at the Plymouth Church and I don't want her to see me slouching and red-eyed.

All the way back to Brooklyn I feel I should return to the hospital but a friend is having an opening night party for his bar, the Clark Street Station. There is music and merry chatter. I stand outside. I can't go in.

When Malachy calls at three in the morning he doesn't have to say the words. All I can do is make a cup of tea the way Mam did at unusual times and sit up in the bed in a dark darker than darkness knowing by now they've moved her to a colder place, that grey fleshly body that carried seven of us into the world. I sip my hot tea for the comfort because there are feelings I didn't expect. I thought I'd know the grief of the grown man, the fine high mourning, the elegiac sense to suit the occasion. I didn't know I'd feel like a child cheated.

I'm sitting up in the bed with my knees pulled to my chest and there are tears that won't come to my eyes but beat instead like a small sea around my heart.

For once, Mam, my bladder is not near my eye and why isn't it?

Here I am looking at my lovely ten-year-old daughter, Maggie, in her white dress, singing Protestant hymns with the choir at the Plymouth Church of the Brethren when I should be at Mass praying for the repose of the soul of my mother, Angela McCourt, mother of seven, believer, sinner, though when I contemplate her seventy-three years on this earth I can't believe the Lord God Almighty on His throne would even dream of consigning her to the flames. A God like that wouldn't deserve the time of day. Her life was Purgatory enough and surely she's in the better place with her three children, Margaret, Oliver, Eugene.

After the service I tell Maggie her grandmother has died and she wonders why I'm dry-eyed. You know, Dad, it's all right if you cry.

My brother Michael has returned to San Francisco and I'm meeting Malachy and Alphie for breakfast on West Seventy-Second Street near the Walter B. Cooke Funeral Home. When Malachy orders a hearty meal Alphie says, I don't know how you can eat so much with your mother dead, and Malachy tells him, I have to sustain my grief, don't I?

Afterwards, at the funeral home, we meet Diana and Lynn, wives of Malachy and Alphie. We sit in a semi-circle at the desk of the funeral counselor. He wears a gold ring, a gold watch, a gold tie clasp, gold spectacles. He wields a gold pen and flashes a consoling golden smile. He places a large book on the desk and tells us the first casket is a very elegant item and would be somewhat less than ten thousand dollars, very nice indeed. We don't linger. We tell him keep turning the pages till he reaches the last item, a coffin for less than three thousand. Malachy inquires, What is the absolute rock bottom price?

Well, sir, will this be interment or cremation?

Cremation.

Before he answers I try to lighten the moment by telling him and my family of the conversation I had with Mam a week ago.

What do you want us to do with you when you go?

Oh, I'd like to be brought back and buried with my family in Limerick.

Mam, do you know the cost of transporting someone your size?

Well, she said, reduce me.

The funeral counselor is not amused. He says we could do it for eighteen hundred dollars, embalming, viewing, cremation. Malachy asks why we have to pay for a coffin if it's going to be burned anyway and the man says it's the law.

Then, says Malachy, why can't we just put her in a Hefty trash bag and leave her outside for collection?

We all laugh and the man has to leave the room for a while.

Alphie observes, There goes a life of extreme unctuousness, and when the man returns he looks puzzled at our laughter.

It is arranged. My mother's body will be laid out in her coffin for a day so that the children can see and say goodbye to a dead grandmother. The man inquires if we'd like to hire a limousine to attend the cremation but no one except for Alphie is inclined to travel to North Bergen, New Jersey, and even he changes his mind.

In Limerick Mam had a friend, Mary Patterson, who said, Do you know what, Angela?

No, what, Mary?

I often wondered what I'd look like when I died and do you know what I did, Angela?

I don't, Mary.

I got myself all dressed up in my brown habit from the Third Order of St Francis and do you know what I did next, Angela?

I don't, Mary.

379

I laid down on the bed with a mirror at the end, crossed my hands with the rosary beads around them, and closed my eyes and do you know what I did next, Angela?

I don't, Mary.

I opened one eye and took a little look at myself in the mirror and do you know what, Angela?

I don't, Mary.

I looked very peaceful.

No one can say my mother looks peaceful in her coffin. All the misery of her life is in the face bloated from hospital drugs and there are stray tufts of hair that escaped her plastic razor.

Maggie kneels by me, looking on her grandmother, the first dead body in her ten years. She has no vocabulary for this, no religion, no prayer, and that's another sadness. She can only look at her grandmother and say, Where is she now, Dad?

If there's a heaven, Maggie, she's there and she's queen of it.

Is there a heaven, Dad?

If there isn't, Maggie, I don't understand God's ways.

She doesn't understand my babbling and neither do I because the tears erupt and she tells me again, It's all right to cry, Dad.

When your mother is dead you can't be sitting around looking mournful, recalling her virtues, receiving the condolences of friends and neighbors. You have to stand before the coffin with your brothers Malachy and Alphie and Malachy's sons, Malachy, Conor, Cormac, link arms and sing the songs your mother loved and the songs your mother hated because that's the only way you can be sure she's dead, and we sang

> *A mother's love is a blessing*
> *No matter where you roam,*
> *Keep her while she's living,*
> *You'll miss her when she's gone.*

and

> *Goodbye, Johnny dear, when you're far away,*
> *Don't forget your dear old mother*

Far across the sea.
Write a letter now and then
And send her all you can
And don't forget where'er you roam
That you're an Irishman.

Visitors look at each other and you know what they're thinking. What kind of mourning is this where sons and grandsons sing and dance before the poor woman's casket? Don't they have any respect for their mother?

We kiss her and I place on her breast a shilling I had borrowed from her long ago and when we walk the long corridor to the elevator I look back at her in the coffin, my gray mother in a cheap gray coffin, the color of beggary.

56

In January 1985 my brother Alphie called to say there was sad news from our cousins in Belfast, that our father, Malachy McCourt, had died early that morning at the Royal Victoria Hospital.

I don't know why Alphie used the word sad. It wouldn't describe how I felt myself and I thought of a line from Emily Dickinson, *After great pain a formal feeling comes*.

I had the formal feeling, but no pain.

My father and mother are dead and I'm an orphan.

As a grown man Alphie had visited our father out of curiosity or love or whatever the reasons he had for wanting to see a father who had abandoned us when I was ten and Alphie barely one. Now Alphie was saying he was taking a flight that night for the funeral next day and there was something in his voice that said, Aren't you coming?

That was softer than, Are you coming? less demanding, because Alphie knew the tangled emotions of himself and his brothers, Frank, Malachy, Michael.

Coming? Why should I fly to Belfast to the funeral of a man who went off to work in England and drank every penny of his wages? If my mother were alive would she go to the funeral of one who had left her in beggary?

No, she might not go to the funeral herself but she'd tell me to go. She'd say no matter what he did to us he had the weakness, the curse of the race, and a father dies and is buried only once. She'd say he wasn't the worst in the world and who are we to judge, that's what God is for, and out of her charitable soul she'd light a candle and offer a prayer.

I flew to my father's funeral in Belfast in the hope I might discover why I was flying to my father's funeral in Belfast.

We drove from the airport through the troubled streets of Belfast, armored cars, military patrols, young men stopped, pushed against walls, searched. My cousins said it was quiet now but one bomb anywhere, Protestant or Catholic, and you'd think you were in a world war. No one remembered anymore what it was like to walk the streets in an ordinary way. If you went out for a pound of butter you might come back without a leg or you might not come back. Once they said this it was better not to talk about it anymore. Some day it would end and they'd all saunter out for the pound of butter or even the saunter for its own sake.

My cousin, Francis MacRory, took us to see our father laid out in his coffin at the Royal Victoria Hospital and when we drove up to the death house I realized I was the oldest son, the chief mourner, and all these cousins were watching me, cousins I scarcely remembered, some I had never known, McCourts, MacRorys, Foxes. Three of my father's living sisters were there, Maggie and Eva and Sister Comgall, whose name before she took the veil was Moya. Aunt Vera, the other sister, was too ill to travel from Oxford.

Alphie and I, the youngest and the oldest sons of that man in the coffin, knelt on the prie-dieu. Our aunts and the cousins looked on these two men who had traveled a long way to a mystery and surely they wondered if there was any grief.

How could there be sorrow with my father shrunken there in the coffin, his teeth gone, his face collapsed and his body in a fancy black suit with a little white silken bow tie he would have scorned, all this giving me the sudden impression I was looking at a seagull so that I shook with spasms of silent laughter so hard that all assembled, including Alphie, must have been convinced I was overcome with a grief beyond control.

A cousin touched my shoulder and I wanted to say thank you but I knew if I removed my hands from my face I'd break into such laughter I'd shock everyone and be drummed out of the clan forever. Alphie blessed himself and rose from his knees. I controlled myself, dried my laugh tears, blessed myself and stood to face the sad looks around the little death house.

Outside in the Belfast night there were tears with the embraces of my frail ageing aunts. Oh, Francis, Francis, Alphie, Alphie, he loved you boys, he did, oh, he did, talked about you all the time.

Oh, he did, indeed, Aunt Eva and Aunt Maggie and Aunt Sister Comgall, and he raised many a glass to us in three countries not that we want to whine and whimper at a time like this, after all it's his funeral, and if I could control myself in the presence of my father, that seagull in the coffin, I can surely keep a bit of dignity before my three sweet aunts and cousins galore.

We milled around ready to drive away but I had to return to my father, to satisfy myself, to tell him that if I hadn't laughed to myself over the seagull my heart might have burst with the piling up of the past, images of the day he left us with high hopes of money coming soon from England, remembrances of my mother by the fire waiting for the money that never came and having to beg from the St Vincent de Paul Society, memories of my brothers asking if they could have one more cut of fried bread. All this was your doing, Dad, and even if we came out of it, your sons, you inflicted a life of misfortune on our mother.

I could only kneel by his coffin again and recall mornings in Limerick when the fire glowed and he talked softly for fear of waking my mother and brothers, telling me of Ireland's sufferings and the great deeds of the Irish in America and those mornings are now pearls that turn into three Hail Marys there by the coffin.

We buried him next day on a hill overlooking Belfast. The priest prayed and as he sprinkled the coffin with holy water shots rang out somewhere in the city. They're at it again, someone said.

There was a gathering at the house of our cousin, Theresa Fox, and her husband, Phil. There was talk about the day, a radio report that three IRA men trying to ram through a British Army barricade had been shot by the troops. In the next world my father would have the escort of his dreams, three IRA men, and he'd envy them the manner of their going.

We had tea and sandwiches and Phil brought out a bottle of whiskey to start the stories and the songs for there's nothing else to do the day you bury your dead.

In August of 1985, the year my father died, we brought my mother's ashes to her last resting place, the graveyard at Mungret Abbey outside Limerick City. My brother Malachy was there with his wife, Diana, and their son, Cormac. My fourteen-year-old daughter, Maggie, was there along with neighbors from the old days in Limerick and friends from New York. We took turns dipping our fingers into the tin urn from the New Jersey crematorium and sprinkling Angela's ashes over the graves of the Sheehans and Guilfoyles and Griffins while watching the breeze eddying her white dust around the grayness of their old bone bits and across the dark earth itself.

We said a Hail Mary and it wasn't enough. We had drifted from the church but we knew that for her and for us in that ancient abbey there would have been comfort and dignity in the prayers of a priest, proper requiem for a mother of seven.

We had lunch at a pub along the road to Ballinacurra and you'd never know from the way we ate and drank and laughed that we'd scattered our mother who was once a grand dancer at the Wembley Hall and known to one and all for the way she sang a good song, oh, if she could only catch her breath.